Durham's Place-N̶
of California Series

- Fourteen volumes cover the state of California by region
- The most complete California place-name series

- *Durham's Place-Names of California's Gold Country Including Yosemite National Park:* **Includes Madera, Mariposa, Tuolumne, Calaveras, Amador, El Dorado, Placer, Sierra & Nevada Counties** ISBN 1-884995-25-X

- *Durham's Place-Names of the California North Coast:* **Includes Del Norte, Humbolt, Lake, Mendocino & Trinity Counties** ISBN 1-884995-26-8

- *Durham's Place-Names of California's Old Wine Country:* **Includes Napa & Sonoma Counties** ISBN 1-884995-27-6

- *Durham's Place-Names of Greater Los Angeles:* **Includes Los Angeles, Orange & Ventura Counties** ISBN 1-884995-28-4

- *Durham's Place-Names of California's Central Coast:* **Includes Santa Barbara, San Luis Obispo, San Benito, Monterey & Santa Cruz Counties** ISBN 1-884995-29-2

- *Durham's Place-Names of California's Eastern Sierra:* **Includes Alpine, Inyo & Mono Counties** ISBN 1-884995-30-6

- *Durham's Place-Names of California's Desert Counties:* **Includes Imperial, Riverside & San Bernadino Counties** ISBN 1-884995-31-4

- *Durham's Place-Names of* **San Diego County** ISBN 1-884995-32-2

- *Durham's Place-Names of Central California:* **Includes Madera, Fresno, Tulare, Kings & Kern Counties** ISBN 1-884995-33-0

- *Durham's Place-Names of California's North Sacramento Valley:* **Includes Butte, Glenn, Shasta, Siskiyou & Tehama Counties** ISBN 1-884995-34-9

- *Durham's Place-Names of the San Francisco Bay Area:* **Includes Marin, San Francisco, San Mateo, Contra Costa, Alameda , Solano & Santa Clara Counties** ISBN 1-884995-35-7

- *Durham's Place-Names of California's South Sacramento Valley:* **Includes Colusa, Sacramento, Sutter, Yuba & Yolo Counties** ISBN 1-884995-36-5

- *Durham's Place-Names of California's North San Joaquin Valley:* **Includes San Joaquin, Stanislaus & Merced Counties** ISBN 1-884995-37-3

- *Durham's Place-Names of Northeastern California:* **Includes Lassen, Modoc & Plumas Counties** ISBN 1-884995-38-1

The above titles are available at better bookstores, on-line bookstores or by calling 1-800-497-4909

Durham's

Place-Names
of the
San Francisco
Bay Area

Durnam's

Place-Names
of the

San Francisco
Bay Area

Includes Marin, San Francisco,
San Mateo, Contra Costa, Alameda,
Solano and Santa Clara Counties

David L. Durham

Word Dancer Press

Printed in the United States of America
Published by
Quill Driver Books/Word Dancer Press, Inc.
8386 N. Madsen
Clovis, CA 93611
559-322-5917
800-497-4909

Word Dancer Press books may be purchased at special prices for educational, fund-raising, business or promotional use. Please contact Special Markets, Quill Driver Books/Word Dancer Press, Inc. at the above address or phone number.

To order another copy of this book or another book in the Durham's Place-Names of California series, please call 1-800-497-4909.

Quill Driver Books/Word Dancer Press, Inc. project cadre:
Doris Hall, Dave Marion, Stephen Blake Mettee

ISBN 1-884995-35-7

Library of Congress Cataloging-in-Publication Data

Durham, David L., 1925-
    Durham's place names of the San Francisco Bay area : includes Marin, San Francisco, San Mateo, Contra Costa, Alameda, Solano & Santa Clara Counties / David L. Durham.
    p. cm.
    Includes bibliographical references.
    ISBN 1-884995-35-7 (trade paper)
    1. Names, Geographical--California--San Francisco Bay Area. 2. San Francisco Bay Area (Calif.)--History, Local. 3. Marin County (Calif.)--History, Local. 4. San Mateo County (Calif.)--History, Local. 5. Contra Costa County (Calif.)--History, Local. 6. Alameda County (Calif.)--History, Local. 7. Solano County (Calif.)--History, Local. 8. Santa Clara County (Calif.)--History, Local. I. Title: Place names of the San Francisco Bay area. II. Title.

F868.S156 D87 2001
917.94'6003--dc21

                                                                00-054636

CONTENTS

CALIFORNIA
SAN FRANCISCO
BAY AREA COUNTIES
SHADED

Introduction

Purpose, organization and scope

This gazetteer, which lists geographic features of Marin, San Francisco, San Mateo, Contra Costa, Alameda, Solano and Santa Clara counties, California, is one of a series of fourteen books that cover the whole state. This series is derived from *California's Geographic Names: A Gazetteer of Historic and Modern Names of the State,* David L. Durham's definitive gazetteer of California. Each book contains all the entries for the counties covered that are included in the larger volume.United States government quadrangle maps, which are detailed, somewhat authoritative, and generally available, are the primary source of information. Included are features that are named on quadrangle maps, or that can be related to features named on the maps. The books list relief features, water features, and most kinds of cultural features, but omit names of streets, parks, schools, churches, cemeteries, dams and the like. Some names simply identify a person or family living at a site because such places are landmarks in sparsely settled parts of the state.

The listing of names is alphabetical, and multiword names are alphabetized as one word. Terms abbreviated on maps are given in full in the alphabetical list, and numerals in names are listed in alphabetical order rather than in numerical order. In addition to the principal entries, the list includes cross references to variant names, obsolete names and key words in multiword English-language names. For each principal entry, the name is followed by the name of the county or counties in which the feature lies, a classifying term, general and specific locations, identification of one or more quadrangle maps that show the name and other information. All features named in an entry generally belong to the same county. The classifying terms are defined under the heading "Geographic Terms" beginning on page *xiii.*

Locations and measurements are from quadrangle maps, distances and directions are approximate, and latitude and longitude generally are to the nearest five seconds. Distances between post offices are measured by road, as the mail would be carried. Other distances are measured in a straight line unless the measurement is given with a qualifying expression such as "downstream" or "by road." For streams, the location given generally is the place that the stream joins another stream, enters the sea or a lake, or debouches into a canyon or valley. For features of considerable areal extent, the location given ordinarily is near the center, except for cities and towns, for which the location given is near the center of the downtown part, or at the city hall or civic center. Measurements to or from areal features usually are to or from the center. Specific locations are omitted for some very large or poorly defined places. Books, articles, and miscellaneous maps are listed under "References Cited." The references identify sources of data and provide leads to additional information. If a name applies to more than one feature in a county, the features are numbered and identified elsewhere in the list by that number in parentheses following the name.

SETTING

General.—The following gazetteer lists geographic features in seven counties—Alameda, Contra Costa, Marin, San Francisco, San Mateo, Santa Clara, and Solano—that touch upon San Francisco Bay and adjacent water bodies. The map on page *viii* shows the location of the counties. Townships (T) and Ranges (R) refer to Mount Diablo Base and Meridian. The counties are in the generally mountainous terrane between California's Central Valley and the sea. Cermeño first applied the name "San Francisco" in California in 1595 to present Drakes Bay (Treutlein, p. 12). Members of the Portola expedition in 1769 used the term "Puerto de San Francisco" for present Gulf of the Farallons before they discovered present San Francisco Bay (Davidson, p. 6); gradually the name "San Francisco" transferred to the bay (Treutlein, p. 14).

Alameda County.—Alameda County extends from San Francisco Bay eastward into and across Diablo Range. The county was organized in 1853 from territory of Contra Costa County and Santa Clara County; the county boundaries have had only minor changes (Coy, p. 61). The county seat first was at Alvarado, it moved in 1856 to San Leandro, and moved again in 1873 to Oakland, where it remains (Hoover, Rensch, and Rensch, p. 1). The county name doubtless is from Alameda Creek (Thompson and West, 1878, p. 15).

Contra Costa County.—Contra Costa County lies east of San Francisco Bay and San Pablo Bay, and south of Suisun Bay and Carquinez Strait. It includes the northernmost part of Diablo Range. The first state legislature created the county in 1850; the southern third of the original territory of the county was lost in 1853 to newly created Alameda County (Coy, p. 91). Martinez is and always has been the county seat; the name "Contra Costa" is from the early designation of land east of San Francisco Bay—*contra costa* means "opposite coast" in Spanish (Hoover, Rensch, and Rensch, p. 50).

Marin County.—Marin County extends from the coast north of San Francisco eastward to San Francisco Bay and San Pablo Bay. The county is one of the original counties that the state legislature created in 1850; the only significant boundary change came in 1854 when the county line in San Francisco Bay was modified (Coy, p. 158-159). San Rafael was designated the seat of government when the county was organized, and has retained the honor (Hoover, Rensch, and Rensch, p. 174). The name "Marin" is thought to be from the word "Marinero," the name given by Spaniards to an Indian ferryman on San Francisco Bay—*marinero* means "mariner" in Spanish (Kroeber, p. 47).

San Francisco County.—San Francisco County is at the north end of the peninsula that separates San Francisco Bay from the sea; the county also includes some rocks and islands in the bay and in the sea. The county was created in 1850; much of the original area of the county was lost in 1856 to newly formed San Mateo County (Coy, p. 225-227). After this loss of territory, the governments of the county and of the city of San Francisco were consolidated; the name "San Francisco" is from San Francisco de Asis mission, started within the limits of the present city in 1776 (Hoover, Rensch, and Rensch, p. 346).

San Mateo County.— San Mateo County is south of San Francisco between San Francisco Bay and the sea, and includes the north part of Santa Cruz Mountains. The county was created in 1856 from the south part of the original San Francisco County; San Mateo County annexed the north part of Santa Cruz County in 1868, but otherwise the boundaries of San Mateo County have changed only slightly (Coy, p. 238-239). Belmont was chosen the first county seat by a fraudulent election; within a year the seat of government moved to Redwood City, where it remains (Hoover, Rensch, and Rensch, p. 389).

Santa Clara County.—Santa Clara County covers most of Santa Clara Valley, which is the south part of the topographic depression occupied by San Francisco Bay. The county extends east to the crest of Diablo Range and west to the crest of Santa Cruz Mountains. It was created when California achieved statehood in 1850; the only significant change in county boundaries came in 1853, when territory was lost to newly organized Alameda County (Coy, p. 245). San Jose was the first, and remains the county seat; the name of the county is from Santa Clara de Asis mission, founded in 1777 (Hoover, Rensch, and Rensch, p. 425).

Solano County.—Solano County lies north of the mouth of Sacramento River and north of the connection of the river with San Pablo Bay through Suisun Bay and Carquinez Strait. The first state legislature created the county in 1850; except for the transfer of Mare Island from Sonoma County to Solano County in 1853, the original counties' boundaries have changed only slightly (Coy, p. 259). The county seat first was at Benicia, but it moved in 1858 to Fairfield; the county name is from an Indian, a friend of the Mexicans, who was baptized Francisco Solano—the Indian's name was taken from San Francisco Solano mission at Sonoma in Sonoma County (Hoover, Rensch, and Rensch, p. 511).

GEOGRAPHIC TERMS

Area —A tract of land, either precisely or indefinitely defined.

Bay —A body of water connected to a larger body of water and nearly surrounded by land.

Beach —An expanse of sandy or pebbly material that borders a body of water.

Bend —A pronounced curve in the course of a stream, and the land partly enclosed therein.

Canyon —A narrow elongate depression in the land surface, generally confined between steep sides and usually drained by a stream.

Channel —The deep part of a moving body of water through which the main current flows, or part of a body of water that affords a suitable passage for ships.

City —An inhabited place that has a population greater than about 25,000 in an urban setting..

District —Part of an inhabited place, either precisely or indefinitely defined.

Embayment —An indentation in the shoreline of a body of water.

Hill —A prominent elevation on the land surface that has a well-defined outline on a map, and that rises less than 1000 feet above its surroundings.

Intermittent lake —A lake that ordinarily contains water only part of the time.

Island —A tract of normally dry land, or of marsh, that is surrounded by water.

Lake —A body of standing water, either natural or artificial.

Land grant —A gift of land made by Spanish or Mexican authority and eventually confirmed by the United States government.

Locality —A place that has past or present cultural associations.

Marsh —A poorly drained wet area.

Military installation —Land or facility used for military purposes.

Narrows —The constricted part of a channel, river, canyon, valley, or pass.

Pass —A saddle or natural depression that affords passage across a range or between peaks.

Peak —A prominent high point on a larger elevated land surface.

Peninsula —An elongate tract of land nearly surrounded by water.

Promontory —A conspicuous, but not necessarily high, elevation of the land surface that protrudes into a body of water or into a lowland.

Range —An elevated land surface of ridges and peaks.

Relief feature —A general term for a recognizable form of the land surface produced by natural causes.

Ridge —A prominent elongate elevation on the land surface; occurs either independently or as part of a larger elevation.

Rock —A rocky mass that lies near or projects above the surface of a body of water.

Settlement —An informal inhabited place.

Shoal —A shallow place in a body of water.

Spring —A natural flow of water from the ground.

Stream —A body of water that moves under gravity in a depression on the land surface; includes watercourses that have intermittent flow and watercourses that are modified by man.

Town —An inhabited place that has a population of about 500 to 25,000 in an urban setting.

Valley —A broad depression in the land surface, or a wide place in an otherwise narrow depression.

Village —An inhabited place that has a compact cluster of buildings and a population less than about 500.

Waterfall —A perpendicular or very steep descent of the water in a stream.

Water feature —A general term for something or some place involving water.

Well —A hole sunk into the ground to obtain water.

Place-Names
of the
San Francisco
Bay Area

– A –

Abbey House: see **Daly City** [SAN MATEO].

Abbotts Lagoon [MARIN]: *lake,* 1.5 miles long, 9.5 miles north-northeast of the lighthouse at Point Reyes (lat. 38°07'15" N, long. 122°56'45" W). Named on Drakes Bay (1953) and Tomales (1954) 7.5' quadrangles. The name recalls John Abbott and his brother, Carlyle S. Abbott, who had a ranch in the neighborhood and took turns as justice of the peace at Point Reyes from 1859 until 1861 (Teather, p. 1).

Acalanes [CONTRA COSTA]: *land grant,* at and west of Lafayette. Named on Briones Valley (1959) and Walnut Creek (1959) 7.5' quadrangles. Candelario Valencia received 1 league in 1834 and Elam Brown claimed 3329 acres patented in 1858 (Cowan, p. 12). The name probably is from an Indian village located on or near the grant (Kroeber, p. 33).

Acelanus: see **Alamo** [CONTRA COSTA].

Adams: see **Corte Madera** [MARIN]; **Moon and Adams Landing**, under **Oakland** [ALAMEDA].

Adeline [ALAMEDA]: *locality,* nearly 3 miles north of downtown Oakland along Southern Pacific Railroad (lat. 37°50'40" N, long. 122°16'25" W). Named on San Francisco (1899) 15' quadrangle.

Adeline [CONTRA COSTA]: *locality,* 6.5 miles north-northeast of the present Walnut Creek civic center along Oakland, Antioch and Eastern Railroad (lat. 37°59'45" N, long. 122°01'45" W). Named on Concord (1915) 15' quadrangle.

Adobe Corner [SAN MATEO]: *locality,* 4.5 miles south-southwest of downtown Redwood City in Woodside (lat. 37°25'35" N, long. 122°15'55" W). Named on Woodside (1961) 7.5' quadrangle. John Coppinger built an adobe house at the site in 1841 (Brown, p. 1).

Adobe Creek [SANTA CLARA]: *stream,* flows 11 miles to flatlands 3 miles east-southeast of downtown Palo Alto near San Francisco Bay (lat. 37°25'50" N, long. 122°06'20" W). Named on Cupertino (1961), Mindego Hill (1961), and Mountain View (1961) 7.5' quadrangles. Called San Antonio Creek on Palo Alto (1899) 15' quadrangle, called Yeguas Cr. on Healy's (1866) map, and called San Antonio or Yeguas Creek on Thompson and West's (1876) map. Juan Prado Mesa gave the name "San Antonio" to the stream after he obtained nearby San Antonio grant in 1839 (Fava, p.

29). West Fork enters from the southwest 9 miles upstream from the flatlands; it is 2 miles long and is named on Mindego Hill (1961) 7.5' quadrangle.

Adobe Gulch [SAN MATEO]: *canyon,* drained by a stream that flows 1 mile to marsh 6.5 miles north-northwest of Skeggs Point near Upper Crystal Springs Reservoir (lat. 37°29'50" N, long. 122°20'45" W; sec. 18, T 5 S, R 4 W). Named on Woodside (1961) 7.5' quadrangle. The name is from an adobe house built in the canyon in 1850 (Brown, p. 1).

Adobe Point [SAN MATEO]: *promontory,* 6 miles north-northwest of Skeggs Point on the west side of Upper Crystal Springs Reservoir (lat. 37°29'45" N, long. 122°20'15" W); the feature is near the mouth of Adobe Gulch. Named on Woodside (1961) 7.5' quadrangle.

Agnes Island: see **Point San Quentin** [MARIN].

Agnew [SANTA CLARA]: *locality,* 2 miles south-southeast of Alviso along Southern Pacific Railroad (lat. 37°23'45" N, long. 121°57'30" W). Named on Milpitas (1961) 7.5' quadrangle. The name commemorates Abram Agnew, who settled in the neighborhood about 1873; the form "Agnews" also was used for the name (Rambo, 1964, p. 30). Postal authorities established Agnew post office in 1884 and discontinued it for a short time in 1890 (Frickstad, p. 172). In 1888 W.H. Peall, a real estate promoter, started a community called Bethlehem across the street from the community of Agnew; Bethlehem had a forty-room hotel, but the promotion failed (Joanne Grant in *San Jose Mercury News,* December 14, 1992). Postal authorities established Bethlehem post office less than 1 mile south of Agnew post office in 1890 and discontinued it the same year (Salley, p. 20).

Agnews: see **Agnew** [SANTA CLARA].

Agua Caliente [ALAMEDA-SANTA CLARA]: *land grant,* at and near Warm Springs district of Fremont on Alameda-Santa Clara county line, mainly in Alameda County. Named on Calaveras Reservoir (1961), Milpitas (1961), and Niles (1961) 7.5' quadrangles. Fulgencio Higuera received 2 leagues in 1834 and claimed 9564 acres patented in 1858 (Cowan, p. 12). Perez (p. 52) gave the year 1839 for the grant. The name is from hot springs— *agua caliente* means "hot water" in Spanish (Arbuckle, p. 13).

Agua Caliente Creek [ALAMEDA]: *stream,* flows 2.25 miles to lowlands 4.5 miles southeast of Fremont civic center (lat. 37°30'10" N, long. 121°54'40" W). Named on Milpitas (1961) and Niles (1961) 7.5' quadrangles. The stream also had the names "Arroyo del Agua Caliente" and "Warm Springs Creek" (Mosier and Mosier, p. 4).

Agua de Vida Springs: see **Mendenhall Springs** [ALAMEDA].

Agua Fria Creek [ALAMEDA]: *stream,* flows 2.5 miles to lowlands 4.5 miles southeast of Fremont civic center (lat. 37°29'50" N, long. 121°55' W). Named on Milpitas (1961) 7.5' quadrangle. The stream first had the name "Arroyo de Agua Fria," and later the names "Agua Frio" and "Cold Springs Creek" (Mosier and Mosier, p. 4).

Agua Frio: see **Agua Fria Creek** [ALAMEDA].

Air Base: see **Travis Air Force Base** [SOLANO].

Airport Channel [ALAMEDA]: *channel,* extends for 2.25 miles southeast from the Tidal Canal through San Leandro Bay to Metropolitan Oakland International Airport 3 miles west of downtown San Leandro (lat. 37°43'55" N, long. 122°12'35" W). Named on Oakland East (1959) and San Leandro (1959) 7.5' quadrangles.

Alambique Creek [SAN MATEO]: *stream,* flows 2.5 miles to marsh 5.5 miles south of downtown Redwood City near Searsville Lake (lat. 37°24'10" N, long. 122°14'15" W). Named on Woodside (1961) 7.5' quadrangle. The stream first was called Arroyo del Alambique for an illegal still built beside the creek in 1842—*alambique* means "stillhouse" in Spanish; the canyon along the upper part of the stream has been called Alambique Gulch, Mountain Home Gulch, and Jones Gulch (Brown, p. 1).

Alambique Gulch: see **Alambique Creek** [SAN MATEO].

Alameda [ALAMEDA]: *city,* 3 miles south-southeast of downtown Oakland on an island separated from the mainland by the Tidal Canal and Oakland Inner Harbor (lat. 37°45'45" N, long. 122°14'30" W). Named on Hunters Point (1956), Oakland East (1959), Oakland West (1959), and San Leandro (1959) 7.5' quadrangles. Postal authorities established Alameda post office in 1854 (Frickstad, p. 1), and the community incorporated the same year. The city was named for the county in the expectation that the name would influence settlers (Bancroft, 1888, p. 478). The site first was known as Bolsa de Encinal, or Encinal de San Antonio; soon after Alameda began on what then was a peninsula, a community called Encinal was laid out near the center of the peninsula and a community called Woodstock was laid out at the west end, but in 1872 the entire peninsula was united as Alameda under a town charter (Bancroft, 1888, p. 478). San Francisco and Alameda Railroad started Encinal Station in 1864 to serve the community of Encinal; the place also

was known as Fasskings Station for Frederick Louis Fassking, a pioneer, and was called Grand Street Station (Mosier and Mosier, p. 35). Postal authorities established Encinal post office 4 miles south of Oakland post office in 1876, changed the name to West End in 1877, and discontinued it in 1891 (Salley, p. 69, 237). The settlement of West End first was called Bowman's Point for Charles C. Bowman, who settled at the place (Mosier and Mosier, p. 16).

Alameda Canyon: see **Niles Canyon** [ALAMEDA].

Alameda Creek [ALAMEDA-SANTA CLARA]: *stream,* heads in Santa Clara County and flow 46 miles to San Francisco Bay 7 miles south-southwest of downtown Hayward in Alameda County (lat. 37°34'55" N, long. 122°08'35" W). Named on Calaveras Reservoir (1961), Eylar Mountain (1955), La Costa Valley (1960), Mount Day (1955), Newark (1959), Niles (1961), and Redwood Point (1959) 7.5' quadrangles. The stream is called Rio de San Clemente and rio de la Alameda in Spanish documents of 1795 (Gudde, 1949, p. 6). The stream also had the local name "Arroyo de las Calaveras" (Mosier and Mosier, p. 11). Present Mount Eden Creek is called North Branch Alameda Creek on Thompson and West's (1878) map.

Alameda Naval Air Station [ALAMEDA]: *military installation,* 2.5 miles southwest of downtown Oakland along San Francisco Bay (lat. 37°47' N, long. 122°18'30" W); the installation is west of Alameda. Named on Oakland West (1959) 7.5' quadrangle.

Alameda Warm Springs: see **Warm Springs** [ALAMEDA].

Alamias Creek [SANTA CLARA]: *stream,* flows 2 miles to lowlands 3.5 miles northeast of Gilroy (lat. 37°02'30" N, long. 121°31' W). Named on Gilroy (1955) 7.5' quadrangle. On Chittenden (1955, photorevised 1968 and 1973) 7.5' quadrangle, the continuation of the stream in the lowlands is called Jones Creek.

Alamitos [SANTA CLARA]: *locality,* 6 miles south of downtown San Jose along Southern Pacific Railroad (lat. 37°15'05" N, long. 121°52' W); the place is near the confluence of Alamitos Creek and Guadalupe River. Named on San Jose East (1961) and Santa Teresa Hills (1953) 7.5' quadrangles.

Alamitos Creek [SANTA CLARA]: *stream,* flows 12 miles to Guadalupe Creek 5.5 miles north-northwest of New Almaden (lat. 37°14'50" N, long. 121°52'10" W). Named on Santa Teresa Hills (1953) 7.5' quadrangle; application of the name to upper reaches of the stream is unclear on the map. Called Arroyo de los Alamitos on Thompson and West's (1876) map.

Alamo [CONTRA COSTA]: *town,* 2.5 miles northwest of Danville (lat. 37°51' N, long. 122°01'50" W). Named on Las Trampas Ridge

(1959) 7.5' quadrangle. Postal authorities established Alamo post office in 1852 (Frickstad, p. 20). The name is from poplar trees that were abundant near the place—*alamo* means "poplar" in Spanish (Hoover, Rensch, and Rensch, p. 56-57). Postal authorities established Acelanus post office 7 miles northwest of Alamo in 1854 and discontinued it in 1855; the name was from Acelanes grant (Salley, p. 1).

Alamo Creek [ALAMEDA-CONTRA COSTA]: *stream,* heads in Contra Costa County and flows 10 miles to Amador Valley 1.5 miles northeast of Dublin in Alameda County (lat. 37°42'50" N, long. 121°54'50" W). Named on Diablo (1953), Dublin (1961), and Tassajara (1953) 7.5' quadrangles. West Branch joins the main stream 6.5 miles southeast of Danville; it is 7.5 miles long and is named on Diablo (1953) 7.5' quadrangle.

Alamo Creek [SOLANO]: *stream,* flows 10 miles to lowlands 2 miles east-southeast of downtown Vacaville (lat. 38°20'35" N, long. 121°57'30" W). Named on Elmira (1953), Fairfield North (1951), and Mount Vaca (1951) 7.5' quadrangles.

Alamo Creek: see **Cottonwood Creek** [ALAMEDA-CONTRA COSTA].

Alamo Oaks [CONTRA COSTA]: *settlement,* 1.5 miles north-northeast of Danville (lat. 37°50'25" N, long. 121°59'30" W; sec. 17, T 1 S, R 1 W). Named on Diablo (1953) 7.5' quadrangle.

Alamo Ridge [CONTRA COSTA]: *ridge,* northwest- to west-northwest-trending, 2.25 miles long, center 1.5 miles north-northwest of Danville (lat. 37°50'40" N, long. 122°00'20" W); the ridge is east-southeast of Alamo. Named on Diablo (1953) and Las Trampas Ridge (1959) 7.5' quadrangles.

Alaska Packers Association Basin: see **Fortmann Basin** [ALAMEDA].

Albany [ALAMEDA]: *town,* 6.25 miles north-northwest of downtown Oakland (lat. 37°53'25" N, long. 122°17'55" W). Named on Richmond (1959) 7.5' quadrangle. Postal authorities established Albany post office in 1926 (Salley, p. 3). The town incorporated in 1908 under the name "Ocean View," but in 1909 the name was changed to Albany after the birthplace in New York of the town's first mayor, Frank J. Roberts (Gudde, 1949, p. 6).

Albany Hill [ALAMEDA]: *hill,* 6.5 miles north-northwest of downtown Oakland (lat. 37°53'40" N, long. 122°18'20" W); the hill is in the town of Albany. Named on Richmond (1959) 7.5' quadrangle. Called Serrito de San Antonio on a diseño of San Pablo [CONTRA COSTA] grant made in 1830 (Becker, 1964). Called Cerritos San Antonio on Thompson and West's (1878) map. The hill also was called Signal Hill, Cerrito de San Antonio, Cerrito Hill, El Cerrito Hill, and Skunk Hill (Bowen, p. 339).

Albert Canyon [SAN MATEO]: *canyon,* drained by a stream that flows 1.5 miles to Pilarcitos Creek 3 miles northeast of downtown Half Moon Bay (lat. 37°29'30" N, long. 122°23' W; sec. 14, T 5 S, R 5 W). Named on Woodside (1961) 7.5' quadrangle. The William C. Albrecht (also called Albert) family ranch was in the canyon from the early 1870's until 1954 (Brown, p. 1; Brown called the feature Albert Gulch).

Albert Gulch: see **Albert Canyon** [SAN MATEO].

Albrae [ALAMEDA]: *locality,* 4 miles south-southwest of Fremont civic center along Southern Pacific Railroad (lat. 37°29'40" N, long. 121°59'15" W; sec. 17, T 5 S, R 1 W). Named on Milpitas (1961) 7.5' quadrangle. The name is from Albrae Gun Club, which incorporated in 1907; the club owned property at the place (Mosier and Mosier, p. 8).

Alcatraces Island: see **Alcatraz Island** [SAN FRANCISCO].

Alcatraz: see **Alcatraz Island** [SAN FRANCISCO]; **Lorin** [ALAMEDA].

Alcatraz Island [SAN FRANCISCO]: *island,* 1800 feet long, 1.25 miles north-northwest of North Point in San Francisco Bay (lat. 37°49'35" N, long. 122°25'20" W). Named on San Francisco North (1956) 7.5' quadrangle. Called Alcatraces on Ringgold's (1850a) map, and called Alcatraces Id. on Williamson's (1853) map. Ringgold (p. 25) referred to the feature as Isle of Alcatraces, and Fremont called it White Island or Bird Island in 1847 (Spence and Jackson, p. 317). The island was fortified in the 1850's, became a military prison in 1907, and a federal prison in 1934 (Frazer, p. 19). Postal authorities established Alcatraz post office in 1874 and discontinued it in 1963 (Salley, p. 4).

Alcatraz Shoal [SAN FRANCISCO]: *shoal,* 1.25 miles northwest of North Point in San Francisco Bay (lat. 37°49'30" N, long. 122°26' W); the shoal is west of Alcatraz Island. Named on San Francisco North (1956, photorevised 1968 and 1973) 7.5' quadrangle.

Alden: see **Oakland** [ALAMEDA].

Alder Creek [CONTRA COSTA]: *stream,* flows 1.25 miles to Curry Canyon nearly 2 miles south-southeast of Mount Diablo (lat. 37°51'30" N, long. 121°53'55" W; sec. 7, T 1 S, R 1 E). Named on Diablo (1953) 7.5' quadrangle.

Aldercroft Creek [SANTA CLARA]: *stream,* flows nearly 2 miles to Lexington Reservoir 3 miles south of downtown Los Gatos (lat. 37°10'40" N, long. 121°59'45" W; sec. 5, T 9 S, R 1 W). Named on Castle Rock Ridge (1955) and Los Gatos (1953) 7.5' quadrangles.

Aldercroft Heights [SANTA CLARA]: *settlement,* 4.25 miles south-southwest of Los Gatos (lat. 37°09'45" N, long. 121°58'15" W; sec. 9, 10, T 9 S, R 1 W); the place is 1.5 miles southeast of the mouth of Aldercroft Creek. Named on Los Gatos 1953 7.5' quadrangle.

Alec Canyon [SANTA CLARA]: *canyon,* drained by a stream that flows 1.25 miles to Uvas Creek 3.5 miles east-southeast of Loma Prieta (lat. 37°05'05" N, long. 121°47' W; sec. 6, T 10 S, R 2 E). Named on Loma Prieta (1955) 7.5' quadrangle.

Alhambra: see **Lake Alhambra** [CONTRA COSTA].

Alhambra Creek [CONTRA COSTA]: *stream,* flows 2.5 miles to Arroyo del Hambre 6 miles northwest of Walnut Creek civic center (lat. 37°58'25" N, long. 122°07'30" W). Named on Briones Valley (1959) and Walnut Creek (1959) 7.5' quadrangles.

Alhambra Creek: see **Arroyo del Hambre** [CONTRA COSTA].

Alhambra Valley [CONTRA COSTA]: *valley,* along Arroyo del Hambre above a point 8.5 miles north-northeast of Orinda (lat. 37° 59'45" N, long. 122°07'50" W). Named on Briones Valley (1959) 7.5' quadrangle. According to Holmes (p. 248-249), Louisiana Strentzel gave the name "Alhambra" to the valley when she moved there in the 1850's. The feature first was called Cañada del Hambre—*Cañada del Hambre* means "Valley of Hunger" in Spanish—and later it was called Hungry Valley (Gudde, 1949, p. 7); this name came from the hunger that a company of Spanish soldiers suffered at the place (Davis, W.H., p. 16).

Alice Eastwood: see **Camp Alice Eastwood,** under **Camp Eastwood** [MARIN].

Alisal: see **Pleasanton** [ALAMEDA].

Allendale [SOLANO]: *settlement,* 6.5 miles north-northeast of Vacaville (lat. 38°26'35" N, long. 121°56'30" W). Named on Allendale (1953) 7.5' quadrangle. Postal authorities established Allendale post office in 1876 and discontinued it in 1884; the name is for Morgan Allen, first postmaster (Salley, p. 4).

Allendale: see **Oakland** [ALAMEDA].

Allen's Landing: see **Mount Eden** [ALAMEDA].

Allison: see **Mount Allison** [ALAMEDA].

Allison Canyon [SANTA CLARA]: *canyon,* drained by a stream that flows 1 mile to Llagas Creek 3.5 miles south-southeast of New Almaden (lat. 37°08' N, long. 121°47'25" W). Named on Loma Prieta (1955) and Santa Teresa Hills (1953) 7.5' quadrangles.

Alma [SANTA CLARA]: *village,* 2.5 miles south of Los Gatos along Los Gatos Creek (lat. 37°11' N, long. 121°59'05" W; sec. 5, T 9 S, R 1 W); water of Lexington Reservoir now covers the site. Named on Los Gatos (1919) 15' quadrangle. The place began in 1862 with the opening there of a hotel called Forest House (Hoover, Rensch, and Rensch, p. 455). Postal authorities established Alma post office in 1873 and discontinued it in 1952 (Frickstad, p. 172). Gudde (1949, p. 8) related the name "Alma" to the first four letters of the name "*Alma*den."

Almaden: see **New Almaden** [SANTA CLARA].

Almaden Canyon [SANTA CLARA]: *canyon,* extends for at least 3 miles along Alamitos Creek at and above New Almaden (lat. 37° 10' N, long. 121°49'45" W). Named on Santa Teresa Hills (1953) 7.5' quadrangle.

Almaden Reservoir [SANTA CLARA]: *lake,* 1 mile long, behind a dam on Alamitos Creek less than 1 mile south-southwest of New Almaden (lat. 37°09'55" N, long. 121°49'40" W); the lake is in Almaden Canyon. Named on Santa Teresa Hills (1953) 7.5' quadrangle.

Alma Soda Spring: see **Soda Spring Canyon** [SANTA CLARA].

Almond Reservoir [ALAMEDA]: *intermittent lake,* 350 feet long, 3 miles north of downtown Hayward (lat. 37°42'50" N, long. 122°04'50" W). Named on Hayward (1959) 7.5' quadrangle. The name is from Almond Road, where the feature is located (Mosier and Mosier, p. 8).

Almonte [MARIN]: *locality,* nearly 6 miles south of downtown San Rafael along Northwestern Pacific Railroad (lat. 37°53'25" N, long. 122°31'25" W). Named on San Rafael (1954) 7.5' quadrangle. Called Mill Valley Junction on Tamalpais (1897) 15' quadrangle. The place first was called Bay Junction in 1890 (Teather, p. 1).

Alms House Canyon: see **Polhemus Creek** [SAN MATEO].

Alpine Creek [SAN MATEO]: *stream,* flows 4.5 miles to join La Honda Creek and form San Gorgonio Creek 0.5 mile south-southwest of La Honda (lat. 37°18'35" N, long. 122°16'35" W; near E line sec. 22, T 7 S, R 4 W). Named on La Honda (1961) and Mindego Hill (1961) 7.5' quadrangles. The name is from Alpine ranch, located at the head of the stream (Brown, p. 2).

Alpine Lake [MARIN]: *lake,* behind a dam on Lagunitas Creek 3.25 miles northwest of Bolinas (lat. 37°56'25" N, long. 122°38'15" W). Named on Bolinas (1954) and San Rafael (1954) 7.5' quadrangles.

Alston: see **Dresser** [ALAMEDA].

Alta Creek: see **Strawberry Creek** [ALAMEDA].

Alta Mesa [SANTA CLARA]: *locality,* 3.5 miles east-southeast of downtown Palo Alto along Southern Pacific Railroad (lat. 37°24'05" N, long. 122°08' W). Named on Palo Alto (1961) 7.5' quadrangle. The rail line no longer reaches the place.

Altamont [ALAMEDA]: *locality,* 7.5 miles northeast of Livermore (lat. 37°44'40" N, long. 121°39'45" W; sec. 20, T 2 S, R 3 E). Named on Altamont (1953) 7.5' quadrangle. Postal authorities established Altamont post office in 1872 and discontinued it in 1955 (Salley, p. 6). Irelan (p. 34) referred to the place as Alta Monte. The site was called The Summit before Central Pacific Railroad reached it in 1869 (Mosier and Mosier, p. 8).

Altamont Creek [ALAMEDA]: *stream,* flows 3.25 miles to Livermore Valley 2.5 miles southwest of Altamont (lat. 37°42'45" N, long. 121°41'45" W; near E line sec. 36, T 2 S, R 2 E); the stream heads near Altamont Pass. Named on Altamont (1953) 7.5' quadrangle.

Alta Monte: see **Altamont** [ALAMEDA].

Altamont Pass [ALAMEDA]: *pass,* 7.5 miles northeast of Livermore (lat. 37°44'50" N, long. 121°39'15" W; near W line sec. 21, T 2 S, R 3 E); the pass is near Altamont. Named on Altamont (1953) 7.5' quadrangle. Called Livermores Pass on Goddard's (1857) map. Williamson (1855, p. 11) called the feature Livermore's Pass, and Whitney (p. 33) called it Livermore Pass—Whitney (p. 32) noted that the name is for "Mr. Livermore, an old settler in the valley."

Alto [MARIN]: *locality,* nearly 5 miles south of downtown San Rafael along Northwestern Pacific Railroad (lat. 37°54'15" N, long. 122°31'30" W). Named on San Rafael (1954) 7.5' quadrangle. The railroad station at the site was called Blithedale during the early 1880's, when carriages from Blithedale resort met trains there (Teather, p. 1).

Alton: see **Maine Prairie** [SOLANO].

Alum Rock [SANTA CLARA]:
(1) *relief feature,* a conspicuous outcrop of alum-bearing rock in Alum Rock Canyon 1 mile east of the mouth of the canyon (lat. 37°23'40" N, long. 121°48'35" W). Named on Calaveras Reservoir (1961) 7.5' quadrangle.
(2) *district,* on the east side of San Jose south of the mouth of Alum Rock Canyon. Named on Calaveras Reservoir (1961) and San Jose East (1961) 7.5' quadrangles. California Mining Bureau's (1917b) map shows a place called Alum Rock located beyond Berryessa at the end of a rail line.

Alum Rock Canyon [SANTA CLARA]: *canyon,* along Upper Penitencia Creek and the lower part of Arroyo Aguague; the name seems to apply to a canyon 3 miles long that opens into lowlands 5 miles northeast of downtown San Jose (lat. 37°23'40" N, long. 121°49'45" W); Alum Rock (1) is in the lower part of the canyon. Named on Calaveras Reservoir (1961) 7.5' quadrangle. Rancher John Martin Ogan named the canyon, and the state legislature used the name in the act that created a park there in 1872 (undated item from *San Jose Mercury*). Crawford (1894, p. 345) called the feature Penitentiary Cañon. Winslow Anderson (p. 78-80) described a resort called Alum Rock Springs that was situated in the canyon.

Alum Rock Springs: see **Alum Rock Canyon** [SANTA CLARA].

Alvarado [ALAMEDA]: *district,* 5 miles north-northwest of downtown Newark in Union City (lat. 37°35'45" N, long. 122°04'45" W). Named on Newark (1959) 7.5' quadrangle. Newark (1948) 7.5' quadrangle has the name for a community that in 1958 joined with the neighboring community of Decoto to form the new city of Union City (Hoover, Rensch, and Rensch, p. 17). Henry C. Smith founded a town at the site in 1851 and named it New Haven after the city in his home state of Connecticut; in 1853 the place became the seat of government of newly formed Alameda County, and took the name "Alvarado" from a nearby community that had been named for Juan B. Alvarado, Mexican governor of California from 1836 until 1842 (Gudde, 1949, p. 9). Postal authorities established Alvarado post office in 1853 (Frickstad, p. 1).

Alvirez Field [SANTA CLARA]: *land grant,* 1.5 miles northwest of Coyote. Named on Santa Teresa Hills (1953) 7.5' quadrangle. The land belonged to Juan Alvirez; title to 78.62 acres was confirmed in 1865 (Arbuckle, p. 37).

Alviso [SANTA CLARA]: *town,* 8 miles northwest of downtown San Jose near the head of navigation at the south end of San Francisco Bay (lat. 37°25'35" N, long. 121°58'30" W). Named on Milpitas (1961) and Mountain View (1961) 7.5' quadrangles. The place has been part of San Jose since 1968. The landing place for Santa Clara mission, called Embarcadero de Santa Clara de Asis, was at the head of present Alviso Slough; Ygnacio Alviso, owner of Ricon de los Esteros grant, settled at the site in 1840 (Hoover, Rensch, and Rensch, p. 428). The town, which was named for the owner of the grant, was laid out in 1849 and incorporated in 1852 (Bancroft, 1888, p. 525). Postal authorities established Alviso post office in 1854, discontinued it in 1855, and reestablished it in 1859 (Salley, p. 6). A city to be called New Chicago was proposed in the 1890's for lowlands north of Alviso, but it failed to develop (Butler, p. 57). San Jose Port Association was formed in 1928 to promote a deep-water port—to be called Port San Jose—at Alviso, but this project also failed (Curtis, p. 33).

Alviso Slough [SANTA CLARA]: *water feature,* extends for 4 miles from Alviso to Coyote Creek near the mouth of that stream (lat. 37°27'40" N, long. 122°01'20" W). Named on Milpitas (1961) and Mountain View (1961) 7.5' quadrangles. Called Steamboat Slough on Thompson and West's (1876) map.

Amador's: see **Dublin** [ALAMEDA].

Amador Valley [ALAMEDA]: *valley,* at and near Pleasanton; the feature is the western extension of Livermore Valley. Named on Dublin (1961) and Livermore (1961) 7.5' quadrangles. The name commemorates Jose Maria Amador, owner of San Ramon grant (Gudde, 1949, p. 9-10). Thompson and West's (1878) map shows Willow Marsh, which covers much of the west part of the valley.

Amador Valley: see **Dublin** [ALAMEDA]; **San Ramon Valley** [ALAMEDA-CONTRA COSTA].

Ambrose [CONTRA COSTA]: *locality,* 3.5 miles west of Pittsburg along Atchison, Topeka and Santa Fe Railroad (lat. 38°02'05" N, long. 121°56'55" W; near W line sec. 11, T 2 N, R 1 W). Named on Honker Bay (1918) 7.5' quadrangle.

American Canyon [SOLANO]: *canyon,* 3.5 miles long, opens into lowlands 1.25 miles southwest of Cordelia (lat. 38°11'45" N, long. 122°09' W; near W line sec. 13, T 4 N, R 3 W); the canyon heads opposite the head of American Canyon in Napa County. Named on Cordelia (1951) 7.5' quadrangle, where the name "American Canyon" applies to the American Canyon in both counties.

Americano Creek [MARIN]: *stream,* forms part of Marin-Sonoma county line, heads in Sonoma County and flows 11 miles to Estero Americano 4.5 miles north-northwest of Tomales in Marin County (lat. 38°18'45" N, long. 122°55'40" W). Named on Two Rock (1954) and Valley Ford (1954) 7.5' quadrangles. United States Board on Geographic Names (1943, p. 9) rejected the names "Ebabias Creek," "Estero Americano," and "Estero Americano Creek" for the stream, or for any part of it.

Ames Beach: see **Miramar Beach** [SAN MATEO].

Amesport: see **Miramar** [SAN MATEO].

Amesport Landing: see **Miramar** [SAN MATEO].

Ancha Vista Spring: see **Red Hill** [MARIN] (2).

Anderson Lake [SANTA CLARA]: *lake,* 5.25 miles long, behind a dam on Coyote Creek nearly 3 miles north-northeast of Morgan Hill (lat. 37°09'55" N, long. 121°37'40" W). Named on Morgan Hill (1955) and Mount Sizer (1955) 7.5' quadrangles.

Anderson's Landing: see **Patterson Landing** [ALAMEDA].

Andrews Landing: see **San Leandro Creek** [ALAMEDA-CONTRA COSTA].

Andy Mason Slough: see **Simmons Island** [SOLANO].

Angel Island [MARIN-SAN FRANCISCO]: *island,* mainly in Marin County, but two promontories on the east side extend into San Francisco County; 1.5 miles long, 3 miles east of downtown Sausalito in San Francisco Bay (lat. 37°51'45" N, long. 122°25'45" W). Named on San Francisco North (1956) 7.5' quadrangle. Called I. de los Angeles on Ringgold's (1850a) map, but in his text Ringgold (p. 11, 24) called the feature Angel Isle and Angel Island. Ayala in 1775 called it Isla de los Angeles, and his chaplain, Vicente Santa Maria, called it la Isla de Santa Maria de los Angeles (Galvin, p. 83). Postal authorities established Angel Island post office in 1875 and discontinued it in 1945 (Salley, p. 7).

Angelo Creek: see **Angelo Slough** [SAN MATEO]; **Belmont Slough** [SAN MATEO].

Angelo House: see **Belmont** [SAN MATEO].

Angelo's Creek: see **Belmont Slough** [SAN MATEO].

Angelo Slough [SAN MATEO]: *water feature,* extends from Seal Creek (present Seal Slough) to Belmont Slough 4 miles east-southeast of downtown San Mateo (lat. 37°32'45" N, long. 122°15'10" W). Named on San Mateo (1947) 7.5' quadrangle. Called Angelo Cr. on San Mateo (1915) 15' quadrangle. The name commemorates Charles Aubrey Angelo, who started Angelo House in 1850 at present Belmont (Brown, p. 2).

Angelo Slough: see **Seal Slough** [SAN MATEO].

Anita Rock [SAN FRANCISCO]: *rock,* 1.25 miles east of Fort Point, and 900 feet offshore in San Francisco Bay (lat. 37°48'30" N, long. 122°27'10" W). Named on San Francisco North (1956) 7.5' quadrangle. Called Annita Rocks on Ringgold's (1850a) map.

Ann: see **Livermore** [ALAMEDA].

Annita Rocks: see **Anita Rock** [SAN FRANCISCO].

Año Nuevo Bay [SAN MATEO]: *embayment,* east of Año Nuevo Point (present Point Año Nuevo) along the coast (lat. 37°06'45" N, long. 122°18'45" W). Named on Año Nuevo (1955) 7.5' quadrangle. Brown (p. 61) used the name "New Year's Bay." United States Board on Geographic Names (1962, p. 4) rejected the name "New Year Bay" for the feature, and rejected the form "Ano Nuevo Bay" for the name. California Mining Bureau's (1917b) map has the name "Steele" for a place near the coast at the embayment.

Año Nuevo Creek [SAN MATEO]: *stream,* heads in Santa Cruz County and flows nearly 4 miles to the sea 1.25 miles east of Año Nuevo Point (present Point Año Nuevo) (lat. 37°07' N, long. 122° 18'20" W). Named on Año Nuevo (1955) and Franklin Point (1955) 7.5' quadrangles. United States Board on Geographic Names (1962, p. 4) rejected the name "New Year Creek" for the feature, and rejected the form "Ano Nuevo Creek" for the name. Brown (p. 61) used the name "New Year's Creek" for the stream, and noted that in Spanish times the creek was called arroyo de Lucia for an incident involving Lucia Bolcof of Santa Cruz, and also was called arroyo de los Lobos—*lobos* is the Spanish term for "sea lion." Davidson (p. 37) stated that the name "Big Gulch" is a local designation for the canyon of the stream. Brown (p. 98) used the name "Waddell Beach" for the beach at and south of the mouth of the creek, and remarked that Waddell's Landing was situated at the north end of the beach from 1864 into the 1870's. Morrall (p. 51) mentioned that lumber was shipped from Waddell's Wharf at Point Año Nuevo.

Año Nuevo Island [SAN MATEO]: *island,* 0.25 mile long, 0.5 mile southwest of Año Nuevo Point (present Point Año Nuevo) (lat. 37° 06'30" N, long. 122°20'10" W). Named on

Año Nuevo (1955) 7.5' quadrangle. Brown (p. 61) used the form "New Year's Island" for the name. United States Board on Geographic Names (1962, p. 5) rejected the name "New Year Island" for the feature, and rejected the form "Ano Nuevo Island" for the name.

Año Nuevo Point [SAN MATEO]: *promontory,* 6 miles southeast of Pigeon Point along the coast (lat. 37°06'45" N, long. 122°19'40" W). Named on Año Nuevo (1955) 7.5' quadrangle. United States Board on Geographic Names (1962, p. 4) approved the name "Point Año Nuevo" for the promontory, and rejected the names "New Years Point," "Año Nuevo Point," "Ano Nuevo Point," "Point Anno Nueva," "Point Anno Nuevo," "Point Ano Nuevo," and "Punta Año Nueva." The Board pointed out that Sebastian Vizcaino gave the name "Punta de Año Nuevo" to the feature on January 3, 1603, because it was the first promontory sighted in the new year—*Punta de Año Nuevo* means "New Year Point" in Spanish. Postal authorities established Point New Year post office 12 miles south of Pescadero in 1872 and discontinued it in 1874 (Salley, p. 175). Grant and Gale (p. 661) used the name "Purisima Rock" for a feature located seven-eighths of a mile east of Año Nuevo Point.

Antioch [CONTRA COSTA]: *city,* 10 miles north-northeast of Mount Diablo (lat. 38°00'40" N, long. 121°48'30" W). Named on Antioch North (1978) and Antioch South (1953) 7.5' quadrangles. Postal authorities established Antioch post office in 1851, discontinued it in 1852, reestablished it in 1855, discontinued it in 1862, and reestablished it in 1863 (Salley, p. 8). The city incorporated in 1872. Brothers W.W. Smith and Joseph Smith settled in 1849 at the site, which was known as Smith's Landing before it was named after the biblical city of Antioch (Gleason, p. 190). The place also was called Marshs Landing because John Marsh used it as a shipping point (Hanna, P.T., p. 14). Postal authorities established Junction post office in 1850 and discontinued it in 1853, when they moved it to Antioch (Salley, p. 108). A place called Horse Haven was situated 6 miles south of Antioch in the 1870's (Davis and Goldman, p. 516).

Antioch: see **East Antioch** [CONTRA COSTA].

Antioch Point [CONTRA COSTA]: *promontory,* 1.25 miles northwest of downtown Antioch along San Joaquin River (lat. 38°01'30" N, long. 121°49'30" W). Named on Antioch North (1978) 7.5' quadrangle.

Antioch Station [CONTRA COSTA]: *locality,* less than 1 mile south-southeast of present downtown Antioch along Southern Pacific Railroad (lat. 38°00'05" N, long. 121°48'20" W). Named on Collinsville (1918) 7.5' quadrangle.

Antonio Mountain [MARIN]: *peak,* 11 miles west-northwest of downtown Novato (lat. 38°11'35" N, long. 122°44' W); the peak is on Laguna de San Antonio grant. Altitude 1171 feet. Named on Petaluma (1953) 7.5' quadrangle.

Anza: see **Lake Anza** [CONTRA COSTA].

Apanolio Creek [SAN MATEO]: *stream,* flows 3.5 miles to Pilarcitos Creek 1.25 miles northeast of downtown Half Moon Bay (lat. 37°28'35" N, long. 122°24'40" W). Named on Half Moon Bay (1961) and Montara Mountain (1956) 7.5' quadrangles. The misspelled name is for Apolonio Rodriguez, who settled by the stream in 1858; the feature also was called Fillmore Creek for another rancher (Brown, p. 28). The stream drains Digges Canyon.

Apperson Creek [ALAMEDA]: *stream,* flows 3.25 miles to San Antonio Creek nearly 3 miles southeast of Sunol (lat. 37°34'20" N, long. 121°50'30" W). Named on La Costa Valley (1960) 7.5' quadrangle. The stream now enters San Antonio Reservoir. The name commemorates Elbert Apperson, who settled in the neighborhood in the 1890's (Mosier and Mosier, p. 10). South Fork enters from the south 1 mile upstream from the mouth of the main creek; it is 2.5 miles long and is named on La Costa Valley (1960) 7.5' quadrangle.

Apperson Ridge [ALAMEDA]: *ridge,* northwest-trending, 3.5 miles long, 5.5 miles southeast of Sunol (lat. 37°32'15" N, long. 121°47'30" W). Named on La Costa Valley (1960) 7.5' quadrangle. Pleasanton (1906) 15' quadrangle shows the feature as part of Valpe Ridge.

Appletree Gulch [SAN MATEO]: *canyon,* drained by a stream that flows 1.25 miles to West Union Creek 2.25 miles northeast of Skeggs Point (lat. 37°25'40" N, long. 122°16'10" W). Named on Woodside (1961) 7.5' quadrangle.

Arastradero Creek [SANTA CLARA]: *stream,* flows 2.25 miles to Matadero Creek 4.25 miles south of downtown Palo Alto (lat. 37°23'05" N, long. 122°09'50" W). Named on Mindego Hill (1961) and Palo Alto (1961) 7.5' quadrangles.

Arch Rock [SAN FRANCISCO]: *rock,* 2 miles northwest of North Point in San Francisco Bay (lat. 37°49'45" N, long. 122°26'20" W). Named on San Francisco North (1956) 7.5' quadrangle. Called Bird Rock on Wackenreuder's (1861) map.

Arden: see **Dumbarton Point** [ALAMEDA].

Arff: see **Baumberg** [ALAMEDA].

Argus Island: see **Point San Pedro** [MARIN].

Armstrong's Creek: see **Kingston Creek** [SAN MATEO].

Army Point [SOLANO]: *promontory,* 1.5 miles east of downtown Benicia along Carquinez Strait (lat. 38°02'40" N, long. 122°17'45" W; sec. 6, T 2 N, R 2 W). Named on Benicia (1959) 7.5' quadrangle. Called Navy Pt. on Ringgold's (1850c) map.

Arroya de la Alameda: see **Arroyo de la Alameda** [ALAMEDA].

Arroya Honda [MARIN]: *stream,* flows 3 miles to the sea 3 miles west-northwest of Bolinas (lat. 37°55'35" N, long. 122°44'10" W). Named on Bolinas (1954) 7.5' quadrangle.

Arroyo Aguague [SANTA CLARA]: *stream,* flows 8.5 miles to Upper Penitencia Creek 7.5 miles northeast of downtown San Jose (lat. 37°24'10" N, long. 121°47'25" W). Named on Calaveras Reservoir (1961), Lick Observatory (1955), and San Jose East (1961) 7.5' quadrangles. Whitney (p. 51) used the names "Arroyo de la Penitencia" and "Arroyo Aguage" for the stream.

Arroyo Arichi: see **Arroyo Avichi** [MARIN].

Arroyo Avichi [MARIN]: *stream,* flows 3 miles to Novato Creek 0.5 mile south-southeast of downtown Novato (lat. 38°05'55" N, long. 122°34' W). Named on Novato (1954) 7.5' quadrangle. Called Arroyo Arichi on Petaluma (1914) 15' quadrangle.

Arroyo Bayo [SANTA CLARA]: *stream,* flows 8 miles to San Antonio Creek 6.25 miles south of Eylar Mountain (lat. 37°23'05" N, long. 121°34'20" W; sec. 30, T 6 S, R 4 E). Named on Eylar Mountain (1955), Isabel Valley (1955), and Mount Stakes (1955) 7.5' quadrangles.

Arroyo Buenos Ayres: see **Corral Hollow** [ALAMEDA].

Arroyo Calero [SANTA CLARA]: *stream,* joins Alamitos Creek 2.5 miles north-northwest of New Almaden (lat. 37°12'50" N, long. 121°50' W). Named on Santa Teresa Hills (1953) 7.5' quadrangle. The stream extends for nearly 2 miles below Calero Reservoir, but application of the name above the reservoir is uncertain on the map. On Thompson and West's (1876) map, the lower part of the stream has the name "Arroyo Seco" and the upper part has the name "Calero Creek."

Arroyo Cañada Verde: see **Cañada Verde** [SAN MATEO].

Arroyo Cavelano: see **Cayetano Creek** [ALAMEDA-CONTRA COSTA].

Arroyo Cayetano: see **Cayetano Creek** [ALAMEDA-CONTRA COSTA].

Arroyo Corte Madera Del Presidio [MARIN]: *stream,* flows 4.5 miles to Richardson Bay 5.5 miles south of downtown San Rafael (lat. 37°53'30" N, long. 122°31'15" W); the stream forms part of the boundary of Corte de Madera del Presidio grant. Named on San Rafael (1954) 7.5' quadrangle. Called Widow Reed Creek on Tamalpais (1897) 15' quadrangle—this name was for Mrs. John Reed, whose husband built the first sawmill in Marin County along the stream in 1834 (Gudde, 1949, p. 389).

Arroyo Covelano: see **Cayetano Creek** [ALAMEDA-CONTRA COSTA].

Arroyo Creek: see **Pulgas Creek** [SAN MATEO].

Arroyo de Agua Fria: see **Agua Fria Creek** [ALAMEDA].

Arroyo de Carnadero: see **Carnadero Creek** [SANTA CLARA].

Arroyo de en Medio [SAN MATEO]: *stream,* flows 2.5 miles to the sea 2.5 miles northwest of downtown Half Moon Bay (lat. 37°29'35" N, long. 122°27'35" W). Named on Half Moon Bay (1961) and Montara Mountain (1956) 7.5' quadrangles. The stream is the boundary between the two Corral de Tierra grants. The name is from an enclosure that was situated by the stream in the early nineteenth century and had the name "rodeo de en Medio" from its position between the two ranches—*rodeo de en medio* has the meaning "middle roundup corral" in Spanish; other names for the stream were Mullen's Creek and Bradley's Creek, both for ranchers (Brown, p. 59-60).

Arroyo de la Alameda [ALAMEDA]: *land grant,* at and near Union City. Named on Hayward (1959), Newark (1959), Niles (1961), and Redwood Point (1959) 7.5' quadrangles. Called Arroya de la Alameda on San Leandro (1959) 7.5' quadrangle. Jose de Jesus Vallejo received 4 leagues in 1842 and claimed 17,705 acres patented in 1858 (Cowan, p. 13-14).

Arroyo de la Bajada: see **Gazos Creek** [SAN MATEO].

Arroyo de la Ballena: see **Yankee Jim Gulch** [SAN MATEO].

Arroyo de la Bocana: see **Strawberry Creek** [ALAMEDA].

Arroyo de la Cienega: see **Cascade Creek** [SAN MATEO].

Arroyo de la Cuesta: see **Martini Creek** [SAN MATEO].

Arroyo de la Encarnation: see **Scott Creek** [ALAMEDA-SANTA CLARA].

Arroyo del Agua Caliente: see **Agua Caliente Creek** [ALAMEDA].

Arroyo de la Harina: see **San Lorenzo Creek** [ALAMEDA].

Arroyo de la Laguna [ALAMEDA]:
(1) *stream,* flows 7.25 miles to Alameda Creek 0.5 mile southwest of Sunol (lat. 37°35'20" N, long. 121°53'25" W; sec. 17, T 4 S, R 1 E). Named on Dublin (1961), La Costa Valley (1960), and Niles (1961) 7.5' quadrangles.
(2) *stream,* heads at The Lagoon (present Stivers Lagoon) near present Fremont civic center (lat. 37°32'30" N, long. 121°57'45" W), and flows south for 3.25 miles before ending. Named on Pleasanton (1906) 15' quadrangle.

Arroyo del Alambique: see **Alambique Creek** [SAN MATEO].

Arroyo de la Penitencia: see **Arroyo Aguague** [SANTA CLARA]; **Upper Penitencia Creek** [SANTA CLARA].

Arroyo de la Purisima: see **Cañada de Verde y Arroyo de la Purisima** [SAN MATEO].

Arroyo de la Purissima: see **Purisima Creek** [SAN MATEO].

Arroyo de las Calaveras: see **Alameda Creek** [ALAMEDA].

Arroyo de las Garzas: see **Gazos Creek** [SAN MATEO].

Arroyo de las Llagas: see **Llagas Creek** [SANTA CLARA].

Arroyo de las Nueces: see **Walnut Creek** [CONTRA COSTA] (1).

Arroyo de las Nueces y Bolbones [CONTRA COSTA]: *land grant,* extends from the city of Walnut Creek to Concord and eastward. Named on Clayton (1953), Diablo (1953), Las Trampas Ridge (1959), and Walnut Creek (1959) 7.5' quadrangles. Juan Sanchez Pacheco received 2 leagues in 1834; Pacheco's heirs claimed 17,782 acres patented in 1866 (Cowan, p. 53; Cowan listed the grant under the name "Arroyo de las Nueces y Sierra de Bolbones"). The term "Bolbones" probably is from the Spanish name for the inhabitants of an Indian village (Kroeber, p. 36).

Arroyo de las Nueces y Sierra de Bolbones: see **Arroyo de las Nueces y Bolbones** [CONTRA COSTA].

Arroyo de las Pulgas: see **Pulgas Creek** [SAN MATEO].

Arroyo de las Trampas: see **Bolinger Creek** [CONTRA COSTA].

Arroyo de las Trancas: see **Corinda Los Trancos Creek** [SAN MATEO].

Arroyo de las Tunitas: see **Tunitas Creek** [SAN MATEO].

Arroyo del Bosque: see **Sausal Creek** [ALAMEDA].

Arroyo del Cerro [CONTRA COSTA]: *stream,* flows nearly 3 miles to Ygnacio Valley 4.5 miles west-northwest of Mount Diablo (lat. 37°54'05" N, long. 121°59'35" W). Named on Clayton (1953) 7.5' quadrangle.

Arroyo del Coyote: see **Coyote Creek** [ALAMEDA-SANTA CLARA].

Arroyo del Hambre [CONTRA COSTA]: *stream,* flows 8 miles to Carquinez Strait at Martinez (lat. 38°01'25" N, long. 122°08'25" W). Named on Benicia (1959), Briones Valley (1959), and Walnut Creek (1959) 7.5' quadrangles. United States Board on Geographic Names (1943, p. 11) rejected the name "Alhambra Creek" for the stream. Whitney (p. 15) called the feature El Hambre Creek.

Arroyo del Ingreto: see **San Ramon Creek** [CONTRA COSTA].

Arroyo del Leona: see **Lion Creek** [ALAMEDA].

Arroyo del Matadero: see **Matadero Creek** [SANTA CLARA].

Arroyo del Monte: see **Frenchmans Creek** [SAN MATEO].

Arroyo del Monte Diablo: see **Mount Diablo Creek** [CONTRA COSTA].

Arroyo de los Alamitos: see **Alamitos Creek** [SANTA CLARA].

Arroyo de los Cadillos: see **Cordilleras Creek** [SAN MATEO].

Arroyo De Los Calabazas: see **Calabazas Creek** [SANTA CLARA].

Arroyo de los Capitancillos: see **Los Capitancillos Creek** [SANTA CLARA].

Arroyo de los Coches [SANTA CLARA]: *stream,* flows 2.25 miles to lowlands 2 miles east-northeast of Milpitas (lat. 37°26'20" N, long. 121°52'05" W), and continues in an artificial watercourse through lowlands to Lower Penitencia Creek. Named on Calaveras Reservoir (1961) and Milpitas (1961) 7.5' quadrangles.

Arroyo de los Frijoles [SAN MATEO]: *stream,* flows 5.5 miles to the sea 3 miles north-northwest of Pigeon Point at Bean Hollow Beach (lat. 37°13'30" N, long. 122°24'30" W). Named on Franklin Point (1955) and Pigeon Point (1955) 7.5' quadrangles. According to Brown (p. 6), the stream should be called Bean Hollow Creek, from the name "Bean Hollow" for the canyon of the stream; the early name for the canyon was Cañada del Frijol—*frijol* means "kidney bean" in Spanish.

Arroyo de Los Gatos: see **Los Gatos Creek** [SANTA CLARA].

Arroyo de los Laureles: see **Laurel Creek** [SAN MATEO].

Arroyo de los Lobitos: see **Lobitos Creek** [SAN MATEO].

Arroyo de los Lobos: see **Año Nuevo Creek** [SAN MATEO].

Arroyo de los Nogales: see **Walnut Creek** [CONTRA COSTA] (1).

Arroyo de los Pilarcitos: see **Miramontes** [SAN MATEO] (1); **Pilarcitos Creek** [SAN MATEO].

Arroyo de los Poblanos: see **Marsh Creek** [CONTRA COSTA].

Arroyo de los Taunamines: see **Arroyo Valle** [ALAMEDA-SANTA CLARA].

Arroyo del Pescadero: see **Pescadero Creek** [SAN MATEO].

Arroyo del Puetro: see **Lobos Creek** [SAN FRANCISCO].

Arroyo del Sanjon: see **Sausal Creek** [SAN MATEO].

Arroyo de Lucia: see **Año Nuevo Creek** [SAN MATEO].

Arroyo del Valle: see **Arroyo Valle** [ALAMEDA-SANTA CLARA].

Arroyo del Viaje: see **Arroyo Valle** [ALAMEDA-SANTA CLARA].

Arroyo de Matadera: see **Matadero Creek** [SANTA CLARA].

Arroyo de Monte Verde: see **Higgins Canyon** [SAN MATEO].

Arroyo de Nuestra Señora de los Dolores: see **Mission District** [SAN FRANCISCO].

Arroyo de Pescadero: see **Pescadero Creek** [SANTA CLARA].

Arroyo de San Antonio: see **San Antonio Creek** [MARIN].

Arroyo de San Bruno: see **Colma Creek** [SAN MATEO].

Arroyo de San Felipe: see **Pacheco Creek** [SANTA CLARA].

Arroyo de San Francisco: see **San Francisquito Creek** [SAN MATEO-SANTA CLARA].

Arroyo de San Francisquito: see **San Francisquito Creek** [SAN MATEO-SANTA CLARA].

Arroyo de San Geronimo: see **Lagunitas Creek** [MARIN].

Arroyo de San Gregorio: see **San Gregorio Creek** [SAN MATEO].

Arroyo de San Jose Cupertino: see **Stevens Creek** [SANTA CLARA].

Arroyo de San Leandro: see **San Leandro Creek** [ALAMEDA-CONTRA COSTA].

Arroyo de San Matheo: see **San Mateo Creek** [SAN MATEO].

Arroyo de San Pedro: see **San Pedro Creek** [SAN MATEO].

Arroyo de San Salvador de Horta: see **San Lorenzo Creek** [ALAMEDA].

Arroyo de San Simon y San Judas: see **Pilarcitos Creek** [SAN MATEO].

Arroyo de Santa Toma Aquino: see **San Tomas Aquinas Creek** [SANTA CLARA].

Arroyo de San Vicente: see **San Vicente Creek** [SAN MATEO].

Arroyo de Soto: see **Whitehouse Creek** [SAN MATEO].

Arroyo Diablo: see **Belmont Creek** [SAN MATEO].

Arroyo Holon: see **Larkspur Creek** [MARIN].

Arroyo Hondo [SANTA CLARA]: *stream,* formed by the confluence of Isabel Creek and Smith Creek, flows 9 miles to Calaveras Reservoir 11 miles northeast of downtown San Jose (lat. 37°27'50" N, long. 121°46'30" W; sec. 29, T 5 S, R 2 E). Named on Calaveras Reservoir (1961) and Mount Day (1955) 7.5' quadrangles.

Arroyo Hondo: see **La Honda Creek** [SAN MATEO].

Arroyo las Positas [ALAMEDA]: *stream,* flows 14 miles to Arroyo Mocho 5 miles west of Livermore (lat. 37°41'40" N, long. 121°51'30" W). Named on Tesla (1907) 15' quadrangle, and on Livermore (1961) 7.5' quadrangle. The stream is called Posita Creek on Land Office maps of the 1850's, and it is called Las Posita Creek on a map of 1873 (Gudde, 1949, p. 270).

Arroyo Leon [SAN MATEO]: *stream,* flows 6.25 miles to Pilarcitos Creek near downtown Half Moon Bay (lat. 37°27'55" N, long. 122°25'30" W). Named on Half Moon Bay (1961) and Woodside (1961) 7.5' quadrangles. Called Leon Creek on Halfmoon Bay (1940) 15' quadrangle. The name commemorates Francisco de Leon, a Chilenian who settled by the stream in the 1850's (Brown, p. 47).

Arroyo Limpio: see **Clear Creek** [SAN MATEO].

Arroyo Mocho [ALAMEDA-SANTA CLARA]: *stream,* heads in Santa Clara County and flows 34 miles to Arroyo de la Laguna 2.25 miles southeast of Dublin in Alameda County (lat. 37°40'40" N, long. 121°54'40" W); the stream heads near Mount

Mocho. Named on Altamont (1953), Cedar Mountain (1956), Dublin (1961), Eylar Mountain (1955), Livermore (1961), and Mendenhall Springs (1956) 7.5' quadrangles. Gudde (1949, p. 218) noted use of the name "Mocho Creek" as early as 1852, and attributed the name to disappearance of the water after the stream forms distributaries—*arroyo mocho* means "cut-off creek" in Spanish.

Arroyo Nicasio: see **Nicasio Creek** [MARIN].

Arroyo Ojo de Agua [SAN MATEO]: *stream,* flows 2 miles to lowlands 1.5 miles south-southwest of downtown Redwood City (lat. 37°27'45" N, long. 122°14'15" W). Named on Palo Alto (1961) and Woodside (1961) 7.5' quadrangles. The name is from a lake called el Ojo de Agua that was near the feature; the stream, or its canyon, also was called Deer Creek, Hawes Gulch—for Horace Hawes, who had a ranch along the stream in the late 1850's, and Schroeder Gulch—for J.B. Schroeder, who lived near the mouth of the canyon in the 1880's (Brown, p. 86).

Arroyo Olemus Loke: see **Olema Creek** [MARIN].

Arroyo Permanente: see **Permanente Creek** [SANTA CLARA].

Arroyo Quito: see **Saratoga Creek** [SANTA CLARA].

Arroyo Rodrigues: see **San Gregorio Creek** [SAN MATEO].

Arroyo Salinas: see **Redwood Creek** [SAN MATEO].

Arroyo San Antonio: see **Chileno Creek** [MARIN]; **Walker Creek** [MARIN].

Arroyo San Jose [MARIN]: *stream,* flows 4 miles to lowlands 3.25 miles south-southeast of downtown Novato at Ignacio (lat. 38°04'05" N, long. 122°32'15" W); the stream is on San Jose grant. Named on Novato (1954) 7.5' quadrangle.

Arroyo San Tomas Aquino: see **San Tomas Aquinas Creek** [SANTA CLARA].

Arroyo Sausal [MARIN]: *stream,* flows 11 miles to join Salmon Creek and form Walker Creek 9 miles southeast of Tomales (lat. 38°09'40" N, long. 122°46'50" W). Named on Petaluma (1953), Point Reyes NE (1954), and San Geronimo (1954) 7.5' quadrangles.

Arroyo Sausal: see **Sausal Creek** [SAN MATEO]; **Walker Creek** [MARIN].

Arroyo Seco [ALAMEDA]: *stream,* flows 7.25 miles to Livermore Valley 5.25 miles south-southwest of Altamont (lat. 37°40'30" N, long. 121°42'04" W; sec. 13, T 3 S, R 2 E). Named on Altamont (1953) and Midway (1953) 7.5' quadrangles. Called Muddy Creek on Thompson and West's (1878) map. The feature was known as Coal Mine Creek in the early 1870's, and also was called Bangs Creek, for Joseph L. Bangs, a local resident (Mosier and Mosier, p. 12). Thomas Harris and Jenkin Richards discovered coal in the canyon of Arroyo Seco 7 miles southeast of Livermore in 1862; a community called Harrisville, for Thomas Harris, flourished there in the 1870's (Mosier, p. 5).

Arroyo Seco: see **Arroyo Calero** [SANTA CLARA].

Arroyo Seco de los Capitancillos: see **Los Capitancillos Creek** [SANTA CLARA].

Arroyo Valle [ALAMEDA-SANTA CLARA]: *stream,* formed by the confluence of Arroyo Bayo and San Antonio Creek in Santa Clara County, flows 24 miles to Arroyo de la Laguna 3.25 miles south-southeast of Dublin in Alameda County (lat. 37°39'40" N, long. 121°54'20" W). Named on Cedar Mountain (1956), Dublin (1961), Eylar Mountain (1955), La Costa Valley (1960), Livermore (1961), and Mendenhall Springs (1956) 7.5' quadrangles. The name is from Valle de San Jose grant (Gudde, 1949, p. 376). Dall and Harris (p. 198) referred to "the Arroyo del Viaja, or Valle." United States Board on Geographic Names (1933, p. 104) rejected the name "Arroyo del Valle" for the feature. The stream first was called Arroyo de los Taunamines for an Indian tribe (Mosier and Mosier, p. 12).

Arroyo Viejo [ALAMEDA]: *stream,* flows 5 miles to Lion Creek 5 miles southeast of downtown Oakland (lat. 37°45'15" N, long. 122° 12' W). Named on Oakland East (1959) 7.5' quadrangle.

Arthur Creek: see **Little Arthur Creek** [SANTA CLARA].

Artist Point [CONTRA COSTA]: *peak,* 2.5 miles south-southwest of Mount Diablo (lat. 37°50'55" N, long. 121°56' W; near E line sec. 14, T 1 S, R 1 W). Named on Diablo (1953) 7.5' quadrangle.

Asco [ALAMEDA]: *locality,* nearly 6 miles west of Livermore along Southern Pacific Railroad (lat. 37°41' N, long. 121°52'20" W). Named on Livermore (1961) 7.5' quadrangle. The name is from <u>A</u>lameda <u>S</u>ugar <u>Co</u>mpany, which raised sugar beets and other crops at the place from 1899 until 1917 (Mosier and Mosier, p. 12).

Ashland [ALAMEDA]: *town,* 2.5 miles northwest of downtown Hayward (lat. 37°41'40" N, long. 122°07' W). Named on Hayward (1959) 7.5' quadrangle. The place developed in the 1940's and was named for an Oregon ash tree growing there (Mosier and Mosier, p. 13).

Aspenwall Bay: see **Paradise Cay** [MARIN].

Associated: see **Avon** [CONTRA COSTA].

Atchison: see **Richmond** [CONTRA COSTA].

Atherton [SAN MATEO]: *town,* center 2 miles southeast of downtown Redwood City (lat. 37°27'45" N, long. 122°12' W). Named on Palo Alto (1961) 7.5' quadrangle. The place, which began as a community of estates around Fair Oaks railroad station, was known as Fair Oaks; the town incorporated in 1923 and took the name "Atherton" for Faxon Dean Atherton, whose estate was there (Brown, p.

3). Postal authorities established Atherton post office in 1947 (Salley, p. 11).

Atherton Peak [SANTA CLARA]: *peak,* 2 miles northwest of Pajaro Gap on Santa Clara-Santa Cruz county line (lat. 36°56'15" N, long. 121°38'50" W). Altitude 1616 feet. Named on Watsonville East (1955) 7.5' quadrangle.

Aurora Creek: see **Stemple Creek** [MARIN].

Ausaymas y San Felipe [SANTA CLARA]: *land grant,* 10 miles east of Gilroy; partly in San Benito County. Named on Gilroy Hot Springs (1955), Pacheco Peak (1955), San Felipe (1955), and Three Sisters (1954) 7.5' quadrangles. Francisco Perez Pacheco received 2 leagues in 1836 and claimed 35,504 acres patented in 1859 (Cowan, p. 17). According to Kroeber (p. 35), the term "Ausaymas" came from the name of Indians who lived near San Juan Bautista mission in San Benito County.

Austin [SANTA CLARA]: *locality,* 1.5 miles northwest of Los Gatos (lat. 37°14'30" N, long. 121°59'50" W). Named on Los Gatos (1919) 15' quadrangle.

Austin: see **Melrose** [ALAMEDA].

Austin Creek [SOLANO]: *stream,* flows 1.25 miles to Napa River 2 miles north-northwest of downtown Vallejo (lat. 38°07'40" N, long. 122°16'20" W). Named on Mare Island (1959) 7.5' quadrangle.

Austrian Gulch [SANTA CLARA]: *canyon,* drained by a stream that flows 2 miles to Lake Elsman 2.25 miles southwest of Mount Umunhum (lat. 37°08'05" N, long. 121°55'20" W; sec. 24, T 9 S, R 1 W). Named on Los Gatos (1953) 7.5' quadrangle. The name commemorates a group of Austro-Germans who settled in the canyon in the 1870's (Hoover, Rensch, and Rensch, p. 457). Water of Lake Elsman now covers the sites of communities called Austrian Gulch and Germantown, built by the settlers (Young, p. 63).

Avalis Beach [MARIN]: *beach,* 4.25 miles west-southwest of Tomales Point at the mouth of Tomales Bay (lat. 38° 13'55" N, long. 122°58'50" W). Named on Tomales (1954) 7.5' quadrangle. The name commemorates an Indian (Mason, 1976a, p. 149).

Avisadero Point: see **Point Avisadero** [SAN FRANCISCO].

Avon [CONTRA COSTA]: *locality,* 3.5 miles east-northeast of Martinez along Southern Pacific Railroad (lat. 38°02' N, long. 122°04'30" W). Named on Vine Hill (1959) 7.5' quadrangle, which also has the name "Associated P.O." at the place. Postal authorities established Marsh post office in 1912, changed the name to Associated in 1913, and discontinued it in 1960; the name "Marsh" was for John Marsh, a pioneer in the region, and the name "Associated" was for Tidewater Associated Oil Company, which owned the site (Salley, p. 11, 134).

Ayala Cove: see **Hospital Cove** [MARIN].

Azule Springs [SANTA CLARA]: *locality,* 1.5 miles west-northwest of Saratoga along Calabazas Creek (lat. 37°15'50" N, long. 122°03'25" W; sec. 2, T 8 S, R 2 W). Named on Palo Alto (1899) 15' quadrangle. Arthur S. Caldwell discovered a soda spring at the site in the early 1850's; the spring was called Caldwell Springs before L.R. Mills bought the property (Cunningham, p. 79). The place was called Mills Seltzer Spring until it received the name "Azule" from the blue appearance of the range to the southwest—*azule* means "blue" in Spanish; the owner sold bottled water and developed the property as a picnic resort (Waring, p. 212-213). Cunningham (p. 80-81) noted that a popular resort called Idlewild was started in the 1870's on the ridge above Azule Springs

– B –

Babb Creek [SANTA CLARA]: *stream,* flows 2.5 miles to lowlands 3 miles east-southeast of Berryessa (lat. 37°22'10" N, long. 121°48'45" W). Named on San Jose East (1961) 7.5' quadrangle.

Babb Creek: see **South Babb Creek** [SANTA CLARA].

Babbs Canyon [SANTA CLARA]: *canyon,* drained by a stream that flows 1 mile to lowlands nearly 2 miles southwest of Gilroy (lat. 36°59' N, long. 121°35'10" W). Named on Chittenden (1955) 7.5' quadrangle.

Baby Peak [SANTA CLARA]: *peak,* 3.5 miles north-northeast of Mount Day (lat. 37°27'45" N, long. 121°39'50" W; at SE cor. sec. 29, T 5 S, R 3 E). Altitude 2766 feet. Named on Mount Day (1955) 7.5' quadrangle.

Bache: see **Mount Bache**, under **Loma Prieta** [SANTA CLARA].

Back Creek [CONTRA COSTA]: *stream,* flows 2 miles to Donner Creek 3 miles north-northwest of Mount Diablo (lat. 37°55'20" N, long. 121°55'35" W; sec. 24, T 1 N, R 1 W). Named on Clayton (1953) 7.5' quadrangle.

Baden: see **South San Francisco** [SAN MATEO].

Baden Creek: see **Twelvemile Creek** [SAN MATEO].

Baden Station [SAN MATEO]: *locality,* 1 mile west of present downtown South San Francisco along Southern Pacific Railroad (lat. 37°39'15" N, long. 122°26' W). Named on San Mateo (1915) 15' quadrangle. Postal authorities established Baden Station post office in 1895 and discontinued it in 1897 (Salley, p. 13).

Bahia [SOLANO]: *locality,* 4.25 miles northeast of Benicia along Southern Pacific Railroad (lat. 38°05'45" N, long. 122°06'10" W). Named on Vine Hill (1959) 7.5' quadrangle. Called Goodyear on Karquines (1898) 15' quadrangle, and called Benicia Junction on

Carquinez (1938) 15' quadrangle. Postal authorities established Goodyear post office in 1907 and discontinued it in 1912; the name was for the operator of a boat landing near the place (Salley, p. 87).

Bahia de Nuestra Señora del Rosario la Marinera: see **San Rafael Bay** [MARIN].

Bahia de San Francisco: see **Drakes Bay** [MARIN].

Bahia de San Pablo: see **San Pablo Bay** [CONTRA COSTA-MARIN-SOLANO].

Bahia de Sonoma: see **San Pablo Bay** [CONTRA COSTA-MARIN-SOLANO].

Bahia Redondo: see **San Pablo Bay** [CONTRA COSTA-MARIN-SOLANO].

Bair Island [SAN MATEO]: *island,* 2.5 miles long, 3.25 miles north of downtown Redwood City along San Francisco Bay (lat. 37°31'50" N, long. 122°13'15" W). Named on Redwood Point (1959) 7.5' quadrangle.

Baker: see **Fort Baker Military Reservation** [MARIN].

Baker Beach [SAN FRANCISCO]: *beach,* 1.25 miles south-southwest of Fort Point along the coast (lat. 37°47'40" N, long. 122°28'55" W). Named on San Francisco North (1956, photorevised 1968 and 1973) 7.5' quadrangle. Called Bakers Beach on San Francisco North (1956) 7.5' quadrangle, but United States Board on Geographic Names (1976a, p. 1) gave this name as a variant. The name commemorates the Baker family, who had a dairy ranch near the beach in the 1860's (Gudde, 1949, p. 20). United States Board on Geographic Names (1979b, p. 5) approved the name "China Beach" for the next beach along the coast southwest of Baker Beach.

Baker Creek: see **Langley Creek** [SAN MATEO].

Bakers Beach: see **Baker Beach** [SAN FRANCISCO].

Baker's Landing: see **Warm Springs Landing**, under **Mud Slough** [ALAMEDA].

Bald Hill [MARIN]: *ridge,* south-southwest-trending, 0.5 mile long, nearly 3 miles west-southwest of downtown San Rafael (lat. 37°57'55" N, long. 122°34'50" W). Named on San Rafael (1954) 7.5' quadrangle.

Bald Knob [SAN MATEO]: *peak,* 3 miles west-northwest of Skeggs Point (lat. 37°25'25" N, long. 122°21'10" W). Altitude 2102 feet. Named on Woodside (1961) 7.5' quadrangle. Brown (p. 4) gave the name "Bald Mountain" as an alternate.

Bald Mountain [SANTA CLARA]: *peak,* 3 miles west-southwest of New Almaden (lat. 37°09'35" N, long. 121°52' W; sec. 9, T 9 S, R 1 E). Altitude 2387 feet. Named on Santa Teresa Hills (1953) 7.5' quadrangle.

Bald Mountain: see **Bald Knob** [SAN MATEO].

Bald Pate: see **Ox Hill** [SAN MATEO].

Bald Peak: see **Volimer Peak** [CONTRA COSTA].

Bald Peaks [SANTA CLARA]: *ridge,* east- to east-northeast-trending, 1 mile long, 2 miles southeast of New Almaden (lat. 37°09'30" N, long. 121°47'40" W). Named on Santa Teresa Hills (1953) 7.5' quadrangle.

Bald Ridge [CONTRA COSTA]: *ridge,* west-northwest-trending, 1 mile long, center 1 mile northwest of Mount Diablo (lat. 37°53'35" N, long 121°55'30" W). Named on Clayton (1953) 7.5' quadrangle.

Bald Ridge: see **Buri Buri Ridge** [SAN MATEO]; **Cahill Ridge** [SAN MATEO].

Baldy Ryan [SANTA CLARA]: *canyon,* drained by a stream that flows 2.5 miles to Llagas Creek 3.5 miles southeast of New Almaden (lat. 37°08'55" N, long. 121°46'15" W). Named on Santa Teresa Hills (1953) 7.5' quadrangle. Called Longwall Canyon on Los Gatos (1919) 15' quadrangle.

Ballenas: see **Bolinas** [MARIN].

Ballenas Bay: see **Bolinas Bay** [MARIN].

Baltimore Canyon [MARIN]: *canyon,* 2 miles long, along Larkspur Creek above a point 3 miles south of downtown San Rafael (lat. 37°55'50" N, long. 122°32'10" W). Named on San Rafael (1954) 7.5' quadrangle. Hoover, Rensch, and Rensch (p. 186) called the feature Baltimore Gulch, and noted that the name is from Baltimore and Frederick Trading Company, which sent a group of men to the region in 1849 to erect a sawmill on Corte de Madera grant.

Baltimore Gulch: see **Baltimore Canyon** [MARIN].

Baltimore Park [MARIN]: *locality,* 3 miles south of downtown San Rafael (lat. 37°55'50" N, long. 122°31'50" W); the place is near the mouth of Baltimore Canyon. Named on San Rafael (1954) 7.5' quadrangle.

Bancroft [CONTRA COSTA]: *locality,* 2.25 miles north-northeast of Walnut Creek civic center along Sacramento Northern Railroad (lat. 37°56'05" N, long. 122°02'45" W). Named on Walnut Creek (1959) 7.5' quadrangle. Concord (1915) 15' quadrangle has the name "Hookston" along Oakland Antioch and Eastern Railroad at present Bancroft, as well as at present Hookston.

Bangs Creek: see **Arroyo Seco** [ALAMEDA].

Bank Mills: see **Saratoga** [SANTA CLARA].

Banks of Braes: see **Los Altos** [SANTA CLARA].

Banta Spring [SANTA CLARA]: *spring,* 10.5 miles north-northeast of Mount Hamilton (lat. 37°28'30" N, long. 121°32'40" W; sec. 28, T 5 S, R 4 E). Named on Eylar Mountain (1955) 7.5' quadrangle.

Bar Channel [SAN FRANCISCO]: *channel,* southeast of Yerba Buena Island in San Francisco Bay (lat. 37°48'10" N, long. 122°21'15" W). Named on Oakland West (1959) 7.5' quadrangle. The feature leads to the entrance channels for harbors in Alameda County.

Barker Slough [SOLANO]: *water feature,* joins Lindsey Slough 10 miles southwest of Elmira (lat. 38°15'40" N, long. 121°46'15" W). Named on Dozier (1952) 7.5' quadrangle.

Barnabe Creek [MARIN]: *stream,* flows 0.5 mile to Lagunita Creek 10.5 miles southwest of downtown Novato (lat. 38°01'10" N, long. 122°43'30" W); the stream heads at Bernabe Mountain. Named on San Geronimo (1954) 7.5' quadrangle.

Barnabe Mountain [MARIN]: *peak,* 10 miles southwest of downtown Novato (lat. 38°01'40" N, long. 122°42'55" W). Altitude 1466 feet. Named on San Geronimo (1954) 7.5' quadrangle. The peak was named for Barnabe, a white mule that grazed there (Teather, p. 6).

Barret Canyon [SANTA CLARA]: *canyon,* drained by a stream that flows nearly 3.5 miles to Alamitos Creek 2 miles southwest of New Almaden (lat. 37°09'20" N, long. 121°50'35" W). Named on Loma Prieta (1955) and Santa Teresa Hills (1953) 7.5' quadrangles. Called Berrocal Canyon on Los Gatos (1919) 15' quadrangle.

Barrett [CONTRA COSTA]: *locality,* 0.5 mile west of present Richmond civic center along Southern Pacific Railroad (lat. 37°56'15" N, long. 122°21'20" W). Named on San Francisco (1899) 15' quadrangle.

Barries Bay [MARIN]: *bay,* opens into Drakes Estero 5.25 miles northeast of the lighthouse at Point Reyes (lat. 38°02'50" N, long. 122°56'55" W). Named on Drakes Bay (1953) 7.5' quadrangle.

Barron Creek [SANTA CLARA]: *stream,* flows 5.25 miles to flatlands near San Francisco Bay 3.5 miles north-northwest of downtown Mountain View (lat. 37°26' N, long. 122°06'30" W). Named on Mountain View (1961) and Palo Alto (1961) 7.5' quadrangles. Called Dry Creek on Mountain View (1953) 7.5' quadrangle. The stream passes through Barron Park, a residential and commercial development named for Edward Barron, a retired stock dealer and mine operator who came to the place in 1878 (Hoover, Rensch, and Rensch, p. 462).

Barron Park: see **Barron Creek** [SANTA CLARA].

Barron's Landing: see **Hayward Landing** [ALAMEDA]; **Mount Eden** [ALAMEDA].

Barry: see **Fort Barry Military Reservation** [MARIN].

Barths Creek [MARIN]: *stream,* flows 0.5 mile to Cataract Creek 6.25 miles southwest of downtown San Rafael (lat. 37°55'20" N, long. 122°37'55" W). Named on San Rafael (1954) 7.5' quadrangle. Teather (p. 7) associated the name with Emil Barth, who hiked and helped build trails in the neighborhood of Mount Tamalpais.

Barths Retreat [MARIN]: *locality,* nearly 6 miles southwest of downtown San Rafael (lat. 37°55'20" N, long. 122°36'55" W); the place is near the head of Barths Creek. Named on San Rafael (1954) 7.5' quadrangle.

Barton's Store: see **Suisun City** [SOLANO].

Barzilla: see **Pescadero** [SAN MATEO].

Basalt Creek [MARIN]: *stream,* 2 miles long, winds through lowlands 2 miles north-north-east of downtown Novato (lat. 38°08' N, long. 122°33'10" W). Named on Petaluma River (1954) 7.5' quadrangle.

Bascome: see **Meridian** [SANTA CLARA].

Bass Lake [MARIN]: *lake,* 1350 feet long, 1 mile east of Double Point (lat. 37°57'05" N, long. 122°45'50" W). Named on Double Point (1954) 7.5' quadrangle.

Batavia [SOLANO]: *locality,* 3.5 miles south-southwest of Dixon along Southern Pacific Railroad (lat. 38°24'25" N, long. 121°51'30" W; at W line sec. 34, T 7 N, R 1 E). Named on Dixon (1952) 7.5' quadrangle.

Batchelder Creek: see **Sinbad Creek** [ALAMEDA].

Bateria San Jose: see **Fort Mason Military Reservation** [SAN FRANCISCO].

Baulenas: see **Bolinas** [MARIN].

Baulenas Bay: see **Bolinas Bay** [MARIN].

Baumberg [ALAMEDA]: *locality,* 7 miles north-northwest of downtown Newark along Southern Pacific Railroad (lat. 37°37'10" N, long. 122°06' W). Named on Newark (1959) 7.5' quadrangle. South Pacific Coast Railroad established a station called Arff at the site in 1877—the name was for Frederic Danieh Arff, who settled at the place in 1856; officials of Southern Pacific Railroad changed the name to Baumberg after that company took over the line in 1887—the name Baumberg was from Baumberger's Salt Works, which was active in the 1880's and 1890's (Mosier and Mosier, p. 10, 14).

Bay Farm Island [ALAMEDA]: *area,* 3.5 miles west of downtown San Leandro along San Francisco Bay (lat. 37°44' N, long. 122°13'15" W). Named on Hunters Point (1956) and San Leandro (1959) 7.5' quadrangles. Haywards (1899) 15' quadrangle has the name for an island, 1.25 miles long, that is separated from shore by mud flats. The area now is largely filled land between the original island and shore, and is the site of Metropolitan Oakland International Airport. The place was called Bay Island in the 1870's, but this name was changed to Bay Farm Island in the 1880's, when farming began there (Mosier and Mosier, p. 14).

Bay Island: see **Bay Farm Island** [ALAMEDA].

Bay Junction: see **Almonte** [MARIN].

Bay of Napa: see **Mare Island Strait** [SOLANO].

Bay of Sir Francis Drake: see **Drakes Bay** [MARIN].

Bay of Suisun: see **Suisin Bay** [CONTRA COSTA-SOLANO].

Bayo Vista [CONTRA COSTA]: *district,* 6 miles east-northeast of Pinole Point in Rodeo (lat. 38°02'15" N, long. 122°15'30" W). Named on Mare Island (1959) 7.5' quadrangle.

Bay Point: see **Port Chicago** [CONTRA COSTA].

Bay Point Yacht Harbor [CONTRA COSTA]: *water feature,* 7 miles east-northeast of Martinez (lat. 38°03'15" N, long. 122°01' W). Named on Carquinez (1938) 15' quadrangle.

Bayshore [SAN MATEO]: *district,* 3.5 miles north of downtown South San Francisco in Visitacion Valley (lat. 37°42'20" N, long. 122°24'50" W). Named on San Francisco South (1956) 7.5' quadrangle. Diller and others' (1915) map has the form "Bay Shore" for the name of the railroad station at the place.

Bay Slough [SAN MATEO]: *water feature,* extends for 1 mile from Belmont Slough to San Francisco Bay 4.5 miles north of downtown Redwood City (lat. 37°32'55" N, long. 122°13'30" W). Named on Redwood Point (1959) 7.5' quadrangle. United States Board on Geographic Names (1961b, p. 8) rejected the names "Seal Creek," "The Cut," and "The Cutoff" for the feature.

Bayview District [SAN FRANCISCO]: *district,* 3.5 miles east of Mount Davidson near San Francisco Bay (lat. 37°44'15" N, long. 122°23'15" W). Named on San Francisco South (1956) 7.5' quadrangle.

Baywood [SAN MATEO]: *district,* 1 mile south-southwest of downtown San Mateo (lat. 37°33'15" N, long. 122°20' W). Named on San Mateo (1947) 7.5' quadrangle.

Bean Hollow: see **Arroyo de los Frijoles** [SAN MATEO].

Bean Hollow Beach [SAN MATEO]: *beach,* 3 miles north-northwest of Pigeon Point along the coast at the mouth of Arroyo de los Frijoles (lat. 37°13'30" N, long. 122°24'30" W). Named on Pigeon Point (1955) 7.5' quadrangle.

Bean Hollow Creek: see **Arroyo de los Frijoles** [SAN MATEO].

Bean Hollow Lagoon: see **Lake Lucerne** [SAN MATEO].

Bean Hollow Lake [SAN MATEO]: *lake,* 1.25 miles long, behind a dam on Arroyo de los Frijoles 2.5 miles north-northeast of Pigeon Point (lat. 37°12'55" N, long. 122°22'20" W). Named on Año Nuevo (1948) 15' quadrangle. The lake is named from the stream—*frijoles* means "kidney beans" in Spanish. Franklin Point (1955) 7.5' quadrangle shows a dam dividing the lake into two nearly equal parts called Upper Bean Hollow Lake and Lower Bean Hollow Lake—together they sometimes are called Hidden Valley Lakes from the name of a hunting club started there after the lakes formed in the early 1930's (Brown, p. 96).

Bear Creek [CONTRA COSTA]: *stream,* flows 6.25 miles to San Pablo Reservoir 2.5 miles northwest of Orinda (lat. 37°54'25" N, long. 122°12'50" W). Named on Briones Valley (1959) 7.5' quadrangle.

Bear Creek [SAN MATEO]:
(1) *stream,* flows 1.25 miles to Peters Creek 3 miles southeast of Mindego Hill (lat. 37°16'35" N, long. 122°11'55" W; sec. 33, T 7 S, R 3 W). Named on Mindego Hill (1961) 7.5' quadrangle.
(2) *stream,* flows 6.5 miles to San Francisquito Creek 5 miles south of downtown Redwood City (lat. 37°24'35" N, long. 122°14'15" W); the stream drains Bear Gulch. Named on Palo Alto (1961) and Woodside (1961) 7.5' quadrangles. Brown (p. 6) used the name "Bear Gulch Creek" for at least part of the stream, and noted that it also was called Coppinger Creek, for John Coppinger, who dammed the creek about 1840.
Bear Creek: see **Tarwater Creek** [SAN MATEO].
Beard Creek [ALAMEDA]: *water feature,* enters San Francisco Bay 4.25 miles west-south-west of downtown Newark (lat. 37°3030" N, long. 122°06'45" W). Named on Haywards (1899) 15' quadrangle. The name commemorates E.L. Beard, who settled near Mission San Jose about 1846 (Gudde, 1949, p. 26).
Beard's Slough: see **Newark Slough** [ALAMEDA].
Bear Gulch [ALAMEDA-SANTA CLARA]: *canyon,* drained by a stream that heads in Alameda County and flows 2.25 miles to Alameda Creek 4.5 miles north-northwest of Mount Day in Santa Clara County (lat. 37°28'50" N, long. 121°42'55" W; sec. 24, T 5 S, R 2 E). Named on Mount Day (1955) 7.5' quadrangle.
Bear Gulch [SAN MATEO]: *canyon,* 3.25 miles long, along Bear Creek (2) above a point 2 miles east-northeast of Skeggs Point (lat. 37°25' N, long. 122°16'05" W). Named on Woodside (1961) 7.5' quadrangle. The canyon first was called El Arroyo de la Presa for a dam that John Coppinger built there—*presa* means "dam" in Spanish; the feature received the name "Bear Gulch" after a bear mauled a man there (Stanger, 1967, p. 35).
Bear Gulch Creek: see **Bear Creek** [SAN MATEO] (2).
Bear Gulch Lake: see **Bear Gulch Reservoir** [SAN MATEO].
Bear Gulch Reservoir [SAN MATEO]: *lake,* 0.25 mile long, 3.5 miles south of downtown Redwood City (lat. 37°26' N, long. 122° 13'35" W). Named on Palo Alto (1961) 7.5' quadrangle. The name is from Bear Gulch Water Company, which piped water from Bear Gulch to the reservoir; the feature also was called Bear Gulch Lake, and before about 1900 it was called Corte Madera Lake (Brown, p. 6).
Bear Mountain [SANTA CLARA]: *peak,* 9 miles north-northeast of Gilroy Hot Springs on Santa Clara-Stanislaus county line (lat. 37° 13'55" N, long. 121°26'10" W; sec. 21, T 8 S, R 5 E). Altitude 2604 feet. Named on Mississippi Creek (1955) 7.5' quadrangle.

Bear Springs [SANTA CLARA]: *spring,* 1 mile south-southeast of Bear Mountain (lat. 37°13'05" N, long. 121°25'50" W; at N line sec. 28, R 8 S, R 5 E). Named on Mississippi Creek (1955) 7.5' quadrangle.
Bear Trap Ridge: see **Mitchell Ravine** [ALAMEDA].
Beartrap Ridge [ALAMEDA-SANTA CLARA]: *ridge,* east-northeast-trending, 2 miles long, 15 miles east-southeast of Sunol on Alameda-Santa Clara county line (lat. 37°29' N, long. 121°38' W). Named on Eylar Mountain (1955) and Mount Day (1955) 7.5' quadrangles.
Bear Valley [MARIN]: *canyons,* two; one canyon extends for 1.25 miles from near Olema to the top of Inverness Ridge 3.5 miles south of Point Reyes Station (lat. 38°01'10" N, long. 122°48' W); the second canyon extends for 2.5 miles from the head of the first to the sea 3.25 miles north-northwest of Double Point (lat. 37°59'10" N, long. 122°48'45" W). Named on Double Point (1954) and Inverness (1954) 7.5' quadrangles. The name is from bears that preyed on cattle in the vicinity in the early days (Gilliam, p. 86).
Beauregard Creek [SANTA CLARA]: *stream,* flows 6.5 miles to San Antonio Creek 5.5 miles northwest of Mount Stakes in San Antonio Valley (lat. 37°22'05" N, long. 121°29'15" W; sec. 36, T 6 S, R 4 E). Named on Mount Boardman (1955) and Mount Stakes (1955) 7.5' quadrangles. Thompson and West's (1876) map has the name "Beauregarde Cañon" along the stream.
Beauregarde Cañon: see **Beauregard Creek** [SANTA CLARA].
Beenar: see **Point Beenar** [CONTRA COSTA].
Beeners Channel: see **Middle Slough** [CONTRA COSTA].
Beldons Landing [SOLANO]: *locality,* 5 miles west-southwest of Denverton along Montezuma Slough (lat. 38°11'20" N, long. 121° 58'30" W; sec. 16, T 4 N, R 1 W). Named on Denverton (1953) 7.5' quadrangle. Pittsburg (1953) 15' quadrangle shows Grizzly Island Ferry at the site.
Belleair [SOLANO]: *locality,* 7 miles southeast of Dixon along Sacramento Northern Railroad (lat. 38°21'45" N, long. 121°44'50" W; near W line sec. 15, T 6 N, R 2 E). Named on Liberty Island (1952) 7.5' quadrangle.
Belle Monte [SAN MATEO]: *district,* 3.5 miles south-southeast of downtown San Mateo in Belmont (lat. 37°31'05" N, long. 122° 18' W). Named on San Mateo (1956) 7.5' quadrangle.
Bello Beach: see **Muir Beach** [MARIN].
Belloma Slough [CONTRA COSTA]: *water feature,* joins Suisun Bay 7 miles east-northeast of Martinez (lat. 38°03'25" N, long. 122°01'05" W). Named on Vine Hill (1959) 7.5' quadrangle.
Bello's Bend: see **Muir Beach** [MARIN].
Bell Station [SANTA CLARA]: *locality,* 15

miles east of Gilroy (lat. 37°02'10" N, long. 121°18'35" W). Named on Pacheco Peak (1955) 7.5' quadrangle. Called Bells Station on Gilroy Hot Springs (1921) 15' quadrangle. The place first was called Hollenbeck's Station (Latta, 1976, p. 212), but after Lafayette F. Bell bought the toll road over Pacheco Pass in the 1860's, the tavern near the toll gate became known as Bell's Station (Shumate, p. 3). Postal authorities established Bell's Station post office in 1873 and discontinued it in 1914 (Frickstad, p. 173).

Bellvale [SAN MATEO]: *village,* 2.25 miles west of La Honda along San Gregorio Creek (lat. 37°18'45" N, long. 122°18'45" W). Named on Santa Cruz (1902) 30' quadrangle. Postal authorities established Bellvale post office in 1897 and discontinued it in 1922 (Frickstad, p. 167).

Belmae Park: see **Lomita Park** [SAN MATEO].

Belmont [SAN MATEO]: *city,* 4.25 miles southeast of downtown San Mateo (lat. 37°31'05" N, long. 122°16'20" W). Named on San Mateo (1956) 7.5' quadrangle. Charles Aubrey Angelo opened a stage station called Angelo House in 1850 at the site of the present city (Hoover, Rensch, and Rensch, p. 406). The community that grew around Angelo House took the name "Belmont" from a beautiful hill nearby (Hynding, p. 123). Postal authorities established Belmont post office in 1854, discontinued it in 1856, and reestablished it in 1857 (Frickstad, p. 167). The city incorporated in 1926.

Belmont Channel [SAN MATEO]: *water feature,* joins Bay Slough 4.5 miles north-northwest of downtown Redwood City (lat. 37° 33' N, long. 122°14'30" W). Named on Redwood Point (1959) and San Mateo (1956) 7.5' quadrangles.

Belmont Creek [SAN MATEO]: *stream,* flows nearly 3 miles to lowlands along San Francisco Bay 4.5 miles southeast of downtown San Mateo in Belmont (lat. 37°31'05" N, long. 122°16'20" W). Named on San Mateo (1956) 7.5' quadrangle. The stream was called Arroyo Diablo in the 1850's, and the canyon of the stream called Cañada del Diablo; Spanish missionaries gave the name "cañada de San Agustin" to the feature in the 1780's (Brown, p. 7, 27).

Belmont Creek: see **Belmont Slough** [SAN MATEO].

Belmont Embarcadero Creek: see **Belmont Slough** [SAN MATEO].

Belmont Hill [SAN MATEO]: *peak,* 4.5 miles southeast of downtown San Mateo (lat. 37°30'35" N, long. 122°16'30" W); the peak is in Belmont. Named on San Mateo (1956) 7.5' quadrangle. The feature has had several names: Hull Hill, for William Hull's brickyard, established in 1858; Van Court's Hill, for Jimmie Van Court, who lived there in the

1870's; and Picnic Hill, for a picnic ground at the base of the peak in the 1870's and 1880's (Brown, p. 7).

Belmont Landing: see **North Belmont Landing**, under **Belmont Slough** [SAN MATEO].

Belmont Slough [SAN MATEO]: *water feature,* enters San Francisco Bay 5 miles north of downtown Redwood City (lat. 37°33'15" N, long. 122°14'35" W). Named on Redwood Point (1959) and San Mateo (1956) 7.5' quadrangles. United States Board on Geographic Names (1961b, p. 8) rejected the names "Angelo Creek" and "Belmont Creek" for the feature. According to Brown (p. 7), it first was called Angelo's Creek, for Charles Aubrey Angelo of Angelo House, and later it was called Belmont Embarcadero Creek for a landing at its head. California Division of Highways (1934) map shows a place called North Belmont Landing located at the mouth of Belmont Slough.

Belvedere [MARIN]: *town,* 1.5 miles northeast of downtown Sausalito across Richardson Bay (lat. 37°52'30" N, long. 122°28' W); the town is on Belvedere Island. Named on San Francisco North (1956) and San Quentin (1959) 7.5' quadrangles. Postal authorities established Belvedere post office in 1897 (Frickstad, p. 87), and the town incorporated in 1896.

Belvedere Cove [MARIN]: *embayment,* 1.5 miles east-northeast of downtown Sausalito off Raccoon Strait (lat. 38°52'15" N, long. 122°27'30" W); the feature is at Belvedere. Named on San Francisco North (1956) 7.5' quadrangle. Called Ensenada del Santo Evangelio on a map of 1775; about 1880 the place sometimes was called Stillwater Bay (Teather, p. 8).

Belvedere Island [MARIN]: *island,* 1.5 miles long, 1.25 miles northeast of downtown Sausalito across the mouth of Richardson Bay (lat. 37°52'15" N, long. 122°27'55" W). Named on San Francisco North (1956, photorevised 1968 and 1973) and San Quentin (1959) 7.5' quadrangles. The island was called El Potrero de la Punta del Tiburon in the early days, and later it was called Kashow's Island, for Israel Kashow and his family, who lived there; the feature also was known as Peninsula Island, Promontory Island, and Still Island (Teather, p. 7-8).

Belvedere Lagoon [MARIN]: *water feature,* 4.5 miles south of Point San Quentin (lat. 37°52'40" N, long. 122°28' W); the feature is at Belvedere. Named on San Quentin (1959) 7.5' quadrangle.

Benecia: see **Benicia** [SOLANO].

Benicia [SOLANO]: *town,* 15 miles south-southwest of Fairfield along Carquinez Strait (near lat. 38°03' N, long. 122°09'30" W). Named on Benicia (1959) 7.5' quadrangle. United States Board on Geographic Names (1933, p. 136) rejected the form "Benecia" for the name. Postal authorities established Benicia post office in 1849 (Frickstad, p. 191), and the town incorporated in 1850. Robert Semple laid out the community in 1847 on land that had belonged to Mariano Guadalupe Vallejo, and gave it the name "Francisca" for Vallejo's wife; when the name of the rival town of Yerba Buena was changed to San Francisco, the name "Francisca" was changed to Benicia, another of Mrs. Vallejo's names (Hoover, Rensch, and Rensch, p. 514) United States Board on Geographic Names (1984a, p. 3) approved the name "Port of Benicia" for the waterfront of Carquinez Strait between Benicia Point and Army Point (lat. 38°02'33" N, long. 122°08' W; sec. 1, T 2 N, R 3 W, and sec. 6, T 2 N, R 2 W). Postal authorities established Dalton Manor post office as a station of Benicia post office in 1944 and discontinued it in 1954; the name was from a real-estate development (Salley, p. 55).

Benicia Junction: see **Bahia** [SOLANO].

Benicia Point [SOLANO]: *promontory,* along Carquinez Strait at Benicia (lat. 38°02'40" N, long. 122°09'40" W). Named on Benicia (1959) 7.5' quadrangle. Ringgold's (1850c) map shows Seal I. off present Benicia Point, and Ringgold (p. 36) mentioned Seal isle.

Benicia Shoals [SOLANO]: *shoal,* 0.25 mile south-southeast of Benicia Point in Carquinez Strait (lat. 38°02'20" N, long. 122°09'35" W). Named on Benicia (1959) 7.5' quadrangle. Called Three fathom Shoal on Ringgold's (1850c) map. Officials of United States Bureau of Lighthouses applied the name "Benicia" to the shoal (Gudde, 1949, p. 28).

Bennett Tract [SANTA CLARA]: *land grant,* 1.5 miles west-southwest of downtown Santa Clara. Named on San Jose West (1961) 7.5' quadrangle. Narciso Bennett received two tracts, one of 1000 varas and the other of 2000 varas, in 1845; Mary S. Bennett claimed 359 acres patented in 1871 (Cowan, p. 92; Cowan listed the grant under the name "Solar en Santa Clara").

Beresford: see **Hillsdale** [SAN MATEO].

Berkeley [ALAMEDA]: *city,* 4.5 miles north of downtown Oakland (lat. 37°52'10" N, long. 122°16'20" W). Named on Briones Valley (1959), Oakland East (1959), Oakland West (1959), and Richmond (1959) 7.5' quadrangles. Postal authorities established Berkeley post office in 1872 (Salley, p. 19), and the city incorporated in 1878. The place was chosen as the site of the new state university and named in 1866 for George Berkeley, Bishop of Cloyne—Frederick Billings proposed the name (Gudde, 1949, p. 29).

Berkeley: see **North Berkeley** [ALAMEDA]; **South Berkeley**, under **Lorin** [ALAMEDA]; **West Berkeley** [ALAMEDA].

Berkeley Hills [ALAMEDA-CONTRA COSTA]: *range,* first range east of San Francisco Bay on Alameda-Contra Costa county line. Named on Briones Valley (1959), Oak-

land East (1959), and Richmond (1959) 7.5' quadrangles. The feature is part of what was known in the early days as Contra Costa Hills (Diller and others, p. 83).

Berkeley Yacht Harbor [ALAMEDA]: *water feature,* 5 miles northwest of downtown Oakland along the Berkeley water front (lat. 37° 52' N, long. 122°18'45" W). Named on Oakland West (1959) 7.5' quadrangle.

Bernal Heights [SAN FRANCISCO]: *ridge,* east-trending, 0.5 mile long, 2.25 miles east of Mount Davidson (lat. 37°44'35" N, long. 122°24'45" W); the ridge is on Rincon de las Salinas y Potrero Viejo grant, which belonged to the Bernal family. Named on San Francisco South (1956) 7.5' quadrangle.

Bernards Landing: see **Jagel Landing** [SANTA CLARA].

Berreyesa: see **Berryessa** [SANTA CLARA].

Berrocal Canyon: see **Barret Canyon** [SANTA CLARA].

Berry Creek [SAN MATEO]: *stream,* flows less than 0.5 mile to Santa Cruz County 6 miles east-northeast of Franklin Point (lat. 37°11'25" N, long. 122°15'35" W; at SE cor. sec. 35, T 8 S, R 4 W). Named on Franklin Point (1955) 7.5' quadrangle. T.G. Berry homesteaded along the stream in 1878 (Brown, p. 7).

Berryessa [SANTA CLARA]: *settlement,* 2 miles west-southwest of the mouth of Alum Rock Canyon (lat. 37°23'10" N, long. 121°51'35" W). Named on Calaveras Reservoir (1961) 7.5' quadrangle. Postal authorities established Berryessa post office in 1889, discontinued it in 1904, and reestablished it in 1976 (Salley, p. 20). The name commemorates Nicolas Berryessa, who claimed land at the place (Rambo, 1973, p. 39). United States Board on Geographic Names (1901, p. 33) rejected the forms "Berreyesa," "Berryesa," and "Beryessa" for the name.

Berryessa Creek [SANTA CLARA]: *stream,* flows 5 miles to lowlands 2.25 miles north of Berryessa (lat. 37°25'10" N, long. 121° 51'15" W). Named on Calaveras Reservoir (1961) 7.5' quadrangle. Called Milpitas Creek on Hare's (1872) map.

Berryessa Siding [SANTA CLARA]: *locality,* 1 mile west of Berryessa along Western Pacific Railroad (lat. 37°23'15" N, long. 121° 52'50" W). Named on Milpitas (1961) 7.5' quadrangle.

Berryman: see **North Berkeley** [ALAMEDA].

Berryman Reservoir [ALAMEDA]: *lake,* 600 feet long, 5.5 miles north of downtown Oakland (lat. 37°53'05" N, long. 122°15'40" W). Named on Richmond (1959) 7.5' quadrangle. The name is for Henry Burpee Berryman, who built the lake in 1884 (Mosier and Mosier, p. 15-16).

Beryessa: see **Berryessa** [SANTA CLARA].

Bessie: see **Camp Bessie** [SANTA CLARA].

Betabel [SANTA CLARA]: *locality,* 7.25 miles south of Gilroy along Southern Pacific Railroad (lat. 36°53'50" N, long. 121°33'45" W). Named on San Juan Bautista (1917) 15' quadrangle.

Bethany Reservoir [ALAMEDA]: *lake,* 1.5 miles long, 11 miles northeast of Livermore along California Aqueduct (lat. 37°46'45" N, long. 121°36'30" W). Named on Clifton Court Forebay (1978) 7.5' quadrangle. The reservoir was built in the 1960's and named for the town of Bethany, located in San Joaquin County (Mosier and Mosier, p. 16).

Bethel Island [CONTRA COSTA]:

(1) *island,* 4 miles long, 8 miles east of Antioch between Piper Slough, Sand Mound Slough, Dutch Slough, and Taylor Slough (lat. 38°01'45" N, long. 121°38'30" W). Named on Bouldin Island (1978) and Jersey Island (1978) 7.5' quadrangles. Called Bethel Tract on Bouldin Island (1952) and Jersey Island (1952) 7.5' quadrangles, but United States Board on Geographic Names (1977, p. 3) approved the designation "Bethel Island" for the feature.

(2) *settlement,* about 9 miles east of Antioch (lat. 38°00'50" N, long. 121°38'20" W); the place is on Bethel Island (1). Named on Jersey Island (1978) 7.5' quadrangle. Bethell post office, named for Franklin C. Bethell, first postmaster, was established in 1897, discontinued in 1902, and reestablished with the name "Bethel Island" in 1947 (Salley, p. 20).

Bethell: see **Bethel Island** [CONTRA COSTA] (2).

Bethel Tract: see **Bethel Island** [CONTRA COSTA] (1).

Bethlehem: see **Agnew** [SANTA CLARA].

Beulah Heights: see **Oakland** [ALAMEDA].

Bielawski Mountain [SANTA CLARA]: *peak,* 4.5 miles southwest of Saratoga on Santa Clara-Santa Cruz county line (lat. 37°13'25" N, long. 122°05'30" W; sec. 21, T 8 S, R 2 W). Altitude 3231 feet. Named on Castle Rock Ridge (1955) 7.5' quadrangle. Whitney (p. 70) gave the name "Mount Bielawski" to the peak to honor C. Bielawski, chief draughtsman of the Surveyor-General's Office. United States Board on Geographic Names (1960b, p. 16) approved this name for the feature, and rejected the names "Bielawski Mountain," "Bielwaski Mountain," and "Mount McPherson."

Big Break [CONTRA COSTA]: *bay,* 4 miles west of the settlement of Bethel Island off San Joaquin River (lat. 38°01' N, long. 121°42'30" W). Named on Jersey Island (1978) 7.5' quadrangle.

Big Bull Valley [CONTRA COSTA]: *canyon,* 1.5 miles long, 3.5 miles west-northwest of Martinez (lat. 38°02'25" N, long. 122°11'30" W); the canyon is 0.5 mile northwest of Little Bull Valley. Named on Benicia (1959) 7.5' quadrangle.

Big Canyon [CONTRA COSTA]: *canyon,* drained by a stream that flows 2.5 miles to lowlands 7.5 miles south-southeast of Danville (lat. 37°43'20" N, long. 121°56'40" W). Named on Dublin (1961) 7.5' quadrangle.

Big Canyon [SANTA CLARA]: *canyon,* formed by the junction of Rough Gulch and Little Rough Gulch, drained by a stream that flows nearly 1 mile to Coyote Creek 2.25 miles south-southeast of Manzanita Point (lat. 37°08'35" N, long. 121°29'10" W; near NW cor. sec. 24, T 9 S, R 4 E). Named on Mississippi Creek (1955) 7.5' quadrangle.

Big Carson Creek [MARIN]: *stream,* flows 1.5 miles to Kent Lake 5.5 miles north of Bolinas (lat. 37°59'30" N, long. 122°40'30" W). Named on Bolinas (1954) 7.5' quadrangle.

Big Chicken Hollow [SAN MATEO]: *canyon,* 1 mile long, 4.5 miles southwest of La Honda on the upper reaches of Honsinger Creek (lat. 37°16'50" N, long. 122°20'15" W); the canyon is south of Little Chicken Hollow. Named on La Honda (1961) 7.5' quadrangle.

Big Coyote: see **Tamalpais**, under **Mill Valley** [MARIN] (2); **The Big Coyote**, under **Coyote Point** [SAN MATEO].

Big Coyote Hill: see **Coyote Point** [SAN MATEO].

Big Coyote Point: see **Coyote Point** [SAN MATEO].

Big Creek Artesian Slough: see **Coyote Creek** [ALAMEDA-SANTA CLARA].

Big Ditch: see **The Big Ditch** [SOLANO].

Big Gulch: see **Año Nuevo Creek** [SAN MATEO].

Big Lagoon [MARIN]: *intermittent lake,* 1100 feet long, 4 miles northwest of Point Bonita near the mouth of Redwood Creek (lat. 37°51'35" N, long. 122°34'30" W). Named on Point Bonita (1954) 7.5' quadrangle.

Big Lagoon [SAN MATEO]: *lake,* 650 feet long, nearly 3 miles southwest of La Honda (lat. 37°17'35" N, long. 122°18'35" W; sec. 28, T 7 S, R 4 W); the lake is 650 feet southwest of Little Lagoon. Named on La Honda (1961) 7.5' quadrangle.

Big Moody Creek: see **Saratoga Creek** [SANTA CLARA].

Big Rock [MARIN]: *relief feature,* 5 miles southwest of downtown Novato (lat. 38°02'55" N, long. 122°37'15" W). Named on Novato (1954) 7.5' quadrangle.

Big Rock Ridge [MARIN]: *ridge,* west-north-west-trending, 5 miles long, 4 miles southsouthwest of downtown Novato (lat. 38°03'05" N, long. 122°36'15" W); the ridge is northeast of Big Rock. Named on Novato (1954) and San Geronimo (1954) 7.5' quadrangles.

Bills Hill [SANTA CLARA]: *peak,* nearly 5 miles south-southeast of Gilroy Hot Springs (lat. 37°02'45" N, long. 121°26'20" W; near SE cor. sec. 20, T 10 S, R 5 E). Altitude 1988 feet. Named on Gilroy Hot Springs (1955) 7.5' quadrangle.

Bill Williams Creek [MARIN]: *stream,* flows

1.25 miles to Phoenix Lake nearly 3 miles southwest of downtown San Rafael (lat. 37° 57' N, long. 122°34'20" W). Named on San Rafael (1954) 7.5' quadrangle.

Binghamton [SOLANO]: *locality,* 5 miles east of Elmira (lat. 38°21'05" N, long. 121°48'55" W; sec. 24, T 6 N, R 1 E). Named on Dozier (1952) 7.5' quadrangle. Postal authorities established Binghamton post office in 1864, discontinued it for a short time in 1874, and discontinued it finally in 1906; the place was named after Binghamton, New York (Salley, p. 22).

Bird Island [CONTRA COSTA]: *island,* 150 feet long, 3 miles south-southwest of Richmond civic center in San Francisco Bay (lat. 37° 53'45" N, long. 122°21'30" W). Named on Richmond (1959) 7.5' quadrangle.

Bird Island [MARIN]: *island,* 500 feet long, less than 1 mile northwest of Point Bonita, and 50 feet offshore (lat. 37°49'25" N, long. 122°32'10" W). Named on Point Bonita (1954) 7.5' quadrangle.

Bird Island: see **Alcatraz Island** [SAN FRANCISCO].

Bird Rock [MARIN]: *island,* 450 feet long, 5 miles west-southwest of Tomales, and 950 feet offshore west of Tomales Point (lat. 38° 13'50" N, long. 122°59'35" W). Named on Tomales (1954) 7.5' quadrangle.

Bird Rock: see **Arch Rock** [SAN FRANCISCO].

Birds Landing [SOLANO]:
(1) *locality,* 1 mile west-southwest of Birds Landing (2) along Montezuma Slough (lat. 38°07'20" N, long. 121°53'10" W). Named on Honker Bay (1918) 7.5' quadrangle. The name is for John Bird, who built a wharf at the place about 1869 and shipped hay and wheat from there (Hoover, Rensch, and Rensch, p. 524).
(2) *village,* 17 miles south-southeast of Vacaville (lat. 38°08' N, long. 121°52'10" W; sec. 4, T 3 N, R 1 E); 1 mile east-northeast of Birds Landing (1). Named on Birds Landing (1953) 7.5' quadrangle. Postal authorities established Birds Landing post office in 1876 (Frickstad, p. 192).

Bivalve [MARIN]: *locality,* 2 miles northwest of Point Reyes Station on the northeast side of Tomales Bay (lat. 38°05'30" N, long. 122° 49'30" W). Named on Inverness (1954) 7.5' quadrangle. Point Reyes (1918) 15' quadrangle shows the place along Northwestern Pacific Railroad. Pacific Oyster Company planted 450 acres of oyster beds in 1907 and shipped oysters (which are bivalves) to San Francisco from the railroad station at the place (Teather, p. 8).

Bixler [CONTRA COSTA]: *locality,* 4 miles east of Brentwood along Atchison, Topeka and Santa Fe Railroad (lat. 37°56'35" N, long. 121°37'30" W; near SE cor. sec. 10, T 1 N, R 3 E). Named on Brentwood (1978) and Woodward Island (1978) 7.5' quadrangles.

Blackberry Spring [SANTA CLARA]: *spring,* 2.5 miles west-southwest of Mount Sizer on Pine Ridge (lat. 37°11'50" N, long. 121°33'15" W). Named on Mount Sizer (1955) 7.5' quadrangle.

Blackbird Valley [SANTA CLARA]: *canyon,* 2.5 miles long, 1.5 miles south of Mount Mocho on upper reaches of Colorado Creek (lat. 37°26'10" N, long. 121°29' W). Named on Eylar Mountain (1955) and Mount Boardman (1955) 7.5' quadrangles. On Mount Hamilton (1897) 15' quadrangle, the name "Blackbird Valley" applies to present South Pocket.

Black Canyon [MARIN]: *canyon,* 1.25 miles long, 1.5 miles northeast of downtown San Rafael (lat. 37°59'30" N, long. 122°30'30" W). Named on San Rafael (1954) 7.5' quadrangle.

Black Creek [SANTA CLARA]: *stream,* flows nearly 0.5 mile to Lexington Reservoir 2.25 miles south of downtown Los Gatos (lat. 37°11'25" N, long. 121°59'40" W; sec. 32, T 8 S, R 1 W). Named on Los Gatos (1953) 7.5' quadrangle.

Black Creek Valley: see **Dry Creek** [ALAMEDA] (1).

Black Diamond: see **Pittsburg** [CONTRA COSTA].

Black Diamond Landing: see **Pittsburg** [CONTRA COSTA].

Blackhawk Canyon [SANTA CLARA]: *canyon,* drained by a stream that flows nearly 2 miles to Bodfish Creek 1.5 miles east-southeast of Mount Madonna (lat. 37°00'10" N, long. 121°40'50" W). Named on Mount Madonna (1955) 7.5' quadrangle.

Black Hawk Creek: see **Mills Creek** [SAN MATEO] (1).

Black Hawk Ridge [CONTRA COSTA]: *ridge,* west-northwest-trending, 1.25 miles long, 3 miles south of Mount Diablo (lat. 37°50'15" N, long. 121°54'15" W). Named on Diablo (1953) 7.5' quadrangle.

Black Head Rock [SAN FRANCISCO]: *rock,* less than 1 mile northeast of Point Lobos, and 500 feet offshore at Lands End (lat. 37°47'20" N, long. 122°30'25" W). Named on San Francisco North (1956) 7.5' quadrangle.

Black Hills [CONTRA COSTA]:
(1) *ridge,* west- to south-trending, 2.5 miles long, 3 miles north of Orinda (lat. 37°55'15" N, long. 122°11'30" W). Named on Briones Valley (1959) 7.5' quadrangle.
(2) *range,* center 5 miles southeast of Mount Diablo (lat. 37°49'45" N, long. 121°51'45" W). Named on Diablo (1953) and Tassajara (1953) 7.5' quadrangles.

Black Hills: see **Candlestick Point** [SAN FRANCISCO].

Black John Slough [MARIN]: *water feature,* enters Petaluma River 3.5 miles northeast of downtown Novato (lat. 38°08'10" N, long. 122°30'55" W). Named on Petaluma River (1954) 7.5' quadrangle. The name commemorates John Henry Pingston, known as Black John, who was an early settler in the neighborhood (Teather, p. 8).

Black Mountain [MARIN]: *peak,* 2.5 miles east-northeast of Point Reyes Station (lat. 38°04'50" N, long. 122°45'50" W). Altitude 1280 feet. Named on Inverness (1954) 7.5' quadrangle. The name commemorates James Black, who owned Nicasio (1) grant., where the peak is located. The feature also was called Black's Peak (Teather, p. 8), Seven Sisters, and Elephant Mountain (Mason, 1976a, p. 149).

Black Mountain [SAN MATEO]: *peak,* 2 miles southwest of downtown San Mateo (lat. 37°32'45" N, long. 122°21'05" W). Altitude 676 feet. Named on San Mateo (1956) 7.5' quadrangle.

Black Mountain [SANTA CLARA]:
(1) *peak,* 4.5 miles south-southwest of Los Altos on Monte Bello Ridge (lat. 37°19'05" N, long. 122°08'45" W; sec. 13, T 7 S, R 3 E). Named on Mindego Hill (1961) 7.5' quadrangle.
(2) *peak,* 1 mile north of Mount Day (lat. 37°26'15" N, long. 121° 42' W). Altitude 3951 feet. Named on Mount Day (1955) 7.5' quadrangle. Called Mt. Day on Mount Hamilton (1897) 15' quadrangle, where present Mount Day is called Black Mountain.
(3) *peak,* nearly 1 mile north of Mount Stakes on Santa Clara-Stanislaus county line (lat. 37°19'55" N, long. 121°24'30" W; at N line sec. 15, T 7 S, R 5 E). Named on Mount Stakes (1955) 7.5' quadrangle.

Black Point [CONTRA COSTA]: *peak,* 3.25 miles northwest of Mount Diablo (lat. 37°54'45" N, long. 121°07'30" W; near N line sec. 27, T 1 N, R 1 W). Altitude 1791 feet. Named on Clayton (1953) 7.5' quadrangle. Members of the Whitney survey named the peak in the 1860's (Whitney, p. 22).

Black Point [MARIN]: *town,* 3.5 miles east of downtown Novato on the west side of Petaluma River (lat. 38°06'40" N, long. 122°30'05" W). Named on Novato (1954) and Petaluma Point (1959) 7.5' quadrangles. Called Grandview on Petaluma (1914) 15' quadrangle, but United States Board on Geographic Names (1950, p. 4) rejected this name for the place. Postal authorities established Black Point post office in 1865 and discontinued it in 1891; they established Grandview post office in 1905, changed the name to Black Point in 1944, and discontinued it in 1952 (Salley, p. 22, 88). They established Fairford post office 4 miles southwest of Black Point in 1879 and discontinued it the same year; the post office was located at Pacheco station of Northwestern Pacific Railroad (Salley, p. 72).

Black Point [SAN FRANCISCO]: *promontory,* nearly 1 mile west of North Point along San Francisco Bay (lat. 37°48'30" N, long. 122° 25'35" W). Named on San Francisco North (1956) 7.5' quadrangle. Called Pta. de San Josef on Ringgold's (1850a) map, and called San Jose or Black Point on Wackenreuder's (1861) map. The feature also was called Punta Medanos in Spanish times (Whiting and Whiting, p. 44). Ringgold's (1850a) map shows a promontory called Tonquin Pt. located about 0.5 mile east of present Black Point.

Blakes Landing [MARIN]: *locality,* 3.5 miles south of Tomales on the northeast side of Tomales Bay (lat. 38°11'40" N, long. 122°55'05" W). Named on Tomales (1954) 7.5' quadrangle. Jeremiah Blake owned the landing (Mason, 1976a, p. 33).

Blake's Ravine: see **Strawberry Creek** [ALAMEDA].

Blenheim: see **Moss Beach** [SAN MATEO].

Blind Point [CONTRA COSTA]: *promontory,* 4.5 miles west-northwest of the settlement of Bethel Island along San Joaquin River at the west end of Jersey Island (lat. 38°01'55" N, long. 121°43'10" W). Named on Jersey Island (1978) 7.5' quadrangle.

Blithedale: see **Alto** [MARIN].

Blithedale Ridge [MARIN]: *ridge,* southeast-to south-southeast-trending, 2 miles long, 3.5 miles south-southwest of downtown San Rafael (lat. 37°55'30" N, long. 122°32'55" W). Named on San Rafael (1954) 7.5' quadrangle. The name recalls a resort near the ridge that was called Blithedale from Hawthorne's novel, *The Blithedale Romance* (Teather, p. 9).

Blodgett Magic Spring: see **Bodfish Creek** [SANTA CLARA].

Blodgett Magnesia Spring: see **Bodfish Creek** [SANTA CLARA].

Blodgett Mineral Spring: see **Bodfish Creek** [SANTA CLARA].

Bloomfield: see **Miller** [SANTA CLARA].

Bloomquist Creek [SAN MATEO]: *stream,* flows 1 mile to Pescadero Creek 3.5 miles south-southwest of La Honda (lat. 37°16'20" N, long. 122°17'50" W; near S line sec. 33, T 7 S, R 4 W). Named on La Honda (1961) 7.5' quadrangle. The Bloomquist family had a sawmill along the creek in the 1870's; the stream also is called Hoffman Creek (Brown, p. 9).

Blossom Hill [SANTA CLARA]: *ridge,* west-northwest-trending, 2.25 miles long, 3 miles east of downtown Los Gatos (lat. 37°13'40" N, long. 121°55'40" W). Named on Los Gatos (1953) 7.5' quadrangle. Postal authorities established a post office called Blossom Hill in 1968 (Salley, p. 23).

Blossom Rock [SAN FRANCISCO]: *rock,* nearly 1 mile northeast of North Point in San Francisco Bay (lat. 37°49'05" N, long. 122°24'05" W). Named on San Francisco North (1956) 7.5' quadrangle. Captain Beechey discovered the rock in 1826 while he was charting the bay, and named the feature for his ship *Blossom,* a British man-of-war (Davis, W.H., p. 138).

Blucher [MARIN]: *land grant,* inland from the

coast along Estero San Antonio and Americano Creek on Marin-Sonoma county line. Named on Two Rock (1954) and Valley Ford (1954) 7.5' quadrangles. Jean Vioget received 6 leagues in 1844; heirs of Stephen Smith claimed 26,759 acres patented in 1858 (Cowan, p. 19). Vioget had the nickname "Blucher" because of his resemblance to Prussian Field Marshall Gebhard von Blucher, famous for his role at the Battle of Waterloo; from the nickname came the designation of the grant (Gudde, 1949, p. 34).

Blue Gums [MARIN]: *locality,* 4.25 miles west-southwest of Tomales on Tomals Point (lat. 38°13'35" N, long. 122°58'35" W). Named on Tomales (1954) 7.5' quadrangle.

Blue Hills [SANTA CLARA]: *locality,* 2 miles north of downtown Saratoga along Southern Pacific Railroad (lat. 37°17'15" N, long. 122°01'50" W; sec. 25, T 7 S, R 2 W). Named on Cupertino (1961) 7.5' quadrangle.

Blue Mountain: see **Mount Davidson** [SAN FRANCISCO]; **Mount Sutro** [SAN FRANCISCO]; **Mount Vaca** [SOLANO].

Blue Mountains: see **Vaca Mountains** [SOLANO].

Blue Ridge [MARIN]: *ridge,* south-southeast-trending, 1 mile long, 4.5 miles west-north-west of San Rafael (lat. 37°59'15" N, long. 122°36'50" W). Named on San Rafael (1954) 7.5' quadrangle. United States Board on Geographic Names (1976a, p. 5) approved the name "Pams Blue Ridge" for the next ridge east of the south part of Blue Ridge; the name "Pam" commemorates Pamela Ettinger, who lived near the ridge and hiked there.

Blue Ridge [SOLANO]: *ridge,* generally south-trending, 15 miles long, extends from Putah Creek along Napa-Solano county line to the southeast corner of Napa County. Named on Capell Valley (1951), Fairfield North (1951), Monticello Dam (1959), and Mount Vaca (1951) 7.5' quadrangles.

Blue Ridge [SANTA CLARA]: *ridge,* northwest-trending, 7.5 miles long, 9 miles northeast of Morgan Hill (lat. 37°13'15" N, long. 121°31'15" W). Named on Isabel Valley (1955), Mississippi Creek (1955), and Mount Sizer (1955) 7.5' quadrangles.

Blue Rocks [SANTA CLARA]: *peak,* 6 miles west-northwest of Mount Sizer (lat. 37°14'55" N, long. 121°36'35" W). Altitude 2441 feet. Named on Mount Sizer (1955) 7.5' quadrangle.

Blue Rock Springs: see **Sulphur Springs** [SOLANO].

Blue Rock Springs Creek [SOLANO[: *stream,* flows 3.5 miles to Lake Chabot 2.5 miles northeast of downtown Vallejo (lat. 38°08'05" N, long. 122°13'45" W; sec. 6, T 3 N, R 3 W). Named on Benicia (1959) 7.5' quadrangle. Called Sulphur Springs Creek on Karquines (1898) 15' quadrangle.

Bluff Point [MARIN]: *promontory,* nearly 5 miles south-southeast of Point San Quentin near the southeast end of Tiburon Peninsula (lat. 37°52'50" N, long. 122°26'15" W). Named on San Quentin (1959) 7.5' quadrangle. Called Pt. Reed on Ringgold's (1850a) map.

Blumbago Canyon [SANTA CLARA]: *canyon,* drained by a stream that flows nearly 2 miles to Arroyo Bayo 7 miles south-southwest of Eylar Mountain (lat. 37°22'50" N, long. 121°34'50" W; sec. 39, T 6 S, R 4 E). Named on Eylar Mountain (1955) 7.5' quadrangle. Thompson and West's (1876) map has the name "Plumbajo Flat" near the canyon.

Blunt Point [MARIN-SAN FRANCISCO]: *promontory,* at the southeast end of Angel Island on Marin-San Francisco county line (lat. 37°51'10" N, long. 122°25'05" W). Named on San Francisco North (1956) 7.5' quadrangle. Called Point Blunt on San Francisco (1942) 15' quadrangle, and United States Board on Geographic Names (1980, p. 3) approved this form of the name, which commemorates Lieutenant Simon F. Blunt, a member of Ringgold's expedition of 1849 (Teather, p. 2).

Blunt Point Rock [SAN FRANCISCO]: *rock,* 3 miles north of North Point in San Francisco Bay (lat. 37°51'10" N, long. 122°25' W); the rock is 100 feet off Blunt Point (present Point Blunt). Named on San Francisco North (1956) 7.5' quadrangle. United States Board on Geographic Names (1980, p. 4) approved the name "Point Blunt Rock" for the feature.

Boardman: see **Mount Boardman** [ALAMEDA-SANTA CLARA].

Boca del Puerto Dulce: see **Carquinez Strait** [CONTRA COSTA-SOLANO].

Bocus Creek: see **Bogess Creek** [SAN MATEO].

Bodega: see **Point Bodega**, under **Tomales Bluff** [MARIN].

Bodega Bay [MARIN]: *embayment,* north-northwest of the mouth of Tomales Bay and southeast of Bodega Head along the coast on Marin-Somoma county line (lat. 38°16' N, long. 123° 00' W). Named on Bodega Head (1972), Tomales (1954) and Valley Ford (1954) 7.5' quadrangles. Called Puerto de la Bodega on Ringgold's (1850b) map. The name is for Juan Francisco Bodega y Quadra, who entered the embayment in 1775 (Wagner, H.R., p. 376-377). Ivan A. Ruskov built the first Russian structure in California at the place, which he called Port Rumyantsev (Schwartz, p. 37).

Bodfish Canon: see **Bodfish Creek** [SANTA CLARA].

Bodfish Creek [SANTA CLARA]: *stream,* flows 8 miles to Uvas Creek 3 miles west of Gilroy (lat. 37°00'50" N, long. 121°37'50" W). Named on Mount Madonna (1955) and Watsonville East (1955) 7.5' quadrangles. Thompson and West's (1876) map has the name

"Bodfish Canon" on upper reaches of the stream. Waring (p. 273) described Blodgett Magic Spring, a summer camp and source of bottled mineral water located along Bodfish Creek nearly 7 miles west of Gilroy; Waring described another spring, called Blodgett Mineral Spring or Magnesia Spring, situated on a hillside above a branch of Bodfish Creek several miles north of Blodgett Magic Spring.

Bogess Creek [SAN MATEO]: *stream,* flows 5 miles to San Gregorio Creek 3.25 miles west of La Honda (lat. 37°18'55" N, long. 122° 19'40" W). Named on La Honda (1961) 7.5' quadrangle. The stream has been called Keiffer's Creek for a rancher of the 1860's; the name "Bogess" also had the forms "Bogus," "Bocus," and "Boggess" (Brown, p. 9).

Boggess Creek: see **Bogess Creek** [SAN MATEO].

Bogus Creek: see **Bogess Creek** [SAN MATEO].

Bolinas [MARIN]: *town,* 10 miles west-south-west of downtown San Rafael along Bolinas Bay (lat. 37°54'35" N, long. 122°41'05" W). Named on Bolinas (1954) 7.5' quadrangle. Postal authorities established Bolinas post office in 1863 (Frickstad, p. 87). United States Board on Geographic Names (1933, p. 155) rejected the forms "Ballenas" and "Baulenas" for the name, which is from an Indian word (Gilliam, p. 86).

Bolinas Bay [MARIN]: *embayment,* between Duxbury Point and Rocky Point along the coast (lat. 37°53'30" N, long. 122°40' W); the feature is at Bolinas. Named on Bolinas (1954) 7.5' quadrangle. Called Rialto Cove on Ringgold's (1850b) map. United States Board on Geographic Names (1933, p. 155) rejected the forms "Ballenas" and "Baulenas" for the name.

Bolinas Creek [ALAMEDA]: *stream,* flows 3 miles to Crow Creek 14 miles east-southeast of downtown Oakland (lat. 37°45'35" N, long. 122°01'40" W; sec. 13, T 2 S, R 2 W). Named on Las Trampas Ridge (1959) 7.5' quadrangle. The name is from Antonio Bolena, who owned land along the stream in the 1870's; the canyon of the stream was called Davis Canyon in 1894 for J.H. Davis, a farmer who had land along the creek (Mosier and Mosier, p. 16, 28).

Bolinas Creek: see **Pine Gulch Creek** [MARIN].

Bolinas Lagoon [MARIN]: *bay,* opens into Bolinas Bay at Bolinas (lat. 37°54'30" N, long. 122°40'50" W). Named on Bolinas (1954) 7.5' quadrangle.

Bolinas Point [MARIN]: *promontory,* 2.25 miles west of Bolinas along the coast (lat. 37°54'15" N, long. 122°43'35" W). Named on Bolinas (1954) 7.5' quadrangle.

Bolinas Ridge [MARIN]: *ridge,* northwest-trending, 23 miles long, extends from Mount Tamalpais northwest to near Tomales. Named

on Bolinas (1954), Inverness (1954), Point Reyes NE (1954), San Geronimo (1954), San Rafael (1954), and Tomales (1954) 7.5' quadrangles.

Bolinger Creek [CONTRA COSTA]: *stream,* flows 5.25 miles to San Ramon Creek 3.25 miles south of Danville (lat. 37°46'25" N, long. 121°59'45" W; sec. 8, T 2 S, R 1 W). Named on Diablo (1953) and Las Trampas Ridge (1959) 7.5' quadrangles. United States Board on Geographic Names (1981a, p. 2) approved the name "Bollinger Canyon Creek" for the feature, and rejected the names "Bolinger Creek" and "Bollinger Creek." At the same time the Board approved the name "Bollinger Canyon" for the canyon of the stream, and noted that the name commemorates Joshua Bollinger, who settled in the canyon in 1855. Becker (1969) identified a feature called Arroyo de las Trampas, shown on a diseño of Laguna de los Palos Colorados grant in 1835, as probably present Bollinger Canyon.

Bolitas Point: see **Bulls Head Point** [CONTRA COSTA].

Bollinger Canyon [SANTA CLARA]: *canyon,* drained by a stream that flows 2 miles to Arroyo Bayo 2.5 miles north-northeast of Isabel Valley (lat. 37°20'30" N, long. 121°31'10" W; sec. 10, T 7 S, R 4 E). Named on Isabel Valley (1955) and Mount Stakes (1955) 7.5' quadrangles.

Bollinger Canyon: see **Bolinger Creek** [CONTRA COSTA].

Bollinger Canyon Creek: see **Bolinger Creek** [CONTRA COSTA].

Bollinger Creek: see **Bolinger Creek** [CONTRA COSTA].

Bollinger Mountain [SANTA CLARA]: *peak,* 4 miles south of Isabel Valley (lat. 37°15'15" N, long. 121°32'40" W; sec. 9, T 8 S, R 4 E); the peak is near the southeast end of Bollinger Ridge. Named on Isabel Valley (1955) 7.5' quadrangle.

Bollinger Ridge [SANTA CLARA]: *ridge,* northwest- to west-trending, 5 miles long, 3.5 miles south of Isabel Valley. Named on Isabel Valley (1955) and Mount Sizer (1955) 7.5' quadrangles. On Morgan Hill (1917) and Mount Hamilton (1897) 15' quadrangles, the ridge is shown as part of a larger feature called Pine Ridge

Bolsa de Encinal: see **Alameda** [ALAMEDA].

Bolsa Point [SAN MATEO]: *promontory,* 1 mile north-northwest of Pigeon Point along the coast (lat. 37°11'45" N, long. 122°24'15" W). Named on Pigeon Point (1955) 7.5' quadrangle.

Bon Air Hill [MARIN]: *hill,* nearly 2 miles south of downtown San Rafael (lat. 37°56'50" N, long. 122°31'55" W). Named on San Rafael (1954) 7.5' quadrangle. The name recalls a resort hotel called Bon Air that was popular from the 1880's until the 1920's (Teather, p. 12).

Bonita [CONTRA COSTA]: *locality,* 1.5 miles

north of present Walnut Creek civic center along Oakland Antioch and Eastern Railroad (lat. 37°55'25" N, long. 122°03'30" W). Named on Concord (1915) 15' quadrangle.

Bonita: see **Point Bonita** [MARIN].

Bonita Channel [MARIN]: *water feature*, northwest of Point Bonita between Potatopatch Shoal and the coast (lat. 37°49'45" N, long. 122°33'25" W). Named on Point Bonita (1954) 7.5' quadrangle.

Bonita Cove [MARIN-SAN FRANCISCO]: *embayment*, east of Point Bonita along Marin County coast (lat. 37°49'20" N, long. 122° 31' W). Named on Point Bonita (1954) 7.5' quadrangle. Marin-San Francisco county line follows the low-water mark of Marin County coast from Point Bonita to Cavallo Point, which places the water area of the embayment in San Francisco County.

Bonita Creek [SANTA CLARA]: *stream*, flows 3.5 miles to Isabel Creek 2 miles north of Mount Hamilton (lat. 37°22'25" N, long. 121°38'25" W; sec. 34, T 6 S, R 3 E). Named on Lick Observatory (1955) and Mount Day (1955) 7.5' quadrangles. Called Bonito Creek on Mount Hamilton (1897) 15' quadrangle.

Bonito Creek: see **Bonita Creek** [SANTA CLARA].

Bonjetti Creek [SANTA CLARA]: *stream*, flows 2 miles to Saratoga Creek 2.25 miles west-southwest of Saratoga (lat. 37°14'55" N, long. 122°04'05" W; sec. 10, T 8 S, R 2 W). Named on Castle Rock Ridge (1955) 7.5' quadrangle. A resort called Long Bridge operated along Saratoga Creek near the mouth of Bonjetti Creek in the 1890's (Cunningham, p. 79).

Bon Tempe Creek [MARIN]: *stream*, flows 0.5 mile to Alpine Lake 4.5 miles west of downtown San Rafael (lat. 37°57'45" N, long. 122°36'40" W). Named on San Rafael (1954) 7.5' quadrangle.

Bon Tempe Lake [MARIN]: *lake*, behind a dam on Lagunitas Creek 4.5 miles west-southwest of downtown San Rafael (lat. 37°57'20" N, long. 122°36'40" W). Named on San Rafael (1954) 7.5' quadrangle. The Americanized name commemorates brothers Guiseppi Bautunpi and Pasquale Bautunpi, who started a dairy at the site of the present lake in 1868; Marin Municipal Water District built the lake in 1948 (Teather, p. 12).

Booker Creek [SANTA CLARA]: *stream*, flows 1.25 miles to Saratoga Creek 3 miles west of Saratoga (lat. 37°15'15" N, long. 122° 05'15" W; sec. 9, T 8 S, R 2 W). Named on Castle Rock Ridge (1955) and Cupertino (1961) 7.5' quadrangles.

Boon Hill [CONTRA COSTA]: *peak*, 1 mile east-northeast of Danville at the west end of Short Ridge (lat. 37°49'40" N, long. 121°58'40" W; sec. 21, T 1 S, R 1 W). Named on Diablo (1953) 7.5' quadrangle.

Bootjack Camp [MARIN]: *locality*, 6 miles southwest of downtown San Rafael (lat. 37°54'30" N, long. 122°36'05" W); the place is near Bootjack Creek. Named on San Rafael (1954) 7.5' quadrangle.

Bootjack Creek [MARIN]: *stream*, flows 1 mile to Rattlesnake Creek nearly 6 miles southwest of downtown San Rafael (lat. 37° 54'20" N, long. 122°35'35" W). Named on San Rafael (1954) 7.5' quadrangle.

Borel Hill [SAN MATEO]: *peak*, 2 miles east-northeast of Mindego Hill on Russian Ridge (lat. 37°19'10" N, long. 122°11'55" W; sec. 16, T 7 S, R 3 W). Altitude 2572 feet. Named on Mindego Hill (1961) 7.5' quadrangle.

Bothin [MARIN]: *locality*, 8 miles south-southwest of downtown Novato along Northwestern Pacific Railroad (lat. 38°00'15" N, long. 122°37'10" W). Named on Petaluma (1914) 15' quadrangle.

Bothin Creek [MARIN]: *stream*, flows less than 1 mile to Fairfax Creek 3.5 miles west-northwest of downtown San Rafael (lat. 37° 59'25" N, long. 122°35'35" W). Named on San Rafael (1954) 7.5' quadrangle.

Boulder Creek: see **Little Boulder Creek** [SAN MATEO].

Bowman Canyon [MARIN]: *canyon*, 1 mile long, opens into the canyon of Novato Creek 3.25 miles west-northwest of downtown Novato (lat. 38°07'20" N, long. 122°37'30" W). Named on Petaluma (1954) 15' quadrangle.

Bowman's Point: see **West End**, under **Alameda** [ALAMEDA].

Boynton Slough [SOLANO]: *water feature*, joins Suisun Slough 2.5 miles south of Fairfield (lat. 38°12'40" N, long. 122°02'15" W). Named on Fairfield South (1949) 7.5' quadrangle.

Bozzo Gulch [SAN MATEO]: *canyon*, drained by a stream that flows 0.5 mile to Sausal Creek 4.25 miles north of Mindego Hill in Portola Valley (1) (lat. 37°22'25" N, long. 122°13'25" W). Named on Mindego Hill (1961) 7.5' quadrangle. Emmanuel Bozzo had a ranch at the head of the canyon in the late 1860's (Brown, p. 10).

Bradford Island [CONTRA COSTA]: *island*, 2.5 miles long, 4.25 miles north-northwest of the settlement of Bethel Island between San Joaquin River, Fishermans Cut, and False River (lat. 38°04'30" N, long. 121°39'45" W). Named on Jersey Island (1978) 7.5' quadrangle. Called Bradford Tract on Davis and Vernon's (1951) map.

Bradford Landing [CONTRA COSTA]: *locality*, 4.5 miles north-northwest of the present settlement of Bethel Island along San Joaquin River (lat. 38°04'35" N, long. 121°40'30" W); the place is on the west side of Bradford Island. Named on Jersey (1910) 7.5' quadrangle.

Bradford Tract: see **Bradford Island** [CONTRA COSTA].

Bradley Beach: see **Sand Beach** [SAN MATEO].

Bradley Creek [SAN MATEO]: *stream,* flows 3 miles to Pescadero Creek 5 miles south of the village of San Gregorio near Pescadero (lat. 37°15'10" N, long. 122°23'15" W). Named on San Gregorio (1961) 7.5' quadrangle. Charles Bradley had a dairy by the stream in the 1880's (Brown, p. 10).

Bradley's Creek: see **Arroyo de en Medio** [SAN MATEO].

Bradleys Store [SANTA CLARA]: *locality,* 4.5 miles west-southwest of Morgan Hill along Little Uvas Creek (lat. 37°06'30" N, long. 121°43'55" W). Named on Morgan Hill (1917) 15' quadrangle. This appears to be the place, or near the place, called Uvas on California Mining Bureau's (1917b) map. Postal authorities established Uvas post office in 1896, moved it 1.5 miles south in 1890, moved it 0.5 mile south in 1899, and discontinued it in 1908; the post office was located 9 miles southwest of Madrone (Salley, p. 228).

Bradmoor Island [SOLANO]: *island,* 2.5 miles south-southwest of Denverton along Nurse Slough (lat. 38°11'30" N, long. 121°55'15" W). Named on Denverton (1953) 7.5' quadrangle. Called Bradtmoor Island on Denverton (1918) 7.5' quadrangle.

Bradtmoor Island: see **Bradmoor Island** [SOLANO].

Braen Canyon [SANTA CLARA]: *canyon,* drained by a stream that flows 2 miles to Hunting Hollow nearly 3 miles south-southeast of Gilroy Hot Springs (lat. 37°04'20" N, long. 121°27'20" W; near N line sec. 18, T 10 S, R 5 E). Named on Gilroy Hot Springs (1955) 7.5' quadrangle.

Brays: see **Fruitvale Station** [ALAMEDA].

Brazil Beach [MARIN]: *beach,* 3 miles west-southwest of Tomales along the northeast side of Tomales Bay (lat. 38°14' N, long. 122°57'15" W). Named on Tomales (1954) 7.5' quadrangle. The name commemorates Antone Brazil, a farmer who shipped his produce by barge from the beach to San Francisco (United States Board on Geographic Names, 1967a, p. 2).

Brazoria: see **Rio Vista** [SOLANO].

Brazos del Rio: see **Rio Vista** [SOLANO].

Brentwood [CONTRA COSTA]: *town,* 12 miles east-northeast of Mount Diablo (lat. 37°55'55" N, long. 121°41'55" W). Named on Brentwood (1978) 7.5' quadrangle. Postal authorities established Brentwood post office in 1878 (Frickstad, p. 21), and the town incorporated in 1948. The name is from the town in England that was the ancestral home of John Marsh, owner of Los Meganos grant (Gudde, 1949, p. 40).

Brewer Island [SAN MATEO]: *island,* 2.5 miles long, 3 miles east of downtown San Mateo along San Francisco Bay (lat. 37°33'45" N, long. 122°16' W). Named on Redwood Point (1959) and San Mateo (1956) 7.5' quadrangles. Frank M. Brewer built levees and

drained the island about 1905 to make a place for his dairy ranch (Brown, p. 11).

Bridgehead [CONTRA COSTA]: *settlement,* 3.25 miles east of downtown Antioch (lat. 38°00'20" N, long. 121°45' W); the place is near the south end of a bridge across San Joaquin River. Named on Antioch North (1978) and Jersey Island (1978) 7.5' quadrangles.

Bridgeport: see **Cordelia** [SOLANO].

Briggs Creek [SANTA CLARA]: *stream,* flows 2.25 miles to Lexington Reservoir 3 miles south of downtown Los Gatos (lat. 37°10'55" N, long. 121°59'25" W; sec. 5, T 9 S, R 1 W). Named on Castle Rock Ridge (1955) and Los Gatos (1953) 7.5' quadrangles.

Briggston [SOLANO]: *locality,* 7 miles north-northeast of Dixon along Southern Pacific Railroad (lat. 38°31'55" N, long. 121°44'50" W; near NW cor. sec. 22, T 8 S, R 2 E). Named on Swingle (1915) 7.5' quadrangle. The name commemorates Charles Briggs, a pioneer of Solano County (Hanna, P.T., p. 41).

Brighton Beach: see **Sharp Park** [SAN MATEO].

Brighton Lake: see **Laguna Salada** [SAN MATEO].

Brightside [ALAMEDA]: *locality,* 2.25 miles west of Sunol along Southern Pacific Railroad in Alameda (present Niles) Canyon (lat. 37°36' N, long. 121°55'25" W; sec. 12, T 4 S, R 1 W). Named on Pleasanton (1906) 15' quadrangle. The name is from the position of the place on the sunny, or bright, side of Alameda Creek (Mosier and Mosier, p. 17).

Briones Hills [CONTRA COSTA]: *ridge,* west-trending, 4.5 miles long, center 5 miles north-northeast of Orinda (lat. 37°56'35" N, long. 122°08'45" W). Named on Briones Valley (1959) and Walnut Creek (1959) 7.5' quadrangles. The name is from the Spanish Briones family (Gudde, 1949, p. 40).

Briones Reservoir [CONTRA COSTA]: *lake,* 3 miles long, behind a dam on Bear Creek 2.5 miles north-northwest of Orinda (lat. 37°54'50" N, long. 122°12'30" W); water of the lake floods part of Briones Valley (1). Named on Briones Valley (1959, photorevised 1968) 7.5' quadrangle.

Briones Valley [CONTRA COSTA]:

(1) *canyon,* along Bear Creek above a point 3.5 miles north-northwest of Orinda (lat. 37°55'35" N, long. 122°12'05" W). Named on Briones Valley (1959) 7.5' quadrangle. Water of Briones Reservoir now covers part of the feature.

(2) *valley,* 8 miles east of Mount Diablo (lat. 37°53'50" N, long. 121°46'30" W). Named on Antioch South (1953) and Brentwood (1978) 7.5' quadrangles.

Brisbane [SAN MATEO]: *town,* 2 miles north-northeast of downtown South San Francisco (lat. 37°40'55" N, long. 122°24' W). Named on San Francisco South (1956) 7.5' quadrangle. Called Visitacion on San Mateo (1915)

15' quadrangle. A subdivision called Visitacion City was started at the place in 1908 to attract refugees from San Francisco after the earthquake of 1906, but the development failed to prosper; more than 20 years later Arthur Ennis, agent for the subdivision, renamed the place Brisbane for Arthur Brisbane, a popular newspaper columnist, and this time the community did prosper (Stanger, 1963, p. 163-164). Postal authorities established Visitacion post office in 1908 and discontinued it in 1914; they established Brisbane post office in 1931 (Frickstad, p. 167, 169), and Brisbane incorporated in 1961.

Brisbane Lagoon: see **Sierra Point** [SAN MATEO].

Brittan Knoll [SAN MATEO]: *peak,* 2.5 miles west-northwest of downtown Redwood City (lat. 37°30' N, long. 122°15'50" W). Named on Woodside (1961) 7.5' quadrangle. Brown (p. 11) called the feature Brittan's Knoll, and noted that Nat Brittan's ranch was there for nearly 70 years after 1856.

Brittan Park [SAN MATEO]: *district,* 5.5 miles south-southeast of downtown San Mateo in San Carlos (lat. 37°30'05" N, long. 122°16'10" W). Named on San Mateo (1947) 7.5' quadrangle.

Broad Slough [CONTRA COSTA]: *water feature,* the lowermost reach of San Joaquin River 3 miles north-northwest of Antioch (lat. 38°02'50" N, long. 121°50'25" W). Named on Antioch North (1978) 7.5' quadrangle.

Broadway Wharf: see **Oakland** [ALAMEDA].

Brooklyn: see **Oakland** [ALAMEDA].

Brooklyn Basin [ALAMEDA]: *water feature,* 1 mile south-southeast of downtown Oakland in the east part of Oakland Inner Harbor (lat. 37°47'10" N, long. 122°15' W). Named on Oakland East (1959) and Oakland West (1959) 7.5' quadrangles. Concord (1897) and San Francisco (1899) 15' quadrangles have the name "Oakland Harbor" at the place. United States Board on Geographic Names (1949b, p. 3) rejected the name "North Channel" for the feature, and later the Board (1984b, p. 2) rejected the name "Embarcadero Cove" for it. The name "Brooklyn" is from the former town of Brooklyn, now part of Oakland (Gudde, 1969, p. 39).

Brooks Island [CONTRA COSTA]: *island,* 3250 feet long, 3 miles south-southwest of Richmond civic center in San Francisco Bay (lat. 37°53'50" N, long. 122°21'15" W). Named on Richmond (1959) 7.5' quadrangle. United States Board on Geographic Names (1933, p. 166) rejected the names "Rocky Island" and "Sheep Island" for the feature. H.R. Wagner (p. 439) listed the early names "Isla del Carmen" or "Isla del Carmel" for it.

Brothers: see **The Brothers** [CONTRA COSTA].

Brown Island: see **Turk Island** [ALAMEDA].

Browns Island [CONTRA COSTA]: *island,* 1.5 miles long, 3.5 miles west-northwest of Antioch (lat. 38°02'20" N, long. 121°51'50" W). Named on Antioch North (1978) and Honker Bay (1953) 7.5' quadrangles, which show the feature as marsh and water. Called Gwin I. on Ringgold's (1850b) map.

Brusha Peak: see **Brushy Peak** [ALAMEDA].

Brush Mountain [SANTA CLARA]: *peak,* 1 mile south of Isabel Valley (lat. 37°17'55" N, long. 121°31'55" W). Altitude 2920 feet. Named on Isabel Valley (1955) 7.5' quadrangle.

Brushy Canyon [SANTA CLARA]: *canyon,* drained by a stream that flows 1.25 miles to Carlin Canyon 6 miles west-northwest of Mount Sizer (lat. 37°13'55" N, long. 121°37'20" W). Named on Mount Sizer (1955) 7.5' quadrangle.

Brushy Creek [ALAMEDA-CONTRA COSTA]: *stream,* heads just inside Alameda County and flows 8 miles to lowlands 7.5 miles south-southeast of Brentwood in Contra Costa County (lat. 37°50'20" N, long. 121°37'30" W; near S line sec. 15, T 1 S, R 3 E); the stream heads near Brushy Peak. Named on Byron Hot Springs (1953) and Clifton Court Forebay (1978) 7.5' quadrangles.

Brushy Peak [ALAMEDA]: *peak,* 7 miles north-northeast of Livermore (lat. 37°46'05" N, long. 121°42'05" W). Altitude 1702 feet. Named on Byron Hot Springs (1953) 7.5' quadrangle. Called Las Cuevas on California Mining Bureau's (1917b) map. Whitney (p. 33) referred to Bushy Knob or Las Cuevas. *Las Cuevas* means "the caves" in Spanish; outlaw Joaquin Murieta supposedly hid in caves at the base of the peak (Mosier and Mosier, p. 18). Hoover, Rensch, and Rensch (p. 1) described "Brushy (Brusha) Peak."

Bryant: see **Orinda** [CONTRA COSTA].

Buckeye Camp [CONTRA COSTA]: *locality,* 2 miles south-southwest of Mount Diablo (lat. 37°51'20" N, long. 121°55'50" W; near SW cor. sec. 12, T 1 S, R 1 W). Named on Diablo (1953) 7.5' quadrangle.

Buckhorn Creek [ALAMEDA-CONTRA COSTA]: *stream,* heads in Contra Costa County and flows 3 miles to Kaiser Creek 10 miles east of downtown Oakland in Alameda County (lat. 37°47'20" N, long. 122°05'35" W; sec. 4, T 2 S, R 2 W). Named on Las Trampas Ridge (1959) 7.5' quadrangle. Called Kaiser Creek on Concord (1897) 15' quadrangle. The name "Buckhorn Creek" is from August Buchhorn and Frederick Buchhorn, who settled at the place in the 1890's (Mosier and Mosier, p. 18).

Buckle Point [CONTRA COSTA]: *ridge,* west-southwest-trending, 0.5 mile long, 2.5 miles west of Mount Diablo (lat. 37°52'50" N, long. 121°57'50" W). Named on Clayton (1953) 7.5' quadrangle.

Buckler: see **Point Buckler** [SOLANO].
Bucks Canyon: see **Mix Canyon** [SOLANO].
Bucktown [SOLANO]: *locality,* 4.5 miles east of Mount Vaca in Vaca Valley (lat. 38°23'25" N, long. 122°01'20" W). Named on Mount Vaca (1951) 7.5' quadrangle.
Buenos Ayres Creek: see **Corral Hollow Creek** [ALAMEDA].
Bullhead Canyon [SANTA CLARA]: *canyon,* drained by a stream that flows 4 miles to North Fork Pacheco Creek 8 miles north-northwest of Pacheco Peak (lat. 37°07'05" N, long. 121°19'05" W; sec. 28, T 9 S, R 6 E). Named on Mustang Peak (1955) and Pacheco Peak (1955) 7.5' quadrangles.
Bull Head Point: see **Bulls Head Point** [CONTRA COSTA].
Bullhead Reservoir [SANTA CLARA]: *lake,* 175 feet long, nearly 3 miles east-southeast of Mustang Peak (lat. 37°09'50" N, long. 121°19' W; sec. 9, T 9 S, R 6 E); the lake is at the head of a branch of Bullhead Canyon. Named on Mustang Peak (1955) 7.5' quadrangle.
Bull Point [MARIN]: *ridge,* south-southeast-trending, nearly 1 mile long, 6.5 miles northeast of the lighthouse at Point Reyes (lat. 38°04' N, long. 122°56'45" W). Named on Drakes Bay (1953) 7.5' quadrangle.
Bull Run [SANTA CLARA]: *area,* nearly 2 miles west of New Almaden (lat. 37°10'50" N, long. 121°51' W). Named on Santa Teresa Hills (1953) 7.5' quadrangle. Workers at New Almaden mine held games and festivities at the place (Hoover, Rensch, and Rensch, p. 435).
Bull Run Creek [SAN MATEO]: *stream,* flows 1.25 miles to Sausal Creek nearly 7 miles south of downtown Redwood City in Portola Valley (1) (lat. 37°23'15" N, long. 122°14' W). Named on Palo Alto (1961) 7.5' quadrangle. A Southern sympathizer named the stream following the Union defeat at the Battle of Bull Run; the stream, or its canyon, has been called Sausal Creek, Willow Creek, and Kelley Gulch (Stanger, 1967, p. 27), as well as Uval Creek, Cañada de Sansevan—for William Nichols Sansevain, and Smith Gulch—for William R. Smith's steam-powered sawmill (Brown, p. 12).
Bulls Head Channel [CONTRA COSTA-SOLANO]: *channel,* 2.25 miles north-northeast of Martinez along Contra Costa-Solano county line near the junction of Suisun Bay and Carquinez Strait (lat. 38°02'30" N, long. 122°06'45" W); the feature is north of Bulls Head Point. Named on Vine Hill (1959) 7.5' quadrangle.
Bulls Head Channel: see **East Bulls Head Channel** [CONTRA COSTA-SOLANO].
Bulls Head Point [CONTRA COSTA]: *promontory,* nearly 2 miles north-northeast of Martinez on the south side of Carquinez Strait (lat. 38°02'10" N, long. 122°06'55" W). Named on Vine Hill (1959) 7.5' quadrangle.

Called Pt. Bolitas on Ringgold's (1850b) map. United States Board on Geographic Names (1933, p. 173) rejected the names "Bolitas Point" and "Bull Head Point" for the feature.
Bull Tail Valley [MARIN]: *valley,* 5.5 miles southwest of downtown Novato (lat. 38°03'45" N, long. 122°39' W). Named on San Geronimo (1954) 7.5' quadrangle.
Bull Valley: see **Big Bull Valley** [CONTRA COSTA]; **Little Bull Valley** [CONTRA COSTA].
Bunker [SOLANO]: *locality,* 8 miles east of Elmira along Sacramento Northern Railroad (lat. 38°21'05" N, long. 121°45'25" W; sec. 21, T 6 N, R 2 E). Named on Dozier (1952) 7.5' quadrangle.
Burbank [SANTA CLARA]: *district,* 2 miles west-southwest of downtown San Jose. Named on San Jose West (1961) 7.5' quadrangle. The name honors Luther Burbank—the district originally was called Rose Lawn (Rambo, 1973, p. 39).
Burdell [MARIN]: *locality,* 3.5 miles north of downtown Novato along Northwestern Pacific Railroad (lat. 38°09'25" N, long. 122°33'50" W); the place is 1.5 miles east-northeast of Burdell Mountain. Named on Petaluma River (1954) 7.5' quadrangle. The name recalls Dr. Burdell, owner of Olompali grant (Teather, p. 13).
Burdell Island [MARIN]: *island,* 3.5 miles north-northeast of downtown Novato in marsh lands (lat. 38°09'20" N, long. 122°33'10" W); the feature is 0.5 mile east of Burdell. Named on Petaluma River (1954) 7.5' quadrangle. James Burdell and his friends built Mira Monte Club on the island in 1895 (Mason, 1976b, p. 117-118).
Burdell Mountain [MARIN]: *ridge,* south-southeast-trending, 1.5 miles long, 3 miles north-northwest of downtown Novato (lat. 38°08'45" N, long. 122°35'25" W). Named on Petaluma River (1954) 7.5' quadrangle. The peak is on Olompali grant, owned by Dr. Galen Burdell; the feature originally was called Mount Olompali (Teather, p. 13).
Buri Buri [SAN MATEO]: *land grant,* mainly between South San Francisco and Burlingame. Named on Montara Mountain (1956), San Francisco South (1956), and San Mateo (1956) 7.5' quadrangles. Jose Sanchez received the land in 1827 and 1835; Jose de la Cruz Sanchez and others claimed 14,639 acres patented in 1872 (Cowan, p. 21). The name is of Indian origin (Davis, W.H., p. 171).
Buri Buri Ridge [SAN MATEO]: *ridge,* southeast-trending, 5 miles long, center 3 miles south of downtown Millbrae (lat. 37°33'30" N, long. 122°22'20" W); the ridge is on Buri Buri grant. Named on Montara Mountain (1956) and San Mateo (1956) 7.5' quadrangles. On San Mateo (1915) 15' quadrangle, the name has the form "Buriburi Ridge." The feature was called Lomas Muertas in Spanish

times because of the lack of vegetation there—
lomas muertas means "bald hills" in Spanish; later it was called Bald Ridge before trees
were planted there (Brown, p. 4).

Burlingame [SAN MATEO]: *city,* 2.5 miles
west-northwest of downtown San Mateo (lat.
37°35' N, long. 122°21'50" W). Named on
Montara Mountain (1956) and San Mateo
(1956) 7.5' quadrangles. William C. Ralston
named the place in 1868 for his friend Anson
Burlingame, United States minister to China
in the 1860's (Gudde, 1949, p. 45). The first
attempt to develop a town failed, but in the
1890's some wealthy San Francisco men organized Burlingame Country Club, and a railroad station called Burlingame was built; the
town began to grow only after the earthquake
of 1906, when refugees relocated there
(Stanger, 1963, p. 151). Postal authorities established Burlingame post office in 1894
(Frickstad, p. 167), and the city incorporated
in 1908. A railroad station called Oak Grove
was at present Burlingame from the middle
1860's until Burlingame station was started
in 1894 (Brown, p. 62).

Burnett: see **Coyote** [SANTA CLARA].

Burns Chalks [SAN MATEO]: *relief feature,* 1.5
miles southwest of La Honda (lat. 37°18' N,
long. 122°17'30" W; near NW cor. sec. 27, T
7 S, R 4 W). Named on La Honda (1961) 7.5'
quadrangle, which shows Burns ranch 1 mile
south of the feature.

Burnt Hills [SANTA CLARA]: *range,* 5.5 miles
south of Eyler Mountain (lat. 37°24' N, long.
121°32'30" W). Named on Eylar Mountain
(1955) and Isabel Valley (1955) 7.5' quadrangles.

Burra Burra Peak [SANTA CLARA]: *peak,* 8
miles north-northwest of Pacheco Peak (lat.
37°06'35" N, long. 121°21'50" W; sec. 31, T
9 S, R 6 E). Altitude 2281 feet. Named on
Pacheco Peak (1955) 7.5' quadrangle.

Burrell: see **Wrights** [SANTA CLARA].

Burton [CONTRA COSTA]: *locality,* 3.5 miles
southwest of present Walnut Creek civic center along Oakland Antioch and Eastern Railroad (lat. 37°51'55" N, long. 122°06' W); the
place is in present Burton Valley. Named on
Concord (1915) 15' quadrangle.

Burton Valley [CONTRA COSTA]: *valley,* 6.25
miles west-northwest of Danville at the
confluence of Grizzly Creek and Las Trampas
Creek (lat. 37°52'15" N, long. 122°05'35" W).
Named on Las Trampas Ridge (1959) 7.5'
quadrangle.

Bush Hill [CONTRA COSTA]: *ridge,* north- to
west-trending, 1 mile long, 4.5 miles west-
northwest of Martinez (lat. 38°02'45" N, long.
122°12'20" W). Named on Benicia (1959) 7.5'
quadrangle.

Bushy Knob: see **Brushy Peak** [ALAMEDA].

Butano [SAN MATEO]: *land grant,* along and
near Butano Creek. Named on Franklin Point
(1955), Pigeon Point (1955), and San

Gregorio (1961) 7.5' quadrangles. Ramona
Sanchez received 1 league in 1844; M.
Rodriguez claimed 4439 acres patented in
1866 (Cowan, p. 21).

Butano Creek [SAN MATEO]: *stream,* flows
15 miles to Pescadero Creek 4.5 miles south-
southwest of the village of San Gregorio (lat.
37°15'50" N, long. 122°24'20" W). Named
on Big Basin (1955), Franklin Point (1955),
Pigeon Point (1955), and San Gregorio (1961)
7.5' quadrangles. South Fork joins the main
stream 7 miles north-northeast of Franklin
Point. It is 4 miles long and is named on Big
Basin (1955) and Franklin Point (1955) 7.5'
quadrangles.

Butano Creek: see **Little Butano Creek** [SAN
MATEO].

Butano Falls [SAN MATEO]: *waterfall,* nearly
7 miles north-northeast of Franklin Point (lat.
37°14'30" N, long. 122°18'55" W; sec. 17, T
8 S, R 4 W); the feature is along Butano Creek.
Named on Franklin Point (1955) 7.5' quadrangle.

Butano Flat: see **Little Butano Flat**, under
Little Butano Creek [SAN MATEO].

Butano Park [SAN MATEO]: *settlement,* 6
miles north-northeast of Franklin Point (lat.
37°14' N, long. 122°19'25" W; sec. 17, T 8 S,
R 4 W); the place is along Butano Creek.
Named on Franklin Point (1955) 7.5' quadrangle.

Butano Ridge [SAN MATEO]: *ridge,* east- to
southeast-trending, 5 miles long, center 4.5
miles south of La Honda (lat. 37°15' N, long.
122°15'50" W). Named on Big Basin (1955),
Franklin Point (1955), and La Honda (1961)
7.5' quadrangles.

Byrnes' Lake: see **Upper Crystal Springs Reservoir** [SAN MATEO].

Byron [CONTRA COSTA]: *town,* 5.5 miles
southeast of Brentwood (lat. 37°52'05" N,
long. 121°38'20" W; near SW cor. sec. 3, T 1
S, R 3 E). Named on Byron Hot Springs
(1953) 7.5' quadrangle. Postal authorities established Byron post office in 1878; the name
is for a railroad employee (Salley, p. 31). They
established Point of Timber post office 2 miles
north of Byron in 1869, discontinued it in
1871, reestablished in 1872, and discontinued it in 1882 (Salley, p. 175). The names
"Point of Timber" and "Eden Plain" were applied to part of the lowlands in the eastern
section of Contra Costa County (Smith and
Elliott, p. 28).

Byron Hot Springs [CONTRA COSTA]: *locality,* 7 miles south-southeast of Brentwood (lat.
37°50'50" N, long. 121°37'55" W; sec. 15, T
1 S, R 3 E); the place is 1.5 miles south-southeast of Byron. Named on Byron Hot Springs
(1953) 7.5' quadrangle. Postal authorities established Byron Hot Springs post office in
1889 and discontinued it in 1930 (Frickstad,
p. 21). More that 50 springs were the basis of
a resort at the site (Anderson, Winslow, p.

105). The place was an interrogation center for prisoners of war during World War II (Hillman and Covello, p. 70).

Byron Hot Springs Station [CONTRA COSTA]: *locality,* 7.5 miles southeast of Brentwood along Southern Pacific Railroad (lat. 37° 50'40" N, long. 121°37' W; sec. 14, T 1 S, R 3 E); the place is 1 mile east-south-east of Byron Hot Springs. Named on Byron (1916) 15' quadrangle.

Byron Tract [CONTRA COSTA]: *area,* 6 miles east-southeast of Brentwood (lat. 37°54' N, long. 121°35'45" W); the place is 3 miles northeast of Byron. Named on Clifton Court Forebay (1978) and Woodward Island (1978) 7.5' quadrangles.

– C –

Caballo Point: see **Cavallo Point** [MARIN].

Cabo de Fortunas: see **Pigeon Point** [SAN MATEO].

Cabo de Pinos: see **Point Reyes** [MARIN] (1).

Cache Slough [SOLANO]: *water feature,* joins Sacramento River 2 miles northeast of Rio Vista (lat. 38°10'45" N, long. 121°39'55" W). Named on Dozier (1952), Liberty Island (1978), and Rio Vista (1978) 7.5' quadrangles.

Cache Slough: see **Maine Prairie Slough** [SOLANO].

Cahill Ridge [SAN MATEO]: *ridge,* northwest-trending, 5 miles long, 5.5 miles east-south-east of Montara Knob (lat. 37°31'45" N, long. 122°23'30" W). Named on Montara Mountain (1956), San Mateo (1956), and Woodside (1961) 7.5' quadrangles. Called Cahil Ridge on San Mateo (1915) 15' quadrangle. On Santa Cruz (1902) 30' quadrangle, the name applies along the ridge southeast as far as Kings Mountain. The feature was called Cuchilla de los Ajos by the 1840's—*ajos* means "garlic" in Spanish, and it was called Bald Ridge in the 1850's and 1860's; the name "Cahill" recalls Joseph Cahill, who started a ranch at the ridge in the late 1850's (Brown, p. 15).

Calabazas Creek [SANTA CLARA]: *stream,* flows 12.5 miles to Guadalupe Slough 1 mile southwest of Alviso (lat. 37°25' N, long. 121°59'10" W). Named on Cupertino (1961), Milpitas (1961), and San Jose West (1961) 7.5' quadrangles. San Jose (1899) 15' quadrangle, made before the lower course of the stream was altered, shows the creek continuing to Guadalupe Slough about 1 mile west-south-west of Alviso (lat. 37°25'10" N, long. 121°59'20" W), and it also shows that the watercourse is interrupted between the upper and lower parts. Called Arroyo De Los Calabazas on Thompson and West's (1876) map, which shows the stream entering Campbell Creek. The name "Calabazas" was given because Indians who lived along the creek raised and sold vegetables to early settlers—*calabazas* means "squash" or "pumpkin" in Spanish (Rambo, 1973, p. 39).

Calaveras Creek [ALAMEDA-SANTA CLARA]: *stream,* flows 5.25 miles in Santa Clara County to Calaveras Reservoir, and from Calaveras Reservoir it flows 1 mile in Alameda County to Alameda Creek 7 miles south-southeast of Sunol (lat. 37°30'15" N, long. 121°49'15" W; sec. 13, T 5 S, R 1 E). Named on Calaveras Reservoir (1961), La Costa Valley (1960), and Mount Day (1955) 7.5' quadrangles. The name probably came after Spaniards discovered Indian skeletons near the stream—*calaveras* means "skulls" in Spanish (Rambo, 1973, p. 40).

Calaveras Point [ALAMEDA]: *promontory,* 5 miles south of downtown Newark on the north side of the mouth of Coyote Creek (lat. 37°28' N, long. 122°03' W). Named on Mountain View (1961) 7.5' quadrangle.

Calaveras Reservoir [ALAMEDA-SANTA CLARA]: *lake,* on Alameda-Santa Clara county line, mainly in Santa Clara County; 3.25 miles long, behind a dam on Calaveras Creek 8 miles south-southeast of Sunol (lat. 37°29'35" N, long. 121°49'10" W; sec. 13, T 5 S, R 1 E); water of the lake floods most of Calaveras Valley. Named on Calaveras Reservoir (1961) 7.5' quadrangle.

Calaveras Valley [ALAMEDA-SANTA CLARA]: *valley,* on Alameda-Santa Clara county line, mainly in Santa Clara County; along Calaveras Creek above a point 8 miles south-southeast of Sunol (lat. 37°29'35" N, long. 121°49'10" W). Named on Calaveras Reservoir (1961) 7.5' quadrangle. San Jose (1899) 15' quadrangle shows the valley before water of Calaveras Reservoir inundated it.

Caldwell Springs: see **Azule Springs** [SANTA CLARA].

Calera: see **Rockaway Beach** [SAN MATEO].

Calera Creek [SANTA CLARA]: *stream,* flows 2.25 miles to lowlands 2.25 miles north-north-east of Milpitas (lat. 37°27'45" N, long. 121°53'40" W), and continues in an artificial watercourse. Named on Calaveras Reservoir (1961) and Milpitas (1961) 7.5' quadrangles. The name records a limekiln built in the neighborhood as early as 1807—*calera* means "limekiln" in Spanish (Gudde, 1949, p. 50).

Calera Hill: see **Lime Hill**, under **Calera Valley** [SAN MATEO].

Calera Valley [SAN MATEO]: *valley,* 4 miles north of Montara Knob near the coast (lat. 37°36'50" N, long. 122°29'10" W). Named on Montara Mountain (1956) 7.5' quadrangle. The valley was called Cañada de la Calera in Spanish times because of a nearby limekiln—*calera* means "limekiln" in Spanish (Gudde, 1949, p. 50). Brown (p. 47) used the name "Lime Hill" for the ridge north of the mouth of the valley, and Eckel (p. 354) used the name

"Calera Hill" for the same feature—limestone was mined at the place.

Calero Creek: see **Arroyo Calero** [SANTA CLARA].

Calero Reservoir [SANTA CLARA]: *lake,* 2.25 miles long, behind a dam on Arroyo Calero 1.5 miles east-northeast of New Almaden (lat. 37°11' N, long. 121°47'30" W). Named on Santa Teresa Hills (1953) 7.5' quadrangle.

Calhoun Cut [SOLANO]: *water feature,* joins Lindsey Slough 9.5 miles southeast of Elmira (lat. 38°15'40" N, long. 121°46'30" W). Named on Dozier (1952) 7.5' quadrangle.

California City: see **Paradise Cove** [MARIN].

California Point: see **Paradise Point** [MARIN].

Callahan Gulch [ALAMEDA]: *canyon,* drained by a stream that flows 3.25 miles to Arroyo Mocho 4.25 miles southeast of Cedar Mountain (lat. 37°31'15" N, long. 121°32'45" W; near SW cor. sec. 4, T 5 S, R 4 E). Named on Cedar Mountain (1956) 7.5' quadrangle. The name commemorates Patrick Callaghan and John Callaghan, brothers who raised sheep in the neighborhood after 1868 (Mosier and Mosier, p. 19).

Calletano Creek: see **Cayetano Creek** [ALAMEDA-CONTRA COSTA].

Cambrian Park: see **Cambrian Village** [SANTA CLARA].

Cambrian Village [SANTA CLARA]: *district,* 3.5 miles north-northeast of downtown Los Gatos (lat. 37°15'25" N, long. 121°55'30" W). Named on San Jose West (1961) 7.5' quadrangle. Postal authorities established Cambrian Park post office in the district in 1954 (Salley, p. 33).

Campbell [SANTA CLARA]: *city,* 5 miles southwest of downtown San Jose (lat. 37°17'15" N, long. 121°57' W). Named on San Jose West (1961) 7.5' quadrangle. Benjamin Campbell subdivided his land and founded the community in 1885 (Butler, p. 124). Postal authorities established Campbell post office in 1885 (Frickstad, p. 173), and the city incorporated in 1952. Peninsular Railway Company's (1912) map shows a station called Hamilton located about one-quarter of the way from Campbell to San Jose, a station called Fairfield located along the railway about halfway, and a station called Lincoln located about three-quarters of the way. The same map shows a station called Union Ave. situated southeast of Campbell along a Southern Pacific Railroad branch line to New Almaden, and a station called LeFranc located farther southeast along the same branch line. MacGregor (p. 124) mentioned a place called Lovelady's that was located along the railroad near present Campbell in 1877, and noted (p. 135) that this station later was called Gravel Pit—a spur line ran from the spot to gravel deposits along Los Gatos Creek.

Campbell Creek: see **Saratoga Creek** [SANTA CLARA].

Campbell Creek Cañon: see **Saratoga Creek** [SANTA CLARA].

Campbell Point [MARIN]: *promontory,* on the north shore of Angel Island (lat. 37°52'20" N, long. 122°25'45" W). Named on San Francisco North (1956) 7.5' quadrangle. United States Board on Geographic Names (1980, p. 3) approved the name "Point Campbell" for the feature. The name commemorates A.H. Campbell, a civil engineer with Ringgold's expedition of 1849 (Teather, p. 2).

Campbells Creek: see **Saratoga Creek** [SANTA CLARA].

Campbell's Gap: see **Saratoga** [SANTA CLARA].

Campbell's Redwoods: see **Saratoga Creek** [SANTA CLARA].

Camp Bessie [SANTA CLARA]: *locality,* 2.5 miles southeast of Eylar Mountain along Arroyo Mocho (lat. 37°27'20" N, long. 121°30'55" W; sec. 34, T 5 S, R 4 E). Named on Eylar Mountain (1955) 7.5' quadrangle.

Camp Cooley [SANTA CLARA]: *locality,* 4 miles southwest of Cupertino near Stevens Creek (lat. 37°16'50" N, long. 122°04'25" W; sec. 34, T 7 S, R 2 W). Named on Cupertino (1961) 7.5' quadrangle.

Camp Eastwood [MARIN]: *locality,* 5.5 miles south-southwest of downtown San Rafael (lat. 37°54'20" N, long. 122°34'50" W). Named on San Rafael (1954) 7.5' quadrangle. Called Eastwood Camp on Mount Tamalpais (1950) 15' quadrangle. Fairley (1987, p. 100) referred to Camp Alice Eastwood, located at the site of Mt. Tamalpais Camp, a former CCC facility.

Camp Fremont: see **Menlo Park** [SAN MATEO].

Camp Grizzly: see **Tanforan**, under **San Bruno** [SAN MATEO].

Camp Herms [CONTRA COSTA]: *locality,* 3 miles east-southeast of Richmond civic center (lat. 37°55'30" N, long. 122°17'20" W). Named on Richmond (1959) 7.5' quadrangle. United States Board on Geographic Names (1988a, p. 2) approved the name "William Rust Summit" for a peak located 0.25 mile northwest of Camp Herms (lat. 37°55'35" N, long. 122°17'23" W); the name is for a pioneer settler who was active in business and community affairs.

Camp Lilienthal [MARIN]: *locality,* 4.25 miles west of downtown San Rafael (lat. 37°58'20" N, long. 122°36'30" W). Named on San Rafael (1954) 7.5' quadrangle.

Camp Parks [ALAMEDA-CONTRA COSTA]: *military installation,* 2 miles east-northeast of Dublin on Alameda-Contra Costa county line, mainly in Alameda County (lat. 37°43' N, long. 121°54' W). Named on Dublin (1961) and Livermore (1961) 7.5' quadrangles. The camp operated from 1943 until 1945 as a naval training and distribution center, and again during the Korean War as an air force base;

the name commemorates Rear Admiral Charles Wellman Parks (Mosier and Mosier, p. 19). A navy replacement center called Camp Shoemaker was situated east of Camp Parks in Livermore Valley (Mosier and Mosier, p. 19). Postal authorities established Shoemaker post office in Alameda County at the place in 1946 and discontinued it the same year (Salley, p. 203).

Camp Pistolesi: see **Camp Tomales** [MARIN].

Camp Pomponio [SAN MATEO]: *locality,* 3.5 miles south-southwest of Mindego Hill along Pescadero Creek (lat. 37°15'50" N, long. 122°14'50" W; sec. 1, T 8 S, R 4 W). Named on Mindego Hill (1961) 7.5' quadrangle.

Camp Reynolds: see **Fort McDowell** [MARIN-SAN FRANCISCO].

Camp Saratoga [SANTA CLARA]: *locality,* 3.25 miles west of Saratoga (lat. 37°15'30" N, long. 122°05'30" W; near SW cor. sec. 4, T 8 S, R 2 W); the place is on upper reaches of Saratoga Creek. Named on Cupertino (1961) 7.5' quadrangle.

Camp Shoemaker: see **Camp Parks** [ALAMEDA-CONTRA COSTA].

Camp Stoneman [CONTRA COSTA]: *military installation,* 1.5 miles south-southeast of Pittsburg (lat. 38°00'30" N, long. 121°52'30" W). Named on Antioch North (1953), Clayton (1953), and Honker Bay (1953) 7.5' quadrangles. War Department officials named the place in 1942 to honor George Stoneman, governor of California from 1883 until 1887, who came to California in 1846 as a lieutenant in the Mormon Battalion (Hanna, P.T., p. 317).

Camp Sycamore [SANTA CLARA]: *locality,* nearly 3 miles west-northwest of Saratoga near Stevens Creek (lat. 37°16'55" N, long. 122°04'20" W; sec. 34, T 7 S, R 2 W). Named on Cupertino (1961) 7.5' quadrangle.

Camp Taylor [MARIN]: *locality,* 10.5 miles southwest of downtown Novato (lat. 38°01'10" N, long. 122°43'45" W). Named on San Geronimo (1954) 7.5' quadrangle. Petaluma (1914) 15' quadrangle shows the place along Northwestern Pacific Railroad. Postal authorities established Camp Taylor post office in 1894 and discontinued it in 1912 (Frickstad, p. 87).

Camp Tomales [MARIN]: *locality,* 1.25 miles south-southwest of Tomales (lat. 38°13'50" N, long. 122°55' W). Named on Tomales (1954) 7.5' quadrangle. Called Camp Pistolesi on Point Reyes (1918) 15' quadrangle. The name "Pistolesi" is for Frank V. Pistolesi, who started a resort at the place in 1902 (Mason, 1976a, p. 149).

Cañada de Apolonio: see **Digges Canyon** [SAN MATEO].

Cañada de Guadalupe la Visitacion y Rodeo Viejo [SAN FRANCISCO-SAN MATEO]: *land grant,* at and near San Bruno Mountain, mainly in San Mateo County, but extends north into San Francisco west of Visitacion Valley. Named on San Francisco South (1956) 7.5' quadrangle. Jacob P. Leese received 2 leagues in 1841, and H.R. Payson claimed 5473 acres patented in 1865 (Cowan, p. 38).

Cañada de Guadalupe y Rodeo Viejo [SAN FRANCISCO-SAN MATEO]: *land grant,* at and near Visitacion Valley on San Francisco-San Mateo county line. Named on San Francisco South (1956) 7.5' quadrangle. Jacob P. Leese received the land in 1841, and William Pierce claimed 943 acres patented in 1865 (Cowan, p. 38).

Cañada de Herrera [MARIN]: *land grant,* around Fairfax. Named on Bolinas (1954), Novato (1954), and San Rafael (1954) 7.5' quadrangles. Domingo Sais received the land in 1839 and his heirs claimed 6648 acres patented in 1876 (Cowan, p. 39; Cowan gave the name "Providencia" as an alternate). According to Perez (p. 58), the grant has 6658.45 acres.

Cañada de la Brea: see **Las Animas** [SANTA CLARA].

Cañada de la Calera: see **Calera Valley** [SAN MATEO].

Cañada de la Dormida [SANTA CLARA]: *stream,* flows 5.5 miles to Cedar Creek 6 miles north-northwest of Pacheco Peak (lat. 37° 05' N, long. 121°20'40" W; near W line sec. 8, T 10 S, R 6 E). Named on Gilroy Hot Springs (1955) and Pacheco Peak (1955) 7.5' quadrangles.

Cañada del Aliso [ALAMEDA]: *stream,* flows 2 miles to lowlands 3 miles southeast of Fremont civic center (lat. 37°30'50" N, long. 121°56'10" W). Named on Niles (1961) 7.5' quadrangle. Pleasanton (1906) 15' quadrangle has the name "Canada del Aliso" for the canyon of the stream. Two large sycamore trees stood near the stream in the early days—*aliso* means "sycamore" in Spanish (Gudde, 1969, p. 7).

Cañada de la Puente: see **Digges Canyon** [SAN MATEO].

Cañada de las Auras: see **Feliz** [SAN MATEO].

Cañada del Cierbo [CONTRA COSTA]: *canyon,* 2.5 miles long, opens into lowlands along San Pablo Bay 7 miles west-northwest of Martinez near Tormey (lat. 38°03'05" N, long. 122°15' W). Named on Benicia (1959) 7.5' quadrangle.

Cañada del Corte de Madera [SAN MATEO-SANTA CLARA]: *land grant,* near Portola Valley (1) on San Mateo-Santa Clara county line, mainly in San Mateo County. Named on Mindego Hill (1961) and Palo Alto (1961) 7.5' quadrangles. Jose D. Peralta and Maximo Martinez received the land in 1833; Cipriano Thurn and H.W. Carpentier claimed 3566 acres patented in 1882 (Perez, p. 60).

Cañada del Diablo: see **Belmont Creek** [SAN MATEO].

Cañada de Leon: see **Nuff Creek** [SAN MATEO].

Cañada del Frijol: see **Arroyo de los Frijoles** [SAN MATEO].

Cañada del Hambre: see **Alhambra Valley** [CONTRA COSTA].

Cañada del Hambre y las Bolsas [CONTRA COSTA]: *land grant,* extends from near Crocket to the city of Walnut Creek. Named on Benicia (1959), Briones Valley (1959), and Walnut Creek (1959) 7.5' quadrangles. Teodora Soto received 2 leagues in 1842 and claimed 13,354 acres patented in 1866 (Cowan, p. 39; Cowan gave the grant the designation "Cañada del Hambre, (or) Las Bolsas del Hambre"). Perez (p. 60) used the name "Canada del Hambre y las Bolsas del Hambre" for the grant.

Cañada de los Capitancillos [SANTA CLARA]: *land grant,* 6 miles east of Los Gatos. Named on Los Gatos (1953) 7.5' quadrangle. Justo Larios received the land in 1842; Guadalupe Mining Company claimed 1110 acres patented in 1871 (Cowan, p. 23-24; Cowan gave the grant the designation "Cañada de los Capitancillos, (or) New Almaden"). According to tradition, the name originated because Indians who lived at the place were small in stature, but brave— *cañada de los capitancillos* means "valley of the little captains" in Spanish (Johnson, p. 35).

Cañada de los Osos [SANTA CLARA]: *stream,* flows 8 miles to Coyote Creek 2.5 miles south of Gilroy Hot Springs (lat. 37°04'20" N, long. 121°28'35" W; near S line sec. 12, T 10 S, R 4 E). Named on Gilroy Hot Springs (1955) 7.5' quadrangle.

Cañada de los Poblanos [CONTRA COSTA]: *valley,* 7 miles east of Mount Diablo along Marsh Creek (lat. 37°53'15" N, long. 121°46'55" W). Named on Antioch South (1953) 7.5' quadrangle. Marsh Creek had the early name "Arroyo de los Poblanos" (Gudde, 1949, p. 206).

Cañada de los Vaqueros [ALAMEDA-CONTRA COSTA]: *land grant,* southwest of Byron on Alameda-Contra Costa county line, mainly in Contra Costa County. Named on Byron Hot Springs (1953) and Tassajara (1953) 7.5' quadrangles. Francisco Alviso received the land in 1844; Robert Livermore and Jose Noriega claimed 17,760 acres patented in 1889 (Cowan, p. 106).

Cañada de Novato: see **Novato Valley** [MARIN].

Cañada de Pala [SANTA CLARA]: *land grant,* in highlands east of San Jose. Named on Calaveras Reservoir (1961), Lick Observatory (1955), Mount Day (1955), and San Jose East (1961) 7.5' quadrangles. Jose Jesus Bernal received the land in 1839 and claimed 15,714 acres patented in 1863 (Cowan, p. 56). The name commemorates an Indian called Pala, who was mentioned in Spanish records as early as 1795 (Gudde, 1949, p. 249).

Cañada de Polonio: see **Digges Canyon** [SAN MATEO].

Cañada de Raimundo: see **Cañada de Raymundo** [SAN MATEO]; **Upper Crystal Springs Reservoir** [SAN MATEO].

Cañada de Raymundo [SAN MATEO]: *land grant,* around Woodside. Named on Palo Alto (1961) and Woodside (1961) 7.5' quadrangles. John Coppinger received 2.5 leagues in 1840; Coppinger's widow and her new husband, Mr. Greer, claimed 12,545 acres patented in 1859 (Cowan, p. 67; Cowan gave the grant the designation "Cañada de Raimundo (or Raymundo)").

Cañada de San Agustin: see **Belmont Creek** [SAN MATEO].

Cañada de San Andres: see **San Andreas Lake** [SAN MATEO].

Cañada de San Felipe y las Animas [SANTA CLARA]: *land grant,* 5 miles north of Morgan Hill. Named on Morgan Hill (1955) and Mount Sizer (1955) 7.5' quadrangles. Thomas Bowen received 2 leagues in 1839; Charles M. Weber claimed 8788 acres patented in 1866 (Cowan, p. 75). Perez (p. 60) named Francisco Garcia as the grantee in 1844. Thompson and West's (1876) map has the name "Las Animas Hills" for the range located east of Coyote along the west edge of the grant.

Cañada de Sansevan: see **Bull Run Creek** [SAN MATEO]; **Neils Gulch** [SAN MATEO].

Cañada de Verde y Arroyo de la Purisima [SAN MATEO]: *land grant,* extends from the crest of Santa Cruz Mountains to the sea between Purisima Creek and Tunitas Creek. Named on Half Moon Bay (1961), San Gregorio (1961), and Woodside (1961) 7.5' quadrangles. Jose M. Alviso received 2 league in 1838; Jose Antonio Alviso claimed 8906 acres patented in 1865 (Cowan, p. 65). Perez (p. 60) listed Jose A. Alviso as the grantee in 1839.

Cañada Garcia [SANTA CLARA]: *canyon,* drained by a stream that flows 2.25 miles to Llagas Creek 4.25 miles west of Morgan Hill (lat. 37°07'35" N, long. 121°43'50" W). Named on Morgan Hill (1955), Mount Madonna (1955), and Santa Teresa Hills (1953) 7.5' quadrangles.

Canada Pomponio [MARIN]: *canyon,* 2.5 miles long, 7.5 miles west of downtown Novato along present Arroyo Sausal (lat. 38°07' N, long. 122°42' W). Named on Petaluma (1914) 15' quadrangle. The name commemorates an outlaw Indian (Mason, 1976b, p. 162).

Cañada Raimundo Creek: see **Upper Crystal Springs Reservoir** [SAN MATEO].

Cañada Verde [SAN MATEO]: *canyon,* drained by a stream that flows 1.5 miles to lowlands along the coast 2.5 miles south of downtown Half Moon Bay (lat. 37°25'35" N, long. 122°25'30" W; sec. 8, T 6 S, R 5 W). Named on Half Moon Bay (1961) 7.5' quadrangle. Brown (p. 16) noted the names "Cañada Verde Creek" and "Arroyo Cañada Verde" for the stream that drains the canyon.

Cañada Verde: see **Green Valley** [CONTRA COSTA].

Cañada Verde Creek: see **Cañada Verde** [SAN MATEO].

Candlestick Cove: see **Sierra Point** [SAN MATEO].

Candlestick Point [SAN FRANCISCO]: *promontory*, 4.25 miles east-southeast of Mount Davidson along San Francisco Bay (lat. 37°42'45" N, long. 122°23' W). Named on San Francisco South (1956) 7.5' quadrangle. San Francisco South (1956, photorevised 1980) 7.5' quadrangle shows the feature flanked by landfill. The name is from Candlestick Rock, a sharp pinnacle, 8 feet high, that was at the spot in the early days (Gudde, 1969, p. 52). Wackenreuder's (1861) map has the name "Black Hills" for the range that extends west from present Candlestick Point.

Candlestick Rock: see **Candlestick Point** [SAN FRANCISCO].

Cannon [SOLANO]: *locality*, 4 miles southeast of Vacaville along Southern Pacific Railroad (lat. 38°18'15" N, long. 121°56'45" W; sec. 2, T 5 N, R 1 W). Named on Elmira (1953) 7.5' quadrangle.

Cannons Resort [SANTA CLARA]: *locality*, 1 mile southwest of New Almaden (lat. 37°09'45" N, long. 121°50'05" W). Named on Los Gatos (1919) 15' quadrangle. Water of Almaden Reservoir now covers the site.

Canoas Creek [SANTA CLARA]: *stream*, flows 7.25 miles to Guadalupe River 3 miles south of downtown San Jose (lat. 37°17'20" N, long. 121°52'50" W). Named on San Jose East (1961), San Jose West (1961), and Santa Teresa Hills (1953) 7.5' quadrangles. The stream originally had the name "El Arroyo Tulares de los Canoas"—*el arroyo tulares de los canoas* means "the rivulet of the tules for canoes" in Spanish (Sawyer, p. 267). United States Board on Geographic Names (1943, p. 10) rejected the name "Cincas Creek" for the feature.

Cape Horn Pass [SANTA CLARA]: *pass*, nearly 1 mile northwest of New Almaden (lat. 37°11' N, long. 121°49'55" W). Named on Santa Teresa Hills (1953) 7.5' quadrangle.

Carey Camp Creek [MARIN]: *stream*, flows 1 mile to San Anselmo Creek 4.5 miles west of downtown San Rafael (lat. 37°58'45" N, long. 122°36'50" W). Named on San Rafael (1954) 7.5' quadrangle.

Carlin Canyon [SANTA CLARA]: *canyon*, drained by a stream that flows nearly 4.5 miles to San Felipe Creek 5 miles east of Coyote (lat. 37°13'20" N, long. 121°38'50" W). Named on Morgan Hill (1955) and Mount Sizer (1955) 7.5' quadrangles.

Carlyle Hills [SANTA CLARA]: *range*, 3.5 miles south of Gilroy near the southeast end of Santa Cruz Mountains (lat. 36°57'10" N, long. 121°34'45" W). Named on Chittenden (1955) 7.5' quadrangle.

Carnadero [SANTA CLARA]: *locality*, 2.5 miles southeast of Gilroy along Southern Pacific Railroad, where the rail line branches to Hollister in San Benito County (lat. 36°58'35" N, long. 121°32'30" W). Named on Chittenden (1955) 7.5' quadrangle.

Carnadero: see **Las Animas** [SANTA CLARA].

Carnadero Creek [SANTA CLARA]: *stream*, joins Pajaro River 5.5 miles south-southeast of Gilroy (lat. 36°55'35" N, long. 121°32'25" W). Named on Chittenden (1955) 7.5' quadrangle, where the name applies to the southern extension for about 4 miles of the stream called Uvas Creek farther north. Morgan Hill (1917) 15' quadrangle has the name "Carnadero Creek" for present Uvas Creek below the confluence of present Uvas Creek and Bodfish Creek. On a diseño of Las Animas grant, present Carnadero Creek is called Arroyo de Carnadero (Becker, 1969). Bancroft's (1864) map has the name "Carniadero Cr." for the whole combined length of present Uvas Creek and present Carnadero Creek. Gudde (1949, p. 57) pointed out that *carnadero* probably refers to "butchering place" in Spanish, and was recorded in the neighborhood of Carnadero Creek as early as 1784. United States Board on Geographic Names (1973a, p. 2) approved the name "Gavilan Creek," from Gavilan College, for a stream that joins Carnadero Creek 4 miles south of Gilroy near the college (lat. 36°56'50" N, long. 121°31'55" W).

Carniadero Creek: see **Carnadero Creek** [SANTA CLARA].

Caroline Livermore: see **Mount Caroline Livermore** [MARIN].

Carpenter [ALAMEDA]: *locality*, nearly 6 miles north of downtown Newark along Western Pacific Railroad (lat. 37°36'50" N, long. 122°02'35" W). Named on Newark (1959) 7.5' quadrangle.

Carpentier's Wharf: see **Oakland** [ALAMEDA].

Carquines Strait: see **Carquinez Strait** [CONTRA COSTA-SOLANO].

Carquinez Heights [SOLANO]: *district*, 2 miles south-southeast of downtown Vallejo along Carquinez Strait (lat. 38°04'35" N, long. 122°14'15" W). Named on Benicia (1959) 7.5' quadrangle. Postal authorities established Carquinez Heights post office in 1944 and discontinued it in 1954 (Salley, p. 38).

Carquinez Point: **Point Carquinez** [CONTRA COSTA].

Carquinez Strait [CONTRA COSTA-SOLANO]: *water feature*, extends for 9 miles from Suisun Bay to San Pablo Bay on Contra Costa-Solano county line; opens into San Pablo Bay 3 miles south of downtown Vallejo (lat. 38°03'35" N, long. 122°16' W). Named on Benicia (1959), Mare Island (1959), and Vine Hill (1959) 7.5' quadrangles. Called Karquines Strait on Karquines (1898) 15' quadrangle, but United States Board on Geographic Names (1933, p. 197) rejected the names "Karquines Strait," "Karquenas Strait," and "Carquines Strait" for the feature. The name "Carquinez" is derived from an Indian tribe or village called Carquin or Karkin (Kroeber, p. 37). Font gave the name "Boca del Puerto Dulce" to the strait in 1776—*boca del puerto dulce* means "mouth of the freshwater port" in Spanish (Gudde, 1949, p. 58). Padre Ramon Abella gave the feature the name "Estrecho de las Karquines" in 1811 (Hanna, P.T., p. 56), and Crespi called it Rio de San Francisco in 1772 (Hoover, Rensch, and Rensch, p. 53). It is called Estrecho de Karquines on Beechey's (1827-1828) map. The name had a variety of forms in the early days: Wilkes (p. 47) called the feature Straits of Kaquines in 1841; Revere (p. 53) called it Straits of Karquin in 1846; Dana (p. 260) called it straits of Caquines in 1849; P.T. Tyson (p. 16) called it straits of Carquinos in 1850; and Ringgold (p. 27) called it Straits of Carquines in 1852. Ringgold's (1850b) map has the name "Vallejo Bay" for the east part of present Carquinez Strait opposite Martinez.

Carriger Creek [SAN MATEO]: *stream,* flows nearly 1 mile to Pescadero Creek 4 miles south-southeast of La Honda (lat. 37°15'50" N, long. 122°15'20" W; sec. 1, T 8 S, R 4 W). Named on La Honda (1961) 7.5' quadrangle. Officials of Santa Cruz Lumber Company named the stream about 1946 for Edward Carriger, secretary-treasurer of the company (Brown, p. 17).

Carson Creek: see **Big Carson Creek** [MARIN]; **Little Carson Creek** [MARIN].

Cascade: see **Lake Cascade** [CONTRA COSTA].

Cascade Creek [MARIN]:
(1) *stream,* flows 1 mile to San Anselmo Creek nearly 5 miles west of downtown San Rafael (lat. 37°58'50" N, long. 122°37'05" W). Named on Bolinas (1954) and San Rafael (1954) 7.5' quadrangles.
(2) *stream,* flows 1 mile to Old Mill Creek 4.5 miles south-southwest of downtown San Rafael (lat. 37°54'45" N, long. 122°33'50" W). Named on San Rafael (1954) 7.5' quadrangle.

Cascade Creek [SAN MATEO]: *stream,* heads in Santa Cruz County and flows 3.25 miles to the sea 1.5 miles southeast of Franklin Point (lat. 37°08'10" N, long. 122°20'15" W). Named on Franklin Point (1955) 7.5' quadrangle. The name is from Cascade dairy, started along the creek in 1863; the lower part of the stream was called Arroyo de la Cienega in Spanish times (Brown, p. 17).

Castillo de San Joaquin: see **Fort Point** [SAN FRANCISCO].

Castle Canyon [SANTA CLARA]: *canyon,* drained by a stream that flows 3.5 miles to Smith Creek nearly 3 miles south of Mount Isabel (lat. 37°17'05" N, long. 121°36'55" W); the canyon heads on Castle Ridge. Named on Isabel Valley (1955) 7.5' quadrangle.

Castle Hill [CONTRA COSTA]: *peak,* 4 miles northwest of Danville (lat. 37°51'35" N, long. 122°03'05" W; sec. 11, T 1 S, R 2 W). Named on Las Trampas Ridge (1959) 7.5' quadrangle.

Castle Ridge [SANTA CLARA]: *ridge,* northwest-trending, 3 miles long, 2 miles southwest of Isabel Valley (lat. 37°17'45" N, long. 121°34' W). Named on Isabel Valley (1955) 7.5' quadrangle. The ridge is part of a larger feature called Pine Ridge on Morgan Hill (1917) and Mount Hamilton (1897) 15' quadrangles.

Castle Rock [CONTRA COSTA]: *peak,* 4 miles west of Mount Diablo (lat. 37°52'50" N, long. 121°59' W). Altitude 972 feet. Named on Clayton (1953) 7.5' quadrangle.

Castle Rock [SANTA CLARA]: *peak,* 0.5 mile north-northwest of Bielawski Mountain on Santa Clara-Santa Cruz county line (lat. 37°13'40" N, long. 122°05'40" W; at SW cor. sec. 16, T 8 S, R 2 W). Altitude 3214 feet. Named on Castle Rock Ridge (1955) 7.5' quadrangle.

Castle Rock Ridge [SANTA CLARA]: *ridge,* northwest-trending, 6 miles long, southeast of Saratoga Gap on Santa Clara-Santa Cruz county line (lat. 37°13'30" N, long. 122°05'30" W); Castle Rock is on the ridge. Named on Castle Rock Ridge (1955) and Cupertino (1961) 7.5' quadrangles.

Castro: see **Castro City** [SANTA CLARA].

Castro City [SANTA CLARA]: *locality,* 1.25 miles northwest of downtown Mountain View along Southern Pacific Railroad (lat. 37°24'10" N, long. 122°05'45" W). Named on Mountain View (1961) 7.5' quadrangle. Palo Alto (1899) 15' quadrangle has the name "Castro" at the place. Castro Station was named for Mariano Castro, owner of Pastoria de las Borregas grant, where the station is situated (Rambo, 1973, p. 40).

Castro Creek [CONTRA COSTA]: *stream,* enters San Pablo Bay 2 miles east-southeast of Point San Pablo (lat. 37°57'30" N, long. 122°23'35" W). Named on San Quentin (1959) 7.5' quadrangle.

Castro Flats: see **Castro Valley** [SANTA CLARA].

Castro Point [CONTRA COSTA]: *promontory,* 2.25 miles south-southeast of Point San Pablo along San Francisco Bay (lat. 37°56'10" N, long. 122°24'45" W). Named on San Quentin (1959) 7.5' quadrangle.

Castro Rocks [CONTRA COSTA]: *rocks,* 2.25 miles south-southeast of Point San Pablo in San Francisco Bay (lat. 37°55'55" N, long. 122°25' W); the rocks are 0.25 mile southwest of Castro Point. Named on San Quentin (1959) 7.5' quadrangle.

Castro Valley [ALAMEDA]:
(1) *valley,* 2 miles north-northeast of Haywards (present Hayward) (lat. 37°41'45" N, long. 122°04'15" W); the valley is on San Lorenzo

(2) grant, which was owned by Guilleremo Castro. Named on Haywards (1899) 15' quadrangle.

(2) *city,* 2 miles north-northeast of downtown Hayward (lat. 37°41'45" N, long. 122°04'15" W); the city is in Castro Valley (1). Named on Hayward (1959) 7.5' quadrangle.

Castro Valley [SANTA CLARA]: *valley,* 3.5 miles south-southwest of Gilroy along upper reaches of Tar Creek (lat. 36°57'45" N, long. 121°36'45" W); the valley is partly on Las Animas grant, which belonged to the Castro family. Named on Chittenden (1955) 7.5' quadrangle. Called Castro Flats on San Juan Bautista (1917) 15' quadrangle.

Cataract Canyon: see **Cataract Creek** [MARIN].

Cataract Creek [MARIN]: *stream,* flows 2.25 miles to Alpine Lake 3.25 miles northeast of Bolinas (lat. 37°56' N, long. 122°38'05" W). Named on Bolinas (1954) and San Rafael (1954) 7.5' quadrangles. The canyon of the stream is called Cataract Canyon on Mount Tamalpais (1950) 15' quadrangle. East Fork, which flows less than 1 mile to join the main stream in Alpine Lake, is named on Bolinas (1954) 7.5' quadrangle.

Cat Slough [SOLANO]: *water feature,* joins Volanti Slough nearly 5 miles south of Fairfield (lat. 38°10'50" N, long. 122°02' W). Named on Fairfield South (1949) 7.5' quadrangle.

Cattle Hill [SAN MATEO]: *peak,* 3.5 miles north of Montara Knob (lat. 37°36'25" N, long. 122°28'50" W). Named on Montara Mountain (1956) 7.5' quadrangle.

Cavallo Point [MARIN]: *promontory,* 2 miles south-southeast of downtown Sausalito along San Francisco Bay (lat. 37°49'55" N, long. 122°28'20" W). Named on San Francisco North (1956) 7.5' quadrangle. Called Pto. Cavallos on Ringgold's (1850a) map. United States Board on Geographic Names (1983a, p. 3) approved the name "Point Cavallo" for the promontory, and rejected the names "Cavallo Point," "Caballo Point," "Plaza de los Caballos," "Punta de los Caballos," and "Punto Cavallos." According to Gudde (1949, p. 61), the name "Cavallo" presumably is from horses that were kept at the place in Spanish times—*caballos* means "horses" in Spanish; the letters "b" and "v" commonly were interchanged.

Cavanaugh Gulch: see **Soda Spring Canyon** [SANTA CLARA].

Cavelano Creek: see **Cayetano Creek** [ALAMEDA].

Cave Point [CONTRA COSTA]: *peak,* 3.25 miles south-southeast of Mount Diablo (lat. 37°50'25" N, long. 121°52'55" W; sec. 17, T 1 S, R 1 E). Named on Diablo (1953) 7.5' quadrangle. Members of the Whitney survey named the feature for hollows in sandstone at the summit; they also gave the name "Tower

Rocks" to outcrops of sandstone in the saddle just south of Cave Point (Whitney, p. 27).

Cayetano Creek [ALAMEDA-CONTRA COSTA]: *stream,* heads in Contra Costa County and flows 8 miles to Arroyo las Positas 1.5 miles northwest of Livermore in Alameda County (lat. 37°42'05" N, long. 121°47'05" W). Named on Livermore (1961) and Tassajara (1953) 7.5' quadrangles. Called Arroyo Cayetano on Mount Diablo (1898) 15' quadrangle. United States Board on Geographic Names (1933, p. 204) rejected the names "Arroyo Cavelano," "Arroyo Covelano," "Calletano Creek," and "Cavelano Creek" for the feature.

Cayle: see **Cayley** [ALAMEDA].

Cayley [ALAMEDA]: *locality,* 2.5 miles west-northwest of Midway along Southern Pacific Railroad (lat. 37°43'50" N, long. 121° 36' W; sec. 25, T 2 S, R 3 E). Named on Midway (1953) 7.5' quadrangle. Called Cayle on Tesla (1907) 15' quadrangle.

Cebada Flat [SANTA CLARA]: *area,* 6 miles northeast of Gilroy (lat. 37°03'40" N, long. 121°30'25" W). Named on Gilroy (1955) 7.5' quadrangle.

Cedar Creek [SANTA CLARA]: *stream,* flows 6.25 miles to Pacheco Creek 2.5 miles east-northeast of Pacheco Peak (lat. 37°01'40" N, long. 121°19'30" W). Named on Pacheco Peak (1955) 7.5' quadrangle.

Cedar Hill: see **Cedar Mountain** [ALAMEDA].

Cedar Mountain [ALAMEDA]: *peak,* 3 miles southeast of Mendenhall Springs (lat. 37°33'35" N, long. 121°36'20" W; near W line sec. 25, T 4 S, R 3 E). Altitude 3675 feet. Named on Cedar Mountain (1956) 7.5' quadrangle. The peak also was known as Cedar Hill (Mosier and Mosier, p. 21).

Cedar Mountain Ridge [ALAMEDA]: *ridge,* northwest-trending, 8 miles long, center 2.25 miles southeast of Mendenhall Springs (lat. 37°33'10" N, long. 121°37'30" W); Cedar Mountain is near the ridge. Named on Cedar Mountain (1956) and Mendenhall Springs (1956) 7.5' quadrangles. The ridge was given the misspelled name "Chapparal Mountains" in 1874, and the name was changed to Cedar Mountain Ridge in 1878 (Mosier and Mosier, p. 22).

Cement [SOLANO]: *locality,* 3.25 miles northeast of Fairfield (lat. 38°17'15" N, long. 122°00'10" W); the place is on the south side of present Cement Hill. Named on Suisun (1918) special quadrangle, which shows a cement mill near the place. Postal authorities established Cement post office in 1903 and discontinued it in 1928 (Frickstad, p. 192). Pacific Portland Cement Company completed a mill at the site in 1902 (Laizure, 1927b, p. 205).

Cement Hill [SOLANO]: *peak,* 4 miles north-northeast of Fairfield (lat. 38°18' N, long.

122°00'05" W; sec. 5, T 6 N, R 1 W). Named on Elmira (1953) and Fairfield North (1951) 7.5' quadrangles.

Cemetery [SANTA CLARA]: *locality,* 3 miles southeast of downtown San Jose along Southern Pacific Railroad (lat. 37°17'50" N, long. 121°51'30" W); the station for Oak Hill Memorial Park was at the site before the railroad was routed farther west. Named on San Jose (1899) 15' quadrangle.

Cemetery Creek: see **Glen Echo Creek** [ALAMEDA].

Center Creek: see **Little Llagas Creek** [SANTA CLARA].

Center Flats [SANTA CLARA]: *area,* 4 miles east of Gilroy Hot Springs (lat. 37°06'40" N, long. 121°24'05" W; sec. 35, T 9 S, R 5 E). Named on Gilroy Hot Springs (1955) 7.5' quadrangle.

Centerville: see **Centerville District** [ALAMEDA].

Centerville District [ALAMEDA]: *district,* 2 miles west-northwest of Fremont civic center in Fremont (lat. 37°33'30" N, long. 122°00'20" W). Named on Newark (1959) and Niles (1961) 7.5' quadrangles. Newark (1948) 7.5' quadrangle has the name "Centerville" for the community that joined with other communities in 1956 to form the new city of Fremont. George Lloyd set up a tent at the site in 1850 and sold cold beer to horsemen and stage passengers; then Captain George Bond built a general store there, and the name "Centerville" was adopted for the place (MacGregor, p. 46). Postal authorities established Centreville post office in 1855, changed the name to Centerville in 1893, and discontinued it in 1956 (Salley, p. 41).

Centissima Reef [MARIN]: *shoal,* 1.5 miles northwest of Point Bonita, and 2200 feet offshore (lat. 37°49'40" N, long. 122°32'55" W). Named on Point Bonita (1954) 7.5' quadrangle.

Central Basin [SAN FRANCISCO]: *water feature,* 1.5 miles south of Rincon Point along San Francisco Bay (lat. 37°45'55" N, long. 122°23' W). Named on San Francisco North (1956) 7.5' quadrangle.

Central Reservoir [ALAMEDA]: *lake,* 1500 feet long, nearly 2.5 miles east-southeast of downtown Oakland (lat. 37°47'50" N, long. 122°13'20" W). Named on Oakland East (1959) 7.5' quadrangle. The lake also was called Highland Park Reservoir (Mosier and Mosier, p. 22).

Centreville: see **Centerville District** [ALAMEDA].

Cerrilo Creek: see **Cerrito Creek** [ALAMEDA-CONTRA COSTA].

Cerrito [CONTRA COSTA]: *hill,* 1 mile south of present Richmond civic center (lat. 37°55'20" N, long. 122°20'40" W). Named on San Francisco (1899) 15' quadrangle.

Cerrito Creek [ALAMEDA-CONTRA COSTA]: *stream,* forms part of Alameda-Contra Costa county line, flows 2 miles to San Francisco Bay 3.25 miles south-southeast of downtown Richmond (lat. 37° 53'50" N, long. 122°18'40" W). Named on Richmond (1959) 7.5' quadrangle. Called Cerritos Creek on Thompson and West's (1978) map. United States Board on Geographic Names (1933, p. 206) rejected the name "Cerrilo Creek" for the feature.

Cerrito de San Antonio: see **Albany Hill** [ALAMEDA].

Cerrito Hill: see **Albany Hill** [ALAMEDA].

Cerritos Creek: see **Cerrito Creek** [ALAMEDA].

Cerritos Hills: see **Coyote Hills** [ALAMEDA].

Cerritos San Antonio: see **Albany Hill** [ALAMEDA].

Cerro [MARIN]: *locality,* 1.25 miles north of downtown San Rafael along Northwestern Pacific Railroad (lat. 37°59'30" N, long. 122° 31'50" W). Named on San Rafael (1954) 7.5' quadrangle.

Cerro Alto de los Bolbones: see **Mount Diablo** [CONTRA COSTA].

Cerro Colorado: see **Red Mountain** [SANTA CLARA].

Cerro de las Calaveras: see **Monument Peak** [ALAMEDA-SANTA CLARA].

Cerro de San Bruno: see **San Bruno Mountain** [SAN MATEO].

Cerro de San Juan: see **Mount Diablo** [CONTRA COSTA].

Chabot: see **Lake Chabot** [ALAMEDA]; **Lake Chabot** [SOLANO]; **Lake Chabot**, under **Lake Temescal** [ALAMEDA].

Chabot Terrace [SOLANO]: *district,* 3 miles north-northeast of downtown Vallejo (lat. 38°08'50" N, long. 122°14'45" W); the district is northwest of Lake Chabot. Named on Cordelia (1951) and Cuttings Wharf (1949) 7.5' quadrangles. Postal authorities established Chabot Terrace post office in 1944 and discontinued it in 1956 (Salley, p. 41).

Chadbourne [SOLANO]: *locality,* 2.25 miles west of Fairfield along Sacramento Northern Railroad (lat. 38°14'40" N, long. 122°05' W). Named on Fairfield South (1949) 7.5' quadrangle.

Chadbourne Slough [SOLANO]: *water feature,* joins Wells Slough 5 miles south-southwest of Fairfield (lat. 38°10'50" N, long. 122° 04'15" W). Named on Fairfield South (1949) 7.5' quadrangle.

Champagne Fountain [SANTA CLARA]: *locality,* nearly 2 miles northeast of downtown Saratoga along Southern Pacific Railroad (lat. 37°16'35" N, long. 122°00'25" W). Named on Cupertino (1961) 7.5' quadrangle. California Mining Bureau's (1909b) map has the name "Congress Jn." [Junction] at the place, which is the nearest railroad station to Congress Springs. The name "Congress Junction" was changed to "Champagne Fountain" in

1959 at the request of the management of a nearby winery (Willys Peck, *San Jose Mercury News*, July 22, 1981). Peninsular Railroad Company's (1912) map shows a railway station called Sorosis situated northeast of Congress Junction, about one-quarter of the way from Congress Junction to Meridian. The name "Sorosis" was from the large Sorosis fruit ranch (Willys Peck, *San Jose Mercury News*, July 22, 1981).

Champion Slough [SOLANO]: *water feature,* on Wheeler Island, joins Suisun Bay about 6 miles southwest of Birds Landing (2) (lat. 38°04'45" N, long. 121°57'30" W). Named on Honker Bay (1953) 7.5' quadrangle.

Chandler Gulch [SAN MATEO]: *canyon,* drained by a stream that flows 1.5 miles to Bradley Creek 3 miles south of the village of San Gregorio (lat. 37°16'55" N, long. 122°22'45" W). Named on La Honda (1961) 7.5' quadrangle. The name commemorates Lafayette Chandler, who had a ranch in the canyon in the late 1870's and 1880's (Brown, p. 18).

Chaparral Peak [ALAMEDA-CONTRA COSTA]: *peak,* 2.5 miles west of Orinda on Alameda-Contra Costa county line (lat. 37°52'40" N, long. 122°13'20" W; sec. 5, T 1 S, R 3 W). Named on Briones Valley (1959) 7.5' quadrangle.

Chaparral Spring [CONTRA COSTA]: *spring,* 3.25 miles north-northeast of Mount Diablo in Goethels Canyon (lat. 37°55'20" N, long. 121°52'55" W). Named on Clayton (1953) 7.5' quadrangle.

Chaplin: see **Dutton** [SOLANO].

Chapman: see **Point Chapman**, under **Steamboat Slough** [SOLANO].

Chapparal Mountains: see **Cedar Mountain Ridge** [ALAMEDA].

Charleston Slough [SANTA CLARA]: *water feature,* meandering waterway that reaches mud flats near San Francisco Bay 4.25 miles north of downtown Mountain View (lat. 37°27'10" N, long. 122°05'25" W). Named on Mountain View (1961) 7.5' quadrangle.

Chase Pond [CONTRA COSTA]: *lake,* 250 feet long, 1.5 miles south of Mount Diablo (lat. 37°51'40" N, long. 121°54'55" W; sec. 12, T 1 S, R 1 W). Named on Diablo (1953) 7.5' quadrangle.

Chauncey Point: see **Point Chauncey** [MARIN].

Chemeketa: see **Chemeketa Park** [SANTA CLARA].

Chemeketa Park [SANTA CLARA]: *settlement,* 4 miles south of Los Gatos (lat. 37°09'45" N, long. 121°58'45" W; sec. 9, T 9 S, R 1 W). Named on Los Gatos (1953) 7.5' quadrangle. The place also is called Chemeketa.

Cherry Canyon [SAN MATEO]: *canyon,* drained by a stream that flows 1.5 miles to lowlands along San Francisco Bay 1.5 miles west of downtown San Mateo (lat. 37°34'10" N, long. 122°21' W). Named on San Mateo (1956) 7.5' quadrangle.

Cherry Canyon [SANTA CLARA]: *canyon,* drained by a stream that flows 2 miles to Calero Reservoir nearly 2 miles east-southeast of New Almaden (lat. 37°10'20" N, long. 121°47'20" W). Named on Santa Teresa Hills (1953) 7.5' quadrangle.

Cherry Flat Reservoir [SANTA CLARA]: *lake,* 0.5 mile long, behind a dam on Upper Penitencia Creek nearly 4 miles east of the mouth of Alum Rock Canyon (lat. 37°23'50" N, long. 121°45'25" W). Named on Calaveras Reservoir (1961) and Mount Day (1955) 7.5' quadrangles.

Cherry Glen [SOLANO]: *valley,* 5.5 miles north of Fairfield along Laguna Creek (lat. 38°20' N, long. 122°02'30" W; near SW cor. sec. 25, T 6 N, R 2 W). Named on Fairfield North (1951) 7.5' quadrangle.

Cherry Springs [SANTA CLARA]: *spring,* 2 miles north-northwest of Mount Umunhum (lat. 37°11'20" N, long. 121°54'45" W). Named on Los Gatos (1953) 7.5' quadrangle.

Chesbro Reservoir [SANTA CLARA]: *lake,* 2.25 miles long, behind a dam on Llagas Creek 2.5 miles west-southwest of Morgan Hill (lat. 37°07' N, long. 121°41'35" W). Named on Morgan Hill (1955) and Mount Madonna (1955) 7.5' quadrangles.

Chicago: see **New Chicago** under **Alviso** [SANTA CLARA]; **Port Chicago** [CONTRA COSTA].

Chicken Hollow: see **Big Chicken Hollow** [SAN MATEO]; **Little Chicken Hollow** [SAN MATEO].

Chilanian Gulch [SANTA CLARA]: *canyon,* drained by a stream that flows 1 mile to Alamitos Creek 0.5 mile northeast of New Almaden (lat. 37°10'55" N, long. 121°48'55" W). Named on Santa Teresa Hills (1953) 7.5' quadrangle.

Chileno: see **Chileno Valley** [MARIN].

Chileno Creek [MARIN]: *stream,* heads at Laguna Lake and flows 6.25 miles to Walker Creek 3.5 miles southeast of Tomales (lat. 38°12'45" N, long. 122°51'30" W); the stream drains Chileno Valley. Named on Point Reyes NE (1954) 7.5' quadrangle. United States Board on Geographic Names (1943, p. 10) rejected the name "Arroyo San Antonio" for the upper part of the stream, and rejected the name "North Fork, San Antonio Creek" for the entire stream.

Chileno Valley [MARIN]: *valley,* on Marin-Sonoma county line, mainly in Marin County, along Chileno Creek above a point 5 miles east-southeast of Tomales (lat. 38°12'50" N, long. 122°49'30" W). Named on Petaluma (1953) and Point Reyes NE (1954) 7.5' quadrangles. The name is from natives of Chili that Adrian Godoy, a Chilean immigrant himself, brought to the place after 1868 (Mason, 1976b, p. 163). Postal authorities established

Offutt post office in Chileno Valley in Marin County in 1895, changed the name to Chileno in 1896, and discontinued it in 1900; the name was for Charles Alex Offutt (Salley, p. 43, 159).

Chimney Canyon [SANTA CLARA]: *canyon,* drained by a stream that flows 4.25 miles to East Fork Pacheco Creek nearly 7 miles north of Pacheco Peak (lat. 37°06'20" N, long. 121°15'50" W; sec. 36, T 9 S, R 6 E). Named on Mustang Peak (1955) and Pacheco Peak (1955) 7.5' quadrangles.

Chimney Gulch [SANTA CLARA]: *canyon,* drained by a stream that flows 2 miles to East Fork Pacheco Creek nearly 7 miles north-northeast of Pacheco Peak (lat. 37°06'30" N, long. 121°15'20" W). Named on Pacheco Pass (1955) and Pacheco Peak (1955) 7.5' quadrangles.

Chimney Ridge [SANTA CLARA]: *ridge,* northwest- to west-northwest-trending, 2.25 miles long, 13 miles east-southeast of Gilroy (lat. 36°58'30" N, long. 121°19' W). Named on Three Sisters (1954) 7.5' quadrangle.

Chimney Rock [MARIN]: *rock,* 3.25 miles east of the lighthouse at Point Reyes, and 100 feet off the east end of Point Reyes (lat. 37° 59'20" N, long. 122°57'45" W). Named on Drakes Bay (1953) 7.5' quadrangle.

Chimney Rock [SANTA CLARA]: *relief feature,* 5.5 miles north of Pacheco Peak (lat. 37°05'25" N, long. 121°17'05" W). Named on Pacheco Peak (1955) 7.5' quadrangle.

China Basin [SAN FRANCISCO]: *water feature,* less than 1 mile south of Rincon Point along San Francisco Bay (lat. 37°46'40" N, long. 122°23'10" W). Named on San Francisco North (1956) 7.5' quadrangle.

China Beach: see **Baker Beach** [SAN FRANCISCO].

China Camp [MARIN]: *locality,* 9.5 miles southeast of downtown Novato along San Pablo Bay (lat. 38°00'05" N, long. 122°27'40" W). Named on Petaluma Point (1959) 7.5' quadrangle. A village of Chinese people who gathered shrimp was at the site (Teather, p. 16).

China Cove: see **Winslow Cove**, under **Simpton Point** [MARIN].

China Flat [SAN MATEO]: *area,* 5.5 miles southwest of La Honda (lat. 37°16'10" N, long. 122°21'10" W; sec. 1, T 8 S, R 5 W). Named on La Honda (1961) 7.5' quadrangle.

China Gulch: see **Old Womans Creek** [SAN MATEO].

Chinamans Cut: see **Chinese Cut** [SOLANO].

Chinatown [SAN FRANCISCO]: *district,* 1.25 miles north-northeast of San Francisco civic center (lat. 37°47'45" N, long. 122°24'20" W). Named on San Francisco North (1956) 7.5' quadrangle. A small valley in the present district was the source of water for San Francisco in early American times; the feature was called Spring Valley and gave its name to

Spring Valley Water Company, which later brought water to the city from outside the present city limits (Gudde, 1969, p. 318).

Chinese Cut [SOLANO]: *water feature,* 4 miles south-southwest of Rio Vista along Sacramento River (lat. 38°06'15" N, long. 121°43'30" W). Named on Jersey Island (1978) 7.5' quadrangle. Called Chinamans Cut on Jersey Island (1952) 7.5' quadrangle.

Chipps [SOLANO]: *locality,* 6.25 miles south-southwest of Birds Landing (2) along Sacramento Northern Railroad at the north end of a railroad ferry (lat. 38°03' N, long. 121°54'50" W); the place is on Chipps Island. Named on Honker Bay (1953) 7.5' quadrangle. Honker Bay (1953, photorevised 1968 and 1973) quadrangle shows the place by an old railroad grade.

Chipps Island [SOLANO]: *island,* 5.5 miles south-southwest of Birds Landing (2) between Honker Bay, Spoonbill Creek, and Suisun Bay (lat. 38°03'30" N, long. 121°54'45" W). Named on Honker Bay (1953) 7.5' quadrangle. Called Knox I. on Ringgold's (1850c) map.

Chisholm Landing: see **Sulphur Creek** [ALAMEDA].

Chisnantuck: see **Mount Chisnantuck**, under **New Almaden** [SANTA CLARA].

Choual: see **Mount Choual**, under **Mount Chual** [SANTA CLARA].

Christie [CONTRA COSTA]: *locality,* 4 miles west-southwest of Martinez along Atchison, Topeka and Santa Fe Railroad (lat. 38° 00' N, long. 122°12'15" W). Named on Benicia (1959) and Briones Valley (1959) 7.5' quadrangles.

Christmas Hill [SANTA CLARA]: *relief feature,* 1.5 miles southwest of Gilroy (lat. 36°59'20" N, long. 121°35'05" W). Named on Chittenden (1955) 7.5' quadrangle.

Chrysopylae: see **Golden Gate** [SAN FRANCISCO].

Chual: see **Mount Chual** [SANTA CLARA].

Church Creek: see **Little Llagas Creek** [SANTA CLARA].

Church Hill [SANTA CLARA]: *peak,* nearly 1 mile west of New Almaden (lat. 37°10'40" N, long. 121°50'10" W). Named on Santa Teresa Hills (1953) 7.5' quadrangle.

Cincas Creek: see **Canoas Creek** [SANTA CLARA].

Clamshell Cut [SOLANO]: *water feature,* joins Miner Slough 10 miles north-northeast of Rio Vista (lat. 38°17'30" N, long. 121°37'15" W). Named on Vorden (1916) 7.5' quadrangle.

Clank Hollow [SOLANO]: *canyon,* 2 miles long, opens into lowlands 1 mile south-southeast of Birds Landing (2) (lat. 38°07'05" N, long. 121°51'55" W; sec. 9, T 3 N, R 1 E). Named on Antioch North (1978) 7.5' quadrangle.

Claremont Creek [ALAMEDA]: *stream,* flows 1.5 miles to lowlands 4 miles north-northeast of downtown Oakland (lat. 37°51'35" N, long. 122°14'25" W). Named on Oakland East (1959) 7.5' quadrangle. The stream was called Harwood Creek as late as 1889, and the canyon of the stream was called Telegraph Canyon until 1886 or 1887 (Mosier and Mosier, p. 23, 87).

Clark Canyon [ALAMEDA]: *canyon,* drained by a stream that flows 1 mile to lowlands 0.5 mile north of Dublin (lat. 37°42'35" N, long. 121°56'20" W). Named on Dublin (1961) 7.5' quadrangle.

Clarks Canyon [SANTA CLARA]: *canyon,* 1 mile long, branches west-northwest from North Fork Otis Canyon 4.5 miles southsouthwest of Mount Sizer (lat. 37°09'25" N, long. 121°33'10" W; sec. 17, T 9 S, R 4 E). Named on Mount Sizer (1955) 7.5' quadrangle.

Clark's Point: see **Telegraph Hill** [SAN FRANCISCO].

Clayburn [CONTRA COSTA]: *locality,* 1 mile southeast of Point San Pablo (lat. 37°57'15" N, long. 122°24'45" W). Named on San Francisco (1942) 15' quadrangle. Postal authorities established Ladrillo post office in 1906, changed the name to Clayburn in 1907, and discontinued it in 1910; the name "Ladrillo" is from bricks that were made at the place— *ladrillo* means "brick" in Spanish; the name "Clayburn" refers to the burning of clay to make bricks (Salley, p. 45, 114).

Clayton [CONTRA COSTA]: *town,* 4.25 miles north-northwest of Mount Diablo (lat. 37°56'25" N, long. 121°56'05" W; near NE cor. sec. 14, T 1 N, R 1 W). Named on Clayton (1953) 7.5' quadrangle. Postal authorities established Clayton post office in 1861 (Frickstad, p. 21), and the town incorporated in 1964. The name commemorates Joel Clayton, who laid out the townsite in 1856 during the early days of the coal boom in the vicinity (Mosier, p. 5). Brewer (p. 198) noted in 1861 that the place first was called Deadfall. The community also was called Clayton's and Claytonville (Gudde, 1949, p. 70).

Clayton's: see **Clayton** [CONTRA COSTA].

Clayton Valley [CONTRA COSTA]: *valley,* 7 miles northwest of Mount Diablo along Mount Diablo Creek (lat. 37°58' N, long. 121°59' W); Clayton is near the southeast end of the valley. Named on Clayton (1953) and Walnut Creek (1959) 7.5' quadrangles.

Claytonville: see **Clayton** [CONTRA COSTA].

Clear Creek [SAN MATEO]: *stream,* flows 3 miles to San Gregorio Creek 4.5 miles west of La Honda (lat. 37°19'30" N, long. 122°21'20" W). Named on La Honda (1961) 7.5' quadrangle. The stream was called Arroyo Limpio and Raynor Creek in the early days—*limpio* means "clear" in Spanish; the name "Raynor" was for a rancher who lived along the stream in the 1860's and 1870's (Brown, p. 19).

Clifton Court Ferry [CONTRA COSTA]: *locality,* 7.5 miles east-southeast of Byron along Old River on Contra Costa-San Joaquin county line (lat. 37°47'35" N, long. 121°33' W). Named on Bethany (1952) 7.5' quadrangle.

Clifton Court Forebay [CONTRA COSTA]: *lake,* 2.5 miles long, 9 miles southeast of Brentwood (lat. 37°50'20" N, long. 121°34'30" W). Named on Clifton Court Forebay (1978) 7.5' quadrangle. Bethany (1952) 7.5' quadrangle shows an area called Clifton Court Tract at the site of the lake.

Clifton Court Tract: see **Clifton Court Forebay** [CONTRA COSTA].

Clima [SOLANO]: *locality,* 1.5 miles west of downtown Fairfield along Sacramento Northern Railroad (lat. 38°14'55" N, long. 122°04'15" W). Named on Fairfield South (1949) 7.5' quadrangle.

Clinton: see **Oakland** [ALAMEDA].

Clinton Basin [ALAMEDA]: *water feature,* 1.5 miles south-southeast of downtown Oakland on the north side of Oakland Inner Harbor (lat. 37°47'20" N, long. 122°15'30" W). Named on Oakland West (1959) 7.5' quadrangle. The feature is at the site of the old community of Clinton.

Clyde [CONTRA COSTA]: *town,* 6 miles east of Martinez (lat. 38°01'40" N, long. 122°01'40" W; on S line sec. 12, T 2 N, R 2 W). Named on Vine Hill (1959) 7.5' quadrangle. The name is from Clyde Shipyard, which was at the place during World War I (Gudde, 1949, p. 71).

Coal Creek [SAN MATEO]: *stream,* flows nearly 1 mile to Corte Madera Creek 2.5 miles north-northeast of Mindego Hill (lat. 37°20'40" N, long. 122°12'20" W). Named on Mindego Hill (1961) 7.5' quadrangle.

Coal Mine Creek: see **Arroyo Seco** [ALAMEDA].

Coal Mine Ridge [SAN MATEO]: *ridge,* northwest-trending, 3 miles long, 3 miles northnortheast of Mindego Hill (lat. 37°20'45" N, long. 122°12'05" W). Named on Mindego Hill (1961) 7.5' quadrangle. A small low-grade coal mine was opened on the ridge in 1855 (Brown, p. 20).

Coast Campground [MARIN]: *locality,* 4.5 miles southwest of Point Reyes Station along the coast (lat. 38°01' N, long. 122°51'15" W). Named on Inverness (1954, photorevised 1971) 7.5' quadrangle.

Coast Guard Island: see **Government Island** [ALAMEDA].

Cochiyunes: see **San Pablo** [CONTRA COSTA] (1).

Codornices Creek [ALAMEDA]: *stream,* flows 1.25 miles to land fill along San Francisco Bay 5.5 miles north-northwest of downtown Oakland (lat. 37°52'55" N, long. 122°18'25" W), and continues in an artificial watercourse around Golden Gate Fields racetrack. Named on Richmond (1959) 7.5' quadrangle. Jose Domingo Peralta named the stream in 1818 after he and his brother found a nest of quail eggs on its bank—*codorniz* means "quail" in Spanish (Gudde, 1949, p. 73). United States Board on Geographic Names (1933, p. 227) rejected the form "Cordonices Creek" for the name.

Coe's Spring: see **Madrone Soda Springs** [SANTA CLARA].

Coffey Mill Gulch [ALAMEDA-SANTA CLARA]: *canyon,* drained by a stream that heads in Santa Clara County and flows nearly 3 miles to Eylar Canyon 4.5 miles south of Cedar Mountain in Alameda County (lat. 37°29'30" N, long. 121°36'05" W; near S line sec. 13, T 5 S, R 3 E). Named on Eylar Mountain (1955) 7.5' quadrangle.

Cold Canyon [SOLANO]: *canyon,* drained by a stream that flows 2.5 miles to Putah Creek 7.5 miles north of Mount Vaca (lat. 38°30'45" N, long. 122°05'45" W; near W line sec. 28, T 8 N, R 2 W). Named on Monticello Dam (1959) and Mount Vaca (1951) 7.5' quadrangles.

Cold Flat [SANTA CLARA]: *area,* nearly 1 mile north of Mount Sizer along East Fork Coyote Creek (lat. 37°13'35" N, long. 121° 30'45" W). Named on Mount Sizer (1955) 7.5' quadrangle.

Cold Springs Creek: see **Agua Fria Creek** [ALAMEDA].

Cold Stream [MARIN]: *stream,* flows 1 mile to the sea 5 miles east-southeast of Bolinas (lat. 37°52'35" N, long. 122°36'15" W). Named on San Rafael (1954) 7.5' quadrangle.

Coldwater Creek: see **Iverson Creek** [SAN MATEO].

College Park [SANTA CLARA]: *district,* 1 mile northwest of downtown San Jose (lat. 37°20'30" N, long. 121°54'15" W). Named on San Jose West (1961) 7.5' quadrangle. The district was named for its proximity to College of the Pacific, which later moved to Stockton, California (Harry Farrell, *San Jose Mercury News,* January 6, 1980). Postal authorities established College Park post office in 1888 and changed the name to Substation No. 1 [of San Jose post office] in 1899 (Salley, p. 48).

College Terrace: see **Palo Alto** [SANTA CLARA].

Collier Canyon [ALAMEDA-CONTRA COSTA]: *canyon,* drained by a stream that heads in Contra Costa County and flows 4 miles to lowlands 3 miles northwest of Livermore in Alameda County (lat. 37°42'40" N, long. 121°48'15" W). Named on Livermore (1961) and Tassajara (1953) 7.5' quadrangles. The name commemorates Michael McCollier, who settled in the canyon in 1856 (Mosier and Mosier, p. 24).

Collier Spring [MARIN]: *spring,* 4.5 miles southwest of downtown San Rafael (lat. 37°55'50" N, long. 122°35'35" W). Named on San Rafael (1954) 7.5' quadrangle. Teather (p. 17) associated the name with John Munro

Colier, who hiked and worked on trails in the neighborhood of Mount Tamalpais.

Collinsville [SOLANO]: *village,* 4 miles south-southeast of Birds Landing (2) near the mouth of Sacramento River (lat. 38°04'40" N, long. 121°51' W). Named on Antioch North (1978) 7.5' quadrangle. Postal authorities established Collinsville post office in 1862, discontinued it the same year, reestablished it in 1864, changed the name to Newport in 1867, and discontinued it in 1868; they reestablished Collinsville post office in 1871, discontinued it for a time in 1876, and discontinued it finally in 1960 (Salley, p. 48, 154). The name commemorates C.F. Collins, who settled in the neighborhood in 1856 and filed a map of the City of Collinsville in 1862 (Hoover, Rensch, and Rensch, p. 513-514). Ringgold's (1850c) map has the name "Montezuma House" east of the site of present Collinsville. In 1846 Lansford W. Hastings laid out a town and erected a building that he called Montezuma House about 1.25 miles east of present Collinsville, but this town failed to develop (Hoover, Rensch, and Rensch, p. 513).

Colma [SAN MATEO]: *village,* 3.5 miles west-northwest of downtown South San Francisco (lat. 37°40'30" N, long. 122°27'15" W). Named on San Francisco South (1956) 7.5' quadrangle. San Mateo (1942) 15' quadrangle has the name "Lawndale" at present Colma, and the name "Colma" at present Daly City. According to Stanger (1963, p. 157-158), a village called Colma began in present Daly City as an American farming center, but little by little it was annexed by Daly City until nothing was left but the name and post office; southeast of the village site some farmers and the proprietors of a group of cemeteries decided in 1924 to incorporate their property to avoid annexation by neighboring towns, and they chose the name "Lawndale" for their incorporated area, but because there already was a Lawndale post office in California, the newly incorporated area could not have a post office by that name; instead, the place took the name "Colma" from the already established post office in nearby Daly City. Postal authorities established Schoolhouse Station post office in 1869, changed the name to Colma Station in 1888, and changed it to Colma in 1943; the name "Colma" was coined from letters in the name of Thomas Coleman, a pioneer settler (Salley, p. 48, 199).

Colma Creek [SAN MATEO]: *stream,* flows nearly 6 miles to San Francisco Bay 1.25 miles east-southeast of downtown South San Francisco (lat. 37°38'55" N, long. 122°23'25" W); the creek goes through Colma. Named on San Francisco South (1956) 7.5' quadrangle. The stream was called Arroyo de San Bruno in Spanish times, and later it was called San Bruno Creek and Twelve Mile Creek (Brown, p. 21-22).

Colma Station: see **Colma** [SAN MATEO].

Colony: see **Moss Beach** [SAN MATEO].

Colorado Camp [SANTA CLARA]: *locality*, 2 miles south of Eylar Mountain (lat. 37°26'40" N, long. 121°32'25" W; near N line sec. 4, T 6 S, R 4 E); the place is along Colorado Creek. Named on Eylar Mountain (1955) 7.5' quadrangle.

Colorado Creek [SANTA CLARA]: *stream*, flows 11 miles to Arroyo Valle 2.5 miles east-southeast of Eylar Mountain (lat. 37°27'55" N, long. 121°35'35" W; sec. 25, T 5 S, R 3 E). Named on Eylar Mountain (1955) 7.5' quadrangle.

Colorado Ledge: see **Point Montara** [SAN MATEO].

Colorado Reef: see **Point Montara** [SAN MATEO].

Commission Rock: see **Mare Island Strait** [SOLANO].

Commodore Jones Point [SOLANO]: *promontory*, 1 mile northwest of downtown Benicia along Carquinez Strait (lat. 38°03'30" N, long. 122°10'25" W). Named on Benicia (1959, photorevised 1980) 7.5' quadrangle. The name commemorates Commodore Thomas ap Catesby Jones, United States Navy, who brought the storeship *Southampton* to Benicia in 1849 (United States Board on Geographic Names, 1975b, p. 4). Ringgold's (1850e) map has the name "Littles Pt." at or near present Commodore Jones Point, and has the name "Coopers Pt." for the next promontory to the southeast.

Comstock Canyon [SANTA CLARA]: *canyon*, drained by a stream that flows 1 mile to Wildcat Canyon (2) 18 miles east of Gilroy (lat. 36°57'35" N, long. 121°14'35" W). Named on Mariposa Peak (1969) 7.5' quadrangle.

Concord [CONTRA COSTA]: *city*, 5.25 miles north-northeast of Walnut Creek civic center (lat. 37°58'40" N, long. 122°01'50" W). Named on Walnut Creek (1959) 7.5' quadrangle. Postal authorities established Concord post office in 1872 (Frickstad, p. 21), and the city incorporated in 1905. Salvio Pacheco, owner of Monte del Diablo grant, founded the community and called it Todos Santos, but the strong New England influence of the population soon changed the name (Gudde, 1949, p. 76).

Cone Rock [MARIN]: *rock*, 1 mile east-northeast of downtown Sausalito near the mouth of Richardson Bay (lat. 37°51'50" N, long. 122°28'10" W). Named on San Francisco North (1956) 7.5' quadrangle.

Coney Island [CONTRA COSTA]: *island*, 2 miles long, 10 miles southeast of Brentwood along Old River (lat. 37°50'45" N, long. 121°32'50" W). Named on Clifton Court Forebay (1978) 7.5' quadrangle.

Congress Heights: see **Congress Springs** [SANTA CLARA].

Congress Junction: see **Champagne Fountain** [SANTA CLARA].

Congress Springs [SANTA CLARA]: *locality*, 1 mile west of Saratoga along Campbell Creek (present Saratoga Creek) (lat. 37°15'05" N, long. 122°03'10" W; sec. 11, T 8 S, R 2 W). Named on Palo Alto (1899, reprinted 1930) 15' quadrangle. Palo Alto (1899) 15' quadrangle has the name "Congress Heights" at the site. A resort at the place opened to the public in 1866 and featured mineral springs discovered in the early 1850's; the resort closed in 1942 (Hoover, Rensch, and Rensch, p. 458). The place also was called Pacific Congress Springs, a name given because the water there was considered similar to water from the noted Congress Springs at Saratoga, New York (Anderson, Winslow, p. 213).

Congress Springs Canyon [SANTA CLARA]: *canyon*, drained by a stream that flows 1.5 miles to Saratoga Creek 1.25 miles west-southwest of Saratoga (lat. 37°15'05" N, long. 122°03'05" W; sec. 11, T 8 S, R 2 W); the mouth of the canyon is near the site of Congress Springs. Named on Castle Rock Ridge (1955) 7.5' quadrangle.

Consolation Cove: see **Horesehoe Bay** [MARIN].

Contra Costa: see **Oakland** [ALAMEDA].

Contra Costa Hills: see **Berkeley Hills** [ALAMEDA-CONTRA COSTA].

Conyer Gulch: see **Soda Spring Canyon** [SANTA CLARA].

Cook: see **Dan Cook Canyon** [CONTRA COSTA].

Cook Canyon [ALAMEDA]: *canyon*, drained by a stream that flows 1.5 miles to Palomares Creek 4 miles southwest of Dublin (lat. 37°39'50" N, long. 121°59'35" W; sec. 20, T 3 S, R 1 W). Named on Dublin (1961) 7.5' quadrangle. The name commemorates Charles Cook and Annie L. Cook, local ranchers (Mosier and Mosier, p. 25).

Cook Canyon [SOLANO]: *canyon*, drained by a stream that flows nearly 2 miles to Green Valley Creek 7 miles west-northwest of Fairfield (lat. 38°16'35" N, long. 122°09'45" W; sec. 14, T 5 N, R 3 W). Named on Mount George (1951) 7.5' quadrangle.

Cook's Pond: see **Santa Clara** [SANTA CLARA].

Cooley: see **Camp Cooley** [SANTA CLARA].

Cooley Landing [SAN MATEO]: *locality*, 5.5 miles east of downtown Redwood City along San Francisco Bay (lat. 37°28'35" N, long. 122°07'15" W). Named on Mountain View (1961) 7.5' quadrangle. Ravenswood Wharf was built at the site in the 1850's (Hoover, Rensch, and Rensch, p. 406).

Coon Creek [SANTA CLARA]: *stream*, flows 5.25 miles to North Fork Pacheco Creek 8.5 miles north-northwest of Pacheco Peak (lat. 37°07'25" N, long. 121°20'25" W; sec. 29, T 9 S, R 6 E). Named on Mustang Peak (1955) 7.5' quadrangle.

Coon Hunters Gulch [SANTA CLARA]: *can-*

yon, drained by a stream that flows nearly 5 miles to Hunting Hollow 3.5 miles southsoutheast of Gilroy Hot Springs (lat. 37°03'50" N, long. 121°26'30" W; sec. 17, T 10 S, R 5 E). Named on Gilroy Hot Springs (1955) 7.5' quadrangle, where the name may apply only to the canyon along the lower 2.5 miles of the stream.

Coopers Point: see **Commodore Jones Point** [SOLANO].

Copernicus Peak [SANTA CLARA]: *peak,* nearly 1 mile east-northeast of Mount Hamilton (lat. 37°20'50" N, long. 121°37'45" W; sec. 10, T 7 S, R 3 E). Named on Lick Observatory (1955) 7.5' quadrangle. The staff of Lick Observatory on nearby Mount Hamilton named the peak in 1895 for Nicolaus Copernicus (Gudde, 1949, p. 78).

Copper Mine Gulch [MARIN]: *canyon,* drained by a stream that heads on Bolinas Ridge and flows southwesterly for 2 miles to Pine Gulch Creek 3 miles north-northwest of Bolinas (lat. 37°56'50" N, long. 122°42'50" W). Named on Bolinas (1954) 7.5' quadrangle. Two or three companies worked on copper prospects in the neighborhood in 1863 (Laizure, 1926, p. 320). United States Board on Geographic Names (1980, p. 3-4) approved names for several canyons that lie parallel to Copper Mine Gulch: Lewis Gulch, located between Copper Mine Gulch and Wilkins Gulch, and named for the Lewis family who lived in the canyon in the late nineteenth century; Cronin Gulch, situated 0.25 mile northwest of Copper Mine Gulch; Cottinham Gulch, located 1.25 miles northwest of Copper Mine Gulch; and Mill Gulch, located 1.5 miles northwest of Copper Mine Gulch and named in 1979 for a sawmill that was at the mouth of the canyon. At the same time the Board approved the name "Pecks Ridge" for the ridge southeast of Cottinham Gulch.

Coppinger Creek: see **Bear Creek** [SAN MATEO] (2).

Corall Hollow: see **Corral Hollow** [ALAMEDA].

Cordelia [SOLANO]: *village,* 6 miles westsouthwest of Fairfield (lat. 38°12'40" N, long. 122°08' W; on W line sec. 7, T 4 N, R 2 W). Named on Cordelia (1951) 7.5' quadrangle. Postal authorities established Cordelia post office in 1854, discontinued it in 1858, reestablished it in 1869, and discontinued it in 1943 (Salley, p. 50). The name was given to honor the wife of the founder of Fairfield, Captain Robert H. Waterman; in 1868 the original community of Cordelia moved a short distance south to a shipping point known as Bridgeport, which was along the railroad (Hoover, Rensch, and Rensch, p. 519). The name "Bridgeport" was for Bridgeport, Connecticut (Gudde, 1949, p. 78).

Cordelia Junction [SOLANO]: *locality,* 0.5 mile north-northwest of Cordelia (lat. 38°13'

N, long. 122°08'15" W; near SE cor. sec. 1, T 4 N, R 3 W). Named on Cordelia (1951) 7.5' quadrangle.

Cordelia Slough [SOLANO]: *water feature,* joins Suisun Slough 8 miles south-southwest of Fairfield (lat. 38°08'10" N, long. 122°04'55" W). Named on Fairfield South (1949) 7.5' quadrangle.

Cordell Bank [MARIN]: *shoal,* 22 miles west of the lighthouse at Point Reyes (lat. 38°02' N, long. 123°26' W). Named on Santa Rosa (1958) 1°x 2° quadrangle. Captain Edward Cordell explored the feature in 1869 and named it Sutter Bank to honor John A. Sutter; members of United States Coast Survey renamed the shoal for Captain Cordell after Cordell's death in 1870 (Gudde, 1969, p. 74-75).

Cordero Junction [SOLANO]: *locality,* 5 miles south-southeast of Vacaville along Sacramento Northern Railroad (lat. 38°17'15" N, long. 121°57'15" W; near S line sec. 10, T 5 N, R 1 W). Named on Elmira (1953) 7.5' quadrangle.

Cordilleras Creek [SAN MATEO]: *stream,* flows 3.5 miles to lowlands along San Francisco Bay 1 mile west-northwest of downtown Redwood City (lat. 37°29'20" N, long. 122°14'45" W). Named on Palo Alto (1961) and Woodside (1961) 7.5' quadrangles. Brown (p. 33) called the stream Finger Creek, and noted that this name commemorates Theodore Finger, who settled near the creek in 1855; other names for the feature were Finger's Arroyo and Arroyo de los Cadillos—*Arroyo de los Cadillos* has the meaning "Cockleburr Creek" in Spanish.

Cordonices Creek: see **Codornices Creek** [ALAMEDA].

Cordoza Canyon [SANTA CLARA]: *canyon,* drained by a stream that flows nearly 2 miles to North Fork Otis Canyon 4.5 miles southsoutheast of Mount Sizer (lat. 37°09'25" N, long. 121°33'10" W; sec. 17, T 9 S, R 4 E); the canyon heads on Cordoza Ridge. Named on Mount Sizer (1955) 7.5' quadrangle.

Cordoza Ridge [SANTA CLARA]: *ridge,* north- to northwest-trending, 1 mile long, 3.5 miles south of Mount Sizer (lat. 37°10' N, long. 121°31'30" W). Named on Mount Sizer (1955) 7.5' quadrangle.

Corinda Los Trancos [SAN MATEO]: *ridge,* southeast- to southwest-trending, 2 miles long, 5.5 miles southeast of Monara Knob (lat. 37°30'45" N, long. 122°24'20" W). Named on Montara Mountain (1956) 7.5' quadrangle.

Corinda Los Trancos Creek [SAN MATEO]: *stream,* flows 2.5 miles to Pilarcitos Creek 1.5 miles northeast of downtown Half Moon Bay (lat. 37°28'45" N, long. 122°24'15" W); the stream is east of the ridge called Corinda Los Trancos. Named on Half Moon Bay (1961) and Montara Mountain (1956) 7.5' quadrangles. According to Brown (p. 95), the stream should be called Trancas Creek—its original name was Arroyo de las Trancas.

Corkscrew Creek: see **Corkscrew Slough** [SAN MATEO].

Corkscrew Slough [SAN MATEO]: *water feature*, extends for nearly 4 miles along a circuitous course from Steinberger Slough to Redwood Creek 3 miles north-northeast of downtown Redwood City (lat. 37°31'25" N, long. 122°12'20" W). Named on Redwood Point (1959) 7.5' quadrangle. Called Corkscrew Cr. on Hayward (1915) 15' quadrangle.

Cornwall: see **Pittsburg** [CONTRA COSTA].

Cornwall Station: see **Pittsburg** [CONTRA COSTA].

Corporal [SANTA CLARA]: *locality*, about 5.5 miles south-southeast of Gilroy along Southern Pacific Railroad (lat. 36°55'45" N, long. 121°32'50" W). Named on Chittenden (1955) 7.5' quadrangle.

Corral de Tierra [SAN MATEO]:
(1) *land grant*, north of the north end of Half Moon Bay (1). Named on Half Moon Bay (1961) and Montara Mountain (1956) 7.5' quadrangles. Francisco Guerrero y Palomares received 1 league in 1839 and his heirs claimed 7766 acres patented in 1866 (Cowan, p. 103). According to Perez (p. 63), Francisco Palomeres was the grantee in 1844, and Josefa Guerrero was the patentee in 1866.
(2) *land grant*, north of the town of Half Moon Bay. Named on Half Moon Bay (1961) and Montara Mountain (1956) 7.5' quadrangles. Tiburcio Vasquez received 1 league in 1839 and claimed 4436 acres patented in 1873 (Cowan, p. 103).

Corral de Tierra: see **Pillar Point** [SAN MATEO].

Corral Hollow [ALAMEDA]: *canyon*, 10 miles long, 5.5 miles south of Midway on Alameda-San Joaquin county line (lat. 37°38'10" N, long. 121°33'20" W). Named on Midway (1953) 7.5' quadrangle. Called Corall Hollow on Goddard's (1857) map, and called Arroyo Buenos Ayres on Thompson and West's (1879) map. The feature is called Portezuela de Buenos Ayres on a Mexican map of 1834 (Gudde, 1949, p. 79). According to Mosier and Mosier (p. 25), the name "Corral" is from horse corrals built in the 1850's to hold captured wild horses, but Latta (1949, p. 234) cited a statement made by Mrs. Mamie Carroll Burns that the canyon was named for her stepfather, Edward Carroll.

Corral Hollow Creek [ALAMEDA]: *stream*, heads in San Joaquin County and flows 11 miles in Alameda County before reentering San Joaquin County 5.5 miles south of Midway (lat. 37°38'10" N, long. 121°33'20" W; at S line sec. 29, T 3 S, R 4 E); the stream goes through Corral Hollow. Named on Cedar Mountain (1956) and Midway (1953) 7.5' quadrangles. United States Board on Geographic Names (1933, p. 237) rejected the name "Buenos Ayres Creek" for the stream.

Corte de Madera Creek: see **Corte Madera Creek** [SAN MATEO]; **Sausal Creek** [SAN MATEO].

Corte de Madera del Presidio [MARIN]: *land grant*, at Corte Madera and Tiburon Peninsula. Named on San Quentin (1959) and San Rafael (1954) 7.5' quadrangles. John Reed received the land in 1834 and his heirs claimed 7845 acres patented in 1885 (Cowan, p. 30). The name is from lumber that was sent from the place to the presidio at San Francisco—*corte de madera* means "place where wood is cut" in Spanish (Gudde, 1949, p. 80).

Corte de Madera de Novato: see **Corte Madera de Novato** [MARIN].

Corte Madera [MARIN]: *town*, 3.25 miles south of downtown San Rafael (lat. 37°55'35" N, long. 122°31'40" W); the town is on Corte de Madera del Presidio grant. Named on San Quentin (1959) and San Rafael (1954) 7.5' quadrangles. Postal authorities established Corte Madera post office in 1878 and discontinued it in 1880; they established Adams post office, named for postmaster Jerry Adams, at the place in 1902 and changed the name to Corte Madera the same year (Salley, p. 1, 51). The town incorporated in 1916.

Corte Madera Channel: see **Corte Madera Creek** [MARIN].

Corte Madera Creek [MARIN]: *stream*, formed by the confluence of San Anselmo Creek and Rose Creek, flows 4.5 miles to San Francisco Bay 2.5 miles southeast of downtown San Rafael (lat. 37°56'35" N, long. 122°30'10" W). Named on San Rafael (1954) 7.5' quadrangle. United States Board on Geographic Names (1983c, p. 4) approved the name "Corte Madera Channel" for the waterway that extends for 2.25 miles from the mouth of Corte Madera Creek into San Francisco Bay.

Corte Madera Creek [SAN MATEO]: *stream*, flows 6.25 miles to marsh near Searsville Lake 6.25 miles south of downtown Redwood City (lat. 37°23'45" N, long. 122°14' W); the stream is on El Corte de Madera grant and on Cañada del Corte Madera grant. Named on Mindego Hill (1961) and Palo Alto (1961) 7.5' quadrangles. United States Board on Geographic Names (1939, p. 11) rejected the name "Corte de Madera Creek" for the feature. It was called Jones Creek in the 1850's and 1860's for Nathan Jones, a rancher (Brown, p. 23).

Corte Madera de Novato [MARIN]: *land grant*, 6 miles west-northwest of downtown Novato along Novato Creek. Named on Petaluma (1953) and San Geronimo (1954) 7.5' quadrangles. John Martin received 1 league in 1839 and claimed 8879 acres patented in 1863 (Cowan, p. 30; Cowan listed the grant under the name "Corte de Madera de Novato"). According to Perez (p. 63), the patent was issued in 1862.

Corte Madera Lake: see **Bear Gulch Reservoir** [SAN MATEO].

Corte Madera Ridge [MARIN]: *ridge*, southeast-trending, 1.25 mile long, 3.5 miles south of downtown San Rafael (lat. 37°55'20" N, long. 122°32'15" W); the ridge is southwest of Corte Madera. Named on San Rafael (1954) 7.5' quadrangle.

Costa: see **Port Costa** [CONTRA COSTA].

Cottinham Gulch [MARIN]: see **Copper Mine Gulch** [MARIN].

Cottonwood Canyon: see **Doolan Canyon** [ALAMEDA].

Cottonwood Creek [ALAMEDA-CONTRA COSTA]: *stream*, heads in Contra Costa County and flows 4.5 miles to lowlands 3.5 miles west-southwest of Livermore in Alameda County (lat. 37°42'10" N, long. 121°49'40" W); the creek drains Doolan Canyon, which originally was called Cottonwood Canyon. Named on Livermore (1961) 7.5' quadrangle. The stream first was called Los Alamos Creek, and then Alamo Creek (Mosier and Mosier, p. 25-26).

Cottrell [SAN MATEO]: *locality*, 3 miles southeast of downtown San Mateo along Southern Pacific Railroad (lat. 37°32' N, long. 122° 17'40" W). Named on San Mateo (1915) 15' quadrangle. The place was called Laurel Creek before about 1890 (Brown, p. 83).

Country Club Branch [ALAMEDA]: *stream*, flows 2 miles to Rifle Range Branch 7.5 miles east-southeast of downtown Oakland (lat. 37°45'25" N, long. 122°08'50" W). Named on Oakland East (1959) 7.5' quadrangle. The name is from Sequoyah Country Club, through which the stream flows (Mosier and Mosier, p. 26).

County Line: see **El Cerito** [CONTRA COSTA].

Cow Canyon [SANTA CLARA]: *canyon*, drained by a stream that flows 4.5 miles to Pine Spring Canyon 7 miles north of Pacheco Peak (lat. 37°06'30" N, long. 121°17'40" W; sec. 34, T 9 S, R 6 E). Named on Mustang Peak (1955) and Pacheco Peak (1955) 7.5' quadrangles.

Cow Creek [SANTA CLARA]: *stream*, flows nearly 4 miles to San Felipe Creek 6 miles south of Mount Hamilton (lat. 37°15'25" N, long. 121°39'20" W); the stream heads at Cow Hill. Named on Isabel Valley (1955) and Lick Observatory (1955) 7.5' quadrangles.

Cowell [CONTRA COSTA]: *locality*, 6.5 miles northwest of Mount Diablo (lat. 37°57'10" N, long. 121°59'20" W). Named on Clayton (1953) 7.5' quadrangle. Postal authorities established Cowell post office in 1922 and discontinued it in 1969; the name is for Joshua Cowell, who gave right of way at the place to Bay Point and Clayton Railroad (Salley, p. 52). Cowell was a company town for a cement operation (Hoover, Rensch, and Rensch, p. 67).

Cow Hill [SANTA CLARA]: *ridge*, north- to northwest-trending, 3 miles long, 4.5 miles south-southeast of Mount Isabel (lat. 37°15'25" N, long. 121°35'55" W). Named on Isabel Valley (1955) and Mount Sizer (1955) 7.5' quadrangles.

Cow Hollow: see **Marina District** [SAN FRANCISCO].

Coyote [SANTA CLARA]: *village*, 12 miles southeast of downtown San Jose along Coyote Creek (lat. 37°13' N, long. 121°44'15" W). Named on Morgan Hill (1955) 7.5' quadrangle. The community now is part of San Jose. Thompson and West's (1876) map has the names "Coyote Station" and "12 Mile House" at the place. Coyote was the site of a travelers stop called Laguna House, or Twelve Mile House, that operated as early as 1853 along the road south from San Jose (Hoover, Rensch, and Rensch, p. 431). Postal authorities established Burnett post office in 1862 and operated it until 1882, when they moved it and changed the name to Coyote; the name "Burnett" was for Peter H. Burnett, first governor of the state (Salley, p. 30).

Coyote: see **South Coyote** [SANTA CLARA]; **The Coyote**, under **Coyote Point** [SAN MATEO].

Coyote Creek [ALAMEDA-SANTA CLARA]: *stream*, formed by the confluence of East Fork and Middle Fork in Santa Clara County, flows 62 miles to the southeast end of San Francisco Bay 5 miles north-northeast of downtown Mountain View (lat. 37°27'30" N, long. 122°03' W). Near the bay, the stream marks part of Alameda-Santa Clara county line. Named on San Francisco (1956) and San Jose (1962) 1°x 2° quadrangles. Called Coyote River on New Almaden (1919) and San Jose (1899) 15' quadrangles, but United States Board on Geographic Names (1943, p. 10-11) decided against the names "Coyote River" and "Coyote Slough" for the feature. Font gave the name "Arroyo del Coyote" to the stream when the Anza expedition reached it in 1776 (Mosier and Mosier, p. 26). East Fork Coyote Creek is 13 miles long and is named on Mississippi Creek (1955) and Mount Stakes (1955) 7.5' quadrangles. United States Board on Geographic Names (1943, p. 11) rejected the names "Coyote Creek," "East Fork," and "East Fork Coyote River" for present East Fork Coyote Creek. Middle Fork Coyote Creek is 18 miles long and is named on Isabel Valley (1955), Mississippi Creek (1955), and Mount Sizer (1955) 7.5' quadrangles. On Thompson and West's (1876) map, Coyote River (present Coyote Creek) divides—about where modern maps show the creek reaching Alameda County—into two waterways, called North Coyote Slough and South Coyote Slough, which rejoin northeast of Alviso to form a single waterway, called Coyote Slough, that goes on to San Francisco

Bay. On Milpitas (1961) 7.5' quadrangle, North Coyote Slough of the older map is called Coyote Creek, and South Coyote Slough of the older map is unnamed. Thompson and West's (1876) map also shows a waterway called Big Creek Artesian Slough that extends across mud flats north and east of Alviso to join Coyote Slough north of Alviso. Mathew William Dixon established Dixon's Landing along Coyote Creek in present Warm Springs district in 1868 (Mosier and Mosier, p. 30).

Coyote Creek [CONTRA COSTA]: *stream,* flows nearly 3 miles to South San Ramon Creek 5.5 miles south-southeast of Danville (lat. 37°45'10" N, long. 121°56'45" W). Named on Diablo (1953) 7.5' quadrangle.

Coyote Creek [MARIN]: *stream,* flows 2.5 miles to Richardson Bay 6.25 miles south of downtown San Rafael (lat. 37°52'55" N, long. 122°31'15" W); the stream heads on Coyote Ridge. Named on Point Bonita (1954) and San Rafael (1954) 7.5' quadrangles.

Coyote Creek [SAN MATEO]: *stream,* flows 2.25 miles to San Gregorio Creek 5.5 miles west of La Honda (lat. 37°19'40" N, long. 122°22'05" W). Named on La Honda (1961) 7.5' quadrangle.

Coyote Creek: see **Little Coyote Creek** [SANTA CLARA].

Coyote Hill [SANTA CLARA]: *hill,* 3 miles south-southeast of downtown Palo Alto (lat. 37°23'55" N, long. 122°08'50" W). Altitude 371 feet. Named on Palo Alto (1961) 7.5' quadrangle.

Coyote Hill: see **Big Coyote Hill**, under **Coyote Point** [SAN MATEO].

Coyote Hill Creek: see **Coyote Hills Slough** [ALAMEDA].

Coyote Hills [ALAMEDA]: *ridge,* northwest- to north-northwest-trending, nearly 3 miles long, 2.5 miles west-northwest of downtown Newark (lat. 37°32'45" N, long. 122°05'15" W). Named on Newark (1959) 7.5' quadrangle. The feature first was called Cerritos Hills, and later it was called Potrero Hills for Potrero de los Cerritos grant; the name "Coyote Hills" was given in the 1880's because coyotes at the place howled in response to the whistling of trains on the nearby tracks (Mosier and Mosier, p. 26). E.H. Dyer, a surveyor, gave the name "Hunter Island" in the 1850's to a hill situated north of Coyote Hills and surrounded by marsh; W.J. Lewis, another surveyor, renamed the feature Salmon Island in 1860 for Daniel E. Salmon, who owned it (Mosier and Mosier, p. 75).

Coyote Hills Slough [ALAMEDA]: *water feature,* enters San Francisco Bay 8 miles south-southwest of downtown Hayward (lat. 37°33'45" N, long. 122°07'50" W); the feature is north of Coyote Hills. Named on Newark (1948) and Redwood Point (1959) 7.5' quadrangles. Called Coyote Hill Creek on

Haywards (1899) 15' quadrangle.

Coyote Lake [SANTA CLARA]: *lake,* 3 miles long, behind a dam on Coyote Creek 4 miles northeast of San Martin (lat. 37°07'05" N, long. 121°32'55" W; sec. 29 T 9 S, R 4 E). Named on Gilroy (1955) 7.5' quadrangle.

Coyote Peak [SANTA CLARA]: *peak,* 3.5 miles northeast of New Almaden (lat. 37°12'30" N, long. 121°46'30" W). Altitude 1155 feet. Named on Santa Teresa Hills (1953) 7.5' quadrangle.

Coyote Point [SAN MATEO]: *promontory,* less than 2 miles north of downtown San Mateo along San Francisco Bay (lat. 37°35'30" N, long. 122°19'10" W). Named on San Mateo (1956) 7.5' quadrangle, which gives the name "Point San Mateo" as an alternate. Called San Mateo Pt. on San Mateo (1915) 15' quadrangle, and called Punta San Matheo on Beechey's (1827-1828) map. United States Board on Geographic Names (1961b, p. 10) rejected the names "San Mateo Point," "Point San Mateo," "Point San Matheo," and "Big Coyote Point" for the feature. The promontory had the names "The Coyote," "The Big Coyote," and "Big Coyote Hill" in the 1850's; the area along the shore for 1.5 miles west of present Coyote Point was called San Mateo Beach until the 1890's or later (Brown, p. 23, 84).

Coyote Point: see **Little Coyote Point** [SAN MATEO].

Coyote Point Yacht Harbor [SAN MATEO]: *water feature,* 1.5 miles north-northeast of downtown San Mateo along San Francisco Bay (lat. 37°35'20" N, long. 122°19' W); the feature is east of Coyote Point. Named on San Mateo (1956) 7.5' quadrangle.

Coyote Ridge [MARIN]: *ridge,* south-trending, 2 miles long, 3.5 miles north-northwest of Point Bonita (lat. 37°51'35" N, long. 122° 33'15" W). Named on Point Bonita (1954) 7.5' quadrangle.

Coyote River: see **Coyote Creek** [ALAMEDA-SANTA CLARA].

Coyote Slough: see **Coyote Creek** [ALAMEDA-SANTA CLARA]; **North Coyote Slough**, under **Coyote Creek** [ALAMEDA-SANTA CLARA]; **South Coyote Slough**, under **Coyote Creek** [ALAMEDA-SANTA CLARA].

Coyote Station: see **Coyote** [SANTA CLARA].

Coyote Valley: see **Tamalpais Valley** [MARIN].

Crandall Creek [ALAMEDA]: *stream,* diverges southwest from Alameda Creek 3.25 miles north-northeast of Newark (lat. 37°34'30" N, long. 122°01'05" W), and continues for another 2.5 miles before ending. Named on Newark (1948) 7.5' quadrangle. The name "Crandall Creek" is for a family that lived along the stream (Mosier and Mosier, p. 26-27).

Crane Ridge [ALAMEDA]: *ridge,* northwest- to west-northwest-trending, 6 miles long, center 2 miles northeast of Mendenhall Springs (lat. 37°36'30" N, long. 121°37'30" W). Named on Altamont (1953), Cedar Mountain (1956), and Mendenhall Springs (1956) 7.5' quadrangles. The name is for Andrew Edward Crane, a settler of 1876 (Mosier and Mosier, p. 27).

Creamery Bay [MARIN]: *bay,* opens into Drakes Estero 6 miles northeast of the lighthouse at Point Reyes (lat. 38°03'35" N, long. 122°57' W). Named on Drakes Bay (1953) 7.5' quadrangle.

Creed [SOLANO]: *locality,* 2.5 miles east-northeast of Denverton along Sacramento Northern Railroad (lat. 38°14'30" N, long. 121° 51'15" W; near S line sec. 27, T 5 N, R 1 E). Named on Birds Landing (1953) 7.5' quadrangle. Called Reservoir on Birds Landing (1918) 7.5' quadrangle.

Creston [SOLANO]: *locality,* 3.5 miles west of Cordelia along Southern Pacific Railroad (lat. 38°12'30" N, long. 122°12' W; sec. 9, T 4 N, R 3 W). Named on Cordelia (1951) 7.5' quadrangle.

Crocker Mountain: see **San Bruno Mountain** [SAN MATEO].

Crockett [CONTRA COSTA]: *town,* 5 miles west-northwest of Martinez (lat. 38°03'15" N, long. 122°12'45" W). Named on Benicia (1959) 7.5' quadrangle. Postal authorities established Crockettville post office in 1883 and changed the name to Crockett the same year (Salley, p. 53). The name commemorates Joseph B. Crockett, who was a justice of California supreme court in 1867 (Hanna, P.T., p. 77). Thomas Edwards, Sr., purchased land from Judge Crockett and built a home in 1867 that became the nucleus of a company town of California and Hawaiian Sugar Refinery (Hoover, Rensch, and Rensch, p. 66-67).

Crockettville: see **Crockett** [CONTRA COSTA].

Cronin Gulch: see **Copper Mine Gulch** [MARIN].

Cronkhite: see **Fort Cronkhite Military Reservation** [MARIN].

Cropley Creek: see **Sweigert Creek** [SANTA CLARA].

Crosley Creek [SANTA CLARA]: *stream,* flows nearly 1 mile to lowlands 1.5 miles north-northeast of Berryessa (lat. 37°24'30" N, long. 121°50'35" W). Named on Calaveras Reservoir (1961) 7.5' quadrangle.

Cross Slough [SOLANO]: *water feature,* extends from Nurse Slough to Montezuma Slough 4.5 miles southwest of Denverton (lat. 38° 11' N, long. 121°57'45" W). Named on Denverton (1953) 7.5' quadrangle.

Crow Canyon: see **Crow Creek** [ALAMEDA].

Crow Creek [ALAMEDA]: *stream,* flows 8 miles to San Lorenzo Creek 2 miles northeast of downtown Hayward (lat. 37°41'35" N, long. 122°03'25" W). Named on Hayward (1959) and Las Trampas Ridge (1959) 7.5' quadrangles. Mosier and Mosier (p. 27) used

the name "Crow Canyon" for the canyon of the creek, and noted that the name is for William Granville Crow, who settled at the place in the 1850's.

Croy Creek [SANTA CLARA]: *stream,* flows 2.5 miles to Uvas Creek 4.5 miles east-southeast of Loma Prieta (lat. 37°05'05" N, long. 121°46'05" W; sec. 5, T 10 S, R 2 E); the stream is west of Croy Ridge. Named on Loma Prieta (1955) 7.5' quadrangle.

Croy Ridge [SANTA CLARA]: *ridge,* north-trending, 2 miles long, 5.5 miles east-southeast of Loma Prieta (lat. 37°04' N, long. 121° 45'15" W). Named on Loma Prieta (1955) 7.5' quadrangle.

Crystal Lake [MARIN]: *lake,* 1750 feet long, nearly 1 mile northeast of Double Point (lat. 37°57'20" N, long. 122°46'10" W). Named on Double Point (1954) 7.5' quadrangle.

Crystal Peak: see **Sveadal** [SANTA CLARA].

Crystal Springs: see **Lower Crystal Springs Reservoir** [SAN MATEO].

Crystal Springs Lake: see **Lower Crystal Springs Reservoir** [SAN MATEO].

Crystal Springs Reservoir: see **Lower Crystal Springs Reservoir** [SAN MATEO]; **Upper Crystal Springs Reservoir** [SAN MATEO].

Cuchilla de Almaden: see **New Almaden** [SANTA CLARA].

Cuchilla de la nema de la Luis Cheavoya: see **New Almaden** [SANTA CLARA].

Cuchilla de los Ajos: see **Cahill Ridge** [SAN MATEO].

Cuchillo de Pomponio: see **Pomponio Creek** [SAN MATEO].

Cuesta de los Gatos: see **Wrights** [SANTA CLARA].

Cull Canyon: see **Cull Creek** [ALAMEDA].

Cull Creek [ALAMEDA]: *stream,* flows 7.5 miles to Crow Creek 2.5 miles northeast of downtown Hayward (lat. 37°42'05" N, long. 122°03'10" W). Named on Hayward (1959) and Las Trampas Ridge (1959) 7.5' quadrangles. Mosier and Mosier (p. 27) used the name "Cull Canyon" for the canyon of the stream, and noted that it was named for William Slead Cull, who settled there in the 1850's.

Cupertino [SANTA CLARA]: *city,* 8 miles west of downtown San Jose (lat. 37°19'25" N, long. 122°01'55" W). Named on Cupertino (1961) 7.5' quadrangle. John T. Doyle purchased land along Stevens Creek in present Monte Vista, and in 1873 he built a house there that in 1882 became the site of Cupertino post office (Hoover, Rensch, and Rensch, p. 459). The name "Cupertino" came from Arroyo de San Jose Cupertino, the original name of Stevens Creek (Butler, p. 108). Postal authorities established this first Cupertino post office in 1882 and discontinued it in 1894 (Frickstad, p. 173). Meanwhile, a settlement called West Side developed in present Cupertino at the intersection of present Stevens Creek Boulevard and Saratoga-Sunnyvale Road—the place is named on Santa Cruz (1902) 30' quadrangle. Postal authorities established West Side post office in 1892 and changed the name to Cupertino in 1900 (Frickstad, p. 175). Cupertino incorporated in 1955.

Cupertino Creek: see **Stevens Creek** [SANTA CLARA].

Curry Canyon [CONTRA COSTA]: *canyon,* drained by a stream that flows 5 miles to Marsh Creek 2.5 miles east of Mount Diablo (lat. 37°52'50" N, long. 121°51'50" W; sec. 4, T 1 S, R 1 E). Named on Antioch South (1953), Diablo (1953), and Tassajara (1953) 7.5' quadrangles. Whitney (p. 26) mentioned Curry's Cañada, and Stanton (p. 1020) referred to Currys Creek, or Currys Cañada.

Curry's Cañada: see **Curry Canyon** [CONTRA COSTA].

Currys Creek: see **Curry Canyon** [CONTRA COSTA].

Curtis: see **Rio Vista Junction** [SOLANO].

Curtis Gulch: see **Liberty Gulch** [MARIN].

Curtner [ALAMEDA]: *locality,* 6 miles southsoutheast of Fremont civic center along Western Pacific Railroad (lat. 37°28'10" N, long. 121°55'20" W). Named on Milpitas (1961) 7.5' quadrangle.

Cut: see **The Cut**, under **Bay Slough** [SAN MATEO].

Cutoff: see **The Cutoff**, under **Bay Slough** [SAN MATEO].

Cutoff Slough [SOLANO]: *water feature,* extends from Montezuma Slough to Suisun Slough 4 miles south of Fairfield (lat. 38°11'35" N, long. 122°02'15" W). Named on Denverton (1953) and Fairfield South (1949) 7.5' quadrangles.

Cygnus [SOLANO]: *locality,* 7 miles southsouthwest of Fairfield along Southern Pacific Railroad (lat. 38°09'10" N, long. 122°05'20" W). Named on Fairfield South (1949) 7.5' quadrangle. Called Drawbridge on Karquines (1898) 15' quadrangle. Postal authorities established Cygnus post office in 1902 and discontinued it in 1907 (Frickstad, p. 192).

Cypress Grove [MARIN]: *locality,* 5.5 miles south of Tomales on the northeast side of Tomales Bay (lat. 38°09'55" N, long. 122°53'55" W). Named on Tomales (1954) 7.5' quadrangle. Point Reyes (1918) 15' quadrangle shows the place along Northwestern Pacific Railroad.

Cypress Point [CONTRA COSTA]: *promontory,* 3.5 miles southeast of Point San Pablo along San Francisco Bay (lat. 37°55'20" N, long. 122°23'25" W). Named on San Quentin (1959) 7.5' quadrangle.

— D —

Dairy Flat [SANTA CLARA]: *area,* 5.5 miles west-southwest of Mount Sizer (lat. 37°11'30"

N, long. 121°36'30" W). Named on Mount Sizer (1955) 7.5' quadrangle.

Dairy Gulch [SAN MATEO]: *canyon,* drained by a stream that flows 1.25 miles to the sea 3 miles south-southwest of the village of San Gregorio (lat. 37°17'10" N, long. 122°24'25" W). Named on San Gregorio (1961, photorevised 1968) 7.5' quadrangle.

Dalton Manor: see **Benicia** [SOLANO].

Daly City [SAN MATEO]: *city,* 4.25 miles northwest of downtown South San Francisco (lat. 37°42'20" N, long. 122°27'40" W). Named on San Francisco South (1956) 7.5' quadrangle. A travelers stop called Abbey House was built at the site of present downtown Daly City in the 1850's, and it was still there when refugees from the 1906 earthquake began settling nearby on John D. Daly's dairy ranch; the citizens of the new community voted in 1911 to incorporate their town and named it for dairyman Daly (Stanger, 1963, p. 65, 157). Postal authorities established Vista Grande post office in 1908 and changed the name to Daly City in 1913 (Salley, p. 233).

Damiani Creek [SAN MATEO]: *stream,* flows less than 1 mile to Corte Madera Creek 3 miles north of Mindego Hill (lat. 37°21'20" N, long. 122°12'55" W). Named on Mindego Hill (1961) 7.5' quadrangle.

Damon Marsh: see **Fitchburg** [ALAMEDA].

Damon's Landing: see **Fitchburg** [ALAMEDA].

Damon Slough: see **Fitchburg** [ALAMEDA].

Dan Cook Canyon [CONTRA COSTA]: *canyon,* drained by a stream that flows 2 miles to Green Valley 3.5 miles south-southwest of Mount Diablo (lat. 37°50'15" N, long. 121°57' W; near NW cor. sec. 23, T 1 S, R 1 W). Named on Diablo (1953) 7.5' quadrangle.

Daniels Creek: see **Lagunitas Creek** [MARIN].

Danielson [SOLANO]: *locality,* 3.5 miles westsouthwest of Fairfield along Sacramento Northern Railroad (lat. 38°14'15" N, long. 122° 06'15" W). Named on Fairfield South (1949) 7.5' quadrangle.

Danville [CONTRA COSTA]: *city,* 6.25 miles southwest of Mount Diablo (lat. 37°49'20" N, long. 121°59'55" W). Named on Diablo (1953) and Las Trampas Ridge (1959) 7.5' quadrangles. Postal authorities established Danville post office in 1860 (Frickstad, p. 21). The name is from Danville, Kentucky (Hoover, Rensch, and Rensch, p. 57).

Dark Canyon [CONTRA COSTA]: *canyon,* 0.5 mile long, 4.25 miles east of Mount Diablo along Marsh Creek (lat. 37°53'05" N, long. 121°50'05" W; sec. 35, T 1 N, R 1 E). Named on Antioch South (1953) 7.5' quadrangle.

Dark Gulch [SAN MATEO]: *canyon,* drained by a stream that flows nearly 1 mile to Pescadero Creek 3.5 miles south-southeast of La Honda (lat. 37°15'55" N, long. 122°15'30" W; near W line sec. 1, T 8 S, R 4 W). Named on La Honda (1961) 7.5' quadrangle.

Davaney Canyon [ALAMEDA]: *canyon,* drained by a stream that flows 2.25 miles to Dublin Creek 0.5 mile southwest of Dublin (lat. 37°41'40" N, long. 121°56'50" W; near SW cor. sec. 2, T 3 S, R 1 W). Named on Dublin (1961) 7.5' quadrangle.

Davidson: see **Mount Davidson** [SAN FRANCISCO].

Davis Canyon: see **Bolinas Creek** [ALAMEDA].

Davis Point [CONTRA COSTA]: *promontory,* 6.25 miles east-northeast of Pinole Point on the south side of the mouth of Carquinez Strait (lat. 38°03'05" N, long. 122°15'35" W). Named on Mare Island (1959) 7.5' quadrangle. Called Pt. Davis on Ringgold's (1850a) map.

Day: see **Mount Day** [SANTA CLARA].

Day Creek: see **Lions Peak** [SANTA CLARA].

Day Island [MARIN]: *hill,* 4.5 miles east of downtown Novato near San Pablo Bay (lat. 38°06'10" N, long. 122°29'20" W). Named on Petaluma Point (1959) 7.5' quadrangle.

Deadfall: see **Clayton** [CONTRA COSTA].

Deadman Gulch [ALAMEDA]: *canyon,* flows 1 mile to Eylar Canyon 4 miles south of Cedar Mountain (lat. 37°29'40" N, long. 121°35'50" W; sec. 13, T 5 S, R 3 E). Named on Eylar Mountain (1955) 7.5' quadrangle.

Deadman Island [SOLANO]: *peninsula,* 2.25 miles south-southeast of Fairfield along Suisun Slough at the mouth of Hill Slough (lat. 38°13'15" N, long. 122°01'40" W). Named on Fairfield South (1949) 7.5' quadrangle.

Deadmans Gulch [MARIN]: *canyon,* drained by a stream that flows 0.5 mile to Lagunitas Creek 10.5 miles southwest of downtown Novato (lat. 38°01'40" N, long. 122°44'05" W). Named on San Geronimo (1954) 7.5' quadrangle.

Dean's Island: see **Wood Island** [MARIN].

Dearborn Gulch: see **Dearborn Park** [SAN MATEO].

Dearborn Park [SAN MATEO]: *settlement,* 5 miles south-southwest of La Honda (lat. 37°15'20" N, long. 122°18'55" W; near NE cor. sec. 8, T 8 S, R 4 W). Named on La Honda (1961) 7.5' quadrangle. Brown (p. 26) used the name "Dearborn Gulch" for the canyon in which the settlement lies, and noted that Henry Dearborn came to the place in the late 1880's.

Decker Island [SOLANO]: *island,* nearly 2 miles long, 4.5 miles south-southwest of Rio Vista in Sacramento River (lat. 38°05'30" N, long. 121°43' W). Named on Jersey Island (1978) 7.5' quadrangle. An artificial waterway across the neck of Horseshoe Bend forms the island.

Decoto [ALAMEDA]: *district,* 5 miles north of downtown Newark in Union City (lat. 37°36' N, long. 122°01'15" W). Named on Newark (1959) 7.5' quadrangle. Newark (1948) 7.5' quadrangle has the name on the community

that joined with the neighboring community of Alvarado in 1958 to form the new city of Union City (Hoover, Rensch, and Rensch, p. 17). Postal authorities established Decoto post office in 1871, discontinued it in 1872, reestablished it in 1875, and discontinued it in 1959 (Salley, p. 56). The name commemorates Ezra Decoto, who sold right-of-way to the railroad in 1867 (Gudde, 1949, p. 90-91).

Deep Gulch [SANTA CLARA]: *canyon,* drained by a stream that flows almost 1 mile to Alamitos Creek near the south end of New Almaden (lat. 37°10'25" N, long. 121°49'25" W). Named on Santa Teresa Hills (1953) 7.5' quadrangle.

Deep Water Channel: see **Oakland Inner Harbor** [ALAMEDA].

Deep Water Ship Channel: see **Sacramento River Deep Water Ship Channel** [SOLANO].

Deepwater Slough [SAN MATEO]: *water feature,* 2.25 miles north of downtown Redwood City off Redwood Creek (lat. 37°31' N, long. 122°13' W). Named on Redwood Point (1959) 7.5' quadrangle.

Deer Creek [CONTRA COSTA]: *stream,* flows 8 miles to Marsh Creek less than 1 mile west-northwest of Brentwood (lat. 37°55'20" N, long. 121°42'40" W); the stream drains Deer Valley. Named on Antioch South (1953) and Brentwood (1954) 7.5' quadrangles. Called Dry Creek on Mount Diablo (1898) 15' quadrangle.

Deer Creek [SANTA CLARA]: *stream,* flows 3.25 miles to Matadero Creek 3 miles south of downtown Palo Alto (lat. 37°24'15" N, long. 122°09'05" W). Named on Palo Alto (1961, photorevised 1968 and 1973) 7.5' quadrangle. Called Purisima Creek on Mindego Hill (1961) and Palo Alto (1961) 7.5' quadrangles. United States Board on Geographic Names (1972, p. 2) listed the variant name "Purisima Creek" for the stream.

Deer Creek: see **Arroyo Ojo de Agua** [SAN MATEO].

Deer Flat [CONTRA COSTA]: *area,* 1 mile west-northwest of Mount Diablo (lat. 37°53'20" N, long. 121°56' W; near E line sec. 35, T 1 N, R 1 W). Named on Clayton (1953) 7.5' quadrangle.

Deer Flat Creek [CONTRA COSTA]: *stream,* flows 1.5 miles to Mitchell Creek nearly 2 miles west-northwest of Mount Diablo (lat. 37°53'45" N, long. 121°56'25" W; sec. 35, T 1 N, R 1 W); the stream is north of Deer Flat. Named on Clayton (1953) 7.5' quadrangle.

Deer Horn Spring [SANTA CLARA]: *spring,* 1.5 miles west of Mount Sizer (lat. 37°12'45" N, long. 121°32'30" W; sec. 28, T 8 S, R 4 E). Named on Mount Sizer (1955) 7.5' quadrangle.

Deer Island [MARIN]: *hill,* 2 miles east-southeast of downtown Novato (lat. 38°05'50" N, long. 122°32'10" W). Named on Novato (1954) 7.5' quadrangle.

Deer Park Creek [MARIN]: *stream,* flows 1.25 miles to San Anselmo Creek 3.25 miles west-northwest of downtown San Rafael (lat. 37°59' N, long. 122°35'20" W). Named on San Rafael (1954) 7.5' quadrangle.

Deer Park Ridge [SAN MATEO]: *ridge,* west-northwest-trending, 2.5 miles long, 3 miles west-southwest of La Honda (lat. 37°18' N, long. 122°19' W). Named on La Honda (1961) 7.5' quadrangle.

Deer Valley [CONTRA COSTA]: *valley,* 7 miles east-northeast of Mount Diablo (lat. 37°55'15" N, long. 121°47'30" W); the valley is along Deer Creek. Named on Antioch South (1953) 7.5' quadrangle.

De Forest: see **San Antonio Valley** [SANTA CLARA].

De Las Pulgas: see **Pulgas** [SAN MATEO].

De Laveaga [CONTRA COSTA]: *locality,* 1 mile northwest of present Orinda along California and Nevada Railroad (lat. 37°53'20" N, long. 122°11'35" W). Named on Concord (1897) 15' quadrangle.

Del Valle: see **Lake Del Valle** [ALAMEDA].

Dennis Martin Creek: see **Martin Creek** [SAN MATEO].

Denniston Creek [SAN MATEO]: *stream,* flows 4.25 miles to the sea 3.5 miles south of Montara Knob at Princeton (lat. 37°30'10" N, long. 122°29'10" W). Named on Montara Mountain (1956) 7.5' quadrangle. The name commemorates James G. Denniston, who came to California with the New York Volunteers, and later settled by the stream (Hanna, P.T., p. 85).

Denverton [SOLANO]: *locality,* 10.5 miles south-southeast of Vacaville (lat. 38°13'30" N, long. 121°53'50" W; near E line sec. 6, T 4 N, R 1 E). Named on Denverton (1953) 7.5' quadrangle. The place first was called Nurse's Landing, for Dr. Stephen K. Nurse, who purchased land there in 1853 and built a house, store, and wharf; the name Denverton was given in 1858 to honor J.W. Denver, congressman from the district (Hoover, Rensch, and Rensch, p. 524). Postal authorities established Denverton post office in 1858 and discontinued it in 1911 (Frickstad, p. 192).

Denverton Creek [SOLANO]: *stream,* flows nearly 2 miles to Denverton Slough near Denverton (lat. 38°13'25" N, long. 121°53'50" W; near E line sec. 6, T 4 N, R 1 E). Named on Denverton (1953) 7.5' quadrangle.

Denverton Slough [SOLANO]: *water feature,* heads near Denverton and joins Nurse Slough 2 miles south-southwest of Denverton (lat. 38°12' N, long. 121°55'05" W). Named on Denverton (1953) 7.5' quadrangle.

Denverton Station [SOLANO]: *locality,* 1.25 miles east-southeast of Denverton along Sacramento Northern Railroad (lat. 38°13'15" N, long. 121°52'25" W; sec. 4, T 4 N, R 1 E). Named on Antioch (1908) 15' quadrangle.

Devils Canyon [SAN MATEO]: *canyon,* on up-per reaches of Peters Creek 3.25 miles east-southeast of Mindego Hill (lat. 37°17'20" N, long. 122°10'30" W). Named on Mindego Hill (1961) 7.5' quadrangle. According to Brown (p. 27), the stream in the canyon should be called Devil's Canyon Creek.

Devil's Canyon Creek: see **Devils Canyon** [SAN MATEO]; **Peters Creek** [SAN MATEO].

Devils Gate [SOLANO]: *narrows,* 7.5 miles north of Mount Vaca along Putah Creek on Solano-Yolo county line (lat. 38°30'45" N, long. 122°06' W; sec. 29, T 8 N, R 2 W). Named on Capay (1945) 15' quadrangle.

Devils Gulch [MARIN]: *canyon,* drained by a stream that flows 3 miles to Lagunitas Creek 10.5 miles west-southwest of downtown Novato (lat. 38°01'45" N, long. 122°44'05" W). Named on San Geronimo (1954) 7.5' quadrangle.

Devils Hole [ALAMEDA]: *relief feature,* 4.5 miles south of Mendenhall Springs (lat. 37°31'25" N, long. 121°37'55" W; sec. 3, T 5 S, R 3 E). Named on Mendenhall Springs (1956) 7.5' quadrangle.

Devils Pit [ALAMEDA]: *relief feature,* 2.25 miles south of Cedar Mountain (lat. 37°31'40" N, long. 121°36'10" W; sec. 1, T 5 S, R 3 E). Named on Cedar Mountain (1956) 7.5' quadrangle.

Devils Pulpit [CONTRA COSTA]: *relief feature,* 0.25 mile east-southeast of Mount Diablo (lat. 37°52'50" N, long. 121°54'30" W; near N line sec. 6, T 1 S, R 1 E). Named on Clayton (1953) 7.5' quadrangle.

Devils Slide [CONTRA COSTA]: *relief feature,* 3 miles south of Mount Diablo on the north side of East Fork Sycamore Creek (1) (lat. 37°50'30" N, long. 121°54'20" W; sec. 18, T 1 S, R 1 E). Named on Diablo (1953) 7.5' quadrangle.

Devils Slide [SAN MATEO]: *promontory,* 2.25 miles west-northwest of Montara Knob along the coast (lat. 37°34'30" N, long. 122°31'10" W). Named on Montara Mountain (1956) 7.5' quadrangle. The feature had the early names "Saddle Rock" and "Striped Rock"; the name "Devils Slide" is used also for the steep slope on the coast just north of the promontory, where slides periodically destroy the highway (Brown, p. 27).

Devils Slough [SANTA CLARA]: *water feature,* opens into mud flats near San Francisco Bay 4.5 miles north-northeast of downtown Mountain View (lat. 37°26'55" N, long. 122°02'45" W). Named on Mountain View (1961, photorevised 1968 and 1973) 7.5' quadrangle, which shows Devils Slough and nearby Jagel Slough as artificial watercourses through salt ponds along opposite sides of a waterway that, together with adjacent marsh, is called Jagel Slough on Mountain View (1953) 7.5' quadrangle. Palo Alto (1899) 15' quadrangle has the name "Devils Slough" for a waterway that winds through tidal marshes to the bay south of the mouth of Coyote Creek (lat. 37°26'55" N, long. 122°02'55" W).

Dewing Park: see **Saranap** [CONTRA COSTA].

Dexter Canyon [SANTA CLARA]: *canyon,* drained by a stream that flows 3 miles to Coyote Creek 2.25 miles south-southwest of Gilroy Hot Springs (lat. 37°04'40" N, long. 121°29'35" W; sec. 11, T 10 S, R 4 E). Named on Gilroy (1955) and Gilroy Hot Springs (1955) 7.5' quadrangles. Called Leesley and Dexter Canyon on Morgan Hill (1917) 15' quadrangle.

Dexter Creek [SANTA CLARA]: *stream,* flows 1.25 miles to Jones Creek 1 mile east-southeast of Old Gilroy (lat. 36°59'30" N, long. 121°30'40" W). Named on Chittenden (1955, photorevised 1968 and 1973) 7.5' quadrangle. The name commemorates the Dexter family, ranchers who came to the neighborhood in the nineteenth century; the stream has the variant name "Furlong Creek" (United States Board on Geographic Names, 1973a, p. 2).

Diablo [CONTRA COSTA]: *settlement,* 2.5 miles east-northeast of Danville in Green Valley (lat. 37°50'05" N, long. 121°57'30" W; sec. 22, T 1 S, E 1 W). Named on Diablo (1953) 7.5' quadrangle. Postal authorities established Diablo post office in 1916 (Frickstad, p. 21).

Diablo: see **Mount Diablo** [CONTRA COSTA]; **Point Diablo** [MARIN].

Diablo Range [ALAMEDA-CONTRA COSTA-SANTA CLARA]: *range,* includes the east part of Alameda County and Santa Clara County, and most of the east part of Contra Costa County. Named on San Jose (1962) and Santa Cruz (1956) 1°x 2° quadrangles. The range extends from Carquinez Strait in Contra Costa County southeast to Antelope Valley in Kern County; Mount Diablo is near the northwest end. Called Sierra del Monte Diablo on Parke's (1854-1855) map. Whitney (p. 2) used the name "Monte Diablo Range," and stated that the range "is so called from the conspicuous point [Mount Diablo] of that name." United States Board on Geographic Names (1933, p. 264) rejected the names "Monte Diablo Range," "Mount Diablo Range," and "Sierra del Monte Diablo" for the feature. Carey and Miller (p. 153) referred to the part of the range east of San Jose in Santa Clara County as Mount Hamilton Range.

Diamond Canyon: see **Dimond Canyon** [ALAMEDA].

Diamond Creek: see **Dimond Canyon** [ALAMEDA].

Diavolo: see **Mount Diavolo**, under **Mount Diablo** [CONTRA COSTA].

Digges Canyon [SAN MATEO]: *canyon,* drained by Apanolio Creek, which flows 3.5 miles to Pilarcitos Creek 1.25 miles northeast of downtown Half Moon Bay (lat. 37°28'35" N, long. 122°24'40" W). Named on Half Moon Bay (1961) and Montara Mountain

(1956) 7.5' quadrangles. R. Montgomery Digges had a ranch in the canyon after 1866 (Brown, p. 27). Other names for the canyon, or for the stream in it, include Cañada de Polonio or Apolonio—Apolonio Rodriguez settled at the mouth of the canyon in 1858—and Cañada de la Puente (Brown, p. 28).

Dillon Beach [MARIN]: *village,* 3.25 miles west of Tomales near the coast (lat. 38°15' N, long. 122°57'50" W). Named on Tomales (1954) and Valley Ford (1954) 7.5' quadrangles. Postal authorities established Dillon Beach post office in 1922 (Frickstad, p. 87). The name commemorates George Dillon, who settled at the place in 1868 (Mason, 1976a, p. 126-127).

Dillon Point [SOLANO]: *promontory,* 2 miles west-northwest of Benicia along Carquinez Strait (lat. 38°03'35" N, long. 122°11'35" W; sec. 33, T 3 N, R 3 W). Named on Benicia (1959) 7.5' quadrangle. Called Ma lek ad el Pt. on Ringgold's (1850a) map; Ringgold (p. 36) also used the hyphenated form "Ma-lek-ad-el Point" for the name.

Dimond: see **Oakland** [ALAMEDA].

Dimond Canyon [ALAMEDA]: *canyon,* about 3 miles east of downtown Oakland along Sausal Creek (lat. 37°48'55" N, long. 122°12'40" W). Named on Oakland East (1959) 7.5' quadrangle. Called Diamond Canyon on Concord (1915) 15' quadrangle. Concord (1897) 15' quadrangle shows Diamond Creek in the canyon.

Dingee Reservoir [ALAMEDA]: *intermittent lake,* 300 feet long, 3 miles east-northeast of downtown Oakland (lat. 37°49'45" N, long. 122°13' W). Named on Oakland East (1959) 7.5' quadrangle. The name commemorates William Jackson Dingee, who founded Oakland Water Company in the late 1890's (Mosier and Mosier, p. 30).

Dini Gulch: see **Milagra Valley** [SAN MATEO].

Divide Ridge [ALAMEDA-CONTRA COSTA]: *ridge,* north- to northwest-trending, 3.5 miles long, 2.5 miles northwest of Dublin, partly on Alameda-Contra Costa county line (lat. 37°43'45" N, long. 121°58'30" W). Named on Pleasanton (1906) 15' quadrangle. The ridge first was called Pita Navaga—*pita navaga* means "knife blade" in Spanish (Mosier and Mosier, p. 30).

Divide Ridge [SANTA CLARA]: *ridge,* west- to northwest-trending, 2.25 miles long, 1.5 miles north of Mount Sizer (lat. 37°14'25" N, long. 121°30'30" W). Named on Mississippi Creek (1955) and Mount Sizer (1955) 7.5' quadrangles.

Divide Springs [SANTA CLARA]: *spring,* 3.5 miles south-southeast of Mount Hamilton (lat. 37°17'25" N, long. 121°37'40" W). Named on Lick Observatory (1955) 7.5' quadrangle.

Dixon [SOLANO]: *town,* 11 miles northeast of Vacaville (lat. 38°26'50" N, long. 121°49'15" W; around SE cor. sec. 14, T 7 N, R 1 E). Named on Dixon (1952) 7.5' quadrangle. Postal authorities established Dixon post office in 1869 (Frickstad, p. 192), and the town incorporated in 1878. The misspelled name commemorates Thomas Dickson, who donated 10 acres at the place for a railroad station (Hoover, Rensch, and Rensch, p. 523). In 1852 Elijah S. Silvey built a house at a site that became a trading center called Silveyville; Silveyville was moved bodily 5 miles east in 1868 to the railroad, where Dixon developed (Hoover, Rensch, and Rensch, p. 523). Postal authorities established Putah post office along Putah Creek 13 miles north of Vacaville in 1854, discontinued it in 1856, re-established it in 1858, changed the name to Silveyville in 1864, and discontinued it in 1871 (Salley, p. 179, 205).

Dixon Creek [SOLANO]: *stream,* flows 2 miles to end in Dixon (lat. 38°27'10" N, long. 121°49'55" W; sec. 14, T 7 N, R 1 E); the stream heads on Dixon Ridge. Named on Dixon (1952) 7.5' quadrangle.

Dixon Ridge [SOLANO]: *ridge,* north-trending, 5 miles long, center 1.25 miles west of Dixon (lat. 38°27' N, long. 121°50'50" W). Named on Dixon (1952) 7.5' quadrangle.

Dixon's Landing: see **Coyote Creek** [ALAMEDA-SANTA CLARA].

Dodonis Landing [SOLANO]: *locality,* 7 miles southwest of Denverton along Land Slough (present Tree Slough) (lat. 38°09'40" N, long. 121°59'50" W). Named on Denverton (1918) 7.5' quadrangle.

Dogtown: see **Woodville** [MARIN].

Doherty Ridge [SAN MATEO]: *ridge,* southwest-trending, 1 mile long, 4 miles southeast of Mindego Hill (lat. 37°16'25" N, long. 122°10'40" W). Named on Mindego Hill (1961) 7.5' quadrangle.

Donlan Canyon [ALAMEDA]: *canyon,* 1 mile long, on upper reaches of Dublin Creek above a point 1 mile west of Dublin (lat. 37°41'55" N, long. 121°57'20" W; sec. 3, T 3 S, R 1 W). Named on Dublin (1961) 7.5' quadrangle. The name commemorates John Donlan, who settled in the neighborhood in 1858 (Mosier and Mosier, p. 30).

Donland Point [ALAMEDA]: *peak,* 1.5 miles west of Dublin (lat. 37°42'05" N, long. 121°58' W; sec. 3, T 3 S, R 1 W); the peak is west of Donlan Canyon. Altitude 1138 feet. Named on Dublin (1961) 7.5' quadrangle.

Donner Canyon [CONTRA COSTA]: *canyon,* 3.25 miles long, along Donner Creek above a point 3 miles north-northwest of Mount Diablo (lat. 37°55'20" N, long. 121°55'35" W; sec. 24, T 1 N, R 1 W). Named on Clayton (1953) 7.5' quadrangle.

Donner Creek [CONTRA COSTA]: *stream,* flows nearly 4 miles to Mount Diablo Creek 4 miles north-northwest of Mount Diablo (lat. 37°56'10" N, long. 121°55'40" W; sec. 13, T 1 N, R 1 W); the stream drains Donner Canyon. Named on Clayton (1953) 7.5' quadrangle.

Doolan Canyon [ALAMEDA-CONTRA COSTA]: *canyon,* drained by Cottonwood Creek, which heads in Contra Costa County and flows 4.5 miles to lowlands 3.5 miles west-northwest of Livermore in Alameda County (lat. 37°42'10" N, long. 121°49'40" W). Named on Livermore (1961) and Tassajara (1953) 7.5' quadrangles. The name commemorates Michael Doolan, who settled in the canyon in 1871; the feature was known as Cottonwood Canyon in 1878 (Mosier and Mosier, p. 30).

Dorenda [CONTRA COSTA]: *locality,* 6 miles north-northeast of present Walnut Creek civic center along Oakland Antioch and Eastern Railroad (lat. 37°59'15" N, long. 122°01'55" W). Named on Concord (1915) 15' quadrangle.

Double Bowknot [MARIN]: *locality;* twisted road 4.25 miles south-southwest of downtown San Rafael (lat. 37°55'10" N, long. 122°34'20"). Named on San Rafael (1954) 7.5' quadrangle.

Double Point [MARIN]: *promontory,* 6 miles west-northwest of Bolinas along the coast (lat. 37°56'50" N, long. 122°46'50" W); the feature has two high spurs less than 0.5 mile apart (United States Coast and Geodetic Survey, p. 124). Named on Double Point (1954) 7.5' quadrangle.

Double Rock [SAN FRANCISCO]: *rock,* 4.25 miles east-southeast of Mount Davidson in South Basin (lat. 37°43'15" N, long. 122°22'50" W). Named on San Francisco South (1956) 7.5' quadrangle.

Dougherty [ALAMEDA]: *locality,* 1.5 miles east-northeast of Dublin along Southern Pacific Railroad (lat. 37°42'35" N, long. 121°54'35" W). Named on Dublin (1961) 7.5' quadrangle.

Dougherty: see **Dublin** [ALAMEDA].

Dougherty Hills [ALAMEDA-CONTRA COSTA]: *ridge,* south-southeast-trending, 3.5 miles long, 7 miles southeast of Danville on Alameda-Contra Costa county line, mainly in Contra Costa County (lat. 37°44'45" N, long. 121°55'20" W). Named on Diablo (1953) and Dublin (1961) 7.5' quadrangles. The name commemorates James Witt Dougherty, who settled in the neighborhood in the 1850's (Mosier and Mosier, p. 31).

Dougherty's Station: see **Dublin** [ALAMEDA].

Dowest Slough: see **New York Slough** [CONTRA COSTA].

Dozier [SOLANO]: *locality,* 7 miles southeast of Elmira along Sacramento Northern Railroad (lat. 38°17'10" N, long. 121°48'55" W; at S line sec. 12, T 5 S, R 1 E). Named on Dozier (1952) 7.5' quadrangle.

Drakes Bay [MARIN]: *embayment,* 7 miles southeast of Point Reyes Station along the coast east of Point Reyes (lat. 38°00'30" N, long. 122°55' W). Named on Drakes Bay (1953) and Inverness (1954) 7.5' quadrangles.

Called Sir Francis Drake's Bay on Ringgold's (1850b) map, and called Bay of Sir F. Drake on Goddard's (1857) map. Sebastian Cermeño visited the embayment in 1595 and named it Puerto de San Francisco, or Bahia de San Francisco; Vizcaino came to the place in 1603—on January 6, the day of Los Reyes—and called it Puerto de los Reyes, or Puerto de Don Gaspar (Hanna, W.L., p. 39; Wagner, H.R., p. 405). Abraham Goos in 1624, and Henry Briggs in 1625, associated Sir Francis Drake's name with the place on maps, using the designation "P. Sr. Francisco Draco" (Wagner, H.R., p. 118, 304). The embayment was known as Jack's Harbor in the 1850's (Soule, Gihon, and Nisbet, p. 32). The present name is from the belief of some people that Francis Drake landed at the place in 1579.

Drakes Beach [MARIN]: *beach,* 4 miles northeast of the lighthouse at Point Reyes (lat. 38°01'40" N, long. 122°57'35" W); the beach is along Drakes Bay. Named on Drakes Bay (1953) 7.5' quadrangle.

Drakes Estero [MARIN]: *bay,* opens into Drakes Bay 5.5 miles east-northeast of the lighthouse at Point Reyes (lat. 38°01'55" N, long. 122°56' W). Named on Drakes Bay (1953) 7.5' quadrangle. Members of United States Coast Survey named the feature in 1860; before that time this bay and the adjoining bays together were called Estero de Limantour for the commander of a Mexican vessel lost at the entrance to the feature in 1841 (Hanna, W.L., p. 40-41).

Drakes Head [MARIN]: *ridge,* south-trending, less than 1 mile long, 6.5 miles east-northeast of the lighthouse at Point Reyes (lat. 38°02'20" N, long. 122°54'50" W). Named on Drakes Bay (1953) 7.5' quadrangle.

Drakes Peak: see **Drakes Point** [SOLANO].

Drakes Point [SOLANO]: *peak,* 5.25 miles south-southwest of Allendale (lat. 38°22'35" N, long. 121°59'15" W). Altitude 624 feet. Named on Allendale (1953) 7.5' quadrangle. United States Board on Geographic Names (1933, p. 272) rejected the name "Drakes Peak" for the feature.

Drawbridge [ALAMEDA]: *locality,* 6 miles south of Fremont civic center along Southern Pacific Railroad on an island between Coyote Creek and Mud Slough (lat. 37°28' N, long. 121°58'25" W). Named on Milpitas (1961) 7.5' quadrangle. The place was called Saline City about 1904, referring no doubt to the nearby salt ponds (Dick Barrett, *San Jose Mercury-News*, August 12, 1973).

Drawbridge: see **Cygnus** [SOLANO].

Dresser [ALAMEDA]: *locality,* 3 miles northnortheast of Fremont civic center along Southern Pacific Railroad in Niles Canyon (lat. 37°35'30" N, long. 121°57'15" W; near N line sec. 15, T 4 S, R 1 W). Named on Niles (1961) 7.5' quadrangle. According to Mosier and Mosier (p. 31), the place was called Merienda

until 1915, and then was called Alston until 1957, when it received the present name.

Driftwood Beach [MARIN]: *beach,* 4.5 miles southwest of Tomales along the sea coast (lat. 38°11'45" N, long. 122°57'50" W). Named on Tomales (1954) 7.5' quadrangle.

Dry Arroyo [SOLANO]: *stream,* flows 5 miles to lowlands 2.5 miles north of Allendale (lat. 38°28'45" N, long. 121°56'45" W). Named on Allendale (1953) and Mount Vaca (1951) 7.5' quadrangles.

Dry Creek [ALAMEDA]:
(1) *stream,* flows 6.5 miles to Alameda Creek 4 miles north of downtown Newark (lat. 37°35'15" N, long. 122°02'15" W). Named on Newark (1959) 7.5' quadrangle. Thompson and West (1878, p. 17) used the designation "Segunda, or Dry Creek" for the feature. Spaniards applied the name "Segunda" to the stream because it was the second stream crossed by a traveler on the way north from San Jose mission—*segunda* means "second" in Spanish; the canyon of the stream has the local name "Black Creek Valley" (Mosier and Mosier, p. 16, 79-80).
(2) *stream,* flows 4.5 miles to Arroyo Valle 3.25 miles south of Livermore (lat. 37°38'10" N, long. 121°45'50" W). Named on Altamont (1953), Livermore (1961), and Mendenhall Springs (1956) 7.5' quadrangles.
(3) *stream,* flows 4.5 miles to Arroyo Mocho 7 miles south-southwest of Altamont (lat. 37°39'35" N, long. 121°43'50" W; near W line sec. 23, T 3 S, R 2 E). Named on Tesla (1907) 15' quadrangle.

Dry Creek [CONTRA COSTA]: *stream,* flows 3.5 miles to Marsh Creek about 1 mile southwest of Brentwood (lat. 37°55'20" N, long. 121°42'40" W). Named on Antioch South (1953) and Brentwood (1978) 7.5' quadrangles.

Dry Creek [SAN MATEO]: *stream,* flows 2.5 miles to Tunitas Creek 2.25 miles north of the village of San Gregorio (lat. 37°21'35" N, long. 122°23'25" W). Named on La Honda (1961) and San Gregorio (1961) 7.5' quadrangles.

Dry Creek [SANTA CLARA]:
(1) *stream,* flows nearly 3.5 miles to Los Gatos Creek 2 miles south-southwest of downtown San Jose (lat. 37°18'25" N, long. 121°54'35" W). Named on San Jose West (1961) 7.5' quadrangle. Called Old Channel Los Gatos [Creek] on Thompson and West's (1876) map.
(2) *stream,* flows nearly 3 miles to Sulphur Springs Creek 5.5 miles south-southeast of Eylar Mountain (lat. 37°23'55" N, long. 121°30'25" W; sec. 23, T 6 S, R 4 E). Named on Eylar Mountain (1955) 7.5' quadrangle. On Mount Hamilton (1897) 15' quadrangle, the stream is shown as part of Sulphur Spring Creek.

Dry Creek: see **Barron Creek** [SANTA CLARA]; **Deer Creek** [CONTRA COSTA];

Martin Creek [SAN MATEO]; **Thompson Creek** [SANTA CLARA].

Dublin [ALAMEDA]: *town,* 9.5 miles west of Livermore at the southwest end of San Ramon Valley (lat. 37°42'05" N, long. 121° 56'15" W). Named on Dublin (1961) 7.5' quadrangle. Pleasanton (1906) 15' quadrangle has both the names "Dublin" and "Dougherty P.O." at the place. James Witt Dougherty purchased a large part of Amador's San Ramon grant in 1852, including a two-story adobe building; the community that grew up around the building generally was known until 1860 as Amador's or Amador Valley, and the post office there was called Dougherty's Station— the south part of the community was called Dublin, supposedly because of the large number of Irish people there (Hoover, Rensch, and Rensch, p. 12-13). Postal authorities established Dougherty's Station post office in 1860, changed the name to Dougherty in 1896, and discontinued it in 1908; they established Dublin post office in 1963 (Salley, p. 61, 62).

Dublin Canyon [ALAMEDA]: *canyons,* two, each heads 2 miles west of Dublin (lat. 37°41'50" N, long. 121°58'30" W; sec. 4, T 3 S, R 1 W). Named on Dublin (1961) and Hayward (1959) 7.5' quadrangles. One canyon extends west for 2.5 miles to a point 4 miles east-northeast of downtown Hayward, and the other extends east for 2 miles to Dublin. The divide between the two canyons is called Haywards Pass on Pleasanton (1906) 15' quadrangle.

Dublin Creek [ALAMEDA]: *stream,* flows 2.25 miles to lowlands at Dublin (lat. 37°42' N, long. 121°56' W). Named on Dublin (1961) 7.5' quadrangle.

Duck Cove [MARIN]: *embayment,* 7 miles south of Tomales on the southwest side of Tomales Bay (lat. 38°08'35" N, long. 122° 54' W). Named on Tomales (1954) 7.5' quadrangle.

Duck Island: see **Hog Island** [MARIN].

Duck Slough [SOLANO]:

(1) *water feature,* joins Hass Slough 10.5 miles north of Rio Vista (lat. 38°18'25" N, long. 121°43'50" W). Named on Liberty Island (1978) 7.5' quadrangle.

(2) *water feature,* joins Hill Slough 2 miles southsoutheast of downtown Fairfield (lat. 38°13'35" N, long. 122°01'20" W). Named on Fairfield South (1949) 7.5' quadrangle.

(3) *water feature,* in Yolo Basin (present Yolo Bypass), joins Miner Slough 10 miles northnortheast of Rio Vista (lat. 38°17'20" N, long. 121°36'45" W). Named on Vorden (1916) 7.5' quadrangle.

Duck Slough: see **Little Duck Slough** [SOLANO].

Dudley Creek [SOLANO]: *water feature,* dry watercourse that lies less than 1 mile northeast of Dixon (lat. 38°27'15" N, long. 121°48'45" W). Named on Dixon (1952) 7.5' quadrangle. Shown as an intermittent stream on Vacaville (1953) 15' quadrangle.

Dug Road Creek [SOLANO]: *stream,* flows 2.5 miles to Wild Horse Creek 7.25 miles west of Fairfield (lat. 38°16'05" N, long. 122°10'10" W; near W line sec. 23, T 5 N, R 3 W). Named on Mount George (1951) 7.5' quadrangle.

Dumbarton [ALAMEDA]: *locality,* 3.25 miles west-southwest of downtown Newark along Southern Pacific Railroad (lat. 37°30'25" N, long. 122°05'35" W). Named on Hayward (1915) 15' quadrangle.

Dumbarton Point [ALAMEDA]: *promontory,* 4 miles west-southwest of downtown Newark at the edge of San Francisco Bay (lat. 37°29'55" N, long. 122°06'10" W). Named on Mountain View (1961) and Newark (1959) 7.5' quadrangles. Called Potrero Pt. on Palo Alto (1899) 15' quadrangle. A Scottish railroad surveyor named the feature for the city and county of Dumbarton in Scotland (Mosier and Mosier, p. 32). A place called Arden was situated along South Coast Railroad between Newark and Dumbarton Point; it was on land belonging to George Patterson, who called his estate Ardenwood (MacGregor, p. 90, 103).

Dunes Beach [SAN MATEO]: *beach,* 2 miles northwest of downtown Half Moon Bay along the coast (lat. 37°29' N, long. 122°27'05" W). Named on Half Moon Bay (1961) 7.5' quadrangle.

Dunn Canyon [SANTA CLARA]: *canyon,* drained by a stream that flows 1 mile to Hay Canyon 5 miles north of Mount Madonna (lat. 37°05'15" N, long. 121°42'15" W). Named on Mount Madonna (1955) 7.5' quadrangle.

Dunne Ridge [SANTA CLARA]: *ridge,* northtrending, 3 miles long, 12 miles east-southeast of Gilroy on Santa Clara-San Benito county line (lat. 36°58' N, long. 121°21'15" W). Named on Three Sisters (1954) 7.5' quadrangle.

Dunns Peak [SOLANO]: *peak,* 5 miles east of Mount Vaca (lat. 38° 23'45" N, long. 122°00'45" W). Altitude 804 feet. Named on Mount Vaca (1951) 7.5' quadrangle.

Du Pont [CONTRA COSTA]: *locality,* 5.5 miles west of the settlement of Bethel Island along Atchison, Topeka and Santa Fe Railroad (lat. 38°00'25" N, long. 121°44'15" W; sec. 22, T 2 N, R 2 E). Named on Jersey Island (1978) 7.5' quadrangle.

Durham Ridge [SAN MATEO]: *ridge,* southwest-trending, 1.5 miles long, 2.5 miles westsouthwest of Skeggs Point (lat. 37°23'45" N, long. 122°20'50" W). Named on Woodside (1961) 7.5' quadrangle. Durham ranch was on the ridge in the middle and late 1850's (Brown, p. 30).

Dutard Creek [SANTA CLARA]: *stream,* flows 1.25 miles to Upper Penitencia Creek nearly 2 miles east-northeast of Berryessa (lat. 37°23'40" N, long. 121°49'40" W). Named on Calaveras Reservoir (1961) 7.5' quadrangle.

Dutchman Slough [SOLANO]: *water feature,*

lies between Island Number 1 and Knight Island from South Slough to Napa River 2 miles northwest of downtown Vallejo (lat. 38°07'15" N, long. 122° 17' W). Named on Cuttings Wharf (1949) and Mare Island (1959) 7.5' quadrangles.

Dutch Slough [CONTRA COSTA]: *water feature,* extends for 6.25 miles from Sand Mound Slough to San Joaquin River 4.5 miles west of the settlement of Bethel Island (lat. 38°01'35" N, long. 121°43'25" W). Named on Brentwood (1954) and Jersey Island (1978) 7.5' quadrangles.

Dutton [SOLANO]: *locality,* 4 miles south of Birds Landing (2) along Sacramento Northern Railroad on Van Sickle Island (lat. 38°04'35" N, long. 121°53' W). Named on Honker Bay (1953) 7.5' quadrangle. Called Chaplin on Honker Bay (1918) 7.5' quadrangle, which shows the place along Oakland Antioch and Eastern Railroad. Honker Bay (1953, photorevised 1968 and 1973) 7.5' quadrangle shows it along an old railroad grade.

Dutton Island [SOLANO]: *island,* 6.5 miles west-southwest of Birds Landing (2) along Suisun Bay (lat. 38°04'50" N, long. 121°58'15" W). Named on Honker Bay (1953) 7.5' quadrangle.

Duttons Landing [SOLANO]: *locality,* 2.25 miles south-southwest of Birds Landing (2) along Montezuma Slough (lat. 38°06'35" N, long. 121°53'20" W). Named on Honker Bay (1918) 7.5' quadrangle. Postal authorities established Duttons Landing post office in 1887 and discontinued it in 1926; the name is from John W. Dutton, who operated the boat landing at the place (Salley, p. 63).

Du Vrees Creek: see **Islais Creek Channel** [SAN FRANCISCO].

Duxbury Point [MARIN]: *promontory,* at Bolinas (lat. 37°53'40" N, long. 122°42' W); the feature is along the coast opposite Duxbury Reef. Named on Bolinas (1954) 7.5' quadrangle. Called Punta de Baulenes on a diseño of Las Baulenes grant made in 1846 (Becker, 1969).

Duxbury Reef [MARIN]: *shoal,* 1.5 miles south-southwest of Bolinas (lat. 37°53'30" N, long. 122°42' W). Named on Bolinas (1954) 7.5' quadrangle. The name is from the ship *Duxbury,* which ran aground at the place in 1849 (Mason, 1976b, p. 103).

Dyer Canyon [SANTA CLARA]: *canyon,* drained by a stream that flows 1 mile to Briggs Creek 3.25 miles south-southwest of Los Gatos (lat. 37°11'10" N, long. 122°00'25" W; near S line sec. 31, T 8 S, R 1 W). Named on Castle Rock Ridge (1955) 7.5' quadrangle.

— E —

Ead's Island: see **Simmons Island** [SOLANO].
Eagle Hill [SAN MATEO]: *hill,* 1 mile south-

west of downtown Redwood City (lat. 37°28'30" N, long. 122°14'35" W). Named on Palo Alto (1961) 7.5' quadrangle.

Eagle Peak [CONTRA COSTA]: *peak,* 2 miles northwest of Mount Diablo (lat. 37°54'05" N, long. 121°56'15" W; sec. 26, T 1 N, R 1 E). Altitude 2369 feet. Named on Clayton (1953) 7.5' quadrangle. Called Eagle Pt. on Mount Diablo (1898) 15' quadrangle—members of the Whitney survey gave this name to the feature (Whitney, p. 21).

Eagle Point: see **Eagle Peak** [CONTRA COSTA].

Eagle Rock [SANTA CLARA]: *relief feature,* 2.5 miles east-northeast of Berryessa near the mouth of Alum Rock Canyon (lat. 37°23'45" N, long. 121°48'50" W). Named on Calaveras Reservoir (1961) 7.5' quadrangle.

East Antioch [CONTRA COSTA]: *settlement,* 2 miles east of downtown Antioch (lat. 38°00'30" N, long. 121°46'15" W). Named on Antioch North (1978) 7.5' quadrangle.

East Bulls Head Channel [CONTRA COSTA-SOLANO]: *channel,* 3.5 miles northeast of Martinez in Suisun Bay along Contra Costa-Solano county line (lat. 38°03' N, long. 122°05'20" W); the feature is east-northeast of Bulls Head Channel. Named on Vine Hill (1959) 7.5' quadrangle.

East Creek: see **Lion Creek** [ALAMEDA].

East Harbor [SAN FRANCISCO]: *water feature,* 1.25 miles west of North Point along San Francisco Bay (lat. 37°48'25" N, long. 122° 25'55" W). Named on San Francisco North (1956, photorevised 1968 and 1973) 7.5' quadrangle. United States Board on Geographic Names (1981b, p. 3) approved the name "Gashouse Cove" for the embayment that includes East Harbor, and noted that the name is from a gas works built near the embayment in the 1890's.

Eastland: see **Mill Valley** [MARIN] (2).

East Landing: see **Southeast Farallon** [SAN FRANCISCO].

Eastman Canyon [SANTA CLARA]: *canyon,* drained by a stream that flows 3.25 miles to Uvas Reservoir 4 miles north of Mount Madonna (lat. 37°04'20" N, long. 121°42'35" W; sec. 12, T 10 S, R 2 E). Named on Mount Madonna (1955, photorevised 1968 and 1973) 7.5' quadrangle.

East Marin Island [MARIN]: *island,* 1350 feet long, nearly 2 miles southwest of Point San Pedro in San Rafael Bay (lat. 37°57'50" N, long. 122°28' W); the feature is 400 feet east-southeast of West Marin Island. Named on San Quentin (1959) 7.5' quadrangle. East Marin Island and West Marin Island together are called Marin Is. on San Francisco (1915) 15' quadrangle.

East Oakland: see **San Antonio**, under **Oakland** [ALAMEDA].

Easton: see **Easton Creek** [SAN MATEO].

Easton Creek [SAN MATEO]: *stream,* flows 1.5 miles to lowlands along San Francisco Bay 2.5

miles east-northeast of downtown San Mateo (lat. 37°35'05" N, long. 122°22'05" W). Named on Montara Mountain (1956) and San Mateo (1956) 7.5' quadrangles. A community called Easton developed near the mouth of present Easton Creek between 1900 and 1910; Burlingame annexed the place in 1910 (Brown, p. 11). Ansel Mills Easton subdivided land at Easton and built a depot that he named Easton Station (Hynding, p. 113). Postal authorities established Easton post office in 1909 and discontinued it in 1916 (Frickstad, p. 167).

East Palo Alto [SAN MATEO]: *town,* 5 miles east-southeast of downtown Redwood City (lat. 37°28'10" N, long. 122°08'10" W); the community is north of Palo Alto [SANTA CLARA]. Named on Palo Alto (1961) 7.5' quadrangle. Palo Alto (1953) 7.5' quadrangle gives the alternate name "Ravenswood" for East Palo Alto. Isaiah Woods laid out a townsite at the place in 1849 and called it Ravenswood; a cooperative colony called Runnymede was at the site from 1916 until the 1930's, but in 1925 residents chose the name "East Palo Alto" for the community (Hynding, p. 133, 135-136). The town incorporated in 1983. California Mining Bureau's (1917b) map shows a place called Sweeney along the railroad in present East Palo Alto at the edge of San Francisco Bay.

East Peak [MARIN]: *peak,* 4 miles southwest of downtown San Rafael on Mount Tamalpais (lat. 37°55'45" N, long. 122°34'35" W). Altitude 2571 feet. Named on San Rafael (1954) 7.5' quadrangle.

East Pleasanton [ALAMEDA]: *locality,* 3.5 miles west of Livermore (lat. 37°40'20" N, long. 121°49'45" W); the place is 2.5 miles east-northeast of Pleasanton. Named on Livermore (1961) 7.5' quadrangle.

Eastport [CONTRA COSTA]: *locality,* 2.5 miles south of Orinda (lat. 37°50'25" N, long. 122°10'50" W; sec. 15, T 1 S, R 3 W). Named on Oakland East (1959) 7.5' quadrangle. Concord (1915) 15' quadrangle shows the place at the east portal of a tunnel along Oakland Antioch and Eastern Railroad.

East San Jose [SANTA CLARA]: *district,* 1.5 miles east-northeast of present downtown San Jose, and east of Coyote Creek (lat. 37°20'30" N, long. 121°52' W). Named on San Jose (1899) 15' quadrangle.

East Slough [ALAMEDA]: *water feature,* enters San Leandro Bay 4.25 miles southeast of downtown Oakland (lat. 37°45'35" N, long. 122°13' W). Named on Oakland East (1959) 7.5' quadrangle.

East Vallejo: see **Vallejo** [SOLANO].

Eastwood Camp: see **Camp Eastwood** [MARIN].

Eastyard: see **Point Richmond** [CONTRA COSTA] (2).

Ebabias Creek: see **Americano Creek** [MARIN].

Eberly [ALAMEDA]: *locality,* 2 miles northwest of Fremont civic center along Western Pacific Railroad (lat. 37°34'20" N, long. 121°59'30" W). Named on Niles (1961) 7.5' quadrangle. The name commemorates William V. Eberly, manager of California Nursery from 1904 until 1917 (Mosier and Mosier, p. 33).

Eckley [CONTRA COSTA]: *locality,* 4.5 miles northwest of Martinez along Southern Pacific Railroad (lat. 38°03'15" N, long. 122°12'05" W). Named on Benicia (1959) 7.5' quadrangle. The name commemorates Commodore John L. Eckley, who bought the cove at the place in the 1870's for a yacht harbor (Gudde, 1949, p. 103).

Eden: see **Mount Eden** [ALAMEDA].

Eden Canyon [ALAMEDA]: *canyon,* 2.5 miles long, on upper reaches of San Lorenzo Creek above a point 4.25 miles northeast of downtown Hayward (lat. 37°42'35" N, long. 122°01'05" W). Named on Dublin (1961) and Hayward (1959) 7.5' quadrangles. The stream in the canyon is called Eden Creek on Haywards (1899) and Pleasanton (1906) 15' quadrangles.

Eden Creek: see **Eden Canyon** [ALAMEDA].

Edendale: see **Mount Eden** [ALAMEDA].

Eden Landing: see **Mount Eden** [ALAMEDA].

Eden Plain: see **Byron** [CONTRA COSTA].

Edenvale [SANTA CLARA]: *locality,* 6 miles southeast of downtown San Jose along Southern Pacific Railroad (lat. 37°15'55" N, long. 121°49' W). Named on San Jose East (1961) 7.5' quadrangle. An inn called Seven Mile House began operating at the place in the 1850's (Hoover, Rensch, and Rensch, p. 431). Another stopping place, called Eight Mile House, was situated about 1 mile farther southeast (*San Jose Mercury-News, California Today Magazine,* October 23, 1977). The names recorded the distance of the places from San Jose. Postal authorities established Eden Vale post office in 1893 and discontinued it in 1916 (Frickstad, p. 173). Rambo (1973, p. 41) attributed the name "Edenvale" to the Edenlike beauty of Hayes Estate, which was at the site. The low range 0.5 mile north of Edenvale is called Los Lagrimas Hills (Carey and Miller, p. 153) or Las Lagrimas (Hoover, Rensch, and Rensch, p. 431).

Edgemar [SAN MATEO]: *district,* 4 miles west of downtown South San Francisco near the coast (lat. 37°39'15" N, long. 122°29'15" W). Named on San Francisco South (1956) 7.5' quadrangle. The residents of the place voted in 1957 to join neighboring communities and form the new city of Pacifica (Gudde, 1969, p. 233).

Edith Point: see **Point Edith** [CONTRA COSTA].

Edson Canyon [SANTA CLARA]: *canyon,* drained by a stream that flows nearly 1 mile to an unnamed stream 3 miles south-southeast of New Almaden (lat. 37°08'05" N, long.

121°48'40" W; near E line sec. 24, T 9 S, R 1 E). Named on Santa Teresa Hills (1953) 7.5' quadrangle.

Eel Rock [SAN MATEO]: *island,* 550 feet long, 4 miles south of downtown Half Moon Bay and 100 feet offshore (lat. 37°24'20" N, long. 122°25'40" W). Named on Half Moon Bay (1961) 7.5' quadrangle.

Egbert Cut [SOLANO]: *water feature,* joins Miner Slough 9.5 miles north-northeast of Rio Vista near Five Points (lat. 38°17'35" N, long. 121°38'40" W). Named on Courtland (1952) and Liberty Island (1952) 7.5' quadrangles.

Eighteen Mile House: see **Madrone** [SANTA CLARA].

Eight Mile House: see **Edenvale** [SANTA CLARA].

El Arroyo de Gallinas: see **Gallinas Creek** [MARIN].

El Arroyo de la Presa: see **Bear Gulch** [SAN MATEO].

El Arroyo Tulares de los Canoas: see **Canoas Creek** [SANTA CLARA].

El Campo [MARIN]: *locality,* 3 miles south-southeast of Point San Quentin on the northeast side of Tiburon Peninsula (lat. 37°53'50" N, long. 122°27'50" W). Named on San Quentin (1959) 7.5' quadrangle. Officials of San Francisco and North Pacific Railroad opened a resort called El Campo at the place in 1891; later the resort site was called Paradise Park (Teather, p. 23).

El Cañada de San Vicente: see **San Antonio Valley** [SANTA CLARA].

El Cerito [CONTRA COSTA]: *town,* 3 miles east-southeast of Richmond civic center (lat. 37°54'45" N, long. 122°17'45" W). Named on Richmond (1959) 7.5' quadrangle. The place first was called County Line (Gudde, 1949, p. 62). Postal authorities established Rust post office at the site in 1909 and changed the name to El Cerito in 1916; the name "Rust" was for William R. Rust, first postmaster (Salley, p 191). The town incorporated in 1917.

El Cerrito Hill: see **Albany Hill** [ALAMEDA].

El Cierbo: see **Tormey** [CONTRA COSTA].

El Corte de Madera [SAN MATEO-SANTA CLARA]: *land grant,* chiefly southwest of Portola Valley (1) on San Mateo-Santa Clara county line, mainly in San Mateo County. Named on La Honda (1961), Mindego Hill (1961), Palo Alto (1961), and Woodside (1961) 7.5' quadrangles. Maximo Martinez received 2 leagues in 1844 and claimed 13,316 acres patented in 1858 (Cowan, p. 30). *El corte de madera* has the meaning "the place where lumber is cut," "the lumber cutting," or "the timber clearing" in Spanish (Arbuckle, p. 15).

El Corte de Madera Creek [SAN MATEO]: *stream,* flows 8.5 miles to San Gregorio Creek nearly 4 miles west of La Honda (lat. 37°18'50" N, long. 122°20'20" W). Named

on La Honda (1961) and Woodside (1961) 7.5' quadrangles.

Elephant Head [SANTA CLARA]: *peak,* nearly 4 miles west-northwest of Pacheco Peak (lat. 37°01'30" N, long. 121°21' W; sec. 31, T 10 S, R 6 E). Altitude 1905 feet. Named on Pacheco Peak (1955) 7.5' quadrangle.

Elephant Head Creek [SANTA CLARA]: *stream,* flows 3.5 miles to Pacheco Creek 4 miles west of Pacheco Peak (lat. 37°00'20" N, long. 121°21'30" W); the stream is southwest of Elephant Head Ridge. Named on Pacheco Peak (1955) 7.5' quadrangle.

Elephant Head Ridge [SANTA CLARA]: *ridge,* north- to west-trending, 3.5 miles long, 5 miles west-northwest of Pacheco Peak (lat. 37°02'35" N, long. 121°21'45" W); Elephant Head is near the southeast end of the ridge. Named on Gilroy Hot Springs (1955) and Pacheco Peak (1955) 7.5' quadrangles.

Elephant Mountain [SANTA CLARA]: *peak,* 2 miles north of Black Mountain (1) (lat. 37°20'55" N, long. 122°09'10" W; sec. 2, T 7 S, R 3 W). Named on Mindego Hill (1961) 7.5' quadrangle.

Elephant Mountain: see **Black Mountain** [MARIN].

Elephant Rock [MARIN]: *island,* 300 feet long, 5.5 miles southwest of Tomales, and 350 feet offshore (lat. 38°10'50" N, long. 122°57'50" W). Named on Tomales (1954) 7.5' quadrangle.

El Granada [SAN MATEO]: *town,* 3.5 miles south-southeast of Montara Knob near the coast (lat. 37°30'15" N, long. 122°28'10" W). Named on Montara Mountain (1956) 7.5' quadrangle. San Mateo (1915) 15' quadrangle shows North Granada along Ocean Shore Railroad at the place. The town had railroad stations called North Granada, Granada, and South Granada; the main stop was North Granada (Wagner, J.R., p. 50). Postal authorities established El Granada post office in 1909, discontinued it in 1945, and reestablished it in 1948 (Frickstad, p. 167).

El Granada Beach [SAN MATEO]: *beach,* 4 miles south of Montara Knob along the coast (lat. 37°30'05" N, long. 122°28'15" W); the beach is at El Granada. Named on Half Moon Bay (1961) and Montara Mountain (1956) 7.5' quadrangles. Brown (p. 36) called the place Granada Beach.

El Hambre Creek: see **Arroyo del Hambre** [CONTRA COSTA].

Elizabeth: see **Lake Elizabeth**, under **Stivers Lagoon** [ALAMEDA].

Elk Horn: see **Mountain House** [ALAMEDA].

Elkhorn Peak [SOLANO]: *peak,* 3.5 miles west-northwest of Cordelia on Napa-Solano county line (lat. 38°13'50" N, long. 122° 11'40" W; near S line sec. 33, T 5 N, R 3 W). Altitude 1330 feet. Named on Cordelia (1951) 7.5' quadrangle.

Elkhorn Slough [SOLANO]: *water feature,* on

Ryer Island (1), joins Cache Slough 4 miles north-north-east of Rio Vista (lat. 38°12'35" N, long. 121°39'15" W). Named on Courtland (1978), Liberty Island (1978), and Rio Vista (1978) 7.5' quadrangles. Called West Fork [Sacramento River] on Ringgold's (1850c) map.

Elk Slough [CONTRA COSTA]: *water feature,* 5.5 miles north-north-east of the settlement of Bethel Island on Webb Track (lat. 38° 05' N, long. 121°35'20" W). Named on Bouldin Island (1952) 7.5' quadrangle.

Elk Valley: see **Tennessee Valley** [MARIN].

Elliot [ALAMEDA]: *locality,* 4 miles west of Livermore along Southern Pacific Railroad (lat. 37°40'25" N, long. 121°50'15" W). Named on Pleasanton (1906) 15' quadrangle.

Elliot: see **Point Elliot**, under **Port Costa** [CONTRA COSTA].

Elliot Cove [SOLANO]: *embayment,* 3.25 miles west-north-west of Benicia along Carquinez Strait (lat. 38°04' N, long. 121°12'45" W). Named on Benicia (1959) 7.5' quadrangle.

Elliot Creek [SAN MATEO]: *stream,* heads in Santa Cruz County and flows 2 miles to the sea 2 miles east of Año Nuevo Point (present Point Año Nuevo) (lat. 37°06'40" N, long. 122°17'45" W). Named on Año Nuevo (1955) and Franklin Point (1955) 7.5' quadrangles.

Ellis Slough: see **Santa Fe Channel** [CONTRA COSTA].

Elmar Beach [SAN MATEO]: *beach,* 1.25 miles northwest of downtown Half Moon Bay along the coast (lat. 37°28'30" N, long. 122° 26'55" W). Named on Half Moon Bay (1961) 7.5' quadrangle.

Elmhurst [ALAMEDA]: *town,* nearly 2 miles north-north-west of downtown San Leandro in present Oakland (lat. 37°44'45" N, long. 122°10'05" W). Named on Haywards (1899) 15' quadrangle. Officials of San Francisco and Oakland Railroad established a station at the place in 1865 and called it Jones, for Edmond Jones; officials of Central Pacific Railroad changed the name of the station to Elmhurst in 1869 (Mosier and Mosier, p. 34). Postal authorities established Elmhurst post office in 1892 and discontinued it in 1911 (Frickstad, p. 1).

Elmira [SOLANO]: *village,* 4.5 miles east of Vacaville (lat. 38°21' N, long. 121°54'25" W; sec. 19, T 6 N, R 1 E). Named on Elmira (1953) 7.5' quadrangle. Postal authorities established Valta post office in 1868, changed the name to Vaca in 1870, and to Elmira in 1873 (Frickstad, p. 193). The name "Vaca" was given to the railroad station at the place because Vacaville was nearby; when the railroad came to Vacaville about 1875, the name of the station at Vaca was changed to Elmira, for the city in New York State (Gudde, 1949, p. 106).

El Pescadero [ALAMEDA-CONTRA COSTA]: *land grant,* mainly in Contra Costa and San Joaquin Counties, but extends into the extreme northeast part of Alameda County 15

miles northeast of Livermore. Named on Clifton Court Forebay (1978) 7.5' quadrangle. Antonio Maria Pico received 8 leagues in 1843; Pico and Henry M. Naglee claimed 35,546 acres patented in 1865 (Cowan, p. 59).

El Pinole: see **Pinole** [CONTRA COSTA] (1) and (2).

El Pinole Point: see **Pinole Point** [CONTRA COSTA] (1) and (2).

El Potrero de la Punta del Tiburon: see **Belvedere Island** [MARIN],

El Potrero de Santa Clara [SANTA CLARA]: *land grant,* 2 miles northwest of downtown San Jose near San Jose Municipal Airport. Named on San Jose West (1961) 7.5' quadrangle. Called Potrero de Santa Clara on San Jose (1899) 15' quadrangle. James Alexander Forbes received 1 league in 1844; Robert F. Stockton claimed 1939 acres patented in 1861 (Cowan, p. 91).

El Pueblo San Jose de Guadalupe: see **San Jose** [SANTA CLARA].

El Sereno [SANTA CLARA]: *peak,* 4 miles east of Castle Rock (lat. 37°13'10" N, long. 122°01'20" W). Named on Castle Rock Ridge (1955) 7.5' quadrangle.

Elsman: see **Lake Elsman** [SANTA CLARA].

El Sobrante [CONTRA COSTA]:

(1) *land grant,* extends from Orinda to the town of El Sobrante. Named on Briones Valley (1959) and Richmond (1959) 7.5' quadrangles. Juan Jose Castro received 11 leagues in 1841; V. Castro and Juan Jose Castro claimed 20,565 acres patented in 1883 (Cowan, p. 98-99). According to Perez (p. 100), the patentees received 19,982.49 acres.

(2) *town,* 4 miles northeast of Richmond civic center (lat. 37°58'40" N, long. 122°17'40" W); the town is on El Sobrante grant. Named on Richmond (1959) 7.5' quadrangle. Postal authorities established El Sobrante post office in 1941 (Salley, p. 68). When the railroad reached the place in 1878, the station there was called Sobrante, and only after the post office was established was the Spanish article "El" added to the name (Gudde, 1949, p. 337).

El Sombroso [SANTA CLARA]: *peak,* 1.5 miles north-north-west of Mount Umunhum (lat. 37°10'40" N, long. 121°54'35" W; sec. 6, T 9 S, R 1 E). Altitude 2999 feet. Named on Los Gatos (1953) 7.5' quadrangle.

El Toro [SANTA CLARA]: *peak,* 1 mile southwest of Morgan Hill (lat. 37°07'15" N, long. 121°40'20" W). Altitude 1420 feet. Named on Mount Madonna (1955) 7.5' quadrangle. Butler (p. 169) noted that the peak was known locally as Murphy's Peak, for Martin Murphy, Sr., whose ranch house was nearby. The peak also was called Oreja del Oso—*oreja del oso* means "bear's ear" in Spanish—and Twenty-one Mile Peak, presumably for Twenty-one Mile House, or for the distance from San Jose (Hoover, Rensch, and Rensch, p. 431).

El Valle de San Jose: see **Livermore Valley** [ALAMEDA].

Embarcadero: see **Redwood City** [SAN MATEO].

Embarcadero Cove: see **Brooklyn Basin** [ALAMEDA].

Embarcadero de San Francisquito: see **Mayfield Slough** [SANTA CLARA].

Embarcadero de Santa Clara [SANTA CLARA]: *land grant,* 1 mile south-southeast of Alviso. Named on Milpitas (1961) 7.5' quadrangle. Barcilla Bernal received the land in 1845, and was patentee for 196.25 acres in 1936—this is the last land grant in California to receive a United States patent (Arbuckle, p. 17; Perez, p. 65).

Embarcadero de Santa Clara de Asis: see **Alviso** [SANTA CLARA].

Emerald Lake: see **Lower Emerald Lake** [SAN MATEO]; **Upper Emerald Lake** [SAN MATEO].

Emerson Slough [CONTRA COSTA]: *water feature,* joins Dutch Slough 2 miles west of the settlement of Bethel Island (lat. 38° 00'40" N, long. 121°40'40" W). Named on Jersey Island (1978) 7.5' quadrangle.

Emery [ALAMEDA]: *locality,* 2 miles north-northwest of downtown Oakland along Southern Pacific Railroad (lat. 37°49'50" N, long. 122°17'30" W). Named on San Francisco (1899) 15' quadrangle.

Emeryville [ALAMEDA]: *town,* 2.5 miles north-northwest of downtown Oakland near San Francisco Bay (lat. 37°50'30" N, long. 122°17'15" W). Named on Oakland West (1959) 7.5' quadrangle. Postal authorities established Emeryville post office in 1884 (Frickstad, p. 1), and the town incorporated in 1896. The name, given in 1897, commemorates Joseph S. Emery, who in 1859 bought the land where the town is situated (Gudde, 1949, p. 107). Postal authorities established Stockyards post office 1.5 miles north of Emeryville in 1898 and discontinued it in 1909; the place was at a shipping point for cattle and sheep (Salley, p. 213).

Emmet: see **Point Emmet** [CONTRA COSTA].

Emmons Canyon [CONTRA COSTA]: *canyon,* drained by a stream that flows 1 mile to Green Valley Creek 4 miles west-southwest of Mount Diablo (lat. 37°51'20" N, long. 121°58'40" W; sec. 9, T 1 S, R 1 W). Named on Diablo (1953) 7.5' quadrangle.

Empire [CONTRA COSTA]: *locality,* less than 1 mile south of present downtown Antioch along Southern Pacific Railroad (lat. 38°00'15" N, long. 121°48'50" W). Named on Collinsville (1918) 7.5' quadrangle.

Encinal: see **Alameda** [ALAMEDA]; **Sunnyvale** [SANTA CLARA].

Encinal Basin [ALAMEDA]: *water feature,* 1.5 miles south-southeast of downtown Oakland on the south side of Oakland Inner Harbor (lat. 37°46'50" N, long. 122°15'35" W).

Named on Oakland West (1959) 7.5' quadrangle.

Encinal de San Antonio: see **Alameda** [ALAMEDA].

Encinal Station: see **Alameda** [ALAMEDA].

Encinosa Creek [SOLANO]: *stream,* flows nearly 4 miles to Alamo Creek 8 miles north of Fairfield in Vacaville (lat. 38°21'35" N, long. 122°00'30" W). Named on Fairfield North (1951) 7.5' quadrangle.

Endor: see **Mountain View** [SANTA CLARA].

English Creek [SOLANO]: *stream,* flows 3.5 miles to Sweany Creek 2.5 miles west-southwest of Allendale (lat. 38°25'30" N, long. 121° 58'50" W; sec. 28, T 7 N, R 1 W); the stream is in English Hills. Named on Allendale (1953) and Mount Vaca (1951) 7.5' quadrangles. South Fork enters from the southwest 5.5 miles east of Mount Vaca; it is 1.5 miles long and is named on Mount Vaca (1951) 7.5' quadrangle.

English Hills [SOLANO]: *range,* north of Vacaville (lat. 38°26'15" N, long. 122°00'30" W). Named on Allendale (1953), Elmira (1953), and Mount Vaca (1951) 7.5' quadrangles.

English Town [SANTA CLARA]: *locality,* 1 mile west-northwest of New Almaden near New Almaden mine (lat. 37°10'45" N, long. 121°50'15" W). Named on Santa Teresa Hills (1953) 7.5' quadrangle. The name is from English, particularly Cornish, miners who lived at the place (Lanyon and Bulmore, p. 63).

Enright Tract [SANTA CLARA]: *land grant,* southeast of Lawrence in Sunnyvale. Named on San Jose West (1961) 7.5' quadrangle. Francisco Garcia received the land in 1845; James Enright claimed 710.14 acres patented in 1866 (Arbuckle, p. 17-18).

Ensenada de Consolacion: see **Sausalito Point** [MARIN].

Ensenada de la Carmelita: see **Richardson Bay** [MARIN].

Ensenada de los Llorones: see **Mission Bay**, under **Mission District** [SAN FRANCISCO].

Ensenada del Santo Evangelio: see **Belvedere Cove** [MARIN].

Encinal de San Antonio: see **Alameda** [ALAMEDA].

Estero Americano [MARIN]: *water feature,* estuary that forms part of Marin-Sonoma county line; heads at the mouth of Americano Creek and extends to Bodega Bay in Sonoma County (1) 6.25 miles west-northwest of Tomales (lat. 38°17'45" N, long. 123°00'05" W). Named on Valley Ford (1954) 7.5' quadrangle. United States Board on Geographic Names (1943, p. 9) rejected the name "Estero de San Antonio" for the feature.

Estero Americano: see **Americano Creek** [MARIN]; **Tomales Bay** [MARIN].

Estero Americano Creek: see **Americano Creek** [MARIN].

Estero de Americano: see **Estero de San Antonio** [MARIN].

Estero de las Mercedes: see **Petaluma River** [MARIN].

Estero de Limantour [MARIN]: *bay*, opens into Drakes Estero near the mouth of that feature 5.5 miles east-northeast of the lighthouse at Point Reyes (lat. 38°02'05" N, long. 122°55'50" W). Named on Drakes Bay (1953) 7.5' quadrangle. The name commemorates Jose Yves Limantour, who was shipwrecked at the mouth of present Drakes Estero in 1841 (Gilliam, p. 86). The name originally applied to present Drakes Estero and to nearby bays together, but after members of United States Coast Survey named Drakes Estero in 1860, the name "Estero de Limantour" was restricted to its present usage (Hanna, W.L., p. 40-41).

Estero de Nuestra Señora de la Merced: see **Petaluma River** [MARIN].

Estero de Petaluma: see **Petaluma River** [MARIN].

Estero de San Antonio [MARIN]: *water feature*, estuary that heads at the mouth of Stemple Creek and extends to Bodega Bay 4.25 miles west-northwest of Tomales (lat. 38°16'10" N, long. 122°58'40" W). Named on Valley Ford (1954) 7.5' quadrangle. United States Board on Geographic Names (1943, p. 12) rejected the names "Estero de Americano," "Stemple Creek," and "Tomales Creek" for all or part of the feature.

Estero de San Antonio: see **Estero Americano** [MARIN]; **Stemple Creek** [MARIN].

Estero de San Francisco: see **San Francisco Bay**.

Estero de San Rafael de Agnanni: see **San Rafael Creek** [MARIN].

Estero de Santa Clara: see **San Francisco Bay**.

Estrecho de Karquines: see **Carquinez Strait** [CONTRA COSTA-SOLANO].

Estrecho de las Karquines: see **Carquinez Strait** [CONTRA COSTA-SOLANO].

Estrecho de San Jose: see **San Francisco Bay**.

Eucalyptus Island [CONTRA COSTA]: *island*, 0.5 mile long, 8.5 miles southeast of Brentwood along Old River (lat. 37°51'35" N, long. 121°34'15" W). Named on Clifton Court Forebay (1978) 7.5' quadrangle, which shows the feature as marsh and water.

Eues Creek: see **Evans Creek** [SAN MATEO].

Eugene Spring [CONTRA COSTA]: *spring*, 7 miles south-southeast of Danville (lat. 37°43'35" N, long. 121°57'50" W; sec. 27, T 2 S, R 1 W). Named on Dublin (1961) 7.5' quadrangle.

Eureka Peak [CONTRA COSTA]: *peak*, 1.5 miles west of Orinda (lat. 37°52'45" N, long. 122°12'40" W; sec. 5, T 1 S, R 3 W). Named on Briones Valley (1959) 7.5' quadrangle.

Eu's Creek: see **Evans Creek** [SAN MATEO].

Eva [SANTA CLARA]: *locality*, 5.5 miles south-southeast of downtown Los Gatos along

Southern Pacific Railroad (lat. 37°09' N, long. 121°57'30" W; sec. 15, T 9 S, R 1 W). Named on Los Gatos (1919) 15' quadrangle.

Evans Creek [SAN MATEO]: *stream*, flows nearly 2 miles to Peters Creek 3.5 miles southsoutheast of Mindego Hill (lat. 37°15'35" N, long. 122°12'50" W; sec. 5, T 8 S, R 3 W). Named on Mindego Hill (1961) 7.5' quadrangle. Called Eues Creek on Palo Alto (1899) 15' quadrangle. The stream also was called Eu's Creek, for Eugenio Soto, whose ranch was near the head of the creek in the 1850's (Brown, p. 33).

Evergreen [SANTA CLARA]: *settlement*, 6 miles east-southeast of downtown San Jose (lat. 37°15'35" N, long. 121°47' W). Named on San Jose East (1961) 7.5' quadrangle. Postal authorities established Evergreen post office in 1870, discontinued it in 1913, reestablished it in 1932, and discontinued it in 1935 (Frickstad, p. 173). Rambo (1973, p. 41) attributed the name to groves of live oaks at the place.

Ewing Hill [SANTA CLARA]: *peak*, 2 miles north of Black Mountain (1) (lat. 37°20'40" N, long. 122°08'50" W; on N line sec. 12, T 7 S, R 3 W). Named on Mindego Hill (1961) 7.5' quadrangle.

Ex Mission San Jose [ALAMEDA]: *land grant*, at and near Fremont. Named on La Costa Valley (1960), Milpitas (1961), Newark (1959), and Niles (1961) 7.5' quadrangles. Andrés Pico and Juan Buatista Alvarado purchased the land in 1846, but their claim was rejected; the Catholic Church patented 28 acres in 1858 (Cowan, p. 80; Cowan listed the grant under the name "San José de Guadalupe Mision").

Eylar Canyon [ALAMEDA]: *canyon*, drained by a stream that flows 5.5 miles to Arroyo Valle 5 miles south of Cedar Mountain (lat. 37°29'25" N, long. 121°36'25" W; near NW cor. sec. 24, T 5 S, R 3 E); the canyon heads on the west side of Man Ridge near Eylar Mountain [SANTA CLARA]. Named on Cedar Mountain (1956) and Eylar Mountain (1955) 7.5' quadrangles. Called Man Gulch on Mount Hamilton (1897) and Tesla (1907) 15' quadrangles.

Eylar Mountain [SANTA CLARA]: *ridge*, west-northwest-trending, 1.5 miles long, 10.5 miles northeast of Mount Hamilton (lat. 37°28'30" N, long. 121°32'50" W). Named on Eylar Mountain (1955) 7.5' quadrangle.

— F —

Fairchild Gulch [ALAMEDA]: *canyon*, drained by a stream that flows 2 miles to Eylar Gulch 4 miles south-southeast of Cedar Mountain (lat. 37°30'15" N, long. 121°35'10" W; at S line sec. 7, T 5 S, R 4 E). Named on Cedar Mountain (1956) and Eylar Mountain (1955) 7.5' quadrangles. The name commemorates

P.R. Fairchild, who owned property in the canyon in 1900 (Mosier and Mosier, p. 36).

Fairfax [MARIN]: *town,* 3.25 miles west-northwest of downtown San Rafael (lat. 37°59'10" N, long. 122°35'30" W). Named on San Rafael (1954) 7.5' quadrangle. Postal authorities established Fairfax post office in 1910 (Frickstad, p. 87), and the town incorporated in 1931. The name commemorates Charles S. Fairfax, who purchased 40 acres in 1856 at the site of the present town (Hanna, P.T., p. 102).

Fairfax Creek [MARIN]: *stream,* flows 3.25 miles to San Anselmo Creek 3.25 miles west-northwest of downtown San Rafael (lat. 37° 59'10" N, long. 122°35'20" W). Named on Novato (1954) and San Rafael (1954) 7.5' quadrangles.

Fairfax Manor: see **Manor** [MARIN].

Fairfield [SOLANO]: *city,* in the west-central part of Solano County (lat. 38°15' N, long. 122°02'30" W). Named on Fairfield North (1951) and Fairfield South (1949) 7.5' quadrangles. Postal authorities established Fairfield post office in 1858, discontinued it in 1861, and reestablished it in 1879 (Frickstad, p. 192). The city incorporated in 1903. R.H. Waterman purchased part of Suisun grant in 1848 and made a gift of land for a new county seat in 1858; the new town was laid out in 1859 and named for Waterman's birthplace, Fairfield, Connecticut (Hoover, Rensch, and Rensch, p. 523). Postal authorities established Waterman Park post office as a station of Fairfield post office in 1944 and discontinued it in 1948; the name was for R.H. Waterman (Salley, p. 235).

Fairfield: see **Campbell** [SANTA CLARA].

Fairfield Unit Number 1: see **Travis Air Force Base** [SOLANO].

Fairford: see **Black Point** [MARIN].

Fair Oaks: see **Atherton** [SAN MATEO].

Fairoaks [SAN MATEO]: *locality,* 2 miles southeast of downtown Redwood City along Southern Pacific Railroad (lat. 37°27'50" N, long. 122°11'55" W). Named on Palo Alto (1899) 7.5' quadrangle. Postal authorities established Fair Oaks post office in 1867 and discontinued it in 1871 (Frickstad, p. 167).

Fall Creek [SAN MATEO]: *stream,* flows 1.25 miles to Pescadero Creek 4 miles south of Mindego Hill (lat. 37°14'55" N, long. 122° 13' W; sec. 8, T 8 S, R 3 W). Named on Big Basin (1955) 7.5' quadrangle.

Fallon [MARIN]: *village,* 2 miles north of Tomales (lat. 38°16'30" N, long. 122°54'15" W). Named on Valley Ford (1954) 7.5' quadrangle. Postal authorities established Fallon post office in 1898 (Salley, p. 72). The name is from Luke Fallon and James Fallon, brothers who were early settlers in the region (Hanna, P.T., p. 103).

False River [CONTRA COSTA]: *water feature,* extends for 6 miles from Old River to San Joaquin River 3.5 miles northwest of the settlement of Bethel Island (lat. 38°03'30" N,

long. 121°40'40" W). Named on Bouldin Island (1978) and Jersey Island (1978) 7.5' quadrangles. Bouldin (1910) 7.5' quadrangle shows an artificial waterway called Washington Slough situated along the north side of False River at the south edge of Webb Tract; the former Washington Slough now is part of the west end of present False River.

Family Farm: see **The Family Farm** [SAN MATEO].

Farallon: see **Middle Farallon** [SAN FRANCISCO]; **North Farallon** [SAN FRANCISCO]; **Southeast Farallon** [SAN FRANCISCO]; **South Farallon**, under **Southeast Farallon** [SAN FRANCISCO].

Farallone [SAN MATEO]: *locality,* 2 miles west-southwest of present Montara Knob along Ocean Shore Railroad (lat. 37°32'25" N, long. 122°31' W). Named on San Mateo (1915) 15' quadrangle. Postal authorities established Farallone post office in 1909 and changed the name to Montara in 1918 (Salley, p. 73).

Farallones del Angel de la Guarda: see **Farallon Islands** [SAN FRANCISCO].

Farallones de los Frayles: see **Farallon Islands** [SAN FRANCISCO].

Farallones de San Francisco: see **Farallon Islands** [SAN FRANCISCO].

Farallones Islands: see **Farallon Islands** [SAN FRANCISCO].

Farallones Rocks: see **Farallon Islands** [SAN FRANCISCO].

Farallon Islands [SAN FRANCISCO]: *islands,* 30 miles west of the Golden Gate; the principal islands are—from northwest to southeast—North Farallon, Isle of St. James, Middle Farallon, and Southeast Farallon. Named on Farallon Islands (1988) 7.5' quadrangle. Called Los Farellones on Costanso's (1771) map, called Farellons of Sn. Francisco on Dalrymple's (1789) map, and called Farallones de los Freyles on Ringgold's (1850b) map. Smith (p. 103) mentioned Farallones Rocks in 1850, and Blake (1856, p. 397) used the name "Farallones Islands" in 1856. United States Board on Geographic Names (1933, p. 298) rejected the names "Farallones" and "Marallone" for the features. Francis Drake landed on the islands in 1579 and called them the Ilands of St. James (Hanna, W.L., p. 263). *Los Farallones* is a Spanish nautical term derived from the word meaning "cliff" or "small, pointed island in the sea" (Hoover, p. 1). In 1602, Vizcaino called the northwest group of the islands the Frayles, from the Spanish term with the meaning "friar" or "monk," but the name "Farallones de los Freyles" dates from Bodega's expedition of 1775; the islands sometimes were called Farallones de San Francisco and Farallones del Angel de la Guarda (Wagner, H.R., p. 387, 426).

Farman Canyon [SANTA CLARA]: *canyon,*

drained by a stream that flows 1 mile to low-lands nearly 2 miles south-southwest of Gilroy (lat. 36°58'50" N, long. 121°34'40" W). Named on Chittenden (1955) 7.5' quadrangle.

Farwell [ALAMEDA]: *locality,* 3.5 miles north-northeast of Fremont civic center along Southern Pacific Railroad in Niles Canyon (lat. 37°35'35" N, long. 121°56'40" W; sec. 11, T 4 S, R 1 W). Named on Niles (1961) 7.5' quadrangle. The name commemorates James Dumaresy Farwell, who owned property north of the site; the place also was called Stonybrook after Stonybrook Creek (Mosier and Mosier, p. 36).

Fasskings Station: see **Alameda** [ALAMEDA].

Federal Terrace: see **Vallejo** [SOLANO].

Felix: see **Feliz** [SAN MATEO].

Feliz [SAN MATEO]: *land grant,* west of Upper Crystal Springs Reservoir and Lower Crystal Springs Reservoir. Named on Montara Mountain (1956), San Mateo (1956), and Woodside (1961) 7.5' quadrangles. Domingo Felix received 1 league in 1844 and claimed 4448 acres patented in 1873 (Cowan, p. 17; Cowan listed the grant under the designation "Cañada de las Auras, (or) Felix").

Felt Lake [SANTA CLARA]: *lake,* 0.5 mile long, behind a dam on a tributary to Los Trancos Creek 4 miles south-southwest of downtown Palo Alto (lat. 37°23'40" N, long. 122°11'05" W). Named on Palo Alto (1961) 7.5' quadrangle. Palo Alto (1899) 15' quadrangle shows a natural lake. Thompson and West's (1876) map indicates that J.H. Felt owned land near the site

Fenton Canyon [SANTA CLARA]: *canyon,* drained by a stream that flows 3 miles to Black Bird Valley 3 miles south of Mount Boardman (lat. 37°26'10" N, long. 121°28'40" W; at W line sec. 6, T 6 S, R 5 E). Named on Mount Boardman (1955) 7.5' quadrangle.

Fern Creek [MARIN]: *stream,* formed by the confluence of East Fork and West Fork, flows 1.5 miles to Redwood Creek 5.5 miles south-southwest of downtown San Rafael (lat. 37°54'05" N, long. 122°34'40" W). Named on San Rafael (1954) 7.5' quadrangle. East Fork and West Fork each are 0.5 mile long; both forks are named on San Rafael (1954) 7.5' quadrangle.

Ferndale Springs: see **Vaca Canyon** [CONTRA COSTA].

Fern Hill: see **Fern Peak** [SANTA CLARA]; **Nob Hill** [SAN FRANCISCO].

Fern Mountain [SOLANO]: *ridge,* northwest-trending, 0.5 mile long, 4.5 miles south of Big Mountain (lat. 38°38'40" N, long. 123°09'05" W). Named on Tombs Creek (1978) 7.5' quadrangle.

Fern Peak [SANTA CLARA]: *peak,* nearly 2 miles south-southeast of New Almaden (lat. 37°09'10" N, long. 121°48'40" W). Altitude 1710 feet. Named on Santa Teresa Hills (1953)

7.5' quadrangle. Called Fern Hill on Los Gatos (1919) 15' quadrangle.

Fifield Ridge [SAN MATEO]: *ridge,* southeast-trending, 1.5 miles long, 3 miles east-north-east of Montara Knob (lat. 37°34'10" N, long. 122°25'55" W). Named on Montara Mountain (1956) 7.5' quadrangle. The name commemorates Albert B. Fifield and Winfield J. Fifield, who in 1859 settled east of the ridge in Fifield Valley (Brown, p. 33)

Fifield Valley: see **Fifield Ridge** [SAN MATEO].

Fifteen Mile House: see **Perry** [SANTA CLARA].

Fillmore Creek: see **Apanolio Creek** [SAN MATEO].

Finger Creek: see **Cordilleras Creek** [SAN MATEO].

Finger's Arroyo: see **Cordilleras Creek** [SAN MATEO].

Finley Ridge [SANTA CLARA]: *ridge,* north-west-trending, 2 miles long, 5 miles south-west of Mount Sizer (lat. 37°09'20" N, long. 121°34' W). Named on Mount Sizer (1955) 7.5' quadrangle.

Finney Creek [SAN MATEO]: *stream,* heads in Santa Cruz County and flows 1.5 miles to the sea 1.5 miles east of Año Nuevo Point (present Point Año Nuevo) (lat. 37°06'50" N, long. 122°18' W). Named on Año Nuevo (1955) and Franklin Point (1955) 7.5' quadrangles. Called Finny Creek on Año Nuevo (1948) 15' quadrangle. The name is for Seldon J. Finney, who lived along the creek; Finney was a state assemblyman from 1869 until 1870, and a state senator from 1871 until 1875 (Gudde, 1949, p. 116).

Finny Creek: see **Finney Creek** [SAN MATEO].

First Mallard Branch [SOLANO]: *water feature,* joins Cutoff Slough nearly 3 miles south of Fairfield (lat. 38°11'40" N, long. 122°01'55" W). Named on Fairfield South (1949) 7.5' quadrangle.

First Slough [SAN MATEO]: *water feature,* joins Westpoint Slough 2.5 miles northeast of downtown Redwood City (lat. 37°30'30" N, long. 122°11'35" W). Named on Redwood Point (1959) 7.5' quadrangle.

Fishermans Bay [SAN FRANCISCO]: *embayment,* on the north side of South Farallon (lat. 37°41'55" N, long. 123°00'35" W). Named on Farallon Islands (1988) 7.5' quadrangle. Hoover (frontispiece map) used the form "Fisherman's Bay" for the name.

Fisherman's Bay: see **Fishermans Bay** [SAN FRANCISCO].

Fishermans Channel: see **Fishermans Cut**, under **Roe Island** [SOLANO].

Fishermans Cut [CONTRA COSTA]: *water feature,* extends for 2 miles between Bradford Island and Webb Tract from San Joaquin River to False River 3 miles north of the community of Bethel Island (lat. 38°03'25" N,

121°38'50" W). Named on Jersey Island (1978) 7.5' quadrangle.

Fishermans Cut: see **Roe Island** [SOLANO].

Fishermans Slough [CONTRA COSTA]: *water feature,* 4.5 miles north of the settlement of Bethel Island on Webb Tract (lat. 38°04'55" N, long. 121°38' W). Named on Jersey Island (1952) 7.5' quadrangle.

Fishermans Wharf [SAN FRANCISCO]: *locality,* near North Point along San Francisco Bay (lat. 37°48'35" N, long. 122°24'55" W). Named on San Francisco North (1956) 7.5' quadrangle.

Fishermen's: see **Marconi** [MARIN].

Fisher's Ranche: see **La Laguna Seca** [SANTA CLARA].

Fish Gulch [MARIN]: *canyon,* drained by a stream that flows 0.5 mile to Phoenix Creek 3 miles west-southwest of downtown San Rafael (lat. 37°57'20" N, long. 122°35' W). Named on San Rafael (1954) 7.5' quadrangle.

Fitchburg [ALAMEDA]: *locality,* 5.5 miles southeast of downtown Oakland (lat. 37°45'25" N, long. 122°11'10" W). Named on Concord (1897) 15' quadrangle. The railroad stop at the place first was called Fitch's Station (Mosier and Mosier, p. 37). Postal authorities established Fitchburg post office in 1908, discontinued it in 1911, and reestablished it in 1954; the name is for Colonel Henry S. Fitch, a land developer (Salley, p. 75). Damon Slough is situated at the mouth of Lion Creek, Damon's Landing was located along the slough on the east side of San Leandro Bay, and Damon Marsh is north of the site of the landing; Nathaniel Damon came to the neighborhood in 1853 and established the landing, which served the community of Fitchburg—the place also was called Fitchburg Landing (Mosier and Mosier, p. 27-28, 36).

Fitchburg Landing: see **Damon's Landing**, under **Fitchburg** [ALAMEDA].

Fitch's Station: see **Fitchburg** [ALAMEDA].

Fitzgerald Ridge [SANTA CLARA]: *ridge,* northwest- to west-trending, 1 mile long, 4.25 miles south-southwest of Mount Sizer (lat. 37°09'25" N, long. 121°32'30" W). Named on Mount Sizer (1955) 7.5' quadrangle.

Five Brooks [MARIN]: *locality,* 5.25 miles south-southeast of Point Reyes Station along Olema Creek (lat. 38°00'05" N, long. 122°45'25" W). Named on Inverness (1954) 7.5' quadrangle.

Five Points [SOLANO]: *locality,* 9.5 miles north-northeast of Rio Vista in Yolo Bypass (lat. 38°17'25" N, long. 121°38'35" W). Named on Liberty Island (1978) 7.5' quadrangle.

Fleming [ALAMEDA]: *locality,* 4.5 miles north-northwest of downtown Oakland along Southern Pacific Railroad (lat. 37°53'05" N, long. 122°18'30" W); the place is 0.5 mile east-northeast of Fleming Point. Named on San Francisco (1915) 15' quadrangle. The name commemorates John J. Fleming, a local meat-market proprietor (Mosier and Mosier, p. 37). The place is called Highland on San Francisco (1899) 15' quadrangle.

Fleming Point [ALAMEDA]: *promontory,* 6 miles north-northwest of downtown Oakland along San Francisco Bay (lat. 37°53'10" N, long. 122°18'55" W). Named on Richmond (1959) 7.5' quadrangle. Called Pt. Fleming on San Francisco (1942) 15' quadrangle, and called Flemings Pt. on San Francisco (1899) 15' quadrangle, which shows the feature as an island separated from the mainland by marsh. The name commemorates J.J. Fleming, who settled near the promontory in 1853 (Gudde, 1949, p. 116).

Flint Creek [SANTA CLARA]: *stream,* flows 3 miles to lowlands 3 miles north of Evergreen (lat. 37°21'10" N, long. 121°47'20" W). Named on San Jose East (1961) 7.5' quadrangle.

Flood Slough [SAN MATEO]: *water feature,* joins Westpoint Slough 3 miles east-northeast of downtown Redwood City (lat. 37°29'55" N, long. 122°10'35" W). Named on Palo Alto (1961) 7.5' quadrangle.

Flosden [SOLANO]: *locality,* 3 miles north of downtown Vallejo along Southern Pacific Railroad (lat. 38°08'45" N, long. 122°15'05" W). Named on Mare Island (1916) 15' quadrangle.

Flosden Acres [SOLANO]: *district,* 2.25 miles north of downtown Vallejo (lat. 38°08'10" N, long. 122°15' W; sec. 1, T 3 N, R 4 W). Named on Cordelia (1951) and Cuttings Wharf (1949) 7.5' quadrangles.

Floyd: see **Harry Floyd Terrace** [SOLANO].

Foam Gulch: see **Spring Bridge Gulch** [SAN MATEO].

Fog Whistle [SAN MATEO]: *locality,* 2.25 miles southwest of present Montara Knob along Ocean Shore Railroad near Montara Point (present Point Montara) (lat. 37°32'05" N, long. 122°31'05" W). Named on San Mateo (1915) 15' quadrangle.

Forbes [MARIN]: *locality,* 7.5 miles southsoutheast of downtown Novato along Northwestern Pacific Railroad (lat. 38°30' N, long. 122°32'20" W). Named on Petaluma (1914) and Tamalpais (1897) 15' quadrangles.

Forbes Mill: see **Los Gatos** [SANTA CLARA].

Forbestown: see **Los Gatos** [SANTA CLARA].

Forest House: see **Alma** [SANTA CLARA].

Forest Knolls [MARIN]: *settlement,* 9 miles southwest of downtown Novato (lat. 38°00'55" N, long. 122°41'15" W). Named on San Geronimo (1954) 7.5' quadrangle. Postal authorities established Forest Knolls post office in 1916 (Frickstad, p. 87).

Fort Baker Military Reservation [MARIN]: *military installation,* 2 miles south of downtown Sausalito at the southeast end of Marin Peninsula (lat. 37°50' N, long. 122°29'15" W).

Named on San Francisco North (1956) 7.5' quadrangle. The federal government bought the property in 1866 and called it Lime Point Military Reservation (Teather, p. 5). A new installation built there in the 1890's was named Fort Baker in 1897 to honor Colonel Edward D. Baker, who was killed in 1861 at the Battle of Ball's Bluff in Virignia (Frazer, p. 20).

Fort Barry: see **Fort Barry Military Reservation** [MARIN].

Fort Barry Military Reservation [MARIN]: *military installation,* at and east of Point Bonita and Rodeo Cove (lat. 37°49'45" N, long. 122°31' W). Named on Point Bonita (1954) and San Francisco North (1956) 7.5' quadrangles. Postal authorities established Fort Barry post office in 1911 and discontinued it in 1918 (Frickstad, p. 87). The name, given in 1904, honors Brevet Major General William F. Barry (Whiting and Whiting, p. 10).

Fort Cronkhite Military Reservation [MARIN]: *military installation,* 1.5 miles north-northwest of Point Bonita (lat. 37°50'20" N, long. 122°32'30" W). Named on Point Bonita (1954) 7.5' quadrangle. The name, given in 1937, honors Major General Adelbert Cronkhite (Whiting and Whiting, p. 19).

Fort Funston Military Reservation [SAN FRANCISCO]: *military installation,* 3 miles west-southwest of Mount Davidson (lat. 37° 43' N, long. 122°30' W). Named on San Francisco South (1956) 7.5' quadrangle. San Mateo (1942) 15' quadrangle shows Fort Funston. The installation was acquired in 1901 and called Laguna Merced Military Reservation; the place was renamed in 1917 to honor Major General Frederick Funston (Whiting and Whiting, p. 28).

Fortmann Basin [ALAMEDA]: *water feature,* 2 miles south-southeast of downtown Oakland on the south side of Oakland Inner Harbor (lat. 37°46'45" N, long. 121°15'20" W). Named on Oakland West (1959) 7.5' quadrangle. The name commemorates Henry F. Fortmann, who was instrumental in formation of Alaska Packers Association, which purchased waterfront land in 1904 and had the basin dredged to accommodate a fishing fleet; the feature was called Alaska Packers Association Basin before 1926 (Mosier and Mosier, p. 37).

Fort Mason Military Reservation [SAN FRANCISCO]: *military installation,* 1 mile west of North Point at Black Point (lat. 37° 48'25" N, long. 122°25'40" W). Named on San Francisco North (1956) 7.5' quadrangle. The place was reserved for military use in 1850 and occupied by the army in 1863; it first was called Fort Point San Jose, from the designation "Bateria San Jose" for the old Spanish installation there, and then in 1882 the name was changed to Fort Mason to honor Brevet Brigadier General Richard B. Mason,

military governor of California in early American times (Whiting and Whiting, p. 44-45).

Fort McDowell [MARIN-SAN FRANCISCO]: *military installation,* on the east shore of Angel Island on Marin-San Francisco county line (lat. 37°51'45" N, long. 122°25'10" W). Named on San Francisco North (1956) 7.5' quadrangle. Camp Reynolds, named for Major General John F. Reynolds, who was killed at the Battle of Gettysburg, was built at the site in 1864; the name of the installation was changed in 1900 to Fort McDowell, for Major General Irvin McDowell, (Frazer, p. 25-26).

Fort Miley Military Reservation [SAN FRANCISCO]: *military installation,* less than 0.5 mile east of Point Lobos (lat. 37°46'55" N, long. 122°30'25" W). Named on San Francisco North (1956) 7.5' quadrangle. The name, given in 1900, commemorates Lieutenant Colonel John D. Miley (Whiting and Whiting, p. 47).

Fort Montgomery: see **Telegraph Hill** [SAN FRANCISCO].

Fort Point [SAN FRANCISCO]: *promontory,* 4 miles northwest of San Francisco civic center on the south side of the Golden Gate (lat. 37°48'40" N, long. 122°28'35" W). Named on San Francisco North (1956) 7.5' quadrangle. Spaniards had a fortification with the name "Castillo de San Joaquin" at the place as early as 1794; Americans built a new fort at the site in the 1850's that first was called Fort Point and then given the name "Fort Winfield Scott" in 1882 (Hoover, Rensch, and Rensch, p. 351). The Spaniards called the promontory Punta del Cantil Blanco—*cantil blanco* means "white cliff" in Spanish—and Punta del Castillo (Davidson, p. 117; Davis, W.H., p. 4). Dalrymple's (1789) map has the designation "Punta del Cantil Blanco (White Cliff Pt.)" for the feature. The anchorage inside Fort Point was known as Presidio Anchorage, or Old Spanish Anchorage, in American times (Treutlein, p. 68).

Fort Point Rock [SAN FRANCISCO]: *rock,* 0.25 mile south-southwest of Fort Point, and 100 feet offshore (lat. 37°48'30" N, long. 122°28'40" W). Named on San Francisco North (1956) 7.5' quadrangle.

Fort Point San Jose: see **Fort Mason Military Reservation** [SAN FRANCISCO].

Fort Scott [SAN FRANCISCO]: *military installation,* 0.5 mile south-southeast of Fort Point on Presidio Military Reservation (lat. 37° 48'10" N, long. 122°28'20" W). Named on San Francisco North (1956) 7.5' quadrangle. This place and Fort Winfield Scott at Fort Point are separate installations.

Fort Winfield Scott: see **Fort Point** [SAN FRANCISCO].

Fossil Ridge [CONTRA COSTA]: *ridge,* west-northwest-trending, 1.5 miles long, 2.5 miles south-southwest of Mount Diablo (lat. 37°50'50" N, long. 121°55'55" W). Named on Diablo (1953) 7.5' quadrangle.

Foster City [SAN MATEO]: *city,* 3 miles east of downtown San Mateo on Brewer Island (lat. 37°33'30" N, long. 122°16'15" W). Named on San Mateo (1956, photorevised 1980) 7.5' quadrangle. Postal authorities established Foster City post office in 1964 (Salley, p. 79), and the city incorporated in 1971. The name is for T. Jack Foster, who developed of the place (Hynding, p. 280).

Four Corners [CONTRA COSTA]: *locality,* nearly 4 miles north-northeast of Walnut Creek civic center (lat. 37°57'25" N, long. 122°02'15" W). Named on Walnut Creek (1959) 7.5' quadrangle.

Four Fathom Bank: see **Potatopatch Shoal** [MARIN].

Four Mile House: see **Lick** [SANTA CLARA].

Fourteenmile House [ALAMEDA]: *locality,* 1.5 miles northeast of Cedar Mountain (lat. 37°34'40" N, long. 121°35'10" W; near NE cor. sec. 24, T 4 S, R 3 E). Named on Cedar Mountain (1956) 7.5' quadrangle.

Fowler Creek [SANTA CLARA]: *stream,* flows 2 miles to lowlands 1.5 miles east-northeast of Evergreen (lat. 37°19' N, long. 121°45'20" W). Named on San Jose East (1961) 7.5' quadrangle.

Francis Beach [SAN MATEO]: *beach,* 1 mile west-northwest of downtown Half Moon Bay along the coast (lat. 37°28'10" N, long. 122°26'45" W). Named on Half Moon Bay (1961) 7.5' quadrangle. The Manuel Francis family settled in the 1870's at the place, which has the alternate name "Half Moon Bay Beach" (Brown, p. 34).

Francisca: see **Benicia** [SOLANO].

Franconia Bay: see **Maintop Bay** [SAN FRANCISCO].

Frank Canyon [MARIN]: *canyon,* drained by a stream that flows 2.5 miles to Walker Creek 6 miles southeast of Tomales (lat. 38°10'55" N, long. 122°50'10" W). Named on Point Reyes NE (1954) 7.5' quadrangle.

Frank Horan Slough [SOLANO]: *water feature,* 6.25 miles south-southwest of Fairfield in marsh lands (lat. 38°10'10" N, long. 122°05'45" W). Named on Fairfield South (1949) 7.5' quadrangle.

Franklin Canyon [CONTRA COSTA]: *canyon,* nearly 3 miles long, along Franklin Creek above a point 8 miles north of Orinda (lat. 37°59'50" N, long. 122°09'10" W). Named on Benicia (1959) and Briones Valley (1959) 7.5' quadrangles. The name commemorates Edward Franklin, who lived in the canyon until 1875 (Gudde, 1969, p. 113).

Franklin Creek [CONTRA COSTA]: *stream,* flows 5 miles to Arroyo del Hambre 8.5 miles north-northeast of Orinda (lat. 37°59'45" N, long. 122°07'50" W); the stream drains Franklin Canyon. Named on Briones Valley (1959) 7.5' quadrangle.

Franklin Point [SAN MATEO]: *promontory,* nearly 3 miles southeast of Pigeon Point along the coast (lat. 37°09' N, long. 122°21'35" W). Named on Franklin Point (1955) 7.5' quadrangle. The name is for the ship *Sir John Franklin,* which was wrecked at the point in 1865; before the wreck, the promontory was called Middle Point (Gudde, 1949, p. 120).

Franklin Ridge [CONTRA COSTA]: *ridge,* northwest-trending, 6 miles long, center 8 miles north of Orinda (lat. 37°59'35" N, long. 122°10'15" W). Named on Benicia (1959) and Briones Valley (1959) 7.5' quadrangles.

Frank's Lagoon: see **Muir Beach** [MARIN].

Franks Tract [CONTRA COSTA]: *area,* center 2.5 miles north-northeast of the settlement of Bethel Island (lat. 38°02'40" N, long. 121°36'45" W). Named on Bouldin Island (1978) and Jersey Island (1978) 7.5' quadrangles, which show the area mainly covered by water. The feature is shown as an island on Bouldin (1910) and Jersey (1910) 7.5' quadrangles.

Frank Valley [MARIN]: *canyon,* 2.5 miles long, along the lower reaches of Redwood Creek, which enters the sea 4 miles northwest of Point Bonita (lat. 37°51'35" N, long. 122°34'40" W). Named on Point Bonita (1954) and San Rafael (1954) 7.5' quadrangles.

Frayles: see **Farallon Islands** [SAN FRANCISCO].

Frazer: see **Glen Frazer** [CONTRA COSTA].

Frazerville: see **Glen Frazer** [CONTRA COSTA].

Freeman Island [SOLANO]: *island,* 3900 feet long, 7.25 miles west-southwest of Birds Landing (2) in Suisun Bay (lat. 38°04'50" N, long. 121°59'10" W). Named on Honker Bay (1953) 7.5' quadrangle. Called Holbrook Id. on Ringgold's (1850c) map.

Fremont [ALAMEDA]: *city;* the civic center is 25 miles southeast of Oakland (lat. 37°33'05" N, long. 121°58'05" W; near SE cor. sec. 28, T 4 S, R 1 W). Named on Milpitas (1961), Mountain View (1961), Newark (1959), Niles (1961), and Redwood Point (1959) 7.5' quadrangles. The communities of Centerville, Irvington, Mission San Jose, Niles, and Warm Springs joined to form the new city of Fremont, incorporated in 1956; the incorporation committee chose the name "Fremont" for the place (Gudde, 1969, p. 114-115). Postal authorities established Fremont post office in 1956 (Salley, p. 80).

Fremont: see **Camp Fremont**, under **Menlo Park** [SAN MATEO].

Fremont House: see **Mountain View** [SANTA CLARA].

Fremont Well [ALAMEDA]: *well,* nearly 2 miles south-southeast of Fremont civic center (lat. 37°31'30" N, long. 121°57'25" W; sec. 3, T 5 S, R 1 W). Named on Niles (1961) 7.5' quadrangle.

French Island [SOLANO]: *island,* 2300 feet

long, 7 miles north of Rio Vista at the junction of Cache Slough and Shag Slough (lat. 38°15'50" N, long. 121°41'35" W). Named on Liberty Island (1978) 7.5' quadrangle.

Frenchmans Creek [SAN MATEO]: *stream,* flows 4 miles to the sea 1.5 miles northwest of downtown Half Moon Bay (lat. 37°28'50" N, long. 122°27'05" W). Named on Half Moon Bay (1961) and Montara Mountain (1956) 7.5' quadrangles. Called Frenchman Cr. on Santa Cruz (1902) 30' quadrangle. The stream was called Arroyo del Monte in the early days; the canyon of the creek was called Jara Canyon for Sebastian Jara, a woodcutter who lived there in the 1860's and 1870's, and now it commonly is called Frenchman's Creek Canyon (Brown, p. 35, 43).

Frenchman's Creek Canyon: see **Frenchmans Creek** [SAN MATEO].

Frenchs Flat [SANTA CLARA]: *area,* nearly 4 miles south-southwest of Pacheco Pass on Santa Clara-Merced county line (lat. 37°00'45" N, long. 121°14'05" W; around NW cor. sec. 5, T 11 S, R 7 E). Named on Pacheco Pass (1955) 7.5' quadrangle.

Freshwater Bay: see **Suisun Bay** [CONTRA COSTA-SOLANO].

Frey: see **Lake Frey** [SOLANO].

Frick Lake [ALAMEDA]: *intermittent lake,* 2000 feet long, 3 miles west-southwest of Altamont (lat. 37°43'50" N, long. 121°42'35" W; sec. 25, T 2 S, R 2 E). Named on Altamont (1953) 7.5' quadrangle. The name is for John Frick, a farmer in the region (Mosier and Mosier, p. 38).

Frog Pond [ALAMEDA]: *lake,* 300 feet long, 9 miles southeast of Sunol along Alameda Creek (lat. 37°30'05" N, long. 121°46'20" W). Named on Pleasanton (1906) 15' quadrangle.

Frog Pond [CONTRA COSTA]: *lake,* 150 feet long, 1.5 miles southeast of Mount Diablo (lat. 37°51'55" N, long. 121°53'50" W; sec. 7, T 1 S, R 1 E). Named on Diablo (1953) 7.5' quadrangle.

Frohm: see **New Almaden** [SANTA CLARA].

Frost Slough [SOLANO]: *water feature,* on Grizzly Island, joins Montezuma Slough 5 miles southwest of Denverton (lat. 38°10'15" N, long. 121°57'15" W). Named on Denverton (1953) 7.5' quadrangle.

Frowning Ridge [ALAMEDA-CONTRA COSTA]: *ridge,* west-northwest-trending, 1 mile long, 2.5 miles west of Orinda on Alameda-Contra Costa county line (lat. 37°52'50" N, long. 122°13'30" W). Named on Briones Valley (1959) 7.5' quadrangle.

Fruitvale: see **Fruitvale Station** [ALAMEDA].

Fruitvale Creek: see **Sausal Creek** [ALAMEDA].

Fruitvale Station [ALAMEDA]: *locality,* 3.5 miles southeast of downtown Oakland along Southern Pacific Railroad (lat. 37°46'30" N, long. 122°13'35" W). Named on Oakland East (1959) 7.5' quadrangle. Concord (1897) 15'

quadrangle shows a community called Fruitvale at the place. Postal authorities established Brays post office in 1891 and changed the name to Fruitvale in 1892; the name "Brays" was for Watson A. Bray, a pioneer rancher (Salley, p. 26).

Funston: see **Fort Funston Military Reservation** [SAN FRANCISCO].

Furlong Creek: see **Dexter Creek** [SANTA CLARA].

– G –

Galindo [CONTRA COSTA]: *locality,* 6.25 miles north of present Walnut Creek civic center along Southern Pacific Railroad (lat. 37° 59'40" N, long. 122°03'05" W). Named on Concord (1943) 15' quadrangle.

Galindo Creek [CONTRA COSTA]: *stream,* flows 8 miles to Pine Creek 4.5 miles northeast of Walnut Creek civic center (lat. 37°58' N, long. 122°02'30" W). Named on Clayton (1953) and Walnut Creek (1959) 7.5' quadrangles.

Gallinas [MARIN]: *locality,* 6.5 miles southeast of downtown Novato along Northwestern Pacific Railroad (lat. 38°01'10" N, long. 122°31'25" W); the place is on San Pedro Santa Margarita y las Gallinas grant. Named on Novato (1954) 7.5' quadrangle. Petaluma (1942) 15' quadrangle shows St. Vincent Station along the railroad about 1 mile north-northeast of Gallinas near St. Vincent School. Postal authorities established Saint Vincent post office in 1896 and discontinued it in 1922—the name was for St. Vincent School for Boys, founded in 1855 by Daughters of Charity of St. Vincent de Paul (Salley, p. 191).

Gallinas Beach [MARIN]: *beach,* 7.25 miles south-southeast of downtown Novato (lat. 38°00'55" N, long. 122°30'15" W); the beach is south of Gallinas Creek. Named on Novato (1954) 7.5' quadrangle.

Gallinas Creek [MARIN]: *water feature,* enters San Pablo Bay 7.5 miles south-southeast of downtown Novato (lat. 38°01' N, long. 122°29'45" W). Named on Novato (1954) and Petaluma Point (1959) 7.5' quadrangles. The diseño for Las Gallinas grant, made in 1844, shows El Arroyo de Gallinas (Becker, 1969). South Fork enters from the southwest about 1 mile above the mouth of the main stream; it is named on Novato (1954) 7.5' quadrangle.

Gallinas Valley [MARIN]: *valley,* 5.5 miles south of downtown Novato along Miller Creek (lat. 38°01'40" N, long. 122°34' W); the valley is on San Pedro Santa Margarita y las Gallinas grant. Named on Novato (1954) 7.5' quadrangle.

Gang Mill Gulch: see **Martin Creek** [SAN MATEO].

Garcia [MARIN]: *locality,* nearly 2 miles east of Point Reyes Station along Northwestern

Pacific Railroad (lat. 38°04'05" N, long. 122° 46'25" W); the place is on Tomales y Bolinas (1) grant, patented to Rafael Garcia. Named on Point Reyes (1918) 15' quadrangle.

Garfield [SOLANO]: *locality,* 3 miles south-southeast of Denverton along Sacramento Northern Railroad (lat. 38°11'05" N, long. 121° 53' W; at S line sec. 17, T 4 N, R 1 E). Named on Denverton (1953) 7.5' quadrangle. Denverton (1918) 7.5' quadrangle has the name for a place located nearly 0.5 mile farther east.

Garnet Point [SOLANO]: *promontory,* 7.25 miles east-northeast of Benicia in Suisun Bay at the northwest end of Ryer Island (2) (lat. 38°05'40" N, long. 122°02'20" W). Named on Vine Hill (1959) 7.5' quadrangle. United States Board on Geographic Names (1933, p. 318) rejected the name "Long Point" for the feature.

Garretson Point: see **Lion Creek** [ALAMEDA].

Garrity Creek [CONTRA COSTA]: *stream,* flows 3 miles to San Pablo Bay 2.25 miles east-southeast of Pinole Point (lat. 38°00'10" N, long. 122°19'40" W). Named on Mare Island (1959) and Richmond (1959) 7.5' quadrangles.

Garrity Ridge [SANTA CLARA]: *ridge,* southsouthwest-trending, nearly 1 mile long, 2 miles west-northwest of Loma Prieta (lat. 37° 07'25" N, long. 121°52'45" W). Named on Laurel (1955) 7.5' quadrangle. The name commemorates an early settler who had a cabin at the head of Los Gatos Creek above present Williams Reservoir (Young, p. 66).

Gashouse Cove: see **East Harbor** [SAN FRANCISCO].

Gateley [CONTRA COSTA]: *locality,* 3 miles east of Pinole Point along Atchison, Topeka and Santa Fe Railroad (lat. 38°00'25" N, long. 122°18'35" W). Named on Mare Island (1959) 7.5' quadrangle.

Gates Canyon [SOLANO]: *canyon,* 3.5 miles long, on upper reaches of Alamo Creek, opens into Vaca Valley 4.5 miles east-southeast of Mount Vaca (lat. 38°22'30" N, long. 122°01'30" W). Named on Mount Vaca (1951) 7.5' quadrangle.

Gavilan Creek: see **Carnadero Creek** [SANTA CLARA].

Gavin [CONTRA COSTA]: *locality,* 3 miles east-northeast of present Walnut Creek civic center along a branch of Oakland Antioch and Eastern Railroad (lat. 37°55'15" N, long. 122°00'40" W). Named on Concord (1915) 15' quadrangle.

Gazos: see **Gazos Creek** [SAN MATEO].

Gazos Creek [SAN MATEO]: *stream,* heads just inside Santa Cruz County and flows 9 miles to the sea 1 mile north of Franklin Point (lat. 37°09'55" N, long. 122°21'40" W). Named on Big Basin (1955) and Franklin Point (1955) 7.5' quadrangles. The stream also had the

names "Arroyo de las Garzas," "Arroyo de la Bajada," and "Rice's Creek" (Brown, p. 35-36). California Mining Bureau's (1917a) map shows a place called Gazos located along the coast at about the position of Gazos Creek. Postal authorities established Gazos post office 10 miles south of Pescadero along Gazos Creek in 1882 and discontinued it in 1883 (Salley, p. 83).

Gelston: see **Point Gelston**, under **Ryer Island** [SOLANO] (1).

Germantown: see **Austrian Gulch** [SANTA CLARA].

Giant [CONTRA COSTA]: *locality,* 3.5 miles north of Richmond civic center along Southern Pacific Railroad (lat. 37°59'25" N, long. 122°21'20" W). Named on Richmond (1959) 7.5' quadrangle. Postal authorities established Giant post office in 1895 and discontinued it in 1936 (Frickstad, p. 21). The name is from Giant Powder Company's plant located at the place (Gudde, 1949, p. 126).

Gibbon Point [ALAMEDA]: *promontory,* 2 miles west of downtown Oakland along San Francisco Bay (lat. 37°48'20" N, long. 122°18'35" W). Named on San Francisco (1899) 15' quadrangle. The name recalls Rodmond Gibbons, who in 1855 planned to build a ferry terminal at the place; the feature now is called Oakland Point (Mosier and Mosier, p. 39).

Gibson Canyon Creek [SOLANO]: *stream,* flows 3.5 miles to lowlands 2 miles south of Allendale (lat. 38°25' N, long. 121°57' W). Named on Allendale (1953) 7.5' quadrangle. On Vacaville (1953) 15' quadrangle, the stream extends through lowlands to Sweany Creek 4.5 miles south-southwest of Dixon.

Gilbert: see **San Antonio Creek** [SANTA CLARA].

Gilbert's Camp: see **Grabtown** [SAN MATEO].

Gillespie Point [SOLANO]: *promontory,* 8 miles east of Benicia along Suisun Bay at the east end of Roe Island (lat. 38°04'15" N, long. 122°01'15" W). Named on Vine Hill (1959) 7.5' quadrangle. Called Pt. Gillespie on Ringgold's (1850c) map.

Gilroy [SANTA CLARA]: *town,* 28 miles southeast of downtown San Jose (lat. 37°00'30" N, long. 121°34'15" W). Named on Chittenden (1955) and Gilroy (1955) 7.5' quadrangles. Scotsman John Gilroy arrived in California in 1814 and married Maria Clara Ortega, who inherited a third part of San Ysidro grant (Butler, p. 177-178). The first village in the neighborhood was called San Isidro (or San Ysidro), for the grant, but gradually it took Gilroy's name; eventually the name "Gilroy" shifted 2.5 miles west-northwest to a settlement around an inn established in 1850 on the main road down the valley—there the present town of Gilroy was laid out in 1868 and incorporated in 1870 (Bancroft, 1888, p. 525). Postal authorities established Gilroy post office in 1851 (Frickstad, p. 173). With the shift of the name to the new site, the old settlement at became known as Old Gilroy. The present site of Gilroy, when the place was only a stage stop, was called Pleasant Valley (Pierce, p. 161).

Gilroy Hot Springs [SANTA CLARA]: *locality,* 8.5 miles northeast of Gilroy along Coyote Creek (lat. 37°06'30" N, long. 121°28'40" W; sec. 36, T 9 S, R 4 E). Named on Gilroy Hot Springs (1955) 7.5' quadrangle. Anza may have camped at the place in 1776, but a Mexican sheepherder made the effective discovery of the springs at the site in 1865 (Rambo, 1973, p. 41). A resort developed at the springs as early as the 1870's, and by 1908 a hotel and other facilities provided rooms for about 125 guests (Waring, p. 80). Postal authorities established Gilroy Hot Springs post office in 1873 and discontinued it in 1934 (Frickstad, p. 173).

Gilroy Valley: see **Santa Clara Valley** [SANTA CLARA].

Giubbini Point: see **Willow Point** [MARIN].

Glenbrook Creek [MARIN]: *stream,* flows 3.5 miles to an arm of Estero de Limantour 7.5 miles east-northeast of the lighthouse at Point Reyes (lat. 38°02'10" N, long. 122°53'30" W). Named on Drakes Bay (1953) 7.5' quadrangle. The name is from Glen Brook ranch (Teather, p. 27).

Glen Cove [SOLANO]: *embayment,* 3 miles west-northwest of Benicia along Carquinez Strait (lat. 38°04' N, long. 122°12'20" W; sec. 33, T 3 N, R 3 W). Named on Benicia (1959) 7.5' quadrangle.

Glencove [SOLANO]: *locality,* 3 miles west-northwest of Benicia (lat. 38°04'05" N, long. 122°12'20" W; near NW cor. sec. 33, T 3 N, R 3 W); the place is at at Glen Cove. Named on Benicia (1959) 7.5' quadrangle.

Glen Echo Creek [ALAMEDA]: *stream,* ends in downtown Oakland 0.25 mile north of Lake Merritt (lat. 37°48'55" N, long. 122°15'45" W). Named on Oakland West (1959) 7.5' quadrangle. Called Hayes Creek on Concord (1897) 15' quadrangle. The stream formerly was called Cemetery Creek and Hays' Creek—Wickham Havens, a developer, gave the present name to the stream in 1905; the canyon of the stream was called Hays Canyon, for John Coffee Hays, who had an estate at the head of the feature (Mosier and Mosier, p. 39, 42).

Glen Frazer [CONTRA COSTA]: *locality,* 8 miles north of Orinda along Atchison, Topeka and Santa Fe Railroad in Franklin Canyon (lat. 37°59'50" N, long. 122°09'40" W; sec. 23, T 2 N, R 3 W). Named on Briones Valley (1959) 7.5' quadrangle. Postal authorities established Frazerville post office at the place in 1898 and discontinued it in 1899; they established Glen Frazer post office in 1906 and discontinued it in 1919—the name "Frazer" is from an early rancher in the neighborhood (Salley, p. 80, 86).

Glen Una: see **Saratoga** [SANTA CLARA].

Glorietta [CONTRA COSTA]: *settlement,* 1.25 miles southeast of Orinda (lat. 37°51'45" N, long. 122°10' W). Named on Oakland East (1959) 7.5' quadrangle.

Goat Hill [SAN MATEO]: *peak,* 4 miles southwest of La Honda (lat. 37°16'55" N, long. 122°19'35" W; sec. 32, T 7 S, R 4 W). Named on La Honda (1961) 7.5' quadrangle.

Goat Island [SOLANO]: *hill,* 2.5 miles south of Fairfield in marsh (lat. 38°12'50" N, long. 122°02' W). Named on Fairfield South (1949) 7.5' quadrangle. United States Board on Geographic Names (1983e, p. 2) approved the name "Japanese Point" for a promontory on Goat Island (lat. 38°12'52" N, long. 122°02' W; sec. 1, T 4 N, R 2 W), and rejected the name "Jap Rock" for the feature.

Goat Island: see **Yerba Buena Island** [SAN FRANCISCO].

Goecken: see **Greenville** [ALAMEDA].

Goethels Canyon [CONTRA COSTA]: *canyon,* drained by a stream that flows 1.25 miles to Mount Diablo Creek nearly 3 miles northnortheast of Mount Diablo (lat. 37°55'10" N, long. 121°53'50" W; sec. 19, T 1 N, R 1 E). Named on Clayton (1953) 7.5' quadrangle.

Gold Creek [ALAMEDA]: *stream,* flows 1.5 miles to lowlands 1 mile south-southeast of Dublin (lat. 37°41'15" N, long. 121°55'45" W). Named on Dublin (1961) 7.5' quadrangle. Prospectors found placer gold in the creek in 1871 (Mosier and Finney, p. 8).

Golden Gate [ALAMEDA]: *locality,* 2.5 miles north-northwest of downtown Oakland along Southern Pacific Railroad (lat. 37°50'20" N, long. 122°17' W). Named on San Francisco (1899) 15' quadrangle. Postal authorities established Klinknerville post office in 1887, changed the name to Golden Gate in 1888, changed it to Goldengate in 1895, and discontinued the post office in 1905; the first name was for Charles A. Klinkner, who built 75 homes at the place (Salley, p. 87, 113).

Golden Gate [SAN FRANCISCO]: *narrows,* water connection between San Francisco Bay and the sea; 1 mile wide north of Fort Point (lat. 37°49'10" N, long. 122°28'40" W). Named on San Francisco North (1956) 7.5' quadrangle. Soldiers of Lieutenant Fages party first sighted the entrance to San Francisco Bay in 1770 from heights east of the bay; the first vessel to traverse Golden Gate was the Spanish ship *San Carlos,* under the command of Lieutenant Ayala, which entered San Francisco Bay in 1775 (Stanger and Brown, p. 19, 34). Fremont's (1848) map has the designation "Chrysopylae or Golden Gate" for the feature. Fremont (p. 29-30) bestowed the name by analogy with the harbor of Byzantium called Chrysoceras, or golden horn.

Golden Rock: see **Red Rock** [CONTRA COSTA-MARIN-SAN FRANCISCO].

Golden Spur: see **Monta Vista** [SANTA CLARA].

Golf [MARIN]: *locality,* 7.25 miles south-southeast of downtown Novato along Northwestern Pacific Railroad (lat. 38°00'20" N, long. 122°31'55" W). Named on Petaluma (1914) 15' quadrangle.

Goodyear: see **Bahia** [SOLANO].

Goodyear Landing: see **Goodyear Slough** [SOLANO].

Goodyear Slough [SOLANO]: *water feature,* joins Cordelia Slough 8 miles south-southwest of Fairfield (lat. 38°08'05" N, long. 122°05'05" W). Named on Fairfield South (1949) and Vine Hill (1959) 7.5' quadrangles. A place called Goodyear Landing was situated along Goodyear Slough in the early days (Hoover, Rensch, and Rensch, p. 525).

Gordon Ridge [SAN MATEO]: *ridge,* southwest- to west-trending, 3.5 miles long, 6 miles west-northwest of La Honda (lat. 37°21'05" N, long. 122°22' W). Named on La Honda (1961) and San Gregorio (1961, photorevised 1968) 7.5' quadrangles. Alexander Gordon settled on the ridge in the late 1860's (Brown, p. 36).

Gordon's Chute: see **Tunitas Creek** [SAN MATEO].

Gordon Valley Creek [SOLANO]: *stream,* heads in Napa County and flows 6.5 miles to Ledgewood Creek 4.5 miles west-northwest of Fairfield in Solano County (lat. 38°17'05" N, long. 122°06'50" W). Named on Fairfield North (1951) 7.5' quadrangle.

Government Island [ALAMEDA]: *island,* 3000 feet long, nearly 2 miles southeast of downtown Oakland in Oakland Inner Harbor (lat. 37°47' N, long. 122°15' W). Named on Oakland East (1959) and Oakland West (1959) 7.5' quadrangles. United States Board on Geographic Names (1985a, p. 3) approved the name "Coast Guard Island" for the feature— the new name is for the continued presence of United States Coast Guard on the island since 1926.

Government Ranch [CONTRA COSTA]: *locality,* 6 miles east of Martinez along Oakland Antioch and Eastern Railroad (lat. 38°01'05" N, long. 122°01'35" W). Named on Carquinez Strait (1896) 15' quadrangle.

Grabtown [SAN MATEO]: *locality,* 2.25 miles west-northwest of Skeggs Point (lat. 37°25'20" N, long. 122°20'35" W). Named on Woodside (1961) 7.5' quadrangle. A settlement called Gilbert's Camp developed at the site in the 1860's, but the place took the nickname "Grabtown," reportedly after one inhabitant "grabbed" the garden plot of another resident and built a barn on it (Morrall, p. 44).

Grabtown Gulch [SAN MATEO]: *canyon,* drained by a stream that flows 0.5 mile to Purisima Creek nearly 3 miles northwest of

Skeggs Point (lat. 37°26'05" N, long. 122°20'50" W); the canyon heads near Grabtown. Named on Woodside (1961) 7.5' quadrangle.

Granada: see **El Granada** [SAN MATEO].

Granada Beach: see **El Granada Beach** [SAN MATEO].

Grand Canyon [MARIN]: *canyon,* drained by a stream that flows 3.25 miles to lowlands along Tomales Bay 1.5 miles north-northwest of Point Reyes Station (lat. 38°05'30" N, long. 122°49'10" W). Named on Inverness (1954) 7.5' quadrangle.

Grand Street Station: see **Alameda** [ALAMEDA].

Grandview: see **Black Point** [MARIN].

Grass Creek: see **Grass Valley** [ALAMEDA].

Grass Valley [ALAMEDA]: *canyon,* drained by a stream that flows 4 miles to Lake Chabot 5 miles north-northwest of downtown Hayward (lat. 37°44'25" N, long. 122°06'50" W). Named on Hayward (1959), Las Trampas Ridge (1959), and Oakland East (1959) 7.5' quadrangles. Haywards (1899) 15' quadrangle shows Grass Creek in the canyon.

Gravel Pit: see **Lovelady's**, under **Campbell** [SANTA CLARA].

Grayson Creek [CONTRA COSTA]: *stream,* flows 8 miles to Walnut Creek (1) 4 miles east of Martinez (lat. 38°00'15" N, long. 122°03'35" W). Named on Vine Hill (1959) and Walnut Creek (1959) 7.5' quadrangles.

Great Beach: see **The Great Beach**, under **Point Reyes Beach** [MARIN].

Great Farallon: see **Southeast Farallon** [SAN FRANCISCO].

Greco Island [SAN MATEO]: *marsh,* 3.25 miles northeast of downtown Redwood City along San Francisco Bay (lat. 37°31'05" N, long. 122°10'55" W). Named on Redwood Point (1959) 7.5' quadrangle. V.C. Greco had a salt works at the place from 1910 until 1923 (Brown, p. 37).

Green: see **Point Green**, under **Preston Point** [SOLANO].

Green Brae [MARIN]: *town,* 1.5 miles south-southeast of downtown San Rafael (lat. 37°56'55" N, long. 122°31'30" W). Named on San Rafael (1954) 7.5' quadrangle. The name is from a huge dairy ranch that James Ross, Jr., started in the 1860's (Teather, p. 27).

Green Canon [SAN MATEO]: *locality,* 1.5 miles west-northwest of present Montara Knob along Ocean Shore Railroad (lat. 37°33'50" N, long. 122°30'40" W); the place is near present Green Valley. Named on San Mateo (1915) 15' quadrangle.

Green Gulch [MARIN]: *canyon,* drained by a stream that flows 2 miles to Big Lagoon 4 miles northwest of Point Bonita (lat. 37°51'35" N, long. 122°34'25" W). Named on Point Bonita (1954) and San Rafael (1954) 7.5' quadrangles.

Green Hill [MARIN]: *peak,* 6 miles north of

69

Bolinas (lat. 37°59'50" N, long. 122°40'15" W). Altitude 1418 feet. Named on Bolinas (1954) 7.5' quadrangle.

Green Oaks Creek [SAN MATEO]: *stream,* heads in Santa Cruz County and flows nearly 4 miles to the sea 2 miles southeast of Franklin Point (lat. 37°07'50" N, long. 122°20'10" W). Named on Año Nuevo (1955) and Franklin Point (1955) 7.5' quadrangles. Called Greenoaks Creek on Año Nuevo (1948) 15' quadrangle. The name is from Green Oaks dairy ranch, started near the stream in 1863 (Brown, p. 37).

Green Point [MARIN]: *promontory,* 3.5 miles east of downtown Novato on the west side of Petaluma River (lat. 38°06'50" N, long. 122°30'25" W). Named on Novato (1954) 7.5' quadrangle.

Green Point Landing: see **Mowry Landing** [ALAMEDA].

Green Valley [CONTRA COSTA]: *valley,* 2.25 miles east-northeast of Danville (lat. 37°50'05" N, long. 121°57'30" W); the valley is along Green Valley Creek and East Branch Green Valley Creek. Named on Diablo (1953) 7.5' quadrangle. Called Cañada Verde on a diseño of San Ramon (2) grant made in 1834 (Becker, 1969).

Green Valley [SAN MATEO]: *canyon,* drained by a stream that flows less than 1 mile to the sea 1.5 miles west-northwest of Montara Knob (lat. 37°33'55" N, long. 122°30'45" W). Named on Montara Mountain (1956) 7.5' quadrangle.

Green Valley [SOLANO]: *valley,* 2.5 miles northwest of Cordelia (lat. 38°14'20" N, long. 122°09'30" W); the valley is along Green Valley Creek. Named on Cordelia (1951) and Mount George (1951) 7.5' quadrangles.

Green Valley Creek [CONTRA COSTA]: *stream,* flows nearly 4 miles to San Ramon Creek at Danville (lat. 37°49'25" N, long. 121°59'50" W); the stream drains Green Valley. Named on Diablo (1953) 7.5' quadrangle. East Branch enters from the east 1.5 miles northeast of Danville; it is 3.5 miles long and is named on Diablo (1953) 7.5' quadrangle.

Green Valley Creek [SOLANO]: *stream,* flows 8.5 miles to Cordelia Slough 0.25 mile east of Cordelia (lat. 38°12'45" N, long. 122°07'40" W); the stream goes through Green Valley. Named on Cordelia (1951) and Mount George (1951) 7.5' quadrangles.

Green Valley Falls [SOLANO]: *waterfall,* 8 miles west-northwest of Fairfield along Wild Horse Creek (lat. 38°16'35" N, long. 122°10'50" W; sec. 15, T 5 N, R 3 W). Named on Mount George (1951) 7.5' quadrangle.

Greenville [ALAMEDA]: *locality,* 2.5 miles southwest of Altamont (lat. 37°43'15" N, long. 121°42' W; sec. 36, T 2 S, R 2 E). Named on Tesla (1907) 15' quadrangle. The name commemorates John Green, who started the first store at the place (Hoover, Rensch, and

Rensch, p. 12). A Southern Pacific Railroad station called Goecken, situated north of Greenville, was named for Herman Bernard Goecken, a local rancher (Mosier and Mosier, p. 39).

Greenwood Creek: see **Honsinger Creek** [SAN MATEO].

Greersburg: see **Woodside** [SAN MATEO].

Greer's Creek: see **West Union Creek** [SAN MATEO].

Gregorio's Creek: see **Pine Gulch Creek** [MARIN].

Greystone [SANTA CLARA]: *locality,* 3.5 miles north-northwest of New Almaden along Southern Pacific Railroad (lat. 37°13'25" N, long. 121°50'45" W). Named on Los Gatos (1919) 15' quadrangle. Santa Teresa Hills (1953) 7.5' quadrangle shows Greystone quarry near the site.

Grizzly: see **Camp Grizzly**, under **San Bruno** [SAN MATEO].

Grizzly Bay [SOLANO]: *embayment,* 8 miles south of Fairfield off Suisun Bay (lat. 38°08' N, long. 122°01' W). Named on Denverton (1953), Fairfield South (1949), Honker Bay (1953), and Vine Hill (1959) 7.5' quadrangles. Karquines (1898) 15' quadrangle and Denverton (1918) 7.5' quadrangle show the embayment as part of Suisun Bay.

Grizzly Creek [CONTRA COSTA]: *stream,* flows 3 miles to Las Trampas Creek 6.25 miles west-northwest of Danville in Burton Valley (lat. 37°52' N, long. 122°05'50" W; near E line sec. 5, T 1 S, R 2 W). Named on Las Trampas Ridge (1959) 7.5' quadrangle.

Grizzly Creek [SANTA CLARA]: *stream,* flows nearly 5 miles to East Fork Coyote Creek 6 miles southwest of Mount Stakes (lat. 37°15'15" N, long. 121°28'35" W; sec. 7, T 8 S, R 5 E). Named on Isabel Valley (1955), Mississippi Creek (1955), Mount Sizer (1955), and Mount Stakes (1955) 7.5' quadrangles. North Fork enters from the northwest 1.5 miles upstream from the mouth of the main stream; it is 2.5 miles long and is named on Isabel Valley (1955) 7.5' quadrangle. The canyon of North Fork is called Skunk Hollow on Mount Hamilton (1897) 15' quadrangle.

Grizzly Flats [SANTA CLARA]: *area,* 4 miles south-southeast of Isabel Valley (lat. 37°15'40" N, long. 121°30' W); the place is at the confluence of Grizzly Creek and North Fork Grizzly Creek. Named on Isabel Valley (1955) and Mount Stakes (1955) 7.5' quadrangles.

Grizzly Island [SOLANO]: *island,* 14 miles south of Fairfield between Montezuma Slough, Grizzly Slough, and Grizzly Bay (lat. 38°09'15" N, long. 121°57'45" W). Named on Denverton (1953), Fairfield South (1949), and Honker Bay (1953) 7.5' quadrangles.

Grizzly Island Ferry: see **Beldons Landing** [SOLANO].

Grizzly Peak [ALAMEDA-CONTRA COSTA]:

peak, 3 miles west of Orinda on Alameda-Contra Costa county line (lat. 37°52'55" N, long. 122°13'55" W). Named on Briones Valley (1959) 7.5' quadrangle. The name is from a grizzly bear killed at the place in the early days (Mosier and Mosier, p. 40).

Grizzly Slough [SOLANO]: *water feature,* joins Montezuma Slough nearly 3 miles south-southwest of Birds Landing (2) (lat. 38°05'45" N, long. 121°53'40" W); the feature is along the southwest side of Grizzly Island. Named on Honker Bay (1953) 7.5' quadrangle.

Guadalcanal Village [SOLANO]: *locality,* 2.25 miles west-northwest of downtown Vallejo adjacent to the naval reservation (lat. 38°07'10" N, long. 122°17'25" W). Named on Mare Island (1959) 7.5' quadrangle.

Guadalupe [SANTA CLARA]: *settlement,* 3.5 miles north of Mount Umunhum (lat. 37°12'45" N, long. 121°54'20" W); the place is along Guadalupe Creek. Named on Los Gatos (1919) 15' quadrangle. Los Gatos (1953) 7.5' quadrangle shows Guadalupe mines near the site.

Guadalupe Creek [SANTA CLARA]: *stream,* flows 10 miles to join Alamitos Creek and form Guadalupe River 5.5 miles north-north-west of New Almaden (lat. 37°14'50" N, long. 121°52'10" W). Named on Los Gatos (1953) and Santa Teresa Hills (1953) 7.5' quadrangles. United States Board on Geographic Names (1960b, p. 17) rejected the name "Los Capitancillos Creek" for the stream.

Guadalupe Reservoir [SANTA CLARA]: *lake,* 1 mile long, behind a dam on Guadalupe Creek nearly 3 miles north-northeast of Mount Umunhum (lat. 37°11'55" N, long. 121°52'40" W). Named on Los Gatos (1953) and Santa Teresa Hills (1953) 7.5' quadrangles.

Guadalupe River [SANTA CLARA]: *stream,* formed by the confluence of Guadalupe Creek and Alamitos Creek, flows 17 miles through San Jose to Alviso Slough at Alviso (lat. 37°25'30" N, long. 121°58'35" W). Named on Mipitas (1961), San Jose East (1961), San Jose West (1961), and Santa Teressa Hills (1953) 7.5' quadrangles. On San Jose (1899) 15' quadrangle, the river joins Guadalupe Slough at Alviso. According to Gudde (1949, p. 137), Anza called the stream Rio de Nuestra Señora de Guadalupe in 1776 to honor the principal patron saint of the Anza expedition. Gudde (1949, p. 306) also noted that the stream is called Rio de San Jose on old maps. United States Board on Geographic Names (1933, p. 342) rejected the forms "Guadaloupe River" and "Guadelupe River" for the name, and later (1943, p. 11) rejected the name "Guadalupe Slough" for the stream.

Guadalupe River: see **Guadalupe Slough** [SANTA CLARA].

Guadalupe Slough [SANTA CLARA]: *water feature,* 4 miles long, enters mud flats near San Francisco Bay 4 miles west-northwest of

Alviso near the mouth of Coyote Creek (lat. 37°27'10" N, long. 122°02'15" W). Named on Milpitas (1961) and Mountain View (1961) 7.5' quadrangles. Called Guadalupe River on Mountain View (1953) 7.5' quadrangle. Water of Guadalupe River once entered San Francisco Bay through Guadalupe Slough, but now reaches the bay about 1 mile farther north through Alviso Slough. United States Board on Geographic Names (1960b, p. 17) rejected the name "Guadalupe River" for present Guadalupe Slough.

Guadalupe Slough: see **Guadalupe River** [SANTA CLARA].

Guadalupe Valley [SAN MATEO]: *valley,* 2.25 miles north of downtown South San Francisco (lat. 37°41'20" N, long. 122°24'35" W); the valley is on Cañada de Guadalupe la Visitacion y Rodeo Viejo grant. Named on San Francisco South (1956) 7.5' quadrangle.

Guano Island: see **Little Coyote Point** [SAN MATEO].

Gubserville [SANTA CLARA]: *village,* 2.5 miles west-northwest of Campbell (lat. 37°17'40" N, long. 121°59'15" W). Named on San Jose (1899) 15' quadrangle. Postal authorities established Gubserville post office in 1882 and discontinued it in 1899 (Frickstad, p. 173). The place had a stage station, post office, and a house or two; the name commemorates Frank Gubser, a Swiss immigrant (undated item from *San Jose Mercury*).

Gudde Ridge: see **Round Top** [CONTRA COSTA].

Gulf of the Farallones [MARIN-SAN FRANCISCO-SAN MATEO]: *embayment,* along the coast between Point Reyes [MARIN] and Point San Pedro [SAN MATEO] (United States Coast and Geodetic Survey, p. 123); Farallon Islands lie west of the embayment. Named on San Francisco (1956) 1°x 2° quadrangle. After Cermeño applied the name "San Francisco" to present Drakes Bay in 1595 (Treutlein, p. 12), members of the Portola expedition used the term "Puerto de San Francisco" for present Gulf of the Farallones in 1769, before they were aware of present San Francisco Bay (Davidson, p. 6).

Gull Rock [MARIN]: *rock,* 4.5 miles east-southeast of Bolinas, and 300 feet offshore (lat. 37°52'35" N, long. 122°36'55" W). Named on San Rafael (1954) 7.5' quadrangle.

Gulnac Peak [SANTA CLARA]: *peak,* 6.5 miles northeast of Pacheco Peak (lat. 37°04'25" N, long. 121°22' W; sec. 12, T 10 S, R 5 E). Altitude 2276 feet. Named on Pacheco Peak (1955) 7.5' quadrangle. The name commemorates the Gulnac family, whose first member in California arrived in 1833 (Hanna, P.T., p. 130).

Gushee Creek: see **Old Womans Creek** [SAN MATEO].

Guth Landing [SANTA CLARA]: *locality,* 3 miles north of downtown Mountain View along Stevens Creek in mud flats near San

Francisco Bay (lat. 37°25'55" N, long. 122°04'30" W). Named on Palo Alto (1899) 15' quadrangle.

Gwin Island: see **Browns Island** [CONTRA COSTA].

— H —

Haakerville: see **Woodside** [SAN MATEO].

Haas Slough: see **Hass Slough** [SOLANO].

Hacienda: see **New Almaden** [SANTA CLARA]; **Pleasanton** [ALAMEDA].

Hagerman Canyon [SANTA CLARA]: *canyon,* drained by a stream that flows 5.25 miles to Cedar Creek 3.25 miles northwest of Pacheco Peak (lat. 37°02'35" N, long. 121°19'25" W). Named on Gilroy Hot Springs (1955) and Pacheco Peak (1955) 7.5' quadrangles. Called Harrigan Canyon on Gilroy Hot Springs (1921) 15' quadrangle.

Hagerman Peak [SANTA CLARA]: *peak,* 3.5 miles north-northwest of Pacheco Pass (lat. 37°06'45" N, long. 121°14'15" W; sec. 31, T 9 S, R 7 E). Altitude 1790 feet. Named on Pacheco Pass (1955) 7.5' quadrangle.

Haggerty Gulch [MARIN]: *canyon,* drained by a stream that flows 1.5 miles to Lagunitas Creek nearly 1 mile west-southwest of Point Reyes Station (lat. 38°03'50" N, long. 122°49'10" W). Named on Inverness (1954) 7.5' quadrangle. Teather (p. 28) associated the name with Martin Haggerty, a rancher in the neighborhood in the 1870's.

Hale Creek [SANTA CLARA]: *stream,* flows 3.25 miles to Permanente Creek 1.5 miles east of downtown Los Altos (lat. 37°23' N, long. 122°05'15" W). Named on Cupertino (1961) and Mountain View (1961) 7.5' quadrangles. The name commemorates Joseph A. Hale, who owned most of San Antonio grant (Mary T. Fortney, *Times Tribune,* October 15, 1988).

Half Moon Bay [SAN MATEO]:

(1) *embayment,* east and southeast of Pillar Point along the coast (lat. 37°29' N, long. 122°28' W). Named on Half Moon Bay (1961) and Montara Mountain (1956) 7.5' quadrangles. Called Halfmoon Bay on Santa Cruz (1902) 30' quadrangle, but United States Board on Geographic Names (1960b, p. 17) rejected this form of the name, which. is from the shape of the feature (Gudde, 1949, p. 140).

(2) *town,* 11 miles west of Redwood City (lat. 37°27'50" N, long. 122°25'40" W); the town is near the coast at Half Moon Bay (1). Named on Half Moon Bay (1961) 7.5' quadrangle. Called Halfmoon Bay on Santa Cruz (1902) 30' quadrangle, but United States Board on Geographic Names (1960b, p. 17) rejected the names "Halfmoon Bay," "Half-Moon Bay," "Spanish Town," and "Spanish-Town" for the place. Postal authorities established Halfmoon Bay post office in 1861, discontinued it for a time in 1862, and changed the name to Half

Moon Bay in 1905 (Salley, p. 92). A village at the site in the 1840's was called San Benito, but Americans began calling it Spanish Town or Spanishtown in the 1850's; this name lasted long after Halfmoon Bay post office opened (Brown, p. 39).

Half Moon Bay Beach: see **Francis Beach** [SAN MATEO].

Half Way House: see **San Mateo** [SAN MATEO] (2).

Halfway House [ALAMEDA]: *locality,* nearly 3 miles southeast of Cedar Mountain along Arroyo Mocho (lat. 37°32'20" N, long. 121° 33'55" W; near W line sec. 32, T 4 S, R 4 E). Named on Tesla (1907) 15' quadrangle.

Hall: see **Hall Station** [ALAMEDA].

Halleck Creek [MARIN]: *stream,* flows 7.5 miles to Nicasio Creek 8 miles west-southwest of downtown Novato (lat. 38°04'05" N, long. 122°42'10" W); the creek is on Nicasio (4) grant, which Henry W. Halleck owned. Named on San Geronimo (1954) 7.5' quadrangle.

Hallidie Gulch: see **Neils Gulch** [SAN MATEO].

Hall Station [ALAMEDA]: *locality,* 4 miles north-northwest of downtown Newark along Southern Pacific Railroad (lat. 37°35'10" N, long. 122°03'45" W). Named on Newark (1959) 7.5' quadrangle. Called Hall on Haywards (1899) 15' quadrangle. The name commemorates John Hall, a farmer who donated land for railroad construction (MacGregor, p. 90).

Halls Valley [SANTA CLARA]: *valley,* 4 miles west of Mount Hamilton on the upper reaches of San Felipe Creek (lat. 37°20'15" N, long. 121°42'50" W). Named on Lick Observatory (1955) 7.5' quadrangle. Called Hall's Valley on Thompson and West's (1876) map. The name commemorates Frederic Hall, San Jose lawyer and historian (Arbuckle, p. 14).

Halo-Chemuck: see **Rio Vista** [SOLANO].

Halvern [ALAMEDA]: *locality,* 3.5 miles southsoutheast of Hayward along Southern Pacific Railroad (lat. 37°37'25" N, long. 122° 03'10" W). Named on Hayward (1915) 15' quadrangle.

Halverson's Landing: see **San Leandro Creek** [ALAMEDA-CONTRA COSTA].

Hamilton: see **Campbell** [SANTA CLARA]; **Hamilton Air Force Base** [MARIN]; **Mount Hamilton** [SANTA CLARA].

Hamilton Air Force Base [MARIN]: *military installation,* 4.5 miles southeast of downtown Novato (lat. 38°03'30" N, long. 122°30'50" W). Named on Novato (1954) and Petaluma Point (1959) 7.5' quadrangles. Postal authorities established Hamilton Field post office in 1936, changed the name to Hamilton in 1949, and changed it to Hamilton Air Force Base in 1956 (Salley, p. 92). The name commemorates Lieutenant Lloyd A Hamilton, an American aviator who was killed in action in World

War I; the site was known as Marin Meadows before it became an air field (Gudde, 1949, p. 141).

Hamilton Field: see **Hamilton Air Force Base** [MARIN].

Hamilton Flat [ALAMEDA]: *area,* 12 miles east-southeast of Sunol (lat. 37°29'50" N, long. 121°41'15" W; sec. 18, T 5 S, R 3 E). Named on Mendenhall Springs (1956) and Mount Day (1955) 7.5' quadrangles.

Hamilton Gulch [ALAMEDA]: *canyon,* drained by a stream that flows 1 mile to Strawberry Creek nearly 5 miles north-northeast of downtown Oakland (lat. 37°52'50" N, long. 122°14'15" W). Named on Oakland East (1959) 7.5' quadrangle.

Hamlet [MARIN]: *locality,* 3 miles south-southwest of Tomales on the northeast side of Tomales Bay (lat. 38°12'25" N, long. 122°55'25" W). Named on Tomales (1954) 7.5' quadrangle. Shown along Northwestern Pacific Railroad on Point Reyes (1918) 15' quadrangle. John Hamlet bought land at the site in 1865 (Teather, p. 28). Postal authorities established Hamlet post office in 1876 and discontinued it in 1886 (Frickstad, p. 88). They established Telmat post office at the place in 1917 after they rejected the name "Hamlet," and discontinued it in 1931—the name "Telmat" was derived from the word "Hamlet" by reversing the order of letters and substituting "t" for "h" (Salley, p. 219).

Hammer Island [ALAMEDA-CONTRA COSTA]: *island,* 15 miles northeast of Livermore in a branch of Old River on Alameda-Contra Costa county line at the extreme northeast corner of Alameda County (lat. 37°49' N, long. 121°33'20" W). Named on Clifton Court Forebay (1978) 7.5' quadrangle.

Hammock Hill [MARIN]: *peak,* 9 miles westnorthwest of downtown Novato (lat. 38°09'50" N, long. 122°43'20" W). Altitude 914 feet. Named on Petaluma (1953) 7.5' quadrangle.

Hammond Island [SOLANO]: *island,* between Grizzly Slough and Roaring River Slough 4 miles southwest of Birds Landing (2) (lat. 38°06'15" N, long. 121°56'30" W). Named on Denverton (1953) and Honker Bay (1953) 7.5' quadrangles.

Hamms Gulch [SAN MATEO]: *canyon,* drained by a stream that flows 1.25 miles to Corte Madera Creek 3.5 miles north of Mindego Hill (lat. 37°21'45" N, long. 122°13'15" W). Named on Mindego Hill (1961) 7.5' quadrangle. Alexander N. Hamm had a ranch at the head of the canyon after 1860 (Brown, p. 39).

Hansen: see **Point Hansen**, under **Van Sickle Island** [SOLANO].

Happersberger Point [MARIN]: *ridge,* east-trending, 1 mile long, nearly 6 miles north-northeast of Bolinas (lat. 37°58'40" N, long. 122°37'35" W). Named on Bolinas (1954) and San Rafael (1954) 7.5' quadrangles.

Happy Valley [CONTRA COSTA]: *valley,* 3 miles northeast of Orinda (lat. 37°54'15" N, long. 122°08'20" W). Named on Briones Valley (1959) 7.5' quadrangle. Called Pleasant Valley on Concord (1897) 15' quadrangle.

Happy Valley: see **Rincon Hill** [SAN FRANCISCO].

Harbor View: see **Yacht Harbor** [SAN FRANCISCO].

Harding Rock [SAN FRANCISCO]: *rock,* 2.5 miles northwest of North Point in San Francisco Bay (lat. 37°50'10" N, long. 122°26'40" W). Named on San Francisco North (1956) 7.5' quadrangle.

Harlan Hill [CONTRA COSTA]: *peak,* 6 miles south-southeast of Danville (lat. 37°44'10" N, long. 121°58'50" W; near N line sec. 28, T 2 S, R 1 W). Altitude 1719 feet. Named on Dublin (1961) 7.5' quadrangle.

Harper Canyon [SANTA CLARA]: *canyon,* drained by a stream that flows 3.5 miles to Pacheco Creek nearly 3 miles west-northwest of Pacheco Peak (lat. 37°01' N, long. 121°20'05" W). Named on Pacheco Peak (1955) and Three Sisters (1954) 7.5' quadrangles.

Harrigan Canyon: see **Hagerman Canyon** [SANTA CLARA].

Harrington Creek [SAN MATEO]: *stream,* flows 4.5 miles to San Gregorio Creek 1.5 miles west of La Honda (lat. 37°19'10" N, long. 122°18'05" W). Named on La Honda (1961) and Woodside (1961) 7.5' quadrangles. The name commemorates George Harrington, who built a cabin at the head of the creek in 1859 (Brown, p. 40).

Harrington's Pond: see **Upper Crystal Springs Reservoir** [SAN MATEO].

Harrisburg: see **Warm Springs District** [ALAMEDA].

Harrison: see **Pescadero** [SAN MATEO].

Harrisville: see **Arroyo Seco** [ALAMEDA].

Harry Floyd Terrace [SOLANO]: *district,* 2 miles north-northwest of downtown Vallejo (lat. 38°07'55" N, long. 122°14'45" W; sec. 6, T 3 N, R 3 W). Named on Cordelia (1951) 7.5' quadrangle.

Hartley [SOLANO]: *locality,* nearly 2 miles south of Allendale along Southern Pacific Railroad (lat. 38°25' N, long. 121°56'45" W). Named on Allendale (1953) 7.5' quadrangle.

Hartley: see **West Hartley** [CONTRA COSTA].

Harvey Slough [SOLANO]: *water feature,* joins Suisun Slough 8 miles south-southwest of Fairfield (lat. 38°08'20" N, long. 122°04'55" W). Named on Fairfield South (1949) 7.5' quadrangle.

Harwood Creek [SAN MATEO]: *stream,* flows 0.5 mile to Pescadero Creek 3.5 miles south of La Honda (lat. 37°16' N, long. 122° 15'45" W; sec. 2, T 8 S, R 4 W). Named on La Honda (1961) 7.5' quadrangle.

Harwood Creek: see **Claremont Creek** [ALAMEDA].

Haskins Hill [SAN MATEO]: *ridge*, east-south-east-trending, 0.5 mile long, 1 mile south-southwest of La Honda (lat. 37°18'10" N, long. 122°16'40" W). Named on La Honda (1961) 7.5' quadrangle. Aaron A. Haskins settled at the place in the early 1860's (Brown, p. 40).

Hass Slough [SOLANO]: *water feature*, joins Cache Slough 9 miles north of Rio Vista (lat. 38°17'30" N, long. 121°43'25" W). Named on Dozier (1952) and Liberty Island (1978) 7.5' quadrangles. Called Haas Slough on Liberty Island (1952) 7.5' quadrangle.

Hastings Creek: see **Hastings Slough** [CONTRA COSTA].

Hastings Cut [SOLANO]: *water feature*, artificial waterway that extends from Lindsey Slough to Cache Slough 9.5 miles north-northwest of Rio Vista (lat. 38°17'30" N, long. 121°44'25" W). Named on Dozier (1952) and Liberty Island (1978) 7.5' quadrangles. Liberty Island (1952) 7.5' quadrangle has the name "McCoy Slough" at the northeast end of present Hastings Cut, where Hastings Cut joins Cache Slough.

Hasting Slough [SOLANO]: *water feature*, joins Cross Slough 4 miles southwest of Denverton (lat. 38°10'50" N, long. 121°56'40" W). Named on Denverton (1953) 7.5' quadrangle.

Hastings Slough [CONTRA COSTA]: *water feature*, enters Suisun Bay 5 miles east-north-east of Martinez (lat. 38°03'05" N, long. 122°03'20" W). Named on Vine Hill (1959) 7.5' quadrangle. Called Hastings Creek on Karquinez (1898) 15' quadrangle.

Hastings Tract [SOLANO]: *area*, 8 miles north-northwest of Rio Vista (lat. 38°16'30" N, long. 121°44' W). Named on Dozier (1952), Liberty Island (1978), and Rio Vista (1978) 7.5' quadrangles.

Hastings Tract: see **Little Hastings Tract** [SOLANO].

Hatfield Canyon [SANTA CLARA]: *canyon*, drained by a stream that flows nearly 2 miles to Pescadero Creek 2.5 miles north of Pajaro Gap (lat. 36°56'55" N, long. 121°38' W). Named on Watsonville East (1955) 7.5' quadrangle.

Havens [ALAMEDA]: *locality*, 4.25 miles east-northeast of downtown Oakland along Oakland Antioch and Eastern Railroad (lat. 37°49'45" N, long. 122°11'45" W). Named on Concord (1915) 15' quadrangle. The name commemorates Frank Colton Havens, a developer (Mosier and Mosier, p. 41-42).

Hawes Gulch: see **Arroyo Ojo de Agua** [SAN MATEO].

Hay Canyon [SANTA CLARA]: *canyon*, drained by a stream that flows 1.5 miles to Uvas Reservoir 5 miles north of Mount Madonna (lat. 37°05' N, long. 121°42'30" W). Named on Mount Madonna (1955, photorevised 1968 and 1973) 7.5' quadrangle.

Hayes Creek [SANTA CLARA]: *stream*, flows 1.5 miles to Llagas Creek nearly 6 miles north-northeast of Mount Madonna (lat. 37°05'05" N, long. 121°39'05" W); the stream drains part of Hayes Valley. Named on Mount Madonna (1955, photorevised 1968 and 1973) 7.5' quadrangle. The name commemorates an early land-owner in the neighborhood (United States Board on Geographic Names, 1973a, p. 2).

Hayes Creek: see **Glen Echo Creek** [ALAMEDA].

Hayes Reach [CONTRA COSTA]: *water feature*, part of San Joaquin River located 5.5 miles northeast of the settlement of Bethel Island on Contra Costa-San Joaquin county line at the mouth of Old River (lat. 38°04'35" N, long. 121°34'10" W). Named on Bouldin Island (1978) 7.5' quadrangle.

Hayes Valley [SANTA CLARA]: *valley*, about 5 miles northeast of Mount Madonna (lat. 37°04'15" N, long. 121°39' W); Hayes Creek drains part of the valley. Named on Mount Madonna (1955) 7.5' quadrangle.

Haynes Gulch [ALAMEDA]: *canyon*, drained by a stream that flows 1.25 miles to Alameda Creek 4.5 miles south-southeast of Sunol (lat. 37°32'05" N, long. 121°51'05" W; near N line sec. 3, T 5 S, R 1 E). Named on La Costa Valley (1960) 7.5' quadrangle.

Hays Camp [ALAMEDA]: *locality*, 4 miles south of Cedar Mountain (lat. 37°29'55" N, long. 121°36'50" W; near E line sec. 14, T 5 S, R 3 E). Named on Eylar Mountain (1955) 7.5' quadrangle.

Hays Canyon: see **Glen Echo Creek** [ALAMEDA].

Hays' Creek: see **Glen Echo Creek** [ALAMEDA].

Hayward [ALAMEDA]: *city*, 13 miles southeast of downtown Oakland (lat. 37°40'15" N, long. 122°04'50" W). Named on Hayward (1959), Redwood Point (1959), and San Leandro (1959) 7.5' quadrangles. Called Haywards on Haywards (1899) 15' quadrangle. United States Board on Geographic Names (1933, p. 358) rejected the names "Haywards," "Hayward's," "Haywards Station," and "Haywood" for the place. Postal authorities established Haywood post office in 1860, changed the name to Haywards in 1880, and changed it to Hayward in 1911 (Frickstad, p. 2). The city incorporated in 1876. The name commemorates William Hayward, an early settler at the site (Hoover, Rensch, and Rensch, p. 18). Postal authorities established Hayward Heath post office in 1916 and discontinued it in 1918, when they moved the service to Hayward; the name was from a real-estate promotion (Salley, p. 95).

Hayward Heath: see **Hayward** [ALAMEDA].

Hayward Landing [ALAMEDA]: *locality*, 4.5 miles west-southwest of downtown Hayward at the edge of San Francisco Bay (lat. 37°38'40" N, long. 122°09'15" W). Named on San Leandro (1959) 7.5' quadrangle. Called

Haywards Landing on Haywards (1899) 15' quadrangle. Richard Barron arrived in the neighborhood in 1855 and established Barron's Landing at the site; the name was changed in the 1860's to Simpson's Landing for John Simpson, who operated the place; Hans Peter Jensen bought the business from Barron in 1884, and for a time the place was known locally as Jensen's Landing (Mosier, and Mosier, p. 43).

Hayward Park [SAN MATEO]: *district,* 1 mile southeast of downtown San Mateo (lat. 37°33'20" N, long. 122°18'40" W). Named on San Mateo (1956) 7.5' quadrangle.

Haywards: see **Hayward** [ALAMEDA].

Haywards Pass: see **Dublin Canyon** [ALAMEDA].

Haywards Station: see **Hayward** [ALAMEDA]; **Hayward Station** [ALAMEDA].

Hayward Station [ALAMEDA]: *locality,* 1 mile southwest of Hayward along Southern Pacific Railroad (lat. 37°39'50" N, long. 122° 05'55" W). Named on Hayward (1915) 15' quadrangle. Called Haywards Station on Haywards (1899) 15' quadrangle.

Haywood: see **Hayward** [ALAMEDA].

Hearst: see **Pleasanton** [ALAMEDA].

Hearts Desire [MARIN]: *locality,* 8 miles south of Tomales on the southwest side of Tomales Bay (lat. 38°08' N, long. 122°53'35" W). Named on Tomales (1954) 7.5' quadrangle.

Hecker Pass [SANTA CLARA]: *pass,* 7.5 miles northwest of Pajaro Gap on Santa Clara-Santa Cruz county line (lat. 36°59'45" N, long. 121°43' W). Named on Watsonville East (1955) 7.5' quadrangle. The name honors Henry Hecker, a Santa Clara County supervisor when the road over the pass was completed in 1928 (Rambo, 1964, p. 36). Because of a change made in the county line in 1971, the pass now lies entirely in Santa Clara County (Clark, D.T., p. 149).

Hedd Canyon [ALAMEDA]: *canyon,* drained by a stream that flows 1 mile to Devaney Canyon 1.25 miles southwest of Dublin (lat. 37° 41'20" N, long. 121°57'30" W; sec. 10, T 3 S, R 1 W). Named on Dublin (1961) 7.5' quadrangle. The misspelled name commemorates William G. Head, who owned land in the canyon in 1879 (Mosier and Mosier, p. 43).

Helen: see **Mount Helen**, under **Martinez** [CONTRA COSTA]; **Mount Helen** [SANTA CLARA].

Helmet Rock [SAN FRANCISCO]: *rock,* 0.5 mile south-southwest of Fort Point, and 600 feet offshore (lat. 37°48'05" N, long. 122°28'50" W). Named on San Francisco North (1956) 7.5' quadrangle.

Hemme Hills [CONTRA COSTA]: *ridge,* south-trending, 1 mile long, 4.5 miles south of Mount Diablo (lat. 37°49'05" N, long. 121°55'35" W). Named on Diablo (1953) 7.5' quadrangle.

Henderson [SAN MATEO]: *locality,* 3.5 miles east of downtown Redwood City along Southern Pacific Railroad (lat. 37°28'45" N, long. 122°09'45" W). Named on Palo Alto (1961) 7.5' quadrangle.

Henderson Ridge [SANTA CLARA]: *ridge,* south-southwest- to west-trending, nearly 4 miles long, 5 miles south of Mount Hamilton (lat. 37°15' N, long. 121°37'30" W). Named on Isabel Valley (1955), Lick Observatory (1955), Morgan Hill (1955), and Mount Sizer (1955) 7.5' quadrangles.

Hendrys Creek [SANTA CLARA]: *stream,* flows 1.5 miles to Lexington Reservoir 4 miles south of downtown Los Gatos (lat. 37°10'10" N, long. 121°58'45" W; sec. 9, T 9 S, R 1 W). Named on Los Gatos (1953) 7.5' quadrangle.

Herbert Creek [SANTA CLARA]: *stream,* flows 2 miles to Alamitos Creek nearly 3 miles southwest of New Almaden (lat. 37°09' N, long. 121°51'30" W; near W line sec. 15, T 9 S, R 1 E). Named on Los Gatos (1953) and Santa Teresa Hills (1953) 7.5' quadrangles.

Hercules [CONTRA COSTA]: *town,* 4 miles east of Point Pinole (lat. 38°01' N, long. 122°17'20" W). Named on Benicia (1959), Briones Valley (1959), Mare Island (1959), and Richmond (1959) 7.5' quadrangles. The town incorporated in 1900. Postal authorities established Hercules post office in 1914 (Frickstad, p. 22). The name is from Hercules Powder Company's plant established at the place in the 1890's (Gudde, 1949, p. 147).

Hercules Wharf [CONTRA COSTA]: *locality,* 4 miles east of Point Pinole along San Pablo Bay (lat. 38°01'20" N, long. 122°17'20" W); the place is at Hercules. Named on Mare Island (1959) 7.5' quadrangle. Called Refugio Ldg. on Mare Island (1916) 15' quadrangle.

Herdlyn [CONTRA COSTA]: *locality,* 10 miles southeast of Brentwood along Southern Pacific Railroad (lat. 37°49'05" N, long. 121° 35'05" W; on E line sec. 25, T 1 S, R 3 E). Named on Bethany (1952) 7.5' quadrangle.

Herman: see **Lake Herman** [SOLANO].

Herms: see **Camp Herms** [CONTRA COSTA].

Herpoco [CONTRA COSTA]: *locality,* 5 miles east of Pinole Point along Atchison, Topeka and Santa Fe Railroad (lat. 38°00'40" N, long. 122°16'10" W). Named on Mare Island (1959) 7.5' quadrangle. Railroad officials coined the name in 1919 from letters of the term "Hercules Powder Company" (Gudde, 1949, p. 147).

Hicks Mountain [MARIN]: *peak,* 9 miles west of downtown Novato (lat. 38°07'45" N, long. 122°43'30" W); the peak is south-southwest of Hicks Valley. Altitude 1532 feet. Named on Petaluma (1953) 7.5' quadrangle.

Hicks Valley [MARIN]: *valley,* 8 miles west-northwest of downtown Novato on the upper reaches of Arroyo Sausal (lat. 38°08'45" N, long. 122°42'30" W); the valley is mainly on Corte Madera de Novato grant. Named on

Petaluma (1953) 7.5' quadrangle. The name is for William Hicks, who bought Corte Madera de Novato grant in 1855 (Mason, 1976b, p. 147).

Hidden Lake [MARIN]: *marsh,* 5 miles west-southwest of downtown San Rafael (lat. 37°56'25" N, long. 122°36'50" W). Named on San Rafael (1954) 7.5' quadrangle.

Hidden Pond [CONTRA COSTA]: *lake,* 200 feet long, 1.5 miles south of Mount Diablo (lat. 37°51'45" N, long. 121°54'35" W; sec. 7, T 1 S, R 1 E). Named on Diablo (1953) 7.5' quadrangle.

Hidden Valley [ALAMEDA]: *canyon,* 1.5 miles long, 5 miles southeast of Fremont civic center along Agua Caliente Creek (lat. 37°30'20" N, long. 121°54' W). Named on Niles (1961) 7.5' quadrangle.

Hidden Valley Lakes: see **Bean Hollow Lake** [SAN MATEO].

Higgins Canyon [SAN MATEO]: *canyon,* along Arroyo Leon above a point 1 mile south-southeast of downtown Half Moon Bay (lat. 37°27'10" N, long. 122°25'15" W). Named on Half Moon Bay (1961) 7.5' quadrangle. John Higgins had a ranch at the place after about 1870; the stream in the canyon had the name "Arroyo de Monte Verde" in the early days (Brown, p. 41).

Highland: see **Fleming** [ALAMEDA].

Highland Park Reservoir: see **Central Reservoir** [ALAMEDA].

Hilarita [MARIN]: *locality,* 4 miles south of Point San Quentin on Tiburon Peninsula (lat. 37°53' N, long. 122°27'55" W). Named on San Quentin (1959) 7.5' quadrangle.

Hillsborough [SAN MATEO]: *town,* 2 miles west of downtown San Mateo (lat. 37°33'45" N, long. 122°21'45" W). Named on Montara Mountain (1956) and San Mateo (1956) 7.5' quadrangles. Postal authorities established Hillsborough post office in 1956 (Salley, p. 97), and the town incorporated in 1910. The name is from a town in New Hampshire that was the ancestral home of W.D.M. Howard, former owner of land at the site (Gudde, 1969, p. 140).

Hillsborough Park [SAN MATEO]: *district,* 2 miles west-southwest of downtown San Mateo in Hillsborough (lat. 37°33'20" N, long. 122°21'45" W). Named on San Mateo (1956) 7.5' quadrangle.

Hillsdale [SAN MATEO]: *district,* 2.25 miles south-southeast of downtown San Mateo (lat. 37°32'15" N, long. 122°18'15" W). Named on San Mateo (1956) 7.5' quadrangle. Called Beresford on San Mateo (1947) 7.5' quadrangle. The name "Beresford" is from Beresford Park subdivision, begun in the 1890's; the name of the railroad station at the place was changed in 1940 to Hillsdale for another subdivision (Brown, p. 83).

Hillsdale: see **Lick** [SANTA CLARA].

Hillside: see **Vallejo** [SOLANO].

Hill Slough [SOLANO]: *water feature,* joins Suisun Slough 2.25 miles south-southeast of Fairfield (lat. 38°13'10" N, long. 122°01'40" W). Named on Denverton (1953) and Fairfield South (1949) 7.5' quadrangles.

Hoffman Creek [SAN MATEO]: *stream,* flows 1 mile to Pescadero Creek 3 miles south of La Honda (lat. 37°16'30" N, long. 122° 17' W; sec. 34, T 7 S, R 4 W). Named on La Honda (1961) 7.5' quadrangle.

Hoffman Creek: see **Bloomquist Creek** [SAN MATEO].

Hog Canyon [CONTRA COSTA]: *canyon,* drained by Sycamore Creek (2), which flows nearly 4 miles to Marsh Creek 5.5 miles east of Mount Diablo (lat. 37°53'10" N, long. 121°48'40" W). Named on Antioch South (1953) and Tassajara (1953) 7.5' quadrangles.

Hog Island [MARIN]: *island,* 650 feet long, nearly 4 miles south-southwest of Tomales in Tomales Bay (lat. 38°11'50" N, long. 122°56'05" W). Named on Tomales (1954) 7.5' quadrangle. The name reportedly came after a barge broke loose and left a number of hogs at the place; a small island of less than an acre located near Hog Island is called Duck Island (Mason, 1976a, p. 57, 59).

Hogsback [SANTA CLARA]: *ridge,* north-trending, 0.25 mile long, 3 miles southwest of Mount Sizer (lat. 37°11'15" N, long. 121°33'15" W; on N line sec. 5, T 9 S, R 4 E). Named on Mount Sizer (1955) 7.5' quadrangle.

Hog Slough [SANTA CLARA]: *stream,* flows nearly 2 miles to Isabel Creek 2.5 miles northwest of Mount Hamilton (lat. 37°22'10" N, long. 121°40'10" W; sec. 32, T 6 S, R 3 E). Named on Lick Observatory (1955) 7.5' quadrangle.

Holbrook Island: see **Freeman Island** [SOLANO].

Holland Cut [CONTRA COSTA]: *water feature,* 3.25 miles east of the settlement of Bethel Island on the east side of Holland Tract (lat. 38°01' N, long. 121°34'50" W). Named on Bouldin Island (1978) 7.5' quadrangle.

Holland Tract [CONTRA COSTA]: *island,* 3.5 miles long, 2.5 miles east-southeast of the settlement of Bethel Island between Sheep Slough, Old River, Rock Slough, and Sand Mound Slough (lat. 38° 00' N, long. 121°36' W). Named on Bouldin Island (1978) and Woodward Island (1978) 7.5' quadrangles.

Holland Tract: see **Little Holland Tract** [SOLANO].

Hollenbeck's Station: see **Bell Station** [SANTA CLARA].

Hollis Canyon [ALAMEDA]: *canyon,* 3.25 miles long, on upper reaches of San Lorenzo Creek above a point 4.25 miles northeast of downtown Hayward (lat. 37°42'25" N, long. 122°01'05" W). Named on Dublin (1961) and Hayward (1959) 7.5' quadrangles. The stream in the canyon is called Hollis Creek on

Haywards (1899) and Pleasanton (1906) 15' quadrangles. The name commemorates James Lyman Hollis, who settled at the head of the canyon in 1853 (Mosier, and Mosier, p. 45).

Hollis Creek: see **Hollis Canyon** [ALAMEDA].

Holy City [SANTA CLARA]: *village,* 4.5 miles south of downtown Los Gatos (lat. 37°09'25" N, long. 121°58'40" W; near S line sec. 9, T 9 S, R 1 W). Named on Los Gatos (1953) 7.5' quadrangle. Postal authorities established Holy City post office in 1927 (Frickstad, p. 173). William E. Riker, leader of a religious cult, founded the place in 1918 (Hoover, Rensch, and Rensch, p. 457).

Home Bay [MARIN]: *bay,* opens into Drakes Estero 6.5 miles northeast of the lighthouse at Point Reyes (lat. 38°03'35" N, long. 122°55'45" W). Named on Drakes Bay (1953) 7.5' quadrangle, which shows Home ranch near the head of the bay.

Home Ranch Creek [MARIN]: *stream,* flows 2 miles to Home Bay 8 miles northeast of the lighthouse at Point Reyes (lat. 38°04'15" N, long. 122°54'40" W). Named on Drakes Bay (1953) 7.5' quadrangle, which shows Home ranch situated along the stream.

Homestead [SAN MATEO]: *settlement,* 1.25 miles south-southeast of downtown San Mateo (lat. 37°32'50" N, long. 122°19'10" W). Named on San Mateo (1915) 15' quadrangle. The name is from San Mateo City Homestead subdivision (Brown, p. 83). Diller and others' (1915) map shows a place called Leslie along the railroad at about the site of Homestead.

Homestead Valley [MARIN]: *canyon,* drained by a stream that flows 1.25 miles to Arroyo Corte Madera Del Presidio 5.25 miles south of downtown San Rafael (lat. 37°53'45" N, long. 122°32' W). Named on San Rafael (1954) 7.5' quadrangle. Teather (p. 29) associated the name with a hunting lodge called The Homestead that Samuel Throckmorton had built in 1866.

Honker Bay [SOLANO]: *embayment,* 5.5 miles southwest of Birds Landing (2) off Suisun Bay (lat. 38°04'15" N, long. 121°55'45" W). Named on Honker Bay (1953) 7.5' quadrangle.

Honker Bay: see **Little Honker Bay** [SOLANO].

Honsinger Creek [SAN MATEO]: *stream,* flows 3.5 miles to Pescadero Creek 7 miles southwest of La Honda (lat. 37°15'10" N, long. 122°22'10" W; sec. 11, T 8 S, R 5 W). Named on La Honda (1961) 7.5' quadrangle. The stream first had the name "Greenwood Creek" for the Green family ranch established about 1859; Mr. A. Honsinger had a dairy ranch along the stream after about 1870 (Brown, p. 41).

Hoodoo Gulch [SANTA CLARA]: *canyon,* drained by a stream that flows 1.5 miles to Colorado Creek 1.5 miles south-southwest of

Eylar Mountain (lat. 37°27'20" N, long. 121°33'50" W; sec. 32, T 5 S, R 4 E). Named on Eylar Mountain (1955) 7.5' quadrangle.

Hooker: see **Mount Hooker**, under **Mount Thayer** [SANTA CLARA].

Hooker Creek [SAN MATEO]: *stream,* flows 1.25 miles to Pescadero Creek 4 miles south of Mindego Hill (lat. 37°15'10" N, long. 122°13'35" W). Named on Big Basin (1955) 7.5' quadrangle. According to Brown (p. 78), the canyon of the stream had the name "Rooter Gulch" in the 1930's from a piece of construction machinery left there; the canyon also had the name "Oil Barrel Gulch" at about the same time because of oil stored there.

Hooker Gulch [SANTA CLARA]: *canyon,* drained by a stream that flows nearly 3 miles to Los Gatos Creek 5 miles south-southeast of Los Gatos (lat. 37°09'15" N, long. 121°57'45" W; sec. 15, T 9 S, R 1 W). Named on Los Gatos (1953) 7.5' quadrangle. The name commemorates Billy Hooker, a lumbermill worker who had a cabin in the canyon (Young, p. 124).

Hookston [CONTRA COSTA]: *locality,* 2.5 miles north of Walnut Creek civic center along Southern Pacific Railroad (lat. 37°56'30" N, long. 122°03'05" W). Named on Walnut Creek (1959) 7.5' quadrangle. Concord (1915) 15' quadrangle also has the name "Hookston" at present Bancroft.

Hooper [CONTRA COSTA]: *locality,* 2.25 miles west of present downtown Antioch along Atchison, Topeka and Santa Fe Railroad (lat. 38°01'10" N, long. 121°51' W). Named on Collinsville (1918) 7.5' quadrangle.

Hoover Creek [SANTA CLARA]: *stream,* flows nearly 3 miles to Packwood Creek 5.25 miles west-southwest of Mount Sizer (lat. 37°11'30" N, long. 121°36'15" W); the stream drains Hoover Valley. Named on Mount Sizer (1955) 7.5' quadrangle.

Hoover Lake [SANTA CLARA]: *lake,* 750 feet long, 3.5 miles north-northeast of Gilroy Hot Springs (lat. 38°09'20" N, long. 120°26'50" W; sec. 17, T 9 S, R 5 E). Named on Mississippi Creek 1955) 7.5' quadrangle.

Hoover Valley [SANTA CLARA]: *valley,* 4.25 miles west-southwest of Mount Sizer (lat. 37°11'30" N, long. 121°35' W); the valley is along Hoover Creek. Named on Mount Sizer (1955) 7.5' quadrangle.

Hopkins Ravine [SOLANO]: *canyon,* drained by a stream that flows 2.5 miles to lowlands at Birds Landing (2) (lat. 38°07'55" N, long. 121°52'20" W; sec. 4, T 3 N, R 1 E). Named on Birds Landing (1953) 7.5' quadrangle.

Horan: see **Frank Horan Slough** [SOLANO].

Horse Haven: see **Antioch** [CONTRA COSTA].

Horse Pasture Creek: see **Old Womans Creek** [SAN MATEO].

Horseshoe Bay [MARIN-SAN FRANCISCO]: *embayment,* nearly 2 miles south-southeast of downtown Sausalito along San Francisco Bay (lat. 37°50' N, long. 122°28'30" W). Named on San Francisco North (1956) 7.5' quadrangle. Because Marin-San Francisco county line follows the low-water line of Marin County coast from Point Bonita to Cavallo Point, the water area of the embayment is in San Francisco County. The name is from the horseshoe shape of the feature (Gudde, 1949, p. 61). Galvin (p. 85) identified Horseshoe Bay as the place that Ayala called Consolation Cove in 1775.

Horseshoe Bend [SOLANO]: *bend,* 5 miles south-southwest of Rio Vista along Sacramento River on Solano-Sacramento county line (lat. 38°05' N, long. 121°42'45" W). Named on Jersey Island (1978) 7.5' quadrangle. An artificial waterway now takes the main channel of the river across the neck of land at the bend. Ringgold's (1850c) map has the name "Sagadehock Reach" along this part of Sacramento River.

Horsethief Canyon [SANTA CLARA]: *canyon,* 0.5 mile long, opens into the canyon of Colorado Creek 3.5 miles southeast of Eylar Mountain (lat. 37°26'10" N, long. 121°30'40" W; near SW cor. sec. 2, T 6 S, R 4 E). Named on Eylar Mountain (1955) 7.5' quadrangle.

Horse Valley [CONTRA COSTA]: *valley,* 7.5 miles east-northeast of Mount Diablo (lat. 37°56'10" N, long. 121°47'40" W). Named on Antioch South (1953) 7.5' quadrangle.

Horse Valley [SANTA CLARA]: *valley,* 4 miles southwest of Isabel Valley on the upper reaches of Smith Creek (2) (lat. 37°16'35" N, long. 121°35'35" W). Named on Isabel Valley (1955) 7.5' quadrangle.

Hospital Cove [MARIN]: *embayment,* on the northwest shore of Angel Island (lat. 37°52'05" N, long. 122°26'05" W); the feature is off Raccoon Strait. Named on San Francisco North (1956) 7.5' quadrangle. Called Raccoon Cove on Ringgold's (1850a) map. United States Board on Geographic Names (1969, p. 8) approved the designation Ayala Cove for the feature, and noted that this name commemorates Don Juan Manuel de Ayala, who based his ship at the place while he explored San Francisco Bay in 1775. The embayment was known as Morgan's Cove before the army built two hospital buildings by it in 1870 (Gudde, 1969, p. 146).

Howard Slough [SOLANO]: *water feature,* on Hammond Island, joins Roaring River Slough 4 miles southwest of Birds Landing (2) (lat. 38°05'35" N, long. 121°55'45" W). Named on Honker Bay (1953) 7.5' quadrangle.

Howell Reservoirs [SANTA CLARA]: *lakes,,* largest 850 feet long, nearly 5 miles east-southeast of Bielawski Mountain (lat. 37°11'55" N, long. 122°00'55" W; sec. 31, T 8 S, R 1 W). Named on Castle Rock Ridge (1955) 7.5' quadrangle. The name commemorates Watkins F. Howell, who settled in the neighborhood in 1856 (Young, p. 21).

Huchones: see **Point Huchones,** under **Point San Pablo** [CONTRA COSTA].

Hull Hill: see **Belmont Hill** [SAN MATEO].

Hungry Valley: see **Alhambra Valley** [CONTRA COSTA].

Hunter Island: see **Coyote Hills** [ALAMEDA].

Hunters Point [SAN FRANCISCO]: *peninsula,* modified by landfill, 4.5 miles east of Mount Davidson along San Francisco Bay (lat. 37°43'45" N, long. 122°22'30" W). Named on Hunters Point (1956, photorevised 1968) and San Francisco South (1956) 7.5' quadrangles. Called Hunter Point on San Mateo (1915) 15' quadrangle. H.R. Wagner (p. 443, 502) listed the obsolete names "Punta de Concha" and "San Juan Capistrano" for the feature.

Hunters Point: see **Point Avisadero** [SAN FRANCISCO].

Hunting Hollow [SANTA CLARA]: *canyon,* drained by a stream that flows 4 miles to Coyote Creek 2.25 miles south-southeast of Gilroy Hot Springs (lat. 37°04'35" N, long. 121°28'05" W; sec. 7, T 10 S, R 5 E). Named on Gilroy Hot Springs (1955) 7.5' quadrangle.

Hurricane Canyon [SANTA CLARA]: *canyon,* 3 miles long, 4 miles north-northwest of Pacheco Peak on lower reaches of Cedar Creek (lat. 37°03'30" N, long. 121°19'40" W). Named on Pacheco Peak (1955) 7.5' quadrangle.

— I —

Ibis Cut [SOLANO]: *water feature,* extends from Cordelia Slough to Frank Horan Slough 6.5 miles south-southwest of Fairfield (lat. 38°10'05" N, long. 122°06'10" W). Named on Fairfield South (1949) 7.5' quadrangle.

Ida: see **Mount Ida,** under **Mount Caroline Livermore** [MARIN].

Idlewild: see **Azule Springs** [SANTA CLARA].

Idlwood: see **Sunol** [ALAMEDA].

Ignacio [MARIN]: *town,* 3 miles southeast of downtown Novato (lat. 38°04'15" N, long. 122°32'15" W); the town is on San Jose grant, owned by Ignacio Pacheco. Named on Novato (1954) 7.5' quadrangle. Postal authorities established Ignacio post office in 1893, discontinued it in 1944, and reestablished it in 1961 (Salley, p. 103). They established Machin post office 4 miles north of Ignacio in 1896 and discontinued it in 1904; the name honored Timothy N. Machin, lieutenant governor of California in 1863, and later a real-estate man at Novato (Salley, p. 130).

India Basin [SAN FRANCISCO]: *embayment,* 4.5 miles east of Mount Davidson along San Francisco Bay on the north side of Hunters Point (lat. 37°44'05" N, long. 122°22' W). Named on Hunters Point (1956, photorevised 1980) 7.5' quadrangle. On San Francisco South (1956) 7.5' quadrangle, the name "India Basin" applies to an embayment located nearly 1 mile farther northwest—this earlier embayment now is filled.

Indian Beach [MARIN]: *beach*, 7.5 miles south of Tomales on the southwest side of Tomales Bay (lat. 38°08'15" N, long. 122°53'45" W). Named on Tomales (1954) 7.5' quadrangle.

Indian Cove: see **Tennessee Cove** [MARIN].

Indian Creek [ALAMEDA]: *stream,* flows 9.5 miles to San Antonio Creek 3.5 miles east of Sunol in La Costa Valley (lat. 37°35'20" N, long. 121°49'15" W). Named on La Costa Valley (1960) and Mendenhall Springs (1956) 7.5' quadrangles. Called South Fork San Antonio Cr. on Thompson and West's (1878) map. The stream now enters San Antonio Reservoir.

Indian Creek [CONTRA COSTA]: *stream,* flows nearly 2 miles to San Leandro Creek 4.5 miles south-southeast of Orinda (lat. 37°49'05" N, long. 122°08'45" W). Named on Oakland East (1959) 7.5' quadrangle.

Indian Creek [SANTA CLARA]: *stream,* flows nearly 1 mile to Stevens Creek 1 mile southwest of Black Mountain (1) (lat. 37°18'40" N, long. 122°09'35" W; sec. 23, T 7 S, R 3 W). Named on Mindego Hill (1961) 7.5' quadrangle.

Indian Gulch [ALAMEDA]: *canyon,* nearly 2 miles long, opens into lowlands 1.5 miles east of downtown Oakland (lat. 37°48'35" N, long. 122°14'45" W). Named on Oakland East (1959) 7.5' quadrangle. After trestles were built in 1893 to enable streetcars to travel to the head of Indian Gulch, the canyon was renamed Trestle Glen; the old name was restored after the trestles were removed (Mosier and Mosier, p. 45). Thompson and West's (1878) map shows a stream called Indian Gulch Creek that flows to Lake Merritt.

Indian Gulch Creek: see **Indian Gulch** [ALAMEDA].

Indian Joe Creek [ALAMEDA]: *stream,* flows 2.5 miles to Alameda Creek 6.25 miles south-southeast of Sunol (lat. 37°30'50" N, long. 121°49'35" W; sec. 11, T 5 S, R 1 E). Named on La Costa Valley (1960) 7.5' quadrangle. The name recalls Indian Joe, thought to be the last Ohlone Indian, who lived and worked in the neighborhood (Mosier and Mosier, p. 45).

Indian Point [SAN MATEO]: *relief feature,* 3 miles south of La Honda on the south side of Pescadero Creek (lat. 37°16'25" N, long. 122°16'40" W; near SE cor. sec. 34, T 7 S, R 4 W). Named on La Honda (1961) 7.5' quadrangle.

Indian Slough [CONTRA COSTA]: *water feature,* joins Old River 7 miles east of Brentwood (lat. 37°54'55" N, long. 121°33'55" W). Named on Woodward Island (1978) 7.5' quadrangle.

Indian Springs [SANTA CLARA]: *springs,* near the southeast end of Isabel Valley (lat.

37°18'05" N, long. 121°30'40" W; sec. 26, T 7 S, R 4 E). Named on Isabel Valley (1955) 7.5' quadrangle.

Indian Valley [MARIN]: *valley,* nearly 2 miles southwest of downtown Novato (lat. 38°05'30" N, long. 122°35'40" W). Named on Novato (1954) 7.5' quadrangle.

Ingleside [SAN FRANCISCO]: *district,* 1 mile south of Mount Davidson (lat. 37°43'20" N, long. 122°27'20" W). Named on San Francisco South (1956) 7.5' quadrangle.

Ingram Flat [SANTA CLARA]: *area,* 2 miles south-southeast of Eyler Mountain (lat. 37°27'10" N, long. 121°31'55" W; sec. 33, T 5 S, R 4 E). Named on Eyler Mountain (1955) 7.5' quadrangle.

Inner Harbor Basin [CONTRA COSTA]: *water feature,* 1.5 miles south-southwest of Richmond civic center off Richmond Inner Harbor (lat 37°54'40" N, long. 122°21' W). Named on Richmond (1959) 7.5' quadrangle. United States Board on Geographic Names (1981b, p. 4) approved the name "Richmond Marina Bay" for the feature.

Inner Signal Station: see **Telegraph Hill** [SAN FRANCISCO].

Inspiration Point [CONTRA COSTA]: *peak,* 4 miles west-northwest of Orinda on San Pablo Ridge (lat. 37°54'20" N, long. 122°14'35" W). Named on Briones Valley (1959) 7.5' quadrangle.

Inverness [MARIN]: *town,* 3.5 miles northwest of Point Reyes Station on the southwest side of Tomales Bay (lat. 38°06' N, long. 122°51'15" W). Named on Inverness (1954) 7.5' quadrangle. Postal authorities established Inverness post office in 1897 (Frickstad, p. 88). The town was named for Inverness, Scotland (Mason, 1972, p. 75). Teather (p. 57) gave the name "Point Julia" for a promontory on the west side of Tomales Bay just north of Inverness—the name commemorates Julia Shaffer Hamilton, daughter of James M. Shaffer, a major landowner in the neighborhood (Mosier and Mosier, p. 45).

Inverness Park [MARIN]: *settlement,* 1 mile west-southwest of Point Reyes Station (lat. 38°03'55" N, long. 122°49'20" W); the place is 3 miles southeast of Inverness. Named on Inverness (1954) 7.5' quadrangle. Development of the place began in 1909 (Mason, 1976a, p. 135).

Inverness Ridge [MARIN]: *ridge,* northwest-trending, 15 miles long, center 2.5 miles west of Point Reyes Station (lat. 38°04'30" N, long. 122°51'30" W); the ridge is west of Inverness. Named on Drakes Bay (1953), Inverness (1954), and Tomales (1954) 7.5' quadrangles.

Invincible Rock [CONTRA COSTA]: *rock,* nearly 1 mile southwest of Point San Pablo in San Francisco Bay (lat. 37°57'20" N, long. 122° 26'20" W). Named on San Quentin (1959) 7.5' quadrangle.

Ione: see **Point Ione** [MARIN].

Irish Canyon [CONTRA COSTA]: *canyon,* drained by a stream that flows nearly 3 miles to an unnamed canyon 4.25 miles north of Mount Diablo (lat. 37°56'35" N, long. 121°54'50" W; near W line sec. 7, T 1 N, R 1 E). Named on Antioch South (1953) and Clayton (1953) 7.5' quadrangles.

Irish Ridge [SAN MATEO]: *ridge,* southwest-trending, 3 miles long, 3.5 miles west of Skeggs Point (lat. 37°24'10" N, long. 122°22'10" W). Named on Half Moon Bay (1961) and Woodside (1961) 7.5' quadrangles. Some Irish families grew potatoes on the ridge (Morrall, p. 28).

Irish Ridge: see Sweeney Ridge [SAN MATEO].

Iron Spring [MARIN]: *spring,* 5 miles west-northwest of downtown San Rafael (lat. 37°59'55" N, long. 122°37'05" W). Named on San Rafael (1954) 7.5' quadrangle.

Irving [MARIN]: *locality,* 10.5 miles southwest of downtown Novato along Northwestern Pacific Railroad (lat. 38°01' N, long. 122°43'20" W). Named on Petaluma (1914) 15' quadrangle.

Irving: see Irvington District [ALAMEDA].

Irvington District [ALAMEDA]: *district,* 1.5 miles south-southeast of Fremont civic center in Fremont (lat. 37°31'45" N, long. 121°57'30" W). Named on Niles (1961) 7.5' quadrangle. On Pleasanton (1906) 15' quadrangle, the name "Irvington" applies to the community that joined with other communities in 1956 to form the new city of Fremont. Postal authorities established Washington Corners post office at Washington College—the first school for industrial education in California—in 1870, changed the name to Irving in 1884, and changed it to Irvington in 1887 (Salley, p. 105, 235).

Isabel: see Mount Isabel [SANTA CLARA].

Isabel Creek [SANTA CLARA]: *stream,* flows 18 miles to join Smith Creek and form Arroyo Hondo 2.5 miles south of Mount Day (lat. 37°23' N, long. 121°41'30" W; sec. 30, T 6 S, R 3 E). Named on Isabel Valley (1955), Lick Observatory (1955), and Mount Day (1955) 7.5' quadrangles. United States Board on Geographic Names (1933, p. 391) rejected the names "San Isabel Creek" and "Santa Ysabel Creek" for the stream.

Isabel Point: see Point Isabel [CONTRA COSTA].

Isabel Valley [SANTA CLARA]: *valley,* 6 miles east-southeast of Mount Hamilton (lat. 37°18'45" N, long. 121°32' W); the valley is along Isabel Creek. Named on Isabel Valley (1955) 7.5' quadrangle. United States Board on Geographic Names (1933, p. 391) rejected the names "San Isabel Valley" and "Santa Ysabel Valley" for the feature.

Isla de Alcatraces: see Yerba Buena Island [SAN FRANCISCO].

Isla de la Yegua: see Mare Island [SOLANO].

Isla del Carmel: see Brooks Island [CONTRA COSTA].

Isla del Carmen: see Brooks Island [CONTRA COSTA].

Isla de los Angeles: see Angel Island [MARIN-SAN FRANCISCO].

Isla de Santa Maria de los Angeles: see Angel Island [MARIN-SAN FRANCISCO].

Islais Creek: see Islais Creek Channel [SAN FRANCISCO].

Islais Creek Channel [SAN FRANCISCO]: *water feature,* 3.5 miles east of Mount Davidson off San Francisco Bay (lat. 37°44'50" N, long. 122°23'15" W). Named on San Francisco South (1956) 7.5' quadrangle. Called Islais Cr. on San Mateo (1915) 15' quadrangle, which shows the feature before it was modified. United States Board on Geographic Names (1983b, p. 5) rejected the names "Du Vrees Creek" and "Islais Creek" for present Islais Creek Channel.

Island Number 1 [SOLANO]: *island,* center 5 miles west-northwest of downtown Vallejo between by Napa Slough, South Slough, Dutchman Slough, and San Pablo Bay on Napa-Solano county line, mainly in Solano County (lat. 38°08'45" N, long. 122° 21' W). Named on Cuttings Wharf (1949), Mare Island (1959), and Sears Point (1951) 7.5' quadrangles.

Island Number 2 [SOLANO]: *island,* 4.5 miles west-southwest of Napa Junction between China Slough and South Slough on Napa-Solano county line (lat. 38°09'20" N, long. 122°19'25" W). Named on Cuttings Wharf (1949) 7.5' quadrangle.

Island of Saint James see Isle of Saint James [SAN FRANCISCO].

Island Slough [SOLANO]: *water feature,* on Grizzly Island, joins Montezuma Slough 5.5 miles west-southwest of Denverton (lat. 38°10'55" N, long. 121°59'15" W). Named on Denverton (1953) 7.5' quadrangle.

Isla Plana: see Mare Island [SOLANO].

Isle Hendida: see Southeast Farallon [SAN FRANCISCO].

Isle of Alcatraces: see Alcatraz Island [SAN FRANCISCO].

Isle of Saint James [SAN FRANCISCO]: *island,* one of Farallon Islands located 0.5 mile southeast of North Farallon (lat. 37°46' N, long. 123°06' W). Named on Farallon Islands (1988) 7.5' quadrangle. United States Board on Geographic Names (1985b, p. 2) noted that the feature is one of the North Farallon group, and used the form "Island of Saint James" for the name; the Board pointed out that Francis Drake gave the name "Iland of Saint James" to Farallon Islands in 1579. United States Coast and Geodetic Survey (p. 123) apparently included this island with nearby North Farallon under the name "North Farallon."

Italian Slough [CONTRA COSTA]: *water feature,* joins Old River 8 miles southeast of Brentwood (lat. 37°51'40" N, long.

121°34'45" W). Named on Clifton Court Forebay (1978) 7.5' quadrangle.

Iverson Creek [SAN MATEO]: *stream,* flows 0.5 mile to Pescadero Creek 4.25 miles south of Mindego Hill (lat. 37°14'45" N, long. 122°12'45" W; near S line sec. 8, T 8 S, R 3 W). Named on Big Basin (1955) 7.5' quadrangle. The stream first was called Coldwater Creek; Chris Iverson settled by the stream in the 1870's (Brown, p. 43).

Ivy Canyon [SANTA CLARA]: *canyon,* drained by a stream that flows 1.25 miles to Jumpoff Creek nearly 4 miles west-northwest of Mount Stakes (lat. 37°20'20" N, long. 121°28'25" W; sec. 7, T 7 S, R 5 E). Named on Mount Stakes (1955) 7.5' quadrangle.

Izabel: see **Point Izabel**, under **Point Isabel** [CONTRA COSTA].

Iverson Creek [SAN MATEO]: *stream,* flows 0.5 mile to Pescadero Creek 4.25 miles south of Mindego Hill (lat. 37°14'45" N, long. 122°12'45" W; near S line sec. 8, T 8 S, R 3 W). Named on Big Basin (1955) 7.5' quadrangle. The stream first was called Coldwater Creek; Chris Iverson settled by it in the 1870's (Brown, p. 43).

Ivy Canyon [SANTA CLARA]: *canyon,* drained by a stream that flows 1.25 miles to Jumpoff Creek nearly 4 miles west-northwest of Mount Stakes (lat. 37°20'20" N, long. 121°28'25" W; sec. 7, T 7 S, R 5 E). Named on Mount Stakes (1955) 7.5' quadrangle.

Izabel: see **Point Izabel**, under **Point Isabel** [CONTRA COSTA].

— J —

Jackass Point [CONTRA COSTA]: *promontory,* 2.25 miles north-northwest of the settlement of Bethel Island on Jersey Island at the confluence of Piper Slough and Taylor Slough (lat. 38°02'50" N, long. 121°39'10" W). Named on Jersey Island (1978) 7.5' quadrangle.

Jack Canyon [SANTA CLARA]: *canyon,* drained by a stream that flows 2 miles to Arroyo Bayo 3 miles north-northwest of Isabel Valley (lat. 37°21'20" N, long. 121°33'35" W; sec. 5, T 7 S, R 4 E). Named on Isabel Valley (1955) 7.5' quadrangle.

Jack's Harbor: see **Drakes Bay** [MARIN].

Jacksnipe [SOLANO]: *locality,* 4.25 miles south-southwest of Fairfield along Southern Pacific Railroad (lat. 38°11'30" N, long. 122° 04'05" W). Named on Fairfield South (1949) 7.5' quadrangle.

Jacques Gulch [SANTA CLARA]: *canyon,* drained by a stream that flows 2 miles to Almaden Reservoir 1.5 miles southwest of New Almaden (lat. 37°09'40" N, long. 121°50'30" W); the canyon is south of Jacques Ridge. Named on Santa Teresa Hills (1953) 7.5' quadrangle.

Jacques Ridge [SANTA CLARA]: *ridge,* north-west-trending, 1.5 miles long, 2 miles west of New Almaden (lat. 37°10'30" N, long. 121°51'35" W); the ridge is north of Jacques Gulch. Named on Santa Teresa Hills (1953) 7.5' quadrangle.

Jagel Landing [SANTA CLARA]: *locality,* 2.5 miles north-northeast of downtown Mountain View near the edge of mud flats along San Francisco Bay (lat. 37°25'30" N, long. 122°03'05" W); the landing is along Jagel Slough. Named on Palo Alto (1899) 15' quadrangle. The place appears to be at or near the site of Bernards Landing, which Thompson and West's (1876) map shows near the head of Whisman Slough (present Jagel Slough).

Jagel Slough [SANTA CLARA]: *water feature,* extends through marsh between salt evaporation ponds to enter San Francisco Bay 4.25 miles north-northeast of downtown Mountain View near the mouth of Coyote Creek (lat. 37°26'55" N, long. 122°02'50" W). Named on Mountain View (1953) 7.5' quadrangle. Called Whisman Slough on Thompson and West's (1876) map. On Mountain View (1961, photorevised 1968 and 1973) 7.5' quadrangle, a salt evaporation pond occupies the former position of the slough, and the name "Jagel Slough" applies to an artificial waterway located along the west side of the salt evaporation pond.

Jagels Slough: see **Moffett Channel** [SANTA CLARA].

Jameson Canyon [SOLANO]: *canyons,* two canyons in Napa County and Solano County that head opposite one another, and that together are 4 miles long; one of the canyons opens into lowlands 1 mile west-southwest of Cordelia (lat. 38°12'25" N, long. 122° 09' W; near W line sec. 12, T 4 N, R 3 W). Named on Cordelia (1951) 7.5' quadrangle.

Japanese Point: see **Goat Island** [SOLANO].

Jap Rock: see **Japanese Point**, under **Goat Island** [SOLANO].

Jara Canyon: see **Frenchmans Creek** [SAN MATEO].

Jarvis Landing [ALAMEDA]: *locality,* 1.25 miles west of downtown Newark along Newark Slough (lat. 37°31'45" N, long. 122°03'45" W). Named on Newark (1959) 7.5' quadrangle. Called Mayhews Landing on Thompson and West's (1878) map. The embarcadero for San Jose mission was at the site—Captain Joseph A. Mayhews bought the landing in 1854 and turned it over to his uncle, Johnathan Mayhews; Francis Carr Jarvis bought the place in 1865 (Mosier and Mosier, p. 55).

Jasper Ridge [SAN MATEO]: *ridge,* east-trending, 1 mile long, 5.25 miles south of downtown Redwood City (lat. 37°24'30" N, long. 122°13'40" W). Named on Palo Alto (1961, photorevised 1968 and 1973) 7.5' quadrangle. Members of Stanford University geology department named the feature about 1901 (Brown, p. 43).

Jays Ridge [SANTA CLARA]: *ridge,* north-trending, 2 miles long, 2 miles south of Isabel Valley (lat. 37°16'45" N, long. 121°31'40" W). Named on Isabel Valley (1955) 7.5' quadrangle.

Jensen's Landing: see **Hayward Landing** [ALAMEDA].

Jersey [CONTRA COSTA]: *locality,* 3.5 miles northwest of the present settlement of Bethel Island along San Joaquin River (lat. 38°02'40" N, long. 121°41'30" W); the place is on Jersey Island. Named on Jersey (1910) 7.5' quadrangle. Postal authorities established Jersey Landing post office in 1878, discontinued it for a time in 1879, discontinued it in 1891, reestablished it with the name "Jersey" in 1898; and discontinued it in 1935 (Salley, p. 107). They established Sand Mound post office 3 miles west of Jersey Landing post office near Sand Mound Slough in 1888 and discontinued it in 1891 (Salley, p. 193).

Jersey Island [CONTRA COSTA]: *island,* 4 miles long, center 2.5 miles west-northwest of the settlement of Bethel Island between San Joaquin River, False River, Piper Slough, Taylor Slough, and Dutch Slough (lat. 38°02' N, long. 121°41' W). Named on Jersey Island (1978) 7.5' quadrangle. Davis and Vernon's (1951) map calls the feature Jersey Island Tract. Hagen and Davis, natives of Jersey Island off England, settled on the island in 1860 (Salley, p. 107).

Jersey Island Tract: see **Jersey Island** [CONTRA COSTA].

Jersey Landing: see **Jersey** [CONTRA COSTA].

Jersey Point [CONTRA COSTA]: *promontory,* 3.5 miles northwest of the settlement of Bethel Island along San Joaquin River (lat. 38°03'05" N, long. 121°41'20" W); the feature is on Jersey Island. Named on Jersey Island (1978) 7.5' quadrangle.

Jewell [MARIN]: *locality,* 11 miles west-southwest of downtown Novato (lat. 38°02'10" N, long. 122°44'40" W). Named on San Geronimo (1954) 7.5' quadrangle The place is near the ranch that Omar Jewell settled on in the 1860's (Teather, p. 32).

Jewel Lake [CONTRA COSTA]: *lake,* 550 feet long, behind a dam on Wildcat Creek 4.5 miles east-southeast of Richmond civic center (lat. 37°54'45" N, long. 122°16'05" W). Named on Richmond (1959) 7.5' quadrangle.

Jim McCall's Gulch: see **Jones Gulch** [SAN MATEO] (2).

Joaquin River: see **San Joaquin River** [CONTRA COSTA].

Johnson Camp [ALAMEDA]: *locality,* 4 miles south-southwest of Midway (lat. 37°39'45" N, long. 121°35'50" W; sec. 24, T 3 S, R 3 E). Named on Midway (1953) 7.5' quadrangle.

Johnson Creek: see **Jones Creek** [SANTA CLARA].

Johnson Landing [ALAMEDA]: *locality,* 6.5 miles south of downtown San Leandro at the edge of San Francisco Bay (lat. 37°37'45" N, long. 122°09'05" W). Named on San Leandro (1959) 7.5' quadrangle. The name commemorates John Johnson, who came to the place in 1856 and built a wharf and warehouses (Mosier and Mosier, p., 47).

Johnston Creek: see **Mills Creek** [SAN MATEO] (2).

Joice Island [SOLANO]: *island,* 5.5 miles south of Fairfield between Cutoff Slough, Montezuma Slough, and Suisun Slough (lat. 38° 10" N, long. 121°03' W). Named on Denverton (1953), Fairfield South (1949), and Vine Hill (1959) 7.5' quadrangles. United States Board on Geographic Names (1933, p. 401) rejected the forms "Joice's Island" and "Joyce Island" for the name.

Joice's Island: see **Joice Island** [SOLANO].

Jones: see **Commodore Jones Point** [SOLANO]; **Elmhurst** [ALAMEDA].

Jones Creek [SANTA CLARA]: *stream,* joins Llagas Creek nearly 4 miles southeast of Gilroy (lat. 36°58'35" N, long. 121°30'40" W); the stream is the continuation in the lowlands of Alamias Creek. Named on Chittenden (1955, photorevised 1968 and 1973) 7.5' quadrangle. According to United States Board on Geographic Names (1973a, p. 2), the name commemorates an early landowner in the region; the Board gave the name "Johnson Creek" as a variant.

Jones Creek: see **Corte Madera Creek** [SAN MATEO]; **Los Gatos Creek** [SANTA CLARA].

Jones Gulch [SAN MATEO]:
(1) *canyon,* drained by a stream that flows 1.5 miles to Pescadero Creek 3 miles south of La Honda (lat. 37°16'30" N, long. 122° 16' W; sec. 35, T 7 S, R 4 W). Named on La Honda (1961) 7.5' quadrangle. J.C. Jones settled in the canyon in the early 1860's (Brown, p. 44).
(2) *canyon,* drained by a stream that flows 1 mile to Corte Madera Creek 3.5 miles north of Mindego Hill (lat. 37°21'45" N, long. 122°13'15" W). Named on Mindego Hill (1961) 7.5' quadrangle. William G. Jones settled near the head of the canyon about 1857; a common name for the feature in the twentieth century is Jim McCall's Gulch, for the owner of a cabin there (Brown, p. 44).

Jones Gulch: see **Alambique Creek** [SAN MATEO].

Jones Island: see **Van Sickle Island** [SOLANO].

Jones Mill: see **Lexington** [SANTA CLARA].

Joyce Island: see **Joice Island** [SOLANO].

Judsonville: see **Stewartville** [CONTRA COSTA].

Julia: see **Point Julia**, under **Inverness** [MARIN].

Jumpoff Creek [SANTA CLARA]: *stream,* flows 9 miles to San Antonio Creek 4 miles north-northeast of Isabel Valley (lat. 37°22'05" N, long. 121°31'05" W; sec. 34, T 6 S, R 4 E). Named on Isabel Valley (1955) and Mount Stakes (1955) 7.5' quadrangles.

Junction: see **Antioch** [CONTRA COSTA]; **New Almaden Station** [SANTA CLARA].

Junction Camp [CONTRA COSTA]: *locality*, 1.5 miles southwest of Mount Diablo (lat. 37°51'55" N, long. 121°55'55" W; near NW cor. sec. 12, T 1 S, R 1 W). Named on Diablo (1953) 7.5' quadrangle.

Juniper Camp [CONTRA COSTA]: *locality*, 1 mile west-southwest of Mount Diablo (lat. 37°52'40" N, long. 121°55'50" W; at W line sec. 1, T 1 S, R 1 W). Named on Clayton (1953) 7.5' quadrangle.

Juristac [SANTA CLARA]: *land grant*, west of Pajaro River at the southernmost tip of Santa Clara County. Named on Chittenden (1955) 7.5' quadrangle. Antonio German and Faustino German received 1 league in 1835; J.L. Sargent claimed 4540 acres patented in 1871 (Cowan, p. 43). Kroeber (p. 44) gave an Indian origin for the name. The grant generally was known as Sargent Ranch for its American owner, James P. Sargent (Arbuckle, p. 18). The grant also was known as Los Germanos, for the original grantees, and as La Brea (Gudde, 1949, p. 169).

– K –

Kaiser Creek [ALAMEDA-CONTRA COSTA]: *stream*, heads in Contra Costa County and flows 3 miles to an arm of Upper San Leandro Reservoir 10 miles east of downtown Oakland in Alameda County (lat. 37°47'15" N, long. 122°05'35" W; sec. 4, T 2 S, R 2 W). Named on Las Trampas Ridge (1959) 7.5' quadrangle. Buckhorn Creek, a tributary of Kaiser Creek, is called Kaiser Creek on Concord (1897) 15' quadrangle.

Karquenas Strait: see **Carquinez Strait** [CONTRA COSTA].

Karquines Point: see **Point Carquinez** [CONTRA COSTA].

Karquines Strait: see **Carquinez Strait** [CONTRA COSTA-SOLANO].

Kashow's Island: see **Belvedere Island** [MARIN].

Kaufman Ridge [SANTA CLARA]: *ridge*, northwest- to west-trending, 2 miles long, 5 miles northwest of Pacheco Peak (lat. 37°03'45" N, long. 121°20'45" W). Named on Pacheco Peak (1955) 7.5' quadrangle.

Keiffer's Creek: see **Bogess Creek** [SAN MATEO].

Keil Cove [MARIN]: *embayment*, nearly 5 miles south-southeast of Point San Quentin near the southeast end of Tiburon Peninsula (lat. 37°52'45" N, long. 122°26'25" W). Named on San Quentin (1959) 7.5' quadrangle. The Keil family lived in the neighborhood (Teather, p. 32).

Keller Ridge [CONTRA COSTA]: *ridge*, generally west-trending, 1.5 miles long, 3.5 miles

north-northeast of Mount Diablo (lat. 37° 55'40" N, long. 121°53'20" W). Named on Clayton (1953) 7.5' quadrangle.

Kelley Gulch: see **Bull Run Creek** [SAN MATEO].

Kellogg Creek [CONTRA COSTA]: *stream*, flows 14 miles to lowlands 2.5 miles south of Brentwood (lat. 37°53'35" N, long. 121° 41'35" W). Named on Brentwood (1978), Byron Hot Springs (1978), and Woodward Island (1978) 7.5' quadrangles.

Kelly Cabin Canyon [SANTA CLARA]: *canyon*, drained by a stream that flows 6.5 miles to East Fork Coyote Creek 4.5 miles north of Gilroy Hot Springs (lat. 37°21'55" N, long. 121°28'50" W; at N line sec. 12, T 9 S, R 4 E). Named on Gilroy Hot Springs (1955) and Mississippi Creek (1955) 7.5' quadrangles.

Kelly Hill [SAN MATEO]: *peak*, 4 miles north-northwest of Mindego Hill (lat. 37°21'55" N, long. 122°14'50" W; sec. 36, T 6 S, R 4 W). Named on Mindego Hill (1961) 7.5' quadrangle.

Kensington [CONTRA COSTA]: *town*, 4 miles east-southeast of Richmond civic center (lat. 37°54'35" N, long. 122°16'45" W). Named on Richmond (1959) 7.5' quadrangle. Robert Bousefield named the place in 1911 for Kensington, England (Gudde, 1949, p. 172; Gudde listed it under the name "Kensington Park").

Kensington: see **Willow Glen** [SANTA CLARA].

Kensington Park: see **Kensington** [CONTRA COSTA].

Kent: see **Kentfield** [MARIN].

Kent Canyon [MARIN]: *canyon*, drained by a stream that flows 1.5 miles to Frank Valley nearly 7 miles south-southwest of downtown San Rafael (lat. 37°52'55" N, long. 122°34'35" W). Named on San Rafael (1954) 7.5' quadrangle. Congressman William Kent had a hunting cabin at the head of the canyon; the feature first was called Rocky Canyon (Teather, p. 32).

Kentfield [MARIN]: *town*, 2 miles southwest of downtown San Rafael (lat. 37°57' N, long. 122°33'15" W). Named on San Rafael (1954) 7.5' quadrangle. Tamalpais (1897) 15' quadrangle has the name "Tamalpais" along Northwestern Pacific Railroad at the place. Postal authorities established Kentfield post office in 1905 (Frickstad, p. 88). Albert Emmet Kent bought land at the place from the estate of James Ross in 1871; Ross Landing was at the site in the early days, when steamers came up Corte Madera Creek (Hoover, Rensch, and Rensch, p. 185). Kent called his home Tamalpais, and the nearby railroad station had that name before it was renamed Kent in the 1890's; the name "Kent" was changed to Kentfield when the post office came (Gudde, 1949, p. 172-173).

Kent Lake [MARIN]: *lake*, behind a dam on

Lagunitas Creek 6 miles north of Bolinas (lat. 37°59'50" N, long. 122°42'10" W). Named on Bolinas (1954) 7.5' quadrangle. Teather (p. 33) associated the name with Thomas T. Kent, a director of Marin Municipal Water District from 1920 until 1959.

Keyes Creek [MARIN]: see **Keys Creek** [MARIN]; **Walker Creek** [MARIN].

Keys Creek [MARIN]: *stream,* flows 3.5 miles to Walker Creek 1 mile south-southwest of Tomales (lat. 38°14' N, long. 122°54'45" W). Named on Point Reyes NE (1954) and Tomales (1954) 7.5' quadrangles. United States Board on Geographic Names (1943, p. 11) rejected the name "Keyes Creek" for the stream, The name "Keys" commemorates John Keys, who took up land along the creek in the 1850's (Gudde, 1949, p. 174).

Keys Creek: see **Walker Creek** [MARIN].

Keys Embarcadero: see **Tomales** [MARIN].

Keyston Creek [SAN MATEO]: *stream,* flows less than 1 mile to Pescadero Creek 3.5 miles south-southwest of Mindego Hill (lat. 37°15'40" N, long. 122°14'55" W; sec. 1, T 8 S, R 4 W). Named on La Honda (1961) and Mindego Hill (1961) 7.5' quadrangles. Employees of Santa Cruz Lumber Company named the stream about 1946 for George N. Keyston, patron of a nearby Boy Scout camp (Brown, p. 44).

Kickham Peak [SANTA CLARA]: *peak,* 6.5 miles southeast of Gilroy Hot Springs on Elephant Head Ridge (lat. 37°02'50" N, long. 121°23'05" W; on W line sec. 24, T 10 S, R 5 E). Named on Gilroy Hot Springs (1955) 7.5' quadrangle.

Kilcare Woods [ALAMEDA]: *settlement,* 5 miles south-southeast of Dublin along Sinbad Creek (lat. 37°37'45" N, long. 121°54'45" W). Named on Dublin (1961) 7.5' quadrangle.

Kilgore [CONTRA COSTA]: *locality,* 4 miles north-northeast of present Walnut Creek civic center along Oakland Antioch and Eastern Railroad (lat. 37°57'20" N, long. 122°01'40" W). Named on Concord (1915) 15' quadrangle.

King: see **Mount King**, under **North Peak** [CONTRA COSTA].

King Canyon [ALAMEDA]: *canyon,* nearly 1 mile long, 8.5 miles east of downtown Oakland (lat. 37°48' N, long. 122°06'55" W; near E line sec. 31, T 1 S, R 2 W). Named on Las Trampas Ridge (1959) 7.5' quadrangle. Water of Upper San Leandro Reservoir nearly fills the canyon. The name commemorates Joaquin King, a stock rancher who settled at the place in the 1850's (Mosier and Mosier, p. 48).

King Mountain [MARIN]: *peak,* 2.5 miles south-southwest of downtown San Rafael (lat. 37°56'10" N, long. 122°32'50" W). Named on San Rafael (1954) 7.5' quadrangle.

King's Island: see **Ryer Island** [SOLANO] (2).

Kings Mountain [SAN MATEO]: *ridge,* northwest-trending, 2 miles long, 2 miles north-northwest of Skeggs Point (lat. 37°26'15" N,

long. 122°19'15" W). Named on Woodside (1961) 7.5' quadrangle. The name is from a travellers stop called Kings Mountain House, operated by Mrs. Honora King (Gudde, 1949, p. 175).

Kings Rock [SAN MATEO]: *rock,* 3.5 miles west-northwest of downtown Half Moon Bay, and about 0.5 mile southeast of Pillar Point (lat. 37°29'15" N, long. 122°29'15" W). Named on Half Moon Bay (1961) 7.5' quadrangle.

Kingston Creek [SAN MATEO]: *stream,* flows nearly 2 miles to San Gregorio Creek 2.5 miles west-southwest of La Honda (lat. 37° 18'35" N, long. 122°19'10" W; sec. 20, T 7 S, R 4 W). Named on La Honda (1961) 7.5' quadrangle. J.R. Kingston had a ranch by the stream in the 1870's; the feature also was called Armstrong's Creek for the previous owner of the ranch (Brown, p. 45).

Kirby Beach: see **Point Diablo** [MARIN].

Kirby Hill [SOLANO]: *hill,* 4 miles south-southwest of Denverton (lat. 38°10'05" N, long. 121°55'10" W). Altitude 361 feet. Named on Denverton (1953) 7.5' quadrangle.

Kirker Creek [CONTRA COSTA]: *stream,* flows 4.25 miles to lowlands 8 miles north of Mount Diablo at Pittsburg (lat. 37°59'50" N, long. 121°53'35" W; near N line sec. 29, T 2 N, R 1 W). Named on Antioch North (1953), Clayton (1953), and Honker Bay (1953) 7.5' quadrangles.

Kirker Pass [CONTRA COSTA]:

(1) *pass,* 5.5 miles north of Mount Diablo (lat. 37°57'40" N, long. 121°55'15" W; sec. 1, T 1 N, R 1 W). Named on Mount Diablo (1898) 15' quadrangle. Whitney (p. 32) mentioned Kirker's Pass. United States Board on Geographic Names (1933, p. 430) rejected the names "Kirkers Pass," "Quercus Pass," and "Quereus Pass" for the feature. James Kirker lived near the place in the 1850's (Gudde, 1969, p. 166).

(2) *locality,* 5.5 miles north of Mount Diablo (lat. 37°57'40" N, long. 121°55'15" W; sec. 1, T 1 N, R 1 W); the place is at Kirker Pass (1). Named on Clayton (1953) 7.5' quadrangle.

Klinknerville: see **Golden Gate** [ALAMEDA].

Knife: see **The Knife** [ALAMEDA-CONTRA COSTA].

Knight Island [SOLANO]: *island,* 3 miles northwest of downtown Vallejo between Napa River, Dutchman Slough, and South Slough (lat. 38°08'15" N, long. 122°18'15" W). Named on Cuttings Wharf (1949) 7.5' quadrangle. On Mare Island (1916) 15' quadrangle, present Russ Island in Napa County has the name "Knight Island."

Knightsen [CONTRA COSTA]: *town,* 3 miles north-northeast of Brentwood (lat. 37°58'10" N, long. 121°39'55" W; near S line sec. 32, T 2 N, R 3 E). Named on Brentwood (1978) 7.5' quadrangle. Postal authorities established Knightsen post office in 1900 (Frickstad, p.

22). G.M. Knight gave right of way at the place to the railroad, and suggested the name to combine his own name with the suffix of his wife's maiden name, Christensen (Gudde, 1949, p. 176).

Knob Hill [MARIN]: *peak,* 3.25 miles southwest of downtown San Rafael (lat. 37°56'05" N, long. 122°33'45" W). Altitude 1091 feet. Named on San Rafael (1954) 7.5' quadrangle.

Knob Point [CONTRA COSTA]: *peak,* 2.5 miles south-southeast of Mount Diablo (lat. 37°50'35" N, long. 121°53'55" W; sec. 18, T 1 S, R 1 E). Named on Diablo (1953) 7.5' quadrangle.

Knopf Canyon: see **Nuff Creek** [SAN MATEO].

Knox Island: see **Chipps Island** [SOLANO].

Knox Point [MARIN]: *promontory,* at the southwest end of Angel Island (lat. 37°51'20" N, long. 122°26'30" W). Named on San Francisco North (1956) 7.5' quadrangle. United States Board on Geographic Names (1980, p. 4) approved the name "Point Knox" for the promontory. The name "Knox" commemorates Lieutenant Samuel R. Knox, who was an officer with Cadwallader Ringgold's expedition of 1849 (Teather, p. 2).

Knuedler Lake [SAN MATEO]: *lake,* 350 feet long, less than 1 mile southwest of Mindego Hill (lat. 37°18'20" N, long. 122°14'25" W; near E line sec. 24, T 7 S, R 4 W). Named on Mindego Hill (1961) 7.5' quadrangle. John Knuedler had a ranch at the place (Brown, p. 45).

Kohler Creek: see **Temescal Creek** [ALAMEDA].

Komandorski Village [ALAMEDA]: *locality,* nearly 2 miles northeast of Dublin (lat. 37°42'55" N, long. 121°54'35" W). Named on Dublin (1961) 7.5' quadrangle.

Koopman Canyon [ALAMEDA-CONTRA COSTA]: *canyon,* on Alameda-Contra Costa county line, mainly in Contra Costa County; drained by a stream that flows 1.5 miles to lowlands nearly 1 mile north of Dublin (lat. 37°42'50" N, long. 121°56'20" W). Named on Dublin (1961) 7.5' quadrangle. The name commemorates Martin Koopman and Mathew Koopman, who farmed in the neighborhood (Mosier and Mosier, p. 48).

Krelling [CONTRA COSTA]: *locality,* 4.5 miles northwest of Danville along Oakland Antioch and Eastern Railroad (lat. 37°52'20" N, long. 122°02'45" W). Named on Concord (1915) 15' quadrangle.

— L —

La Boca de la Cañada del Pinole [CONTRA COSTA]: *land grant,* between Martinez and Lafayette. Named on Briones Valley (1959) and Walnut Creek (1959) 7.5' quadrangles. Manuel Valencia received the land in 1842

and claimed 13,316 acres patented in 1878 (Cowan, p. 61).

La Brea: see **Juristac** [SANTA CLARA]; **Las Animas** [SANTA CLARA]; **Sargent** [SANTA CLARA].

La Brea Creek: see **Tar Creek** [SANTA CLARA].

La Costa Creek [ALAMEDA]: *stream,* flows 7 miles to San Antonio Creek 6 miles east of Sunol (lat. 37°34'40" N, long. 121°46'25" W; sec. 20, T 4 S, R 2 E); the mouth of the stream is at the head of La Costa Valley. Named on La Costa Valley (1960) and Mendenhall Springs (1956) 7.5' quadrangles. The misspelled name is for Juan F. La Coste, who raised livestock in the region in the 1850's; the stream also was called San Antonio Creek (Mosier and Mosier, p. 48).

La Costa Valley [ALAMEDA]: *valley,* 4 miles east of Sunol along San Antonio Creek (lat. 37°35' N, long. 121°48'45" W). Named on La Costa Valley (1960) 7.5' quadrangle. Water of San Antonio Reservoir now covers part of the valley.

La Cuchilla de la Mina de Louis Chabolla: see **New Almaden** [SANTA CLARA].

Laddville: see **Livermore** [ALAMEDA].

Ladrillo: see **Clayburn** [CONTRA COSTA].

Lafayette [CONTRA COSTA]: *town,* 3.25 miles west-southwest of Walnut Creek civic center (lat. 37°53'30" N, long. 122°07' W). Named on Briones Valley (1959), Las Trampas Ridge (1959), and Walnut Creek (1959) 7.5' quadrangles. Called La Fayette on California Mining Bureau's (1909b) map. Postal authorities established La Fayette post office in 1857 and changed the name to Lafayette in 1932 (Salley, p. 114). The town incorporated in 1968. Elam Brown, who settled at the place in 1846 and built a grist mill there in 1853, is considered the founder of the community (Smith and Elliott, p. 23).

Lafayette Branch: see **Lafayette Creek** [CONTRA COSTA].

Lafayette Creek [CONTRA COSTA]: *stream,* flows 3.25 miles to Las Trampas Creek 3 miles west-southwest of Walnut Creek civic center in Lafayette (lat. 37°53'35" N, long. 122°06'35" W). Named on Briones Valley (1959) and Walnut Creek (1959) 7.5' quadrangles. On Concord (1897) 15' quadrangle, present Lafayette Creek and Las Trampas Creek below their confluence have the name "Lafayette Branch."

Lafayette Reservoir [CONTRA COSTA]: *lake,* 4100 feet long, 2.25 miles east of Orinda (lat. 37°52'55" N, long. 122°08'25" W). Named on Briones Valley (1959) 7.5' quadrangle.

Lafayette Ridge [CONTRA COSTA]: *ridge,* east-southeast-trending, 2.5 miles long, center 3.25 miles west of Walnut Creek civic center (lat. 37°54'30" N, long. 122°07' W). Named on Briones Valley (1959) and Walnut Creek (1959) 7.5' quadrangles.

Lagoon [SOLANO]: *intermittent lake,* 5.5 miles north-northeast of Fairfield in Lagoon Valley (lat. 38°19'45" N, long. 122°00'40" W). Named on Fairfield North (1951) 7.5' quadrangle, which shows two perennial lakes in the intermittent lake.

Lagoon: see **The Lagoon**, under **Stivers Lagoon** [ALAMEDA].

Lagoon Valley [SOLANO]: *valley,* 6.25 miles north of Fairfield (lat. 38°20'30" N, long. 122°01'15" W); Laguna Creek drains the valley. Named on Elmira (1953) and Fairfield North (1951) 7.5' quadrangles.

Laguna: see **The Laguna**, under **Upper Crystal Springs Reservoir** [SAN MATEO].

Laguna Alta [SAN MATEO]: *lake,* 1550 feet long, 3.5 miles west of downtown South San Francisco (lat. 37°39'35" N, long. 122°28'40" W). Named on San Francisco South (1956) 7.5' quadrangle. The lake now is filled, and the filled area is covered by buildings.

Laguna Creek [MARIN]: *stream,* flows 0.5 mile to Fern Creek 5 miles south-southwest of downtown San Rafael (lat. 37°54'40" N, long. 122°34'50" W). Named on San Rafael (1954) 7.5' quadrangle.

Laguna Creek [SOLANO]: *stream,* flows 4.5 miles to Alamo Creek less than 1 mile south-southwest of downtown Vacaville (lat. 38°20'35" N, long. 121°59'55" W); the stream goes through Lagoon Valley. Named on Fairfield North (1951) 7.5' quadrangle.

Laguna Creek: see **Lower Crystal Springs Reservoir** [SAN MATEO].

Laguna de la Merced [SAN FRANCISCO-SAN MATEO]: *land grant,* around Lake Merced on San Francisco-San Mateo county line, mainly in San Francisco. Named on San Francisco South (1956) 7.5' quadrangle. Jose Antonio Galindo received 1.5 leagues in 1835; Josefa de Haro and others claimed 2219 acres patented in 1872 (Cowan, p. 47-48).

Laguna de la Merced: see **Lake Merced** [SAN FRANCISCO].

Laguna del Corazon: see **Mindego Lake** [SAN MATEO].

Laguna de los Dolores: see **Mission District** [SAN FRANCISCO].

Laguna de los Palos Colorados [ALAMEDA-CONTRA COSTA]: *land grant,* mainly near and north of Moraga; almost entirely in Contra Costa County, but the southernmost tip of the grant extends into Alameda County. Named on Briones Valley (1959), Las Trampas Ridge (1959), Oakland East (1959), and Walnut Creek (1959) 7.5' quadrangles. Joaquin Moraga and Juan Bernal received 3 leagues in 1835 and 1841; Moraga and others claimed 13,316 acres patented in 1878 (Cowan, p. 57). The name is from a lake and some redwood trees on the grant (Gudde, 1949, p. 251).

Laguna del Presidio: see **Mountain Lake** [SAN FRANCISCO].

Laguna de Manantial: see **Mission District** [SAN FRANCISCO].

Laguna de Nuestra Señora de la Merced: see **Lake Merced** [SAN FRANCISCO].

Laguna de Nuestra Señora de los Dolores: see **Mission District** [SAN FRANCISCO].

Laguna de Raimundo: see **Upper Crystal Springs Reservoir** [SAN MATEO].

Laguna de San Antonio [MARIN]: *land grant,* around Laguna Lake on Marin-Sonoma county line. Named on Cotati (1954), Petaluma (1953), Point Reyes NE (1954), and Two Rock (1954) 7.5' quadrangles. Bartolo Bojorquez received 6 leagues in 1845 and claimed 24,903 acres patented in 1871 (Cowan, p. 72).

Laguna de San Antonio: see **Laguna Lake** [MARIN].

Laguna de San Benvenuto: see **Laguna Seca** [SANTA CLARA].

Laguna Grande: see **Upper Crystal Springs Reservoir** [SAN MATEO].

Laguna Honda [SAN FRANCISCO]: *lake,* 1200 feet long, 0.5 mile south-southwest of Mount Sutro (lat. 37°45'10" N, long. 122°27'40" W). Named on San Francisco North (1956) 7.5' quadrangle. Called Laguna Honda Reservoir on Wackenreuder's (1861) map.

Laguna Honda Reservoir: see **Laguna Honda** [SAN FRANCISCO].

Laguna House: see **Coyote** [SANTA CLARA].

Laguna Lake [MARIN]: *intermittent lake,* 2 miles long, 6 miles west-southwest of the city of Petaluma on Marin-Sonoma county line (lat. 38°12'45" N, long. 122°44'50" W). Named on Petaluma (1953) and Point Reyes NE (1954) 7.5' quadrangles. Mason (1976b, p. 163) called the feature Laguna de San Antonio.

Laguna Merced Military Reservation: see **Fort Funston Military Reservation** [SAN FRANCISCO].

Laguna Puerca [SAN FRANCISCO]: *lake,* 1250 feet long, nearly 2 miles east of Mount Davidson (lat. 37°44'05" N, long. 122°29'15" W). Named on San Mateo (1915) 15' quadrangle.

Laguna Ranch Canyon: see **Rough Gulch** [SANTA CLARA].

Laguna Salada [SAN MATEO]: *lake,* 1850 feet long, nearly 5 miles west-southwest of downtown South San Francisco near the coast (lat. 37°37'35" N, long. 122°29'30" W). Named on Montara Mountain (1956) and San Francisco South (1956) 7.5' quadrangles. Brown (p. 78) used the name "Salt Lake" for the feature, and gave the name "Salt Lake Valley" to the valley that extends east from the lake; Brown also noted that the lake has the popular name "Brighton Lake" from Brighton Beach subdivision.

Laguna Seca [SANTA CLARA]: *marsh,* 1 mile south-southwest of Coyote (lat. 37°12'20" N, long. 121°44'40" W); the feature is on La Laguna grant. Named on Morgan Hill (1917) 15' quadrangle. Morgan Hill (1940) 15' quadrangle has the name, but shows no marsh. Morgan Hill (1955) 7.5' quadrangle omits the name and shows a drainage ditch through the place. Crespi called the feature Laguna de San Benvenuto in 1772 (Hoover, Rensch, and Rensch, p. 431).

Laguna Seca: see **La Laguna Seca** [SANTA CLARA].

Lagunita [SANTA CLARA]: *intermittent lake,* 1850 feet long, 4 miles south-southwest of downtown Palo Alto (lat. 37°25'20" N, long. 122°10'30" W). Named on Palo Alto (1961) 7.5' quadrangle. Called Lake Lagunita on Palo Alto (1940) 15' quadrangle.

Lagunitas [MARIN]: *settlement,* 10 miles southwest of downtown Novato (lat. 38°00'45" N, long. 122°42' W). Named on San Geronimo (1954) 7.5' quadrangle. Postal authorities established Lagunitas post office in 1906 (Frickstad, p. 88).

Lagunitas: see **Lake Lagunitas** [MARIN].

Lagunitas Creek [MARIN]: *stream,* heads at Lake Lagunitas, where East Fork, Middle Fork, and West Fork meet, flows 23 miles to marsh 1.5 miles northwest of Point Reyes Station at the southeast end of Tomales Bay (lat. 38°04'50" N, long. 122°49'35" W). Named on Bolinas (1954), Inverness (1954), and San Geronimo (1954) 7.5' quadrangles. Called Daniels C. on Goddard's (1857) map. United States Board on Geographic Names (1933, p. 444) rejected the name "Paper Mill Creek" for the stream. Samuel P. Taylor established the first paper mill on the Pacific Coast along the creek in 1856 (Gudde, 1949, p. 253). In Spanish times the stream was called Arroyo de San Geronimo, but the name "San Geronimo" now is restricted to San Geronimo Creek, a branch of Lagunitas Creek (Gudde, 1949, p. 180). East Fork is 1.5 miles long, Middle Fork is 1 mile long, and West Fork is nearly 1 mile long; all three forks are named on San Rafael (1954) 7.5' quadrangle. Postal authorities established Paper Mill post office 5.5 miles southeast of Olema at Taylor's paper mill in 1881, discontinued it in 1882, re-established it with the name "Paperville" in 1884, and discontinued it in 1894 (Salley, p. 166).

La Honda [SAN MATEO]: *town,* 13 miles southeast of the town of Half Moon Bay (lat. 37°19'10" N, long. 122°16'15" W). Named on La Honda (1961) 7.5' quadrangle. John H. Sears built a store at the place about 1877 and named it for nearby Arroyo Hondo (present La Honda Creek) (Hoover, Rensch, and Rensch, p. 410). Postal authorities established La Honda post office in 1873, changed the name to Lahonda in 1894, and changed it back to La Honda in 1905 (Salley, p. 115). United States Board on Geographic Names (1974, p.

3) approved the name "Pearsons Pond" for a lake, 165 feet long, located 2.5 miles north of La Honda (lat. 37°21'08" N, long. 122°15'20" W); the name commemorates Charles A. Pearson and Edward J. Pearson, former owners of the feature.

La Honda Canyon: see **La Honda Creek** [SAN MATEO].

La Honda Creek [SAN MATEO]: *stream,* flows 7.5 miles to join Alpine Creek and form San Gregorio Creek 0.5 mile south-southwest of La Honda (lat. 37°18'35" N, long. 122°16'35" W; near E line sec. 22, T 7 S, R 4 W). Named on La Honda (1961) and Woodside (1961) 7.5' quadrangles. The stream first was called Arroyo Hondo; the canyon of the stream below Woodruff Creek is called La Honda Canyon (Brown , p. 46).

Lairds Landing [MARIN]: *locality,* 6 miles south of Tomales on the southwest side of Tomales Bay (lat. 38°09'35" N, long. 122°54'40" W). Named on Tomales (1954) 7.5' quadrangle. George Laird and Charles Laird leased the place in 1858 (Mason, 1976a, p. 33).

Lake Alhambra [CONTRA COSTA]: *lake,* 0.5 mile long, 1 mile east-southeast of downtown Antioch (lat. 38°00'30" N, long. 121°47'30" W). Named on Antioch North (1978) 7.5' quadrangle.

Lake Anza [CONTRA COSTA]: *lake,* 1000 feet long, behind a dam on Wildcat Creek 4 miles west-northwest of Orinda (lat. 37°53'50" N, long. 122°15' W). Named on Briones Valley (1959) and Richmond (1959) 7.5' quadrangles.

Lake Cascade [CONTRA COSTA]: *lake,* 0.25 mile long, less than 1 mile north-northwest of Orinda (lat. 37°53'35" N, long. 122°11'05" W). Named on Briones Valley (1959) 7.5' quadrangle.

Lake Chabot [ALAMEDA]: *lake,* 2.25 miles long, behind a dam on San Leandro Creek 4.5 miles north-northwest of downtown Hayward (lat. 37°43'45" N, long. 122°07'15" W). Named on Hayward (1959) 7.5' quadrangle. The dam was built in 1868 and 1869; the name of the lake is for Anthony Chabot, a pioneer capitalist (Gudde, 1949, p. 63).

Lake Chabot [SOLANO]: *lake,* 3700 feet long, 2.5 miles north-northeast of downtown Vallejo (lat. 38°08'10" N, long. 122°14'10" W; sec. 6, T 3 N, R 3 W). Named on Cordelia (1951) 7.5' quadrangle.

Lake Chabot: see **Lake Temescal** [ALAMEDA].

Lake Creek: see **Lower Crystal Springs Reservoir** [SAN MATEO].

Lake Del Valle [ALAMEDA]: *lake,* 5.5 miles long, behind a dam on Arroyo Valle nearly 6 miles west-northwest of Mendenhall Springs (lat. 37°36'50" N, long. 121°44'40" W). Named on Mendenhall Springs (1956, photorevised 1971) 7.5' quadrangle.

Lake Elizabeth: see **Stivers Lagoon** [ALAMEDA].

Lake Elsman [SANTA CLARA]: *lake,* nearly 1.5 miles long, behind a dam on Los Gatos Creek 7 miles south-southeast of downtown Los Gatos (lat. 37°07'50" N, long. 121°55'55" W; on W line sec. 24, T 9 S, R 1 W). Named on Laurel (1955) and Los Gatos (1953) 7.5' quadrangles.

Lake Frey [SOLANO]: *lake,* 3700 feet long, 8.5 miles west-northwest of Fairfield (lat. 38°17'35" N, long. 122°11'20" W; on W line sec. 10, T 5 N, R 3 W). Named on Mount George (1951) 7.5' quadrangle.

Lake Herman [SOLANO]: *lake,* 4400 feet long, behind a dam on Sulphur Springs Creek 3 miles north of Benicia (lat. 38°05'35" N, long. 122°09' W; sec. 24, T 3 N, R 3 W). Named on Benicia (1959) 7.5' quadrangle. Herman Schussler had the dam built to form the lake by 1905 (Dillon, p. 217).

Lake Lagunita: see **Lagunita** [SANTA CLARA].

Lake Lagunitas [MARIN]: *lake,* behind a dam on Lagunitas Creek 4 miles west-southwest of downtown San Rafael (lat. 37°56'50" N, long. 122°35'45" W). Named on San Rafael (1954) 7.5' quadrangle.

Lake Lucerne [SAN MATEO]: *lake,* nearly 1 mile long, 3 miles north of Pigeon Point along Arroyo de la Frijoles (lat. 37°13'25" N, long. 122°24'05" W). Named on Pigeon Point (1955) 7.5' quadrangle. Called Bean Hollow Lagoon on California Division of Highways' (1934) map. The lake called Bean Hollow Lagoon was made into a reservoir in 1923 and renamed Lucerne Lake by F.L. Lathrop, manager of the land company at the place (Brown, p. 50).

Lake Madigan [SOLANO]: *lake,* 1 mile long, 9 miles west-northwest of Fairfield (lat. 38°18'35" N, long. 122°11'35" W; sec. 4, T 5 N, R 3 W). Named on Mount George (1951) 7.5' quadrangle.

Lake Mathilde [SAN MATEO]: *lake,* 650 feet long, 3 miles north-northwest of present Montara Knob (lat. 37°35'40" N, long. 122° 30'05" W). Named on San Mateo (1899) 15' quadrangle.

Lake McCoppin: see **Mission District** [SAN FRANCISCO].

Lake Merced [SAN FRANCISCO]: *lake,* 1.5 miles long, 2.5 miles west-southwest of Mount Davidson (lat. 37°43'10" N, long. 122° 29'35" W). Named on San Francisco South (1956) 7.5' quadrangle. A causeway divides the feature into two parts. Called Merced Lake on San Mateo (1915) 15' quadrangle, and called Laguna de la Merced on San Mateo (1942) 15' quadrangle, although United States Board on Geographic Names (1933, p. 513) rejected this name for the feature. Captain Heceta gave the name "Laguna de Nuestra Señora de la Merced" to the lake in 1775

(Davidson, p. 117). A United States Coast and Geodetic Survey map dated 1869 shows a tidal channel connecting the north end of the lake to the sea (Miller, R.C., p. 378).

Lake Merritt [ALAMEDA]: *lake,* nearly 1 mile long, in downtown Oakland (lat. 37°48'15" N, long. 122°15'15" W). Named on Oakland East (1959) and Oakland West (1959) 7.5' quadrangles. The feature originally was part of a tidal slough—called San Antonio Creek or San Antonio Slough—that forms present Oakland Inner Harbor; Dr. Samuel B. Merritt, mayor of Oakland in 1868, was instrumental in having a dam built to impound the tidal water and form present Lake Merritt, a salt-water lake with a broad causeway and a movable floodgate (Hoover, Rensch, and Rensch, p. 20). The lake first was called Lake Peralta, but was renamed Lake Merritt in 1891 (Gudde, 1969, p. 199).

Lake Mountain [SANTA CLARA]: *peak,* 6 miles north-northwest of Pacheco Peak (lat. 37°05'15" N, long. 121°19'15" W; near SW cor. sec. 4, T 10 S, R 6 E); the peak is 0.25 mile south-southwest of Shaeirn Lake. Named on Pacheco Peak (1955) 7.5' quadrangle.

Lake Peralta: see **Lake Merritt** [ALAMEDA].

Lake Ranch Reservoir [SANTA CLARA]: *lake,* 2000 feet long, 2.25 miles east of Bielawski Mountain (lat. 37°13'10" N, long. 122° 03' W; sec. 23, T 8 S, R 2 W). Named on Castle Rock Ridge (1955) 7.5' quadrangle.

Lake Temescal [ALAMEDA]: *lake,* 0.25 mile long, behind a dam on Temescal Creek 3.25 miles northeast of downtown Oakland (lat. 37°50'50" N, long. 122°13'50" W). Named on Oakland East (1959) 7.5' quadrangle. Called Temescal Lake on Concord (1897) 15' quadrangle. The feature first was called Lake Chabot, for Anthony Chabot (Mosier and Mosier, p. 49-50). The dam that forms the lake was built in 1866 (Hoover, Rensch, and Rensch, p. 4).

La Laguna: see **Stivers Lagoon** [ALAMEDA].

La Laguna Seca [SANTA CLARA]: *land grant,* mainly between Coyote and Madrone. Named on Morgan Hill (1955), Mount Sizer (1955), and Santa Teresa Hills (1953) 7.5' quadrangles. Juan Alvirez received 4 leagues in 1834; L.C. Bull and others claimed 19,973 acres patented in 1865 (Cowan, p. 44). The lake called Laguna Seca is on the grant. The place also was known as Refugio de la Laguna Seca; after Alvirez sold the land to William Fisher in 1845, American travelers often referred to it as Fisher's Ranche (Arbuckle, p. 18). Postal authorities established Laguna Seca post office on the grant in 1853 and discontinued it in 1855 (Salley, p. 114).

Lambert Creek [SAN MATEO]: *stream,* flows 1.25 miles to Peters Creek 2.5 miles east-southeast of Mindego Hill (lat. 37°17'45" N, long. 122°11'05" W; sec. 27, T 7 S, R 3 W). Named on Mindego Hill (1961) 7.5' quadrangle. The name recalls Lambert Dornberger, who started a ranch at the head of the creek in the 1850's (Brown, p. 46).

Lamb Ridge [SANTA CLARA]: *ridge,* northwest-trending, 2.5 miles long, 5 miles northeast of Mount Day (lat. 37°28'15" N, long. 121° 37' W). Named on Eylar Mountain (1955) and Mount Day (1955) 7.5' quadrangles.

Lands End [SANTA CLARA]: *locality,* 4.5 miles southeast of Loma Prieta, where the land surface slopes abruptly into the canyon of Uvas Creek (lat. 37°03'55" N, long. 121°47'10" W; sec. 18, T 10 S, R 2 E). Named on Loma Prieta (1955) 7.5' quadrangle. Los Gatos (1919) 15' quadrangle shows a building situated at the end of the road leading to the place.

Lands End [SAN FRANCISCO]: *promontory,* 0.5 mile northeast of Point Lobos along the coast (lat. 37°47'20" N, long. 122°30'20" W). Named on San Francisco North (1956) 7.5' quadrangle.

Lands End: see **Point Bonita** [MARIN].

Land Slough: see **Tree Slough** [SOLANO].

Lane Hill [SAN MATEO]: *peak,* 5 miles southwest of La Honda (lat. 37°16'25" N, long. 122°20'25" W; near SE cor.sec. 36, T 7 S, R 5 W). Altitude 1240 feet. Named on La Honda (1961) 7.5' quadrangle.

Lang Canyon [ALAMEDA]: *canyon,* drained by a stream that flows 3 miles to Arroyo Valle 2.5 miles south-southwest of Mendenhall Springs (lat. 37°33'10" N, long. 121°39'55" W; sec. 29, T 4 S, R 3 E). Named on Cedar Mountain (1956) and Mendenhall Springs (1956) 7.5' quadrangles. The name commemorates Henry W. Lang, who worked in the neighborhood about 1900 (Mosier and Mosier, p. 50).

Langley Creek [SAN MATEO]: *stream,* flows 1.5 miles to La Honda Creek less than 1 mile north of La Honda (lat. 37°19'50" N, long. 122°16'10" W; near N line sec. 14, T 7 S, E 4 W); the stream heads near Langley Hill. Named on La Honda (1961) and Mindego Hill (1961) 7.5' quadrangles. The stream also was called Baker Creek for a rancher who had land along it during and after the 1860's (Brown, p. 46).

Langley Hill [SAN MATEO]: *peak,* 1.5 miles north-northwest of Mindego Hill (lat. 37°19'55" N, long. 122°14'25" W; near SW cor. sec. 7, T 7 S, R 3 W). Altitude 2256 feet. Named on Mindego Hill (1961) 7.5' quadrangle. Langley ranch was on the northeast side of the peak after 1857 (Brown, p. 46).

Lang's Landing: see **Patterson Landing** [ALAMEDA].

Lansdale: see **San Anselmo** [MARIN].

La Polka [SANTA CLARA]: *land grant,* 4.5 miles northeast of Gilroy. Named on Gilroy (1955) 7.5' quadrangle. Isabel Ortega received the land in 1833 as her share of San Ysidro

grant; Bernard Murphy acquired the land in 1849 and reportedly gave it the name of the popular dance—the land was patented to Martin J.C. Murphy in 1860 (Arbuckle, p. 19).

La Punta de las Barrancas blancas: see **Point Reyes** [MARIN] (1).

La Purisima Concepcion [SANTA CLARA]: *land grant,* 5 miles south of downtown Palo Alto. Named on Cupertino (1961), Mindego Hill (1961), Mountain View (1961), and Palo Alto (1961) 7.5' quadrangles. Jose Gorgonio and others received 1 league in 1840; Juana Briones claimed 4439 acres patented in 1871 (Cowan, p. 65). United States Board on Geographic Names (1933, p. 449) rejected the form "La Purissima Concepcion" for the name.

Larios Canyon [SANTA CLARA]: *canyon,* drained by a stream that flows nearly 3.5 miles to Coyote Lake 4.25 miles east-northeast of San Martin (lat. 37°07'10" N, long. 121°32'40" W; near E line sec. 29, T 9 S, R 4 E). Named on Gilroy (1955) and Mount Sizer (1955) 7.5' quadrangle.

Larios Peak [SANTA CLARA]: *peak,* 5.5 miles east-northeast of San Martin (lat. 37°07'20" N, long. 121°31'10" W; sec. 27, T 9 S, R 4 E); the peak is south of Larios Canyon. Altitude 2766 feet. Named on Gilroy (1955) 7.5' quadrangle.

Larkin's Landing: see **Mowry Landing** [ALAMEDA].

Larkspur [MARIN]: *city,* 3 miles south of downtown San Rafael (lat. 38°55'50" N, long. 122°32' W). Named on San Rafael (1954) 7.5' quadrangle. Postal authorities established Larkspur post office in 1891 (Frickstad, p. 88), and the city incorporated in 1908. Charles W. Wright bought the land in 1887 and laid out the town; Mrs. Wright is credited with naming the place for flowers in the neighborhood—she mistook native lupine for larkspur (Teather, p. 35).

Larkspur Creek [MARIN]: *stream,* flows 3.5 miles to Corte Madera Creek 2.5 miles south-southeast of downtown San Rafael (lat. 37° 56'25" N, long. 122°31'05" W). Named on San Rafael (1954) 7.5' quadrangle. Teather (p. 3) gave the alternate name "Arroyo Holon" for the stream, which drains Baltimore Canyon.

Larrabee Gulch [SANTA CLARA]: *canyon,* drained by a stream that flows 1.25 miles to Almaden Reservoir 1.25 miles south-southwest of New Almaden (lat. 37°09'30" N, long. 121°49'40" W). Named on Santa Teresa Hills (1953) 7.5' quadrangle.

Las Animas [SANTA CLARA]: *land grant,* mainly west and south of Gilroy. Named on Chittenden (1955), Gilroy (1955), Mount Madonna (1955), and Watsonville East (1955) 7.5' quadrangles. Mariano Castro received the land in 1802 and Josefa Romero de Castro received it in 1835; heirs of Jose Maria

Sanchez claimed 26,519 acres patented in 1873 (Cowan, p. 15). *Las Animas* means "the souls" in Spanish and refers to All Souls' Day; the grant also was known by the names "Carnadero" and "La Brea" (Gudde, 1949, p. 12). American pioneers often referred to the grant by the name of its augmentation, Sitio de la Brea or Cañada de la Brea (Arbuckle, p. 19).

Las Animas: see **Cañada de San Felipe y las Animas** [SANTA CLARA].

Las Animas Creek [SANTA CLARA]: *stream,* flows 6.25 miles to Anderson Lake nearly 4.5 miles east-southeast of Coyote (lat. 37° 12'15" N, long. 121°39'40" W); the stream is partly on Cañada de San Felipe y las Animas grant. Named on Lick Observatory (1955) and Morgan Hill (1955) 7.5' quadrangles.

Las Animas Hills: see **Cañada de San Felipe y las Animas** [SANTA CLARA].

Las Baulines [MARIN]: *land grant,* around Bolinas Lagoon. Named on Bolinas (1954) and San Rafael (1954) 7.5' quadrangles. Gregorio Briones received the land in 1846 and claimed 8911 acres patented in 1866 (Cowan, p. 18).

Las Bolsas del Hambre: see **Cañada del Hambre y las Bolsas** [CONTRA COSTA].

Las Cuevas: see **Brushy Peak** [ALAMEDA].

Las Gallinas [MARIN]: *locality,* 6.25 miles south-southeast of downtown Novato (lat. 38°01'15" N, long. 122°32'15" W); the place is on San Pedro Santa Margarita y las Gallinas grant. Named on Novato (1954) 7.5' quadrangle.

Las Gallinas: see **San Pedro Santa Margarita y las Gallinas** [MARIN].

Lash Lighter Basin [SAN FRANCISCO]: *water feature,* 4.5 miles east of Mount Davidson along San Francisco Bay north of Hunters Point (lat. 37'44'20" N, long. 122°22' W). Named on Hunters Point (1956, photorevised 1980) 7.5' quadrangle. United States Board on Geographic Names (1976b, p. 2) gave the name "Lighter Basin" as a variant.

Las Juntas [CONTRA COSTA]:
(1) *land grant,* extends from the city of Walnut Creek to Martinez. Named on Benicia (1959), Briones Valley (1959), Vine Hill (1959), and Walnut Creek (1959) 7.5' quadrangles. William Welsh received 3 leagues in 1844; Welsh's estate claimed 13,293 acres patented in 1870 (Cowan, p. 43).
(2) *locality,* 2 miles north of Walnut Creek civic center along Southern Pacific Railroad (lat. 37°55'55" N, long. 122°03'10" W); the place is on Las Juntas grant. Named on Walnut Creek (1959) 7.5' quadrangle. Called Oakleigh on Concord (1915) 15' quadrangle.

Las Lagrimas: see **Edenvale** [SANTA CLARA].

Las Llagas de Nuestro Padre San Francisco: see **San Francisco de las Llagas** [SANTA CLARA].

Las Lomas Bajas: see **New Almaden** [SANTA CLARA].

Las Papas: see **Twin Peaks** [SAN FRANCISCO].

Las Papas Hill: see **Twin Peaks** [SAN FRANCISCO].

Las Posita Creek: see **Arroyo Las Positas** [ALAMEDA].

Las Positas [ALAMEDA]: *land grant,* at and near Livermore. Named on Altamont (1953), Livermore (1961), and Tassajara (1953) 7.5' quadrangles. Salvic Pacheco received 2 leagues in 1839; Jose Noriega and Robert Livermore claimed 8880 acres patented in 1872 (Cowan, p. 63; Cowan used the form "Pozitas" for the name).

Las Pulgas: see **Pulgas** [SAN MATEO].

Las Tampas Peak: see **Las Trampas Peak** [CONTRA COSTA].

Las Trampas Creek [CONTRA COSTA]: *stream,* flows 11.5 miles to join San Ramon Creek and form Walnut Creek (1) near Walnut Creek civic center (lat. 37°53'50" N, long. 122°03'30" W). Named on Las Trampas Ridge (1959) and Walnut Creek (1959) 7.5' quadrangles.

Las Trampas Peak [CONTRA COSTA]: *peak,* 3.5 miles west-northwest of Danville (lat. 37°50' N, long. 122°03'50" W; sec. 22, T 1 S, R 2 W); the peak is near the northwest end of Las Trampas Ridge. Altitude 1827 feet. Named on Las Trampas Ridge (1959) 7.5' quadrangle. United States Board on Geographic Names (1933, p. 450) rejected the names "Las Tampas Peak" and "Sugarloaf Peak" for the feature.

Las Trampas Ridge [CONTRA COSTA]: *ridge,* northwest-trending, 6 miles long, center 2 miles west-southwest of Danville (lat. 37°48'45" N, long. 122°01'35" W). Named on Diablo (1953) and Las Trampas Ridge (1959) 7.5' quadrangles. Gudde (1969, p. 173) reported testimony that traps were set on or near the ridge to catch elk—*trampa* means "trap" or "snare" in Spanish.

Las Uvas [SANTA CLARA]: *land grant,* west of Morgan Hill and San Martin. Named on Loma Prieta (1955), Morgan Hill (1955), Mount Madona (1955), and Santa Teresa Hills (1953) 7.5' quadrangles. Lorenzo Pineda received the land in 1842; M.J.C. Murphy claimed 11,080 acres patented in 1860 (Cowan, p. 106). The name is from the abundance of wild grapes along watercourses in the neighborhood—*las uvas* means "the grapes" in Spanish (Arbuckle, p. 21).

Laurel Creek [ALAMEDA]: *stream,* flows less than 1 mile to Amador Valley 0.5 mile southeast of Dublin (lat. 37°41'30" N, long. 121°55'50" W). Named on Dublin (1961) 7.5' quadrangle.

Laurel Creek [SAN MATEO]: *stream,* flows 2.5 miles to lowlands along San Francisco Bay 2.5 miles southeast of downtown San Mateo (lat. 37°32'10" N, long. 122°17'45" W). Named on San Mateo (1956) 7.5' quadrangle. The stream was called Arroyo de los Laureles in Spanish times, and Laureles Creek in early American times (Brown, p. 47).

Laurel Creek [SOLANO]: *stream,* flows 4 miles to lowlands 3 miles north-northeast of Fairfield (lat. 38°17'15" N, long. 122°01'10" W). Named on Fairfield North (1951) and Fairfield South (1949) 7.5' quadrangles.

Laurel Creek: see **Cottrell** [SAN MATEO].

Laurel Dell Camp [CONTRA COSTA]: *locality,* nearly 1 mile west-southwest of Mount Diablo (lat. 37°52'30" N, long. 121°55'35" W; sec. 1, T 1 S, R 1 W). Named on Clayton (1953) 7.5' quadrangle.

Laurel Dell Campground [MARIN]: *locality,* 3.5 miles east-northeast of Bolinas (lat. 37°55'25" N, long. 122°37'35" W). Named on Bolinas (1954) 7.5' quadrangle.

Laureles Creek: see **Laurel Creek** [SAN MATEO].

Laurel Hill [SANTA CLARA]: *peak,* 3.5 miles west of Madrone (lat. 37°09'15" N, long. 121°44' W). Altitude 1145 feet. Named on Morgan Hill (1955) 7.5' quadrangle.

Lauterwasser Creek [CONTRA COSTA]: *stream,* flows 2.5 miles to San Pablo Creek 1 mile northwest of Orinda (lat. 37°53'25" N, long. 122°11'40" W). Named on Briones Valley (1959) 7.5' quadrangle. The name commemorates F.P. Lauterwasser, an early settler in the neighborhood (Gudde, 1969, p. 174).

Laverne: see **Mill Valley** [MARIN] (2).

Lawler Ravine [CONTRA COSTA]: *canyon,* drained by a stream that flows 2.25 miles to lowlands along Suisun Bay 3 miles west-southwest of Pittsburg (lat. 38°01'10" N, long. 121°56'05" W). Named on Clayton (1953) and Honker Bay (1953) 7.5' quadrangles.

Lawndale: see **Colma** [SAN MATEO].

Lawrence [SANTA CLARA]: *locality,* 6.5 miles west-northwest of downtown San Jose along Southern Pacific Railroad (lat. 37°22'15" N, long. 121°59'45" W; sec. 32, T 6 S, R 1 W). Named on San Jose West (1961) 7.5' quadrangle. Postal authorities established Lawrence post office in 1887 and discontinued it in 1935; the name is for Albert C. Lawrence, a settler in the 1850's (Salley, p. 120).

Lawson Hill [CONTRA COSTA]: *peak,* 4.5 miles north of Orinda (lat. 37°56'35" N, long. 122°11'30" W). Named on Briones Valley (1959) 7.5' quadrangle.

Ledgewood Creek [SOLANO]: *stream,* heads in Napa County and flows 12 miles to marsh 1.5 miles south-southwest of downtown Fairfield in Solano County (lat. 38°13'45" N, long. 122°03'15" W). Named on Fairfield North (1951) and Fairfield South (1949) 7.5' quadrangles.

Leesley and Dexter Canyon: see **Dexter Canyon** [SANTA CLARA].

Le Franc: see **Campbell** [SANTA CLARA].

Leisure Town [SOLANO]: *locality,* 3 miles east-northeast of downtown Vacaville (lat. 38°22'10" N, long. 121°56'45" W). Named on Allendale (1953, photorevised 1968 and 1973) and Elmira (1953, photorevised 1980) 7.5' quadrangles.

Lejuanjelua Bay: see **Point San Quentin** [MARIN].

Leona [ALAMEDA]: *locality,* 5 miles east-southeast of downtown Oakland (lat. 37°46'55" N, long. 122°10'40" W). Named on Concord (1915) 15' quadrangle.

Leona Creek: see **Lion Creek** [ALAMEDA].

Leon Creek: see **Arroyo Leon** [SAN MATEO].

Leslie: see **Homestead** [SAN MATEO].

Lewis: see **Mococo** [CONTRA COSTA]; **Mount Lewis** [SANTA CLARA].

Lewis Gulch: see **Copper Mine Gulch** [MARIN].

Lexington [SANTA CLARA]: *locality,* 2 miles south of Los Gatos along Los Gatos Creek (lat. 37°11'50" N, long. 121°59'15" W; sec. 32, T 8 S, R 1 W). Named on Los Gatos (1919) 15' quadrangle. Water of Lexington Reservoir now covers the site. Postal authorities established Lexington post office in 1861 and discontinued it in 1873 (Frickstad, p. 174). Zachariah Jones bought a sawmill at the place and laid out a town that he called Jones Mill, but in 1860 he sold the mill and 480 acres; John P. Hennings bought some of the property and changed the name of the community to Lexington for his home town of Lexington, Kentucky (Bruntz, p. 7).

Lexington Reservoir [SANTA CLARA]: *lake,* 2.5 miles long, behind a dam on Los Gatos Creek 1.5 miles south-southwest of Los Gatos (lat. 37°12'05" N, long. 121°59'20" W; sec. 29, T 8 S, R 1 W); water of the lake covers the site of Lexington. Named on Castle Rock Ridge (1955) and Los Gatos (1953) 7.5' quadrangles.

Leyden Creek [ALAMEDA]: *stream,* flows 2.5 miles to Alameda Creek 6.5 miles south-southeast of Sunol (lat. 37°30'35" N, long. 121°49'40" W; sec. 11, T 5 S, R 1 E). Named on La Costa Valley (1960) 7.5' quadrangle. The name commemorates James Lydon, who settled near the mouth of the stream in the 1870's (Mosier and Mosier, p. 51).

Liberty [MARIN]: *locality,* 4.5 miles northeast of Bolinas along Lagunitas Creek (lat. 37°57'15" N, long. 122°37'30" W). Named on Tamalpais (1897) 15' quadrangle. Water of Alpine Lake now covers the site. Vincent Liberty built a house for his family and accommodations for guests at the place in 1881 (Fairley, 1985, p. 38).

Liberty Cut [SOLANO]: *water feature,* extends south from Yolo County into Solano County, where it joins Prospect Slough 9 miles north of Rio Vista (lat. 38°17'10" N, long. 121°39'50" W); the feature is east of Liberty Island. Named on Liberty Island (1978) 7.5' quadrangle.

Liberty Farms [SOLANO]: *locality,* 10.5 miles north of Rio Vista (lat. 38°18'45" N, long. 121°41'35" W). Named on Liberty Island (1978) 7.5' quadrangle. Postal authorities established Liberty Farms post office in 1952 (Frickstad, p. 192).

Liberty Gulch [MARIN]: *canyon,* drained by a stream that flows less than 1 mile to Alpine Lake 4.5 miles northeast of Bolinas (lat. 37° 57'35" N, long. 122°37'40" W); the place called Liberty was near the mouth of the canyon. Named on Bolinas (1954) 7.5' quadrangle. The feature first was called Curtis Gulch, for Loomis Curtis, who had a dairy ranch there in the 1850's before Vincent Liberty took over the property (Fairly, 1985, p. 38).

Liberty Island [SOLANO]: *area,* 9 miles north of Rio Vista in Yolo Bypass on Solano-Yolo county line, mainly in Solano County (lat. 38°17' N, long. 121°40'45" W). Named on Liberty Island (1978) and Rio Vista (1978) 7.5' quadrangles.

Liberty Island Ferry [SOLANO]: *locality,* 5.5 miles north of Rio Vista along Cache Slough (lat. 38°14'20" N, long. 121°41' W); the place is at the south end of Liberty Island. Named on Rio Vista (1978) 7.5' quadrangle.

Libfarm [SOLANO]: *locality,* 6.5 miles east-southeast of Dixon along Sacramento Northern Railroad (lat. 38°24'05" N, long. 121° 42'45" W; near NE cor. sec. 2, T 6 N, R 2 E). Named on Saxon (1952) 7.5' quadrangle.

Lick [SANTA CLARA]: *locality,* 4 miles southeast of downtown San Jose along Southern Pacific Railroad, where a rail line branches to Alamitos (lat. 37°17'10" N, long. 121°50'40" W). Named on San Jose East (1961) 7.5' quadrangle. Called Hillsdale on San Jose (1899) 15' quadrangle. Postal authorities established Hillsdale post office in 1887 and discontinued it in 1899 (Frickstad, p. 173). A stopping place called Four Mile House, named for its distance from San Jose, was near the site of Hillsdale before construction of the railroad (*San Jose Mercury-News, California Today Magazine,* October 23, 1977).

Lighter Basin: see **Lash Lighter Basin** [SAN FRANCISCO].

Lilienthal: see **Camp Lilienthal** [MARIN].

Lily Gulch [MARIN]: *canyon,* drained by a stream that flows less than 1 mile to Alpine Lake 4 miles northeast of Bolinas (lat. 37° 57'10" N, long. 122°37'55" W). Named on Bolinas (1954) 7.5' quadrangle.

Lily Lake [MARIN]: *lake,* 50 feet long, 4 miles northeast of Bolinas (lat. 37°57'15" N, long. 122°38'05" W); the feature is in Lily Gulch. Named on Bolinas (1954) 7.5' quadrangle.

Limantour Spit [MARIN]: *relief feature,* sand spit, 2.5 miles long, that separates Estero de Limantour from Drakes Bay 7 miles east-northeast of the lighthouse at Point Reyes (lat. 38°01'45" N, long. 122°54'15" W). Named on Drakes Bay (1953) 7.5' quadrangle. The name recalls Jose Yves Limantour, who wrecked the bark *Ayacucho* on the spit in 1841 (Teather, p. 36-37).

Lime Hill: see **Calera Valley** [SAN MATEO].

Limekiln Canyon [SANTA CLARA]:
(1) *canyon,* drained by a stream that flows 2.25 miles to Lexington Reservoir 1.5 miles south of Los Gatos (lat. 37°12'05" N, long. 121°58'35" W). Named on Los Gatos (1953) 7.5' quadrangle.
(2) *canyon,* drained by a stream that flows 1.25 miles to Llagas Creek 3.25 miles south-southeast of New Almaden (lat. 37°08'20" N, long. 121°47'05" W). Named on Santa Teresa Hills (1953) 7.5' quadrangle.

Lime Point [MARIN]: *promontory,* 2.25 miles south of downtown Sausalito along San Francisco Bay (lat. 37°49'30" N, long. 122°28'40" W). Named on San Francisco North (1956) 7.5' quadrangle. Called Lime Rks. on Ringgold's (1850a) map. Ayala named the feature Punta de San Carlos in 1775 for his ship (Galvin, p. 85; Wagner, H.R., p. 497).

Lime Point Military Reservation: see **Fort Baker Military Reservation** [MARIN].

Limerick: see **San Ramon** [CONTRA COSTA] (3).

Lime Ridge [CONTRA COSTA]: *ridge,* north-to northwest-trending, 4 miles long, 6 miles northwest of Mount Diablo (lat. 37°56'30" N, long. 121°59'30" W). Named on Clayton (1953) and Walnut Creek (1959) 7.5' quadrangles. Burned lime was produced from limestone that crops out on the ridge (Laizure, 1927a, p. 15).

Lime Rocks: see **Lime Point** [MARIN].

Lincoln: see **Campbell** [SANTA CLARA].

Linda Mar: see **Pedro Valley** [SAN MATEO].

Lindsey Slough [SOLANO]: *water feature,* joins Cache Slough 6 miles north of Rio Vista (lat. 38°14'40" N, long. 121°41'20" W). Named on Dozier (1952), Liberty Island (1978), and Rio Vista (1978) 7.5' quadrangles.

Lingos Landing [SOLANO]: *locality,* 4.5 miles south-southwest of Denverton along Montezuma Slough (lat. 38°09'35" N, long. 121° 55'30" W). Named on Denverton (1953) 7.5' quadrangle.

Lion Canyon [SANTA CLARA]: *canyon,* drained by a stream that flows 1 mile to Grizzly Creek 4 miles south-southeast of Isabel Valley (lat. 37°15'30" N, long. 121°30'35" W; sec. 11, T 8 S, R 4 E). Named on Isabel Valley (1955) 7.5' quadrangle.

Lion Creek [ALAMEDA]: *stream,* enters San Leandro Bay 5 miles southeast of downtown Oakland (lat. 37°45'05" N, long. 122°12'40" W). Named on Oakland East (1959) 7.5' quadrangle, which does not show the stream through the urban area. Called East Creek on Concord (1897) 15' quadrangle. The stream first was called Arroyo del Leona, and then Leona Creek—*leona* means "lion" in Spanish (Mosier and Mosier, p. 51). A promontory at the mouth of Lion Creek was given the name "Garretson Point" in 1982 to honor Frederick Van Hon Garretson, a reporter for *Oakland Tribune*, who publicized the need for saving San Francisco Bay (Mosier and Mosier, p. 39).

Lions Peak [SANTA CLARA]: *peak*, 5 miles south-southeast of Morgan Hill (lat. 37°03'25" N, long. 121°37'50" W). Named on Mount Madonna (1955) 7.5' quadrangle. United States Board on Geographic Names (1973a, p. 2) approved the name "Day Creek" for a stream that heads east of Lions Peak and flows 2 miles to an unnamed stream 2.2 miles northwest of Gilroy (lat. 37°02'09" N, long. 121°35'45" W); the name "Day" commemorates an early landowner in the neighborhood.

Little Arthur Creek [SANTA CLARA]: *stream*, flows 6.25 miles to Uvas Creek 3 miles eastnortheast of Mount Madonna (lat. 37°01'40" N, long. 121°39'20" W). Named on Loma Prieta (1955) and Mount Madonna (1955) 7.5' quadrangles.

Little Boulder Creek [SAN MATEO]: *stream*, heads in Santa Cruz County and flows 1.5 miles to Pescadero Creek nearly 7 miles southsoutheast of Mindego Hill (lat. 37°13'05" N, long. 122°11'05" W; sec. 22, T 8 S, R 3 W). Named on Big Basin (1955) 7.5' quadrangle.

Little Bull Valley [CONTRA COSTA]: *canyon*, 1 mile long, 3 miles west-northwest of Martinez (lat. 38°02' N, long. 122°11'05" W); the feature is 0.5 mile southeast of Big Bull Valley. Named on Benicia (1959) 7.5' quadrangle.

Little Butano Creek [SAN MATEO]: *stream*, flows 4.5 miles to Butano Creek 4.5 miles north of Franklin Point (lat. 37°13' N, long. 122°21'05" W). Named on Franklin Point (1955) 7.5' quadrangle. Brown (p. 48) noted that an area located where Little Butano Creek leaves the highlands is called Little Butano Flat.

Little Butano Flat: see **Little Butano Creek** [SAN MATEO].

Little Carson Creek [MARIN]: *stream*, flows 2 miles to Lagunitas Creek 3.5 miles northnortheast of Bolinas (lat. 37°57'50" N, long. 122°39'50" W); the junction with Lagunitas Creek now is in Kent Lake. Named on Mount Tamalpais (1950) 15' quadrangle. On a map of 1873, the canyon of the stream is called Puerto Zuelo Lagunitas (Gudde, 1949, p. 180).

Little Chicken Hollow [SAN MATEO]: *canyon*, 1 mile long, 4.25 miles west-southwest of La Honda on the upper reaches of Honsinger Creek (lat. 37°17'15" N, long. 122°20'15" W); the canyon is north of Big Chicken Hollow. Named on La Honda (1961) 7.5' quadrangle.

Little Coyote Creek [SANTA CLARA]: *stream*, flows nearly 5 miles to Middle Fork Coyote Creek 2.25 miles south of Mount Sizer (lat.

37°10'55" N, long. 121°30'20" W; sec. 2, T 9 S, R 4 E). Named on Mount Sizer (1955) 7.5' quadrangle.

Little Coyote Point [SAN MATEO]: *promontory*, 3.5 miles east of downtown San Mateo along San Francisco Bay on Brewer Island (lat. 37°34'25" N, long. 122°15'50" W; sec. 23, T 4 S, R 4 W). Named on San Mateo (1956) 7.5' quadrangle. San Mateo (1915) 15' quadrangle shows Guano Island at the place.

Little Duck Slough [SOLANO]: *water feature*, extends east from Suisun (present Suisun City) 1 mile south-southeast of downtown Fairfield (lat. 38°14'10" N, long. 122°02'10" W). Named on Suisun (1918) special quadrangle.

Little Hastings Tract [SOLANO]: *area*, 6.5 miles north of Rio Vista (lat. 38°15' N, long. 121°41'30" W); Wright Cut separates the area from Hastings Tract. Named on Liberty Island (1978) and Rio Vista (1978) 7.5' quadrangles.

Little Holland Tract [SOLANO]: *area*, 11 miles north of Rio Vista in Yolo Bypass on Solano-Yolo county line (lat. 38°19' N, long. 121°39'15" W). Named on Liberty Island (1978) 7.5' quadrangle.

Little Honker Bay [SOLANO]: *bay*, 3 miles south-southwest of Denverton off of Nurse Slough (lat. 38°10'55" N, long. 121°54'45" W). Named on Denverton (1953) 7.5' quadrangle.

Little Lagoon [SAN MATEO]: *lake*, 150 feet long, 2.5 miles southwest of La Honda (lat. 37°17'40" N, long. 122°18'30" W; sec. 28, T 7 S, R 4 W); the lake is 650 feet northeast of Big Lagoon. Named on La Honda (1961) 7.5' quadrangle.

Little Llagas Creek [SANTA CLARA]: *stream*, flows 8.5 miles to Llagas Creek 2.5 miles southeast of San Martin (lat. 37°03'35" N, long. 121°34'25" W). Named on Gilroy (1955) and Mount Madonna (1955) 7.5' quadrangles. United States Board on Geographic Names (1973a, p. 2-3) approved names for several streams tributary to Little Llagas Creek: Church Creek, named for a pioneer landowner in the region, flows 3 miles to Little Llagas Creek 2 miles southeast of San Martin (lat. 37°04'05" N, long. 121°34'42" W); San Martin Creek flows 3.2 miles to Little Llagas Creek 1.2 miles west of San Martin (lat. 37°04'51" N, long. 121°35'15" W); Center Creek flows 2 miles to San Martin Creek 1.4 miles east-northeast of San Martin (lat. 37°15'25" N, long. 121° 35'01" W); and New Creek flows 2.5 miles to San Martin Creek 1.3 miles east of San Martin (lat. 37°05'04" N, long. 121°35'02" W).

Little Medora Lake [SOLANO]: *lake*, 1900 feet long, 11 miles north-northeast of Rio Vista in Yolo Basin (present Yolo Bypass) (lat. 38°18'25" N, long. 122°37'55" W); the lake is 0.5 mile east-southeast of Madora Lake.

Named on Cache Slough (1916) 7.5' quadrangle.

Little Mile Rock [SAN FRANCISCO]: *rock,* less than 1 mile north-northeast of Point Lobos, and 1950 feet offshore at Lands End (lat. 37°47'35" N, long. 122°30'30" W); the feature is 100 feet southeast of Mile Rock. Named on San Francisco North (1956) 7.5' quadrangle. This rock and Mile Rock together are called Mile Rocks on San Francisco (1915) 15' quadrangle.

Little Mountain [MARIN]: *peak,* 3 miles west of downtown Novato (lat. 38°07' N, long. 122°37'45" W). Named on Novato (1954) and San Geronimo (1954) 7.5' quadrangles.

Little Peak Canyon [SANTA CLARA]: *canyon,* drained by a stream that flows nearly 2 miles to San Benito County 15 miles east-southeast of Gilroy (lat. 36°57'35" N, long. 121°18'05" W). Named on Three Sisters (1954) 7.5' quadrangle.

Little Pine Creek [CONTRA COSTA]: *stream,* flows 3.25 miles to Pine Creek 4.5 miles west of Mount Diablo (lat. 37°53'45" N, long. 121°59'30" W). Named on Clayton (1953) 7.5' quadrangle.

Little Rough Gulch [SANTA CLARA]: *canyon,* drained by a stream that flows nearly 2 miles to Rough Gulch 2.5 miles north-northwest of Gilroy Hot Springs (lat. 37°08'25" N, long. 121°29'50" W; sec. 23, T 9 S, R 4 E). Named on Mississippi Creek (1955) and Mount Sizer (1955) 7.5' quadrangles.

Littles Point: see **Commodore Jones Point** [SOLANO].

Little Uvas Creek [SANTA CLARA]: *stream,* flows 5 miles to Uvas Creek 6.25 miles north of Mount Madonna (lat. 37°06'05" N, long. 121°43'15" W). Named on Loma Prieta (1955) and Mount Madonna (1955) 7.5' quadrangles.

Live Oak Camp [CONTRA COSTA]: *locality,* 2.5 miles south-southwest of Mount Diablo (lat. 37°51'05" N, long. 121°56'10" W; sec. 14, T 1 S, R 1 W). Named on Diablo (1953) 7.5' quadrangle.

Live Oak Creek [SANTA CLARA]: *stream,* flows 3.25 miles to Llagas Creek nearly 2.5 miles northeast of Gilroy (lat. 37°02'10" N, long. 121°32'35" W). Named on Gilroy (1955) 7.5' quadrangle.

Livermore [ALAMEDA]: *city,* 27 miles east-southeast of Oakland (lat. 37°40'55" N, long. 121°46' W); the city is in Livermore Valley. Named on Livermore (1961) 7.5' quadrangle. The name is for Robert Livermore, an English sailor who settled at the site in the 1830's; his home there was known as Livermore's after the American acquisition of California (Gudde, 1949, p. 189). Postal authorities established Livermore Ranch post office in 1851 and discontinued it in 1853 (Frickstad, p. 2). Alphonso Ladd built a hotel within the present city limits of Livermore in 1855 and the community that grew around the hotel was called Laddville, but when the railroad came through Livermore Valley, a station was built about 0.5 mile west of Laddville, and there in 1869 William M. Mendenhall had the present city of Livermore surveyed (Hoover, Rensch, and Rensch, p. 14-15). The first post office at present Livermore was called Nottingham, for Robert Livermore's home town in England (Gudde, 1949, p. 189); postal authorities established it in 1869 and changed the name to Livermore in 1870 (Frickstad, p. 3). The city incorporated in 1876. Postal authorities established Ann post office 11 miles southeast of Livermore in 1896 and discontinued it the same year (Salley, p. 8). A Military installation called Livermore Naval Air Station, and also called Wagoner Field, opened east of Livermore in 1942; the site now is occupied by Lawrence Livermore Laboratory (Mosier and Mosier, p. 51).

Livermore: see **Mount Caroline Livermore** [MARIN].

Livermore Naval Air Station: see **Livermore** [ALAMEDA].

Livermore Ranch: see **Livermore** [ALAMEDA].

Livermore's Pass: see **Altamont Pass** [ALAMEDA].

Livermore's Plain: see **Livermore Valley** [ALAMEDA].

Livermore Valley [ALAMEDA]: *valley,* at and near Livermore. Named on Altamont (1953) and Livermore (1961) 7.5' quadrangles. Williamson (1855, p. 10) called the feature Livermore's valley, and Parke (p. 7) called it Livermore's plain. Crespi called the place Santa Coleta in 1772, and it was known as El Valle de San Jose when Robert Livermore settled there in 1837 (Mosier and Mosier, p. 52). The range north of Livermore Valley was called Lomas de las Cuevas on a map of 1839 for the caves in weathered sandstone there— *lomas de las cuevas* means "small hills of the caves" in Spanish (Mosier and Mosier, p. 52).

Llagas: see **Llagas Creek** [SANTA CLARA].

Llagas Creek [SANTA CLARA]: *stream,* flows 30 miles to Pajaro River 4.5 miles southeast of Gilroy (lat. 36°57'50" N, long. 121°30'25" W). Named on Chittenden (1955), Gilroy (1955), Loma Prieta (1955), Morgan Hill (1955), Mount Madonna (1955), and Santa Teresa Hills (1953) 7.5' quadrangles. Called Arroyo de las Llagas on a diseño of Las Animas grant (Becker, 1969). West Branch flows 7 miles to Miller Slough at Gilroy and is named on Gilroy (1955) 7.5' quadrangle— Miller Slough joins Llagas Creek 2.25 miles east-southeast of Gilroy. California Mining Bureau's (1917b) map shows a place called Llagas located near Llagas Creek about where Morgan Hill (1917) 15' quadrangle shows Llagas school situated 4.25 west of Madrone (lat. 37°09'05" N, long. 121°44'40" W). Postal authorities established Llagas post office in 1892 and discontinued it in 1911 (Frickstad, p. 174). United States Board on Geographic Names (1973a, p. 3) approved names for several streams tributary to Llagas Creek: Panther Creek, which flows 2.3 miles to Llagas Creek 2.5 miles north-northeast of Gilroy (lat. 37°02'31" N, long. 121°32'57" W); South Panther Creek, which flows 1.5 miles nearly to Panther Creek 2.7 miles north-northeast of Gilroy (lat. 37°02'37" N, long. 121°32'50" W)—on Gilroy (1955) 7.5' quadrangle the stream stops short of Panther Creek, but on Morgan Hill (1917) 15' quadrangle it connects with Llagas Creek; Skillet Creek, which flows 3 miles to Llagas Creek 2.8 miles north of Gilroy (lat. 37°02'58" N, long. 121°33'35" W); and Rucker Creek, which flows 2.5 miles to Skillet Creek 3 miles north of Gilroy (lat. 37°03'03" N, long. 121°33'34" W).

Llagas Creek: see **Little Llagas Creek** [SANTA CLARA].

Llano de las Llagas: see **Santa Clara Valley** [SANTA CLARA].

Llano del Tequisquita [SANTA CLARA]: *land grant,* mainly in San Benito County, but extends into Santa Clara County 7 miles east of Gilroy. Named on Gilroy Hot Springs (1955) and San Felipe (1955) 7.5' quadrangles. Jose Maria Sanchez received the land in 1835; Vicente Sanchez and others claimed 16,016 acres patented in 1871 (Cowan, p. 102; Cowan listed the grant under the name "Tequisquite"). Arbuckle (p. 23) used the form "Llano del Tequisquite" for the name.

Lleguas Valley: see **Sheridan Creek** [ALAMEDA].

Lloyd Lake [SAN FRANCISCO]: *lake,* 500 feet long, nearly 2 miles east-southeast of Point Lobos (lat. 37°46'15" N, long. 122°28'50" W). Named on San Francisco North (1956) 7.5' quadrangle.

Lobatos Creek: see **Lobitos Creek** [SAN MATEO].

Lobitas Creek: see **Lobitos Creek** [SAN MATEO].

Lobitos [SAN MATEO]: *locality,* 5.5 miles south-southeast of downtown Half Moon Bay (lat. 37°23' N, long. 122°23'55" W); the place is along Lobitos Creek. Named on Half Moon Bay (1961) 7.5' quadrangle.

Lobitos Creek [SAN MATEO]: *stream,* flows 5 miles to the sea 6 miles south of downtown Half Moon Bay (lat. 37°23'30" N, long. 122°24'30" W). Named on Half Moon Bay (1961) and Woodside (1961) 7.5' quadrangles. United States Board on Geographic Names (1933, p. 468) rejected the forms "Lobatos," "Lobitas," and "Lobitus" for the name. The stream was called Arroyo de los Lobitos in Spanish times (Gudde, 1949, p. 190).

Lobitus Creek: see **Lobitos Creek** [SAN MATEO].

Lobos: see **Point Lobos** [SAN FRANCISCO].

Lobos Creek [SAN FRANCISCO]: *stream,* flows nearly 1 mile to the sea 1.5 miles southsouthwest of Fort Point (lat. 37°47'25" N, long. 122°29'05" W). Named on San Francisco North (1956) 7.5' quadrangle. Anza called the stream Arroyo del Puerto in 1776 (Davidson, p. 119).

Lobos Rock [SAN FRANCISCO]: *rock,* 0.5 mile north-northeast of Point Lobos, and 700 feet offshore (lat. 37°47'15" N, long. 122°30'35" W). Named on San Francisco North (1956) 7.5' quadrangle.

Locks Creek [SAN MATEO]: *stream,* flows nearly 2 miles to Frenchmans Creek 4 miles southeast of Montara Knob (lat. 37° 31' N, long. 122°25'55" W; sec. 8, T 5 S, R 5 W). Named on Montara Mountain (1956) 7.5' quadrangle. Called Lock Creek on San Mateo (1915) 15' quadrangle. John B. Lock had a ranch near the stream in 1864 (Brown, p. 49).

Locust [CONTRA COSTA]: *locality,* 1 mile north of present Walnut Creek civic center along Oakland Antioch and Eastern Railroad (lat. 37°55' N, long. 122°03'50" W). Named on Concord (1915) 15' quadrangle. Concord (1943) 15' quadrangle shows a place called Walden at or near the site.

Locust: see **Mill Valley** [MARIN] (2).

Loma Alta [MARIN]: *peak,* 6 miles southsouthwest of downtown Novato (lat. 38°01'30" N, long. 122°36'40" W). Altitude 1592 feet. Named on Novato (1954) 7.5' quadrangle.

Loma Alta: see **Telegraph Hill** [SAN FRANCISCO].

Loma Alta Cove: see **Yerba Buena Cove**, under **Telegraph Hill** [SAN FRANCISCO].

Loma Chiquita [SANTA CLARA]: *peak,* 1.25 miles east-southeast of Loma Prieta (lat. 37°06'20" N, long. 121°49'20" W; sec. 35, T 9 S, R 1 E). Altitude 2607 feet. Named on Loma Prieta (1955) 7.5' quadrangle.

Loma Mar [SAN MATEO]: *village,* nearly 4 miles south-southwest of La Honda along Pescadero Creek (lat. 37°16'20" N, long. 122° 18'15" W). Named on La Honda (1961) 7.5' quadrangle. Postal authorities established Loma Mar post office in 1931 (Frickstad, p. 168).

Loma Prieta [SANTA CLARA]: *peak,* 15 miles south of downtown San Jose (lat. 37°06'40" N, long. 121°50'35" W). Altitude 3791 feet. Named on Loma Prieta (1955) 7.5' quadrangle. Called Loma Prieto on Goddard's (1857) map. United States Coast Survey used the peak as a primary triangulation station in 1854 and named it in honor of Alexander D. Bache, superintendent of the survey at the time (Gudde, 1949, p. 192). Whitney (p. 65) used the name "Mount Bache," but pointed out that *loma prieta,* which means "black mountain" in Spanish, was the name commonly given by the Spanish-speaking population to any high chaparral-covered point that appears black from a distance, including this one. On some maps, the name "Loma Prieta" applies mistakenly to present Mount Umunhum (Hoover, Rensch, and Rensch, p. 457).

Lomas de las Cuevas: see **Livermore Valley** [ALAMEDA].

Lomas Muertas: see **Buri Buri Ridge** [SAN MATEO].

Lomita [SANTA CLARA]: *peak,* 3.5 miles south of Mount Umunhum on Santa Clara-Santa Cruz county line (lat. 37°06'40" N, long. 121°53'40" W). Named on Laurel (1955) 7.5' quadrangle.

Lomita de la Linares: see **Rucker** [SANTA CLARA].

Lomita Park [SAN MATEO]: *district,* 1 mile northwest of downtown Millbrae in San Bruno (lat. 37°37' N, long. 122°24'15" W). Named on Montara Mountain (1956) 7.5' quadrangle. Postal authorities established Belmae Park post office in 1927, changed the name to Lomita Park in 1933, and discontinued it in 1957—the name "Belmae" was coined from the names "Belmont" and "Millbrae" (Salley, p. 18, 125).

Lone Hill [SANTA CLARA]: *hill,* 4 miles east-northeast of Los Gatos (lat. 37°14'40" N, long. 121°54'35" W; near NW cor. sec. 18, T 8 S, R 1 E). Named on Los Gatos (1953) 7.5' quadrangle. Housing development has destroyed the feature.

Lone Lake [SANTA CLARA]: *lake,* 250 feet long, 6.25 miles west-southwest of Mount Sizer (lat. 37°11'35" N, long. 121°37'20" W). Named on Mount Sizer (1955) 7.5' quadrangle. Called Lost Lake on Morgan Hill (1917) 15' quadrangle.

Lone Mountain [SAN FRANCISCO]: *peak,* 2.5 miles south-southeast of Fort Point (lat. 37°46'45" N, long. 122°27'05" W). Named on San Francisco North (1956) 7.5' quadrangle.

Lone Point: see **Long Point** [SANTA CLARA].

Lone Tree Creek [MARIN]: *stream,* flows nearly 1.5 miles to the sea 4.5 miles east-southeast of Bolinas (lat. 37°52'40" N, long. 122°36'45" W). Named on San Rafael (1954) 7.5' quadrangle.

Lone Tree Creek: see **Scott Creek** [ALAMEDA-SANTA CLARA].

Lone Tree Island [SOLANO]: *island,* 1200 feet long, 6.25 miles southeast of Birds Landing (2) along Sacramento River (lat. 38°03'55" N, long. 121°47'15" W). Named on Collinsville (1918) 7.5' quadrangle.

Lone Tree Point [CONTRA COSTA]: *promontory,* 5.25 miles east-northeast of Pinole Point along San Pablo Bay at Rodeo (lat. 38°02'20" N, long. 122°16'20" W). Named on Mare Island (1959) 7.5' quadrangle.

Lone Tree Valley [CONTRA COSTA]: *valley,* 9 miles east-northeast of Mount Diablo along

Sand Creek (lat. 37°57' N, long. 121°46'30" W). Named on Antioch South (1953) and Brentwood (1978) 7.5' quadrangles. Mendenhall's (1908) map has the form "Lonetree" for the name.

Long Branch [SANTA CLARA]: *stream,* flows 3.25 miles to Isabel Creek 2.5 miles northwest of Mount Hamilton (lat. 37°22'10" N, long. 121°40'10" W; sec. 32, T 6 S, R 3 E). Named on Lick Observatory (1955) and Mount Day (1955) 7.5' quadrangles.

Long Bridge: see **Bonjetti Creek** [SANTA CLARA]; **Princeton** [SAN MATEO]; **Tunitas Creek** [SAN MATEO].

Long Canyon [CONTRA COSTA]: *canyon,* drained by a stream that flows nearly 3 miles to Marsh Creek 5.5 miles east of Mount Diablo (lat. 37°53'15" N, long. 121°48'55" W; sec. 36, T 1 N, R 1 E). Named on Antioch South (1953) 7.5' quadrangle.

Long Canyon [SANTA CLARA]: *canyon,* 5 miles long, along East Fork Coyote Creek above the mouth of Grizzly Creek, which is 6 miles southeast of Mount Stakes (lat. 37°15'15" N, long. 121°28'35" W). Named on Mount Stakes (1955) 7.5' quadrangle.

Long Gulch [SAN MATEO]: *canyon,* drained by a stream that flows 1 mile to the sea 2.5 miles south-southwest of the village of San Gregorio at Pomponio Beach (lat. 37°17'30" N, long. 122°24'20" W). Named on San Gregorio (1961, photorevised 1968) 7.5' quadrangle.

Long Gulch [SANTA CLARA]: *canyon,* drained by a stream that flows 2 miles to San Antonio Creek nearly 7 miles south of Eylar Mountain (lat. 37°22'40" N, long. 121°31'50" W; near SW cor. sec. 27, T 6 S, R 4 E). Named on Eylar Mountain (1955) 7.5' quadrangle.

Long Point [MARIN]: *promontory,* 5.5 miles southeast of downtown Novato along lowlands adjacent to San Pablo Bay (lat. 38°02'45" N, long. 122°30'20" W). Named on Novato (1954) 7.5' quadrangle.

Long Point [SANTA CLARA]: *promontory,* 4 miles north of downtown Mountain View at the edge of mud flats along San Francisco Bay (lat. 37°27' N, long. 122°04' W). Named on Mountain View (1961) 7.5' quadrangle. Called Lone Point on Thompson and West's (1876) map.

Long Point: see **Garnet Point** [SOLANO].

Long Point Island: see **Ryer Island** [SOLANO] (2).

Long Ridge [CONTRA COSTA]: *ridge,* west-trending, 1.5 miles long, 2.5 miles west of Mount Diablo (lat. 37°53'15" N, long. 121°57'45" W). Named on Clayton (1953) 7.5' quadrangle.

Long Ridge [SAN MATEO]: *ridge,* generally west-trending, 2.5 miles long, 3.5 miles east-southeast of Mindego Hill (lat. 37°17' N, long. 122°10'20" W). Named on Mindego Hill (1961) 7.5' quadrangle.

Long's Landing: see **Plummer Landing** [ALAMEDA].

Long Valley [CONTRA COSTA]: *canyon,* 1.25 miles long, 5.25 miles east-northeast of Mount Diablo (lat. 37°55' N, long. 121°49'45" W). Named on Mount Diablo (1898) 15' quadrangle.

Longwall Canyon: see **Baldy Ryan** [SANTA CLARA].

Lonoke [SANTA CLARA]: *locality,* 1.25 miles north-northwest of Gilroy along Southern Pacific Railroad (lat. 37°01'30" N, long. 121°34'35" W). Named on Gilroy (1955) 7.5' quadrangle.

Lookout Point [ALAMEDA]: *peak,* 5 miles south of Mendenhall Springs (lat. 37°30'50" N, long. 121°39'55" W; near E line sec. 8, T 5 S, R 3 E). Named on Mendenhall Springs (1956) 7.5' quadrangle.

Lookout Slough [SOLANO]: *water feature,* joins Shag Slough 10.5 miles north of Rio Vista (lat. 38°18'50" N, long. 121°41'35" W). Named on Liberty Island (1978) 7.5' quadrangle.

Lorenzo Station [ALAMEDA]: *locality,* 2.5 miles south-southeast of downtown San Leandro along Southern Pacific Railroad (lat. 37° 41'35" N, long. 122°07'45" W). Named on San Leandro (1959) 7.5' quadrangle.

Lorin [ALAMEDA]: *locality,* 3 miles north of downtown Oakland along Southern Pacific Railroad (lat. 37°50'50" N, long. 122°16'20" W). Named on San Francisco (1899) 15' quadrangle. Residents of the community applied for a post office under the name "Garfield," but the postal authorities assigned the name "Lorin" instead; Berkeley annexed Lorin in 1892 (Mosier and Mosier, p. 15, 82). Postal authorities established Lorin post office in 1882 and changed the name to South Berkeley in 1902 (Salley, p. 126). The railroad station at the place first was called Alcatraz, for Alcatraz Avenue (Mosier and Mosier, p. 53).

Los Alamos Creek: see **Cottonwood Creek** [ALAMEDA-CONTRA COSTA].

Los Altos [SANTA CLARA]: *city,* 13 miles west-northwest of downtown San Jose (lat. 37°22'55" N, long. 122°07' W). Named on Cupertino (1961) and Mountain View (1961) 7.5' quadrangles. When workmen for Southern Pacific Railroad began laying tracks to the place in 1906, Paul Shoup, a railroad executive, and some of his friends organized Los Altos Land Company, bought 100 acres, and laid out a town to be called Banks of Braes; after the railroad began operations in 1908, they changed the name of the place to Los Altos—*los altos* means "the heights" in Spanish (Butler, p. 43). Postal authorities established Los Altos post office in 1908 (Frickstad, p. 174), and the city incorporated in 1952. Healy's (1866) map has the name "Oak Grove" for a group of buildings situated in Los Altos at about the present intersection of El Camino Real and San Antonio Road.

Los Altos Hills [SANTA CLARA]: *locality,* the city hall is situated 14 miles west-northwest of downtown San Jose (lat. 37°23' N, long. 122°08'15" W). Named on Cupertino (1961), Mindego Hill (1961), Mountain View (1961), and Palo Alto (1961) 7.5' quadrangles. The community, which incorporated in 1956, has a rural setting.

Los Buellis Hills [SANTA CLARA]: *range,* 2.5 miles northeast of the mouth of Alum Rock Canyon (lat. 37°25'30" N, long. 121°48' W). Named on Calaveras Reservoir (1961) 7.5' quadrangle. According to Gudde (1949, p. 194), the name is from a misspelling of *bueyes,* which means "oxen" in Spanish.

Los Capitancillos [SANTA CLARA]: *land grant,* west-northwest of New Almaden. Named on Los Gatos (1953) and Santa Teresa Hills (1953) 7.5' quadrangles. Justo Larios received 4470.15 acres in 1842 (Arbuckle, p. 21).

Los Capitancillos Creek [SANTA CLARA]: *stream,* flows 1.25 miles to Guadalupe Creek nearly 3 miles west of New Almaden (lat. 37° 11'05" N, long. 121°52'15" W); the stream forms part of the border of Los Capitancillos grant. Named on Santa Teresa Hills (1953) 7.5' quadrangle. United States Board on Geographic Names (1943, p. 10) applied the name "Los Capitancillos Creek" to this stream and to Guadalupe Creek below their junction, while rejecting the names "Arroyo de los Capitancillos," "Arroyo Seco de los Capitancillos," and "Guadalupe Creek" for the combined streams. Later the Board (1960b, p. 17) decided against application of the name "Los Capitancillos Creek" to present Guadalupe Creek.

Los Capitancillos Ridge: see **New Almaden** [SANTA CLARA].

Los Coches [SANTA CLARA]: *land grant,* 2 miles west-southwest of downtown San Jose. Named on San Jose West (1961) 7.5' quadrangle. An Indian called Roberto received 0.5 league in 1844; Antonio Maria Suñol and others claimed 2219 acres patented in 1857 (Cowan, p. 28). The name is from use of the land as the swine range for Santa Clara mission—*los coches* means "the pigs" in colloquial Spanish (Hoover, Rensch, and Rensch, p. 440).

Los Farellones: see **Farallon Islands** [SAN FRANCISCO].

Los Gatos [SANTA CLARA]: *city,* 8.5 miles south-southwest of downtown San Jose (lat. 37°13'30" N, long. 121°58'55" W); the city is at the entrance of Los Gatos Creek to lowlands—partly on Rinconada de los Gatos grant. Named on Los Gatos (1953) and San Jose West (1961) 7.5' quadrangles. Postal authorities established Los Gatos post office in 1864 and discontinued it for a time in 1867 (Frickstad, p. 174). The city incorporated in 1887. After James Alexander Forbes built a flour mill there in the early 1850's, the place was known as Forbes Mill; the town that grew around the mill was called Forbestown first, and then Los Gatos (Hoover, Rensch, and Rensch, p. 454-455).

Los Gatos Creek [SANTA CLARA]: *stream,* flows 24 miles to Guadalupe River in downtown San Jose (lat. 37°20' N, long. 121°53'50" W). Named on Laurel (1955), Loma Prieta (1955), Los Gatos (1953), and San Jose West (1961) 7.5' quadrangles. Called Arroyo de Los Gatos on Hare's (1872) map. Zachariah Jones called the stream Jones Creek at the time that he laid out a town that he named Jones Mill, and that later was called Lexington (Bruntz, p. 7).

Los Gatos Creek, Old Channel: see **Dry Creek** [SANTA CLARA] (1).

Los Germanos: see **Juristac** [SANTA CLARA].

Los Huecos [SANTA CLARA]: *land grant,* southeast of Mount Hamilton. Named on Isabel Valley (1955), Lick Observatory (1955), Morgan Hill (1955), and Mount Sizer (1955) 7.5' quadrangles. Luis Arenas and John Roland received 9 leagues in 1846; Roland and Hornsby claimed 39,951 acres patented in 1876 (Cowan, p. 40).

Los Lagrimas Hills: see **Edenvale** [SANTA CLARA].

Los Medanos [CONTRA COSTA]:

(1) *land grant,* at and near Pittsburg and Antioch. Named on Antioch North (1978), Antioch South (1953), Clayton (1953), and Honker Bay (1953) 7.5' quadrangles. Jose Antonio Mesa and others received 2 leagues in 1839; Johnathan D. Stevenson claimed 8859 acres patented in 1872 (Cowan, p. 47). The name is from sand dunes located on the grant along San Joaquin River—*medanos* means "sand banks" in Spanish (Hoover, Rensch, and Rensch, p. 59).

(2) *locality,* 2.5 miles west of downtown Antioch along Southern Pacific Railroad (lat. 38°00'50" N, long. 121°51'10" W); the place is on Los Medanos grant. Named on Antioch North (1978) 7.5' quadrangle.

Los Meganos [CONTRA COSTA]: *land grant,* between Brentwood and Mount Diablo. Named on Brentwood (1978) and Byron Hot Springs (1953) 7.5' quadrangles. Jose Noriega received 4 leagues in 1835; John Marsh got the land in 1837 and claimed 13,316 acres patented in 1867 (Cowan, p. 47).

Los Putos [SOLANO]: *land grant,* at and north of Vacaville. Named on Allendale (1953), Davis (1952), Dixon (1952), Elmira (1953), Fairfield North (1951), Merritt (1952), Mount Vaca (1951), and Winters (1953) 7.5' quadrangles. Manuel Vaca and Juan Felipe Peña received 10 leagues in 1843 and claimed 44,384 acres patented in 1858 (Cowan, p. 65; Cowan listed the grant under the designation "Putas (or Putos, or Putah)").

Los Stancos Creek: see **Los Trancos Creek** [SAN MATEO-SANTA CLARA].

Lost Canyon [SANTA CLARA]: *canyon,* drained by a stream that flows 1.5 miles to San Antonio Creek 6.5 miles south-southeast of Eyler Mountain (lat. 37°22'55" N, long. 121°30'35" W; sec. 26, T 6 S, R 4 E). Named on Eylar Mountain (1955) 7.5' quadrangle.

Lost Lake: see **Lone Lake** [SANTA CLARA].

Los Trancos Creek [SAN MATEO-SANTA CLARA]: *stream,* flows 7 miles along part of San Mateo-Santa Clara county line to San Francisquito Creek nearly 3 miles southwest of downtown Palo Alto (lat. 37°24'50" N, long. 122°11'30" W). Named on Mindego Hill (1961) and Palo Alto (1961) 7.5' quadrangles. Called Stancos Creek on Thompson and West's (1876) map, but United States Board on Geographic Names (1933, p. 475) rejected the names "Los Stancos Creek" and "Stancos Creek" for the feature. The stream was called Maximo Creek in the 1850's for Maximo Martinez, a landholder near the feature, and was called Reynolds Creek for another early settler (Brown, p. 50).

Los Trancos Woods [SAN MATEO]: *settlement,* 3 miles north-northeast of Mindego Hill (lat. 37°20'55" N, long. 122°11'55" W); the place is near Los Trancos Creek. Named on Mindego Hill (1961) 7.5' quadrangle.

Los Ulpinos [SOLANO]: *land grant,* at and west of Rio Vista. Named on Antioch North (1978), Jersey Island (1978), and Rio Vista (1978) 7.5' quadrangles. John Bidwell received the land in 1845 and claimed 17,726 acres patented in 1866 (Cowan, p. 106). The name is from the designation of a group of Indians (Kroeber, p. 65).

Lovelady's: see **Campbell** [SANTA CLARA].

Lovely Glen Resort: see **Twin Creeks** [SANTA CLARA].

Lovers Leap [SANTA CLARA]: *peak,* 2 miles north-northwest of Pacheco Peak (lat. 37°02'05" N, long. 121°17'55" W). Altitude 1160 feet. Named on Pacheco Peak (1955) 7.5' quadrangle.

Lower Bean Hollow Lake: see **Bean Hollow Lake** [SAN MATEO].

Lower Crystal Springs Reservoir [SAN MATEO]: *lake,* 3.5 miles long, behind a dam on San Mateo Creek 3.25 miles southwest of downtown San Mateo (lat. 37°31'45" N, long. 122°21'40" W); the feature is northeast of Upper Crystal Springs Reservoir, and separated from it by a low dam that forms a causeway. Named on Montara Mountain (1956) and San Mateo (1956) 7.5' quadrangles. Upper Crystal Springs Reservoir and Lower Crystal Springs Reservoir together are called Crystal Springs Lake on San Mateo (1915) 15' quadrangle. These two lakes and nearby San Andreas Lake commonly are called Spring Valley Lakes for Spring Valley Water Company, which owned them; the name "Crystal

Springs" is from the settlement of Crystal Springs that grew at a resort hotel of the same name—water of Lower Crystal Springs Reservoir now covers the site of the settlement (Brown, p. 24). Water of the reservoir also covers the site of San Felix Station, a stage stop of the 1870's (Hoover, Rensch, and Rensch, p. 398). A stream called Lake Creek, or Laguna Creek, was located at the south end of present Lower Crystal Springs Reservoir; it received its name because it drained what was called The Laguna (Brown, p. 46).

Lower Emerald Lake [SAN MATEO]: *lake,* 550 feet long, 2.25 miles west-southwest of downtown Redwood City (lat. 37°28' N, long. 122°15'45" W); the lake is 0.5 mile north-northwest of Upper Emerald Lake. Named on Woodside (1961) 7.5' quadrangle.

Lower Penitencia Creek [SANTA CLARA]: *stream,* flows 5.5 miles to Coyote Creek nearly 2 miles north-northwest of Milpitas (lat. 37°27'15" N, long. 121°55'25" W). Named on Milpitas (1961) 7.5' quadrangle. Both Upper Penitencia Creek and Lower Penitencia Creek have the name "Penitencia Creek" on San Jose (1899) 15' quadrangle, although they are shown as separate streams. United States Board on Geographic Names (1962, p. 13, 18) rejected the name "Penitencia Creek" for both features. According to tradition, the creek was named for a house of penitence that priests used to hear confession (Hoover, Rensch, and Rensch, p. 444).

Loyola: see **Loyola Corners** [SANTA CLARA].

Loyola Corners [SANTA CLARA]: *locality,* 2.25 miles southeast of downtown Los Altos near Southern Pacific Railroad (now the route of Foothill Expressway) crossing of Permanente Creek (lat. 37°21'10" N, long. 122°05'10" W). Named on Cupertino (1961) 7.5' quadrangle. Palo Alto (1940) 15' quadrangle shows a place called Loyola in hills 1 mile west-southwest of Loyola Corners. Peninsular Railway Company's (1912) map has the name "Loyola" along the rail line at present Loyola Corners. University of Santa Clara acquired 650 acres near present Loyola Corners for a new campus, but the 1906 earthquake disrupted the project; the site of the proposed campus was given the name "Loyola" to honor one of the founders of the Society of Jesus, and Loyola Corners received its name from the campus site (Fava, p. 56-59).

Lucas Valley [MARIN]: *canyon,* 2.25 miles long, 6 miles southwest of downtown Novato along Nicasio Creek (lat. 38°03'25" N, long. 122°39'30" W); the canyon is on San Pedro Santa Margarita y las Gallinas grant. Named on San Geronimo (1954) 7.5' quadrangle. The name probably is from John Lucas, who inherited the grant (Gudde, 1949, p. 196).

Lucerne Lake: see **Lake Lucerne** [SAN MATEO].

Luco Hill [SOLANO]: *peak,* 2.5 miles west-southwest of Denverton near the east end of Potrero Hills (lat. 38°12'20" N, long. 121°56'15" W; sec. 11, T 4 N, R 1 W); the peak is west of Luco Slough. Altitude 303 feet. Named on Denverton (1953) 7.5' quadrangle.

Lucol Hollow [SOLANO]: *canyon,* drained by a stream that flows 3.5 miles to lowlands at Birds Landing (2) (lat. 38°07'55" N, long. 121°52'20" W; sec. 4, T 3 N, R 4 E). Named on Birds Landing (1953) 7.5' quadrangle.

Luco Slough [SOLANO]: *water feature,* joins Nurse Slough nearly 2 miles southwest of Denverton (lat. 38°12'20" N, long. 121°55'20" W); the feature is east of Luco Hill. Named on Denverton (1953) 7.5' quadrangle.

Luffley's: see **Barzilla**, under **Pescadero** [SAN MATEO].

Luzon [CONTRA COSTA]: *locality,* 6.25 miles west of Martinez along Atchison, Topeka and Santa Fe Railroad (lat. 38°00'55" N, long. 122°15' W). Named on Benicia (1959) and Mare Island (1959) 7.5' quadrangles. The place was named at the time of the Spanish-American War, when names from the Philippines were popular (Gudde, 1949, p. 197).

Lynchville: see **San Ramon** [CONTRA COSTA] (3).

Lyndon Canyon [SANTA CLARA]: *canyon,* drained by a stream that flows 3 miles to Lexington Reservoir 2.25 miles south-southwest of downtown Los Gatos (lat. 37°11'45" N, long. 122°00'05" W; sec. 32, T 8 S, R 1 W). Named on Castle Rock Ridge (1955) 7.5' quadrangle.

Lynn: see **Oakland** [ALAMEDA].

– M –

Machado Creek [SANTA CLARA]: *stream,* flows 2 miles to Llagas Creek 2.5 miles south-southwest of Morgan Hill (lat. 37°05'30" N, long. 121°39'50" W). Named on Mount Madonna (1955, photorevised 1968 and 1973) 7.5' quadrangle. The name commemorates a pioneer family (United States Board on Geographic Names, 1973a, p. 2).

Machin: see **Ignacio** [MARIN].

Maclaytown: see **Saratoga** [SANTA CLARA].

Madera Creek: see **Matadero Creek** [SANTA CLARA].

Madigan: see **Lake Madigan** [SOLANO].

Madonna: see **Mount Madonna** [SANTA CLARA].

Madrone [SANTA CLARA]: *settlement,* 1.5 miles northwest of Morgan Hill (lat. 37°09' N, long. 121°40'10" W). Named on Morgan Hill (1955) 7.5' quadrangle. The community now is part of Morgan Hill. A stopping place called Madrone Station, or Eighteen Mile House, was on the stage route between Coyote and Morgan Hill (Hoover, Rensch, and Rensch, p. 431). Postal authorities established

Sherman post office in 1867, discontinued it in 1870, reestablished it in 1871, changed the name to Madrone in 1882, and discontinued it in 1959 (Salley, p. 130, 203).

Madrone Mineral Springs: see **Madrone Soda Springs** [SANTA CLARA].

Madrone Soda Springs [SANTA CLARA]: *spring,* nearly 3.5 miles south of Mount Sizer (lat. 37°10' N, long. 121°30'45" W; sec. 10, T 9 S, R 4 E); the spring is in Soda Springs Canyon. Named on Mount Sizer (1955) 7.5' quadrangle. Morgan Hill (1917) 15' quadrangle shows a group of buildings at the site. Several cottages and a small hotel were built there as early as 1880; in 1892 and subsequent years, water from the spring was taken in barrels to San Jose and bottled (Waring, p. 214). Winslow Anderson (p. 191) referred to Madrone Mineral Springs. Postal authorities established Madrone Springs post office in 1883 and discontinued it in 1895 (Frickstad, p. 174). Crawford (1896, p. 518) noted that Coe's Spring was located 1 mile west of Madrone Soda Springs.

Madrone Springs: see **Madrone Soda Springs** [SANTA CLARA].

Madrone Station: see **Madrone** [SANTA CLARA].

Maguire Peaks [ALAMEDA]: *peaks,,* 4.25 miles southeast of Sunol (lat. 38°32'45" N, long. 121°50' W; sec. 35, T 4 S, R 1 E). Altitude of highest, 1688 feet. Named on La Costa Valley (1960) 7.5' quadrangle. The name commemorates Peter Maguire, an Irish farmer who settled in the neighborhood in the 1870's (Mosier and Mosier, p. 54).

Mailliard [MARIN]: *locality,* 8 miles southsouthwest of downtown Novato along Northwestern Pacific Railroad (lat. 38°00'25" N, long. 122°38'10" W). Named on Petaluma (1914) 15' quadrangle.

Maine Prairie [SOLANO]: *locality,* 9 miles east-southeast of Elmira (lat. 38°18'25" N, long. 121°45'20" W; sec. 4, T 5 N, R 2 E). Site named on Dozier (1952) 7.5' quadrangle. Postal authorities established Maine Prairie post office in 1861 and discontinued it in 1913 (Frickstad, p. 192). In the early days, the place was at the head of navigation on present Maine Prairie Slough, and was a shipping point for wild-oat hay and for wheat before 1859; after a flood destroyed the community in 1862, many residents moved to a new town called Alton that was built on higher ground about 0.25 mile from the flooded site, but some of the flooded-out residents rebuilt at the original place (Hoover, Rensch, and Rensch, p. 524).

Maine Prairie Slough [SOLANO]: *water feature,* joins Cache Slough 9 miles east-southeast of Elmira at the site of Maine Prairie (lat. 38°18'30" N, long. 121°45'30" W; sec. 4, T 5 N, R 2 E). Named on Dozier (1952) 7.5' quadrangle. The feature was called Cache Slough

about 1877 (Hoover, Rensch, and Rensch, p. 524).

Maine Prairie Station: see **Vale** [SOLANO].

Main Ridge [ALAMEDA]: *ridge,* west- to north-trending, nearly 3 miles long, 2.5 miles south-southwest of Dublin (lat. 37°40' N, long. 121°57' W). Named on Dublin (1961) 7.5' quadrangle.

Maintop Bay [SAN FRANCISCO]: *embayment,* on the northwest side of Southeast Farallon (lat. 37°42'05" N, long. 123°00'30" W). Named on Farallon Islands (1988) 7.5' quadrangle. Hoover (p. 14-15) gave the name "Franconia Bay" as an alternate designation for the embayment, and noted that this name commemorates a ship that was wrecked at the place.

Maintop Island [SAN FRANCISCO]: *island,* 1800 feet long, west of Southeast Farallon and only slightly separated from it (lat. 37°41'55" N, long. 123°00'35" W). Named on Farallon Islands (1988) 7.5' quadrangle.

Maladero Creek: see **Matadero Creek** [SANTA CLARA].

Ma-lek-ad-el Point: see **Dillon Point** [SOLANO].

Mallard [ALAMEDA]: *locality,* less than 1 mile east-southeast of present Fremont civic center along Southern Pacific Railroad (lat. 37°32'45" N, long. 121°57'20" W). Named on Pleasanton (1906) 15' quadrangle. Another station called Mallard was located along South Pacific Coast Railroad north of Drawbridge (Mosier and Mosier, p. 54).

Mallard [CONTRA COSTA]: *locality,* 2.25 miles west-northwest of Pittsburg along Suisun Bay at the end of a spur of Sacramento Northern Railroad (lat. 38°02'35" N, long. 121°55'10" W); the place is on Mallard Island. Named on Pittsburg (1953) 15' quadrangle.

Mallard Branch: see **First Mallard Branch** [SOLANO]; **Second Mallard Branch** [SOLANO].

Mallard Island [CONTRA COSTA]: *island,* nearly 1 mile long, 2 miles west-northwest of Pittsburg in Suisun Bay (lat. 38°02'30" N, long. 121°55'10" W). Named on Honker Bay (1953) 7.5' quadrangle.

Mallard Lake [SAN FRANCISCO]: *lake,* 600 feet long, nearly 2 miles east-southeast of Point Lobos (lat. 37°46' N, long. 122°29'05" W). Named on San Francisco North (1956) 7.5' quadrangle.

Mallard Reservoir [CONTRA COSTA]: *lake,* 4500 feet long, 5 miles east of Martinez (lat. 38°01' N, long. 122°02'20" W). Named on Vine Hill (1959) 7.5' quadrangle.

Mallard Slough [CONTRA COSTA]: *water feature,* 2 miles west-northwest of Pittsburg between Mallard Island and the mainland (lat. 38°02'30" N, long. 121°55'15" W). Named on Honker Bay (1953) 7.5' quadrangle.

Maloney Reservoir [CONTRA COSTA]: *lake,*

550 feet long, nearly 5 miles north-northeast of Richmond civic center (lat. 37°59'55" N, long. 122°17'50" W; sec. 21, T 2 N, R 4 W). Named on Richmond (1959) 7.5' quadrangle.

Maloney's Hill: see **Ox Hill** [SAN MATEO].

Maltby [CONTRA COSTA]: *locality,* 3.5 miles east of Martinez along Atchison, Topeka and Santa Fe Railroad (lat. 38°00'55" N, long. 122°04'10" W). Named on Vine Hill (1959) 7.5' quadrangle.

Man Gulch: see **Eylar Canyon** [ALAMEDA].

Manhattan Beach [SAN MATEO]: *beach,* 2.25 miles south-southwest of downtown Half Moon Bay along the coast (lat. 37°25'55" N, long. 122°26'20" W). Named on Halfmoon Bay (1940) 15' quadrangle.

Manka: see **Mankas Corner** [SOLANO].

Mankas Corner [SOLANO]: *locality,* 4.25 miles northwest of Fairfield (lat. 38°17'10" N, long. 122°06'20" W). Named on Fairfield North (1951) 7.5' quadrangle. California Mining Bureau's (1909a) map shows a place called Manka located at or near present Mankas Corner. Postal authorities established Manka post office in 1895 and discontinued it in 1902 (Frickstad, p. 192).

Manor [MARIN]: *locality,* 3.5 miles west-north-west of downtown San Rafael (lat. 37°59'30" N, long. 122°35'30" W). Named on San Rafael (1954) 7.5' quadrangle. Postal authorities established Manor post office in 1915 and discontinued it in 1953; the name was from a real-estate promotion called Fairfax Manor (Salley, p. 131).

Man Ridge [ALAMEDA]: *ridge,* north- to west-northwest-trending, 4 miles long, 4.5 miles southeast of Cedar Mountain (lat. 37°30'20" N, long. 121°33'20" W). Named on Cedar Mountain (1956) and Eylar Mountain (1955) 7.5' quadrangles. The misspelled name commemorates George Mann, who settled at the place in 1855 (Mosier and Mosier, p. 54).

Manzanita [MARIN]: *locality,* 6.25 miles south of downtown San Rafael along Northwestern Pacific Railroad (lat. 37°52'55" N, long. 122°31' W). Named on San Rafael (1954) 7.5' quadrangle.

Manzanita Point [SANTA CLARA]: *ridge,* east-trending, nearly 1 mile long, 9 miles east-northeast of Morgan Hill (lat. 37°10'30" N, long. 121°30' W). Named on Mississippi Creek (1955) and Mount Sizer (1955) 7.5' quadrangles.

Manzanita Ridge [SANTA CLARA]: *ridge,* north-northwest- to west-trending, 2.5 miles long, 5 miles west of Morgan Hill (lat. 37° 08'20" N, long. 121°45'10" W). Named on Morgan Hill (1955) and Santa Teresa Hills (1953) 7.5' quadrangles.

Marallone Islands: see **Farallon Islands** [SAN FRANCISCO].

Marconi [MARIN]: *locality,* 7 miles south-southeast of Tomales on the northeast side of Tomales Bay (lat. 38°08'40" N, long. 122°

52'35" W). Named on Tomales (1954) 7.5' quadrangle. An Indian village called Fishermen's was at the site in the early days when trains stopped there to take on clams and fish; in 1913 Marconi Wireless Company bought land at the place to build a trans-Pacific receiving station (Mason, 1976a, p. 120-121).

Mare Island [SOLANO]: *peninsula,* center 1 mile southwest of downtown Vallejo between Mare Island Strait and San Pablo Bay (lat. 38°05'45" N, long. 122°16'15" W). Named on Benicia (1959) and Mare Island (1959) 7.5' quadrangles. Mare Island (1916) 15' quadrangle shows marsh separating the feature from the mainland at the north end. Juan Manuel de Ayala called the place Isla Plana in 1775 (Hoover, Rensch, and Rensch, p. 522). It also was known in the early days as Isla de la Yegua—*isla de la yegua* means "mare island" in Spanish—either from a lone mare stranded there after a boat wreck, or from horses pastured there by Victor Castro, owner of the place (Bancroft, 1888, p. 475, 630). Ringgold (p. 26) referred to Napa or Mare Island. Ringgold's (1850a) map shows Spear Pt. at the southwest end of Mare Island, and shows Pt. Thompson at the southeast end. Postal authorities established Mare Island post office in 1854, changed the name to Mare Island Naval in 1917, and it changed back to Mare Island in 1924 (Salley, p. 132).

Mare Island Naval: see **Mare Island** [SOLANO].

Mare Island Strait [SOLANO]: *water feature,* estuary of Napa River that opens into Carquines Strait 2 miles south-southeast of downtown Vallejo (lat. 38°04'30" N, long. 122°14'30" W); the feature is between Mare Island and the mainland. Named on Benicia (1959) and Mare Island (1959) 7.5' quadrangles. Ringgold (p. 26) noted that Mare Island forms "the Strait and Bay of Napa, in connection with a stream of the same name." Ringgold's (1850a) map shows Commission Rk. [Rock] in present Mare Island Strait about opposite the site of present downtown Vallejo.

Mare Pasture Ridge [SANTA CLARA]: *ridge,* east-trending, 1.5 miles long, 4 miles west-southwest of Mount Sizer (lat. 37°12'05" N, long. 121°34'50" W). Named on Mount Sizer (1955) 7.5' quadrangle.

Marin: see **Point Reyes Station** [MARIN].

Marina District [SAN FRANCISCO]: *district,* 2 miles north-northwest of San Francisco civic center along San Francisco Bay (lat. 37°48'10" N, long. 122°26'15" W). Named on San Francisco North (1956) 7.5' quadrangle. A small fresh-water lake located in present Marina District in the 1850's was called Washerwoman's Lagoon because San Francisco housewives washed their clothes there (O'Brien, p. 191). Davidson (p. 130) identified Washerwoman's Lagoon as the lake that the Spaniards called Pequeña Laguna. At least 30 dairies that were in present Marina District in the 1870's gave it the name "Cow Hollow" (O'Brien, p. 192).

Marin City [MARIN]: *town,* 1.5 miles northwest of downtown Sausalito (lat. 37°52'20" N, long. 122°30'40" W). Named on Point Bonita (1954) and San Rafael (1954) 7.5' quadrangles. In 1851 Benjamin R. Buckelew laid out a town that he called Marin City at a site near Point San Quintin, but the place failed to develop; modern Marin City started during World War II as housing for workers in shipyards near Sausalito (Teather, p. 39).

Marine [SAN MATEO]: *locality,* 2.5 miles south-southwest of present Montara Knob along Ocean Shore Railroad at present Moss Beach (lat. 37°31'15" N, long. 122°12'35" W). Named on San Mateo (1915) 15' quadrangle. Morrall (p. 155) called the place Marine View.

Marine View: see **Marine** [SAN MATEO].

Marin Island: see **East Marin Island** [MARIN]; **West Marin Island** [MARIN].

Marin Islands: see **East Marin Island** [MARIN].

Marin Meadows: see **Hamilton Air Force Base** [MARIN].

Marin Peninsula [MARIN]: *peninsula,* at the extreme southeast end of Marin County between Richardson Bay and the sea. Named on Point Bonita (1954) and San Francisco North (1956) 7.5' quadrangles.

Markley Canyon [CONTRA COSTA]: *canyon,* 3 miles long, opens into lowlands 8 miles north-northeast of Mount Diablo (lat. 37°59'10" N, long. 121°51'10" W; sec. 27, T 2 N, R 1 E). Named on Antioch North (1953) and Antioch South (1953) 7.5' quadrangles.

Marsh: see **Avon** [CONTRA COSTA].

Marshall [MARIN]: *village,* 6 miles south of Tomales on the northeast side of Tomales Bay (lat. 38°09'40" N, long. 122°53'35" W). Named on Tomales (1954) 7.5' quadrangle. Postal authorities established Marshall post office in 1872 (Frickstad, p. 88). The name commemorates the Marshall brothers, who had a wharf and warehouse at the place (Mason, 1976a, p. 33). United States Board on Geographic Names (1973b, p. 3) approved the name "Marshall Beach" for a beach located 1.2 miles west of Marshall on the west shore of Tomales Bay (lat. 38°09'45" N, long. 122°54'50" W).

Marshall Beach: see **Marshall** [MARIN].

Marshall Cut [SOLANO]: *water feature,* joins Sacramento River 4.5 miles south-southeast of Birds Landing (2) (lat. 38°04'20" N, long. 121°49'55" W). Named on Antioch North (1953) 7.5' quadrangle. Collinsville (1918) 7.5' quadrangle shows a place called Montezuma Landing located at the mouth of the feature.

Marsh Creek [CONTRA COSTA]: *stream,* flows 22 miles to lowlands 3 miles south-

west of Brentwood (lat. 37°53'40" N, long. 121°43'05" W). Named on Antioch South (1953), Brentwood (1954), Byron Hot Springs (1953), Jersey Island (1978), and Tassajara (1953) 7.5' quadrangles. The name commemorates John Marsh, who lived by the stream; the Spaniards called the feature Arroyo de los Poblanos (Gudde, 1949, p. 206).

Marsh Creek Reservoir [CONTRA COSTA]: *lake,* behind a dam on Marsh Creek 3.25 miles south-southwest of Brentwood (lat. 37°53'25" N, long. 121°43'30" W). Named on Brentwood (1978) 7.5' quadrangle.

Marsh Creek Springs [CONTRA COSTA]: *locality,* 3.25 miles east of Mount Diablo (lat. 37°53'30" N, long. 121°51'20" W; sec. 34, T 1 N, R 1 E). Named on Antioch South (1953) 7.5' quadrangle.

Marsh Landing [CONTRA COSTA]: *locality,* 2.5 miles east of present downtown Antioch along San Joaquin River (lat. 38°01'10" N, long. 121°45'45" W). Named on Collinsville (1918) 7.5' quadrangle. Ringgold's (1850b) map shows Marsh's Landing situated about 3 miles farther west. According to Gudde (1949, p. 206), John Marsh's shipping point was 4 miles west of Antioch, and was known as Marsh's Landing. Postal authorities established Marsh's Landing post office in 1852 and discontinued it in 1854 (Salley, p. 134).

Marsh Point: see **Redwood Point** [SAN MATEO].

Marsh's Landing: see **Marsh Landing** [CONTRA COSTA].

Marshs Landing: see **Antioch** [CONTRA COSTA].

Martin Canyon [ALAMEDA]: *canyon,* drained by a stream that flows 2.5 miles to lowlands at Dublin (lat. 37°42'20" N, long. 121° 56'35" W). Named on Dublin (1961) 7.5' quadrangle. The name commemorates William Henry Martin, John Samuel Martin, and Denis David Martin, who settled at the head of the canyon in the late 1850's (Mosier and Mosier, p. 55).

Martin Creek [SAN MATEO]: *stream,* flows 1.25 miles to Portola Valley (1) 6 miles south of downtown Redwood City (lat. 37°23'45" N, long. 122°14'45" W). Named on Palo Alto (1961) and Woodside (1961) 7.5' quadrangles. Brown (p. 26) called the stream Dennis Martin Creek, and noted that the name is for a lumberman who settled by the creek in 1851; Dry Creek was another name for the feature, and the canyon of a north fork was called Gang Mill Gulch.

Martinez [CONTRA COSTA]: *town,* 14 miles west-northwest of Mount Diablo (lat. 38°00'50" N, long. 122°08' W). Named on Benicia (1959), Briones Valley (1959), Vine Hill (1959), and Walnut Creek (1959) 7.5' quadrangles. Postal authorities established Martinez post office in 1851 (Frickstad, p. 22), and the town incorporated in 1876. Colonel William M. Smith laid out the community in

1849 and named it for Ignacio Martinez, who owned the land there (Gudde, 1949, p. 206). United States Board on Geographic Names (1995, p. 5) approved the name "Mount Helen" for a peak located 1.2 miles south of Martinez in John Muir National Historic Site (lat. 37°58'54" N, long. 122°07'56" W); the name is for Helen Lillian Muir Funk, youngest daughter of John Muir. The Board at the same time approved the name "Mount Wanda" for another peak located 1.2 miles south of Martinez in John Muir National Historic Site (lat. 37°59'01" N, long. 122°08'09" W; the name is for Annie Wanda Muir Hanna, eldest daughter of John Muir.

Martinez Reservoir [CONTRA COSTA]: *lake,* 1200 feet long, 1.5 miles east of downtown Martinez (lat. 38°00'35" N, long. 122°06'25" W). Named on Vine Hill (1959) 7.5' quadrangle. United States Board on Geographic Names (1948, p. 5) rejected the name "Mountain View Reservoir" for the feature.

Martinez Ridge [CONTRA COSTA]: *ridge,* northwest-trending, 0.5 mile long, 6.5 miles north-northwest of Walnut Creek civic center (lat. 37°59'25" N, long. 122°07'05" W); the ridge is south of Martinez. Named on Walnut Creek (1959) 7.5' quadrangle.

Martini Creek [SAN MATEO]: *stream,* flows 1.5 miles to the sea 1.5 miles west-southwest of Montara Knob (lat. 37°33'10" N, long. 122°30'45" W; sec. 28, T 4 S, R 6 W). Named on Montara Mountain (1956) 7.5' quadrangle. Martini ranch was along the creek after the early 1890's; before then the stream was called Arroyo de la Cuesta (Brown, p. 51).

Martin Ridge [SAN MATEO]: *ridge,* south-trending, 1.25 miles long, 4.5 miles southwest of La Honda (lat. 37°16'20" N, long. 122°19'35" W). Named on La Honda (1961) 7.5' quadrangle. The name commemorates Andrew Martin, who had a ranch at the place in the 1860's and 1870's (Brown, p. 51).

Martins Beach [SAN MATEO]: *settlement,* 6.25 miles south of downtown Half Moon Bay (lat. 37°22'30" N, long. 122°24'25" W). Named on Half Moon Bay (1961) and San Gregorio (1961) 7.5' quadrangles. The name commemorates Nicholas Martin, who owned land at the site (Gudde, 1949, p. 206).

Mason: see **Andy Mason Slough,** under **Simmons Island** [SOLANO]; **Fort Mason Military Reservation** [SAN FRANCISCO].

Mason Ridge: see **Mesa Ridge** [SANTA CLARA].

Massachusetts: see **Point Massachusetts,** under **Point Edith** [CONTRA COSTA].

Masters Hill [SANTA CLARA]: *peak,* 5.25 miles west of Mount Hamilton (lat. 37°20'15" N, long. 121°44'10" W). Named on Lick Observatory (1955) 7.5' quadrangle.

Matadera Creek: see **Matadero Creek** [SANTA CLARA].

Matadero Creek [SANTA CLARA]: *stream,* flows 4 miles to lowlands 1 mile north-northeast of Coyote Hill (lat. 37°24'45" N, long. 122°08'15" W), and continues to San Francisco Bay in an artificial watercourse. Named on Mindego Hill (1961) and Palo Alto (1961) 7.5' quadrangles. Called Madera Creek on Santa Cruz (1902) 30' quadrangle, and called Matadera Creek on Palo Alto (1899) 15' quadrangle, which shows the stream ending short of San Francisco Bay near Mayfield. Called Arroyo de Matadera on Healy's (1866) map, and called Maladero Creek on Thompson and West's (1876) map. Gudde (1949, p. 201) noted that the name "Arroyo del Matadero" appears on maps of the 1830's and 1840's—*matadero* means "slaughtering place" in Spanish.

Mathilde: see **Lake Mathilde** [SAN MATEO].

Mattos [ALAMEDA]: *locality,* 1.5 miles northeast of downtown Newark (lat. 37°32'40" N, long. 122°01' W). Named on Hayward (1915) 15' quadrangle. The name commemorates John Garcia Mattos, Sr., who settled at the place in 1879 (Mosier and Mosier, p. 55).

Maxmo Creek: see **Los Trancos Creek** [SAN MATEO].

Mayfield [SANTA CLARA]: *town,* nearly 2 miles southeast of downtown Palo Alto, and now part of Palo Alto (lat. 37°25'30" N, long. 122°08'30" W). Named on Palo Alto (1899) 15' quadrangle. A village developed around a public house that James Otterson built at the site in 1853, and the town was laid out in 1867 (Hoover, Rensch, and Rensch, p. 462). The place took its name from nearby Mayfield farm (Butler, p. 11). Postal authorities established Mayfield post office in 1855 and changed the name to Palo Alto Station "A" in 1930 (Salley, p. 135). Palo Alto annexed Mayfield in 1925, and the name of the railroad station at Mayfield was changed to South Palo Alto (Brown, p. 52).

Mayfield Slough [SANTA CLARA]: *water feature,* consists of a series of elongate lakes and intermittent lakes that extend to flatlands near San Francisco Bay 5 miles north-northwest of downtown Mountain View (lat. 37°26'50" N, long. 122°06'15" W). Named on Mountain View (1961) 7.5' quadrangle. A landing called Embarcadero de San Francisquito was on a side channel of the slough in the 1850's; it was the shipping point for Mayfield (Brown, p. 52).

Mayhews Landing: see **Jarvis Landing** [ALAMEDA].

Mayhew Spring: see **Niles District** [ALAMEDA].

Mayhew's Sulphur Spring: see **Mayhew Spring,** under **Niles District** [ALAMEDA].

McAvoy [CONTRA COSTA]: *locality,* 4.25 miles west of Pittsburg along Atchison, Topeka and Santa Fe Railroad (lat. 38°02'20" N, long. 121°57'30" W). Named on Honker Bay (1953) 7.5' quadrangle.

McAvoy Boat Harbor [CONTRA COSTA]:

water feature, 4 miles west of Pittsburg along Suisun Bay (lat. 38°02'25" N, long. 121°57'25" W); the harbor is at McAvoy. Named on Honker Bay (1953) 7.5' quadrangle.

McCall: see **Jim McCall's Gulch**, under **Jones Gulch** [SAN MATEO] (2).

McCartysville: see **Saratoga** [SANTA CLARA].

McClures Beach [MARIN]: *beach,* 5.25 miles southwest of Tomales along the coast (lat. 38°11'15" N, long. 122°57'50" W). Named on Tomales (1954) 7.5' quadrangle. James McClure and Margaret McClure bought the beach in 1929 (Teather, p. 45).

McCoppin: see **Lake McCoppin**, under **Mission District** [SAN FRANCISCO].

McCormick Creek [MARIN]: *stream,* flows 2 miles to Pine Gulch Creek 2.25 miles northwest of Bolinas (lat. 37°56'05" N, long. 122°42'50" W). Named on Bolinas (1954) 7.5' quadrangle.

McCormick Creek [SAN MATEO]: *stream,* flows nearly 2 miles to Pescadero Creek 3 miles south-southwest of La Honda (lat. 37° 16'35" N, long. 122°17'05" W; sec. 34, T 7 S, R 4 W). Named on La Honda (1961) 7.5' quadrangle.

McCoy Creek [SOLANO]: *stream,* flows 1.5 miles to Laurel Creek 3 miles north-north-east of Fairfield (lat. 38°17'20" N, long. 122°01'10" W). Named on Mount Vaca (1942) 15' quadrangle.

McCoy Slough: see **Hastings Cut** [SOLANO].

McCune Creek [SOLANO]:
(1) *stream,* flows 3.5 miles to Putah Creek 4.5 miles northwest of Allendale (lat. 38°29'50" N, long. 121°59'50" W). Named on Allendale (1953) and Mount Vaca (1951) 7.5' quadrangles.
(2) *water feature,* artificial watercourse that joins Sweany Creek 3.5 miles southwest of Dixon (lat. 38°24'35" N, long. 121°52'50" W; sec. 33, T 7 N, R 1 E). Named on Dixon (1952, photorevised 1968 and 1975) 7.5' quadrangle. On Vacaville (1953) 15' quadrangle, the name applies to a stream that heads 9 miles west-northwest of Dixon and flows 11.5 miles to Sweany Creek 3.5 miles southwest of Dixon.

McCutchin Canyon [SANTA CLARA]: *canyon,* drained by a stream that flows 1 mile to lowlands 1.5 miles west-southwest of Gilroy (lat. 36°59'50" N, long. 121°35'45" W). Named on Chittenden (1955) 7.5' quadrangle.

McDowell: see **Fort McDowell** [MARIN-SAN FRANCISCO].

McElroy Creek [SANTA CLARA]: *stream,* flows 1.25 miles to Bonjetti Creek 1.5 miles north-northeast of Bielawski Mountain (lat. 37°14'35" N, long. 122°05' W; near N line sec. 16, T 8 S, R 2 W). Named on Castle Rock Ridge (1955) 7.5' quadrangle.

McGarvey Gulch [SAN MATEO]: *canyon,* drained by a stream that flows nearly 2 miles

to West Union Creek 2.5 miles north-north-east of Skeggs Point (lat. 37°26'40" N, long. 122°17'25" W). Named on Woodside (1961) 7.5' quadrangle. Owen McGarvey had a claim and cut wood in the canyon about 1860 (Brown, p. 53).

McGill's Wharf: see **Miramar** [SAN MATEO].

McGlinchey Spring [SANTA CLARA]: *spring,* 4 miles west of Eylar Mountain (lat. 37°28'55" N, long. 121°37'15" W; sec. 23, T 5 S, R 3 E). Named on Eylar Mountain (1955) 7.5' quadrangle.

McKinnan Gulch [MARIN]: *canyon,* drained by a stream that flows 1.25 miles to Bolinas Lagoon 1.25 miles east of Bolinas (lat. 37° 54'45" N, long. 122°39'45" W). Named on Bolinas (1954) 7.5' quadrangle. The name commemorates Hugh McKennan, who bought land at Bolinas in 1867 and raised ducks there (Teather, p. 46).

McNear: see **McNears Beach** [MARIN].

McNear Landing: see **McNears Beach** [MARIN].

McNears Beach [MARIN]: *locality,* 0.5 mile north-northwest of Point San Pedro along San Pablo Bay (lat. 37°59'35" N, long. 122° 07'10" W). Named on San Quentin (1959) 7.5' quadrangle. United States Board on Geographic Names (1968a, p. 5) rejected the names "McNear" and "McNear Landing" for the place. California Mining Bureau's (1909a) map shows a place called McNear located at or near present Point San Pedro. Postal authorities established McNear post office 6 miles northeast of San Rafael in 1897 and discontinued it in 1910; the name was from McNears Point and McNears Landing (Salley, p. 136). The place developed as a fishing center in the 1870's; the name was taken from the firm of McNear and Brothers, owners of the land (Gudde, 1949, p. 200).

McNears Point: see **Point San Pedro** [MARIN].

McPherson: see **Mount McPherson**, under **Bielawski Mountain** [SANTA CLARA].

Meadowsweet [MARIN]: *locality,* 3.5 miles south-southeast of downtown San Rafael along Northwestern Pacific Railroad (lat. 37°55'25" N, long. 122°30'35" W). Named on San Rafael (1954) 7.5' quadrangle.

Medora Lake [SOLANO]: *lake,* 900 feet long, 11 miles north-northeast of Rio Vista in Yolo Bypass (lat. 38°18'35" N, long. 121°38'25" W). Named on Liberty Island (1978) 7.5' quadrangle.

Medora Lake: see **Little Medora Lake** [SOLANO].

Meinert [CONTRA COSTA]: *locality,* 3.25 miles north-northeast of Walnut Creek civic center along Sacramento Northern Railroad (lat. 37°56'40" N, long. 122°01'35" W). Named on Walnut Creek (1959) 7.5' quadrangle.

Meins Landing [SOLANO]: *locality,* 6 miles south of Denverton along Montezuma Slough (lat. 38°08'25" N, long. 121°54'25" W; at N line sec. 6, T 3 N, R 1 E). Named on Denverton (1953) 7.5' quadrangle.

Melita: see **Oakland** [ALAMEDA].

Melrose [ALAMEDA]: *locality,* 4 miles southeast of downtown Oakland (lat. 37°46' N, long. 122°13' W). Named on Concord (1897) 15' quadrangle. Postal authorities established Melrose post office in 1881, discontinued it for a time in 1887, and discontinued it finally in 1908 (Frickstad, p. 2). Officials of San Francisco and Oakland Railroad had a station called Austin built at the place in 1862; the station was renamed for the community of Melrose in 1906—it also was called Simpson's for Robert Simson, who owned land at the place; Oakland annexed Melrose in 1909 (Mosier and Mosier, p. 56).

Melville: see **Mount Melville** [SAN MATEO].

Mendenhall Springs [ALAMEDA]: *spring,* 9 miles southeast of Livermore (lat. 37°35'15" N, long. 121°38'45" W; sec. 16, T 4 S, R 3 E). Named on Mendenhall Springs (1956) 7.5' quadrangle. Tesla (1907) 15' quadrangle has the name for a group of buildings at the spring. William M. Mendenhall opened a health resort at the place in the 1870's (Mosier and Mosier, p. 56). The resort had accommodations for 75 people in 1909; water that seeps from two short tunnels, dug to prospect for gold, is mineralized and was bottled under the name "Ague de Vida Springs Water" (Waring, p. 309-310).

Menlo Park [SAN MATEO]: *city,* 3.25 miles southeast of downtown Redwood City (lat. 37°27'15" N, long. 122°10'55" W). Named on Mountain View (1961) and Palo Alto (1961) 7.5' quadrangles. Dennis J. Oliver and his brother-in-law, D.C. McGlynn, built a wooden arch at the entrance to their property in present Menlo Park in the 1850's, and put the name "Menlo Park" on the arch in memory of their former home at Menlough, Ireland; when the railroad reached the place in 1863, the station there was called Menlo Park and the community around the station took that name—the city incorporated in 1874 and again in 1927 (Hoover, Rensch, and Rensch, p. 408-409). Postal authorities established Menlo Park post office in 1870 (Frickstad, p. 168). An army post called Camp Fremont occupied thousands of acres of leased land west of present downtown Menlo Park during World War I (Hynding, p. 199).

Menzesville: see **Redwood City** [SAN MATEO].

Merced Lake: see **Lake Merced** [SAN FRANCISCO].

Meridian [SANTA CLARA]: *locality,* 4.5 miles west of downtown San Jose (lat. 37°19'25" N, long. 121°58'10" W). Named on San Jose West (1961) 7.5' quadrangle. Peninsular Railway Company's (1912) map shows a station called Meridian located where a branch line

to Saratoga leaves the main line between Cupertino and San Jose. The same map shows a place called Scotts Spur located just west of Meridian, a station called Bascome located about halfway from Meridian to downtown San Jose, a station called Moreland located about half way from Meridian to Congress Junction, and a place called Prospect Spur located a short distance beyond Moreland .

Meridian Ridge [CONTRA COSTA]: *ridge,* north-trending, 1.5 miles long, 2 miles northnorthwest of Mount Diablo (lat. 37°54'30" N, long. 121°55'35" W); the ridge is 0.5 mile west of Mount Diablo Meridian. Named on Clayton (1953) 7.5' quadrangle.

Merienda: see **Dresser** [ALAMEDA].

Merritt: see **Lake Merritt** [ALAMEDA].

Mesa: see **The Mesa** [SAN MATEO].

Mesa Ridge [SANTA CLARA]: *ridge,* easttrending, 2.5 miles long, 2 miles southwest of Eylar Mountain (lat. 37°27' N, long. 121°34' W). Named on Eylar Mountain (1955) 7.5' quadrangle. Called Mason Ridge on Mount Hamilton (1897) 15' quadrangle.

Metcalfe Canyon [SANTA CLARA]: *canyon,* drained by a stream that flows nearly 2 miles to lowlands 1 mile north-northwest of Coyote (lat. 37°13'50" N, long. 121°44'45" W). Named on Morgan Hill (1955) 7.5' quadrangle.

Mexican Camp [SANTA CLARA]: *locality,* 1.25 miles west of New Almaden near New Almaden mine (lat. 37°10'30" N, long. 121°50'35" W). Site named on Santa Teresa Hills (1953) 7.5' quadrangle. Lanyon and Bulmore (p. 45) called the place Spanishtown.

Middle Farallon [SAN FRANCISCO]: *island,* 2.5 miles northwest of Southeast Farallon (lat. 37°43'40" N, long. 123°01'50" W); the island is between Southeast Farallon and North Farallon. Named on Farallon Islands (1988) 7.5' quadrangle. According to United States Coast and Geodetic Survey (p. 123), the feature consists of a single 20-foot rock 150 feet in diameter.

Middlefield Reservoir [ALAMEDA]: *lake,* 450 feet long, 2 miles southeast of Fremont civic center (lat. 37°31'45" N, long. 121°56'45" W; sec. 2, T 5 S, R 1 W). Named on Niles (1961) 7.5' quadrangle. The reservoir, built in the 1950's, is named for Middlefield Avenue (Mosier and Mosier, p. 56).

Middle Ground Island [SOLANO]: *island,* 7.5 miles southwest of Birds Landing (2) in Suisun Bay (lat. 38°03'45" N, long. 121°58'50" W). Named on Honker Bay (1953) 7.5' quadrangle.

Middle Lake [SAN FRANCISCO]: *lake,* 350 feet long, 1.25 miles southeast of Point Lobos (lat. 37°46'05" N, long. 122°29'55" W); the feature is between North Lake and South Lake. Named on San Francisco North (1956) 7.5' quadrangle.

Middle Pass: see **Patterson Pass** [ALAMEDA].

Middle Peak [MARIN]: *peak,* 4.5 miles southwest of downtown San Rafael on Mount Tamalpais (lat. 37°55'40" N, long. 122°35'15" W). Named on San Rafael (1954) 7.5' quadrangle.

Middle Point [CONTRA COSTA]: *promontory,* 6 miles west-northwest of Pittsburg along Suisun Bay (lat. 38°03'20" N, long. 121°59'30" W). Named on Honker Bay (1953) 7.5' quadrangle. Called Pt. Stephenson on Ringgold's (1850b) map.

Middle Point: see **Franklin Point** [SAN MATEO].

Middle Ridge [SANTA CLARA]: *ridge,* northwest-trending, 3.5 miles long, nearly 1.5 miles southwest of Mount Sizer (lat. 37°12' N, long. 121°31'45" W). Named on Mount Sizer (1955) 7.5' quadrangle.

Middle Slough [CONTRA COSTA]: *water feature,* extends for 1.25 miles, between Browns Island and Winter Island, from New York Slough to Suisun Bay 3.5 miles northwest of Antioch (lat. 38°02'50" N, long. 121°51'35" W). Named on Antioch North (1978) 7.5' quadrangle. Called Beeners Channel on Ringgold's (1850b) map.

Midway [ALAMEDA]: *locality,* 6 miles east-southeast of Altamont along Southern Pacific Railroad (lat. 37°42'55" N, long. 121°33'30" W; sec. 32, T 2 S, R 4 E). Named on Midway (1953) 7.5' quadrangle. Postal authorities established Midway post office in 1870 and discontinued it in 1918 (Frickstad, p. 2).

Midway Siding [ALAMEDA]: *locality,* less than 1 mile south-southwest of Midway along Western Pacific Railroad (lat. 37°42'20" N, long. 121°34' W; at W line sec. 5, T 3 S, R 4 E). Named on Midway (1953) 7.5' quadrangle.

Miguelita Creek [SANTA CLARA]: *stream,* flows 0.5 mile to lowlands 2.5 miles east of Berryessa (lat. 37°23'05" N, long. 121°48'50" W); the same name applies to a stream that joins Coyote Creek in central San Jose (lat. 37°21'20" N, long. 121°52'20" W), but the two streams are unconnected through the intervening urban area. Named on Calaveras Reservoir (1961) and San Jose East (1961) 7.5' quadrangles.

Milagra Ridge [SAN MATEO]: *ridge,* northwest- to west-northwest-trending, 1.25 miles long, 4 miles west-southwest of downtown South San Francisco (lat. 37°38'25" N, long. 122°28'45" W); the ridge is south of Milagra Valley. Named on San Francisco South (1956) 7.5' quadrangle.

Milagra Valley [SAN MATEO]: *canyon,* drained by a stream that flows nearly 2 miles to the sea 4.5 miles west-southwest of downtown South San Francisco (lat. 37°38'40" N, long. 122°29'35" W). Named on San Francisco South (1956) 7.5' quadrangle. Brown (p. 58) gave the names "Morrissey's Gulch" and "Dini Gulch" as alternates, and noted that

Lawrence Morrissey and Patrick Morrissey had a ranch at the place after 1900.

Mile Rock [SAN FRANCISCO]: *rock,* less than 1 mile north-northeast of Point Lobos, and 2100 feet offshore at Lands End (lat. 37°47'35" N, long. 122°30'35" W). Named on San Francisco North (1956) 7.5' quadrangle. This rock and nearby Little Mile Rock are called Mile Rocks on San Francisco (1915) 15' quadrangle. Beechey gave the two rocks the name "One-mile Rocks" in 1826 because they are 1 mile south of the channel leading to the Golden Gate (Gudde, 1949, p. 214). Ringgold (p. 24) used the form "One Mile Rocks" for the name.

Mile Rock: see **Little Mile Rock** [SAN FRANCISCO].

Mile Rocks: see **Mile Rock** [SAN FRANCISCO].

Miley: see **Fort Miley Military Reservation** [SAN FRANCISCO].

Millar [SOLANO]: *locality,* 6 miles east-southeast of Dixon along Oakland Antioch and Eastern Railroad (lat. 38°23'30" N, long. 121°43'15" W; sec. 2, T 6 N, R 2 E). Named on Saxon (1916) 7.5' quadrangle.

Millbrae [SAN MATEO]: *town,* 4 miles southsoutheast of downtown South San Francisco (lat. 37°36'05" N, long. 122°23'25" W). Named on Montara Mountain (1956) and San Mateo (1956) 7.5' quadrangles. Darius Ogden Mills bought land at the place in 1860 and built an estate that he called Millbrae (Hoover, Rensch, and Rensch, p. 403). The name later was applied to the railroad station there (Gudde, 1949, p. 215). Postal authorities established Millbrae post office in 1866, discontinued it in 1874, and reestablished it in 1875 (Frickstad, p. 168). The town incorporated in 1948.

Millbrae Meadows [SAN MATEO]: *district,* 1.5 miles west of downtown Millbrae (lat. 37°36'15" N, long. 122°25' W). Named on Montara Mountain (1956) 7.5' quadrangle.

Miller [MARIN]: *locality,* 6 miles south-southeast of downtown Novato along Northwestern Pacific Railroad (lat. 38°01'40" N, long. 122°31'20" W); the place is near the railroad crossing of present Miller Creek. Named on Petaluma (1914) 15' quadrangle. The name is for James Miller, who settled in present Marin County in 1845 (Gudde, 1949, p. 215).

Miller [SANTA CLARA]: *locality,* 3.5 miles south-southeast of Gilroy along Southern Pacific Railroad (lat. 36°57'25" N, long. 121°32'40" W). Named on Chittenden (1955) 7.5' quadrangle. Thompson and West's (1876) map shows a place called Miller's Station at the site, and shows Bloomfield farm nearby to the northwest. Miller-Lux ranch had its headquarters at Bloomfield, 3 miles south of Gilroy, where a self-contained community included a railroad station (Pierce, p. 177).

Miller Canyon [SOLANO]: *canyon,* 4.5 miles

long, opens into Pleasants Valley 4 miles northeast of Mount Vaca (lat. 38°26'35" N, long. 122°03'30" W; near W line sec. 23, T 7 N, R 2 W); the feature is along upper reaches of Pleasants Creek. Named on Mount Vaca (1951) 7.5' quadrangle. United States Board on Geographic Names (1933, p. 520) rejected the name "Pleasants Canyon" for the feature. The stream in the canyon is called Miller Canyon Creek on Mount Vaca (1942) 15' quadrangle.

Miller Canyon: see **Miller Creek** [ALAMEDA].

Miller Canyon Creek: see **Miller Canyon** [SOLANO].

Miller Creek [ALAMEDA]: *stream,* flows 1.5 miles to San Leandro Creek 10.5 miles east-southeast of downtown Oakland (lat. 37°45'50" N, long. 122°05'30" W; sec. 16, T 2 S, R 2 W). Named on Las Trampas Ridge (1959) 7.5' quadrangle. The name commemorates William Hunt Miller, who settled at the head of the canyon of the stream—called Miller Canyon—in 1856 (Mosier and Mosier, p. 57).

Miller Creek [MARIN]: *stream,* flows 7 miles to lowlands 5.5 miles south-southeast of downtown Novato (lat. 38°01'55" N, long. 122° 31'30" W). Named on Novato (1954) 7.5' quadrangle.

Miller Slough [SANTA CLARA]: *stream,* the continuation of West Branch Llagas Creek has this name for 3.5 miles south from Gilroy to where it joins Llagas Creek (lat. 36°59'25" N, long. 121°31'50" W). Named on Chittenden (1955) and Gilroy (1955) 7.5' quadrangles.

Millers Peak: see **Putnam Peak** [SOLANO].

Miller's Station: see **Miller** [SANTA CLARA].

Millerton [MARIN]: *locality,* 3.5 miles northwest of Point Reyes Station (lat. 38°06'30" N, long. 122°50'40" W); the place is near the mouth of Millerton Gulch. Named on Inverness (1954) 7.5' quadrangle. James Miller had a large wharf at the place (Mason, 1976a, p. 33).

Millerton Gulch [MARIN]: *canyon,* drained by a stream that flows nearly 4 miles to Tomales Bay 3.5 miles northwest of Point Reyes Station (lat. 38°06'20" N, long. 122°50'25" W). Named on Inverness (1954) and Point Reyes NE (1954) 7.5' quadrangles.

Millerton Point [MARIN]: *promontory,* 3.5 miles northwest of Point Reyes Station on the northeast side of Tomales Bay (lat. 38°06'30" N, long. 122°51'05" W); the promontory is near Millerton. Named on Inverness (1954) 7.5' quadrangle.

Mill Gulch: see **Copper Mine Gulch** [MARIN].

Mills College: see **Oakland** [ALAMEDA].

Mills Creek [SAN MATEO]:

(1) *stream,* flows 2.25 miles to San Francisco Bay 3 miles northwest of downtown San Mateo (lat. 37°35'50" N, long. 122°21'50" W).

Named on Montara Mountain (1956) and San Mateo (1956) 7.5' quadrangles. The stream also has been called Black Hawk Creek for Black Hawk ranch, which was started in 1858 (Brown, p. 56).

(2) *stream,* flows 3.5 miles to Arroyo Leon nearly 2 miles southeast of downtown Half Moon Bay (lat. 37°26'45" N, long. 122°24'15" W). Named on Half Moon Bay (1961) and Woodside (1961) 7.5' quadrangles. Robert Mills had a ranch along the stream in the middle 1860's; the stream also had the names "Woods Creek," "Johnston Creek," and "Savage Creek," all for ranchers in the neighborhood (Brown, p. 56).

Mills Seltzer Spring: see **Azule Springs** [SANTA CLARA].

Mills Seminary: see **Oakland** [ALAMEDA].

Mills Switch Station: see **San Martin** [SANTA CLARA].

Mill Valley [MARIN]:

(1) *valley,* 5 miles south of downtown San Rafael along Arroyo Corte Madera Del Presidio (lat. 37°54'10" N, long. 122°32'15" W). Named on San Rafael (1954) 7.5' quadrangle. The name is from the sawmill that John Reed built in the valley in 1834 (Gudde, 1949, p. 214-215).

(2) *town,* 4.5 miles south of downtown San Rafael (lat. 37°54'25" N, long. 122°32'45" W); the town is in and around Mill Valley (1). Named on San Rafael (1954) 7.5' quadrangle. Postal authorities established Mill Valley post office in 1890, changed the name to Eastland in 1892, and changed it back to Mill Valley in 1904; the name "Eastland" was for Joseph G. Eastland, president of Tamalpais Land and Water Company, which developed the site (Salley, p. 64, 141). The town incorporated in 1900. Postal authorities established Tamalpais post office 8 miles west of Mill Valley post office in 1906 and discontinued it in 1929 (Salley, p. 218); according to Gudde (1969, p. 330), the place was known as Big Coyote before the post office came, and as Tamalpais Valley after 1908. Postal authorities established Laverne post office 1.5 miles west of Mill Valley post office in 1909 and discontinued it in 1914; they established Locust post office as a station of Mill Valley post office in 1938 and discontinued it in 1948 (Salley, p. 119, 124).

Mill Valley Junction: see **Almonte** [MARIN].

Millwood [MARIN]: *locality,* 5 miles south of downtown San Rafael (lat. 37°53'50" N, long. 122°32'20" W). Named on Tamalpais (1897) 15' quadrangle.

Milpitas [SANTA CLARA]:

(1) *land grant,* at and east of the city of Milpitas. Named on Calaveras Reservoir (1961) and Milpitas (1961) 7.5' quadrangles. Jose Maria Alviso received the land in 1835 and his heirs claimed 4458 acres patented in 1871 (Cowan, p. 48). According to Arbuckle (p. 23), the

name is from an Aztec word that means "corn patches" or "little corn fields."

(2) *city,* 7 miles north of downtown San Jose (lat. 37°25'45" N, long. 121°54'20" W); the city is partly on Milpitas grant. Named on Calaveras Reservoir (1961) and Milpitas (1961) 7.5' quadrangles. Postal authorities established Milpitas post office in 1856 (Frickstad, p. 174), and the city incorporated in 1954. The first structure at the place was built in 1855; the settlement that developed there was called Penitencia, presumably for nearby Penitencia Creek (present Lower Penitencia Creek), but the name "Penitencia" was changed to Milpitas, which already was in use for the post office (Hoover, Rensch, and Rensch, p. 453-454).

Milpitas Creek: see **Berryessa Creek** [SANTA CLARA].

Mimulus Spring [CONTRA COSTA]: *spring,* nearly 0.5 mile north-northeast of Mount Diablo (lat. 37°53'10" N, long. 121°54'35" W). Named on Clayton (1953) 7.5' quadrangle.

Mindego Creek [SAN MATEO]: *stream,* flows 4.25 miles to Alpine Creek 1.5 miles southeast of La Honda (lat. 37°17'50" N, long. 122°15'10" W; sec. 25, T 7 S, R 4 W); the stream goes past Mindego Hill. Named on La Honda (1961) and Mindego Hill (1961) 7.5' quadrangles. The stream also is called Wilbur's Creek (Brown, p. 53).

Mindego Hill [SAN MATEO]: *peak,* 12 miles south of Redwood City (lat. 37°18'40" N, long. 122°13'45" W; sec. 19, T 7 S, R 3 W). Altitude 2143 feet. Named on Mindego Hill (1961) 7.5' quadrangle. The misspelled name commemorates Juan Mendico, a Basque who settled at the place in 1859 (Brown, p. 53).

Mindego Lake [SAN MATEO]: *lake,* 650 feet long, 0.25 mile north-northwest of Mindego Hill (lat. 37°18'55" N, long. 122°13'50" W; near N line sec. 19, T 7 S, R 3 W). Named on Mindego Hill (1961) 7.5' quadrangle. The feature first had the name "Laguna del Corazon" for its shape—*corazon* means "heart" in Spanish (Brown, p. 53).

Mine Hill [SANTA CLARA]: *peak,* 1.5 miles west of New Almaden (lat. 37°10'35" N, long. 121°50'40" W); the feature is at New Almaden mine. Named on Santa Teresa Hills (1953) 7.5' quadrangle.

Mine Ridge: see **New Almaden** [SANTA CLARA].

Miner Slough [SOLANO]: *water feature,* extends from Sutter Slough to Cache Slough 5.25 miles north of Rio Vista (lat. 38°14' N, long. 121°40'25" W). Named on Courtland (1978), Liberty Island (1978), and Rio Vista (1978) 7.5' quadrangles.

Mining Hills: see **New Almaden** [SANTA CLARA].

Miramar [SAN MATEO]: *district,* 2.5 miles northwest of downtown Half Moon Bay (lat. 37°29'35" N, long. 122°27'25" W). Named on Half Moon Bay (1961) 7.5' quadrangle. Josiah P. Ames and his partners constructed a wharf at the place in 1868, and the village that developed there was called Amesport (Morrall, p. 48-49). The wharf at the place was called Amesport Landing (Hoover, Rensch, and Rensch, p. 394), and later it was called McGill's Wharf (Wagner, J.R., p. 13).

Miramar Beach [SAN MATEO]: *beach,* 2.5 miles northwest of downtown Half Moon Bay along the coast (lat. 37°29'35" N, long. 122°27'35" W); the beach is at Miramar. Named on Half Moon Bay (1961) 7.5' quadrangle. The place sometimes is called Ames Beach, for J.P. Ames, for whom Amesport was named (Brown, p. 56).

Miramontes [SAN MATEO]:
(1) *land grant,* at and near the town of Half Moon Bay. Named on Half Moon Bay (1961) 7.5' quadrangle. Candelario Miramontes received 1 league in 1841; J.C. Miramontes claimed 4424 acres patented in 1882 (Cowan, p. 60; Cowan gave the names "Arroyo de los Pilarcitos" and "San Benito" as alternates). According to Perez (p. 73), Vincente Miramontes was the patentee in 1882.
(2) *ridge,* northwest-trending, 1.5 miles long, 3.5 miles south-southwest of present Montara Knob (lat. 37°30'20" N, long. 122° 30'15" W). Named on San Mateo (1915) 15' quadrangle.

Miramontes Point [SAN MATEO]: *promontory,* 2.25 miles south-southwest of downtown Half Moon Bay along the coast (lat. 37° 26' N, long. 122°26'30" W); the feature is on Miramontes grant. Named on Half Moon Bay (1961) 7.5' quadrangle.

Misery: see **Mount Misery** [SANTA CLARA].

Mission Bay: see **Mission District** [SAN FRANCISCO].

Mission Creek [ALAMEDA]: *stream,* flows 4.5 miles to lowlands 3 miles east-southeast of Fremont civic center (lat. 37°32'10" N, long. 121°55' W; sec. 36, T 4 S, R 1 W); the stream reaches lowlands at San Jose de Guadalupe mission. Named on Niles (1961) 7.5' quadrangle.

Mission Creek: see **Mission District** [SAN FRANCISCO]; **Santa Clara** [SANTA CLARA].

Mission District [SAN FRANCISCO]: *district,* 1.25 miles south of San Francisco civic center (lat. 37°45'40" N, long. 122°25' W); Mission Dolores is in the northwest part of the district. Named on San Francisco North (1956) 7.5' quadrangle. In 1776 Anza chose the site for San Francisco de Asis mission by a lake called Laguna de Manantial that covered much of present Mission District; the lake was fed by a stream that Anza called Arroyo de Nuestra Señora de los Dolores because he examined it on Friday of Our Lady of Sorrows—the mission became known popularly as Mission Dolores (Hoover, Rensch, and

Rensch, p. 349). The lake also was called Laguna de Nuestra Señora de los Dolores; the word "Manantial" has to do with running water (Davidson, p. 121). The lake also had the names "Laguna de los Dolores"—as shown on Dalrymple's (1789) map)—and "Lake McCoppin" (Hansen and Condon, p. 24). Mission Creek flowed from the lake, and a nearby embayment was called Mission Bay; earlier the embayment was called Ensenada de los Llorones (Davidson, p. 120). The earlier name dates from 1775, when Aguirre found three Indians weeping copiously at the place—*los llorones* means "the weepers" in Spanish (Bolton, p. 252). Wackenreuder's (1861) map shows Mission Bay between Rincon Point and Point San Quentin near present Mission Rock Terminal and China Basin. Soule, Gihon, and Nisbet's (1855) map shows the configuration of Mission Bay before the bay was filled.

Mission Mountains: see **Twin Peaks** [SAN FRANCISCO].

Mission Pass [ALAMEDA]: *pass,* 3.25 miles east of Fremont civic center (lat. 37°33'35" N, long. 121°54'40" W; near W line sec. 30, T 4 S, R 1 E); the pass is nearly 2 miles north-northeast of San Jose de Guadalupe mission. Named on Niles (1961) 7.5' quadrangle. The feature also had the name "Stockton Pass" because it was on the road to Stockton in San Joaquin County (Mosier and Mosier, p. 57)

Mission Peak [ALAMEDA]: *peak,* 5.5 miles east-southeast of Fremont civic center (lat. 37°30'45" N, long. 121°52'50" W; sec. 8, T 5 S, R 1 E); the peak is 2.5 miles southeast of San Jose de Guadalupe mission. Altitude 2517 feet. Named on Niles (1961) 7.5' quadrangle.

Mission Peaks: see **Twin Peaks** [SAN FRANCISCO].

Mission Reservoir [ALAMEDA]: *lake,* 400 feet long, 3.5 miles east-southeast of Fremont civic center (lat. 37°31'50" N, long. 121°54'35" W; sec. 6, T 5 S, R 1 E); the lake is 0.5 mile east-southeast of San Jose de Guadalupe mission. Named on Niles (1961) 7.5' quadrangle.

Mission Rock [SAN FRANCISCO]: *island,* 850 feet long, 1 mile south-southeast of Rincon Point (lat. 37°46'25" N, long. 122°22'55" W). Named on San Francisco North (1947) 7.5' quadrangle. San Francisco North (1956) 7.5' quadrangle shows Mission Rock Terminal at the place, and indicates that the island is enlarged by landfill and is connected to shore by a causeway.

Mission Rock Terminal: see **Mission Rock** [SAN FRANCISCO].

Mission San Jose: see **Mission San Jose District** [ALAMEDA].

Mission San Jose District [ALAMEDA]: *district,* 3 miles east-southeast of Fremont civic center in Fremont (lat. 37°32' N, long. 121°55'15" W); San Jose de Guadalupe mission is in the district. Named on Niles (1961) 7.5'

quadrangle. Pleasanton (1906) 15' quadrangle has the name "Mission San Jose" for the community that in 1956 joined with neighboring communities to form the new city of Fremont. Postal authorities established Mission San Jose post office before April 9, 1850 (Salley, p. 143).

Mission San Jose Hot Springs: see **Warm Springs** [ALAMEDA].

Mississippi Creek [SANTA CLARA]: *stream,* flows 9 miles to North Fork Pacheco Creek nearly 6 miles east-northeast of Gilroy Hot Springs (lat. 37°08' N, long. 121°22'40" W; sec. 24, T 9 S, R 5 E). Named on Mississippi Creek (1955) 7.5' quadrangle.

Mitchell Canyon [CONTRA COSTA]: *canyon,* 4 miles long, opens into lowlands 4 miles north-northwest of Mount Diablo near Clayton (lat. 37°56'10" N, long. 121°56'15" W; sec. 14, T 1 N, R 1 W); Mitchell Creek drains the canyon. Named on Clayton (1953) 7.5' quadrangle. Captain Mitchell located a claim in the canyon in 1853 (Gudde, 1969, p. 205). Whitney (p. 24) mentioned Mitchell's Cañon.

Mitchell Creek [CONTRA COSTA]: *stream,* flows 4.5 miles to Mount Diablo Creek nearly 4.5 miles north-northwest of Mount Diablo at Clayton (lat. 37°56'35" N, long. 121°56'05" W; near SE cor. sec. 11, T 1 N, R 1 W); the stream drains Mitchell Canyon. Named on Clayton (1953) 7.5' quadrangle.

Mitchell Creek [SAN MATEO]: *stream,* flows 1.25 miles to Tunitas Creek 2.5 miles west of Skeggs Point (lat. 37°24'30" N, long. 122° 21' W). Named on Woodside (1961) 7.5' quadrangle. The name is from the operator of a sawmill along the creek from 1910 until 1915 (Brown, p. 57).

Mitchell Ravine [ALAMEDA]: *canyon,* drained by a stream that heads in San Joaquin County and flows 6 miles to Corral Hollow Creek 5.5 miles south of Midway (lat. 37°38'10" N, long. 121°34'30" W; near S line sec. 30, T 3 S, R 4 E). Named on Cedar Mountain (1956) and Midway (1953) 7.5' quadrangles. A ridge known locally as Bear Trap Ridge is on the west side of Mitchell Ravine south of Corral Hollow; the name is from a bear trap that E.B. Carrell, Horatio P. Wright, and Grizzly Adams put on the ridge in 1856 (Mosier and Mosier, p. 14).

Mitchell Rock [CONTRA COSTA]: *peak,* 2.5 miles northwest of Mount Diablo (lat. 37°54'45" N, long. 121°56'25" W; near N line sec. 26, T 1 N, R 1 W). Altitude 1507 feet. Named on Clayton (1953) 7.5' quadrangle.

Mitchell's Cañon: see **Mitchell Canyon** [CONTRA COSTA].

Mix Canyon [SOLANO]: *canyon,* 4 miles long, on upper reaches of Ulatis Creek, opens into lowlands 3.5 miles east of Mount Vaca (lat. 38°24'30" N, long. 122°02'30" W). Named on Mount Vaca (1951) 7.5' quadrangle. Called Weldon Canyon on Napa (1902) 30' quadrangle. United States Board on Geographic Names (1933, p. 807) once approved the name "Weldon Canyon" for the feature, and at the same time rejected the names "Bucks Canyon," "Mix Canyon," and "Mixs Canyon."

Mixs Canyon: see **Mix Canyon** [SOLANO].

Mocho: see **Mount Mocho** [SANTA CLARA].

Mocho Creek: see **Arroyo Mocho** [ALAMEDA-SANTA CLARA].

Mococo [CONTRA COSTA]: *locality,* 1.25 miles northeast of Martinez along Southern Pacific Railroad (lat. 38°01'35" N, long. 122°06'50" W). Named on Vine Hill (1959) 7.5' quadrangle. The name was coined in 1912 from letters in the term "Mountain Copper Company"—the company had a copper smelter at Bulls Head Point; the place first was called Lewis for the general manager of the company (Gudde, 1949, p. 218).

Moffett Channel [SANTA CLARA]: *water feature,* artificial waterway, nearly 1 mile long, that reaches Guadalupe Slough 3 miles southeast of the mouth of that slough (lat. 37°25'40" N, long. 122° 30' W). Named on Mountain View (1961, photorevised 1968 and 1973) 7.5' quadrangle. United States Board on Geographic Names (1968b, p. 8) rejected the names "Jagels Slough" and "Sunnyvale West Outfall Channel" for the feature.

Moffett Field [SANTA CLARA]: *military installation,* between downtown Sunnyvale and San Francisco Bay (lat. 37°25' N, long. 122°03' W). Named on Mountain View (1961) 7.5' quadrangle. According to an undated item from *San Jose Mercury,* the installation was commissioned in 1931 under the name "United States Naval Air Station, Sunnyvale, Mountain View, Calif.," and was a base for navy dirigibles; then in 1935 the army took charge of the place and used it as an air base until 1942, when the installation reverted to the navy as a base for lighter-than-air craft conducting anti-submarine activities off the West Coast—the name "Moffett" honors Admiral William A. Moffett, who was killed in the crash of the navy dirigible *Akron* in 1933. Postal authorities established Naval Air Station post office in 1933 and changed the name after a few months to Moffett Field (Frickstad, p. 174).

Molate Island: see **Red Rock** [CONTRA COSTA-MARIN-SAN FRANCISCO].

Molate Point: see **Point Molate** [CONTRA COSTA].

Molena [SOLANO]: *locality,* nearly 7 miles south of Denverton along Sacramento Northern Railroad (lat. 38°07'30" N, long. 121°52'35" W; at S line sec. 4, T 3 N, R 1 E). Named on Denverton (1953) and Honker Bay (1953) 7.5' quadrangles.

Monclair: see **Thornhill** [ALAMEDA].

Monsanto [CONTRA COSTA]: *locality,* 4.5 miles east of Martinez along Atchison, Topeka and Santa Fe Railroad (lat. 38°01'35" N, long.

122°03'20" W). Named on Vine Hill (1959) 7.5' quadrangle.

Montalvo [SANTA CLARA]: *locality,* 1 mile south of downtown Saratoga (lat. 37°14'35" N, long. 122°01'45" W; near S line sec. 12, T 8 S, R 2 W). Named on Castle Rock Ridge (1955) 7.5' quadrangle.

Montaña de San Juan Bautista: see **Mount Diablo** [CONTRA COSTA].

Montara [SAN MATEO]: *town,* 2 miles southwest of Montara Knob near the coast (lat. 37°32'30" N, long. 122°30'45" W). Named on Montara Mountain (1956) 7.5' quadrangle. Postal authorities established Montara post office in 1908 and discontinued it in 1918; later in 1918, they changed the name of Farallone post office to Montara (Salley, p. 144).

Montara Beach [SAN MATEO]: *beach,* nearly 2 miles west-southwest of Montara Knob along the coast (lat. 37°32'50" N, long. 122°13'20" W); the beach is at Montara. Named on Montara Mountain (1956) 7.5' quadrangle.

Montara Creek: see **Point Montara** [SAN MATEO].

Montara Knob [SAN MATEO]: *peak,* 7.5 miles north-northwest of the town of Half Moon Bay (lat. 37°33'25" N, long. 122°29'05" W; sec. 26, T 4 S, R 6 W); the peak is on Montara Mountain. Named on Montara Mountain (1956) 7.5' quadrangle.

Montara Mountain [SAN MATEO]: *ridge,* northwest- to west-northwest-trending, 8 miles long, 13 miles west-northwest of Redwood City near the coast (lat. 37°33' N, long. 122°27' W). Named on Montara Mountain (1956) 7.5' quadrangle. United States Board on Geographic Names (1933, p. 528) rejected the form "Montora Mountain" for the name.

Montara Point: see **Point Montara** [SAN MATEO].

Monta Vista [SANTA CLARA]: *district,* 1.5 miles west of downtown Cupertino near Stevens Creek (lat. 37°19'20" N, long. 122°03'15" W). Named on Cupertino (1961) 7.5' quadrangle. Called Monte Vista on California Mining Bureau's (1909b) map. Rambo (1964, p. 38) described the place as "a turn of the century subdivision." Postal authorities established Monta Vista post office in 1946 (Salley, p. 144). Peninsular Railway Company's (1912) map shows a place called Simla located along the rail line about halfway from Monta Vista to Loyola, and a place called Golden Spur located about halfway from Monta Vista to Cupertino.

Monte Bello Ridge [SANTA CLARA]: *ridge,* northwest-trending, 6 miles long, 5 miles south of downtown Los Altos (lat. 37°18'30" N, long. 122°07'45" W). Named on Cupertino (1961) and Mindego Hill (1961) 7.5' quadrangles.

Monte del Diablo [CONTRA COSTA]: *land grant,* extends from Clayton Valley to Pacheco and Suisun Bay Named on Clayton (1953),

Honker Bay (1953), Vine Hill (1959), and Walnut Creek (1959) 7.5' quadrangles. Salvio Pacheco received the land in 1834 and 1844; he claimed 17,922 acres patented in 1859 (Cowan, p. 32).

Monte Diablo: see **Mount Diablo** [CONTRA COSTA].

Monte Diablo Creek: see **Mount Diablo Creek** [CONTRA COSTA].

Monte Diablo Range: see **Diablo Range** [ALAMEDA-CONTRA COSTA-SANTA CLARA].

Monte San Bruno: see **San Bruno Mountain** [SAN MATEO].

Monte Sereno [SANTA CLARA]: *town,* between Los Gatos and Saratoga (lat. 37°14'15" N, long. 121°59'15" W). Named on Los Gatos (1953, photorevised 1968 and 1973) 7.5' quadrangle. Postal authorities established Monte Sereno post office in 1957 (Salley, p. 145), and the town incorporated in 1957.

Monte Vista: see **Monta Vista** [SANTA CLARA]; **Oakland** [ALAMEDA].

Montezuma [SOLANO]:
(1) *locality,* nearly 4 mile south of Denverton (lat. 38°10'10" N, long. 121°53'20" W; at N line sec. 29, T 4 N, R 1 E); the place is near the west end of Montezuma Hills. Named on Denverton (1953) 7.5' quadrangle.
(2) *locality,* nearly 3 miles south of Birds Landing (2) along Sacramento Northern Railroad (lat. 38°05'30" N, long. 121°52'30" W; sec. 21, T 3 N, R 1 E). Named on Antioch North (1978) and Honker Bay (1953) 7.5' quadrangles.

Montezuma Creek: see **Montezuma Slough** [SOLANO].

Montezuma Hills [SOLANO]: *range,* north of Sacramento River between Rio Vista and Birds Landing (2). Named on Antioch North (1978), Birds Landing (1953), Denverton (1953), Jersey Island (1978), and Rio Vista (1978) 7.5' quadrangles. Called Montezuma Range on Ringgold's (1850c) map.

Montezuma House: see **Collinsville** [SOLANO].

Montezuma Landing: see **Marshall Cut** [SOLANO].

Montezuma Range: see **Montezuma Hills** [SOLANO].

Montezuma Slough [SOLANO]: *water feature,* extends from Suisun Bay near the mouth of Sacramento River to Grizzly Bay 8 miles south of Fairfield (lat. 38°08' N, long. 122°03'30" W). Named on Antioch North (1978), Denverton (1953), Fairfield South (1949), and Honker Bay (1953) 7.5' quadrangles. Called Montezuma Creek on Karquines (1898) 15' quadrangle, but United States Board on Geographic Names (1943, p. 12) rejected this name.

Montgomery: see **Fort Montgomery** and **Point Montgomery**, under **Telegraph Hill** [SAN FRANCISCO].

Montgomery Hill [SANTA CLARA]: *peak,* 2 miles east-southeast of Evergreen (lat. 37°17'55" N, long. 121°45' W). Named on San Jose East (1961, photorevised 1968 and 1973) 7.5' quadrangle. The name honors Professor John Joseph Montgomery, known for his research in aviation between 1879 and 1911 (United States Board on Geographic Names, 1964, p. 13).

Montora: see **Point Montora**, under **Point Montara** [SAN MATEO].

Montora Mountain: see **Montara Mountain** [SAN MATEO].

Monument Peak [ALAMEDA-SANTA CLARA]: *peak,* 7.5 miles south of Sunol on Alameda-Santa Clara county line (lat. 37°29'05" N, long. 121°51'50" W; sec. 21, T 5 S, R 1 E). Altitude 2594 feet. Named on Calaveras Reservoir (1961) 7.5' quadrangle. The name is from stone monuments that mark the county line (Mosier and Mosier, p. 58). The peak first was known as Cerro de las Calaveras (Gudde, 1949, p. 49).

Moody Creek: see **Big Moody Creek**, under **Saratoga Creek** [SANTA CLARA].

Moody Gulch [SANTA CLARA]: *canyon,* drained by a stream that flows 1.25 miles to Los Gatos Creek 4 miles south of downtown Los Gatos (lat. 37°10' N, long. 121°58'40" W; sec. 9, T 9 S, R 1 W). Named on Los Gatos (1953) 7.5' quadrangle. According to Rambo (1973, p. 24), David B. Moody owned part of an oil strike made in 1872 in what still is known as Moody's Gulch.

Moon and Adams Landing: see **Oakland** [ALAMEDA].

Moore Hill [MARIN]: *ridge,* east-trending, 0.25 mile long, 0.5 mile west of downtown San Rafael (lat. 37°58'20" N, long. 122°32'25" W). Named on San Rafael (1954) 7.5' quadrangle.

Moore Tract [SOLANO]: *area,* 11 miles north of Rio Vista (lat. 38° 18'50" N, long. 121°43' W). Named on Liberty Island (1978) 7.5' quadrangle.

Moraga [CONTRA COSTA]: *town,* 4.25 miles southeast of Orinda (lat. 37°50'05" N, long. 122°07'45" W). Named on Las Trampas Ridge (1959) and Oakland East (1959) 7.5' quadrangles. Postal authorities established Moraga post office in 1886, discontinued it in 1887, and reestablished it in 1915 (Frickstad, p. 22). The town incorporated in 1974. The name is for Joaquin Moraga, a grantee of Laguna de los Palos Colorados grant (Gudde, 1949, p. 224). Postal authorities established Saint Mary's College post office 1 mile northeast of Moraga post office in 1928 (Salley, p. 191).

Moraga Center: see **Moraga Valley** [CONTRA COSTA].

Moraga Valley [CONTRA COSTA]: *valley,* 4 miles southeast of Orinda at Moraga (lat. 37°50' N, long. 122°08' W). Named on Las Trampas Ridge (1959) and Oakland East (1959) 7.5' quadrangles. Postal authorities established Moraga Center post office in 1955 and discontinued it in 1956; the name was from the location of the post office in the center of Moraga Valley (Salley, p. 146).

Moreland: see **Meridian** [SANTA CLARA].

Morgan Hill [SANTA CLARA]: *town,* 19 miles southeast of downtown San Jose (lat. 37°07'45" N, long. 121°39'10" W). Named on Morgan Hill (1955) and Mount Madonna (1955) 7.5' quadrangles. Hiram Morgan Hill married Diana Murphy, who inherited 4900 acres of Ojo de Agua de la Coche grant; the couple built their home on the land, and when Hill subdivided the property in 1892, the community laid out there was named for him (Wyman, p. ix). Postal authorities established Morgan Hill post office in 1893 (Frickstad, p. 174), and the town incorporated in 1906.

Morgan's Cove: see **Hospital Cove** [MARIN].

Morgan Territory [CONTRA COSTA]: *area,* 3 miles east-southeast of Mount Diablo (lat. 37°52'15" N, long. 121°51'30" W). Named on Antioch South (1953) and Tassajara (1953) 7.5' quadrangles. The name commemorates Jeremiah Morgan, a Cherokee Indian who claimed 10,000 acres of unsurveyed land at the place in 1856 (Gudde, 1949, p. 225).

Mori Point [SAN MATEO]: *promontory,* 4.25 miles north of Montara Knob along the coast (lat. 37°37'10" N, long. 122°29'50" W). Named on Montara Mountain (1956) 7.5' quadrangle.

Morrison Canyon [ALAMEDA]: *canyon,* drained by a stream that flows 1.25 miles to lowlands 1.5 miles north-northeast of Fremont civic center (lat. 37°34'10" N, long. 121°57'15" W; sec. 22, T 4 S, R 1 W). Named on Niles (1961) 7.5' quadrangle. Perry Morrison and William Morrison settled in the canyon in 1849 (Mosier and Mosier, p. 58).

Morrissey's Gulch: see **Milagra Valley** [SAN MATEO].

Morrow Cove [SOLANO]: *embayment,* nearly 3 miles south-southeast of downtown Vallejo along Carquinez Strait (lat. 38°04'05" N, long. 122°13'50" W). Named on Benicia (1959) 7.5' quadrangle.

Morrow Island [SOLANO]: *area,* 6 miles northeast of Benicia (lat. 38°07' N, long. 122°05'15" W). Named on Fairfield South (1949) and Vine Hill (1959) 7.5' quadrangles.

Morses Gulch [MARIN]: *canyon,* drained by a stream that flows 1.5 miles to Bolinas Lagoon 1 mile northeast of Bolinas (lat. 37°55'05" N, long. 122°40'10" W). Named on Bolinas (1954) 7.5' quadrangle. Teather (p. 47) associated the name with Benjamin G. Morse, a local carpenter and rancher.

Moses Rock Ridge [CONTRA COSTA]: *ridge,* northwest- to west-trending, 1 mile long, 1.25 miles west of Mount Diablo (lat. 37°52'55" N, long. 121°56'05" W). Named on Clayton (1953) 7.5' quadrangle.

Moses Rock Spring [CONTRA COSTA]: *spring,* 2 miles west of Mount Diablo (lat. 37°53'05" N, long. 121°56'55" W); the spring is near the west end of Moses Rock Ridge. Named on Clayton (1953) 7.5' quadrangle.

Moss Beach [SAN MATEO]: *town,* 2.5 miles southwest of Montara Knob near the coast (lat. 37°31'45" N, long. 122°30'45" W). Named on Montara Mountain (1956) 7.5' quadrangle. The name is from a marine plant found on rocks at the place, and goes back to the opening of Moss Beach hotel in 1880 (Brown, p. 59). Postal authorities established Colony post office at the place in 1894, changed the name to Blenheim in 1895, and discontinued it in 1901—the name "Colony" was from Half Moon Bay Colony Tract of 1881; they established Moss Beach post office in 1910 (Salley, p. 23, 48, 147).

Mountain Home [SANTA CLARA]: *locality,* nearly 3 miles east-northeast of Loma Prieta along Llagas Creek (lat. 37°07'15" N, long. 121°47'40" W; sec. 30, T 9 S, R 2 E). Named on Los Gatos (1919) 15' quadrangle.

Mountain Home Gulch: see **Alambique Creek** [SAN MATEO].

Mountain House [ALAMEDA]: *locality,* 12 miles east-northeast of Livermore (lat. 37°45'15" N, long. 121°34'30" W; sec. 18, T 2 S, R 4 E). Named on Clifton Court Forebay (1978) 7.5' quadrangle. Whitney (p. 33) referred to the place as Zimmerman's Mountain House. Postal authorities established Elk Horn post office at or near present Mountain House in 1852 and discontinued it in 1853; the post office was at a combined home, store, stage stop, and hotel that was decorated with the horns of tule elk (Salley, p. 67).

Mountain House: see **Pacheco Pass** [SANTA CLARA].

Mountain House Creek [ALAMEDA]: *stream,* flows 8 miles to San Joaquin County 13 miles east-northeast of Livermore (lat. 37° 46'20" N, long. 121°33'25" W; sec. 8, T 2 S, R 4 E). Named on Altamont (1953), Clifton Court Forebay (1978), and Midway (1953) 7.5' quadrangles. Called Mountainhouse Creek on Byron (1916) and Tesla (1907) 15' quadrangles.

Mountain Lake [SAN FRANCISCO]: *lake,* 650 feet long, 1.5 miles south-southeast of Fort Point (lat. 37°47'20" N, long. 122°28'10" W). Named on San Francisco North (1956) 7.5' quadrangle. The Spaniards called the feature Laguna del Presidio (Wagner, H.R., p. 486).

Mountain Springs Creek [CONTRA COSTA]: *stream,* flows nearly 2 miles to Curry Canyon 2 miles south-southeast of Mount Diablo (lat. 37°51'25" N, long. 121°54'05" W; sec. 7, T 1 S, R 1 E). Named on Diablo (1953) 7.5' quadrangle.

Mountain View [SANTA CLARA]: *city,* 11 miles west-northwest of downtown San Jose (lat. 37°23'30" N, long. 122°04'45" W). Named on Cupertino (1961) and Mountain

View (1961) 7.5' quadrangles. James Campbell established a stage stop at the place in 1852, and nearby was an inn called Fremont House that was so well known that when the county organized in 1850, the area containing present Mountain View, Los Altos, and Palo Alto was named Fremont Township; Jacob Shumway, who had a store in the community, reportedly looked across the valley to the mountains and gave the name "Mountain View" to the place (Butler, p. 35). Postal authorities established Mountain View post office in 1854 (Frickstad, p. 174), and the city incorporated in 1902. With the coming of the railroad in 1865, a station called Mountain View was built about 1 mile north-northwest of the original community; the first site became known as Old Mountain View, and the village that developed around the railroad station became known as New Mountain View (Rambo, 1973, p. 43). Thompson and West's (1876) map shows both Old Mountain View and New Mountain View. Palo Alto (1899) 15' quadrangle has the name "Mountain View" near the railroad and the name "Old Mountain View" about 1 mile farther south-southeast—both places are in the present city. Peninsular Railroad Company's (1912) map shows a station called Endor along Southern Pacific Railroad less than halfway from Mountain View to Sunnyvale.

Mountain View Landing [SANTA CLARA]: *locality,* 2.5 miles north of downtown Mountain View near the edge of mud flats along San Francisco Bay (lat. 37°25'50" N, long. 122°04'50" W). Named on Palo Alto (1899) 15' quadrangle.

Mountain View Reservoir: see **Martinez Reservoir** [CONTRA COSTA].

Mountain View Slough [SANTA CLARA]: *water feature,* nearly 1.5 miles long, enters San Francisco Bay tidelands 2 miles southwest of the mouth of Coyote Creek (lat. 37°27' N, long. 122°04'35" W). Named on Mountain View (1961) 7.5' quadrangle. The feature is the outlet of Permanente Creek to San Francisco Bay.

Mount Allison [ALAMEDA]: *peak,* 6.5 miles south of Sunol (lat. 37° 29'55" N, long. 121°52'10" W; sec. 16, T 5 S, R 1 E). Altitude 2658 feet. Named on Calaveras Reservoir (1961) 7.5' quadrangle.

Mount Bache: see **Loma Prieta** [SANTA CLARA].

Mount Bielawski: see **Bielawski Mountain** [SANTA CLARA].

Mount Boardman [ALAMEDA-SANTA CLARA]: *peak,* 9 miles east-southeast of Cedar Mountain, where Alameda, San Joaquin, Santa Clara, and Stanislaus Counties meet (lat. 37°28'55" N, long. 121° 28'15" W; sec. 19, T 5 S, R 5 E). Altitude 3593 feet. Named on Mount Boardman (1955) 7.5' quadrangle. The name commemorates W.F.

Boardman, county surveyor of Alameda County and city engineer of Oakland from 1864 until 1868 (Gudde, 1969, p. 33).

Mount Caroline Livermore [MARIN]: *peak, 3* miles east of downtown Sausalito on Angel Island (lat. 37°51'40" N, long. 122°25'45" W). Altitude 781 feet. Named on San Francisco North (1956, photorevised 1968 and 1973) 7.5' quadrangle. Called Mount Ida on San Francisco North (1956) 7.5' quadrangle, but the peak—the highest point on the island—was renamed in 1959 for a Marin County conservation leader (Mason, 1976b, p. 214).

Mount Chisnantuck: see **New Almaden** [SANTA CLARA].

Mount Choual: see **Mount Chual** [SANTA CLARA].

Mount Chual [SANTA CLARA]: *peak,* nearly 1 mile northeast of Loma Prieta (lat. 37°07'10" N, long. 121°49'50" W; sec. 26, T 9 S, R 1 E). Altitude 3562 feet. Named on Loma Prieta (1955) 7.5' quadrangle. Gudde (1949, p. 67-68) traced the name back to a map of 1848, where it appeared as Picacho de Chual—*chual* is an Indian word for common pigweed. Whitney (p. 62) referred to Mount Choual.

Mount Davidson [SAN FRANCISCO]: *peak,* 5 miles south-southeast of Fort Point (lat. 37°44'20" N, long. 122°27'10" W). Named on San Francisco South (1956) 7.5' quadrangle. First called Blue Mountain, but San Francisco Board of Supervisors officially renamed the peak in 1911 to honor George Davidson, who had surveyed it in the 1860's (Lewis, p. 92-93).

Mount Day [SANTA CLARA]: *peak,* 6 miles north-northwest of Mount Hamilton (lat. 37°25'15" N, long. 122°41'55" W; near W line sec. 7, T 6 S, R 3 E). Altitude 3869 feet. Named on Mount Day (1955) 7.5' quadrangle. Called Black Mountain on Mount Hamilton (1897) 15' quadrangle, where Black Mountain (2) is called Mt. Day. The name probably is for Sherman Day, state senator representing Alameda and Santa Clara Counties from 1855 until 1856, and United States surveyor general for California from 1868 until 1871 (Gudde, 1949, p. 89).

Mount Diablo [CONTRA COSTA]: *peak,* near the center of Contra Costa County (lat. 37°52'55" N, long. 121°54'50" W; at NE cor. sec. 1, T 1 S, R 1 W). Altitude 3849 feet. Named on Clayton (1953) 7.5' quadrangle. Called Monte Diablo on Smith and Elliott's (1879) map. H.R. Wagner (p. 502) noted the early names "Cerro de San Juan" and "Montaña de San Juan Bautista" for the peak. According to Gudde (1949, p. 94), the feature also was known to the Spaniards by the names "Sierra de los Bolbones" and "Cerro Alto de los Bolbones" from Indians called Bolbones who lived near the base of the peak. Wilkes (p. 71) called the feature Mount Diavolo in 1841. According to one account, the name "Diablo" is from an incident following a battle between Spaniards and Indians in 1806, when an Indian appeared dressed in a devilish costume—*diablo* means "devil" in Spanish (Hanna, P.T., p. 86).

Mount Diablo Creek [CONTRA COSTA]: *stream,* flows 13 miles to marsh along Suisun Bay 5.25 miles east of Martinez (lat. 38°01'40" N, long. 122°02'20" W); the stream heads near Mount Diablo. Named on Clayton (1953) and Vine Hill (1959) 7.5' quadrangles. Ringgold (p. 27) called it Monte Diablo Creek, and Whitney (p. 23) called it Arroyo del Monte Diablo.

Mount Diablo Range: see **Diablo Range** [ALAMEDA-CONTRA COSTA-SANTA CLARA].

Mount Diavolo: see **Mount Diablo** [CONTRA COSTA].

Mount Eden [ALAMEDA]: *village,* 2.5 miles south-southwest of downtown Hayward (lat. 37°38'10" N, long. 122°05'55" W). Named on Hayward (1959) 7.5' quadrangle. The place was founded in 1850 by an association of farmers from Mount Eden, Kentucky; postal authorities established Mount Eden post office in 1862 and discontinued it for a short time in 1953 (Salley, p. 148). Thompson and West's (1878) map shows Eden Landing situated west-southwest of Mount Eden on Richard Barron's land along North Branch Alameda Creek (present Mount Eden Creek). Postal authorities established Edendale post office at Eden Landing in 1873 and discontinued it in 1875 (Salley, p. 65). Eden Landing was started in 1854 by farmers who were dissatisfied with freight charges at Allen's Landing, which was located 0.25 mile farther west; Richard Barron bought Eden Landing in 1855 (Mosier and Mosier, p. 33). Thompson and West's (1878) map shows Barrons Landing situated west of Mount Eden at the edge of San Francisco Bay; Thompson and West (1878, p. 25) noted that Barron's Landing also was called Mount Eden Landing. Eden Landing also was known locally as Peterman's Landing for Henry Louis Peterman and Mary F. Peterman, who operated Peterman's Salt Works (Mosier and Mosier, p. 33). James Johnstone Stokes established Stokes Landing east of Barron's Landing along Alameda Creek in 1858 (Mosier and Mosier, p. 84).

Mount Eden Creek [ALAMEDA]: *water feature,* enters San Francisco Bay 6 miles southwest of downtown Hayward (lat. 37°36'10" N, long. 122°08'40" W). Named on Newark (1959) and Redwood Point (1959) 7.5' quadrangles. Called North Branch Alameda Creek on Thompson and West's (1878) map.

Mount Eden Landing: see **Mount Eden** [ALAMEDA].

Mount Eden Station [ALAMEDA]: *locality,* 3 miles southwest of downtown Hayward along

Southern Pacific Railroad (lat. 37°38'10" N, long. 122°07'05" W); the place is 1 mile west of Mount Eden. Named on Hayward (1959) 7.5' quadrangle.

Mount Ellen [SAN MATEO]: *peak,* 3 miles south-southwest of La Honda (lat. 37°16'45" N, long. 122°17'20" W; sec. 34, T 7 S, R 4 W). Named on La Honda (1961) 7.5' quadrangle. The name was given about 1890 to honor Miss Ellen Wurr by one of her admirers (Brown, p. 32).

Mount Hamilton [SANTA CLARA]: *peak,* 15 miles east of downtown San Jose (lat. 37°20'30" N, long. 121°38'30" W; sec. 9, T 7 S, R 3 E). Altitude 4213 feet. Named on Lick Observatory (1955) 7.5' quadrangle. William H. Brewer of the Whitney survey named the peak for Laurentine Hamilton, a San Jose clergyman who climbed the peak with Brewer in 1861 (Farquhar *in* Brewer, p. 167, 189). According to Irelan (p. 540), the feature first had the name "Mount Santa Isabel" and consists of a group of peaks, including one called Observatory Peak that has the principal building of Lick Observatory. Postal authorities established Mt. Hamilton post office in 1884 and discontinued it in 1886; they established Mount Hamilton post office in 1890 (Frickstad, p. 174).

Mount Hamilton Range: see **Diablo Range** [SANTA CLARA].

Mount Hamilton Springs [SANTA CLARA]: *spring,* 2.5 miles northwest of Mount Hamilton (lat. 37°22'15" N, long. 121°40' W; sec. 32, T 6 S, R 3 E). Named on Lick Observatory (1955) 7.5' quadrangle.

Mount Helen [SANTA CLARA]: *peak,* 2.5 miles south of Isabel Valley (lat. 37°16'35" N, long. 121°31'40" W; sec. 34, T 7 S, R 4 E). Altitude 3001 feet. Named on Isabel Valley (1955) 7.5' quadrangle.

Mount Helen: see **Martinez** [CONTRA COSTA].

Mount Hooker: see **Mount Thayer** [SANTA CLARA].

Mount Ida: see **Mount Caroline Livermore** [MARIN].

Mount Isabel [SANTA CLARA]: *peak,* 4 miles west of Isabel Valley (lat. 38°19'35" N, long. 121°37'10" W; sec. 14, T 7 S, R 3 E). Altitude 4230 feet. Named on Isabel Valley (1955) 7.5' quadrangle. The name, originally given to Mount Hamilton, was applied to the peak after Mount Hamilton received its present name (Gudde, 1949, p. 141). United States Board on Geographic Names (1933, p. 391) rejected the names "Mount San Isabel" and "Mount Santa Ysabel" for the peak.

Mount King: see **North Peak** [CONTRA COSTA].

Mount Lewis [SANTA CLARA]: *peak,* 4.25 miles north-northeast of Mount Day near Santa Clara-Alameda county line (lat. 37°28'50" N, long. 121°40'45" W; sec. 20, T

5 S, R 3 E). Altitude 3768 feet. Named on Mount Day (1955) 7.5' quadrangle.

Mount Madonna [SANTA CLARA]: *peak,* 7.5 miles west of Gilroy (lat. 37°00'45" N, long. 121°42'15" W). Altitude 1897 feet. Named on Mount Madonna (1955) 7.5' quadrangle. Hiram Wentworth, a pioneer in the neighborhood, named the peak (Gudde, 1949, p. 201).

Mount McPherson: see **Bielawski Mountain** [SANTA CLARA].

Mount Melville [SAN MATEO]: *peak,* 2 miles north-northeast of Mindego Hill (lat. 37°20'15" N, long. 122°13'05" W; sec. 8, T 7 S, R 3 W). Named on Mindego Hill (1961) 7.5' quadrangle. The name honors Dr. Melville Best Anderson, who was professor of English literature at Stanford University (United States Board on Geographic Names, 1933, p. 512).

Mount Misery [SANTA CLARA]: *peak,* 5.5 miles southwest of Mount Hamilton (lat. 37°16'40" N, long. 121°42'20" W). Altitude 2502 feet. Named on Lick Observatory (1955) 7.5' quadrangle.

Mount Mocho [SANTA CLARA]: *peak,* 2.25 miles southwest of Mount Boardman (lat. 37°27'20" N, long. 121°29'35" W; near E line sec. 35, T 5 S, R 4 E). Altitude 3664 feet. Named on Mount Boardman (1955) 7.5' quadrangle. The name is from Arroyo Mocho (Gudde, 1949, p. 218).

Mount Olompali: see **Burdell Mountain** [MARIN].

Mount Olympus [SAN FRANCISCO]: *peak,* nearly 1 mile east-northeast of Mount Sutro (lat. 37°45'50" N, long. 122°26'40" W). Named on San Francisco North (1956) 7.5' quadrangle.

Mount Pajaro [SANTA CLARA]: *peak,* nearly 1 mile north of Pajaro Gap on Santa Clara-Santa Cruz county line (lat. 36°55'25" N, long. 121°37'40" W). Altitude 1573 feet. Named on Watsonville East (1955) 7.5' quadrangle.

Mount Palermo: see **Mount Tamalpais** [MARIN].

Mount San Isabel: see **Mount Isabel** [SANTA CLARA].

Mount Santa Ysabel: see **Mount Isabel** [SANTA CLARA].

Mount Sizer [SANTA CLARA]: *peak,* 9.5 miles northeast of Morgan Hill (lat. 37°12'50" N, long. 121°30'45" W). Altitude 3216 feet. Named on Mount Sizer (1955) 7.5' quadrangle.

Mount Stakes [SANTA CLARA]: *peak,* 12 miles south-southeast of Mount Boardman on Santa Clara-Stanislaus county line (lat. 37°19'20" N, long. 121°24'25" W; sec. 15, T 7 S, R 5 E). Altitude 3804 feet. Named on Mount Stakes (1955) 7.5' quadrangle.

Mount Sutro [SAN FRANCISCO]: *peak,* 2.5 miles southwest of San Francisco civic center (lat. 37°45'30" N, long. 122°27'20" W). Altitude 908 feet. Named on San Francisco North (1956) 7.5' quadrangle. Called Blue Mt.

on San Francisco (1899, reprinted 1906) 15' quadrangle, but United States Board on Geographic Names (1933, p. 731) rejected the names "Blue Mountain" and "Sutro Crest" for the peak. The name "Sutro" commemorates Adolph Sutro, mayor of San Francisco from 1894 until 1898 (Gudde, 1949, p. 348).

Mount Tamalpais [MARIN]: *ridge,* west-south-west-trending, 2 miles long, center 4.5 miles southwest of downtown San Rafael (lat. 37°55'40" N, long. 122°35'30" W). Named on San Rafael (1954) 7.5' quadrangle. Called Table Hill on Beechey's (1827-1828) map. The feature was called Pico y Cerro de Reyes and Picacho Prieto in Spanish times; it was called Table Hill, Table Mountain, and Table Butte after Beechey's survey of San Francisco Bay in 1826, and it was called Mount Palermo by members of Wilkes' expedition in 1841 (Gudde, 1949, p. 353). The name "Tamalpais" is of Indian origin (Kroeber, p. 61).

Mount Tamalpais Camp: see **Camp Eastwood** [MARIN].

Mount Thayer [SANTA CLARA]: *peak,* 5.5 miles southeast of downtown Los Gatos (lat. 37°09'50" N, long. 121°55'05" W; sec. 12, T 9 S, R 1 W). Altitude 3483 feet. Named on Los Gatos (1953) 7.5' quadrangle. The peak first was called Mount Hooker (Young, p. 62).

Mount Umunhum [SANTA CLARA]: *peak,* 6.5 miles southeast of downtown Los Gatos (lat. 37°09'40" N, long. 121°53'50" W; sec. 7, T 9 S, R 1 E). Altitude 3486 feet. Named on Los Gatos (1953) 7.5' quadrangle. Gudde (1969, p. 350) related the name to an Indian word for hummingbird, and noted that the names "Picacho de Umunhum" and "Picacho de Umurhum" occur on maps of 1848. The peak mistakenly is called Loma Prieta on some maps (Hoover, Rensch, and Rensch, p. 457).

Mount Vaca [SOLANO]: *peak,* 12 miles northeast of Napa on Blue Ridge (2) on Napa-Solano county line (lat. 38°24' N, long. 122°06'20" W; sec. 5, T 6 N, R 2 W); the peak is in Vaca Mountains. Altitude 2819 feet. Named on Mount Vaca (1951) 7.5' quadrangle. United States Board on Geographic Names (1970a, p. 3) gave the names "Blue Mountain" and "Vaca Peak" as variants, and pointed out that the feature is the highest point in Vaca Mountains.

Mount Vision [MARIN]: *peak,* 4 miles west-northwest of Point Reyes Station on Inverness Ridge (lat. 38°05'20" N, long. 122°52'20" W). Altitude 1282 feet. Named on Inverness (1954) 7.5' quadrangle. F.M. Anderson (p. 123) referred to Vision Hill.

Mount Wallace [ALAMEDA]: *peak,* 3.5 miles east-southeast of Cedar Mountain on Alameda-San Joaquin county line (lat. 37°32'20" N, long. 121°33' W; sec. 32, T 4 S, R 4 E). Altitude 3112 feet. Named on Cedar Mountain (1956) 7.5' quadrangle. The name commemorates John Wallace, county surveyor of San Joaquin County, who helped establish Alameda-San Joaquin county line in 1868 (Mosier and Mosier, p. 59).

Mount Wanda: see **Martinez** [CONTRA COSTA].

Mount Wittenberg [MARIN]: *peak,* 2.25 miles south-southwest of Point Reyes Station on Inverness Ridge (lat. 38°02'20" N, long. 122°49'15" W). Altitude 1407 feet. Named on Inverness (1954) 7.5' quadrangle. United States Board on Geographic Names (1968b, p. 10) rejected the form "Mount Wittenburg" for the name, which commemorates Peter Wittenberg and Newton M. Wittenberg, who leased land in the neighborhood for a dairy ranch in the 1860's (Teather, p. 88). F.M. Anderson (p. 123) referred to Wittenberg Hill.

Mount Zion [CONTRA COSTA]: *peak,* 3.5 miles northwest of Mount Diablo (lat. 37°55'25" N, long. 121°57'10" W; near NE cor. sec. 22, T 1 N, R 1 W). Altitude 1635 feet. Named on Clayton (1953) 7.5' quadrangle. This apparently is the feature that members of the Whitney survey called Pyramid Hill (Whitney, p. 22).

Mowry Camp [SANTA CLARA]: *locality,* 1.25 miles west-southwest of Eylar Mountain (lat. 37°28'15" N, long. 121°34'05" W; sec. 30, T 5 S, R 4 E). Named on Eylar Mountain (1955) 7.5' quadrangle.

Mowry Landing [ALAMEDA]: *locality,* 2 miles southeast of downtown Newark (lat. 37°30'20" N, long. 122°00'45" W); the place is along Mowry Slough. Named on Newark (1959) 7.5' quadrangle. E.B. Perrin bought land on the north side of the mouth of Mowry Slough in 1870 and started Green Point Dairy Landing and Transportation Company; he built Green Point Landing there and named it for his company (Mosier and Mosier, p. 40). A place called Larkin's Landing was situated east of Mowry Landing along Mowry Slough; it was named for Stephen Larkin, who came to the neighborhood in 1851 (Mosier and Mosier, p. 50).

Mowry Slough [ALAMEDA]: *water feature,* joins San Francisco Bay 2.5 miles south-southwest of downtown Newark (lat. 37°29'30" N, long. 122°03'10" W). Named on Mountain View (1961) and Newark (1959) 7.5' quadrangles. The name commemorates Origin Mowry, who settled along the slough in 1850 (Mosier and Mosier, p. 59).

Mowry Station [ALAMEDA]: *locality,* 2.25 miles southeast of downtown Newark along Southern Pacific Railroad (lat. 37°30'35" N, long. 122°00'15" W). Named on Haywards (1899) 15' quadrangle.

Mowry Well [ALAMEDA]: *well,* 1 mile northwest of Fremont civic center (lat. 37°33'45" N, long. 121°58'45" W; sec. 28, T 4 S, R 1 W). Named on Niles (1961) 7.5' quadrangle.

Mud Creek: see **Mud Slough** [ALAMEDA].

Muddy Creek: see **Arroyo Seco** [ALAMEDA].

Muddy Hollow [MARIN]: *locality,* 3.5 miles west-southwest of Point Reyes Station (lat. 38°03' N, long. 122°52'05" W). Named on Inverness (1954) 7.5' quadrangle.

Mud Lake [MARIN]: *lake,* 550 feet long, 2.25 miles northeast of Double Point (lat. 37°58'25" N, long. 122°45'20" W). Named on Double Point (1954) 7.5' quadrangle.

Mud Lake [SANTA CLARA]: *lake,* 200 feet long, 6 miles south-southwest of Mount Sizer (lat. 37°08'20" N, long. 121°34'30" W; sec. 19, T 9 S, R 4 E). Named on Mount Sizer (1955) 7.5' quadrangle.

Mud Slough [ALAMEDA]: *water feature,* joins Coyote Creek 6 miles south of Fremont civic center (lat. 37°27'55" N, long. 121° 59'15" W). Named on Milpitas (1961) 7.5' quadrangle. Thompson and West's (1878) map calls the slough Mud Creek, and shows a place called Warm Springs Landing situated near the head of the feature in present Warm Springs District—brothers Waitsell Baker and Joseph Baker started Baker's Landing at the place in 1857; the name was changed to Warm Springs Landing in 1860 (Mosier and Mosier, p. 13, 92).

Mud Slough [MARIN]: *water feature,* 0.5 mile long, connects two reaches of San Antonio Creek through marsh 5.25 miles north of downtown Novato (lat. 38°10'50" N, long. 122°34'05" W). Named on Petaluma River (1954) 7.5' quadrangle.

Mud Slough [SOLANO]: *water feature,* joins Roaring River Slough 5.5 miles west-southwest of Birds Landing (2) (lat. 38°05'50" N, long. 121°57'25" W). Named on Honker Bay (1953) 7.5' quadrangle.

Mud Springs [ALAMEDA]:
(1) *spring,* 1.5 miles northwest of Mendenhall Springs (lat. 37°36'20" N, long. 121°39'50" W; sec. 8, T 4 S, R 3 E). Named on Mendenhall Springs (1956) 7.5' quadrangle.
(2) *spring,* 5 miles south of Mendenhall Springs (lat. 37°30'45" N, long. 121°39'15" W; sec. 9, T 5 S, R 3 E). Named on Mendenhall Springs (1956) 7.5' quadrangle.

Mud Springs [SANTA CLARA]: *spring,* 3.5 miles east-southeast of New Almaden near the head of Pine Tree Canyon (lat. 37°09'30" N, long. 121°45'50" W). Named on Santa Teresa Hills (1953) 7.5' quadrangle.

Muir [CONTRA COSTA]: *locality,* 8 miles north-northeast of Orinda along Atchison, Topeka and Santa Fe Railroad in Alhambra Valley (lat. 37°59'25" N, long. 122°07'35" W). Named on Briones Valley (1959) 7.5' quadrangle.

Muir Beach [MARIN]: *beach,* 4 miles northwest of Point Bonita along the coast (lat. 37°51'35" N, long. 122°34'40" W); the beach is at the mouth of Redwood Creek. Named on Point Bonita (1954) 7.5' quadrangle. The name is from Muir Woods National Monument, located on the upper reaches of Redwood Creek (Gudde, 1949, p. 228). The place earlier was called Bello Beach, or Bello's Bend, for Anthony Nunes Bello, who filed a subdivision map in 1923 (Teather, p. 48). A lagoon, now filled, called Frank's Lagoon was at present Muir Beach in the 1850's (Teather, p. 26).

Muir Camp [CONTRA COSTA]: *locality,* 0.5 mile southwest of Mount Diablo (lat. 37°52'35" N, long. 121°55'15" W; sec. 1, T 1 S, R 1 W). Named on Clayton (1953) 7.5' quadrangle.

Mulford: see **West San Leandro** [ALAMEDA].

Mulford Gardens [ALAMEDA]: *district,* 2 miles southwest of downtown San Leandro (lat. 37°42'10" N, long. 122°10'45" W); the district is northeast of Mulford Landing. Named on San Leandro (1959) 7.5' quadrangle.

Mulford Landing [ALAMEDA]: *locality,* 2.5 miles southwest of downtown San Leandro at the edge of San Francisco Bay (lat. 37° 41'50" N, long. 122°11'10" W). Named on San Leandro (1959) 7.5' quadrangle. In 1853 Moses Wicks, Thomas W. Mulford, and others started business at the site, which was called Wicks Landing; Mulford bought the place in 1868 and renamed it—the landing is at what is known as Mulford Point (Mosier and Mosier, p. 60).

Mulford Point: see **Mulford Landing** [ALAMEDA].

Mulholland Hill [CONTRA COSTA]: *peak,* 2.5 miles southeast of Orinda (lat. 37°51'35" N, long. 122°08'40" W; sec. 12, T 1 S, R 3 W). Altitude 1157 feet. Named on Oakland East (1959) 7.5' quadrangle.

Mullen's Creek: see **Arroyo de en Medio** [SAN MATEO].

Mulligan Hill [CONTRA COSTA]: *ridge,* east-trending, nearly 1 mile long, 7 miles north of Mount Diablo (lat. 37°58'55" N, long. 121° 55'55" W). Altitude 1438 feet. Named on Clayton (1953) 7.5' quadrangle.

Munroe: see **Point Munroe**, under **Paradise Cay** [MARIN].

Murphy: see **Sunnyvale** [SANTA CLARA].

Murphy Canyon [SANTA CLARA]: *canyon,* 2 miles long, 2.5 miles north-northwest of Mount Madonna on upper reaches of Little Arthur Creek (lat. 37°02'45" N, long. 121°43'45" W). Named on Mount Madonna (1955) 7.5' quadrangle.

Murphy Rock [MARIN]: *rock,* 1.5 miles north-northwest of Point San Quentin in San Rafael Bay (lat. 37°57'40" N, long. 122°29'25" W). Named on San Quentin (1959) 7.5' quadrangle. Called Murphys Rock on Ringgold's (1850a) map, and called San Rafael Rock on San Francisco (1915) 15' quadrangle. The feature now is at the edge of filled land.

Murphy's Peak: see **El Toro** [SANTA CLARA].

Murray Park [MARIN]: *district,* 2.25 miles south-southwest of downtown San Rafael (lat.

37°56'50" N, long. 122°33'05" W). Named on San Rafael (1954) 7.5' quadrangle.

Mussel Rock [SAN MATEO]:

(1) *rock,* 4.5 miles west of downtown South San Francisco, and 225 feet offshore (lat. 37°40' N, long. 122°29'45" W). Named on San Francisco South (1956) 7.5' quadrangle. The beach north from Mussel Rock to San Francisco-San Mateo-county line was called Seven Mile Beach (Brown, p. 88).

(2) *rock,* 1.5 miles north-northwest of the village of San Gregorio, and 250 feet offshore (lat. 37°20'50" N, long. 122°24'05" W). Named on San Gregorio (1961, photorevised 1968) 7.5' quadrangle.

Mustang Peak [SANTA CLARA]: *peak,* 8 miles northeast of Gilroy Hot Springs on Santa Clara-Stanislaus county line (lat. 37°11'10" N, long. 121°21'35" W; sec. 6, T 9 S, R 6 E). Altitude 2263 feet. Named on Mustang Peak (1955) 7.5' quadrangle.

Mustang Ridge [SANTA CLARA]: *ridge,* north-trending, nearly 4 miles long, 6 miles north of Pacheco Peak (lat. 37°07'10" N, long. 121°16'45" W). Named on Mustang Peak (1955) and Pacheco Peak (1955) 7.5' quadrangles.

– N –

Nacio [CONTRA COSTA]: *locality,* 5 miles north of present Walnut Creek civic center along Southern Pacific Railroad (lat. 37°58'15" N, long. 122°02'50" W). Named on Concord (1943) 15' quadrangle.

Napa Island: see **Mare Island** [SOLANO].

Napa River [SOLANO]: *stream,* heads in Napa County and flows 58 miles to Carquinez Strait (by way of Mare Island Strait) 2 miles south-southeast of downtown Vallejo in Solano County (lat. 38°04'30" N, long. 122°14'40" W). Named on Calistoga (1958), Cuttings Wharf (1949), Mare Island (1959), Napa (1951), Rutherford (1951), Saint Helena (1960), and Yountville (1951) 7.5' quadrangles. Called Nappa C.[Creek] on Trask's (1853) map, and called Napa Cr. on Eddy's (1854) map. United States Board on Geographic Names (1933, p. 544) rejected the name "Napa Creek" for the stream.

Napland [CONTRA COSTA]: *locality,* 2 miles south-southwest of present Walnut Creek civic center along Oakland Antioch and Eastern Railroad (lat. 37°52'35" N, long. 122°04'20" W). Named on Concord (1915) 15' quadrangle.

Naples Beach [SAN MATEO]: *beach,* 2.25 miles northwest of downtown Half Moon Bay along the coast (lat. 37°29'20" N, long. 122° 27'20" W). Named on Half Moon Bay (1961) 7.5' quadrangle. The name is from an unsuccessful subdivision (Brown, p. 60).

Nappa Creek: see **Napa River** [SOLANO].

Narrows: see **The Narrows** [SANTA CLARA].

Naval Air Station: see **Moffett Field** [SANTA CLARA].

Navy Point: see **Army Point** [SOLANO]; **Voltani Slough** [SOLANO].

Neal [SANTA CLARA]: *locality,* 2.5 miles south-southeast of downtown Palo Alto along Southern Pacific Railroad (lat. 37°24'50" N, long. 122°08'25" W). Named on Palo Alto (1961) 7.5' quadrangle. Palo Alto (1961, photorevised 1968 and 1973) 7.5' quadrangle shows the rail line ending before it reaches Neal.

Needles [SAN FRANCISCO]: *rocks,* 1.25 miles north of Fort Point, and 150 feet off of Marin County coast (lat. 37°49'45" N, long. 122°28'35" W). Named on San Francisco North (1956) 7.5' quadrangle.

Neel Gulch: see **Neils Gulch** [SAN MATEO].

Neils Gulch [SAN MATEO]: *canyon,* drained by a stream that flows 1.25 miles to Sausal Creek 7 miles south of downtown Redwood City in Portola Valley (1) (lat. 37°22'50" N, long. 122°13'40" W). Named on Mindego Hill (1961) and Palo Alto (1961) 7.5' quadrangles. The stream in the canyon is called Sausal Cr. on Palo Alto (1899) 15' quadrangle. Brown (p. 60) called the feature Neel Gulch, and noted that it was named for David H. Neel, a settler in the neighborhood in the 1850's; the canyon also had the names "Cañada de Sansevan" and "Hallidie Gulch."

Nema [SANTA CLARA]: *locality,* at the end of a half-mile-long spur of Southern Pacific Railroad that branches southwest from the main line 3 miles south-southeast of Gilroy (lat. 36°57'30" N, long. 121°33' W). Named on San Juan Bautista (1917) 15' quadrangle.

Neroly [CONTRA COSTA]: *locality,* 4.25 miles northwest of Brentwood along Southern Pacific Railroad (lat. 37°58'55" N, long. 121° 44'25" W; near N line sec. 34, T 2 N, R 2 E). Named on Brentwood (1954) 7.5' quadrangle.

Nesbit Ridge [SANTA CLARA]: *ridge,* U-shaped, 2.25 miles long, 6 miles south-south-west of Mount Sizer (lat. 37°07'55" N, long. 121° 32'15" W). Named on Mount Sizer (1955) 7.5' quadrangle.

Nevada Dock [CONTRA COSTA]: *locality,* 2.5 miles northwest of Martinez along Southern Pacific Railroad (lat. 38°02'10" N, long. 122°10'25" W). Named on Benicia (1959) 7.5' quadrangle.

New Almaden [SANTA CLARA]: *village,* 11 miles south-southeast of downtown San Jose (lat. 37°10'30" N, long. 121°49'15" W). Named on Santa Teresa Hills (1953) 7.5' quadrangle, which has both the names "New Almaden" and "Almaden P.O." at the place. Postal authorities established New Almaden post office in 1861, discontinued it the same year, reestablished it in 1873, and discontinued it in 1921; they established Almaden post office in 1934 and changed the name back to New Almaden in 1953 (Frickstad, p.

173, 174). The community name is for nearby New Almaden mine, which itself was named in 1848 after a famous quicksilver mine in Spain—*almaden* means "mine" or "mineral" in Spanish (Gudde, 1969, p. 7-8). The company that began producing quicksilver at New Almaden mine in 1847 selected a site along Alamitos Creek for its headquarters and furnaces; the place was referred to as Hacienda de Beneficio, or Reduction Works; the community that grew there was long called Hacienda, but eventually it became known as New Almaden (Lanyon and Bulmore, p. 91, 99). New Almaden mine is west of the village on a ridge that is unnamed on modern maps, but the name by which the ridge was known to Spanish-speaking residents in the vicinity was of considerable importance in legal proceedings that established ownership of the mine. Depositions of a number of witnesses in 1857 (United States Supreme Court, p. 30, 35, 46, 89) touched upon the question: Jose Fernandez stated that the ridge was called Cuchilla de Almaden, but previously had the name "Cuchilla de la nema [mina] de la Luis Cheavoya"; Jose Noriega testified that the ridge was called Las Lomas Bajas de las Minas, but before discovery of the mine it was called Las Lomas Bajas; James Alexander Forbes said that he first knew the ridge by the name "La Cuchilla de la Mina de Louis Chabolla," but later he knew it by the names "Mining Hills" or "Hills of the Mines"; and William J. Lewis referred to Sierra del Encino or Mine ridge. Davis and Jennings (p. 342) called the feature Los Capitancillos Ridge, and Whitney (p. 65-66) noted the name "Mount Chisnantuck" for the highest point on the ridge. A small mineral spring called Vichy Spring was on the south bank of the stream at New Almaden (Irelan, p. 549-550). Winslow Anderson (p. 208-209) used the name "New Almaden Vichy Springs" for the resort at the spring, but reported that the water had ceased to flow because of deep mine workings. Postal authorities established Frohm post office 4 miles north of New Almaden in 1887 and discontinued it in 1902; the name was for Chester C. Frohm, first postmaster (Salley, p. 81).

New Almaden: see **Cañada de los Capitanicillos** [SANTA CLARA].

New Almaden Station [SANTA CLARA]: *locality,* 2 miles north-northwest of New Almaden at the end of a branch line of Southern Pacific Railroad (lat. 37°12'05" N, long. 121°49'55" W). Named on Los Gatos (1919) 15' quadrangle. California Mining Bureau's (1909b) map shows a place called Junction located 1.5 miles northwest of New Almaden Station, where the rail line branches; Los Gatos (1919) 15' quadrangle shows the rail line branching only 0.5 mile north of New Almaden Station. California Mining Bureau's

(1917b) map shows a place called Thona situated along the railroad about halfway between New Almaden Station and Campbell.

New Almaden Vichy Springs: see **New Almaden** [SANTA CLARA].

Newark [ALAMEDA]: *city,* 22 miles southeast of Oakland (lat. 37° 31'45" N, long. 122°02'20" W). Named on Newark (1959) and Niles (1961) 7.5' quadrangles. Postal authorities established Newark post office in 1878 (Frickstad, p. 3), and the city incorporated in 1955. The name is from the city in New Jersey, home state of the Davis brothers, who were involved in founding the California city (Thompson and West, 1878, p. 27).

Newark Creek: see **Newark Slough** [ALAMEDA].

Newark Slough [ALAMEDA]: *water feature,* enters San Francisco Bay 3 miles southwest of downtown Newark (lat. 37°30'10" N, long. 122°05'05" W). Named on Newark (1959) 7.5' quadrangle. Called Newark Creek on Haywards (1899) 15' quadrangle. The feature was called Beard's Slough in the 1870's (Mosier and Mosier, p. 61).

New Camp [SANTA CLARA]: *locality,* 4.25 miles east-northeast of Mount Day (lat. 37°26'45" N, long. 121°37'45" W; sec. 3, T 6 S, R 3 E); the place is 2.25 miles southeast of Old Camp. Named on Mount Day (1955) 7.5' quadrangle.

New Chicago: see **Alviso** [SANTA CLARA].

New Creek: see **Little Llagas Creek** [SANTA CLARA].

Newell Gulch [SAN MATEO]: *canyon,* drained by a stream that flows nearly 1 mile to Pescadero Creek 5.5 miles southwest of La Honda (lat. 37°15'25" N, long. 122°20'25" W; near N line sec. 12, T 8 S, R 5 W). Named on La Honda (1961) 7.5' quadrangle. Frank Newell lived in the canyon in the 1880's and 1890's (Brown, p. 60).

New Haven: see **Alvarado** [ALAMEDA]; **Union City** [ALAMEDA].

Newlove [CONTRA COSTA]: *locality,* 11.5 miles northeast of Mount Diablo along Southern Pacific Railroad (lat. 37°59'35" N, long. 121°45'45" W; sec. 28, T 2 N, R 2 E). Named on Antioch South (1953) 7.5' quadrangle.

New Mountain View: see **Mountain View** [SANTA CLARA].

Newport: see **Collinsville** [SOLANO].

Newtown [SOLANO]: *locality,* 1 mile north-northeast of Rio Vista along Sacramento River (lat. 38°10'10" N, long. 121°40'45" W). Named on Rio Vista (1910) 7.5' quadrangle.

New Year Bay: see **Año Nuevo Bay** [SAN MATEO].

New Year Creek: see **Año Nuevo Creek** [SAN MATEO].

New Year Island: see **Año Nuevo Island** [SAN MATEO].

New Year's Bay: see **Año Nuevo Bay** [SAN MATEO].

New Year's Creek: see **Año Nuevo Creek** [SAN MATEO].

New Year's Island: see **Año Nuevo Island** [SAN MATEO].

New Years Point: see **Año Nuevo Point** [SAN MATEO].

New York Landing: see **Pittsburg** [CONTRA COSTA].

New York of the Pacific: see **Pittsburg** [CONTRA COSTA].

New York Point [CONTRA COSTA]: *promontory,* 0.5 mile north of downtown Pittsburg along Suisun Bay (lat. 38°02'30" N, long. 121°53'05" W); the feature is on the west side of the mouth of New York Slough. Named on Honker Bay (1953) 7.5' quadrangle.

New York Slough [CONTRA COSTA]: *water feature,* separates Browns Island and Winter Island from the mainland, extends for 3.5 miles from San Joaquin River to Suisun Bay 0.5 mile north of downtown Pittsburg (lat. 38°02'25" N, long. 121°52'55" W). Named on Antioch North (1978) and Honker Bay (1953) 7.5' quadrangles. United States Board on Geographic Names (1979a, p. 6) approved the name "Dowest Slough" for an inlet situated on the south shore of New York Slough 3 miles north-northwest of Antioch (lat. 38°01'30" N, long. 121°50'35" W).

Nibbs Knob [SANTA CLARA]: *peak,* 2.5 miles southeast of Loma Prieta (lat. 37°05'10" N, long. 121°48'40" W; sec. 1, T 10 S, R 1 E). Altitude 2694 feet. Named on Loma Prieta (1955) 7.5' quadrangle. The name also has the form "Nibs Knob" (Young, p. 64).

Nibs Knob: see **Nibbs Knob** [SANTA CLARA].

Nicasio [MARIN]:

(1) *land grant,* at and northeast of Point Reyes Station. Named on Inverness (1954), Point Reyes NE (1954), and San Geronimo (1954) 7.5' quadrangles. Pablo de la Guerra and John Bautista Roger Cooper received the land in 1844; James Black claimed 9479 acres patented in 1861 (Cowan, p. 52).

(2) *land grant,* 9 miles west-southwest of downtown Novato. Named on Inverness (1954) and San Geronimo (1954) 7.5' quadrangles. Pablo de la Guerra and John Bautista Roger Cooper received the land in 1844; B.R. Bucklew claimed 8695 acres patented in 1861 (Cowan, p. 52).

(3) *land grant,* 8 miles south-southeast of Tomales on the northeast side of Tomales Bay. Named on Inverness (1954), Point Reyes NE (1954), and Tomales (1954) 7.5' quadrangles. Pablo de la Guerra and John Bautista Roger Cooper received the land in 1844; Frink and Reynolds claimed 7598 acres patented in 1861 (Cowan, p. 52).

(4) *land grant,* in two parcels, one located 3 miles southeast of Tomales and the other located 6 miles west-southwest of downtown Novato. Named on Inverness (1954), Novato (1954), Petaluma (1953), Petaluma River (1954),

Point Reyes NE (1954), San Geronimo (1954), and Tomales (1954) 7.5' quadrangles. Pablo de la Guerra and John Bautista Roger Cooper received the land in 1844; Henry W. Halleck claimed 30,843 acres patented in 1861 (Cowan, p. 52).

(5) *village,* 8 miles west-southwest of downtown Novato (lat. 38° 03'40" N, long. 122°41'50" W); the village is on Nicasio (2) grant. Named on San Geronimo (1954) 7.5' quadrangle. Postal authorities established Nicasio post office in 1871, discontinued it in 1899, and reestablished it in 1900 (Frickstad, p. 88).

Nicasio: see **San Geronimo** [MARIN] (2).

Nicasio Creek [MARIN]: *stream,* flows 11 miles to Lagunitas Creek 2 miles east of Point Reyes Station (lat. 38°04'10" N, long. 122°46'10" W). Named on Inverness (1954) and San Geronimo (1954) 7.5' quadrangles. Called Arroyo Nicasio on Petaluma (1914) 15' quadrangle.

Nicasio Reservoir [MARIN]: *lake,* behind a dam on Nicasio Creek 3 miles east-northeast of Point Reyes Station (lat. 38°04'35" N, long. 122°45'15" W). Named on Inverness (1954, photorevised 1971) and San Geronimo (1954, photorevised 1971) 7.5' quadrangles.

Nichols [CONTRA COSTA]: *locality,* 5.5 miles west of Pittsburg (lat. 38°02'30" N, long. 121°59'15" W; near SE cor. sec. 5, T 2 N, R 1 W). Named on Honker Bay (1953) 7.5' quadrangle. Officials of Atchison, Topeka and Santa Fe Railroad named the siding at the place in 1909 for William H. Nichols Syndicate, principal landholder there (Gudde, 1949, p. 236).

Nickols Knob [CONTRA COSTA]: *peak,* 4 miles southeast of Point San Pablo (lat. 37°55'15" N, long. 122°22'50" W). Altitude 371 feet. Named on San Quentin (1959) 7.5' quadrangle.

Nicks Cove [MARIN]: *locality,* 3.25 miles south-southwest of Tomales on the northeast side of Tomales Bay (lat. 38°11'55" N, long. 122°55'10" W). Named on Tomales (1954) 7.5' quadrangles. The name is from Nick Kojich, who opened a seafood restaurant by Tomales Bay in 1931 (Teather, p. 49).

Niles: see **Niles District** [ALAMEDA].

Niles Canyon [ALAMEDA]: *canyon,* 5 miles long, along Alameda Creek above a point 2 miles north of Fremont civic center (lat. 37° 34'45" N, long. 121°58' W). Named on Niles (1961) 7.5' quadrangle. Called Alameda Canyon on Pleasanton (1906) 15' quadrangle.

Niles District [ALAMEDA]: *district,* 2 miles north-northwest of Fremont civic center in Fremont (lat. 37°34'35" N, long. 121°59' W); the district is near the mouth of Niles Canyon. Named on Niles (1961) 7.5' quadrangle. Pleasanton (1906) 15' quadrangle has the name "Niles" for the community that joined in 1956 with neighboring communities to form the new city of Fremont. Postal authori-

ties established Niles post office in 1873 (Salley, p. 154). Officials of Central Pacific Railroad named the place in 1869 for Judge Addison C. Niles, who was elected to the state supreme court in 1871 (Gudde, 1949, p. 236). The site first was known as Vallejo's Mills for the water-powered flouring mill that Jose Vallejo built there in 1853 (Thompson and West, 1878, p. 27). Mayhew Spring is about 600 feet north of the railroad depot at Niles (Waring, p. 270); it was owned by H.A. Meyhew, and also was called Meyhew's Sulphur Spring (Crawford, 1896, p. 508).

Niles Junction [ALAMEDA]: *locality,* nearly 2 miles north of Fremont civic center along Western Pacific Railroad (lat. 37°34'35" N, long. 121°57'50" W; sec. 22, T 4 S, R 1 W); the place is in Niles District. Named on Niles (1961) 7.5' quadrangle.

Nitro [CONTRA COSTA]: *locality,* at Pinole Point (lat. 38°00'35" N, long. 122°21'50" W). Named on Mare Island (1959) 7.5' quadrangle. The name is from a nitroglycerin works at the place (Gannett, p. 225).

Nob Hill [CONTRA COSTA]: *peak,* 3.5 miles east of Pinole Point (lat. 38°00'20" N, long. 122°18' W). Named on Mare Island (1959) 7.5' quadrangle.

Nob Hill [SAN FRANCISCO]: *peak,* 1 mile south of North Point (lat. 37°47'35" N, long. 122°24'50" W). Named on San Francisco North (1956) 7.5' quadrangle. The feature originally was called Fern Hill; the name "Nob" may be from the so-called nabob's who built pretentious mansions on the peak (Hoover, Rensch, and Rensch, p. 364).

Nob Hill [SANTA CLARA]: *ridge,* northeast-trending, 200 feet long, in Morgan Hill (lat. 37°07'30" N, long. 121°39'15" W). Named on Morgan Hill (1955) and Mount Madonna (1955) 7.5' quadrangles.

Noble [ALAMEDA]: *locality,* 5 miles north-northwest of downtown Oakland along Southern Pacific Railroad (lat. 37°53'35" N, long. 122°18'35" W). Named on San Francisco (1899) 15' quadrangle.

Nooday Rock [SAN FRANCISCO]: *rock,* 3.5 miles northwest of North Farallon (lat. 37°48'05" N, long. 123°08'30" W). Named on San Francisco (1947) 1°x 2° quadrangle. The name is from a clipper ship that struck the rock in 1862 (United States Coast and Geodetic Survey, p. 123).

Norris Canyon: see **Norris Creek** [ALAMEDA].

Norris Creek [ALAMEDA]: *stream,* flows 2 miles to Crow Creek 5 miles north-northeast of downtown Hayward (lat. 37°43'55" N, long. 122°01'55" W). Named on Hayward (1959) and Las Trampas Ridge (1959) 7.5' quadrangles. The stream first was called Wisener Creek for Joseph Hopson Wisenor, who settled along it in the 1850's; the canyon of the feature is called Norris Canyon for Leo

Norris, who settled there in 1850 (Mosier and Mosier, p. 62, 95).

North Bay: see **North Point** [SAN FRANCISCO].

North Beach [SAN FRANCISCO]: *district,* 2 miles north of San Francisco civic center (lat. 37°48'20" N, long. 122°24'35" W). Named on San Francisco North (1956) 7.5' quadrangle.

North Belmont Landing: see **Belmont Slough** [SAN MATEO].

North Bend [MARIN]: *locality,* 1.5 miles northeast of Point Reyes Station along Northwestern Pacific Railroad (lat. 38°04'50" N, long. 122°46'50" W). Named on Point Reyes (1918) 15' quadrangle.

North Berkeley [ALAMEDA]: *district,* 5.5 miles north of downtown Oakland and north of University of California campus in Berkeley (lat. 37°52'50" N, long. 122°16'15" W). Named on San Francisco (1899) 15' quadrangle. Officials of Southern Pacific Railroad put a station at the place in 1878 and named it Berryman for Henry Burpee Berryman, of Berryman Reservoir; the station now is called North Berkeley (Mosier and Mosier, p. 16).

North Channel: see **Brooklyn Basin** [ALAMEDA]; **Oakland Inner Harbor** [ALAMEDA].

North Coyote Slough: see **Coyote Creek** [ALAMEDA-SANTA CLARA].

North Creek [ALAMEDA]: *water feature,* joins Alameda Creek 6.25 miles northwest of downtown Newark (lat. 37°35'35" N, long. 122° 09'20" W). Named on Newark (1948) 7.5' quadrangle.

Norther Slough [SOLANO]: *water feature,* 7 miles west-southwest of Birds Landing (2) on Simmons Island (lat. 38°05'40" N, long. 121°59' W). Named on Honker Bay (1953) 7.5' quadrangle.

North Farallon [SAN FRANCISCO]: *island,* 7 miles northwest of Southeast Farallon (lat. 37°46'20" N, long. 123°06'25" W); the feature is the northwesternmost of Farallon Islands. Named on Farallon Islands (1988) 7.5' quadrangle. Called N.W. Farallon on Ringgold's (1850b) map. United States Coast and Geodetic Survey (p. 123) described the feature as "two clusters of bare precipitous islets and rocks" 0.9 mile in extent—by this description, the Survey apparently includes present Isle of Saint James under the name "North Farallon."

North Granada: see **El Granada** [SAN MATEO].

North Lake [SAN FRANCISCO]: *lake,* 1050 feet long, 1 mile southeast of Point Lobos (lat. 37°46'10" N, long. 122°30'05" W). Named on San Francisco North (1956) 7.5' quadrangle.

North Peak [CONTRA COSTA]: *peak,* 1 mile northeast of Mount Diablo (lat. 37°53'35" N, long. 121°53'55" W; sec. 31, T 1 N, R 1 E).

Altitude 3557 feet. Named on Clayton (1953) 7.5' quadrangle. Brewer (p. 267) called the peak Mount King in 1862, but Whitney (p. 24) called it North Peak in 1865.

North Peak [SAN MATEO]: *peak,* 0.5 mile northeast of Montara Knob on Montara Mountain (lat. 37°33'40" N, long. 122°28'35" W; on W line sec. 25, T 4 S, R 6 W); the feature is nearly 0.5 mile north-northeast of South Peak. Altitude 1898 feet. Named on Montara Mountain (1956) 7.5' quadrangle.

North Point [SAN FRANCISCO]: *promontory,* 2 miles north of San Francisco civic center along San Francisco Bay (lat. 37°48'35" N, long. 122°24'40" W). Named on San Francisco North (1956) 7.5' quadrangle. Ringgold's (1850a) map has the name "North Bay" for the embayment west of present North Point.

North Reservoir [CONTRA COSTA]: *lake,* 850 feet long, 2.5 miles north-northwest of Richmond civic center (lat. 37°58'25" N, long. 122°19'35" W). Named on Richmond (1959) 7.5' quadrangle.

North Richmond [CONTRA COSTA]: *district,* nearly 2 miles northwest of Richmond civic center (lat. 37°57'25" N, long. 122°21'45" W). Named on Richmond (1959) 7.5' quadrangle.

North Temescal: see **Oakland** [ALAMEDA].

Northwest Farallon: see **North Farallon** [SAN FRANCISCO].

Nortonville [CONTRA COSTA]: *locality,* 5.5 miles north-northeast of Mount Diablo along Kirker Creek (lat. 37°57'30" N, long. 121°52'45" W; near SE cor. sec. 5, T 1 N, R 1 E). Site named on Clayton (1953) 7.5' quadrangle. Postal authorities established Nortonville post office in 1874, discontinued it briefly in 1887, discontinued it in 1890, reestablished it in 1891, and discontinued it finally in 1910 (Frickstad, p. 22). The name was for Noah Norton, who started Black Diamond coal mine in 1861, and built the first house at the place (Hoover, Rensch, and Rensch, p. 65; Mosier, p. 6).

Nortonville Pass [CONTRA COSTA]: *pass,* 5.5 miles north-northeast of Mount Diablo (lat. 37°57'20" N, long. 121°52'25" W; sec. 4, T 1 N, R 1 E); the pass is 2000 feet east-southeast of Nortonville. Named on Antioch South (1953) 7.5' quadrangle.

Norwood Creek [SANTA CLARA]: *stream,* flows 1.5 miles to lowlands nearly 2 miles north-northeast of Evergreen (lat. 37°20' N, long. 121°46' W). Named on San Jose East (1961) 7.5' quadrangle.

Notley Junction [SAN MATEO]: *locality,* nearly 6 miles northeast of Franklin Point (lat. 37°11'40" N, long. 122°16'10" W). Named on Año Nuevo (1948) 15' quadrangle. Franklin Point (1955) 7.5' quadrangle shows Sandy Point guard station at the site. George Notley, Sr., settled at the place, which then was called Sandy Point, about 1910 (Brown, p. 62).

Nottingham: see **Livermore** [ALAMEDA].

Novato [MARIN]:
(1) *land grant,* at and near the city of Novato.
Named on Petaluma (1953), Petaluma Point
(1959), and Petaluma River (1954) 7.5' quadrangles. Fernando Felix received 2 leagues in
1839; assignees of B. Simmons claimed 8971
acres patented in 1866 (Cowan, p. 53). Perez
(p. 79) gave the size of the grant as 8870.62
acres.
(2) *city,* 10 miles north-northwest of San Rafael
along Novato Creek (lat. 38°06'30" N, long.
122°34'10" W). Named on Novato (1954) and
Petaluma River (1954, photorevised 1968 and
1973) 7.5' quadrangles. Postal authorities established Novato post office in 1856, discontinued it in 1860, and reestablished it in 1891
(Salley, p. 157). The city incorporated in 1960.
Novato Creek [MARIN]: *stream,* flows 18 miles
to San Pablo Bay 4.5 miles east of downtown
Novato (lat. 38°05'40" N, long. 122° 29'15"
W). Named on Novato (1954), Petaluma Point
(1959), and San Geronimo (1954) 7.5' quadrangles.
Novato Heights [MARIN]: *ridge,* east-trending,
1 mile long, 1.25 miles southwest of downtown Novato (lat. 38°05'35" N, long. 122°
35'10" W). Named on Novato (1954) 7.5'
quadrangle.
Novato Point: see **Petaluma Point** [MARIN].
Novato Valley [MARIN]: *valley,* at and west of
the city of Novato along Novato Creek (lat.
38°06'30" N, long. 122°35'30" W). Named
on Novato (1954) 7.5' quadrangle. Cañada de
Novato of Spanish times was named for an
Indian (Gudde, 1949, p. 239).
Noyce Slough [SOLANO]: *water feature,* joins
Suisun Bay 7 miles west-southwest of Birds
Landing (2) (lat. 38°04'45" N, long. 121°
58'35" W). Named on Honker Bay (1953) 7.5'
quadrangle.
Nuff Creek [SAN MATEO]: *stream,* flows 2
miles to Pilarcitos Creek 2.5 miles northeast
of downtown Half Moon Bay (lat. 37°29'20"
N, long. 122°23'30" W; sec. 22, T 5 S, R 5
W). Named on Half Moon Bay (1961) and
Montara Mountain (1956) 7.5' quadrangles.
Brown (p. 45) called the canyon of the stream
Knopf Canyon—Knopf ranch was there in the
middle 1870's. The stream was called Toll-
house Creek on a map made about 1868, and
the canyon was called Cañada de Leon for
Jose Maria Leon, who had a sheep ranch there
about 1860 (Brown, p. 45).
Nurse's Landing: see **Denverton** [SOLANO].
Nurse Slough [SOLANO]: *water feature,* joins
Montezuma Slough 4.5 miles south-southwest
of Denverton (lat. 38°10'05" N, long. 121°56'
W). Named on Denverton (1953) 7.5' quadrangle. The name is from Nurse's Landing
(present Denverton) (Gudde, 1949, p. 239).
Nut Tree: see **Vacaville** [SOLANO].

– O –

Oak Grove: see **Burlingame** [SAN MAETO];
Los Altos [SANTA CLARA].
Oakland [ALAMEDA]: *city,* in the north part
of Alameda County near San Francisco Bay
(lat. 37°48'15" N, long. 122°16'15" W).
Named on Hayward (1959), Hunters Point
(1956), Las Trampas Ridge (1959), Oakland
East (1959), Oakland West (1959), and San
Leandro (1959) 7.5' quadrangles. Andres
Moon, Edson Adams, and Horace W.
Carpentier built a cabin in 1850 on land belonging to Vincent Peralta; when Peralta
threatened to eject these squatters, they each
leased 160 acres from him and laid out a townsite that they called Oakland (Hoover, Rensch,
and Rensch, p. 20). Oakland incorporated in
1852; the magnificent live-oak trees of the
place suggested the name (Thompson and
West, 1878, p. 17). In 1852, Moon and Adams built a wharf, called Moon and Adams
Landing, at the foot of present Broadway; the
same year, Carpentier built a wharf at the site
that became known as Carpentier's Wharf, and
that later was called Broadway Wharf (Mosier
and Mosier, p. 17). In 1850, the Patten brothers leased land from Peralta, and in 1852 the
brothers joined with other landholders to lay
out a town that they called Clinton located on
the east side of San Antonio Slough (Hoover,
Rensch, and Rensch, p. 20). In 1851, J.B.
Larue squatted on land west of Clinton across
San Antonio Creek, where he started a store
and built a wharf; the settlement that grew
there was called San Antonio, after the creek
and land grant (Bancroft, 1888, p. 478). San
Francisco and Oakland Railroad built a station called San Antonio at the place; in 1870
Central Pacific Railroad took over the station
and changed the name to Brooklyn, and in
1883 Southern Pacific Railroad changed the
name to East Oakland (Mosier and Mosier,
p. 17). Clinton and San Antonio joined in 1856
to form a new community called Brooklyn,
named for the ship that brought Mormon pioneers to California in 1846; Brooklyn and a
settlement located to the northeast known as
Lynn incorporated under the name "Brooklyn" in 1870—residents of Brooklyn voted for
annexation to Oakland in 1872 (Bancroft,
1888, p. 478). Lynn was named for Lynn,
Massachusetts, because like the New England
town, it had a large shoe and boot factory
(Mosier and Mosier, p. 53). Postal authorities
established Contra Costa post office at present
Jack London Square section of Oakland in
1851, and changed the name to Oakland in
1855 (Salley, p. 49). They established Brooklyn post office in 1855 and it became a station of Oakland post office in 1878 (Frickstad, p. 1). They established Monte Vista post
office 2.5 miles northeast of Oakland post

office in 1865 and discontinued it in 1868 (Salley, p. 145). They established Melita post office 3.5 miles southwest of Brooklyn post office (SW quarter sec. 16, T 2 S, R 3 W) in 1869 and discontinued it in 1871 (Salley, p. 137). They established West Oakland post office in 1873 and discontinued it in 1966 (Salley, p. 238). They established North Temescal post office 2 miles north of the main Oakland post office in 1877, changed the name to Alden in 1899, and discontinued it in 1908—the name "Alden" was for S.E. Alden, a pioneer farmer who owned land at the site (Salley, p. 4, 156). They established Dimond post office 1.5 miles northeast of Alameda post office in 1891 and it became a station of Oakland post office in 1908—the name was for Hugh Dimond, a mine owner (Salley, p. 59). According to Mosier and Mosier (p. 29), the settlement of Dimond was in Dimond Canyon. Postal authorities established Allendale post office 1.5 miles northeast of Fruitvale in 1903 and it became a station of Oakland post office in 1908 (Salley, p. 4). Mosier and Mosier (p. 8) noted that Allendale probably was named for Charles E. Allen, a real-estate broker. Dr. Cyrus Mills and his wife moved their seminary for young ladies to the Oakland environs in 1871; in 1885 they changed the name of the school from Mills Seminary to Mills College (Hoover, Rensch, and Rensch, p. 22). Postal authorities established Mills Seminary post office in 1879 and changed the name to Mills College in 1888 (Frickstad, p. 2). They established Beulah Heights post office 2 miles northwest of Mills College post office in 1907 and discontinued it in 1911 (Salley, p. 20).

Oakland Estuary: see **Oakland Inner Harbor** [ALAMEDA].

Oakland Harbor: see **Brooklyn Basin** [ALAMEDA]; **Oakland Inner Harbor** [ALAMEDA].

Oakland Hills: see **San Leandro Hills** [ALAMEDA].

Oakland Inner Harbor [ALAMEDA]: *water feature,* between Oakland and Alameda, extends for 5 miles from San Francisco Bay to Tidal Canal (center near lat. 37°47'40" N, long. 122°17' W). Named on Oakland West (1959) 7.5' quadrangle. The feature includes what is called San Antonio Creek on San Francisco (1899) 15' quadrangle. United States Board on Geographic Names (1949b, p. 3) rejected the names "San Antonio Creek," "San Antonio Estuary," "Deep Water Channel," "North Channel," "Oakland Estuary," "Oakland Harbor," and "South Channel" for the place

Oakland Middle Harbor [ALAMEDA]: *water feature,* 3 miles west of downtown Oakland along the Oakland waterfront just north of the entrance to Oakland Inner Harbor (lat. 37°48'15" N, long. 122° 19'45" W). Named

on Oakland West (1959) 7.5' quadrangle. United States Board on Geographic Names (1949b, p. 3) rejected the name "Southern Pacific Basin" for the feature.

Oakland Outer Harbor [ALAMEDA]: *water feature,* 3 miles west-northwest of downtown Oakland along Oakland water front 1 mile north of the entrance to Oakland Inner Harbor (lat. 37°49' N, long. 122°19' W). Named on Oakland West (1959) 7.5' quadrangle. Outer Harbor Entrance Channel leads to the place from San Francisco Bay.

Oakland Point: see **Gibbon Point** [ALAMEDA].

Oakleigh: see **Las Juntas** [CONTRA COSTA].

Oakley [CONTRA COSTA]: *town,* 4.5 miles north-northwest of Brentwood (lat. 37°59'45" N, long. 121°42'40" W; around NW cor. sec. 25, T 2 N, R 2 E). Named on Brentwood (1978) 7.5' quadrangle. Postal authorities established Oakley post office in 1898 (Frickstad, p. 22). R.C. Marsh, first postmaster, named the place for the native oak trees (Gudde, 1949, p. 240).

Oak Ridge [ALAMEDA-SANTA CLARA]: *ridge,* northwest- to west-trending, 6 miles long, 4 miles northwest of Mount Day on Alameda-Santa Clara county line, mainly in Santa Clara County (lat. 37°28' N, long. 121°44' W). Named on Calaveras Reservoir (1961) and Mount Day (1955) 7.5' quadrangles.

Oak Ridge [SANTA CLARA]: *ridge,* north-northwest-trending, 1 mile long, 3.5 miles southeast of Mount Day (lat. 37°22'55" N, long. 121°39'30" W). Named on Mount Day (1955) 7.5' quadrangle.

Oak Springs: see **Orinda** [CONTRA COSTA].

Oak Springs Reservoir [SANTA CLARA]: *lake,* 1000 feet long, 6 miles east-southeast of Mustang Peak near Santa Clara-Stanislaus county line (lat. 37°08'55" N, long. 122°15'55" W; sec. 13, T 9 S, R 6 E). Named on Mustang Peak (1955) 7.5' quadrangle.

Oakwood Valley [MARIN]: *canyon,* 1 mile long, 3.5 miles north of Point Bonita (lat. 37°52' N, long. 122°31'20" W). Named on Point Bonita (1954) 7.5' quadrangle.

Oat Hill [MARIN]: *peak,* 3.5 miles northeast of Bolinas (lat. 37°56'50" N, long. 122°38'20" W). Named on Bolinas (1954) 7.5' quadrangle.

Observatory Peak: see **Mount Hamilton** [SANTA CLARA].

Ocean Beach [SAN FRANCISCO]: *beach,* south of Point Lobos along the coast (lat. 37°45'30" N, long. 122°30'35" W). Named on San Francisco North (1956) 7.5' quadrangle.

Ocean House [SAN FRANCISCO]: *locality,* 3 miles west of Mount Davidson near the coast (lat. 37°44'20" N, long. 122°30'25" W). Named on San Mateo (1915) 15' quadrangle.

Ocean Lake [MARIN]: *lake,* 725 feet long, 1

mile north-northwest of Double Point (lat. 37°57'40" N, long. 122°47'05" W). Named on Double Point (1954) 7.5' quadrangle.

Ocean Roar [MARIN]: *locality,* 2.25 miles south-southwest of Tomales (lat. 38°13' N, long. 122°55'20" W). Named on Tomales (1954) 7.5' quadrangle. Point Reyes (1918) 15' quadrangle shows the place along Northwestern Pacific Railroad.

Ocean View: see **Albany** [ALAMEDA]; **Thornton** [SAN MATEO].

Oceanview [SAN FRANCISCO]: *locality,* 2 miles south-southeast of Mount Davidson (lat. 37°42'45" N, long. 122°27'15" W); the place is on San Miguel grant. Named on San Mateo (1915) 15' quadrangle. Postal authorities established San Miguel post office in 1878, changed the name to Ocean View in 1881, and discontinued it in 1895 (Frickstad, p. 159).

Offutt: see **Chileno Valley** [MARIN].

Ohmer [CONTRA COSTA]: *locality,* 6 miles east of Martinez along Oakland Antioch and Eastern Railroad (lat. 38°00'10" N, long. 122°01'20" W). Named on Carquinez Strait (1896) 15' quadrangle.

Oil Barrel Gulch: see **Hooker Creek** [SAN MATEO].

Oil Canyon [CONTRA COSTA]: *canyon,* 2.5 miles long, opens into the canyon of Sand Creek 6 miles northeast of Mount Diablo (lat. 37°56'35" N, long. 121°50'10" W; sec. 11, T 1 N, R 1 E). Named on Antioch South (1953) 7.5' quadrangle. Mount Diablo (1898) 15' quadrangle shows Oil Creek in the canyon.

Oil Creek [SAN MATEO]: *stream,* heads in Santa Cruz County and flows 5 miles to Pescadero Creek 6 miles south-southeast of Mindego Hill (lat. 37°13'45" N, long. 122°11'25" W; at N line sec. 21, T 8 S, R 3 W). Named on Big Basin (1955) and Mindego Hill (1961) 7.5' quadrangles. Oil from natural seepages is noticeable in the water (Brown, p. 62).

Oil Creek: see **Oil Canyon** [CONTRA COSTA].

Ojo de Agua de la Coche: [SANTA CLARA]: *land grant,* near Morgan Hill. Named on Gilroy (1955), Morgan Hill (1955), Mount Madonna (1955), and Mount Sizer (1955) 7.5' quadrangles. Juan Maria Hernandez received 2 leagues in 1835; M.J.C. Murphy claimed 8927 acres patented in 1860 (Cowan, p. 54). Perez (p. 79) used the form "Ojo de Agua de la Coches" for the name.

Olcott [SOLANO]: *locality,* 7 miles southeast of Elmira along Sacramento Northern Railroad (lat. 38°16'35" N, long. 121°49'25" W; near E line sec. 14, T 5 N, R 1 E). Named on Dozier (1952) 7.5' quadrangle.

Old Camp [SANTA CLARA]: *locality,* 4.25 miles north-northeast of Mount Day (lat. 37°28'15" N, long. 121°39'20" W; sec. 28, T 5 S, R 3 E); the place is 2.25 miles northwest of New Camp. Named on Mount Day (1955) 7.5' quadrangle.

Old Gilroy [SANTA CLARA]: *settlement,* 2.25 miles east-southeast of Gilroy (lat. 37°00' N, long. 121°31'30" W). Named on Chittenden (1955) and Gilroy (1955) 7.5' quadrangles. The place first was called San Ysidro or San Isidro, then Gilroy or Gilroy's, and finally Old Gilroy (Bancroft, 1888, p. 525). Postal authorities established San Isidro post office in 1866 and discontinued it in 1877 (Frickstad, p. 175).

Old Landing: see **Princeton** [SAN MATEO].

Old Mill Creek [MARIN]: *stream,* flows 2.25 miles to Arroyo Corte Madera Del Presidio nearly 5 miles south of downtown San Rafael in the town of Mill Valley (lat. 37°54'20" N, long. 122°32'45" W). Named on San Rafael (1954) 7.5' quadrangle.

Old Mountain View: see **Mountain View** [SANTA CLARA].

Old River [CONTRA COSTA]: *stream,* heads in San Joaquin County and flows 33 miles along Contra Costa-San Joaquin county line to San Joaquin River 5.5 miles northeast of the settlement of Bethel Island (lat. 38°04'20" N, long. 121°34'15" W). Named on Bouldin Island (1978), Clifton Court Forebay (1978), and Woodward Island (1978) 7.5' quadrangles.

Old Spanish Anchorage: see **Fort Point** [SAN FRANCISCO].

Old Town [MARIN]: *settlement,* nearly 1 mile south of downtown Novato (lat. 38°05'45" N, long. 122°34'10" W). Named on Petaluma (1914) 15' quadrangle. The place is in the present city of Novato.

Old Womans Creek [SAN MATEO]: *stream,* heads in Santa Cruz County and flows 2.5 miles to Gazos Creek 2.5 miles north-northeast of Franklin Point (lat. 37°11'10" N, long. 122°20'20" W). Named on Franklin Point (1955) 7.5' quadrangle. Año Nuevo (1948) 15' quadrangle has the name on a tributary of Gazos Creek that is located 3.5 miles farther upstream. Brown (p. 18-19) noted that the name "Old Woman Creek" was an early designation of this second tributary of Gazos Creek, and mentioned that the canyon of that tributary was called China Gulch for Chinese laborers who built a sawmill there in 1882. Brown (p. 19) also noted that present Old Womans Creek was called Horse Pasture Creek or Gushee Creek before the name "Old Woman Creek" was applied to it by mistake on early maps.

Olema [MARIN]: *village,* 2.25 miles southsoutheast of Point Reyes Station (lat. 38°02'25" N, long. 122°47'10" W); the place is along Olema Creek. Named on Inverness (1954) 7.5' quadrangle. Postal authorities established Olema post office in 1859, discontinued it in 1860, and reestablished it in 1864 (Frickstad, p. 88). Benjamin Winslow built a hotel called Olema House at the place, and is credited with naming the village (Mason,

1976a, p. 88). The name "Olema" probably is from an Indian village, and is derived from the Indian word for coyote (Kroeber, p. 51-52).

Olema Creek [MARIN]: *stream,* flows 10.5 miles to Lagunitas Creek nearly 0.5 mile south-southwest of Point Reyes Station (lat. 38°03'50" N, long. 122°48'35" W); the stream goes past Olema. Named on Bolinas (1954), Double Point (1954), and Inverness (1954) 7.5' quadrangles. Whitney (p. 84) called the stream Arroyo Olemus Loke.

Olema Station: see **Point Reyes Station** [MARIN].

Oleum [CONTRA COSTA]: *locality,* 6 miles east-northeast of Pinole Point along Southern Pacific Railroad (lat. 38°02'50" N, long. 122° 15'40" W). Named on Mare Island (1959) 7.5' quadrangle. On Benicia (1959) 7.5' quadrangle, the name applies to a group of oil tanks in the hills east of the place. Postal authorities established Oleum post office in 1910 and discontinued it in 1951 (Frickstad, p. 22). The name is from the word "petroleum"—an oil refinery is at the site (Gudde, 1949, p. 242).

Olofson Ridge [CONTRA COSTA]: *ridge,* north-northwest-trending, 1 mile long, 2.5 miles west-northwest of Mount Diablo (lat. 37°53'45" N, long. 121°57'15" W). Named on Clayton (1953) 7.5' quadrangle.

Olompali [MARIN]: *land grant,* 4 miles northwest of downtown Novato. Named on Petaluma (1953) and Petaluma River (1954) 7.5' quadrangles. Camilo Ynitia received 2 leagues in 1843 and claimed 8877 acres patented in 1862 (Cowan, p. 55). According to Perez (p. 79), Jose Ynitia was the grantee in 1843. The name is from the designation of an Indian village (Kroeber, p. 52).

Olompali: see **Mount Olompali**, under **Burdell Mountain** [MARIN].

Olympus: see **Mount Olympus** [SAN FRANCISCO].

O'Neill Creek: see **O'Neill Slough** [SAN MATEO].

O'Neill Slough [SAN MATEO]: *water feature,* extends from Seal Slough to Belmont Slough 4 miles southeast of downtown San Mateo (lat. 37°31'45" N, long. 122°16'05" W). Named on San Mateo (1956) 7.5' quadrangle. San Mateo (1915) 15' quadrangle has the name "O'Neill Creek," but United States Board on Geographic Names (1961b, p. 13) rejected the names "O'Neill Creek," "O'Neil Slough," and "San Mateo Slough" for the feature. Captain Owen O'Neill started a landing place along the slough in the early 1860's (Brown, p. 63).

O'Neil Slough: see **O'Neill Slough** [SAN MATEO].

One Mile Rocks: see **Mile Rock** [SAN FRANCISCO].

Oreja del Oso: see **El Toro** [SANTA CLARA].

Orient: see **Point Orient** [CONTRA COSTA].

Orinda [CONTRA COSTA]: *town,* 7 miles west-southwest of Walnut Creek civic center (lat. 37°52'45" N, long. 122°10'50" W). Named on Briones Valley (1959) and Oakland East (1959) 7.5' quadrangles. Concord (1897) 15' quadrangle shows a place called Bryant at the site of present Orinda, and has the name "Orinda" at present Orinda Village. Bryant was the eastern terminus of California and Nevada Railroad in 1893 (Hildebrand, p. 157). Theodore Wagner, United States surveyor general for California, had an estate in the 1880's that lay between Bear Creek and Lauterwasser Creek; he called the place Orinda Park (Gudde, 1969, p. 230). Postal authorities established Orinda Park post office in 1888, changed the name to Orinda in 1895, moved it 0.5 mile southeast to the site of Bryant in 1898, discontinued it in 1903, and reestablished it in 1927 (Salley, p. 162). United States Board on Geographic Names (1933, p. 575) rejected the name "Orinda Park" for the town. Bowen (p. 347) used the name "Orinda Crossroads" for the place formerly called Bryant. Oak Springs, located near Orinda (S half sec. 3, T 1 S, R 3 W), provided water for domestic use that was carried to Oakland by truck and bottled there (Davis and Vernon, p. 577).

Orinda Crossroads: see **Orinda** [CONTRA COSTA].

Orinda Park: see **Orinda** [CONTRA COSTA].

Orinda Village [CONTRA COSTA]: *town,* 1.5 miles northwest of Orinda (lat. 37°53'30" N, long. 122°12' W). Named on Briones Valley (1959) 7.5' quadrangle. Concord (1897) 15' quadrangle has the name "Orinda" at the place.

Ortega Creek [SANTA CLARA]: *stream,* flows 1.5 miles to lowlands near San Felipe (lat. 36°58'20" N, long. 121°24'55" W). Named on San Felipe (1955, photorevised 1971) 7.5' quadrangle. The name commemorates Ygnacio Ortega, original owner of San Ysidro grant (United States Board on Geographic Names, 1973a, p. 3).

Orwood [CONTRA COSTA]: *locality,* 7 miles east of Brentwood along Atchison, Topeka and Santa Fe Railroad (lat. 37°56'25" N, long. 121°34' W). Named on Woodward Island (1978) 7.5' quadrangle. Postal authorities established Orwood post office in 1913 and discontinued it in 1921; the name is from Orville Y. Woodward, the promoter of Orwood Tract (Salley, p. 163).

Orwood Tract [CONTRA COSTA]: *area,* 6 miles east of Brentwood (lat. 37°55'40" N, long. 121°35' W). Named on Woodward Island (1978) 7.5' quadrangle.

Osage [CONTRA COSTA]: *locality,* 1.5 miles south-southeast of Danville along Southern Pacific Railroad (lat. 37°47'55" N, long. 121°58'55" W). Named on Mount Diablo (1898) 15' quadrangle.

Otis Canyon [SANTA CLARA]: *canyon,* 1 mile long, drained by a stream that joins Coyote Creek 6 miles south-southwest of Mount Sizer (lat. 37°08'15" N, long. 121°33'50" W; near W line sec. 20, T 9 S, R 4 E). Named on Mount Sizer (1955) 7.5' quadrangle. The canyon splits at the head into North Fork and South Fork. North Fork is nearly 1 mile long and divides at its head into Clarks Canyon and Cordoza Canyon. South Fork is nearly 1.25 miles long. Both forks are named on Mount Sizer (1955) 7.5' quadrangle.

Oursan Ridge [CONTRA COSTA]: *ridge,* north- to northwest-trending, 2 miles long, 5.5 miles north-northwest of Orinda (lat. 37°57'15" N, long. 122°13' W). Named on Briones Valley (1959) 7.5' quadrangle.

Ousley Canyon [SANTA CLARA]: *canyon,* drained by a stream that flows nearly 2 miles to Uvas Creek 2.5 miles west of Gilroy (lat. 37°00'30" N, long. 121°36'45" W). Named on Chittenden (1955) and Gilroy (1955) 7.5' quadrangles.

Outer Harbor Entrance Channel: see **Oakland Outer Harbor** [ALAMEDA].

Outer Signal Station: see **Telegraph Hill** [SAN FRANCISCO].

Oxford [SOLANO]: *locality,* 11 miles northnortheast of Rio Vista along Sacramento Northern Railroad (lat. 38°18'25" N, long. 121° 37'10" W). Named on Courtland (1978) 7.5' quadrangle.

Ox Hill [SAN MATEO]: *peak,* 4 miles southeast of Montara Knob on Montara Mountain (lat. 37°31'25" N, long. 122°25'20" W; near E line sec. 5, T 5 S, R 5 W). Named on Montara Mountain (1956) 7.5' quadrangle. The peak was known locally as Bald Pate in the 1860's; the next peak north of Ox Hill is called Maloney's Hill—Michael Maloney had a ranch at the place in the 1860's (Brown, p. 51, 63).

Oxley [CONTRA COSTA]: *locality,* less than 1 mile north-northeast of present Walnut Creek civic center (lat. 37°54'50" N, long. 122° 03'15" W). Named on Concord (1943) 15' quadrangle.

Oyster Point [CONTRA COSTA]: *peak,* 4 miles south-southeast of Mount Diablo (lat. 37°49'50" N, long. 121°52'35" W; on E line sec. 20, T 1 S, R 1 E). Altitude 2106 feet. Named on Diablo (1953) and Tassajara (1953) 7.5' quadrangles.

Oyster Point [SAN MATEO]: *promontory,* 1.5 miles east-northeast of downtown South San Francisco along San Francisco Bay (lat. 37° 40' N, long. 122°23' W). Named on San Francisco South (1956) 7.5' quadrangle. Oyster beds were present near the point after the late 1860's (Brown, p. 63). The feature now is modified by filled land.

Oyster Point Channel [SAN MATEO]: *channel,* extends across San Francisco Bay north of Oyster Point to the shore 1.5 miles north-

northeast of downtown South San Francisco (lat. 37°40' N, long. 122°23'15" W). Named on Hunters Point (1956) 7.5' quadrangle.

Ozol [CONTRA COSTA]: *locality,* about 1.5 miles west-north-west of Martinez along Southern Pacific Railroad (lat. 38°01'35" N, long. 122°09'45" W). Named on Benicia (1959) 7.5' quadrangle.

– P –

Pablo Bay: see **San Pablo Bay** [CONTRA COSTA-MARIN-SOLANO].

Pablo Point [MARIN]: *ridge,* south-southeast-trending, 1 mile long, 3 miles northwest of Bolinas (lat. 37°56'30" N, long. 122°43'20" W). Named on Bolinas (1954) 7.5' quadrangle.

Pabrico [ALAMEDA]: *locality,* 4 miles northnortheast of downtown Newark along Western Pacific Railroad (lat. 37°35' N, long. 122° 00'20" W). Named on Newark (1959) 7.5' quadrangle. The name is from Oakland Paving Brick Company, which operated at the site from 1910 until 1912 (Mosier and Mosier, p. 65).

Pacheco [CONTRA COSTA]: *town,* 5.5 miles north of Walnut Creek civic center (lat. 37°59'05" N, long. 122°04' W). Named on Walnut Creek (1959) 7.5' quadrangle. Postal authorities established Pacheco post office in 1859, discontinued it in 1913, and reestablished it in 1955 (Salley, p. 164). The name is for Salvio Pacheco; Dr. J.H. Carothers laid out the town (Smith and Elliott, p. 23-24).

Pacheco: see **Fairford**, under **Black Point** [MARIN].

Pacheco Canyon [SANTA CLARA]: *canyon,* drained by a stream that flows nearly 1 mile to Anderson Lake 4.5 miles north-northeast of Morgan Hill (lat. 37°11'30" N, long. 121°37'20" W). Named on Morgan Hill (1955) 7.5' quadrangle.

Pacheco Creek [CONTRA COSTA]: *stream,* flows 4 miles in an artificial watercourse to Suisun Bay 3 miles northeast of Martinez (lat. 38°02'35" N, long. 122°05'30" W). Named on Vine Hill (1959) 7.5' quadrangle. The stream is called San Ramon Creek on some early maps (Gudde, 1949, p. 313).

Pacheco Creek [SANTA CLARA]: *stream,* flows 15 miles to San Benito County 11 miles east-southeast of Gilroy (lat. 36°57'35" N, long. 121°22'15" W); the creek heads near Pacheco Pass. Named on Pacheco Peak (1955), San Felipe (1955), and Three Sisters (1954) 7.5' quadrangles. Called Arroyo de S. Felipe on a diseño of San Joaquin grant (which is in San Benito County) made in 1836 (Becker, 1964). Francisco Perez Pacheco had his ranch headquarters near the stream that bears his name (Shumate, p. 12). North Fork enters from the north 10 miles upstream from the entrance of Pacheco Creek into San Benito County; it is 18 miles long and is named on Mississippi Creek (1955), Mustang Peak (1955), and Pacheco Peak (1955) 7.5' quadrangles. North Fork is called Pacheco Creek on Gilroy Hot Springs (1921) 15' quadrangle. South Fork enters from the southeast 11 miles upstream from the entrance of Pacheco Creek into San Benito County; it heads in San Benito County, is 8 miles long, and is named on Pacheco Peak (1955) and Three Sisters (1954) 7.5' quadrangles. East Fork joins North Fork from the northeast nearly 4 miles upstream from the mouth of North Fork; it is 5 miles long and is named on Crevison Peak (1955) and Pacheco Peak (1955) 7.5' quadrangles.

Pacheco Hill [MARIN]: *peak,* 5 miles south-southeast of downtown Novato (lat. 38°02'35" N, long. 122°31'50" W); the peak is on San Jose grant, which Ignacio Pacheco owned. Altitude 454 feet. Named on Novato (1954) 7.5' quadrangle.

Pacheco Lake [SANTA CLARA]: *lake,* 2 miles long, behind a dam on North Fork Pacheco Creek 3 miles north of Pacheco Peak (lat. 37° 03' N, long. 121°17'25" W). Named on Pacheco Peak (1955) 7.5' quadrangle.

Pacheco Pass [SANTA CLARA]: *pass,* 20 miles east-northeast of Gilroy on Santa Clara-Merced county line (lat. 37°03'50" N, long. 121°12'30" W). Named on Pacheco Pass (1955) 7.5' quadrangle. The name commemorates Francisco Perez Pacheco, who owned San Luis Gonzaga grant where the pass lies; the pass has the name "San Luis Gonzaga" in early records (Shumate, p. 1). Called Pacheco's Pass on Williamson's (1853) map. Mountain House station was at the summit of the pass (Latta, 1976, p. 246).

Pacheco Peak [SANTA CLARA]: *peak,* 16 miles east of Gilroy (lat. 37°00'30" N, long. 121°17'15" W). Altitude 2770 feet. Named on Pacheco Peak (1955) 7.5' quadrangle. Antisell (p. 17) used the form "Pacheco's Peak" for the name.

Pacifica [SAN MATEO]: *city,* center about 4.5 miles west-southwest of downtown South San Francisco (lat. 37°37'30" N, long. 122° 29' W). Named on Montara Mountain (1956, photorevised 1980) and San Francisco South (1956, photorevised 1980) 7.5' quadrangles. Residents of several communities in the vicinity voted in 1957 to form a new incorporated city called Pacifica (Gudde, 1969, p. 233). Postal authorities established Pacifica post office in 1959 (Salley, p. 164).

Pacific Congress Springs: see **Congress Springs** [SANTA CLARA].

Pacific Manor [SAN MATEO]: *district,* 4 miles west of downtown South San Francisco near the coast (lat. 37°39' N, long. 122°29'05" W). Named on San Francisco South (1956) 7.5' quadrangle. Residents of the place voted in 1957 to join neighboring communities and form the new city of Pacifica.

Packard Ridge [SANTA CLARA]: *ridge,* west-to north-northwest-trending, nearly 3 miles long, 4 miles east-southeast of Mount Day (lat. 37°23'45" N, long. 121°38' W). Named on Eylar Mountain (1955) and Mount Day (1955) 7.5' quadrangles.

Packwood Creek [SANTA CLARA]: *stream,* flows 7.5 miles to Anderson Lake 6.25 miles west-southwest of Mount Sizer (lat. 37° 10'30" N, long. 121°37' W). Named on Mount Sizer (1955) 7.5' quadrangle.

Packwood Valley [SANTA CLARA]: *valley,* 5 miles west of Mount Sizer (lat. 37°12'20" N, long. 121°36' W); the valley is along upper Packwood Creek. Named on Mount Sizer (1955) 7.5' quadrangle.

Paddy Lake [SOLANO]: *lake,* 1050 feet long, 4 miles north-northeast of Benicia (lat. 38°06'15" N, long. 122°08'10" W; sec. 13, T 3 N, R 3 W). Named on Benicia (1959) 7.5' quadrangle.

Page Flat [SOLANO]: *area,* 4.5 miles southwest of Cordelia (lat. 38° 09'25" N, long. 122°10'55" W; near S line sec. 27, T 4 N, R 3 W). Named on Cordelia (1951) 7.5' quadrangle.

Page Mill [SAN MATEO]: *locality,* 4.25 miles southeast of Mindego Hill along Slate Creek (lat. 37°15'40" N, long. 122°11'10" W; sec. 3, T 8 S, R 3 W). Site named on Mindego Hill (1961) 7.5' quadrangle.

Pajaro: see **Mount Pajaro** [SANTA CLARA].

Pajaro River [SANTA CLARA]: *stream,* heads near the south end of Santa Clara Valley and flows 10 miles along Santa Clara-San Benito county line to the southeast end of Santa Cruz Mountains, where it leaves Santa Clara County and continues to the sea. Named on Chittenden (1955) and San Felipe (1955) 7.5' quadrangles. Called Sanjon de la Brea on a diseño of Llano de Tequesquet grant made in 1834 (Becker, 1969), called Payharo R. on Baker's (1855) map, and called R. Pajaros on Mitchell's (1856) map. Taylor (v. I, p. 175) called the stream Rio del Pajaro. Soldiers of the Portola expedition gave the name "Pajaro" to the stream in 1769 because of a huge stuffed bird displayed there by natives (Wagner, H.R., p. 401)—*pajaro* means "bird" in Spanish.

Pala [SANTA CLARA]: *land grant,* in Alum Rock district of San Jose. Named on Calaveras Reservoir (1961) 7.5' quadrangle. Jose Higuera received 1 league in 1835; Ellen E. White and others claimed 4454 acres patented in 1866 (Cowan, p. 56). According to Gudde (1949, p. 249), the name is from an Indian called Pala, who was mentioned in records as early as 1795.

Palassou Ridge [SANTA CLARA]: *ridge,* north-northwest-trending, 6 miles long, 9 miles east of Morgan Hill (lat. 37°07' N, long. 121° 29'45" W). Named on Gilroy (1955), Gilroy Hot Springs (1955), Mississippi Creek (1955), and Mount Sizer (1955) 7.5' quadrangles. Called Pellisier Ridge on Morgan Hill (1917) 15' quadrangle.

Palermo: see **Mount Palermo**, under **Mount Tamalpais** [MARIN].

Palmentto Landing [SOLANO]: *locality,* 2 miles west-southwest of Birds Landing (2) along Montezuma Slough (lat. 38°07'15" N, long. 121°54'10" W). Named on Honker Bay (1918) 7.5' quadrangle.

Palmer Gulch [SAN MATEO]: *canyon,* drained by a stream that flows 0.5 mile to San Gregorio Creek at the village of San Gregorio (lat. 37°19'35" N, long. 122°23'05" W). Named on San Gregorio (1961, photorevised 1968) 7.5' quadrangle.

Palm Hill [MARIN]: *ridge,* east-southeast-trending, 0.5 mile long, 3 miles south of downtown San Rafael (lat. 37°55'55" N, long. 122° 31'35" W). Named on San Rafael (1954) 7.5' quadrangle.

Palm Tract [CONTRA COSTA]: *area,* 6 miles east-northeast of Brentwood (lat. 37°57'15" N, long. 121°35'15" W). Named on Woodward Island (1978) 7.5' quadrangle. Called Palms Tract on Davis and Vernon's (1951) map.

Palo Alto [SANTA CLARA]: *city,* 15 miles west-northwest of downtown San Jose (lat. 37°26'45" N, long. 122°09'30" W). Named on Mindego Hill (1961), Mountain View (1961), and Palo Alto (1961) 7.5' quadrangles. During construction of Stanford University campus in 1889 on Leland Stanford's Palo Alto farm, Mr. Stanford had a new town, to be called University Park, laid out next to the campus, but a developer bought 120 acres adjoining Stanford's land on the south and laid out another town, to be called Palo Alto; Stanford brought suit to prevent use of the name "Palo Alto" for the second town, and the matter was settled when the name of the second town was changed to College Terrace— Stanford's University Park was renamed Palo Alto (Butler, p. 11). The name "Palo Alto" is from a large redwood tree noted by early Spanish explorers near San Francisquito Creek—*palo alto* means "tall tree" in Spanish (Gudde, 1949, p. 250-251). Postal authorities established Palo Alto post office in 1892 (Frickstad, p. 174), and the town incorporated in 1894. According to Newhall (p. 21), present Palo Alto was the site of Twin Trees Station along the railroad in 1865.

Palo Alto: see **East Palo Alto** [SAN MATEO]; **South Palo Alto**, under **Mayfield** [SANTA CLARA].

Palo Alto Island: see **Snag Island** [SOLANO].

Palo Alto Point: see **Point Palo Alto** [SOLANO].

Palomares Canyon: see **Palomares Creek** [ALAMEDA].

Palomares Creek [ALAMEDA]: *stream,* flows 5.25 miles to San Lorenzo Creek 3.5 miles east-northeast of downtown Hayward (lat.

37°41'45" N, long. 122°01'30" W). Named on Dublin (1961) and Hayward (1959) 7.5' quadrangles. The name commemorates Francisco Palomares, who lived along the stream; the canyon of the creek is called Palomares Canyon (Mosier and Mosier, p. 66).

Palomar Park [SAN MATEO]: *district,* 2.25 miles west of downtown Redwood City (lat. 37°28'50" N, long. 122°15'50" W). Named on Woodside (1961) 7.5' quadrangle.

Palo Seco Creek [ALAMEDA]: *stream,* flows 2 miles to join Shephard Creek and form Sausal Creek 3.5 miles east-northeast of downtown Oakland (lat. 37°49'10" N, long. 122°12'25" W). Named on Oakland East (1959) 7.5' quadrangle.

Pams Blue Ridge: see **Blue Ridge** [MARIN].

Panochita Hill [SANTA CLARA]: *peak,* nearly 4 miles southwest of Mount Hamilton (lat. 37°18'15" N, long. 121°41'30" W). Altitude 1871 feet. Named on Lick Observatory (1955) 7.5' quadrangle.

Panther Creek [SANTA CLARA]: see **Llagas Creek** [SANTA CLARA].

Paper Mill: see **Lagunitas Creek** [MARIN].

Paper Mill Creek: see **Lagunitas Creek** [MARIN].

Paperville: see **Lagunitas Creek** [MARIN].

Paradise Cay [MARIN]: *locality,* 2 miles south of Point San Quentin along the northeast side of Tiburon Peninsula (lat. 37°54'45" N, long. 122°28'30" W). Named on San Quentin (1959) 7.5' quadrangle. Ringgold's (1850a) map shows Pt. Munroe at the place, and has the name "Aspinwall Bay" for the embayment between Point Munroe and Point Chauncey. San Francisco (1915) 15' quadrangle shows a promontory called California Point at the site, but United States Board on Geographic Names (1968a, p. 6) rejected this name.

Paradise Cove [MARIN]: *embayment,* 3.5 miles south-southeast of Point San Quentin on the northeast side of Tiburon Peninsula (lat. 37°53'40" N, long. 122°27'20" W). Named on San Quentin (1959) 7.5' quadrangle. San Francisco (1942) 15' quadrangle shows a place called California City located along San Francisco Bay 0.5 mile south-southeast of present Paradise Cove. Benjamin Buckelew laid out a townsite near Paradise Cove about 1850 and called it California City (Mason, 1976b, p. 62).

Paradise Creek [SANTA CLARA]: *stream,* flows 1 mile to Llagas Creek 2.25 miles west-southwest of Morgan Hill (lat. 37°06'50" N, long. 121°41'10" W). Named on Morgan Hill (1955, photorevised 1968 and 1973) and Mount Madonna (1955, photorevised 1968 and 1973) 7.5' quadrangles. The name is from Paradise Valley, which is at the mouth of the stream (United States Board on Geographic Names, 1973a, p. 3).

Paradise Park: see **El Campo** [MARIN].

Paradise Valley [MARIN]: *valley,* 1.25 miles northwest of Bolinas along Pine Gulch Creek (lat. 37°55'40" N, long. 122°42'10" W). Named on Bolinas (1954) 7.5' quadrangle.

Paradise Valley [SANTA CLARA]: *valley,* 2.25 miles south-southwest of Morgan Hill along Llagas Creek (lat. 37°06' N, long. 121° 40'30" W). Named on Mount Madonna (1955) 7.5' quadrangle.

Parks: see **Camp Parks** [ALAMEDA-CONTRA COSTA].

Passionate Spring [SANTA CLARA]: *spring,* 2 miles south of Mount Boardman (lat. 37°27'05" N, long. 121°28'35" W; sec. 36, T 5 S, R 4 E). Named on Mount Boardman (1955) 7.5' quadrangle.

Pastoria de las Borregas [SANTA CLARA]: *land grant,* in Mountain View and Sunnyvale. Named on Cupertino (1961), Milpitas (1961), and Mountain View (1961) 7.5' quadrangles. Francisco Estrada received 2 leagues in 1842; Martin Murphy, Jr., claimed 4894 acres patented in 1865; Mariano Castro claimed 4172 acres, which he called Refugio, patented in 1881 (Cowan, p. 58).

Patapsco Point: see **Point Molate** [CONTRA COSTA].

Patchen Pass: see **Wrights** [SANTA CLARA].

Patchin: see **Wrights** [SANTA CLARA].

Patterson Creek [ALAMEDA]: *water feature,* joins Coyote Hills Slough 4.5 miles northwest of downtown Newark (lat. 37°34'05" N, long. 122°06'25" W). Named on Newark (1959) 7.5' quadrangle. The name commemorates George Washington Patterson, a local rancher; the feature first had the misspelled name "Sundburg Creek," for Edward Sundberg, who had a landing there in 1863 (Mosier and Mosier, p. 66).

Patterson Landing [ALAMEDA]: *locality,* 3.5 miles northwest of downtown Newark (lat. 37°34'05" N, long. 122°04'50" W); the place is near the head of Patterson Creek. Named on Haywards (1899) 15' quadrangle. Edward Lang built Lang's Landing at the site in the 1850's, and after Edward Sundberg bought the place, it had the misspelled name "Sundburg Landing" until Edward A. Anderson and Edward Anderson, Jr., bought it in 1870 and changed the name to Anderson's Landing; then George W. Patterson bought the landing before 1878 (Mosier and Mosier, p. 67).

Patterson Pass [ALAMEDA]: *pass,* 4.25 miles south-southeast of Altamont (lat. 37°41'15" N, long. 121°37'45" W; sec. 10, T 3 S, R 3 E). Named on Altamont (1953) 7.5' quadrangle. Thompson and West (1878, p. 17) referred to "Middle Pass, or Patterson Road" as a route east from Livermore Valley. The pass is said to have received its name after Mrs. Andrew Jackson Patterson broke her leg in an accident there in the 1850's (Gudde, 1949, p. 255).

Patterson Run [ALAMEDA]: *stream,* flows about 5.5 miles to San Joaquin County 0.5 mile north-northeast of Midway (lat. 37°43'20" N, long. 121°33'20" W; near S line

sec. 29, T 2 S, R 4 E). Named on Midway (1953) 7.5' quadrangle.

Peach Tree Springs [CONTRA COSTA]: *springs,* 3 miles west-northwest of Mount Diablo (lat. 37°54' N, long. 121°57'50" W). Named on Clayton (1953) 7.5' quadrangle. Called Peachtree Springs on Mount Diablo (1898) 15' quadrangle. The name supposedly is from a tree that grew by the springs (Waring, p. 355).

Peacock Creek [CONTRA COSTA]: *stream,* flows 2.5 miles to Mount Diablo Creek at Clayton (lat. 37°56'30" N, long. 121°56'05" W; near SE cor. sec. 11, T 1 N, R 1 W). Named on Mount Diablo (1898) 15' quadrangle.

Peacock's: see **Harrisburg**, under **Warm Springs District** [ALAMEDA].

Peak: see **The Peak** [SANTA CLARA].

Peak Canyon: see **Little Peak Canyon** [SANTA CLARA].

Peak Mountain [SAN MATEO]: *peak,* about 0.25 mile north of Montara Knob on Montara Mountain (lat. 37°33'40" N, long. 122° 29' W; sec. 26, T 4 S, R 6 W). Named on Montara Mountain (1956) 7.5' quadrangle.

Pearsons Pond: see **La Honda** [SAN MATEO].

Pebble Beach [MARIN]: *beach,* 8 miles south of Tomales on the southwest side of Tomales Bay (lat. 38°07'45" N, long. 122°53'10" W). Named on Tomales (1954) 7.5' quadrangle.

Pebble Beach [SAN MATEO]: *beach,* 4 miles north-northwest of Pigeon Point along the coast (lat. 37°14'10" N, long. 122°24'55" W). Named on Pigeon Point (1955) 7.5' quadrangle.

Pecks Ridge: see **Copper Mine Gulch** [MARIN].

Pedro Mountain: see **San Pedro Mountain** [SAN MATEO].

Pedro Point: see **Point San Pedro** [SAN MATEO].

Pedro Valley [SAN MATEO]: *district,* 2.5 miles north-northwest of Montara Knob in San Pedro Valley (lat. 37°35'30" N, long. 122°29'45" W); residents of the place voted in 1957 to join with neighboring communities to form the new city of Pacifica. Named on Montara Mountain (1956) 7.5' quadrangle. San Mateo (1915) 15' quadrangle shows a place called Tobin situated along Ocean Shore Railroad at the mouth of San Pedro Valley, and San Mateo (1942) 15' quadrangle shows a place called San Pedro Terrace at about the same site. Postal authorities established Tobin post office in 1894, moved it 1 mile east in 1897, discontinued it in 1901, reestablished it in 1908, changed the name to Pedro Valley in 1915, discontinued it in 1918, reestablished it in 1937, and discontinued it in 1960—the name "Tobin" was for a San Francisco financier who built a summer home at the site (Salley, p. 169, 222). Modern growth of the place began in 1953 with a large subdivision called Linda Mar (Hynding, p. 185).

Pelican Lake [MARIN]: *lake,* 1400 feet long, 750 feet from the coast at Double Point (lat. 37°57' N, long. 122°46'25" W). Named on Double Point (1954) 7.5' quadrangle.

Pelican Point [MARIN]: *promontory,* 4.25 miles south-southwest of Tomales on the southwest side of Tomales Bay (lat. 38°11'15" N, long. 122°55'50" W). Named on Tomales (1954) 7.5' quadrangle.

Pelican Point [SOLANO]: *promontory,* 7 miles west-southwest of Birds Landing (2) along Grizzly Bay (lat. 38°06'35" N, long. 121°59'35" W). Named on Honker Bay (1953) 7.5' quadrangle.

Pellisier Ridge: see **Palassou Ridge** [SANTA CLARA].

Peltier Slough [SOLANO]: *water feature,* 5 miles southwest of Fairfield (lat. 38°11'25" N, long. 122°05'40" W). Named on Fairfield South (1949) 7.5' quadrangle.

Peninsula Island: see **Belvedere Island** [MARIN].

Peninsula Point [MARIN]: *promontory,* 1.5 miles east of downtown Sausalito at the southeast end of Belvedere Island (lat. 37°51'45" N, long. 122°27'30" W). Named on San Francisco North (1956) 7.5' quadrangle.

Penitencia: see **Milpitas** [SANTA CLARA] (2).

Penitencia Creek: see **Lower Penitencia Creek** [SANTA CLARA]; **Upper Penitencia Creek** [SANTA CLARA].

Penitentiary Cañon: see **Alum Rock Canyon** [SANTA CLARA].

Penole: see **Pinole** [CONTRA COSTA] (1) and (2); **Point Penole**, under **Pinole Point** [CONTRA COSTA].

Pequeña Laguna: see **Washerwoman's Lagoon**, under **Marina District** [SAN FRANCISCO].

Peralta [ALAMEDA]: *locality,* 5.5 miles north of downtown Oakland (lat. 37°52'55" N, long. 122°17' W). Named on San Francisco (1899) 15' quadrangle. Postal authorities established Peralta post office in 1890, discontinued it in 1901, reestablished it in 1949, and discontinued it in 1954 (Salley, p. 169).

Peralta: see **Lake Peralta**, under **Lake Merritt** [ALAMEDA].

Peralta Creek [ALAMEDA]: *stream,* flows nearly 2 miles to end in flatlands 3 miles east-southeast of downtown Oakland (lat. 37° 47' N, long. 122°13'05" W). Named on Oakland East (1959) 7.5' quadrangle. The name commemorates Don Luis Peralta, owner of San Antonio grant (Mosier and Mosier, p. 67).

Perkins Canyon [CONTRA COSTA]: *canyon,* drained by a stream that flows 2 miles to Marsh Creek 2.5 miles east-northeast of Mount Diablo (lat. 37°53'45" N, long. 121°52'10" W; near N line sec. 33, T 1 N, R 1 E). Named on Antioch South (1953) and Clayton (1953) 7.5' quadrangles.

Permanent Creek: see **Permanente Creek** [SANTA CLARA].

Permanente Creek [SANTA CLARA]: *stream,* flows 12 miles to Mountain View Slough 3 miles north of downtown Mountain View (lat. 37°26' N, long. 122°05'05" W). Named on Cupertino (1961), Mindego Hill (1961), and Mountain View (1961) 7.5' quadrangles. The stream is called Arroyo Permanente on a map of 1839 (Gudde, 1949, p. 258), and is called Permanent Creek on Thompson and West's (1876) map. The Spanish word *permanente* describes a stream that flows all year (Rambo, 1964, p. 40).

Perry [SANTA CLARA]: *locality,* 3 miles southeast of Coyote along Southern Pacific Railroad (lat. 37°10'55" N, long. 121°42'10" W). Named on Morgan Hill (1955) 7.5' quadrangle. Called Perrys on Morgan Hill (1917) 15' quadrangle. Perry Station was on the stage route between Coyote and Morgan Hill (Hoover, Rensch, and Rensch, p. 431). The hotel there was called Fifteen Mile House for its distance from San Jose (*San Jose Mercury-News, California Today Magazine,* October 23, 1977).

Perry Station: see **Perry** [SANTA CLARA].

Peruvian Island: see **Turk Island** [ALAMEDA].

Pescadero [SAN MATEO]: *town,* 5 miles south of the village of San Gregorio (lat. 37°15'20" N, long. 122°22'50" W); the town is along Pescadero Creek. Named on San Gregorio (1961) 7.5' quadrangle. Postal authorities established Pescadero post office in 1859 (Frickstad, p. 168). They established Harrison post office 7 miles northeast of Pescadero in 1889, moved it 1 mile west in 1896, discontinued it in 1899, reestablished it in 1909, discontinued it in 1916, reestablished it in 1917, and discontinued it in 1919; the name was for the operator of a logging camp at the place (Salley, p. 94). They established Barzilla post office 3 miles west of Harrison post office in 1891 and discontinued it in 1892; the name was for the operator of a combination lumber, shingle, and grist mill at the site—the place was known as Luffley's before 1874 (Salley, p. 15). They established Torquay post office 12 miles south of Pescadero in 1908 and discontinued it in 1911 (Salley, p. 223).

Pescadero: see **San Antonio or Pescadero** [SAN MATEO].

Pescadero Beach [SAN MATEO]: *beach* 4.5 miles south-southwest of the village of San Gregorio along the coast (lat. 37°15'45" N, long. 122°24'45" W); the beach is south of the mouth of Pescadero Creek. Named on San Gregorio (1961) 7.5' quadrangle.

Pescadero Creek [SAN MATEO]: *stream,* flows 25 miles to the sea 4.25 miles south-southwest of the village of San Gregorio, and 2 miles west-northwest of Pescadero (lat. 37°16' N, long. 122°24'40" W). Named on Big Basin (1955), Franklin Point (1955), La Honda (1961), Mindego Hill (1961), and San

Gregorio (1961) 7.5' quadrangles. The stream was called Arroyo del Pescadero in Spanish times (Brown, p. 67).

Pescadero Creek [SANTA CLARA]: *stream,* flows nearly 6 miles to Pajaro River 7 miles south of Gilroy at the junction of Santa Clara County, Santa Cruz County, and San Benito County (lat. 36°54'05" N, long. 121°35'05" W). Named on Chittenden (1955) and Watsonville East (1955) 7.5' quadrangles. Called Arroyo de Pescadero on a diseño of Las Animas grant (Becker, 1969). According to Gudde (1949, p. 259), the name refers to the catching of fish in the stream—*pescadero* means "fishing place" in Spanish.

Pescadero Point [SAN MATEO]: *promontory,* 4.25 miles north-northwest of Pigeon Point along the coast (lat. 37°14'30" N, long. 122°25'05" W). Named on Pigeon Point (1955) 7.5' quadrangle.

Petaluma Creek: see **Petaluma River** [MARIN].

Petaluma Point [MARIN]: *promontory,* 4.5 miles east of downtown Novato on Day Island (lat. 38°06'20" N, long. 122°29'15" W); the feature is south of the mouth of Petaluma River. Named on Petaluma Point (1959) 7.5' quadrangle. Called Novato Pt. on Ringgold's (1850a) map.

Petaluma River [MARIN]: *stream,* heads in Sonoma County and flows 21 miles to San Pablo Bay 3.5 miles southwest of Sears Point (lat. 38°06'40" N, long. 122°29'30" W). Named on Cotati (1954), Novato (1954), Petaluma (1953), Petaluma Point (1959), and Petaluma River (1954) 7.5' quadrangles. Called Petaluma Creek on Mare Island (1916) and Petaluma (1914) 15' quadrangles, but United States Board on Geographic Names (1959b, p. 7) rejected this form of the name. The feature is called Estero de Petaluma on the diseño of Olompali grant made in 1843 (Becker, 1964). The stream also had the Spanish names "Estero de las Mercedes" and "Estero de Nuestra Señora de la Merced" (Wagner, H.R., p. 472, 478). The river forms the Marin-Sonoma county line below the mouth of San Antonio Creek

Petaluma Valley [MARIN]: *valley,* along Petaluma River from north of the city of Petaluma to San Pablo Bay; on Marin-Sonoma county line. Named on Santa Rosa (1958) 1°x 2° quadrangle. P.T. Tyson (p. 19) referred to Petaloma valley in 1850.

Peterman's Landing: see **Eden Landing**, under **Mount Eden** [ALAMEDA].

Peters Creek [SAN MATEO]: *stream,* heads just inside Santa Cruz County and flows 7 miles to Pescadero Creek 4 miles south of Mindego Hill (lat. 37°15'05" N, long. 122°13' W; sec. 8, T 8 S, R 3 W); the stream drains Devils Canyon. Named on Mindego Hill (1961) 7.5' quadrangle. Brown (p. 27) used the name "Devil's Canyon Creek" for the stream in

Devils Canyon, and noted (p. 68) that the name "Peters" is for Jean Peter, who settled near the creek in 1860.

Peterson Creek [SAN MATEO]: *stream,* flows 1 mile to Pescadero Creek 3.25 miles southsouthwest of La Honda (lat. 37°16'25" N, long. 122°17'30" W; sec. 34, T 7 S, R 4 W). Named on La Honda (1961) 7.5' quadrangle.

Peters Pocket [SOLANO]: *area,* 10 miles northnorthwest of Rio Vista between Hass Slough and Cache Slough (lat. 38°18' N, long. 121°44'10" W). Named on Liberty Island (1978) 7.5' quadrangle.

Peytonia Slough [SOLANO]: *water feature,* joins Suisun Slough 1.5 miles south-southeast of downtown Fairfield (lat. 38°13'35" N, long. 122°02' W). Named on Fairfield South (1949) 7.5' quadrangle.

Pheasant Creek [SANTA CLARA]: *stream,* flows 1.5 miles to Guadalupe Creek nearly 4.5 miles north-northwest of Mount Umunhum (lat. 37°12'50" N, long. 121°54'40" W). Named on Los Gatos (1953) 7.5' quadrangle.

Phegley Ridge [SANTA CLARA]: *ridge,* northnorthwest-trending, nearly 2 miles long, 5 miles southeast of Gilroy Hot Springs (lat. 37°03'45" N, long. 121°24'40" W). Named on Gilroy Hot Springs (1955) 7.5' quadrangle.

Phelps: see **Point Phelps**, under **Point Carquinez** [CONTRA COSTA].

Phelps Slough [SAN MATEO]: *water feature,* enters Steinberger Slough nearly 3 miles north-northwest of downtown Redwood City (lat. 37°31'15" N, long. 122°14'50" W; sec. 1, T 5 S, R 4 W). Named on Redwood Point (1959) and San Mateo (1956) 7.5' quadrangles. Timothy Guy Phelps built a landing at the head of the slough in the late 1850's (Brown, p. 68).

Phoenix Creek [MARIN]: *stream,* flows 1 mile to Phoenix Lake 3 miles west-southwest of downtown San Rafael (lat. 37°57'20" N, long. 122°34'55" W). Named on San Rafael (1954) 7.5' quadrangle.

Phoenix Lake [MARIN]: *lake,* behind a dam on Ross Creek 2.5 miles west-southwest of downtown San Rafael (lat. 37°57'20" N, long. 122°34'30" W). Named on San Rafael (1954) 7.5' quadrangle.

Picacho de Chual: see **Mount Chual** [SANTA CLARA].

Picacho de Umunhum: see **Mount Umunhum** [SANTA CLARA].

Picacho de Umurhum: see **Mount Umunhum** [SANTA CLARA].

Picacho Prieto: see **Mount Tamalpais** [MARIN].

Picket: see **Point Picket**, under **Stake Point** [CONTRA COSTA].

Picnic Hill: see **Belmont Hill** [SAN MATEO].

Pico y Cerro de Reyes: see **Mount Tamalpais** [MARIN].

Piedmont [ALAMEDA]: *town,* 2.5 miles east-northeast of downtown Oakland (lat. 37°49'30" N, long. 122°13'45" W). Named on Oakland East (1959) 7.5' quadrangle. Piedmont Springs Company bought land at the site about 1876 and built a hotel to exploit a sulphur spring located on the property; a community developed at the place about 1900 (Gudde, 1949, p. 261), and postal authorities established Piedmont post office in 1901 (Frickstad, p. 3). The town incorporated in 1907. Winslow Anderson (p. 222) referred to Piedmont White Sulphur Springs at the place.

Piedmont Creek [SANTA CLARA]: *stream,* formed by the confluence of North Branch and South Branch, flows 1 mile in an artificial watercourse to Berryessa Creek nearly 1 mile east of downtown Milpitas (lat. 37°25'35" N, long. 121°53'20" W). Named on Milpitas (1961) 7.5' quadrangle. North Branch is 1.25 miles long and South Branch is 1 mile long; both branches are named on Calaveras Reservoir (1961) 7.5' quadrangle.

Piedmont White Sulphur Springs: see **Piedmont** [ALAMEDA].

Pierce [SOLANO]: *locality,* 9 miles south-southwest of Fairfield along Southern Pacific Railroad (lat. 38°07'35" N, long. 122° 06' W). Named on Fairfield South (1949) 7.5' quadrangle.

Pierce Point: see **Tomales Point** [MARIN].

Pigeon Point [SAN MATEO]: *promontory,* 20 miles south of the town of Half Moon Bay along the coast (lat. 37°10'55" N, long. 122°23'35" W). Named on Pigeon Point (1955) 7.5' quadrangle. The name is for the clipper ship *Carrier Pigeon,* which was wrecked at the place in 1853; in Spanish times the promontory was called Punta de la Ballena, or Cabo de Fortunas (Reinstedt, p. 12). A small port community that developed at the place by the 1860's also was called Pigeon Point (Morrall, p. 60). Postal authorities established Pigeon Point post office in 1874 and discontinued it in 1875 (Frickstad, p. 168). The embayment on the coast under Pigeon Point is called Pigeon Point Cove; a rock in the cove was called Storehouse Rock in the 1850's, and was called Pirate's Rock during Prohibition times (Brown, p. 69, 70).

Pigeon Point [SANTA CLARA]:
(1) *ridge,* west-northwest-trending, 1 mile long, 3.25 miles north of Morgan Hill (lat. 37°10'40" N, long. 121°38'50" W). Named on Morgan Hill (1955) 7.5' quadrangle. On Morgan Hill (1917) 15' quadrangle, the name applies to a peak on the ridge.
(2) *peak,* 4 miles south of Gilroy Hot Springs (lat. 37°03'10" N, long. 121°29'35" W; sec. 23, T 10 S, R 4 E). Named on Gilroy Hot Springs (1955) 7.5' quadrangle.

Pigeon Point Cove: see **Pigeon Point** [SAN MATEO].

Pike County Gulch [MARIN]: *canyon,* drained by a stream that flows 1.5 miles to Bolinas

Lagoon 1.5 miles north of Bolinas (lat. 37°55'55" N, long. 122°41'15" W). Named on Bolinas (1954) 7.5' quadrangle. Settlers reportedly named it for Pike County, Texas (Teather, p. 55).

Pilarcitos Canyon: see **Pilarcitos Creek** [SAN MATEO].

Pilarcitos Creek [SAN MATEO]: *stream,* flows 12.5 miles to the sea 1.25 miles northwest of downtown Half Moon Bay (lat. 37°28'30" N, long. 122°26'50" W). Named on Half Moon Bay (1961) and Montara Mountain (1956) 7.5' quadrangles. United States Board on Geographic Names (1933, p. 603) rejected the form "Pillarcitos" for the name. Crespi called the stream Arroyo de San Simon y San Judas in 1769, and later it was called Arroyo de los Pilarcitos (Gudde, 1949, p. 261). The canyon of the creek below Pilarcitos Lake is called Pilarcitos Canyon (Brown, p. 69).

Pilarcitos Lake [SAN MATEO]: *lake,* 1.25 miles long, behind a dam on Pilarcitos Creek 3.5 miles east of Montara Knob (lat. 37°32'55" N, long. 122°25'20" W; near NW cor. sec. 33, T 4 S, R 5 W). Named on Montara Mountain (1956) 7.5' quadrangle. United States Board on Geographic Names (1933, p. 603) rejected the form "Pillarcitos" for the name.

Pillar Point [SAN MATEO]: *promontory,* 4.25 miles west-northwest of downtown Half Moon Bay along the coast (lat. 37°29'45" N, long. 122°29'45" W). Named on Half Moon Bay (1961) 7.5' quadrangle. The feature is on a peninsula that was called Corral de Tierra in Spanish times, and was called Snake's Head in early American times (Brown, p. 69).

Pillar Point Harbor [SAN MATEO]: *water feature,* 3.5 miles south of Montara Knob at the north end of Half Moon Bay (1) (lat. 37° 30'10" N, long. 122°29' W); the feature is east of Pillar Point. Named on Montara Mountain (1956, photorevised 1980) 7.5' quadrangle.

Pillar Rock: see **Sail Rock** [SAN MATEO].

Pilot Knob [MARIN]: *peak,* 2.5 miles west of downtown San Rafael (lat. 37°56'55" N, long. 122°35'15" W). Altitude 1187 feet. Named on San Rafael (1954) 7.5' quadrangle.

Pine Canyon [CONTRA COSTA]: *canyon,* 4.25 miles long, along Pine Creek above a point 4.5 miles west of Mount Diablo (lat. 37° 53'35" N, long. 122°59'35" W). Named on Clayton (1953) and Diablo (1953) 7.5' quadrangles.

Pine Creek [CONTRA COSTA]: *stream,* flows 12.5 miles to Walnut Creek (1) 5 miles north of Walnut Creek civic center (lat. 37°58'35" N, long. 122°03'05" W); the stream drains Pine Canyon. Named on Clayton (1953) and Walnut Creek (1959) 7.5' quadrangles.

Pine Creek: see **Little Pine Creek** [CONTRA COSTA].

Pine Gulch Creek [MARIN]: *stream,* flows 7.5 miles to Bolinas Lagoon nearly 1 mile north of Bolinas (lat. 37°55'20" N, long. 122° 41'10"

W). Named on Bolinas (1954) 7.5' quadrangle. Teather (p. 12) used the name "Bolinas Creek" for the stream, and noted that the feature also is called Gregorio's Creek, for Gregorio Briones, who received Las Baulines grant.

Pine Lake [SOLANO]: *lake,* 1400 feet long, 1 mile east of downtown Benicia (lat. 38°03'05" N, long. 122°08'10" W; sec. 1, T 2 N, R 3 W). Named on Benicia (1959) 7.5' quadrangle.

Pine Mountain [MARIN]: *peak,* 5 miles north-northeast of Bolinas (lat. 37°58'40" N, long. 122°39'05" W). Altitude 1762 feet. Named on Bolinas (1954) 7.5' quadrangle.

Pine Mountain Ridge [MARIN]: *ridge,* west- to northwest-trending, 2.25 miles long, 5 miles north of Bolinas (lat. 37°58'45" N, long. 122°40'10" W); Pine Mountain is at the east end of the ridge. Named on Bolinas (1954) 7.5' quadrangle.

Pine Ridge [CONTRA COSTA]: *ridge,* south-southeast-trending, 1 mile long, 3.25 miles west-southwest of Mount Diablo (lat. 37° 52' N, long. 121°58'20" W); the ridge is southwest of Pine Canyon. Named on Diablo (1953) 7.5' quadrangle.

Pine Ridge [SANTA CLARA]: *ridge,* northwest-trending, 4 miles long, 2.5 miles west-southwest of Mount Sizer (lat. 37°11'45" N, long. 121°33'15" W). Named on Mount Sizer (1955) 7.5' quadrangle.

Pine Ridge: see **Bollinger Ridge** [SANTA CLARA]; **Castle Ridge** [SANTA CLARA]; **Valpe Ridge** [ALAMEDA-SANTA CLARA].

Pine Spring Canyon [SANTA CLARA]: *canyon,* drained by a stream that flows 6.25 miles to North Fork Pacheco Creek nearly 7 miles north of Pacheco Peak (lat. 37°06'20" N, long. 121°17'40" W; sec. 34, T 9 S, R 6 E). Named on Mustang Peak (1955) and Pacheco Peak (1955) 7.5' quadrangles.

Pine Springs Hill [SANTA CLARA]: *peak,* 4 miles east of Mustang Peak on Santa Clara-Stanislaus county line (lat. 37°10'50" N, long. 121°16'50" W; sec. 2, T 9 S, R 6 E); the peak is at the head of Pine Spring Canyon. Named on Mustang Peak (1955) 7.5' quadrangle.

Pine Tree Canyon [SANTA CLARA]: *canyon,* drained by a stream that flows 1 mile to an unnamed stream 3.5 miles east-southeast of New Almaden (lat. 37°09'50" N, long. 121°45'25" W). Named on Santa Teresa Hills (1953) 7.5' quadrangle.

Pine Tree Gulch [SAN MATEO]: *canyon,* drained by a stream that flows 0.5 mile to El Corte de Madera Creek 4 miles west-northwest of La Honda (lat. 37°21'05" N, long. 122°20' W). Named on La Honda (1961) 7.5' quadrangle.

Pino Creek [SANTA CLARA]: *stream,* flows 2 miles to Arroyo Valle 5 miles south-southwest of Eylar Mountain (lat. 37°24'25" N, long. 121°35' W; sec. 18, T 6 S, R 4 E). Named on

Eylar Mountain (1955) 7.5' quadrangle.

Pinole [CONTRA COSTA]:

(1) *land grant,* extends from the town of Pinole to Martinez. Named on Benicia (1959), Briones Valley (1959), Mare Island (1959), Richmond (1959), and Walnut Creek (1959) 7.5' quadrangles. United States Board on Geographic Names (1933, p. 606) rejected the names "El Pinole" and "Penole" for the grant. Ignacio Martinez held the land in 1829 and received 4 leagues in 1842; M.A. Martinez de Richardson claimed 17,761 acres patented in 1868 (Cowan, p. 61). The name "Pinole" is from the Spanish term for parched corn that the Mexicans ground up and used (Davis, W.H., p. 23).

(2) *town,* 4 miles east of Pinole Point (lat. 38°00'20" N, long. 122° 17'25" W). Named on Mare Island (1959), Petaluma Point (1959), and Richmond (1959) 7.5' quadrangles. United States Board on Geographic Names (1933, p. 606) rejected the names "El Pinole" and "Penole" for the town. Postal authorities established Pinole post office in 1878 (Frickstad, p. 23), and the town incorporated in 1903. Dr. Samuel J. Tennant founded the town, which is named for Pinole grant—Tennant was the son-in-law of the owner of the grant (Hanna, P.T., p. 236-237).

Pinole Creek [CONTRA COSTA]: *stream,* flows 10 miles to San Pablo Bay nearly 4 miles east of Pinole Point in the town of Pinole (lat. 38°00'50" N, long. 122°17'45" W). Named on Briones Valley (1959), Mare Island (1959), and Richmond (1959) 7.5' quadrangles.

Pinole Point [CONTRA COSTA]: *promontory,* 26 miles west-northwest of Mount Diablo along San Pablo Bay (lat. 38°00'45" N, long. 122°21'50" W). Named on Mare Island (1959) 7.5' quadrangle. Called Punta de Almejas on a diseño of San Pablo grant made in 1830 (Becker, 1969). Called Pt. Penole on Ringgold's (1850a) map, but United States Board on Geographic Names (1933, p. 606) rejected the forms "Penole" and "El Pinole" for the name.

Pinole Ridge [CONTRA COSTA]: *ridge,* northwest- to west-trending, 3.25 miles long, 6.25 miles northeast of Richmond civic center (lat. 37°59'30" N, long. 122°15' W). Named on Briones Valley (1959) and Richmond (1959) 7.5' quadrangles.

Pinole Shoal [CONTRA COSTA]: *shoal,* 3.5 miles northeast of Pinole Point in San Pablo Bay just west of Carquinez Strait (lat. 38°02'45" N, long. 122°18'45" W). Named on Mare Island (1959) 7.5' quadrangle.

Pioneer: see **Robertsville** [SANTA CLARA].

Pioneer Camp [CONTRA COSTA]: *locality,* less than 1 mile southwest of Mount Diablo (lat. 37°52'20" N, long. 121°55'20" W; sec. 1, T 1 S, R 1 W). Named on Diablo (1953) 7.5' quadrangle.

Piper Slough [CONTRA COSTA]: *water fea-*

ture, extends for 5 miles, mainly between Bethel Island (1) and Franks Tract, from Sand Mound Slough to False River 3 miles north-northwest of the settlement of Bethel island (lat. 38°03'20" N, long. 121°39'20" W). Named on Bouldin Island (1978) and Jersey Island (1978) 7.5' quadrangles.

Pirate Creek [ALAMEDA]: *stream,* flows 2.5 miles to Alameda Creek 3 miles south-south-east of Sunol (lat. 37°33'20" N, long. 121°51'50" W). Named on La Costa Valley (1960) and Niles (1961) 7.5' quadrangles. Mosier and Mosier (p. 68) suggested stream piracy as the probable source of the name; the stream flowed to Sheridan Creek before it was captured by a tributary of Alameda Creek.

Pirates Cove [MARIN]: *embayment,* 3 miles northwest of Point Bonita along the coast (lat. 37°51'05" N, long. 122°33'40" W). Named on Point Bonita (1954) 7.5' quadrangle.

Pirate's Cove: see **Shelter Cove** [SAN MATEO].

Pirate's Rock: see **Pigeon Point** [SAN MATEO].

Pistolesi: see **Camp Pistolesi**, under **Camp Tomales** [MARIN].

Pita Navaga: see **Divide Ridge** [ALAMEDA-CONTRA COSTA].

Pittsburg [CONTRA COSTA]: *city,* 10 miles north of Mount Diablo (lat. 38°01'55" N, long. 121°52'55" W). Named on Antioch North (1978), Clayton (1953), and Honker Bay (1953) 7.5' quadrangles. Ringgold's (1850b) map shows a town called New York of the Pacific at the site. Postal authorities established Black Diamond post office in 1868 and changed the name to Pittsburg in 1911 (Frickstad, p. 21). The city incorporated in 1903. Colonel Jonathan D. Stevenson of the New York Volunteers bought Los Medanos grant in 1849 and had a town laid out that he called New York of the Pacific (Hoover, Rensch, and Rensch, p. 64), but after 1850 the development was recognized as a failure (Bancroft, 1888, p. 528). With the discovery of coal in Diablo Range, the place became a shipping point for coal and was called Black Diamond until 1909, when the name was changed to Pittsburg in recognition of the industrial potential of the place (Hanna, P.T., p. 238). The site also was known as Black Diamond Landing (MacMullen, p. 78) and New York Landing (Mosier, p. 4). The name "Black Diamond" was from Black Diamond coal mine, located about 4 miles south of the center of Pittsburg (in and near SE quarter sec. 5, T 1 N, R 1 E) (Davis and Goldman, p. 520). California Mining Bureau's (1909b) map shows a place called Cornwall located near Black Diamond 7.25 miles east-southeast of Baypoint along a railroad. Postal authorities established Cornwall Station post office 1 mile south of Black Diamond in 1881, discontinued it in 1888, reestablished it with the name "Cornwall" in 1890, and discontinued

it in 1911 (Salley, p. 50).

Pittsburg: see **West Pittsburg** [CONTRA COSTA].

Pittsburg Landing [CONTRA COSTA]: *locality,* 2.25 miles west-northwest of Antioch near the east end of New York Slough (lat. 38°01'40" N, long. 121°50'50" W). Named on Collinsville (1918) 7.5' quadrangle. Coal from mines in Diablo Range was shipped from the place, which was connected to the mines by Pittsburg Railroad (Mosier, p. 6).

Pittsburg Point [CONTRA COSTA]: *promontory,* 2.5 miles west-northwest of Antioch along New York Slough (lat. 38°01'50" N, long. 121°51'05" W). Named on Antioch North (1978) 7.5' quadrangle.

Pittsburg Station [CONTRA COSTA]: *locality,* less than 1 mile south-southwest of present downtown Pittsburg (lat. 38°01'25" N, long. 121°53'10" W). Named on Honker Bay (1918) 7.5' quadrangle.

Planiel: see **Plantel** [SANTA CLARA].

Plantel [SANTA CLARA]: *locality,* 3 miles southeast of Gilroy along Southern Pacific Railroad (lat. 36°58' N, long. 121°31'50" W). Named on San Juan Bautista (1917) 15' quadrangle. Santa Cruz (1956) 1°x 2° quadrangle has the name "Planiel" at the place.

Plaza de los Caballos: see **Cavallo Point** [MARIN].

Pleasant Creek [SOLANO]: *stream,* flows 4.5 miles to McCune Creek (1) 3.5 miles northwest of Allendale (lat. 38°28'40" N, long. 121°59'20" W). Named on Allendale (1953) and Mount Vaca (1951) 7.5' quadrangles.

Pleasant Hill [CONTRA COSTA]: *city,* 2.5 miles north of Walnut Creek civic center (lat. 37°56'20" N, long. 122°04' W). Named on Walnut Creek (1959) 7.5' quadrangle. Postal authorities established Pleasant Hill post office in 1948 (Salley, p. 174), and the city incorporated in 1961.

Pleasanton [ALAMEDA]: *city,* 6 miles west-southwest of Livermore (lat. 37°39'45" N, long. 121°52'30" W). Named on Dublin (1961) and Livermore (1961) 7.5' quadrangles. The place first was called Alisal, but John Kottinger named the city in 1867 for General Alfred Pleasonton (Mosier and Mosier, p. 69). Postal authorities established the post office there with the misspelled name "Pleasanton" in 1867 (Frickstad, p. 3), and the city incorporated in 1894. A station along Western Pacific Railroad south of Pleasanton was called Hacienda because it served the Hearst estate called La Hacienda del Pozo de Verona; the station also was called Hearst (Mosier and Mosier, p. 40).

Pleasanton: see **East Pleasanton** [ALAMEDA].

Pleasanton Ridge [ALAMEDA]: *ridge,* northwest- to north-northwest-trending, 5.25 miles long, center 4.5 miles south-southeast of Dublin (lat. 37°38'15" N, long. 121°54'45" W); the ridge is 2.5 miles southwest of Pleasanton.

Named on Dublin (1961) and Niles (1961) 7.5' quadrangles.

Pleasants Canyon: see **Miller Canyon** [SOLANO].

Pleasants Creek [SOLANO]: *stream,* flows 10 miles to Putah Creek 7.5 miles northeast of Mount Vaca (lat. 38°29'25" N, long. 122°01'10" W); the stream drains Pleasants Valley. Named on Mount Vaca (1951) 7.5' quadrangle. United States Board on Geographic Names (1933, p. 609) rejected the name "Pleasant Valley Creek" for the feature.

Pleasants Ridge [SOLANO]: *ridge,* north-trending, 4 miles long, 5.5 miles north-northeast of Mount Vaca (lat. 38°28'30" N, long. 122°04'40" W); the ridge is northwest of Pleasants Valley. Named on Monticello Dam (1959) and Mount Vaca (1951) 7.5' quadrangles.

Pleasants Valley [SOLANO]: *valley,* 4.5 miles northeast of Mount Vaca along Pleasants Creek (lat. 38°27'15" N, long. 122°03'15" W). Named on Mount Vaca (1951) 7.5' quadrangle. The name commemorates James Marshall Pleasants and his son William James Pleasants, who arrived in the valley in 1850 and farmed there (Gudde, 1969, p. 251).

Pleasant Valley: see **Gilroy** [SANTA CLARA]; **Happy Valley** [CONTRA COSTA]; **Rincon Hill** [SAN FRANCISCO].

Pleasant Valley Creek: see **Pleasants Creek** [SOLANO].

Plumbajo Flat: see **Blumbago Canyon** [SANTA CLARA].

Plummer Creek [ALAMEDA]: *water feature,* joins Newark Slough 3 miles southwest of downtown Newark (lat. 37°30'20" N, long. 122°05' W). Named on Newark (1959) 7.5' quadrangle. The stream first was called Salt Work Slough for Crystal Salt Works, which John A. Plummer established in 1864 (Mosier and Mosier, p. 69).

Plummer Landing [ALAMEDA]: *locality,* 1.5 miles south-southwest of downtown Newark (lat. 37°30'35" N, long. 122°03'05" W); the place is along Plummer Creek. Named on Newark (1948) 7.5' quadrangle. Isaac Long established Long's Landing along present Plummer Creek in 1852; Long sold his landing to John Plummer in 1855 (Mosier and Mosier, p. 53).

Point Anno Nuevo: see **Año Nuevo Point** [SAN MATEO].

Point Año Nuevo: see **Año Nuevo Point** [SAN MATEO].

Point Avisadero [SAN FRANCISCO]: *promontory,* 5.5 miles east of Mount Davidson along San Francisco Bay at the east end of Hunters Point (lat. 37°43'45" N, long. 122°21'20" W). Named on Hunters Point (1956) 7.5' quadrangle. Called Pta. Avisadera on Beechey's (1827-1828) map, and called Avisadero Pt. on San Mateo (1915) 15' quadrangle. United States Board on Geographic Names (1967b, p. 2) rejected the names "Avisadero Point,"

"Avisadera Point," and "Hunters Point" for the feature.

Point Beenar [CONTRA COSTA]: *promontory,* 2 miles northwest of Antioch along San Joaquin River at the southeast end of Winter Island (lat. 38°01'50" N, long. 121°50'10" W). Named on Antioch North (1978) 7.5' quadrangle.

Point Blunt: see **Blunt Point** [MARIN-SAN FRANCISCO].

Point Blunt Rock: see **Blunt Point Rock** [SAN FRANCISCO].

Point Bodega: see **Tomales Bluff** [MARIN].

Point Bolitas: see **Bulls Head Point** [CONTRA COSTA].

Point Boneta: see **Point Bonita** [MARIN].

Point Bonita [MARIN]: *promontory,* 11 miles south of downtown San Rafael along the coast (lat. 37°48'55" N, long. 122°31'40" W). Named on Point Bonita (1954) 7.5' quadrangle. Ayala called the promontory Punta de Santiago in 1775; the feature also was known as Punta Bonete and Punta de Bonetas in Spanish times (Gudde, 1949, p. 37). United States Board on Geographic Names (1933, p. 156) rejected the form "Point Boneta" for the name. The top of the promontory was called Lands End in the 1860's (Shanks and Shanks, p. 36).

Point Buckler [SOLANO]: *promontory,* 8 miles east-northeast of Benicia at the west end of Simmons Island (lat. 38°05'50" N, long. 122°01'10" W). Named on Vine Hill (1959) 7.5' quadrangle.

Point Campbell: see **Campbell Point** [MARIN].

Point Carquinez [CONTRA COSTA]: *promontory,* nearly 3 miles northwest of Martinez (lat. 38°02'20" N, long. 122°10'30" W); the promontory is along Carquinez Strait. Named on Benicia (1959) 7.5' quadrangle. Called Pt. Phelps on Ringgold's (1850a) map, Karquines Pt. on Karquines (1898) 15' quadrangle, and Carquinez Point on Carquinez Strait (1896) 15' quadrangle.

Point Cavallo: see **Cavallo Point** [MARIN].

Point Chapman: see **Steamboat Slough** [SOLANO].

Point Chauncey [MARIN]: *promontory,* 3.5 miles south-southeast of Point San Quentin on the northeast side of Tiburon Peninsula (lat. 37°53'40" N, long. 122°26'55" W). Named on San Quentin (1959) 7.5' quadrangle. Called Chauncey Pt. on San Francisco (1915) 15' quadrangle.

Point Davis: see **Davis Point** [CONTRA COSTA].

Point Diablo [MARIN]: *promontory,* nearly 3 miles south-southwest of downtown Sausalito along the coast (lat. 37°49'10" N, long. 122°29'50" W). Named on San Francisco North (1956) 7.5' quadrangle. Called Punta Diablo on Beechey's (1827-1828) map, and Kelley (p. 162) called it Punto Diavolo. United

States Board on Geographic Names (1979a, p. 7) approved the name "Kirby Beach" for the beach, 1.7 miles long, that is situated about halfway between Point Diablo and Lime Point (west end at lat. 37°49'36" N, long. 122°29'25" W).

Point Edith [CONTRA COSTA]: *promontory,* 4.5 miles northeast of Martinez along Suisun Bay (lat. 38°03'10" N, long. 122°04'10" W). Named on Vine Hill (1959) 7.5' quadrangle. Called Edith Point on Karquines (1898) 15' quadrangle. Ringgold's (1850b) map shows Pt. Massachusetts situated about 0.5 mile east of Pt. Edith.

Point Edith Crossing Range [CONTRA COSTA-SOLANO]: *channel,* nearly 5 miles northeast of Martinez in Suisun Bay on Contra Costa-Solano county line (lat. 38°03'35" N, long. 122°04' W); the feature is north of Point Edith. Named on Vine Hill (1959) 7.5' quadrangle.

Point Elliot: see **Port Costa** [CONTRA COSTA].

Point Emmet [CONTRA COSTA]: *promontory,* 0.5 mile north of downtown Pittsburg at the west end of Browns Island on the west side of the mouth of New York Slough (lat. 38°02'25" N, long. 121°52'50" W). Named on Honker Bay (1953) 7.5' quadrangle.

Point Fleming: see **Fleming Point** [ALAMEDA].

Point Gelston: see **Ryer Island** [SOLANO] (1).

Point Gillespie: see **Gillespie Point** [SOLANO].

Point Green: see **Preston Point** [SOLANO].

Point Hansen: see **Van Sickle Island** [SOLANO].

Point Huchones: see **Point San Pablo** [CONTRA COSTA].

Point Ione [MARIN]: *promontory,* on the west side of Angel Island (lat. 37°52'05" N, long. 122°26'15" W). Named on San Francisco North (1956, photorevised 1968 and 1973) 7.5' quadrangle.

Point Isabel [CONTRA COSTA]: *promontory,* nearly 3 miles south-southeast of Richmond civic center along San Francisco Bay (lat. 37°53'55" N, long. 122°19'25" W). Named on Richmond (1959) 7.5' quadrangle. Called Isabel Pt. on San Francisco (1899) 15' quadrangle. United States Board on Geographic Names (1933, p. 392) rejected the names "Point Izabel" and "Point Potero" for the feature.

Point Izabel: see **Point Isabel** [CONTRA COSTA].

Point Julia: see **Inverness** [MARIN].

Point Knox: see **Knox Point** [MARIN].

Point Lobos [SAN FRANCISCO]: *promontory,* 3 miles southwest of Fort Point along the coast (lat. 37°46'50" N, long. 122°30'50" W). Named on San Francisco North (1956) 7.5' quadrangle. Called Pta. del Angel de la Guarda on Dalrymple's (1789) map, and called Punta de los Lobos on Ringgold's (1850a) map.

Point Massachusetts: see **Point Edith** [CONTRA COSTA].

Point Molate [CONTRA COSTA]: *promontory,* 1.25 miles south-southeast of Point San Pablo along San Francisco Bay (lat. 37°56'50" N, long. 122°25'15" W). Named on San Quentin (1959) 7.5' quadrangle. Called Patapsco Pt. on Ringgold's (1850a) map, and called Molate Pt. on San Francisco (1899) 15' quadrangle.

Point Montara [SAN MATEO]: *promontory,* 2.5 miles southwest of Montara Knob along the coast (lat. 37°32'15" N, long. 122°31'05" W). Named on Montara Mountain (1956) 7.5' quadrangle. Called Montara Pt. on San Mateo (1915) 15' quadrangle. United States Board on Geographic Names (1933, p. 528) rejected the form "Point Montora" for the name. Brown (p. 57) used the name "Montara Creek" for the stream that enters the sea on the north side of Point Montara. A rock situated offshore south of Point Montara is called Colorado Reef or Colorado Ledge for the steamship *Colorado,* which was wrecked there in 1868; before this wreck, the feature was called Uncle Sam Rock for a ship wrecked there in 1855 (Brown, p. 22).

Point Montgomery: see **Telegraph Hill** [SAN FRANCISCO].

Point Montora: see **Point Montara** [SAN MATEO].

Point Munroe: see **Paradise Cay** [MARIN].

Point New Year: see **Año Nuevo Point** [SAN MATEO].

Point of Timber: see **Byron** [CONTRA COSTA].

Point Orient [CONTRA COSTA]: *promontory,* 0.5 mile south-southeast of Point San Pablo along San Francisco Bay (lat. 37°57'25" N, long. 122°25'25" W). Named on San Quentin (1959) 7.5' quadrangle.

Point Palo Alto [SOLANO]: *promontory,* 7 miles southwest of Birds Landing (2) at the east end of Snag Island (lat. 38°04'20" N long. 123°58'20" W). Named on Honker Bay (1953) 7.5' quadrangle. Called Palo Alto Pt. on Ringgold's (1850c) map, which has the name "Palo Alto Id." for present Snag Island.

Point Penole: see **Pinole Point** [CONTRA COSTA].

Point Picket: see **Stake Point** [CONTRA COSTA].

Point Phelps: see **Point Carquinez** [CONTRA COSTA].

Point Potrero [CONTRA COSTA]: *promontory,* 2.5 miles south-southwest of Richmond civic center (lat. 37°54'15" N, long. 122° 22' W). Named on Richmond (1959) 7.5' quadrangle. Called Shoal Pt. on San Francisco (1915) 15' quadrangle.

Point Potrero: see **Point Isabel** [CONTRA COSTA].

Point Reed: see **Bluff Point** [MARIN].

Point Reyes [MARIN]:

(1) *promontory,* 12 miles west-southwest of Point

Reyes Station at the west end of Drakes Bay (the lighthouse at the end of the promontory is near lat. 37°59'45" N, long. 123°01'20" W). Named on Drakes Bay (1953) 7.5' quadrangle. Called Pta. de los Reyes on Costanso's (1771) map, called Punta de Reyes on Crespi's (1772) map, and called Punto de los Reyes on Ringgold's (1850b) map. Cabrillo discovered the promontory in 1542 and named it Cabo de Pinos; the present name comes from the Vizcaino expedition, which rounded the point and took shelter in present Drakes Bay on January 6, 1603, the day of Los Reyes (Wagner, H.R., p. 405). Vizcaino gave the name "La Punta de las Barrancas blancas" to the east end of present Point Reyes—*barrancas blancas* means "white cliffs" in Spanish (Davidson, p. 22-23), and no doubt refers to cliffs along present Drakes Bay.

(2) *locality,* 7.25 miles north-northeast of the lighthouse at Point Reyes (lat. 38°05'05" N, long. 122°57'15" W). Named on Point Reyes (1918) 15' quadrangle. Postal authorities established Point Reyes post office in 1891 at what was known as "F" Ranch, moved it 4 miles southeast in 1919 to "D" Ranch, moved it 4 miles southwest to the lighthouse at Point Reyes about 1942, and discontinued it in 1948 (Salley, p. 175).

Point Reyes: see **Point Reyes Station** [MARIN].

Point Reyes Beach [MARIN]: *beach,* extends for 10 miles along the coast north-northeast from Point Reyes (1) to a spot 6.5 miles south-southwest of Tomales (lat. 38°09'30" N, long. 122°56'55" W). Named on Drakes Bay (1953) and Tomales (1954) 7.5' quadrangles. The feature also is known as Ten Mile Beach and as The Great Beach (Mason, 1972, p. 62).

Point Reyes Hill [MARIN]: *peak,* 3.5 miles west-northwest of Point Reyes Station on Inverness Ridge (lat. 38°04'50" N, long. 122°52'05" W); the peak is 10 miles northeast of the lighthouse at Point Reyes. Altitude 1336 feet. Named on Inverness (1954) 7.5' quadrangle.

Point Reyes Station [MARIN]: *village,* 13 miles south-southeast of Tomales (lat. 38°04'10" N, long. 122°08'20" W); the village is 13 miles east-northeast of the lighthouse at Point Reyes. Named on Inverness (1954) 7.5' quadrangle. The place was called Olema Station when the railroad reached the site in 1875 (Mason, 1976b, p. 116). Postal authorities established Point Reyes post office at the place in 1882, changed the name to Marin by mistake in 1891, changed it back to Point Reyes the same year, and changed it to Point Reyes Station later in 1891 (Salley, p. 175).

Point Richmond [CONTRA COSTA]:

(1) *promontory,* 4.25 miles south-southeast of Point San Pablo along San Francisco Bay (lat. 37°54'35" N, long. 122°23'15" W). Named on San Quentin (1959) 7.5' quadrangle. Called Pt. Stephens on Ringgold's (1850a) map, and

called Richmond Pt. on San Francisco (1899) 15' quadrangle.

(2) *district,* 3.5 miles southeast of Point San Pablo in Richmond (lat. 37°55'40" N, long. 122°23'10" W); the district is north of Point Richmond (1). Named on San Quentin (1959) 7.5' quadrangle. Atchison, Topeka and Santa Fe Railroad established a terminal at the place in 1897, and the community that developed there was called Santa Fe (Gudde, 1949, p. 286). Postal authorities established Eastyard post office in 1901 and changed the name to Point Richmond in 1902 (Salley, p. 65).

Point San Bruno [SAN MATEO]: *promontory,* 2 miles east of downtown South San Francisco along San Francisco Bay (lat. 37°39'10" N, long. 122°22'35" W). Named on San Francisco South (1956) 7.5' quadrangle, which shows that landfill modifies the feature. Called San Bruno Pt. on San Mateo (1915) 15' quadrangle, and called Punta San Bruno on Beechey's (1827-1828) map.

Point San Joaquin [CONTRA COSTA]: *promontory,* 4 miles northwest of Antioch at the north end of Winter Island (lat. 38°03'35" N, long. 121°51'20" W); the feature is west of the mouth of San Joaquin River. Named on Antioch North (1978) 7.5' quadrangle.

Point San Mateo: see **Coyote Point** [SAN MATEO].

Point San Matheo: see **Coyote Point** [SAN MATEO].

Point San Pablo [CONTRA COSTA]: *promontory,* 5 miles west-northwest of Richmond civic center along San Francisco Bay (lat. 37°57'55" N, long. 122°25'40" W). Named on San Quentin (1959) 7.5' quadrangle. Called San Pablo Pt. on San Francisco (1899) 15' quadrangle. Dalrymple's (1789) map has the name "Pta. de Sn. Antonio" for this or a nearby promontory, and Beechey's (1827-1828) map has the name "pta. San Pablo" for it. A diseño of San Pablo grant made in 1830 has the name "Punta de Sn. Pablo" (Becker, 1969). The feature was called Pt. Huchones before 1811—the Huchones Indians lived there (Bancroft, 1886, p. 321).

Point San Pablo Yacht Harbor [CONTRA COSTA]: *water feature,* 0.5 mile east-southeast of Point San Pablo along San Pablo Bay (lat. 37°57'45" N, long. 122°25'05" W). Named on San Quentin (1959) 7.5' quadrangle.

Point San Pedro [MARIN]: *promontory,* 4.5 miles east-northeast of downtown San Rafael on the northwest side of San Pablo Strait (lat. 37°59'05" N, long. 122°26'45" W). Named on San Quentin (1959) 7.5' quadrangle. Called Pta. San Pedro on Beechey's (1827-1828) map, and called San Pedro Pt. on San Francisco (1915) 15' quadrangle. The promontory was called Punta de San Pedro as early as 1811, and in the 1870's it was known as McNears Point from the firm of McNear and

Brothers, which owned land there (Gudde, 1949, p. 200). Ringgold's (1850a) map shows a feature called Argus I. situated just off Pt. San Pedro.

Point San Pedro [SAN MATEO]: *promontory,* 3.25 miles northwest of Montara Knob along the coast (lat. 37°35'40" N, long. 122°31'10" W); the feature is on San Pedro grant. Named on Montara Mountain (1956) 7.5' quadrangle. Called San Pedro Pt. on San Mateo (1915) 15' quadrangle, and called Punta de Almejas on Font's (1777) map. Members of the Portola expedition in 1769 gave the name "Punta de Almejas" to the feature for mussels found nearby—*almejas* means "mussels" in Spanish; at the same time, Crespi gave it the name "Punta del Angel Custodio" (Wagner, H.R., p. 412). Brown (p. 65) called it Pedro Point.

Point San Quentin [MARIN]: *promontory,* 3.5 miles southeast of downtown San Rafael along San Francisco Bay (lat. 37°56'35" N, long. 122°28'35" W). Named on San Quentin (1959) 7.5' quadrangle. The promontory was called Punta de Quintin in Spanish times for an Indian named Quintin, who was captured there; members of United States Coast Survey Americanized the name and added the word "San" when they surveyed San Francisco Bay in 1850 (Gudde, 1949, p. 312). Ringgold's (1850a) map has the name "Lejuanjelua Bay" for the embayment south of Point San Quentin, and shows Agnes I. located just off of the point—landfill now connects the island to the promontory.

Point San Quentin: see **Potrero Point** [SAN FRANCISCO].

Point Semple: see **Semple Point** [SOLANO].

Point Sherman: see **Port Chicago** [CONTRA COSTA].

Point Simmons: see **Simmons Point** [SOLANO].

Point Simpton: see **Simpton Point** [MARIN].

Point Smith: see **Quarry Point** [MARIN-SAN FRANCISCO].

Point Stephens: see **Point Richmond** [CONTRA COSTA] (1).

Point Stephenson: see **Middle Point** [CONTRA COSTA].

Point Stuart: see **Stuart Point** [MARIN].

Point Thompson: see **Mare Island** [SOLANO].

Point Tiburon [MARIN]: *promontory,* 2 miles east-northeast of downtown Sausalito on the northwest side of Raccoon Strait (lat. 37°52'20" N, long. 122°26'55" W); the promontory is at Tiburon. Named on San Francisco North (1956) 7.5' quadrangle. Called Punta de Tiburon in Spanish times—*tiburon* means "shark" in Spanish (Gudde, 1949, p. 361).

Point Wall [SOLANO]: *promontory,* 5.5 miles south-southwest of Birds Landing (2) along Suisun Bay on Van Sickle Island (lat. 38° 03'10" N, long. 121°53'20" W). Named on Honker Bay (1953) 7.5' quadrangle. Called Wall Pt. on Ringgold's (1850c) map.

Point Wise [SOLANO]: *promontory,* 6 miles south-southwest of Birds Landing (2) along Suisun Bay on Chipps Island (lat. 38° 03' N, long. 121°53'50" W). Named on Honker Bay (1953) 7.5' quadrangle.

Polhemus Creek [SAN MATEO]: *stream,* flows 1.5 miles to San Mateo Creek 2.5 miles south-southwest of downtown San Mateo (lat. 37°31'55" N, long. 122°21'W). Named on San Mateo (1956) 7.5' quadrangle. The canyon of the stream is called Alms House Canyon on San Mateo (1915) 15' quadrangle, which shows an alms house near the head of the canyon. C.B. Polhemus had a ranch along the stream in the 1860's and 1870's (Brown, p. 70).

Pomar [SANTA CLARA]: *locality,* nearly 3 miles northwest of Coyote along Southern Pacific Railroad (lat. 37°14'30" N, long. 121°46'40" W). Named on Los Gatos (1919) 15' quadrangle.

Pomponio: see **Camp Pomponio** [SAN MATEO].

Pomponio Beach [SAN MATEO]: *beach,* 2.5 miles south-southwest of the village of San Gregorio along the coast (lat. 37°17'30" N, long. 122°24'20" W); the beach is south of the mouth of Pomponio Creek. Named on San Gregorio (1961) 7.5' quadrangle.

Pomponio Creek [SAN MATEO]: *stream,* flows 7 miles to the sea 2.25 miles south-southwest of the village of San Gregorio (lat. 37° 17'50" N, long. 122°24'20" W). Named on La Honda (1961) and San Gregorio (1961) 7.5' quadrangles. The name commemorates Jose Pomponio Lupugrim, a renegade neophyte Indian of Spanish times; the ridge at the head of the stream was called Cuchillo de Pomponio, or Pomponio Ridge (Stanger, 1963, p. 29).

Pomponio Reservoir [SAN MATEO]: *lake,* 1250 feet long, behind a dam on Pomponio Creek 3 miles southwest of La Honda (lat. 37° 17'25" N, long. 122°18'45" W; near W line sec. 28, T 7 S, R 4 W). Named on La Honda (1961) 7.5' quadrangle.

Pomponio Ridge: see **Pomponio Creek** [SAN MATEO].

Port Chicago [CONTRA COSTA]: *town,* 6.5 miles east-northeast of Martinez (lat. 38°02'45" N, long. 122°01'10" W). Named on Port Chicago (1959) 7.5' quadrangle. The site is abandoned and unnamed on Vine Hill (1959) 7.5' quadrangle. Karquines (1898) 15' quadrangle shows a place called Bay Point situated along Southern Pacific Railroad at the place, but United States Board on Geographic Names (1934, p. 3) rejected this name. Postal authorities established Baypoint post office in 1901, changed the name to Port Chicago in 1931, and discontinued it in 1969 (Salley, p. 16, 176). Ringgold's (1850b) map shows Pt. Sherman on the coast north of the later site of Port Chicago.

Port Chicago Reach [CONTRA COSTA-SOL-ANO]: *channel*, 7.5 miles east-northeast of Martinez in Suisun Bay on Contra Costa-Solano county line (lat. 38°03'30" N, long. 122°00'15" W); the feature is northeast of the site of Port Chicago. Named on Vine Hill (1959) 7.5' quadrangle.

Port Costa [CONTRA COSTA]: *village*, 3.5 miles northwest of Martinez (lat. 38°02'45" N, long. 122°11' W). Named on Benicia (1959) 7.5' quadrangle. Postal authorities established Port Costa post office in 1881 (Frickstad, p. 23). Ringgold's (1850a) map shows Pt. Elliot located along the shore at or near the site of present Port Costa.

Portezuel [SANTA CLARA]: *pass*, 4 miles southeast of New Almaden at the head of Cañada Garcia (lat. 37°08'15" N, long. 121°45'50" W). Named on Santa Teresa Hills (1953) 7.5' quadrangle.

Portezuela de Buenos Ayres: see **Corral Hollow** [ALAMEDA].

Port of Benicia: see **Benicia** [SOLANO].

Port of Redwood City [SAN MATEO]: *locality*, 2 miles north-northeast of downtown Redwood City along Redwood Creek (lat. 37°30'45" N, long. 122°12'30" W). Named on Redwood Point (1959) 7.5' quadrangle.

Portola: see **Portola Valley** [SAN MATEO] (2).

Portola-Crespi Valley: see **Portola Valley** [SAN MATEO] (1).

Portola Valley [SAN MATEO]:

(1) *valley*, 7 miles south of downtown Redwood City along Sausal Creek (lat. 37°23' N, long. 122°13'45" W). Named on Mindego Hill (1961) and Palo Alto (1961) 7.5' quadrangles. The name stems from the designation "Portola-Crespi Valley" proposed in 1886 for the series of valleys between Crystal Springs and Searsville (Hoover, Rensch, and Rensch, p. 402).

(2) *town*, 7 miles south of downtown Redwood City in Portola Valley (1) (lat. 37°23' N, long. 122°13'45" W). Named on Mindego Hill (1961) and Palo Alto (1961) 7.5' quadrangles. Palo Alto (1953) 7.5' quadrangle has the name "Portola" at the place. Postal authorities established Portola post office in 1894 and discontinued it in 1901; they established Portola Valley post office in 1955 (Salley, p. 176). The town incorporated in 1964.

Port Rumyantsev: see **Bodega Bay** [MARIN].

Port San Jose: see **Alviso** [SANTA CLARA].

Posita Creek: see **Arroyo las Positas** [ALAMEDA].

Posolmi [SANTA CLARA]: *land grant*, at Moffett Field. Named on Mountain View (1961) 7.5' quadrangle. An Indian called Lupe (or Lopez) Iñigo received the land in 1844; the Indian and Robert Walkinshaw claimed 1696 acres patented in 1881 (Cowan, p. 62; Cowan listed the grant under the designation "Posolmi, (or Posolomi, or) y Pozitas de las Animas").

Potatoe Cove: see **Tennessee Cove** [MARIN].

Potato Patch: see **The Potato Patch** [SAN MATEO].

Potatopatch Shoal [MARIN]: *shoal*, west of Point Bonita beyond Bonita Channel (lat. 37°49'20" N, long. 122°34'45" W). Named on Point Bonita (1954) 7.5' quadrangle. Mount Tamalpais (1950) 15' quadrangle has both the names "Potato Patch Shoal" and "Four Fathom Bank" for the feature. The name "Potatopatch Shoal" is said to have originated from the loss of potatoes from the decks of schooners from Bodega Bay as they crossed the feature (United States Coast and Geodetic Survey, p. 124).

Potrero: see **Point Potrero** [CONTRA COSTA]; **Point Potrero**, under **Point Isabel** [CONTRA COSTA].

Potrero de los Cerritos [ALAMEDA]: *land grant*, at and near Fremont. Named on Newark (1959) 7.5' quadrangle. Tomas Pacheco Alviso and Agustin Alviso received 3 leagues in 1844 and claimed 10,610 acres patented in 1866 (Cowan, p. 26).

Potrero de Santa Clara: see **El Potrero de Santa Clara** [SANTA CLARA].

Potrero District [SAN FRANCISCO]: *district*, 2 miles southeast of San Francisco civic center (lat. 37°45'30" N, long. 121°24' W); the district is around Potrero Hill. Named on San Francisco North (1956) 7.5' quadrangle.

Potrero Hill [SAN FRANCISCO]: *hill*, 2.25 miles south-southwest of Rincon Point (lat. 37°45'25" N, long. 122°23'55" W); the hill is west of Potrero Point. Named on San Francisco North (1956) 7.5' quadrangle. Called Potrero Nuevo on San Francisco (1899, reprinted 1913) 15' quadrangle.

Potrero Hills [SOLANO]: *range*, center 4.5 miles west-southwest of Denverton (lat. 38°12'30" N, long. 121°58'45" W). Named on Denverton (1953) and Fairfield South (1949) 7.5' quadrangles.

Potrero Hills: see **Coyote Hills** [ALAMEDA].

Potrero Meadows [MARIN]: *area*, 5.25 miles southwest of downtown San Rafael (lat. 37°55'30" N, long. 122°36'25" W). Named on San Rafael (1954) 7.5' quadrangle.

Potrero Nuevo: see **Potrero Hill** [SAN FRANCISCO].

Potrero Point [SAN FRANCISCO]: *promontory*, 2 miles south of Rincon Point along San Francisco Bay (lat. 37°45'35" N, long. 122°22'50" W). Named on San Francisco North (1956) 7.5' quadrangle. Called Pt. San Quentin on Wackenreuder's (1861) map.

Potrero Point: see **Dumbarton Point** [ALAMEDA].

Potrero San Pablo [CONTRA COSTA]: *ridge*, extends 5.5 miles southeast from San Pablo Point to Potrero Point (present Point Potrero) (center near lat. 37°56' N, long. 122°23'45" W). Named on San Francisco (1899) 15' quadrangle. Before fences were common, the ridge was a convenient place to pasture horses because it was separated from the mainland by marshes (Dilller and others, p. 82)—*potrero* means "pasture-ground" in Spanish.

Potter's Beach: see **Tunitas Beach** [SAN MATEO].

Pottery [ALAMEDA]: *locality,* 5.25 miles south of Midway in Corral Hollow (lat. 37°38'20" N, long. 121°34'15" W; sec. 30, T 3 S, R 4 E). Site named on Midway (1953) 7.5' quadrangle. John Treadwell and James Treadwell built a brick and pottery plant at the site in the 1890's; they gave the name "Pottery" to the place, which was situated at Walden Spur on the rail line in Corral Hollow (Hoover, Rensch, and Rensch, p. 377).

Poverty Flat [SANTA CLARA]: *area,* 2.25 miles south-southeast of Mount Sizer along Little Coyote Creek (lat. 37°10'50" N, long. 121°30' W; sec. 2, T 9 S, R 4 E). Named on Mississippi Creek (1955) and Mount Sizer (1955) 7.5' quadrangles.

Poverty Ridge [SANTA CLARA]: *ridge,* northwest-trending, 5 miles long, 2.5 miles west-northwest of Mount Day (lat. 37°25'45" N, long. 121°44'15" W). Named on Calaveras Reservoir (1961) and Mount Day (1955) 7.5' quadrangles.

Presidio: see **Presidio Military Reservation** [SAN FRANCISCO].

Presidio Anchorage: see **Fort Point** [SAN FRANCISCO].

Presidio Military Reservation [SAN FRANCISCO]: *military installation,* south of the Golden Gate at Fort Point (lat. 37°48' N, long. 122°28' W). Named on San Francisco North (1956) 7.5' quadrangle. Called Presidio of San Francisco on San Francisco (1942) 15' quadrangle. Spaniards established the presidio in 1776 and it became a permanent United States military installation in 1847 (Frazer, p. 30). Postal authorities established Presidio post office in 1888 (Frickstad, p. 159).

Presidio of San Francisco: see **Presidio Military Reservation** [SAN FRANCISCO].

Presidio Shoal [SAN FRANCISCO]: *shoal,* 1 mile east-northeast of Fort Point at the east end of the Golden Gate (lat. 37°48'55" N, long. 122°27'20" W). Named on San Francisco North (1956) 7.5' quadrangle.

Preston: see **Preston Point** [MARIN].

Preston Island: see **Roe Island** [SOLANO].

Preston Point [MARIN]: *promontory,* 3 miles south-southwest of Tomales on the northeast side of Tomales Bay (lat. 38°12'40" N, long. 122°56' W). Named on Tomales (1954) 7.5' quadrangle. Postal authorities established Preston post office at the place in 1863 and discontinued it in 1866; the name was for Robert J. Preston, first postmaster, who operated a wharf and store (Salley, p. 178).

Preston Point [SOLANO]: *promontory,* 6.5 miles east-northeast of Benicia along Suisun Bay at the west end of Roe Island (lat. 38°04'15" N, long. 122°02'45" W). Named on Vine Hill (1959) 7.5' quadrangle. Called Pt. Green on Ringgold's (1850c) map, which has the name "Preston I." for present Roe Island.

Preston Point Reach [CONTRA COSTA-SOLANO]: *channel,* 5.5 miles northeast of Martinez in Suisun Bay on Contra Costa-Solano county line (lat. 38°03'50" N, long. 122°03'10" W); the feature is southeast of Preston Point. Named on Vine Hill (1959) 7.5' quadrangle.

Priest Rock [SANTA CLARA]: *peak,* 2 miles south-southeast of Los Gatos (lat. 37°11'45" N, long. 121°57'50" W). Altitude 1762 feet. Named on Los Gatos (1953) 7.5' quadrangle.

Princeton [SAN MATEO]: *town,* 3.5 miles south of Montara Knob at the north end of Half Moon Bay (1) (lat. 37°30'15" N, long. 122° 29'10" W). Named on Montara Mountain (1956) 7.5' quadrangle. The place also was known as Old Landing—produce was shipped from there by schooner to San Francisco (Hoover, Rensch, and Rensch, p. 394). The name "Princeton" came from the Princeton-by-the-Sea subdivision of 1905 to 1906; the place sometimes was called Long Bridge in the early days (Brown, p. 73).

Promontory Island: see **Belvedere Island** [MARIN].

Prospect Creek [SANTA CLARA]: *stream,* flows nearly 2 miles to Calabazas Creek 2 miles north of downtown Saratoga (lat. 37°17'20" N, long. 122°02'05" W). Named on Cupertino (1961, photorevised 1968 and 1973) 7.5' quadrangle.

Prospect Island [SOLANO]: *area,* 7 miles north-northeast of Rio Vista in Yolo Bypass (lat. 38°15'45" N, long. 121°39'25" W); the place is east of Prospect Slough. Named on Liberty Island (1978) and Rio Vista (1978) 7.5' quadrangles.

Prospectors Gap [CONTRA COSTA]: *pass,* less than 0.5 mile north-northeast of Mount Diablo (lat. 37°53'10" N, long. 121°54'35" W; sec. 31, T 1 N, R 1 E). Named on Clayton (1953) 7.5' quadrangle.

Prospect Slough [SOLANO]: *water feature,* joins Cache Slough 5.5 miles north of Rio Vista (lat. 38°14'15" N, long. 121°40'45" W); the feature is west of Prospect Island. Named on Liberty Island (1978) and Rio Vista (1978) 7.5' quadrangles.

Prospect Spur: see **Meridian** [SANTA CLARA].

Providencia: see **Cañada de Herrera** [MARIN].

Pueblo Saint Joseph: see **San Jose** [SANTA CLARA].

Puerto de Don Gaspar: see **Drakes Bay** [MARIN].

Puerto de la Asunta: see **Southampton Bay** [SOLANO].

Puerto de la Bodega: see **Bodega Bay** [MARIN].

Puerto de los Balleneros: see **Richardson Bay** [MARIN].

Puerto de los Reyes: see **Drakes Bay** [MARIN].

Puerto de San Francisco: see **Drakes Bay** [MARIN]; **Gulf of the Farallones** [MARIN-SAN FRANCISCO-SAN MATEO].

Puerto Dulce: see **Suisun Bay** [CONTRA COSTA-SOLANO].

Puerto Zuelo Lagunitas: see **Little Carson Creek** [MARIN].

Pulgas [SAN MATEO]: *land grant,* near Belmont, Redwood City, and Menlo Park. Named on Mountain View (1961), Palo Alto (1961), Redwood Point (1959), and Woodside (1961) 7.5' quadrangles. United States Board on Geographic Names (1933, p. 623) rejected the names "De Las Pulgas," "Las Pulgas," and "Rancho de las Pulgas" for the grant. Luis Antonio Arguello received 4 leagues about 1824 and 1835; Maria Arguello claimed 35,240 acres patented in 1857 (Cowan, p. 64; Perez, p. 84).

Pulgas Creek [SAN MATEO]: *stream,* flows 2 miles to lowlands along San Francisco Bay 5.5 miles southeast of downtown San Mateo in San Carlos (lat. 37°30'10" N, long. 122°15'25" W). Named on Redwood Point (1959), San Mateo (1956), and Woodside (1961) 7.5' quadrangles. The stream was called Arroyo de las Pulgas in Spanish times, and more recently it was called San Carlos Creek and Arroyo Creek (Brown, p. 73).

Pulgas Ranch Embarcadero: see **Redwood City** [SAN MATEO].

Pulgas Ridge [SAN MATEO]: *ridge,* northwest-trending, 2 miles long, 3.5 miles south-south-west of downtown San Mateo (lat. 37° 31'05" N, long. 122°20'50" W). Named on San Mateo (1956) 7.5' quadrangle.

Pullman [CONTRA COSTA]: *locality,* less than 1 mile south-southeast of present Richmond civic center along Southern Pacific Railroad (lat. 37°55'30" N, long. 122°20'25" W). Named on San Francisco (1915) 15' quadrangle.

Pulse Canyon [SANTA CLARA]: *canyon,* drained by a stream that flows 1.5 miles to Arroyo Mocho 2 miles east-southeast of Eylar Mountain (lat. 37°27'40" N, long. 121°31' W; at N line sec. 34, T 5 S, R 4 E). Named on Eylar Mountain (1955) and Mount Boardman (1955) 7.5' quadrangles.

Punta Alvisadera: see **Point Avisadero** [SAN FRANCISCO].

Punta Año Nueva: see **Año Nuevo Point** [SAN MATEO].

Punta Bonete: see **Point Bonita** [MARIN].

Punta de Almejas: see **Pinole Point** [CONTRA COSTA]; **Point San Pedro** [SAN MATEO].

Punta de Año Nuevo: see **Año Nuevo Point** [SAN MATEO].

Punta de Baulenes: see **Duxbury Point** [MARIN].

Punta de Bonetas: see **Point Bonita** [MARIN].

Punta de Concha: see **Hunters Point** [SAN FRANCISCO].

Punta de la Ballena: see **Pigeon Point** [SAN MATEO].

Punta de la Loma Alta: see **Telegraph Hill** [SAN FRANCISCO].

Punta del Angel Custodio: see **Point San Pedro** [SAN MATEO].

Punta del Angel de la Guarda: see **Point Lobos** [SAN FRANCISCO].

Punta del Ano Nuevo [SAN MATEO]: *land grant,* at and north of Año Nuevo Point near the coast. Named on Año Nuevo (1955), Franklin Point (1955), and Pigeon Point (1955) 7.5' quadrangles. Simon Castro received 4 leagues in 1842; Maria A. Pico claimed 17,753 acres patented in 1857 (Cowan, p. 16; Perez, p. 84).

Punta del Cantil Blanco: see **Fort Point** [SAN FRANCISCO].

Punta del Castillo: see **Fort Point** [SAN FRANCISCO].

Punta del Embarcadero: see **Telegraph Hill** [SAN FRANCISCO].

Punta de los Caballos: see **Cavallo Point** [MARIN].

Punta de los Lobos: see **Point Lobos** [SAN FRANCISCO].

Punta de los Reyes: see **Point Reyes** [MARIN] (1).

Punta de Quintin: see **Point San Quentin** [MARIN].

Punta de Reyes: see **Point Reyes** [MARIN] (1).

Punta de San Antonio: see **Point San Pablo** [CONTRA COSTA].

Punta de San Carlos: see **Lime Point** [MARIN].

Punta de San Josef: see **Black Point** [SAN FRANCISCO].

Punta de San Pablo: see **Point San Pablo** [CONTRA COSTA].

Punta de San Pedro: see **Point San Pedro** [MARIN].

Punta de Santiago: see **Point Bonita** [MARIN].

Punta de Tiburon: see **Point Tiburon** [MARIN].

Punta Diablo: see **Point Diablo** [MARIN].

Punta Medanos: see **Black Point** [SAN FRANCISCO].

Punta Rena: see **Sand Point** [MARIN].

Punta San Bruno: see **Point San Bruno** [SAN MATEO].

Punta San Matheo: see **Coyote Point** [SAN MATEO].

Punta San Pablo: see **Point San Pablo** [CONTRA COSTA].

Punta San Pedro: see **Point San Pedro** [MARIN].

Punto Cavallos: see **Cavallo Point** [MARIN].

Punto de los Reyes: see **Point Reyes** [MARIN] (1).

Punto Diavolo: see **Point Diablo** [MARIN].

Purisima [SAN MATEO]: *settlement,* 4 miles south of the town of Half Moon Bay (lat.

37°24'20" N, long. 122°25'05" W); the place is near the mouth of Purisima Creek. Named on Santa Cruz (1902) 30' quadrangle. United States Board on Geographic Names (1960a, p. 18) rejected the form "Purissima" for the name. Postal authorities established Purissama (also called Purisima) post office in 1868, discontinued it in 1869, reestablished it in 1872, and discontinued it in 1901 (Salley, p. 179).

Purisima Creek [SAN MATEO]: *stream,* flows 7.5 miles to the sea 4 miles south of downtown Half Moon Bay (lat. 37°24'15" N, long. 122°25'30" W). Named on Half Moon Bay (1961) and Woodside (1961) 7.5' quadrangles. United States Board on Geographic Names (1933, p. 624) rejected the form "Purissima Creek" for the name. Spaniards called the stream Arroyo de la Purissima; the lower part of the canyon of the creek is called Purissima Valley (Brown, p. 74).

Purisima Creek: see **Deer Creek** [SANTA CLARA].

Purisima Rock: see **Año Nuevo Point** [SAN MATEO].

Purissima: see **Purisima** [SAN MATEO].

Purissima Valley: see **Purisima Creek** [SAN MATEO].

Puta Creek: see **Putah Creek** [SOLANO].

Putah: see **Dixon** [SOLANO].

Putah Creek [SOLANO]: *stream,* heads in Lake County and flows 60 miles through Napa County and along Solano-Yolo county line to Yolo County 8.5 miles northeast of Dixon (lat. 38° 32'15" N, long. 121°42'35" W). Named on Aetna Springs (1958), Allendale (1953), Chiles Valley (1958), Davis (1952), Jericho Valley (1958), Lake Berryessa (1959), Merritt (1952), Monticello Dam (1959), Mount Vaca (1951), Walter Springs (1959) and Winters (1953) 7.5' quadrangles. Called Puta Cr. on Eddy's (1854) map, but United States Board on Geographic Names (1933, p. 625) rejected this form of the name. Williamson (1857, p. 39) referred to Putos creek. According to Gudde (1949, p. 276), the name "Putah" is from the designation of Indians who lived along the stream, but Kroeber (p. 56) rejected an Indian origin for the name, and attributed it to *puta,* which means "harlot" in Spanish. South Fork diverges southeast from the main stream 6 miles north-northeast of Dixon and flows 5 miles to Yolo County 8.5 miles northeast of Dixon; it is named on Davis (1952) and Merritt (1952) 7.5' quadrangles.

Putnam Peak [SOLANO]: *peak,* 4.5 miles northeast of Mount Vaca (lat. 38°26'45" N, long. 122°02'30" W); near NE cor. sec. 23, T 7 N, R 2 W). Altitude 1224 feet. Named on Mount Vaca (1951) 7.5' quadrangle. United States Board on Geographic Names (1933, p. 625) rejected the names "Millers Peak" and "Putnams Peak" for the feature. According to Gudde (1949, p. 276), the name "Putnam"

Peak" probably is for Ansel W. Putnam, who settled at Vacaville before 1867.

Putnams Peak: see **Putnam Peak** [SOLANO].

Putos Creek: see **Putah Creek** [SOLANO].

Pyramid Hill: see **Mount Zion** [CONTRA COSTA].

Pyramid Point: see **Selby** [CONTRA COSTA].

Pyramid Rock [SAN FRANCISCO]: *rock,* less than 1 mile northeast of Point Lobos, and 500 feet offshore at Lands End (lat. 37°47'25" N, long. 122°30'20" W). Named on San Francisco North (1956) 7.5' quadrangle.

Pyramid Rock [SANTA CLARA]: *peak,* 3.25 miles west of Isabel Valley (lat. 37°18'20" N, long. 121°35'45" W). Altitude 4026 feet. Named on Isabel Valley (1955) 7.5' quadrangle.

– Q –

Quarry Beach: see **Quarry Point** [MARIN].

Quarry Point [MARIN-SAN FRANCISCO]: *promontory,* along the east shore of Angel Island on Marin-San Francisco county line (lat. 37°51'45" N, long. 122°25'05" W). Named on San Francisco North (1956) 7.5' quadrangle. Called Pt. Smith on Ringgold's (1850a) map. Army engineers opened a stone quarry at the point about 1890 (Bradley, p. 254). United States Board on Geographic Names (1980, p. 4) approved the name "Quarry Beach" for the beach that lies southeast of Quarry Point (lat. 37°51'33" N, long. 122°25'12" W).

Quercus Pass: see **Kirker Pass** [CONTRA COSTA] (1).

Quereus Pass: see **Kirker Pass** [CONTRA COSTA] (1).

Quimby Creek [SANTA CLARA]: *stream,* flows 1.25 miles to lowlands 1.5 miles northeast of Evergreen (lat. 37°19' N, long. 121°45'45" W). Named on San Jose East (1961) 7.5' quadrangle.

Quimby Island [CONTRA COSTA]: *island,* 2.25 miles long, 3.5 miles east-northeast of the settlement of Bethel Island between Old River and Sheep Slough (lat. 38°01'30" N, long. 121°34'15" W). Named on Bouldin Island (1978) 7.5' quadrangle.

Quito [SANTA CLARA]: *land grant,* northeast of Saratoga. Named on Cupertino (1961) and San Jose West (1961) 7.5' quadrangles. Jose Zenon Fernandez and Jose Noriega received 3 leagues in 1841; Jose M. Alviso and others claimed 13,310 acres patented in 1866 (Cowan, p. 66). According to Butler (p. 95), the grant originally was known by the name "Tito" for a neophyte Indian who ran a Santa Clara mission dairy ranch in the neighborhood in the 1830's.

Quito Creek: see **Saratoga Creek** [SANTA CLARA].

– R –

Raccoon Cove: see **Hospital Cove** [MARIN].

Raccoon Strait [MARIN]: *water feature,* 2.5 miles east-northeast of downtown Sausalito between Angel Island and Tiburon Peninsula (lat. 37°52'05" N, long. 122°26'35" W). Named on San Francisco North (1956) and San Quentin (1959) 7.5' quadrangles. The name commemorates the British ship *Racoon,* which visited San Francisco Bay in 1814 (Mason, 1976b, p. 214), but United States Board on Geographic Names (1933, p. 630) rejected the form "Racoon Strait" for the name.

Rack Creek [SOLANO]: *water feature,* joins Honker Bay 4 miles south-southwest of Birds Landing (2) (lat. 38°05' N, long. 121°54'35" W). Named on Honker Bay (1953) 7.5' quadrangle.

Rafael Village [MARIN]: *district,* nearly 3 miles south-southeast of downtown Novato (lat. 38°04'10" N, long. 122°33'15" W). Named on Novato (1954) 7.5' quadrangle.

Raleez Creek: see **Reliez Valley** [CONTRA COSTA].

Raliez [CONTRA COSTA]: *locality,* 2.25 miles west-southwest of present Walnut Creek civic center (lat. 37°53'15" N, long. 122°05'45" W); the place is near the mouth of present Reliez Valley. Named on Concord (1943) 15' quadrangle.

Ramage Peak [ALAMEDA]: *peak,* 11 miles east of downtown Oakland (lat. 37°47'25" N, long. 122°04'05" W; sec. 3, T 2 S, R 2 W). Altitude 1401 feet. Named on Las Trampas Ridge (1959) 7.5' quadrangle. The name commemorates Charles Ramage, who owned the place (Mosier and Mosier, p. 70).

Rancho de las Pulgas: see **Pulgas** [SAN MATEO].

Ransome [SAN MATEO]: *locality,* 3 miles northwest of present Montara Knob and 0.25 mile southeast of San Pedro Point (present Point San Pedro) along Ocean Shore Railroad (lat. 37°35'20" N, long. 122°31'05" W). Named on San Mateo (1915) 15' quadrangle.

Ransom Point [CONTRA COSTA]: *ridge,* extends 0.5 mile north-northwest from Mount Diablo (lat. 37°53'05" N, long. 121°54'50" W). Named on Clayton (1953) 7.5' quadrangle. The name commemorates Colonel Leander Ransom, who as deputy United States surveyor established Mount Diablo Base and Meridian lines in 1851 (United States Board on Geographic Names, 1933, p. 633).

Rat Rock [MARIN]: *rock,* 9.5 miles southeast of downtown Novato, and 300 feet offshore in San Pablo Bay (lat. 38°00'15" N, long. 122°27'40" W). Named on Petaluma Point (1959) 7.5' quadrangle.

Rattlesnake Butte [SANTA CLARA]: *peak,* 3.5

miles east-southeast of Mount Day (lat. 37°23'50" N, long. 121°38'40" W; on E line sec. 21, T 6 S, R 3 E). Named on Mount Day (1955) 7.5' quadrangle.

Rattlesnake Creek [MARIN]: *stream,* flows 1.25 miles to Redwood Creek 5.5 miles south-southwest of downtown San Rafael (lat. 37° 54'15" N, long. 122°35'20" W). Named on San Rafael (1954) 7.5' quadrangle.

Ravenswood [SAN MATEO]: *locality,* 5 miles east of downtown Redwood City along Southern Pacific Railroad in East Palo Alto (lat. 37°28'35" N, long. 122°08'05" W). Named on Palo Alto (1961) 7.5' quadrangle. The name is from a town laid out in 1853 that failed to develop (Hoover, Rensch, and Rensch, p. 406). Palo Alto (1953) 7.5' quadrangle gives the alternate name "Ravensswood" for present East Palo Alto.

Ravenswood Point [SAN MATEO]: *promontory,* 5 miles east-northeast of downtown Redwood City along San Francisco Bay (lat. 37° 30'30" N, long. 122°08'15" W). Named on Redwood Point (1959) 7.5' quadrangle. The feature also was called West Point (Brown, p. 75, 99).

Ravenswood Slough [SAN MATEO]: *water feature,* enters San Francisco Bay 3.5 miles east-northeast of downtown Redwood City (lat. 37°30'10" N, long. 122°09'45" W). Named on Palo Alto (1961) and Redwood Point (1959) 7.5' quadrangles.

Ravenswood Wharf: see **Cooley Landing** [SAN MATEO].

Ray Hill: see **Rays Peak** [SAN MATEO].

Raynor Creek: see **Clear Creek** [SAN MATEO].

Rays Peak [SAN MATEO]: *peak,* 1.5 miles west-northwest of La Honda (lat. 37°19'45" N, long. 122°17'45" W). Altitude 1037 feet. Named on La Honda (1961) 7.5' quadrangle. Brown (p. 75) called the feature Ray Hill, and noted that Ray ranch was situated just east of the peak during and after the late 1860's.

Red Hill [ALAMEDA]: *peak,* 3.5 miles west-northwest of downtown Newark (lat. 37°33'05" N, long. 122°05'35" W). Named on Newark (1948) 7.5' quadrangle.

Red Hill [MARIN]:

(1) *peak,* 7 miles west-northwest of downtown Novato (lat. 38° 09' N, long. 122°40'40" W). Altitude 1257 feet. Named on Petaluma (1953) 7.5' quadrangle.

(2) *peak,* 1.5 miles west-northwest of downtown San Rafael (lat. 37°58'45" N, long. 122°33'35" W). Altitude 464 feet. Named on San Rafael (1954) 7.5' quadrangle. Water from a mineral spring called Ancha Vista Spring, located on the slope of this peak, was used therapeutically at a resort (Bradley, p. 249).

Redmond Cut [ALAMEDA]: *locality,* 2.25 miles east-southeast of Altamont along Western Pacific Railroad (lat. 37°43'45" N, long. 121°37'15" W; at E line sec. 27, T 2 S, R 3 E).

Named on Altamont (1953) and Midway (1953) 7.5' quadrangles.

Red Mountain [SANTA CLARA]: *ridge,* northwest-trending, nearly 2 miles long, 4.5 miles south of Mount Boardman on Santa Clara-Stanislaus county line (lat. 37°24'55" N, long. 121°27'45" W). Named on Mount Boardman (1955) 7.5' quadrangle. Thompson and West's (1876) map has the label "Red Mountains or Cerro Colorado" along the crest of Diablo Range—including present Red Mountain—for a distance of about 11 miles south of Mount Boardman.

Red Mountains: see **Red Mountain** [SANTA CLARA].

Redondo Beach [SAN MATEO]: *beach,* 1.5 miles southwest of downtown Half Moon Bay along the coast (lat. 37°26'35" N, long. 122°26'35" W). Named on Halfmoon Bay (1940) 15' quadrangle.

Red Rock [CONTRA COSTA-MARIN-SAN FRANCISCO]: *island,* 850 feet long, 2.5 miles south of point San Pablo [CONTRA COSTA] in San Francisco Bay at the junction of Contra Costa, Marin, and San Francisco Counties (lat. 37°55'45" N, long. 122°25'50" W). Named on San Quentin (1959) 7.5' quadrangle. Called Molate I. on Ringgold's (1850a) map—the island is 1.25 miles south-south-west of Point Molate [CONTRA COSTA]. The feature also was called Treasure Rock and Golden Rock; these names were from a tradition that Spanish navigators buried a large treasure at the place (Smith and Elliott, p. 4). The name "Molate" is a misspelling by Beechey in 1826 of *moleta,* the Spanish word for the conical stone used by painters to grind colors (Gudde, 1949, p. 220).

Redwood: see **Redwood City** [SAN MATEO].

Redwood Canyon [ALAMEDA]: *canyon,* drained by a stream that flows 2.25 miles to Redwood Creek nearly 7 miles east of downtown Oakland (lat. 37°48'05" N, long. 122°08'35" W); the canyon heads near Redwood Peak [CONTRA COSTA]. Named on Oakland East (1959) 7.5' quadrangle.

Redwood Canyon [MARIN]:
(1) *canyon,* drained by a stream that flows 2.5 miles to Halleck Creek nearly 5 miles west-southwest of downtown Novato (lat. 38° 04'45" N, long. 122°38'55" W). Named on Novato (1954) and San Geronimo (1954) 7.5' quadrangles.
(2) *canyon,* 2 miles long, along Redwood Creek above a point 6 miles south-southwest of downtown San Rafael (lat. 37°53'20" N, long. 122°33'55" W). Named on San Rafael (1954) 7.5' quadrangle.

Redwood City [SAN MATEO]: *city,* in the southeast part of San Mateo County near San Francisco Bay (lat. 37°29' N, long. 122°13'30" W). Named on Palo Alto (1961) and Woodside (1961) 7.5' quadrangles. Called Redwood on Palo Alto (1899) 15' quadrangle. Simon

Menzes laid out the community along Redwood Creek in the 1850's and named it Menzesville, but this name failed to last; the place also was known in the early 1850's as Redwood Embarcadero, Red Woods Landing, Pulgas Ranch Embarcadero, Redwood Landing, and Embarcadero (Brown, p. 75-76; Hynding, p. 89-90). Postal authorities established Redwood post office in 1852, changed the name to Steinbergers in 1853, and changed it to Redwood City in 1856—the name "Steinbergers" was for the owner of the stage stop at the place (Salley, p. 183, 212). The city incorporated in 1868. Postal authorities established Redwood Park post office 11 miles southwest of Redwood City in 1940 and discontinued it in 1942 (Salley, p. 183).

Redwood Creek [ALAMEDA-CONTRA COSTA]: *stream,* heads in Contra Costa County and flows 4 miles to Upper San Leandaro Reservoir 7.5 miles east of downtown Oakland in Alameda County (lat. 37°47'30" N, long. 122°07'50" W; sec. 6, T 2 S, R 2 W). Named on Oakland East (1959) 7.5' quadrangle.

Redwood Creek [MARIN]: *stream,* flows 5.25 miles to the sea 4 miles northwest of Point Bonita at Muir Beach (lat. 37°51'35" N, long. 122°34'40" W). Named on Point Bonita (1954) and San Rafael (1954) 7.5' quadrangles.

Redwood Creek [SAN MATEO]: *water feature,* enters San Francisco Bay 3.25 miles north-northeast of downtown Redwood City (lat. 37°31'35" N, long. 122°11'45" W). Named on Palo Alto (1961) and Redwood Point (1959) 7.5' quadrangles. Brown (p. 76) used the name "Redwood Slough" for lower reaches of the feature, and noted that in the 1850's the creek or slough was called Arroyo Salinas and Redwoods Embarcadero Creek—the name "Redwood Creek" is from redwood lumber stacked along the stream for shipment in the early days.

Redwood Embarcadero: see **Redwood City** [SAN MATEO].

Redwood Estates [SANTA CLARA]: *settlement,* 4.5 miles south of downtown Los Gatos (lat. 37°09'25" N, long. 121°59' W). Named on Los Gatos (1953) 7.5' quadrangle. Postal authorities established Redwood Estates post office in 1927 (Frickstad, p. 175).

Redwood Junction [SAN MATEO]: *locality,* 0.5 mile southeast of downtown Redwood City along Southern Pacific Railroad (lat. 37° 28'40" N, long. 122°13' W). Named on Palo Alto (1961) 7.5' quadrangle.

Redwood Landing: see **Redwood City** [SAN MATEO].

Redwood Mills: see **Saratoga** [SANTA CLARA].

Redwood Park: see **Redwood City** [SAN MATEO].

Redwood Peak [CONTRA COSTA]: *peak,* 4.25 miles south of Orinda (lat. 37°49'05" N, long.

122°10'30" W). Altitude 1619 feet. Named on Oakland East (1959) 7.5' quadrangle.

Redwood Point [SAN MATEO]: *promontory,* 4 miles north-northeast of downtown Redwood City along San Francisco Bay (lat. 37°32'05" N, long. 122°11'35" W); the feature is near the mouth of Redwood Creek. Named on Redwood Point (1959) 7.5' quadrangle. United States Board on Geographic Names (1943, p. 12) rejected the name "Marsh Point" for the promontory.

Redwood Retreat [SANTA CLARA]: *settlement,* 2.5 miles north-northwest of Mount Madonna along Little Arthur Creek (lat. 37°02'30" N, long. 121°43' W; near SE cor.sec. 23, T 10 S, R 2 E). Named on Mount Madonna (1955) 7.5' quadrangle.

Red Woods City: see **Redwood City** [SAN MATEO].

Redwoods Embarcadero Creek: see **Redwood Creek** [SAN MATEO].

Redwood Slough: see **Redwood Creek** [SAN MATEO].

Redwood Terrace [SAN MATEO]: *settlement,* 1.25 miles west-southwest of La Honda (lat. 37°18'55" N, long. 122°17'35" W; near NW cor. sec. 22, T 7 S, R 4 W). Named on La Honda (1961) 7.5' quadrangle.

Reed [MARIN]: *locality,* 5 miles south-southeast of downtown San Rafael along Northwestern Pacific Railroad (lat. 37°54'20" N, long. 122°29'55" W). Named on San Quentin (1959) 7.5' quadrangle. The name commemorates John Reed, who owned Corte de Madera del Presidio grant, where the place is situated (Gudde, 1949, p. 283).

Reed: see **Point Reed**, under **Bluff Point** [MARIN]; **Widow Reed Creek**, under **Arroyo Corte Madera Del Presidio** [MARIN].

Reesley Valley: see **Reliez Valley** [CONTRA COSTA].

Reflection Lake [SAN MATEO]: *lake,* 650 feet long, at La Honda (lat. 37°19'05" N, long. 122°16'10" W; near S line sec. 14, T 7 S, R 4 W). Named on La Honda (1961) 7.5' quadrangle.

Refugio: see **Pastoria de las Borregas** [SANTA CLARA].

Refugio Creek [CONTRA COSTA]: *stream,* flows 4 miles to San Pablo Bay 4.5 miles east of Pinole Point (lat. 38°01'20" N, long. 122°17'05" W). Named on Briones Valley (1959) and Mare Island (1959) 7.5' quadrangles.

Refugio de la Laguna Seca: see **La Laguna Seca** [SANTA CLARA].

Refugio Landing: see **Hercules Wharf** [CONTRA COSTA].

Refugio Valley [CONTRA COSTA]: *valley,* 5 miles east of Pinole Point (lat. 38°00'50" N, long. 122°16'15" W); Refugio Creek and its tributaries drain the valley. Named on Mare Island (1959) 7.5' quadrangle.

Regnart Creek [SANTA CLARA]: *stream,*

flows 1 mile to lowlands nearly 1.5 miles south of Monta Vista (lat. 37°18'10" N, long. 122° 03'10" W; sec. 23, T 7 S, R 2 W). Named on Cupertino (1961) 7.5' quadrangle.

Reliez Valley [CONTRA COSTA]: *valley,* 2.25 miles west-northwest of Walnut Creek civic center (lat. 37°55'05" N, long. 122°06'20" W). Named on Walnut Creek (1959) 7.5' quadrangle. Called Reesley Valley on Concord (1897) 15' quadrangle. Smith and Elliott (p. 23) referred to Raleez Creek.

Remillard [ALAMEDA]: *locality,* nearly 5 miles west of Livermore along Southern Pacific Railroad (lat. 37°40'15" N, long. 121°51'20" W). Named on Pleasanton (1906) 15' quadrangle. The name is from Remillard brick works, which was in business from 1889 until 1935 (Mosier and Mosier, p. 73).

Rengstorff Gulch [SAN MATEO]: *canyon,* drained by a stream that flows 0.5 mile to Corte Madera Creek 2.5 miles north-northeast of Mindego Hill (lat. 37°20'35" N, long. 122°12'20" W). Named on Mindego Hill (1961) 7.5' quadrangle. Rengstorff's ranch and silver mine were near the canyon in the 1870's and 1880's (Brown, p. 77).

Renz Gulch [SANTA CLARA]: *canyon,* drained by a stream that flows 1 mile to Bodfish Creek 2 miles east-southeast of Mount Madonna (lat. 37°00'10" N, long. 121°40'15" W). Named on Mount Madonna (1955) 7.5' quadrangle.

Reservoir: see **Creed** [SOLANO].

Reservoir Canyon [SANTA CLARA]: *canyon,* drained by a stream that flows nearly 1.5 miles to lowlands 1.5 miles southwest of Gilroy (lat. 36°59'35" N, long. 121°35'15" W). Named on Chittenden (1955) 7.5' quadrangle.

Reyes: see **Point Reyes** [MARIN].

Reynolds [MARIN]: *locality,* nearly 7 miles south of Tomales on the northeast side of Tomales Bay (lat. 38°08'55" N, long. 122°52'55" W); the place is on Nicasio (3) grant, which belonged to Messrs. Frank and Reynolds. Named on Tomales (1954) 7.5' quadrangle. On Point Reyes (1918) 15' quadrangle, the place is shown along Northwestern Pacific Railroad.

Reynolds: see **Camp Reynolds**, under **Fort McDowell** [MARIN].

Reynolds Creek: see **Los Trancos Creek** [SAN MATEO].

Rheem [CONTRA COSTA]:
(1) *locality,* 2.5 miles north-northwest of Richmond civic center along Southern Pacific Railroad (lat. 37°58'35" N, long. 122°21'25" W). Named on Richmond (1959) 7.5' quadrangle.
(2) *locality,* 7.5 miles west-northwest of Danville (lat. 37°51'35" N, long. 122°07'25" W; sec. 7, T 1 S, R 2 W). Named on Las Trampas Ridge (1959) and Oakland East (1959) 7.5' quadrangles. Donald I. Rheem started a development at the place in 1944 and called it Rheem Center (Gudde, 1969, p. 267).

Rheem Center: see **Rheem** [CONTRA COSTA] (2).

Rhine Canyon [CONTRA COSTA]: *canyon,* drained by a stream that flows nearly 2 miles to Curry Canyon 2 miles southeast of Mount Diablo (lat. 37°51'35" N, long. 121°53'35" W; sec. 8, T 1 S, R 1 E). Named on Clayton (1953) and Diablo (1953) 7.5' quadrangles.

Rhode Island [CONTRA COSTA]: *island,* 0.5 mile long, 3.5 miles east-southeast of the settlement of Bethel Island between Old River and Sheep Slough (lat. 38°00'05" N, long. 121°34'25" W). Named on Bouldin Island (1978) and Woodward Island (1978) 7.5' quadrangles.

Rhododendron Creek [SAN MATEO]: *stream,* flows 1 mile to Pescadero Creek 3.5 miles south of Mindego Hill (lat. 37°15'35" N, long. 122°14'20" W; near SW cor. sec. 6, T 8 S, R 3 W). Named on Mindego Hill (1961) 7.5' quadrangle.

Rialto Cove: see **Bolinas Bay** [MARIN].

Rice's Creek: see **Gazos Creek** [SAN MATEO].

Richardson Bay [MARIN]: *bay,* opens into San Francisco Bay at the town of Sausalito (lat. 37°51'30" N, long. 122°28' W). Named on Point Bonita (1954), San Francisco North (1956), San Quentin (1959), and San Rafael (1954) 7.5' quadrangles. Cañizares explored the bay in 1775 and called it Ensenada de la Carmelita because of a rock there that resembled a Carmelite nun (Bolton, p. 252). The bay also was known as Puerto de los Balleneros, a name later translated to Whaler's Harbor—the name "Richardson" commemorates William A. Richardson, who owned Sausalito grant (Gudde, 1969, p. 268).

Richardson Island [MARIN]: *hill,* 2.5 miles south-southeast of downtown San Rafael (lat. 37°56'10" N, long. 122°31' W). Named on San Rafael (1954) 7.5' quadrangle.

Richmond [CONTRA COSTA]: *city,* 23 miles west of Mount Diablo (civic center near lat. 37°56'15" N, long. 122°20'30" W). Named on Mare Island (1959), Petaluma Point (1959), Richmond (1959), and San Quentin (1959) 7.5' quadrangles. Postal authorities established Richmond post office in 1900 (Frickstad, p. 23), and the city incorporated in 1905. The community began when officials of Atchison, Topeka and Santa Fe Railroad made the place the western terminus of the rail line (Gleason, p. 189). Postal authorities established Atchison post office, named for the railroad, 1 mile southeast of Richmond post office in 1903 and discontinued it in 1912—it was at the local headquarters of the railroad (Salley, p. 11).

Richmond: see **North Richmond** [CONTRA COSTA].

Richmond District [SAN FRANCISCO]: *district,* 3 miles west of San Francisco civic center (lat. 37°46'45" N, long. 122°28'30" W). Named on San Francisco North (1956) 7.5' quadrangle.

Richmond Inner Harbor [CONTRA COSTA]: *water feature,* 2.5 miles south of Richmond civic center off of San Francisco Bay (lat. 37°54'10" N, long. 122°20'30" W). Named on Richmond (1959) 7.5' quadrangle.

Richmond Marina Bay: see **Inner Harbor Basin** [CONTRA COSTA].

Richmond Point: see **Point Richmond** [CONTRA COSTA] (1).

Richs Island: see **Simmons Island** [SOLANO].

Rifle Camp [MARIN]: *locality,* 5.25 miles southwest of downtown San Rafael (lat. 37°55'35" N, long. 122°36'20" W). Named on San Rafael (1954) 7.5' quadrangle.

Rifle Range Branch [ALAMEDA]: *stream,* flows 3 miles to Arroyo Viejo 7.5 miles east-southeast of downtown Oakland (lat. 37°45'15" N, long. 122°09' W). Named on Oakland East (1959) 7.5' quadrangle. The name is from Oakland Pistol Club's range (Mosier and Mosier, p. 73).

Riggs Canyon [CONTRA COSTA]: *canyon,* drained by a stream that flows 2.25 miles to Tassajara Creek 5.25 miles southeast of Mount Diablo (lat. 37°49'10" N, long. 121°51'15" W; sec. 27, T 1 S, E 1 E). Named on Tassajara (1953) 7.5' quadrangle.

Riley Canyon [ALAMEDA]: *canyon,* 0.5 mile long, 10 miles east of downtown Oakland (lat. 37°46'40" N, long. 122°05'45" W). Named on Las Trampas Ridge (1959) 7.5' quadrangle. The name commemorates Eugene Riley, who settled at the place before 1889 (Mosier and Mosier, p. 73-74). Water of Upper San Leandro Reservoir floods the lower part of the canyon.

Riley Ridge [ALAMEDA]: *ridge,* west- to southwest-trending, 2 miles long, 10 miles east of downtown Oakland (lat. 37°46'45" N, long. 122°05'15" W). Named on Las Trampas Ridge (1959) 7.5' quadrangle.

Rinconada [SANTA CLARA]: *locality,* nearly 1 mile east of downtown Los Gatos (lat. 37°13'40" N, long. 121°58' W). Named on Los Gatos (1919) 15' quadrangle.

Rinconada del Arroyo de San Francisquito [SANTA CLARA]: *land grant,* extends from downtown Palo Alto to San Francisco Bay. Named on Mountain View (1961) and Palo Alto (1961) 7.5' quadrangles. Maria Antonio Mesa received 0.5 league in 1841 and claimed 2229 acres patented in 1872 (Cowan, p. 77— Cowan listed the grant under the name "Rinconada del San Francisquito"; Perez, p. 86).

Rinconada de los Gatos [SANTA CLARA]: *land grant,* at Los Gatos. Named on Castle Rock Ridge (1955), Los Gatos (1953), and San Jose West (1961) 7.5' quadrangles. Sebastian Peralta and Jose Hernandez received 1.5 leagues in 1840 and claimed 6631 acres patented in 1860 (Cowan, p. 37). *Rincon* means "corner" in Spanish; according to Arbuckle (p. 29), this word in the name of the grant comes from a sharp bend, or corner, made by Los Gatos Creek.

Rinconada del San Francisquito: see **Rinconada del Arroyo de San Francisquito** [SANTA CLARA].

Rincon Creek [SANTA CLARA]: *stream,* flows 2.5 miles to Guadalupe Creek nearly 3 miles west of New Almaden (lat. 37°10'55" N, long. 121°52'20" W). Named on Los Gatos (1953) and Santa Teresa Hills (1953) 7.5' quadrangles.

Rincon de las Salinas y Potrero Viejo [SAN FRANCISCO-SAN MATEO]: *land grant,* at and near Hunters Point and Bernal Heights; a small part is in San Mateo County. Named on Hunters Point (1956, photorevised 1968) and San Francisco South (1956) 7.5' quadrangles. Jose Cornelio Bernal received 1 league in 1839 and 1840; his heirs claimed 4446 acres patented in 1857 (Cowan, p. 63). Perez (p. 85), gave the grant date as 1845.

Rincon de los Esteros [SANTA CLARA]: *land grant,* east of Alviso. Named on Milpitas (1961) 7.5' quadrangle. Ignacio Alviso received the land in 1838; Rafael Alviso and others claimed 2200 acres patented in 1872; Ellen E. White claimed 2308 acres patented in 1862; Francisco Berryessa and others claimed 1845 acres patented in 1873 (Cowan, p. 35).

Rincon de San Francisquito [SANTA CLARA]: *land grant,* in Palo Alto from the foothills to San Francisco Bay. Named on Mountain View (1961) and Palo Alto (1961) 7.5' quadrangles. Jose Peña received the land in 1841; Teodoro Robles and Secundino Robles claimed 8418 acres patented in 1868 (Cowan, p. 77).

Rincon Hill [SAN FRANCISCO]: *hill,* nearly 0.5 mile southwest of Rincon Point (lat. 37°47'10" N, long. 122°23'30" W). Named on San Francisco North (1956) 7.5' quadrangle. Soule, Gihon, and Nisbet's (1855) map shows two small valleys that were well known in the early days—Happy Valley, located northwest of present Rincon Hill, and Pleasant Valley, located southwest of the hill.

Rincon Point [SAN FRANCISCO]: *promontory,* nearly 2 miles east-northeast of San Francisco civic center along San Francisco Bay (lat. 37°47'25" N, long. 122°23'15" W). Named on San Francisco North (1956) 7.5' quadrangle.

Rindler Creek [SOLANO]: *stream,* flows 2.25 miles to an artificial watercourse 3 miles northeast of downtown Vallejo (lat. 38°08'15" N, long. 122°13'15" W; sec. 5, T 3 N, R 3 W). Named on Cordelia (1951) 7.5' quadrangle. Carquinez (1938) 15' quadrangle shows the stream extending to Lake Chabot.

Rings Gulch [SAN MATEO]: *canyon,* drained by a stream that flows 0.5 mile to Tunitas Creek 4 miles west-southwest of Skeggs Point (lat. 37°23'20" N, long. 122°22'10" W).

Named on Woodside (1961) 7.5' quadrangle. Mr. E. Ring had a ranch in the canyon in the 1860's (Brown, p. 77).

Rio de la Alameda: see **Alameda Creek** [ALAMEDA].

Rio de la Harina: see **San Lorenzo Creek** [ALAMEDA].

Rio de los Putos [SOLANO]: *land grant,* north of Allendale on Solano-Yolo county line. Named on Allendale (1953), Merritt (1952), Mount Vaca (1951), and Winters (1953) 7.5' quadrangles. Francisco Guerrero y Palomares received 4 leagues in 1842; William Wolfskill claimed 17,755 acres patented in 1858 (Cowan, p. 66). According to Perez (p. 87), Wolfskill was the grantee in 1842.

Rio del Pajaro: see **Pajaro River** [SANTA CLARA].

Rio de Nuestra Señora de Guadalupe: see **Guadalupe River** [SANTA CLARA].

Rio de San Clemente: see **Alameda Creek** [ALAMEDA].

Rio de San Francisco: see **Carquinez Strait** [CONTRA COSTA-SOLANO]; **San Francisquito Creek** [SAN MATEO-SANTA CLARA].

Rio de San Jose: see **Guadalupe River** [SANTA CLARA].

Rio de San Matheo: see **San Mateo Creek** [SAN MATEO].

Rio Farms [SOLANO]: *locality,* 7.5 miles north-northeast of Rio Vista on Ryer Island (1) (lat. 38°16' N, long. 121°38'20" W). Named on Liberty Island (1952) 7.5' quadrangle.

Rio Grande de San Sebastian: see **Tomales Bay** [MARIN].

Rio Pajaro: see **Pajaro River** [SANTA CLARA].

Rio Sacramento: see **Sacramento River** [SOLANO].

Rio San Joaquin: see **San Joaquin River** [CONTRA COSTA].

Rio San Leandro: see **San Leandro Creek** [ALAMEDA-CONTRA COSTA].

Rio Tulare: see **San Joaquin River** [CONTRA COSTA].

Rio Vista [SOLANO]: *town,* 21 miles southeast of Vacaville along Sacramento River (lat. 38°09'20" N, long. 121°41'20" W). Named on Rio Vista (1978) 7.5' quadrangle. Postal authorities established Rio Vista post office in 1858 (Salley, p. 186), and the town incorporated in 1894. Colonel N.H. Davis first laid out the community near the entrance of Cache Slough into Sacramento River and called it Brazos del Rio—*brazos del rio* means "arms of the river" in Spanish; the name was changed to Rio Vista before a flood destroyed the town in 1862 and the inhabitants rebuilt on higher ground at the present site (Hoover, Rensch, and Rensch, p. 523-524). According to Bancroft (1888, p. 500), Bidwell and Hopps tried unsuccessfully to start a town in 1848 at or near the original site of Rio Vista; they called the place Brazoria, Sacramento Brazoria, or Halo-Chemuck. Ringgold's (1850c) map shows a place called Suisun City at the site of present Rio Vista.

Rio Vista Junction [SOLANO]: *locality,* 1.5 miles southeast of Denverton along Sacramento Northern Railroad (lat. 38°12'25" N, long. 121°52'30" W; sec. 9, T 4 N, R 1 E). Named on Birds Landing (1953) and Denverton (1953) 7.5' quadrangles. Called Curtis on Denverton (1918) 7.5' quadrangle, which shows the place along Oakland Antioch and Eastern Railroad.

Roaring River Slough [SOLANO]: *water feature,* along the southwest side of Hammond Island, joins Montezuma Slough 3 miles south-southwest of Birds Landing (2) (lat. 38°05'25" N, long. 121°53'05" W). Named on Honker Bay (1953) 7.5' quadrangle.

Roberts Landing [ALAMEDA]: *locality,* nearly 4 miles south of downtown San Leandro at the edge of San Francisco Bay (lat. 37° 40'20" N, long. 122°09'50" W). Named on San Leandro (1959) 7.5' quadrangle. Robert Thompson, William Roberts, and Peter Anderson started the place in 1850, when it was known as Thompson's Landing; it was called Roberts Landing after Thompson sold out in 1856 (Mosier and Mosier, p. 74).

Robertsville [SANTA CLARA]: *locality,* 5 miles south of downtown San Jose near Guadalupe River (lat. 37°15'45" N, long. 121°52'35" W). Named on San Jose West (1961) 7.5' quadrangle. A village at the site was named for John Griffith Roberts, who farmed the surrounding land in the nineteenth century (Harry Farrell, *San Jose Mercury-News*, January 6, 1980). Thompson and West's (1876) map shows Pioneer P.O. near the site of Robertsville. Postal authorities established Pioneer post office in 1875 and discontinued it in 1886 (Frickstad, p. 175).

Rockaway: see **Rackaway Beach** [SAN MATEO].

Rockaway Beach [SAN MATEO]: *district,* 3.5 miles north of Montara Knob near the coast at the mouth of Calera Valley (lat. 37°36'30" N, long. 122°29'40" W). Named on Montara Mountain (1956) 7.5' quadrangle. Called Rockaway on San Mateo (1915) 15' quadrangle. Postal authorities established Rockaway post office in 1908, changed the name to Rockaway Beach the same year, discontinued it in 1922, reestablished it in 1923, and discontinued it in 1959 (Salley, p. 187). Eckel (p. 354) used the designation "Calera or Rockaway Beach" for the community. Residents of the place voted in 1957 to join neighboring communities and form the new city of Pacifica.

Rock City [CONTRA COSTA]: *relief feature,* 2.5 miles south-southwest of Mount Diablo (lat. 37°51' N, long. 121°56'05" W; near E line sec. 14, T 1 S, R 1 W). Named on Diablo (1953) 7.5' quadrangle.

Rock Creek: see **Slate Creek** [SAN MATEO].

Rock Cut [ALAMEDA]: *locality,* 2 miles west-northwest of Midway along Southern Pacific Railroad (lat. 37°43'35" N, long. 121°35'45" W; sec. 25, T 2 S, R 3 E). Named on Tesla (1907) 15' quadrangle.

Rock House Ridge [SANTA CLARA]: *ridge,* west-northwest-trending, 2 miles long, just east of Mount Sizer (lat. 37°12'45" N, long. 121°29'30" W). Named on Mississippi Creek (1955) and Mount Sizer (1955) 7.5' quadrangles.

Rock Slough [CONTRA COSTA]: *water feature,* joins Old River 7 miles east-northeast of Brentwood (lat. 37°58'20" N, long. 121°34'35" W). Named on Brentwood (1978) and Woodward Island (1978) 7.5' quadrangles.

Rock Springs [MARIN]: *spring,* 6 miles southwest of downtown San Rafael (lat. 37°54'40" N, long. 122°36'40" W). Named on San Rafael (1954) 7.5' quadrangle.

Rock Springs Peak [SANTA CLARA]: *peak,* 5 miles east-southeast of Gilroy Hot Springs (lat. 37°05'05" N, long. 121°23'40" W; sec. 11, T 10 S, R 5 E). Named on Gilroy Hot Springs (1955) 7.5' quadrangle.

Rockville [SOLANO]: *village,* 4.25 miles west of Fairfield (lat. 38° 14'40" N, long. 122°07'15" W). Named on Fairfield South (1949) 7.5' quadrangle. Postal authorities established Rockville post office in 1858, discontinued it in 1870, reestablished it in 1898, and discontinued it in 1902; the name is from a nearby rock quarry (Salley, p. 187).

Rocky Canyon: see **Kent Canyon** [MARIN].

Rocky Island: see **Brooks Island** [CONTRA COSTA].

Rocky Point [MARIN]: *promontory,* 3.5 miles east-southeast of Bolinas along the coast (lat. 37°52'55" N, long. 122°37'40" W). Named on Bolinas (1954) 7.5' quadrangle. A spring of warm water known as Rocky Point Spring rises on the beach near the promontory (Waring, p. 80).

Rocky Point Spring: see **Rocky Point** [MARIN].

Rocky Ridge [ALAMEDA]: *ridge,* northwest-trending, 5.5 miles long, 4 miles west-southwest of Mendenhall Springs (lat. 37°33'45" N, long. 121°42'30" W). Named on Mendenhall Springs (1956) 7.5' quadrangle.

Rocky Ridge [ALAMEDA-CONTRA COSTA]: *ridge,* northwest-trending, 5 miles long, on Alameda-Contra Costa county line, mainly in Contra Costa County; center 3 miles southwest of Danville (lat. 37°48' N, long. 122°02'45" W). Named on Las Trampas Ridge (1959) 7.5' quadrangle.

Rocky Ridge [MARIN]: *ridge,* north-northwest-to-northwest-trending, 2 miles long, 4.5 miles west-southwest of downtown San Rafael (lat. 37°56'35" N, long. 122°36'25" W). Named on San Rafael (1954) 7.5' quadrangle.

Rodeo [CONTRA COSTA]: *town*, 5.5 miles east-northeast of Pinole Point (lat. 38°02'05" N, long. 122°16' W); the town is along Rodeo Creek. Named on Mare Island (1959) 7.5' quadrangle. Postal authorities established Rodeo post office in 1892 (Frickstad, p. 23).

Rodeo Cove [MARIN]: *embayment*, 1 mile north-northwest of Point Bonita (lat. 37°49'45" N, long. 122°32'15" W). Named on Point Bonita (1954) 7.5' quadrangle.

Rodeo Creek [CONTRA COSTA]: *stream*, flows 8 miles to San Pablo Bay 5.5 miles east-northeast of Pinole Point (lat. 38°02'20" N, long. 122°16' W); the mouth of the stream is at Rodeo. Named on Benicia (1959), Briones Valley (1959), and Mare Island (1959) 7.5' quadrangles.

Rodeo Flat [SANTA CLARA]: *area*, 3.25 miles west of Mount Sizer (lat. 37°12'40" N, long. 121°34'15" W). Named on Mount Sizer (1955) 7.5' quadrangle.

Rodeo Lagoon [MARIN]: *lake*, 4400 feet long, 1 mile north of Point Bonita (lat. 37°49'50" N, long. 122°31'45" W); the lake is inland from Rodeo Cove. Named on Point Bonita (1954) 7.5' quadrangle. According to Teather (p. 62), the name appears to be derived from the word "Rodier"—the name "Rodier Lagoon" is on a Coast Survey chart of 1856.

Rodeo Viejo: see **Cañada de Guadalupe y Rodeo Viejo** [SAN FRANCISCO-SAN MATEO]; **Cañada de Guadalupe la Visitacion y Rodeo Viejo** [SAN FRANCISCO-SAN MATEO].

Rodgers Gulch [SAN MATEO]: *canyon*, drained by a stream that flows 1.25 miles to Alpine Creek 1.5 miles southwest of Mindego Hill (lat. 37°17'50" N, long. 122°14'55" W; sec. 25, T 7 S, R 4 W). Named on Mindego Hill (1961) 7.5' quadrangle. Benjamin Rodgers had a ranch in the canyon in the 1860's (Brown, p. 78).

Rodier Lagoon: see **Rodeo Lagoon** [MARIN].

Roe Island [SOLANO]: *island*, nearly 1.5 miles long, 7 miles east-northeast of Benicia in Suisun Bay (lat. 38°04'20" N, long. 122° 02' W). Named on Vine Hill (1959) 7.5' quadrangle. Called Preston I. on Ringgold's (1850c) map. United States Board on Geographic Names (1989, p. 4) approved the name "Fishermans Cut" for a channel, 0.5 mile long, situated off of the east end of Roe Island in Suisun Bay (lat. 38°04'15" N, long. 121°01'02" W, at NE end) and rejected the name "Fishermans Channel" for the feature.

Roe Island Channel [CONTRA COSTA-SOLANO]: *channel*, 6.5 miles east-northeast of Martinez in Suisun Bay on Contra Costa-Solano county line (lat. 38°03'50" N, long. 122°01'45" W); the feature is south of Roe Island. Named on Vine Hill (1959) 7.5' quadrangle.

Rogers Canyon [SANTA CLARA]: *canyon*, drained by a stream that flows 3 miles to Sulphur Springs Creek 6.5 miles south-southwest of Mount Boardman (lat. 37°23'20" N, long. 121°29'45" W; sec. 26, T 6 S, R 4 E). Named on Eylar Mountain (1955) and Mount Boardman (1955) 7.5' quadrangles.

Rogers Gulch [SAN MATEO]: *canyon*, drained by a stream that flows 0.5 mile to Lobitos Creek 5.25 miles south-southeast of downtown Half Moon Bay (lat. 37°23'35" N, long. 122°23'35" W). Named on Half Moon Bay (1961) 7.5' quadrangle. Michael Rogers had a ranch in the canyon in the 1860's (Brown, p. 78).

Roos Cut [SOLANO]: *water feature*, joins Suisun Slough 6.5 miles south-southwest of Fairfield (lat. 38°09'25" N, long. 122°04'15" W). Named on Fairfield South (1949) 7.5' quadrangle.

Rooter Gulch: see **Hooker Creek** [SAN MATEO].

Rose Flat [ALAMEDA]: *area*, 6 miles south-southwest of Mendenhall Springs (lat. 37°30'50" N, long. 121°42'05" W; near E line sec. 12, T 5 S, R 2 E). Named on Mendenhall Springs (1956) 7.5' quadrangle. The name commemorates Antonio Rose and Manuel Rose, landowners in the region (Mosier and Mosier, p. 74).

Rose Lawn: see **Burbank** [SANTA CLARA].

Roosevelt Cut [CONTRA COSTA]: *water feature*, 1.5 miles east of the settlement of Bethel Island near Sand Mound Slough (lat. 38°01'10" N, long. 121°36' W). Named on Bouldin Island (1978) 7.5' quadrangle.

Ross [MARIN]: *town*, 1.5 miles west-southwest of downtown San Rafael (lat. 37°57'45" N, long. 122°33'30" W). Named on San Rafael (1954) 7.5' quadrangle. Postal authorities established Ross post office in 1887 (Frickstad, p. 89), and the town incorporated in 1908. The name commemorates James Ross, who settled at the place in 1859 (Hoover, Rensch, and Rensch, p. 185). The railroad station at the site first was called Sunnyside (Teather, p. 62).

Ross Creek [MARIN]: *stream*, flows 1.25 miles from Phoenix Lake to join San Anselmo Creek and form Corte Madera Creek 1.5 miles west-southwest of downtown San Rafael in Ross (lat. 37°58' N, long. 122°33'30" W). Named on San Rafael (1954) 7.5' quadrangle.

Ross Creek [SANTA CLARA]: *stream*, flows 6.5 miles to Guadalupe River 5 miles south of downtown San Jose (lat. 37°15'55" N, long. 121°52'40" W). Named on Los Gatos (1953, photorevised 1968 and 1973) and San Jose West (1961) 7.5' quadrangles. The name is for John E. Ross, who settled in the vicinity in 1856 and farmed along the stream for nearly 40 years (Patricia Loomis, *San Jose Mercury*, January 21, 1980).

Ross Hill [MARIN]: *ridge*, northeast- to east-trending, 1 mile long, 2.25 miles southwest of downtown San Rafael (lat. 37°57'20" N, long. 122°33'55" W); the ridge is south of Ross. Named on San Rafael (1954) 7.5' quadrangle.

Ross Landing: see **Kentfield** [MARIN].

Ross Valley [MARIN]: *valley,* 1.5 miles west of downtown San Rafael along San Anselmo Creek and Corte Madera Creek (lat. 37° 58'30" N, long. 122°33'45" W). Named on San Rafael (1954) 7.5' quadrangle.

Rough Gulch [SANTA CLARA]: *canyon,* drained by a stream that flows 2 miles to Big Canyon 2.5 miles north-northwest of Gilroy Hot Springs (lat. 37°08'25" N, long. 121°29'50" W; sec. 23, T 9 S, R 4 E). Named on Mississippi Creek (1955) and Mount Sizer (1955) 7.5' quadrangles. Called Laguna Ranch Canyon on Morgan Hill (1917) 15' quadrangle.

Rough Gulch: see **Little Rough Gulch** [SANTA CLARA].

Round Hill [SAN MATEO]: *hill,* 4.5 miles south of the village of San Gregorio near Pescadero Creek (lat. 37°15'40" N, long. 122°23'55" W). Named on San Gregorio (1961, photorevised 1968) 7.5' quadrangle.

Round Mountain [SANTA CLARA]: *peak,* 2 miles south-southwest of Isabel Valley (lat. 37°17'20" N, long. 121°32'55" W; near SW cor. sec. 28, T 7 S, R 4 E). Altitude 3085 feet. Named on Isabel Valley (1955) 7.5' quadrangle.

Round Top [CONTRA COSTA]: *peak,* 3 miles south-southwest of Orinda (lat. 37°51' N, long. 122°11'30" W; on S line sec. 9, T 1 S, R 3 W). Altitude 1763 feet. Named on Oakland East (1959) 7.5' quadrangle. United States Board on Geographic Names (1970b, p. 1) approved the name "Gudde Ridge" for the ridge on which Round Top is a high point; the name "Gudde" honors Erwin G. Gudde, professor at University of California, Berkeley, and author of California place-name books.

Round Valley [CONTRA COSTA]: *valley,* 8 miles east-southeast of Mount Diablo (lat. 37°51'10" N, long. 121°46'30" W). Named on Tassajara (1953) 7.5' quadrangle.

Roy Gulch [SAN MATEO]: *canyon,* drained by a stream that flows 1.25 miles to Pescadero Creek 5.25 miles southwest of La Honda (lat. 37°15'40" N, long. 122°20' W; sec. 6, T 8 S, R 4 W). Named on La Honda (1961) 7.5' quadrangle. Louis Roy had a ranch in the canyon in the late 1860's and 1870's (Brown, p. 78).

Ruby Canyon [SANTA CLARA]: *canyon,* 0.25 mile long, 4 miles northeast of Gilroy along Alamias Creek (lat. 37°02'40" N, long. 121°30'50" W). Named on Gilroy (1955) 7.5' quadrangle.

Ruckels Island: see **Winter Island** [CONTRA COSTA].

Rucker [SANTA CLARA]: *locality,* 3.25 miles north-northwest of Gilroy along Southern

Pacific Railroad (lat. 37°03'15" N, long. 121°35'30" W). Named on Gilroy (1955) 7.5' quadrangle. Postal authorities established Rucker post office in 1894, moved it 0.5 mile west in 1896, and discontinued it in 1900; the name commemorates William B. Rucker, a pioneer settler (Salley, p. 190). According to tradition, a low hill on the west side of Santa Clara Valley between Rucker and Gilroy was called Lomita de la Linares for Señora Linares, who rested there when the first settlers bound for San Jose stopped to hunt elk (Hoover, Rensch, and Rensch, p. 431).

Rucker Creek: see **Llagas Creek** [SANTA CLARA].

Rumyantsev: see **Port Rumyantsev**, under **Bodega Bay** [MARIN].

Runnymede: see **East Palo Alto** [SAN MATEO].

Rush Creek [MARIN]: *stream,* flows 1.5 miles to Black John Slough 2.5 miles north-northeast of downtown Novato (lat. 38°08' N, long. 122°33'05" W). Named on Novato (1954) and Petaluma River (1954) 7.5' quadrangles. Teather (p. 63) associated the name "Rush Creek" with Peter Rush, who bought land near present Novato in 1862.

Rush Landing [SOLANO]: *locality,* 2.25 miles south-southeast of Fairfield along Suisun Slough (lat. 38°13' N, long. 122°01'45" W; sec. 1, T 4 N, R 2 W). Named on Fairfield South (1949) 7.5' quadrangle.

Russell [SOLANO]: *locality,* 3 miles west-southwest of Fairfield along Sacramento Northern Railroad (lat. 38°14'20" N, long. 122° 05'40" W). Named on Fairfield South (1949) 7.5' quadrangle.

Russell: see **Russell City** [ALAMEDA].

Russel City [ALAMEDA]: *district,* 5.25 miles south-southeast of downtown San Leandro (lat. 37°39' N, long. 122°08' W). Named on San Leandro (1959) 7.5' quadrangle. United States Board on Geographic Names (1961a, p. 19) rejected the name "Russell" for the place. Frederick James Russell laid out the community in 1907 (Mosier and Mosier, p. 75).

Russellmann Creek [CONTRA COSTA]: *stream,* flows nearly 1 mile to Mount Diablo Creek 3 miles north of Mount Diablo (lat. 37°55'20" N, long. 121°54'20" W; sec. 19, T 1 N, R 1 E). Named on Clayton (1953) 7.5' quadrangle.

Russian Hill [SAN FRANCISCO]: *ridge,* northwest- to north-trending, 0.5 mile long, less than 1 mile south-southwest of North Point (lat. 37°47'55" N, long. 122°25' W). Named on San Francisco North (1956) 7.5' quadrangle. The name probably is from a graveyard for Russian sailors that was located on the hill in the early days (Hoover, Rensch, and Rensch, p. 363).

Russian Ridge [SAN MATEO]: *ridge,* west-northwest-trending, 2 miles long, 1.5 miles

east-northeast of Mindego Hill (lat. 37°19'15"
N, long. 122°12' W). Named on Mindego Hill
(1961) 7.5' quadrangle.

Russ Island [SOLANO]: *island,* 3.25 miles
west-southwest of Napa Junction between
Napa River, South Slough, China Slough, and
Devils Slough on Napa-Solano county line,
mainly in Napa County (lat. 38°10'10" N,
long. 122°18'30" W). Named on Cuttings
Wharf (1949) 7.5' quadrangle. Called Knight
Island on Mare Island (1916) 15' quadrangle.

Rust: see **El Cerito** [CONTRA COSTA]; **William Rust Summit**, under **Camp Herms**
[CONTRA COSTA].

Ryer Island [SOLANO]:
(1) *island,* 6.5 miles north-northeast of Rio Vista
between Miner Slough, Sutter Slough, Steamboat Slough, and Cache Slough (lat. 38°14'
N, long. 121°38' W). Named on Courtland
(1978), Isleton (1978), Liberty Island (1978),
and Rio Vista (1978) 7.5' quadrangles. On
Ringgold's (1850c) map, the part of the feature east of present Elkhorn Slough is called
Sutter I., and the part west of the slough is
called Taylor I. The same map has the name
"Pt. Gelston" for the promontory at the south
tip of present Ryer Island (1).
(2) *island,* 8 miles east-northeast of Benicia between Suisun Bay and Suisun Cutoff (lat.
38°05' N, long. 122°01' W). Named on
Honker Bay (1953) and Vine Hill (1959) 7.5'
quadrangles. Called Kings I. on Ringgold's
(1850c) map, but United States Board on
Geographic Names (1933, p. 654) rejected the
names "King's Island," "Long Point Island,"
and "Ryer's Island" for the feature. The name
commemorates Dr. W.M. Ryer, a pioneer physician who owned the island (Gudde, 1949,
p. 293).

Ryer Island Ferry [SOLANO]: *locality,* 2.5
miles northeast of Rio Vista on Cache Slough
near the south tip of Ryer Island (1) (lat.
38°11'10" N, long. 121°39'30" W). Named
on Rio Vista (1978) 7.5' quadrangle.

Ryer's Island: see **Ryer Island** [SOLANO] (2).

– S –

Sacramento Brazoria: see **Rio Vista** [SOL-
ANO].

Sacramento Deep Water Channel: see **Sacramento River Deep Water Ship Channel**
[SOLANO].

Sacramento Landing [MARIN]: *locality,* 6.5
miles south of Tomales on the southwest side
of Tomales Bay (lat. 38°09' N, long.
122°54'20" W). Named on Tomales (1954)
7.5' quadrangle. The place probably was
named for an Indian (Mason, 1976a, p. 149).

Sacramento River [SOLANO]: *stream,* flows
15 miles along Solano-Sacramento county
line to Suisun Bay 4.5 miles south of Birds
Landing (2) (lat. 38°03'50" N, long. 121°51'

W). Named on Antioch North (1978), Jersey
Island (1978), and Rio Vista (1978) 7.5' quadrangles. Called Rio Sacramento on Fremont's
(1845) map. In 1808 Gabriel Moraga applied
the name "Sacramento" to present Feather
River, a tributary of Sacramento River in
Sutter County; present Sacramento River was
called San Francisco and Buenaventura or
Bonaventura before the name "Sacramento"
shifted to it—*Sacramento* means "Holy Sac-
rament" in Spanish (Hart, p. 364). Present
Elkhorn Slough is called West Fork [Sacra-
mento River] on Ringgold's (1850c) map,
present Steamboat Slough [SOLANO] is
called Middle Fork [Sacramento River] on the
same map, and present Sutter Slough [SOL-
ANO] is called West Fork [Sacramento River]
on Ringgold's (1850d) map.

Sacramento River: see **Suisun Bay** [CONTRA
COSTA].

Sacramento River Deep Water Ship Channel
[SOLANO]: *channel,* extends along Sacramento River from Suisun Bay past Rio Vista,
and then along Cache Slough to Prospect Island, from which the channel follows an artificial waterway through Yolo Bypass to Yolo
County. Named on Antioch North (1978),
Jersey Island (1978), Liberty Island (1978),
and Rio Vista (1978) 7.5' quadrangles. United
States Board on Geographic names (1978, p.
7) rejected the names "Deep Water Ship Channel," "Sacramento Deep Water Channel,"
"Sacramento Ship Channel," and "Ship Channel" for the feature.

Sacramento Ship Channel: see **Sacramento
River Deep Water Ship Channel** [SOL-
ANO].

Saddle Rock: see **Devils Slide** [SAN MATEO];
Seal Rock [SAN FRANCISCO].

Sagadehock Reach: see **Horseshoe Bend** [SOL-
ANO].

Sail Rock [SAN MATEO]: *rock,* 4.5 miles west-
northwest of downtown Half Moon Bay off
Pillar Point (lat. 37°29'35" N, long. 122° 29'55"
W). Named on Half Moon Bay (1961) 7.5'
quadrangle. United States Board on Geographic
Names (1933, p. 656) rejected the names "Pillar Rock," "Seal Rock," and "Steeple Rock"
for the feature. The name "Sail Rock" is from
the shape of the rock (Brown, p. 78).

Saint Josephs Hill [SANTA CLARA]: *peak,* 1.5
miles south of downtown Los Gatos (lat.
37°12'20" N, long. 121°58'35" W; sec. 28, T
8 S, R 1 W). Named on Los Gatos (1953) 7.5'
quadrangle.

Saint Marys Bay [CONTRA COSTA]: *water
feature,* 6 miles east of Brentwood along Indian Slough (lat. 37°55'15" N, long.
121°35'15" W). Named on Woodward Island
(1978) 7.5' quadrangle.

Saint Mary's College: see **Moraga** [CONTRA
COSTA].

Saint Vincent: see **Gallinas** [MARIN].

Salada: see **Sharp Park** [SAN MATEO].

Salada Beach: see **Sharp Park** [SAN MATEO].
Saline City: see **Drawbridge** [ALAMEDA].
Salmon Creek [MARIN]: *stream,* flows 5 miles to join Arroyo Sausal and form Walker Creek 9 miles southeast of Tomales (lat. 38°09'40" N, long. 122°46'50" W). Named on Petaluma (1953) and Point Reyes NE (1954) 7.5' quadrangles.
Salmon Creek: see **Walker Creek** [MARIN].
Salmon Island: see **Coyote Hills** [ALAMEDA].
Salsipuedes [SANTA CLARA]: *land grant,* mainly in Santa Cruz County, but extends into Santa Clara County along the crest of Santa Cruz Mountains southwest of Gilroy. Named on Chittenden (1955), Mount Madonna (1955), and Watsonville East (1955) 7.5' quadrangles. Manuel Jimeno Casarin received 8 leagues in 1834 and 1840; James Blair and John P. Davidson claimed 31,201 acres patented in 1861 (Cowan, p. 71; Perez, p. 87). *Salsipuedes* means "get out if you can" in Spanish, and refers to rugged terrain on the grant (Arbuckle, p. 29-30).
Salt Lake: see **Laguna Salada** [SAN MATEO].
Salt Lake Valley: see **Laguna Salada** [SAN MATEO].
Salt Marsh Creek [MARIN]: *stream,* flows 1.25 miles to San Francisco Bay 3.25 miles south-southeast of downtown San Rafael (lat. 37°55'55" N, long. 122°30'10" W). Named on San Rafael (1954) 7.5' quadrangle.
Salt Valley [SAN MATEO]: *valley,* 4.5 miles north of present Montara Knob at the south end of Laguna Salada (lat. 37°37'10" N, long. 122°29'15" W). Named on San Mateo (1915) 15' quadrangle.
Salt Work Slough: see **Plummer Creek** [ALAMEDA].
Sams Canyon [SANTA CLARA]: *canyon,* drained by a stream that flows nearly 4 miles to Arroyo Valle 3.25 miles southwest of Eylar Mountain (lat. 37°26'15" N, long. 121°35' W; sec. 6, T 6 S, R 4 E). Named on Eylar Mountain (1955) 7.5' quadrangle.
Samson Canyon [SANTA CLARA]: *canyon,* drained by a stream that flows nearly 2 miles to Hoover Valley 4.25 miles west-southwest of Mount Sizer (lat. 37°11'35" N, long. 121°35' W); the canyon is south of Samson Ridge. Named on Mount Sizer (1955) 7.5' quadrangle.
Samson Ridge [SANTA CLARA]: *ridge,* west-northwest-trending, 1.5 miles long, 3.5 miles southwest of Mount Sizer (lat. 37°11'05" N, long. 121°34' W). Named on Mount Sizer (1955) 7.5' quadrangle.
San Andreas Lake [SAN MATEO]: *lake,* nearly 3 miles long, behind a dam 2 miles southwest of downtown Millbrae (lat. 37°34'50" N, long. 122°24'35" W). Named on Montara Mountain (1956) 7.5' quadrangle. United States Board on Geographic Names (1933, p. 664) rejected the form "San Andres Lake" for the name. The reservoir was created in 1875 in the valley that Palou called Cañada de San Andres in 1774 (Gudde, 1949, p. 297).

San Andres Lake: see **San Andreas Lake** [SAN MATEO].
San Anselmo [MARIN]: *town,* 1.5 miles west of downtown San Rafael (lat. 37°58'30" N, long. 122°33'45" W); the town is along San Anselmo Creek. Named on San Rafael (1954) 7.5' quadrangle. Postal authorities established San Anselmo post office in 1892 (Frickstad, p. 89), and the town incorporated in 1907. Postal authorities established Yolanda post office as a station of San Anselmo post office in 1924 and discontinued it in 1954; they established Lansdale post office as a station of San Anselmo post office in 1924 and discontinued it in 1962 (Salley, p. 117, 244).
San Anselmo Creek [MARIN]: *stream,* flows 6 miles to join Ross Creek and form Corte Madera Creek 1.5 miles west-southwest of downtown San Rafael (lat. 37°58' N, long. 122°33'30" W). Named on Bolinas (1954) and San Rafael (1954) 7.5' quadrangles.
San Antone Creek: see **San Antonio Creek** [SANTA CLARA].
San Antone Valley: see **San Antonio Valley** [SANTA CLARA].
San Antonio [ALAMEDA]:
(1) *land grant,* at and near Berkeley. Named on Briones Valley (1959), Oakland East (1959), Oakland West (1959), and Richmond (1959) 7.5' quadrangles. Luis Peralta received 11 leagues in 1820; his sons Domingo and Vicente claimed 18,849 acres patented in 1877 (Cowan, p. 71).
(2) *land grant,* at Oakland. Named on Oakland East (1959) 7.5' quadrangle. Luis Peralta received 11 leagues in 1820; his son Antonio Maria Peralta claimed 15,207 acres patented in 1874 (Cowan, p. 71).
(3) *land grant,* at and near San Leandro. Named on Hayward (1959), Las Trampas Ridge (1959), and San Leandro (1959) 7.5' quadrangles. Luis Peralta received 11 leagues in 1820; his son Ignacio Peralta claimed 9417 acres patented in 1858 (Cowan, p. 71). Perez (p. 88) gave the size of this grant as 9400.16 acres.
San Antonio [SANTA CLARA]: *land grant,* in Los Altos and Los Altos Hills. Named on Cupertino (1961) and Mindego Hill (1961) 7.5' quadrangles. Juan Prado Mesa received the land in 1839; Encarnacion Mesa and others claimed 4440 acres patented in 1866; William A. Dana and others claimed 3542 acres patented in 1857 (Cowan, p. 72).
San Antonio: see **Oakland** [ALAMEDA].
San Antonio Creek [ALAMEDA]: *stream,* flows 11.5 miles to Alameda Creek 1.5 miles south-southeast of Sunol (lat. 37°34'35" N, long. 121°52'10" W). Named on La Costa Valley (1960) and Mendenhall Springs (1956) 7.5' quadrangles. The stream, or part of it, also was called La Costa Creek (Mosier and Mosier, p. 76). Present Indian Creek, a tributary of San Antonio Creek, is called South

Fork San Antonio Cr. on Thompson and West's (1878) map.

San Antonio Creek [MARIN]: *stream,* heads in Sonoma County and flows 17 miles, mainly along along Marin-Sonoma county line, to Petaluma River nearly 4 miles north-north-east of downtown Novato (lat. 38°09'30" N, long. 122°32'40" W). Named on Petaluma (1953) and Petaluma River (1954) 7.5' quadrangles. The stream was called Arroyo de San Antonio in Spanish days (Teather, p. 65).

San Antonio Creek [SANTA CLARA]: *stream,* flows 15 miles to Arroyo Bayo 6.25 miles south-southwest of Eylar Mountain (lat. 37°23'05" N, long. 121°34' W; sec. 30, T 6 S, R 4 E). Named on Eylar Mountain (1955), Isabel Valley (1955), Mount Boardman (1955), and Mount Stakes (1955) 7.5' quadrangles. Called San Antone Creek on Mount Boardman (1942) 15' quadrangle. Postal authorities established Gilbert post office along San Antonio Creek (T 7 S, R 4 E) in 1888 and discontinued it in 1889; the post office was on Charles Gilbert's ranch (Salley, p. 85).

San Antonio Creek: see **Adobe Creek** [SANTA CLARA]; **La Costa Creek** [ALAMEDA]; **Lake Merritt** [ALAMEDA]; **Oakland Inner Harbor** [ALAMEDA].

San Antonio Creek, North Fork: see **Chileno Creek** [MARIN].

San Antonio Estuary: see **Oakland Inner Harbor** [ALAMEDA].

San Antonio or Pescadero [SAN MATEO]: *land grant,* along the coast near Pescadero. Named on Pigeon Point (1955) and San Gregorio (1961) 7.5' quadrangles. Joaquin Solis and Jose Antonio Botiller received 4 leagues in 1829; Juan Jose Gonzales received three-quarters of a league in 1833 and claimed 3282 acres patented in 1866 (Cowan, p. 59).

San Antonio Reservoir [ALAMEDA]: *lake,* 3 miles long, behind a dam on San Antonio Creek 2.5 miles southeast of Sunol in La Costa Valley (lat. 37°34'20" N, long. 121°50'50" W). Named on La Costa Valley (1960, photorevised 1968) 7.5' quadrangle.

San Antonio Slough: see **Lake Merritt** [ALAMEDA].

San Antonio Valley [SANTA CLARA]: *valley,* 5 miles northwest of Mount Stakes (lat. 37°22' N, long. 121°28'45" W); the valley is on upper reaches of San Antonio Creek. Named on Mount Boardman (1955) and Mount Stakes (1955) 7.5' quadrangles. Called San Antone Valley on Mount Boardman (1942) 15' quadrangle. Anza traveled through the valley in 1776 and his soldiers called it El Cañada de San Vicente (Davidson, p. 123). Clark's (1924) map has the name "Deforest" for a group of buildings along San Antonio Creek, apparently in the northwest part of present San Antonio Valley. Postal authorities established DeForest post office in 1892, moved it 0.5 mile northwest in 1897, moved it 8 miles

southeast in 1906, and discontinued it in 1909; the name was for Ransford S. DeForest, first postmaster (Salley, p. 56).

San Antonio Valley: see **Upper San Antonio Valley** [SANTA CLARA].

San Benito: see **Half Moon Bay** [SAN MATEO] (2); **Miramontes** [SAN MATEO] (1).

San Bernardino Valley: see **Santa Clara Valley** [SANTA CLARA].

San Bruno [SAN MATEO]: *city,* 2 miles south of downtown South San Francisco (lat. 37°37'40" N, long. 122°24'35" W). Named on Montara Mountain (1956) and San Francisco South (1956) 7.5' quadrangles. A travelers stop called San Bruno House opened at the place about 1852 and eventually it housed a railroad depot, post office, telegraph office, and freight station (Hynding, p. 53). Postal authorities established San Bruno post office in 1875, discontinued it for a time in 1890, discontinued it again for a time in 1891, discontinued it in 1893, and reestablished it in 1898 (Frickstad, p. 169). The city incorporated in 1914. A railroad station in present San Bruno was named Tanforan for nearby Tanforan Park race track—the track opened in the 1890's; the misspelled name is from Torribio Tanfaran, who inherited the land at the site; during World War I the race track was converted into a military installation called Camp Grizzly for an artillery regiment that had the name "California Grizzlies" (Brown, p. 93; Hynding, p. 120, 201).

San Bruno Canal [SAN MATEO]: *water feature,* opens into San Francisco Bay 1.25 miles east-southeast of downtown South San Francisco (lat. 37°39' N, long. 122°23'15" W). Named on San Francisco South (1956) 7.5' quadrangle. The feature now is filled.

San Bruno Canyon [SANTA CLARA]: *canyon,* drained by a stream that flows 1.25 miles to lowlands nearly 4 miles south-southeast of Coyote (lat. 37°09'55" N, long. 121°42'50" W). Named on Morgan Hill (1955) 7.5' quadrangle.

San Bruno Channel [SAN MATEO]: *channel,* extends through shallow water of San Francisco Bay south of Point San Bruno to the shore 1.5 miles southeast of downtown South San Francisco (lat. 37°38'30" N, long. 122°23'35" W). Named on Hunters Point (1956) 7.5' quadrangle.

San Bruno Creek [SAN MATEO]: *stream,* flows 2 miles to lowlands along San Francisco Bay less than 2 miles south of downtown South San Francisco (lat. 37°37'45" N, long. 122°25'05" W); the stream is on Buri Buri grant. Named on Montara Mountain (1956) and San Francisco South (1956) 7.5' quadrangles. The stream was called Sanjon de Buriburi in Spanish times (Brown, p. 80).

San Bruno Creek: see **Colma Creek** [SAN MATEO].

San Bruno House: see **San Bruno** [SAN MATEO].

San Bruno Mountain [SAN MATEO]: *ridge,* east-southeast-trending, 3.5 miles long, center 2 miles north-northwest of downtown South San Francisco (lat. 37°41' N, long. 122°25'45" W). Named on San Francisco South (1956) 7.5' quadrangle. The feature was called Sierra de San Bruno (Gudde, 1949, p. 299) and Cerro de San Bruno in Spanish times; later it also was called Crocker Mountain (Brown, p. 80). Blake (1856, p. 378) referred to San Bruno range, Antisell (p. 16) mentioned Monte San Bruno, and Whitney (p. 62) used the name "San Bruno Mountains."

San Bruno Point: see **Point San Bruno** [SAN MATEO].

San Bruno Range: see **San Bruno Mountain** [SAN MATEO].

San Bruno Shoal [SAN MATEO]: *shoal,* 7 miles east of downtown South San Francisco in San Francisco Bay (lat. 37°38'45" N, long. 122°17'20" W). Named on Hunters Point (1956) 7.5' quadrangle.

San Carlos [SAN MATEO]: *city,* 5.5 miles southeast of downtown San Mateo (lat. 37°30'15" N, long. 122°15'40" W). Named on Palo Alto (1961), Redwood Point (1959), San Mateo (1956), and Woodside (1961) 7.5' quadrangles. Postal authorities established San Carlos post office in 1895 (Frickstad, p. 169), and the city incorporated in 1925.

San Carlos Creek: see **Pulgas Creek** [SAN MATEO].

San Catanio Creek [CONTRA COSTA]: *stream,* flows 2.5 miles to San Ramon Creek 3.5 miles south-southeast of Danville (lat. 37° 46'25" N, long. 121°59' W). Named on Diablo (1953) 7.5' quadrangle.

Sanchez Creek [SAN MATEO]: *stream,* flows 2.5 miles to San Francisco Bay 2.5 miles northwest of downtown San Mateo (lat. 37°35'20" N, long. 122°21'25" W). Named on San Mateo (1956) 7.5' quadrangle.

San Clemente [MARIN]: *locality,* 4 miles south-southeast of downtown San Rafael along Northwestern Pacific Railroad (lat. 37°55'10" N, long. 122°30'35" W); the place is near present San Clemente Creek. Named on Mount Tamalpais (1950) 15' quadrangle.

San Clemente Creek [MARIN]: *stream,* flows 1.25 miles to San Francisco Bay 1.5 miles southwest of Point San Quentin (lat. 37° 55'35" N, long. 122°29'55" W). Named on San Quentin (1959) and San Rafael (1954) 7.5' quadrangles.

Sand Beach [SAN MATEO]: *beach,* 4 miles south-southwest of the village of San Gregorio along the coast north of the mouth of Pescadero Creek (lat. 37°16'15" N, long. 122°24'35" W). Named on San Gregorio (1961, photorevised 1968) 7.5' quadrangle. The place also was called Bradley Beach (Brown, p. 81).

Sand Creek [CONTRA COSTA]: *stream,* flows 10.5 miles to Marsh Creek 0.5 mile west-northwest of Brentwood (lat. 37°56'20" N, long. 121°42'20" W). Named on Antioch South (1953) and Brentwood (1978) 7.5' quadrangles.

Sand Hill [CONTRA COSTA]: *settlement,* 3 miles north of Brentwood (lat. 37°58'30" N, long. 121°41'35" W). Named on Brentwood (1978) 7.5' quadrangle.

Sand Mound: see **Jersey** [CONTRA COSTA].

Sand Mound Slough [CONTRA COSTA]: *water feature,* extends for 5.5 miles from Rock Slough to Old River 3.5 miles east-northeast of the settlement of Bethel Island (lat. 38°01'50" N, long. 121°34'50" W). Named on Bouldin Island (1978), Jersey Island (1978), and Woodward Island (1978) 7.5' quadrangles.

Sando [CONTRA COSTA]: *locality,* less than 1 mile east of downtown Antioch along Atchison, Topeka and Santa Fe Railroad (lat. 38°00'50" N, long. 121°47'40" W; sec. 18, T 2 N, R 2 E). Named on Antioch North (1953) 7.5' quadrangle.

Sand Point [MARIN]: *promontory,* nearly 4 miles west-southwest of Tomales on the east side of the entrance to Tomales Bay (lat. 38° 13'55" N, long. 122°58'15" W). Named on Tomales (1954) 7.5' quadrangle. The feature also was called Punta Rena (Teather, p. 65).

Sand Point [SANTA CLARA]: *promontory,* 5 miles north-northwest of downtown Mountain View at the edge of mud flats along San Francisco Bay (lat. 37°27'45" N, long. 122°06'05" W). Named on Mountain View (1961) 7.5' quadrangle.

Sandy Point: see **Notley Junction** [SAN MATEO].

San Felipe [SANTA CLARA]: *locality,* 6 miles east-southeast of Gilroy (lat. 36°58'15" N, long. 121°25'05" W); the place is on Ausaymas y San Felipe grant. Named on San Felipe (1955) 7.5' quadrangle. Postal authorities established Felipe post office in 1868 and discontinued it in 1902 (Frickstad, p. 175).

San Felipe: see **Ausaymas y San Felipe** [SANTA CLARA].

San Felipe Creek [SANTA CLARA]: *stream,* flows 14 miles to Las Animas Creek nearly 6 miles north of Morgan Hill (lat. 37°12'50" N, long. 121°39'20" W). Named on Lick Observatory (1955) and Morgan Hill (1955) 7.5' quadrangles.

San Felipe Hills [SANTA CLARA]: *ridge,* northwest-trending, 2.25 miles long, 3 miles south-southeast of Mount Hamilton (lat. 37°17'50" N, long. 121°37'45" W). Named on Isabel Valley (1955) and Lick Observatory (1955) 7.5' quadrangles.

San Felipe Valley [SANTA CLARA]: *valley,* 5 miles south-southwest of Mount Hamilton (lat. 37°16'30" N, long. 121°40'35" W); the valley is along San Felipe Creek. Named on

Lick Observatory (1955) 7.5' quadrangle.

San Felix Station: see **Lower Crystal Springs Reservoir** [SAN MATEO].

San Francisco [SAN FRANCISCO]: *city,* south of the Golden Gate between San Francisco Bay and the sea (civic center near lat. 37° 46'45" N, long. 122°25' W). Named on Hunters Point (1956, photorevised 1968), Oakland West (1959), Richmond (1959), San Francisco North (1956), San Francisco South (1956), and San Quentin (1959) 7.5' quadrangles. Postal authorities established San Francisco post office in 1848 (Frickstad, p. 159), and the city incorporated in 1850. Captain William A. Richardson built a house in 1835 near San Francisco Bay at Yerba Buena Cove, and the building became the nucleus of a village called Yerba Buena (Hoover, Rensch, and Rensch, p. 352). *Californian* newspaper for August 22, 1846, called the place Yerbabuano. *The California Star* newspaper for March 20, 1847, noted that the name "Yerba Buena" had been changed legally to San Francisco.

San Francisco: see **South San Francisco** [SAN MATEO].

San Francisco Bay: *bay,* lies between Contra Costa and Alameda Counties on the east side, and Marin, San Francisco, San Mateo and Santa Clara Counties on the west side. Named on San Francisco (1956) 1°x 2° quadrangle. Called Estero de S. Francisco on Costanso's (1771) map. Cermeño first applied the name "San Francisco" in the region to present Drakes Bay in 1595 (Treutlein, p. 12). Members of the Portola expedition used the term "Puerto de San Francisco" in 1769 for present Gulf of the Farallons before they discovered present San Francisco Bay (Davidson, p. 6), and gradually the name "San Francisco" transferred from the gulf to the bay (Treutlein, p. 14). On some old maps, the south arm of the bay is called Estrecho de San Jose and Estero de Santa Clara (Gudde, 1949, p. 306, 315).

San Francisco de las Llagas [SANTA CLARA]: *land grant,* near San Martin and Morgan Hill. Named on Gilroy (1955), Mount Madonna (1955), and Mount Sizer (1955) 7.5' quadrangles. Carlos Castro received 6 leagues in 1834; J. Murphy and M. Murphy claimed 22,283 acres patented in 1868 (Cowan, p. 76). Fages gave the name "Las Llagas de Nuestro Padre San Francisco" to his stopping place north of present San Martin in 1772; the name has the meaning "Stigmata of Our Father Saint Francis" in Spanish (Hoover, Rensch, and Rensch, p. 442).

San Francisquito [SANTA CLARA]: *land grant,* southwest of downtown Palo Alto at Stanford University. Named on Palo Alto (1961) 7.5' quadrangle. Antonio Buelna received 8 suertes in 1839; M. Concepcion V. de Rodrigues and others claimed 1471 acres patented in 1868 (Cowan, p. 77).

San Francisquito Creek [SAN MATEO-

SANTA CLARA]: *stream,* heads in San Mateo County and flows 11.5 miles, mainly along San Mateo-Santa Clara county line, to mud flats along San Francisco Bay 2.25 miles east-northeast of downtown Palo Alto (lat. 37°27'55" N, long. 122°06'50" W). Named on Mountain View (1961) and Palo Alto (1961) 7.5' quadrangles. Called R. de Sn. Francisco on Font's (1777) map. Palou camped on the bank of the creek in 1774 and selected a spot there for a mission to be dedicated to St. Francis of Assisi; Anza mentioned the name "Arroyo de San Francisco" in 1776, and later the stream was called Arroyo de San Francisquito (Gudde, 1949, p. 304).

San Geronimo [MARIN]:

(1) *land grant,* 6 miles north of Bolinas. Named on Bolinas (1954), Novato (1954), and San Geronimo (1954) 7.5' quadrangles. Rafael Cacho received 2 leagues in 1844; Joseph Warren Revere claimed 8701 acres patented in 1860 (Cowan, p. 78).

(2) *village,* 8 miles southwest of downtown Novato (lat. 38°00'50" N, long. 122°39'50" W); the village is on San Geronimo grant. Named on San Geronimo (1954) 7.5' quadrangle. Postal authorities established San Geronimo post office in 1895, discontinued it in 1910, and reestablished it in 1911 (Frickstad, p. 89). The railroad station at the place first was called Nicasio, but the name was changed to San Geronimo in 1877 (Teather, p. 67).

San Geronimo Creek [MARIN]: *stream,* flows 5.25 miles to Lagunitas Creek 10.5 miles southwest of Novato (lat. 38°00'20" N, long. 122°42'25" W); the stream is on San Geronimo grant. Named on San Geronimo (1954) 7.5' quadrangle.

San Gregorio [SAN MATEO]:

(1) *land grant,* near La Honda. Named on La Honda (1961) 7.5' quadrangle. Antonio Buelna received 4 leagues in two parcels in 1839; Salvador Castro claimed one parcel of 4439 acres patented in 1861 (Cowan, p. 78).

(2) *land grant,* along the coast near San Gregorio Creek, and inland into nearby highlands. Named on La Honda(1961), San Gregorio (1961), and Woodside (1961) 7.5' quadrangles. Antonio Buelna received 4 leagues in two parcels in 1839; M. Concepcion V. de Rodriguez claimed one parcel of 13,344 acres patented in 1861 (Cowan, p. 78). According to Perez (p. 91), Encarnacion Buelna was the patentee in 1861.

(3) *village,* 10 miles south-southeast of the town of Half Moon Bay (lat. 37°19'35" N, long. 122°23'10" W); the village is along San Gregorio Creek on San Gregorio (2) grant. Named on San Gregorio (1961) 7.5' quadrangle. Postal authorities established San Gregorio post office in 1870 (Frickstad, p. 169).

San Gregorio Beach [SAN MATEO]: *beach,* 1

mile west-southwest of the village of San Gregorio (lat. 37°19'25" N, long. 122°24'10" W); the beach is at the mouth of San Gregorio Creek. Named on San Gregorio (1961) 7.5' quadrangle.

San Gregorio Creek [SAN MATEO]: *stream,* formed by the confluence of La Honda Creek and Alpine Creek, flows 10.5 miles to the sea 1 mile west-southwest of the village of San Gregorio (lat. 37° 19'20" N, long. 122°24'10" W). Named on La Honda (1961) and San Gregorio (1961) 7.5' quadrangles. The stream was called Arroyo de San Gregorio in Spanish times, and it was called Arroyo Rodrigues in the 1850's (Brown, p. 82-83).

San Isabel: see **Mount San Isabel**, under **Mount Isabel** [SANTA CLARA].

San Isabel Creek: see **Isabel Creek** [SANTA CLARA].

San Isabel Valley: see **Isabel Valley** [SANTA CLARA].

San Isidro: see **Gilroy** [SANTA CLARA]; **Old Gilroy** [SANTA CLARA]; **San Ysidro** [SANTA CLARA].

San Joachin River: see **San Joaquin River** [CONTRA COSTA].

San Joaquin: see **Point San Joaquin** [CONTRA COSTA].

San Joaquin River [CONTRA COSTA]: *stream,* flows for 22 miles along Contra Costa-Sacramento county line to Suisun Bay 4 miles north-northwest of Antioch (lat. 38°03'45" N, long. 121°50'55" W). Named on Antioch North (1978), Bouldin Island (1978), and Jersey Island (1978) 7.5' quadrangles. Called R. San Joachim on Wilkes' (1841) map, Rio San Joaquin on Fremont's (1848) map, San Joachin R. on Wilkes' (1849) map, Joaquin River on Jefferson's (1849) map, River San Joarquin on Derby's (1850) map, and Rio Tulare or San Joaquin on Sage's (1846) map. Gabriel Moraga named the river about 1805 for St. Joaquim, father of the Virgin Mary (Hart, p. 379).

San Jon Creek: see **Saratoga Creek** [SANTA CLARA].

Sanjon Creek: see **Sausal Creek** [SAN MATEO].

Sanjon de Buriburi: see **San Bruno Creek** [SAN MATEO].

Sanjon de la Brea: see **Pajaro River** [SANTA CLARA].

Sanjon de los Alisos [ALAMEDA]: *stream,* flows 5.25 miles to Newark Slough 1.25 miles west of downtown Newark (lat. 37°31'40" N, long. 122°03'35" W). Named on Newark (1948) 7.5' quadrangle. Called Sanjen de los Alisos on Hayward (1899) 15' quadrangle.

San Jose [MARIN]: *land grant,* south of the city of Novato at and around Ignacio. Named on Novato (1954) 7.5' quadrangle. Ignacio Pacheco received 1.5 leagues in 1840 and claimed 6659 acres patented in 1861 (Cowan, p. 80).

San Jose [SANTA CLARA]: *city,* in the north part of Santa Clara Valley (downtown near lat. 37°20' N, long. 121°53' W). Named on Calaveras Reservoir (1961), Cupertino (1961), Milpitas (1961), San Jose East (1961), and San Jose West (1961) 7.5' quadrangles. Postal authorities established San Jose post office in 1849 (Frickstad, p. 175), and the city incorporated in 1850. The place was founded in 1777 on the bank of Guadalupe River and named El Pueblo San Jose de Guadalupe; floods caused removal of the community to higher ground within a couple of years (Hoover, Rensch, and Rensch, p. 427-428). Bidwell (p. 38) used the name "Pueblo of St. Joseph" in 1841, and Jefferson's (1849) map shows Pueblo St. Joseph.

San Jose: see **East San Jose** [SANTA CLARA]; **Port San Jose**, under **Alviso** [SANTA CLARA].

San Jose de Guadalupe Mision: see **Ex Mission San Jose** [ALAMEDA].

San Jose Point: see **Black Point** [SAN FRANCISCO].

San Jose Valley: see **Santa Clara Valley** [SANTA CLARA].

San Juan Bautista [SANTA CLARA]: *land grant,* south of downtown San Jose. Named on Los Gatos (1953), San Jose East (1961), San Jose West (1961) and Santa Teresa Hills (1953) 7.5' quadrangles. Jose Agustin Narvaez received 2 leagues in 1844 and claimed 8880 acres patented in 1865 (Cowan, p. 81). Thompson and West's (1876) map has the name "San Juan Bautista Hills" for highlands near the east edge of the grant and west of present Lick.

San Juan Bautista Hills: see **San Juan Bautista** [SANTA CLARA].

San Juan Capistrano: see **Hunters Point** [SAN FRANCISCO].

San Leandro [ALAMEDA]:
(1) *land grant,* at the city of San Leandro. Named on Hayward (1959) and San Leandro (1959) 7.5' quadrangles. Jose Joaquin Estudillo received 1 league in 1839 and 1842; he claimed 6830 acres patented in 1863 (Cowan, p. 83).
(2) *city,* 8 miles southeast of downtown Oakland (lat. 37°43'30" N, long. 122°09'20" W). Named on San Leandro (1959) 7.5' quadrangle. The Estudillo family, who owned the grant where the town lies, gave land for county buildings and reserved 200 acres for the community of San Leandro, which was surveyed in 1855; an election in 1854 brought the county seat to San Leandro from Alvarado (Hoover, Rensch, and Rensch, p. 15). Postal authorities established San Leandro post office in 1853 (Frickstad, p. 3), and the city incorporated in 1872.

San Leandro: see **West San Leandro** [ALAMEDA].

San Leandro Bay [ALAMEDA]: *embayment,* 4 miles west-northwest of downtown San

Leandro off of San Francisco Bay (lat. 37°45' N, long. 122°13'30" W). Named on Oakland East (1959) and San Leandro (1959) 7.5' quadrangles.

San Leandro Creek [ALAMEDA-CONTRA COSTA]: *stream,* heads in Contra Costa County and flows 21 miles to San Leandro Bay 3 miles west-northwest of downtown San Leandro in Alameda County (lat. 37°44'35" N, long. 122°12'25" W). Named on Hayward (1959), Las Trampas Ridge (1959), Oakland East (1959), and San Leandro (1959) 7.5' quadrangles. The names "Arroyo de San Leandro" and "Rio San Leandro" were used in the 1820's and 1830's (Gudde, 1949, p. 308). Concord (1897) 15' quadrangle shows West Branch extending north from San Leandro Creek through Moraga Valley. Peter Andrews Halverson established Halverson's Landing at the mouth of San Leandro Creek in 1856—the place also was called Andrews Landing (Mosier and Mosier, p. 41).

San Leandro Hills [ALAMEDA]: *range,* 3.5 miles east-northeast of downtown San Leandro (lat. 37°45'30" N, long. 122°06'15" W). Named on Hayward (1959) and Las Trampas Ridge (1959) 7.5' quadrangles. The range also had the name "Oakland Hills" (Mosier and Mosier, p. 77).

San Leandro Reservoir: see **Upper San Leandro Reservoir** [ALAMEDA-CONTRA COSTA].

San Leandro Valley [ALAMEDA]: *area,* lowlands along San Francisco Bay at and near the city of San Leandro (lat. 37°41'45" N, long. 122°09'30" W). Named on San Leandro (1959) 7.5' quadrangle.

San Lorenzo [ALAMEDA]:
(1) *land grant,* at the town of San Lorenzo. Named on Hayward (1959) and San Leandro (1959) 7.5' quadrangles. Francisco Soto received 1.5 leagues in 1842 and 1844; Barbara Soto and others claimed 6686 acres patented in 1877 (Cowan, p. 83).
(2) *land grant,* at the city of Castro Valley. Named on Hayward (1959) and Las Trampas Ridge (1959) 7.5' quadrangles. Guillermo Castro received the land in 1841 and 1843; he claimed 26,724 acres patented in 1865 (Cowan, p. 83).
(3) *town,* center 2.25 miles west-northwest of downtown Hayward (lat. 37°40'45" N, long. 122°07'15" W). Named on Hayward (1959) and San Leandro (1959) 7.5' quadrangles. American squatters came to San Lorenzo (1) grant in 1851 and settled along San Lorenzo Creek at what they called Squattersville, now the town of San Lorenzo (Hanna, P.T., p. 279). Postal authorities established San Lorenzo post office in 1854 (Frickstad, p. 3).

San Lorenzo: see **West San Lorenzo** [ALAMEDA].

San Lorenzo Creek [ALAMEDA]: *stream,* flows 13 miles to San Francisco Bay 4 miles

south of downtown San Leandro (lat. 37°40'15" N, long. 122°09'45" W). Named on Hayward (1959) and San Leandro (1959) 7.5' quadrangles. Called "R. de la Harina." on Font's (1777) map. Crespi called the stream Arroyo de San Salvador de Horta in 1772; the name "Arroyo de la Harina" for the feature was from a load of flour that got wet there—*harina* means "flour" in Spanish (Gudde, 1949, p. 308).

San Luis Gonzaga [SANTA CLARA]: *land grant,* mainly in Merced County, but extends over the crest of Diablo Range into Santa Clara County near Pacheco Pass. Named on Pacheco Pass (1955) and Pacheco Peak (1955) 7.5' quadrangles. Jose Ramon Estrada received the land in 1834 and Francisco Rivera received it in 1843; Francisco Perez Pacheco claimed 48, 821 acres patented in 1871 (Cowan, p. 83-84). According to Perez (p. 93), Juan Pacheco and Jose Mijira were the grantees in 1843.

San Martin [SANTA CLARA]: *town,* 5.5 miles north-northwest of Gilroy (lat. 37°05'05" N, long. 121°36'35" W). Named on Gilroy (1955) 7.5' quadrangle. According to Butler (p. 170), Martin Murphy built a chapel 2 miles east of the present town and named it San Martin for his patron saint; the name later was applied to the town that grew around a place called Mills Switch Station that was located along the railroad at present San Martin. Postal authorities established San Martin post office in 1894, discontinued it in 1900, and reestablished it in 1902 (Frickstad, p. 175).

San Martin Creek: see **Little Llagas Creek** [SANTA CLARA].

San Mateo [SAN MATEO]:
(1) *land grant,* at and west of the city of San Mateo. Named on Montara Mountain (1956) and San Mateo (1956) 7.5' quadrangles. Cayetano Arenas received 2 leagues in 1846; executors of W.D.M. Howard's estate claimed 6439 acres patented in 1857 (Cowan, p. 84-85).
(2) *city,* 7 miles northwest of downtown Redwood City (city hall near lat. 37°34' N, long. 122°19'25" W). Named on San Mateo (1956) 7.5' quadrangle. Nicholas de Peyster built a hostelry at the place in the early 1850's and called it San Mateo House, or Half Way House for its location halfway from San Francisco to San Jose (Stanger, 1963, p. 65). C.B. Polhemus laid out the modern city in 1863 (Gudde, 1949, p. 310). Postal authorities established San Mateo post office in 1857, discontinued it in 1858, and reestablished it in 1861 (Frickstad, p. 169). The city incorporated in 1894.

San Mateo Beach: see **Coyote Point** [SAN MATEO].

San Mateo Creek [SAN MATEO]: *stream,* flows 12 miles to San Francisco Bay 1.25 miles east-northeast of downtown San Mateo (lat. 37°34'05" N, long. 122°18'55" W).

Named on Montara Mountain (1956) and San Mateo (1956) 7.5' quadrangles. Called R. de Sn. Matheo on Font's (1777) map. Anza and Font used the name "Arroyo de San Matheo" in 1776 (Gudde, 1949, p. 310), but United States Board on Geographic Names (1961b, p. 15) rejected the name "San Matheo Creek" for the stream.

San Mateo House: see **San Mateo** [SAN MATEO] (2).

San Mateo Park [SAN MATEO]: *district,* 1 mile west of downtown San Mateo (lat. 37°34'05" N, long. 122°20'30" W). Named on San Mateo (1956) 7.5' quadrangle.

San Mateo Point: see **Coyote Point** [SAN MATEO].

San Mateo Slough: see **O'Neill Slough** [SAN MATEO]; **Seal Slough** [SAN MATEO].

San Matheo Creek: see **San Mateo Creek** [SAN MATEO].

San Miguel [SAN FRANCISCO]: *land grant,* near Twin Peaks and Mount Davidson. Named on San Francisco North (1956) and San Francisco South (1956) 7.5' quadrangles. Jose de Jesus Noe received 1 league in 1845 and claimed 4443 acres patented in 1857 (Cowan, p. 85).

San Miguel: see **Oceanview** [SAN FRANCISCO].

San Miguel Hills [SAN FRANCISCO]: *range,* at and east of Mount Davidson (lat. 37°44'25" N, long. 122°26'30" W); the range is on San Miguel grant. Named on San Francisco South (1956) 7.5' quadrangle.

San Pablo [CONTRA COSTA]:
(1) *land grant,* extends from El Cerrito nearly to Pinole. Named on Mare Island (1959), Richmond (1959), and San Quentin (1959) 7.5' quadrangles. Francisco Maria Castro received the land in 1823 and 1834; Joaquin Isidro Castro claimed 17,939 acres patented in 1873 (Cowan, p. 86; Cowan listed the grant under the designation "San Pablo, (or) Cochiyunes"). Perez (p. 94) listed Joaquin Y. Castro as both the grantee in 1835, and as the patentee in 1873.
(2) *town,* 1.5 miles north-northwest of Richmond civic center (lat. 37°57'30" N, long. 122°20'55" W). Named on Richmond (1959) 7.5' quadrangle. Postal authorities established San Pablo post office in 1854 (Frickstad, p. 23), and the town incorporated in 1948.

San Pablo Bay [CONTRA COSTA-MARIN-SOLANO]: *bay,* between San Francisco Bay and Carquinez Strait in Contra Costa County, Marin County, Solano County, and Sonoma County. Named on Cuttings Wharf (1949), Mare Island (1959), Petaluma Point (1959), Richmond (1959), San Quentin (1959), and Sears Point (1951) 7.5' quadrangles. Called Bahia de San Pablo on Beechey's (1827-1828) map, and called Pablo Bay on Wilkes' (1849) map. Canizares named the feature Bahia Redondo in 1775—*bahia redondo* means

"round bay" in Spanish (Hanna, W.L., p. 44). Gudde (1969, p. 291) gave the names "Bahia Redonda" and "Bahia de Sonoma" as early designations of the feature.

San Pablo Creek [CONTRA COSTA]: *stream,* flows 17 miles to San Pablo Bay 2.5 miles east-northeast of Point San Pablo (lat. 37°58'35" N, long. 122°22'55" W). Named on Briones Valley (1959), Oakland East (1959), Richmond (1959), and San Quentin (1959) 7.5' quadrangles. Concord (1915) 15' quadrangle shows West Branch, which is 3 miles long, joining the main stream from the southwest at Bryant (present Orinda).

San Pablo Point: see **Point San Pablo** [CONTRA COSTA].

San Pablo Reservoir [CONTRA COSTA]: *lake,* 4 miles long, behind a dam on San Pablo Creek 4.5 miles east of Richmond civic center (lat. 37°56'35" N, long. 122°15'40" W). Named on Briones Valley (1959) and Richmond (1959) 7.5' quadrangles.

San Pablo Ridge [CONTRA COSTA]: *ridge,* northwest-trending, 8 miles long, center 4 miles east of Richmond civic center (lat. 37°56' N, long. 122°16' W). Named on Briones Valley (1959) and Richmond (1959) 7.5' quadrangles.

San Pablo Station [CONTRA COSTA]: *locality,* 1.25 miles north-northwest of present Richmond civic center along Southern Pacific Railroad (lat. 37°57'30" N, long. 122°21'35" W); the place is west of the town of San Pablo. Named on San Francisco (1899) 15' quadrangle.

San Pablo Strait [CONTRA COSTA-MARIN]: *water feature,* between San Francisco Bay and San Pablo Bay on Contra Costa-Marin county line (lat. 37°58'30" N, long. 122°26'15" W); the feature is northwest of Point San Pablo. Named on San Quentin (1959) 7.5' quadrangle. Called Straits of San Pablo on Ringgold's (1850a) map.

San Pedro [SAN MATEO]: *land grant,* near the coast at Pacifica. Named on Montara Mountain (1956) and San Francisco South (1956) 7.5' quadrangles. Francisco Sanchez received 2 leagues in 1839 and claimed 8926 acres patented in 1870 (Cowan, p. 87).

San Pedro Creek [SAN MATEO]: *stream,* formed by the confluence of Middle Fork and South Fork, flows 2.5 miles through San Pedro Valley to the sea 3 miles north-northwest of Montara Knob (lat. 37°35'45" N, long. 122°30'15" W). Named on Montara Mountain (1956) 7.5' quadrangle. Called Arroyo de San Pedro on maps of about 1860 (Brown, p. 65). Middle Fork is 1.5 miles long and South Fork is 1.25 miles long. North Fork, which enters from the northeast less than 0.5 mile downstream from the junction of South Fork and Middle Fork, is 1.5 miles long. All three forks are named on Montara Mountain (1956) 7.5' quadrangle.

San Pedro Hill [MARIN]: *peak,* 0.25 mile west-northwest of Point San Pedro (lat. 37°59'15" N, long. 122°27' W). Named on San Quentin (1959) 7.5' quadrangle.

San Pedro Mountain [SAN MATEO]: *ridge,* west- to northwest-trending, 1.25 miles long, 1.5 miles northwest of Montara Knob (lat. 37°34'30" N, long. 122°30'30" W). Named on Montara Mountain (1956) 7.5' quadrangle. Brown (p. 65) listed the names "Pedro Mountain," "Sierra de San Pedro," and "Sierra de Santa Clara" as former designations of the feature.

San Pedro Point: see **Point San Pedro** [MARIN]; **Point San Pedro** [SAN MATEO].

San Pedro Rock [SAN MATEO]: *island,* 1050 feet long, 3.25 miles northwest of Montara Knob and 300 feet offshore at Point San Pedro (lat. 37°35'40" N, long. 122°31'20" W). Named on Montara Mountain (1956) 7.5' quadrangle.

San Pedro Santa Margarita y las Gallinas [MARIN]: *land grant,* extends west-northwest from San Pablo Bay nearly to the village of Nicasio. Named on Novato (1954), Petaluma Point (1959), San Geronimo (1954), San Quentin (1959), and San Rafael (1954) 7.5' quadrangles. Timothy Murphy received 5 leagues in 1844 and claimed 21,679 acres patented in 1866 (Cowan, p. 87).

San Pedro Terrace: see **Pedro Valley** [SAN MATEO].

San Pedro Valley [SAN MATEO]: *valley,* 2 miles north-northwest of Montara Knob (lat. 37°35'15" N, long. 122°29'40" W); San Pedro Creek drains the valley. Named on Montara Mountain (1956) 7.5' quadrangle.

San Quentin [MARIN]: *town,* west of Point San Quentin (lat. 37°56'30" N, long. 122°29' W); the town is on Punta de Quentin point. Named on San Quentin (1959) 7.5' quadrangle. Postal authorities established San Quentin post office in 1859, discontinued it the same year, and reestablished it in 1862 (Frickstad, p. 89). They established Tamal post office as a station of San Quentin post office in 1960·(Salley, p. 218).

San Quentin: see **Point San Quentin** [MARIN]; **Point San Quentin**, under **Potrero Point** [SAN FRANCISCO].

San Rafael [MARIN]: *city,* near the center of the east part of Marin County (lat. 37°58'25" N, long. 122°31'50" W). Named on Petaluma Point (1959), San Quentin (1959), and San Rafael (1954) 7.5' quadrangles. Postal authorities established San Rafael post office in 1851, discontinued it in 1853, and reestablished it in 1854 (Frickstad, p. 89). The city incorporated in 1874. Franciscan missionaries founded San Rafael Arcangel mission at the place in 1817; Timothy Murphy, who assumed charge of the mission estate and Indians there in 1837, built the first house at the site of the city in 1839 (Hoover, Rensch, and Rensch, p.

176-177). Postal authorities established Terra Linda post office 3 miles north of San Rafael post office in 1961; the name is from a residential development (Salley, p. 220)—Mrs. Joseph Rose, who as a child had lived on a ranch at the place, suggested the name "Terra Linda" (Teather, p. 81).

San Rafael Bay [MARIN]: *embayment,* off of San Francisco Bay between Point San Pedro and Point San Quentin (lat. 37°58' N, long. 122°28'30" W). Named on San Quentin (1959) 7.5' quadrangle. According to H.R. Wagner (p. 478), this probably is the feature that Ayala called Bahia de Nuestra Señora del Rosario la Marinera in 1775.

San Rafael Creek [MARIN]: *stream,* flows 3 miles through San Rafael to San Rafael Bay 2 miles east of downtown San Rafael (lat. 37°58'10" N, long. 122°29'35" W). Named on San Quentin (1959) and San Rafael (1954) 7.5' quadrangles. The stream was called Estero de San Rafael de Agnanni in Spanish days (Teather, p. 71).

San Rafael Hill [MARIN]: *ridge,* east-southeast-trending, 2.5 miles long, center 1 mile northwest of downtown San Rafael (lat. 37°59'15" N, long. 122°32'40" W). Named on San Rafael (1954) 7.5' quadrangle.

San Rafael Rock: see **Murphy Rock** [MARIN].

San Ramon [ALAMEDA-CONTRA COSTA]: *land grant,* southeast of the town of San Ramon on Alameda-Contra Costa county line. Named on Diablo (1953), Dublin (1961) Livermore (1961), and Tassajara (1953) 7.5' quadrangles. Jose Maria Amador received 4 leagues in 1835 and claimed 16,517 acres patented in 1865 (Cowan, p. 88).

San Ramon [CONTRA COSTA]:

(1) *land grant,* at and near Danville and Alamo. Named on Diablo (1953), Las Trampas Ridge (1959), and Walnut Creek (1959) 7.5' quadrangles. Rafael Soto de Pacheco received 2 leagues in 1833; H.W. Carpentier claimed 8917 acres patented in 1866 (Cowan, p. 88). According to Perez (p. 95), Bartolo Pacheco and Mariano Castro were the grantees in 1833, and Rafaela Pacheco and others were the patentees in 1866.

(2) *land grant,* in San Ramon Valley at and near the town of San Ramon. Named on Diablo (1953) and Dublin (1961) 7.5' quadrangles. Jose Maria Amador received 1 league in 1834; Leo Norris claimed 4451 acres patented in 1882 (Cowan, p. 88). According to Perez (p. 95), Jose M. Amador was the grantee in 1835.

(3) *town,* 3 miles south-southeast of Danville (lat. 37°46'45" N, long. 121°58'35" W); the town is in San Ramon Valley. Named on Diablo (1953) 7.5' quadrangle. Postal authorities established San Ramon post office in 1852 and discontinued it in 1859; they established San Ramoon post office in 1873 and changed the name to San Ramon in 1883 (Frickstad, p. 23). The place first was called Lynchville,

and later Limerick—the last name for the preponderance of Irish settlers there (Hanna, P.T., p. 286).

San Ramon Creek [CONTRA COSTA]: *stream,* flows 12 miles to join Las Trampas Creek and form Walnut Creek (1) near Walnut Creek (2) civic center (lat. 37°53'50" N, long. 122°03'30" W); the stream goes through San Ramon Valley. Named on Diablo (1953), Las Trampas Ridge (1959), and Walnut Creek (1959) 7.5' quadrangles. Called Arroyo del Ingreto on a diseño of Arroyo de las Nueces y Bolbones grant made in 1834; the Spanish word *ingreto* refers to a grafted tree—here the reference is to an oak tree with a willow ingrafted on it (Becker, 1969). Gudde (1949, p. 313) cited testimony that San Ramon Creek was named not for a saint but for a Spaniard who ran sheep near the creek in the early days.

San Ramon Creek: see **Pacheco Creek** [CONTRA COSTA]; **South San Ramon Creek** [ALAMEDA-CONTRA COSTA].

San Ramon Siding [CONTRA COSTA]: *locality,* 3.5 miles southeast of Danville along Southern Pacific Railroad (lat. 37°46'45" N, long. 121°57'55" W). Named on Diablo (1953) 7.5' quadrangle.

San Ramon Valley [ALAMEDA-CONTRA COSTA]: *valley,* along San Ramon Creek southeast of Alamo on Alameda-Contra Costa county line, mainly in Contra Costa County. Named on Diablo (1953), Dublin (1961), and Las Trampas Ridge (1959) 7.5' quadrangles. The south part of the feature is called Amador Valley on Diablo (1953) 7.5' quadrangle. Pleasanton (1906) 15' quadrangle shows present San Ramon Valley as part of Amador Valley.

San Ramon Village [ALAMEDA]: *district,* north-northeast of Dublin in San Ramon Valley (lat. 37°43'15" N, long. 121°55'45" W). Named on Dublin (1961, photorevised 1980) 7.5' quadrangle.

San Ramoon: see **San Ramon** [CONTRA COSTA] (3).

Santa Clara [SANTA CLARA]: *city,* 3 miles west-northwest of downtown San Jose (lat. 37°21' N, long. 121°56'30" W). Named on Cupertino (1961), Milpitas (1961), and San Jose West (1961) 7.5' quadrangles. Postal authorities established Santa Clara post office in 1851 (Frickstad, p. 175), and the city incorporated in 1857. The name is from Santa Clara de Asis mission, founded in 1777 within the limits of the modern city about 2 miles from the present site of the mission; the original mission was by a stream called Mission Creek (Hoover, Rensch, and Rensch, p. 426-427). According to Rambo (1964, p. 38), Mission Creek headed at a large spring in the present Hanchett Park neighborhood, fed Cook's Pond, and joined Guadalupe River near the pear orchard of the original mission. Thompson and West's (1876) map shows

Cooks Pond on the north side of The Alameda near present Hilmar Street on land belonging to Jane B. Cook. Rambo (1973, p. 40) noted that Cooks Pond was both a lake and a resort park.

Santa Clara Shoal [CONTRA COSTA]: *shoal,* 5.25 miles north of the settlement of Bethel Island in San Joaquin River on Contra Costa-Sacramento county line (lat. 38°05'25" N, long. 121°38'45" W). Named on Jersey Island (1978) 7.5' quadrangle.

Santa Clara Valley [SANTA CLARA]: *valley,* extends for 60 miles southeast from San Francisco Bay between Santa Cruz Mountains and Diablo Range. Drainage from the north part of the valley is to San Francisco Bay, mainly by way of Coyote Creek; drainage from the south part is to the sea by way of Pajaro River. Named on San Jose (1962) and Santa Cruz (1956) 1°x 2° quadrangles. Parke (p. 7) noted that the "entire valley is known by the general name Santa Clara, whilst that portion enveloping the head of the bay retains the name of the *pueblo* or town, San José." Antisell (p. 32) mentioned "The Santa Clara, or, as it is sometimes called, the San José valley." Blake (1854, p. 438) wrote that the Valley of San Jose is properly the south end of the great valley occupied by San Francisco Bay. Gudde (1949, p. 190) stated that Llano de las Llagas was the Spanish name for Gilroy Valley, meaning presumably the south part of present Santa Clara Valley near Gilroy. Bolton (p. 271) mentioned that Font referred to Gilroy Valley in 1766 by the name "San Bernardino Valley."

Santa Coleta: see **Livermore Valley** [ALAMEDA].

Santa Cruz Mountains [SAN MATEO-SANTA CLARA]: *range,* between the sea and the lowlands along San Francisco Bay in San Mateo, Santa Clara, and Santa Cruz Counties. Named on San Francisco (1956), San Jose (1962), and Santa Cruz (1956) 1°x 2° quadrangles. Called Sierra de la Santa Cruz on Parke's (1854-1855) map. Blake (1856, p. 378) used the name "Santa Cruz Range."

Santa Cruz Range: see **Santa Cruz Mountains** [SAN MATEO].

Santa Fe: see **Point Richmond** [CONTRA COSTA] (2).

Santa Fe Channel [CONTRA COSTA]: *channel,* 1.5 miles southwest of Richmond civic center (lat. 37°55'15" N, long. 122°22'05" W). Named on Richmond (1959) 7.5' quadrangle. United States Board on Geographic Names (1943, p. 13) rejected the name "Ellis Slough" for the feature.

Santa Isabel: see **Mount Santa Isabel**, under **Mount Hamilton** [SANTA CLARA].

Santa Margarita Valley [MARIN]: *valley,* 6.5 miles south of downtown Novato (lat. 38°00'50" N, long. 122°33'30" W); the valley is on San Pedro Santa Margarita y las

Gallinas grant. Named on Novato (1954) 7.5' quadrangle.

Santa Rita [ALAMEDA]: *land grant,* north of Pleasanton in Amador Valley. Named on Dublin (1961) and Livermore (1961) 7.5' quadrangles. Dolores Pacheco received the land in 1839; Yountz, administrator, claimed 8994 acres patented in 1865 (Cowan, p. 94).

Santa Teresa [SANTA CLARA]: *land grant,* north of Santa Teresa Hills around Edenvale. Named on San Jose East (1961) and Santa Teresa Hills (1953) 7.5' quadrangles. Joaquin Bernal received 1 league in 1834; Agustin Bernal claimed 9647 acres patented in 1867 (Cowan, p. 96).

Santa Teresa Hills [SANTA CLARA]: *range,* west-northwest-trending, 7 miles long, 3 miles north of New Almaden (lat. 37°13' N, long. 121°49' W). Named on Santa Teresa Hills (1953) 7.5' quadrangle.

Santa Teresa Spring [SANTA CLARA]: *spring,* 3.5 miles north-northeast of New Almaden (lat. 37°13'35" N, long. 121°47'35" W); the spring is on Santa Teresa grant. Named on Santa Teresa Hills (1953) 7.5' quadrangle.

Santa Venetia [MARIN]: *town,* 1.5 miles north of downtown San Rafael (lat. 37°59'55" N, long. 122°31'30" W). Named on Novato (1954) and San Rafael (1954) 7.5' quadrangles. Mabry McMahon coined the name in 1914 for a development that he intended to have a resemblance to Venice, Italy; the project failed, but the name endured (Teather, p. 71).

Santa Ysabel: see **Mount Santa Ysabel,** under **Mount Isabel** [SANTA CLARA].

Santa Ysabel Creek: see **Isabel Creek** [SANTA CLARA].

Santa Ysabel Valley: see **Isabel Valley** [SANTA CLARA].

San Tomas [SANTA CLARA]: *district,* 2 miles southwest of downtown Campbell (lat. 37°16'10" N, long. 121°58'35" W); the place is near San Tomas Aquinas Creek. Named on San Jose West (1961) 7.5' quadrangle.

San Tomas Aquinas Creek [SANTA CLARA]: *stream,* flows 15 miles to Saratoga Creek nearly 3 miles south of Alviso (lat. 37°23'20" N, long. 121°58'05" W). Named on Castle Rock Ridge (1955), Los Gatos (1953), Milpitas (1961), and San Jose West (1961) 7.5' quadrangles. Called Arroyo San Tomas Aquino and Arroyo de Santa Toma Aquino on Tompson and West's (1876) map, and called Arroyo San Tomas Aquinas on Hare's (1872) map.

San Vicente [SANTA CLARA]: *land grant,* mainly between Santa Teresa Hills and New Almaden. Named on Santa Teresa Hills (1953) 7.5' quadrangle. Jose de los Reyes Berreyesa received 1 league in 1842 and Maria Berreyesa claimed 4438 acres patented in 1868 (Cowan, p. 89; Perez, p. 95).

San Vicente Creek [SAN MATEO]: *stream,* flows nearly 4 miles to the sea 3 miles south-west of Montara Knob at Moss Beach (lat. 37° 31'25" N, long. 122°31' W). Named on Montara Mountain (1956) 7.5' quadrangle. According to Brown (p. 85), the stream also is called Arroyo de San Vicente and Vicente Creek, and the canyon of the stream is called Torello Canyon, from Torello ranch.

San Ysidro [SANTA CLARA]: *land grant,* near Gilroy. Named on Chittenden (1955), Gilroy (1955), Gilroy Hot Springs (1955), and San Felipe (1955) 7.5' quadrangles. According to Arbuckle (p. 19, 34), Ygnacio Ortega received the land about 1809 or 1810 and divided it into thirds for this three children: Jose Quintin claimed 4439 acres patented in 1868; Clara, wife of John Gilroy, claimed 4461 acres patented in 1867; Ysabel got 4167 acres that Bernard Murphy bought in 1849 and gave the name "La Polka"—Martin J.C. Murphy claimed this part of the grant, patented in 1860. Cowan (p. 79) used the form "San Isidro" for the name of the grant.

San Ysidro: see **Gilroy** [SANTA CLARA]; **Old Gilroy** [SANTA CLARA].

San Ysidro Creek [SANTA CLARA]: *stream,* flows 5 miles to a point in lowlands 1.25 miles east-southeast of Old Gilroy (lat. 36° 59'40" N, long. 121°30'15" W). Named on Chittenden (1955, photorevised 1968 and 1973) 7.5' quadrangle. The stream flows through San Ysidro grant, and is named for the grant (United States Board on Geographic Names, 1973a, p. 3).

Saranap [CONTRA COSTA]: *locality,* 1.5 miles south-southwest of present Walnut Creek civic center along Oakland Antioch and Eastern Railroad (lat. 37°53'05" N, long. 122°04'35" W). Named on Concord (1915) 15' quadrangle. The place first was called Dewing Park, but in 1913 the new name was coined from the name of Sara Naphthaly, mother of Samuel Naphthaly, vice-president of the railroad (Gudde, 1949, p. 320).

Saratoga [SANTA CLARA]: *city,* 9 miles southwest of downtown San Jose (lat. 37°15'30" N, long. 122°01'55" W). Named on Cupertino (1961) and San Jose West (1961) 7.5' quadrangles. After William Campbell and his sons built a sawmill in the canyon of present Saratoga Creek in 1848, the little settlement that developed at the mouth of the canyon was identified on an early map by the name "Campbell's Gap" (Cunningham, p. 27). After lumberman Martin McCarty built a toll road up the canyon in 1850 and 1851, the settlement was called Toll Gate, and later the post office there was called McCartysville; in 1854 William Haun and John Whisman built a gristmill, called Redwood Mills, at the settlement (Hoover, Rensch, and Rensch, p. 457-458). Charles Maclay purchased the mill and renamed it Bank Mills in 1863; Maclay also planned a settlement, known as Maclaytown, around the mill (Cunningham,

p. 51, 88). The place finally was named Saratoga because water at nearby Congress Springs was likened to water at Saratoga, New York (Butler, p. 95-96). Postal authorities established McCartysville post office in 1855, changed the name to Bank Mills in 1863, and changed it to Saratoga in 1865 (Frickstad, p. 173, 174). Saratoga incorporated in 1956. Peninsular Railway Company's (1912) map shows a station called Glen Una located nearly one-third of the way along the rail line from Saratoga to Los Gatos.

Saratoga: see **Camp Saratoga** [SANTA CLARA].

Saratoga Creek [SANTA CLARA]: *stream,* flows 18 miles to Alviso Slough at Alviso (lat. 37°25'20" N, long. 121°58'45" W); the stream leaves highlands at Saratoga. Named on Castle Rock Ridge (1955), Cupertino (1961), Milpitas (1961), and San Jose West (1961) 7.5' quadrangles. Thompson and West's (1876) map has the label "San Jon or Campbell Cr." on the lower part of present Saratoga Creek near Alviso, has the name "Campbells Creek" on the stream nearer the highlands, and has the name "Arroyo Quito" on the stream in the highlands. The feature is called Campbell Creek on Palo Alto (1899) 15' quadrangle. Until the early 1850's the stream was called Campbell Creek for William Campbell and his sons, who began construction of a sawmill along the creek in 1847 about 3 miles west of present Saratoga (Hoover, Rensch, and Rensch, p. 457). For many years the neighborhood around the sawmill was called Campbell's Redwoods (Cunningham, p. 27). Crawford (1896, p. 519) referred to Pacific Congress Springs as being in Campbell Creek Cañon. United States Board on Geographic Names (1933, p. 189) approved the name "Campbell Creek" for the stream, and rejected the names "Quito Creek" and "Arroyo Quito," but later the Board (1954, p. 3-4) approved the name "Saratoga Creek" for the stream, and rejected the names "Big Moody Creek" and "Campbell Creek" for it.

Saratoga Gap [SANTA CLARA]: *pass,* 5 miles west of Saratoga on Santa Clara-Santa Cruz county line (lat. 37°15'30" N, long. 122° 07'10" W; near S line sec. 6, T 8 S, R 2 W). Named on Cupertino (1961) 7.5' quadrangle.

Sargent [SANTA CLARA]: *locality,* 6 miles south of Gilroy along Southern Pacific Railroad (lat. 36°55'10" N, long. 121°32'50" W). Named on Chittenden (1955) 7.5' quadrangle. J.P. Sargent owned a ranch at the place (Rambo, 1964, p. 42); a popular picnic resort called Sargent's was on the bank of Pajaro River there in 1895 (Pierce, p. 151-152). Postal authorities established La Brea post office along Tar Creek in 1874, changed the name to Sargent in 1876, discontinued it for a time in 1878, and discontinued it finally in 1933 (Salley, p. 114, 198).

Sargent Creek [SANTA CLARA]: *stream,* flows nearly 3 miles to Pajaro River 7.5 miles south of Gilroy (lat. 36°53'50" N, long. 121° 34'10" W); the stream is in Sargent Hills. Named on Chittenden (1955, photorevised 1968 and 1973) 7.5' quadrangle.

Sargent Hills [SANTA CLARA]: *range,* 6 miles south of Gilroy (lat. 36°55'15" N, long. 121°34'25" W); the range is west of Sargent. Named on Chittenden (1955) 7.5' quadrangle.

Sargent Ranch: see **Juristac** [SANTA CLARA].

Saucelito: see **Sausalito** [MARIN] (1) and (2).

Sausal Creek [ALAMEDA]: *stream,* formed by the confluence of Shephard Creek and Palo Seco Creek, flows 3 miles to end in lowlands 3 miles east-southeast of downtown Oakland (lat. 37°47'15" N, long. 122°13'35" W). Named on Oakland East (1959) 7.5' quadrangle. Crespi called the stream Arroyo del Bosque in 1772—*bosque* means "woods" in Spanish; the stream also was known as Fruitvale Creek from the place called Fruitvale (Mosier and Mosier, p. 79).

Sausal Creek [SAN MATEO]: *stream,* flows 2.5 miles through Portola Valley (1) to marsh 6 miles south of downtown Redwood City near Searsville Lake (lat. 37°23'50" N, long. 122°14'30" W). Named on Mindego Hill (1961) and Palo Alto (1961) 7.5' quadrangles. Called Corte de Madera Creek on Palo Alto (1899) 15' quadrangle, but United States Board on Geographic Names (1968a, p. 7) rejected this designation for the feature. The stream also had the names "Arroyo Sausal," "Arroyo del Sanjon," and "Sanjon Creek" (Brown, p. 85).

Sausal Creek: see **Bull Run Creek** [SAN MATEO]; **Neils Gulch** [SAN MATEO].

Sausalito [MARIN]:

(1) *land grant,* covers the south end of Marin Peninsula, including the town of Sausalito. Named on Point Bonita (1954) and San Francisco North (1950) 7.5' quadrangles. Called Saucelito on Bolinas (1954), San Francisco North (1956), and San Rafael (1954) 7.5' quadrangles. Jose Antonio Galindo received 3 leagues in 1835; William A. Richardson claimed 19,572 acres patented in 1879 (Cowan, p. 96-97; Cowan gave the forms "Sauzalito" and "Saucelito" as alternates). According to Perez (p. 98), Richardson was the grantee in 1838. The name is from *sausal,* the Spanish term for willows that grew around springs on the grant (Hoover, Rensch, and Rensch, p. 179).

(2) *town,* 8 miles south-southeast of downtown San Rafael (lat. 37° 51'30" N, long. 122°29' W); the town is on Sausalito grant. Named on Point Bonita (1954) and San Francisco North (1956) 7.5' quadrangles. United States Board on Geographic Names (1933, p. 674) rejected the form "Saucelito" for the name. Postal authorities established Saucelito post

office in 1870 and changed the name to Sausalito in 1887 (Salley, p. 198). The town incorporated in 1893. The name took a number of forms in the 1840's and 1850's: San Saulito (Rogers and Johnston's (1857) map); San Salita (Agassiz, p. 380); San Solito (Kelly, p. 162); Sancolito (Tyson, J.L., p. 62); Sancilito (Delavan, p. 34); Sousolito (Taylor, volume I, p. 52); Sousalita (Bidwell, p. 39); Sousilito (*The California Star*, January 30, 1847); Sausilito (Dana, p. 261); Sauz Saulita (White, p. 61).

Sausalito Cove: see **Sausalito Point** [MARIN].

Sausalito Point [MARIN]: *promontory,* southwest of the mouth of Richardson Bay at the town of Sausalito (lat. 37°51'25" N, long. 122°28'40" W). Named on San Francisco North (1956) 7.5' quadrangle. Ringgold's (1850a) map has the name "Saucelito Bay" for the embayment south of present Sausalito Point—this embayment appears to be the Sausalito Cove that H.R. Wagner (p. 444) identified as the feature called Ensenada de Consolacion in Spanish times.

Sauselito Bay: see **Sausalito Point** [MARIN].

Sauzalito: see **Sausalito** [MARIN] (1).

Savage Creek: see **Mills Creek** [SAN MATEO] (2).

Sawtooth Canyon [SANTA CLARA]: *canyon,* nearly 1 mile long, drained by a stream that joins San Antonio Creek 4 miles north-northeast of Isabel Valley (lat. 37°22'05" N, long. 121°31'05" W; sec. 34, T 6 S, R 4 E). Named on Isabel Valley (1955) 7.5' quadrangle.

Sawyer Ridge [SAN MATEO]: *ridge,* generally southeast-trending, 5.5 miles long, center 4 miles east of Montara Knob (lat. 37°33'30" N, long. 122°24'35" W). Named on Montara Mountain (1956) 7.5' quadrangle. Leander Sawyer trained performing horses in the 1860's and 1870's at a camp east of the ridge and near the north end of Lower Crystal Springs Lake; another name for the feature was Tunnel Ridge, for an aqueduct tunnel dug about 1860 (Brown, p. 85-86).

Sawyers Crossing [SANTA CLARA]: *locality,* 4 miles southeast of Gilroy along Southern Pacific Railroad (lat. 36°57'30" N, long. 121°31'15" W). Named on San Juan Bautista (1917) 15' quadrangle.

Scarpa Hill: see **Scarper Peak** [SAN MATEO].

Scarper Peak [SAN MATEO]: *peak,* 3.5 miles east-southeast of Montara Knob on Montara Mountain (lat. 37°31'45" N, long. 122° 25'35" W; sec. 5, T 5 S, R 5 W). Altitude 1944 feet. Named on Montara Mountain (1956) 7.5' quadrangle. Brown (p. 86) listed the peak under the name "Scarpa Hill," and noted that Giorgio Scarpa settled in the neighborhood in 1859; the feature also was called Spanish Peak in the early 1860's.

Schilling Lake [SAN MATEO]: *intermittent lake,* 375 feet long, 3 miles east-southeast of Skeggs Point (lat. 37°23'25" N, long. 122° 15'20" W). Named on Woodside (1961) 7.5' quadrangle. Brown (p. 86) called the feature Schilling's Lake, and noted that August Schilling had it built in the 1930's.

Schmidt [CONTRA COSTA]: *locality,* 2 miles east-southeast of present Richmond civic center along Atchison, Topeka and Santa Fe Railroad (lat. 37°55'10" N, long. 122°18'50" W). Named on San Francisco (1915) 15' quadrangle.

Schmidtville: see **Stege** [CONTRA COSTA].

Schoolhouse Creek [SAN MATEO]: *stream,* flows 0.5 mile to Lobitos Creek nearly 6 miles south-southeast of downtown Half Moon Bay at Lobitos (lat. 37°23' N, long. 122°24' W). Named on Half Moon Bay (1961) 7.5' quadrangle, which shows Tunitas Sch. near the head of the stream.

Schoolhouse Ridge [SANTA CLARA]: *ridge,* east-northeast-trending, 1 mile long, 3.5 miles southwest of Mount Sizer (lat. 37°10'30" N, long. 121°33'15" W). Named on Mount Sizer (1955) 7.5' quadrangle.

Schoolhouse Station: see **Colma** [SAN MATEO].

Schooner Bay [MARIN]: *bay,* opens into Drakes Estero 6.5 miles northeast of the lighthouse at Point Reyes (lat. 38°03'45" N, long. 122°56'15" W). Named on Drakes Bay (1953) 7.5' quadrangle, which shows the site of a schooner landing on the west shore of the bay.

Schroeder Gulch: see **Arroyo Ojo de Agua** [SAN MATEO].

Schwerin Valley: see **Visitacion Valley** [SAN FRANCISCO-SAN MATEO].

Scott: see **Fort Scott** [SAN FRANCISCO]; **Fort Winfield Scott**, under **Fort Point** [SAN FRANCISCO].

Scott Creek [ALAMEDA-SANTA CLARA]: *stream,* forms part of Alameda-Santa Clara county line, flows 2.5 miles to lowlands 7 miles southeast of the Fremont civic center (lat. 37°28' N, long. 121°53'50" W). Named on Calaveras Reservoir (1961) and Milpitas (1961) 7.5' quadrangles. Thompson and West's (1876) map has the label "Lone Tree Creek or Scotts Ravine" on the feature. The name "Scott" commemorates Joseph Scott, who settled by the creek in 1852; the name "Lone Tree Creek" was for a single sycamore tree that stood near the stream—Font called the feature Arroyo de la Encarnation in 1776 (Mosier and Mosier, p. 79).

Scotts Corner [ALAMEDA]: *locality,* 1 mile east-southeast of Sunol (lat. 37°35'20" N, long. 121°52'10" W). Named on La Costa Valley (1960) 7.5' quadrangle. Thomas Scott, Sr., opened a store at the place in the 1850's (Mosier and Mosier, p. 79). Thompson and West's (1878) map shows Scotts store situated east of Sunol beyond present Scotts Corner.

Scotts Ravine: see **Scott Creek** [ALAMEDA-SANTA CLARA].

Scotts Spur: see **Meridian** [SANTA CLARA].

Scow Canyon [CONTRA COSTA]: *canyon,* 1 mile long, 5.5 miles northwest of Orinda (lat. 37°56'35" N, long. 122°14'30" W). Named on Briones Valley (1959) 7.5' quadrangle. Water of San Pablo Reservoir floods a large part of the canyon.

Seal Bluff Landing [CONTRA COSTA]: *locality,* 6 miles east-northeast of Martinez along Suisun Bay (lat. 38°03'15" N, long. 122°02'20" W); the place is east of Seal Islands. Named on Karquines (1898) 15' quadrangle.

Seal Cove [SAN MATEO]: *settlement,* 3 miles south-southwest of Montara Knob near the coast (lat. 37°31'10" N, long. 122°13'10" W). Named on Montara Mountain (1956) 7.5' quadrangle.

Seal Creek [CONTRA COSTA]: *water feature,* enters Hastings Slough 5 miles east-northeast of Martinez (lat. 38°02'10" N, long. 122°02'55" W); the feature is south of Seal Islands. Named on Vine Hill (1959) 7.5' quadrangle. On Karquines (1898) 15' quadrangle, the name extends up present Mount Diablo Creek.

Seal Creek: see **Bay Slough** [SAN MATEO]; **Seal Slough** [SAN MATEO].

Sea Lion Rock: see **Seal Rock** [SAN FRANCISCO]; **Seal Rock** [SAN MATEO].

Seal Islands [CONTRA COSTA]: *islands,* two, largest 2100 feet long, 5.5 miles east-northeast of Martinez in Suisun Bay (lat. 38°03'20" N, long. 122°02'45" W). Named on Vine Hill (1959) 7.5' quadrangle, which shows the islands as marsh.

Seal Isle: see **Benicia Point** [SOLANO].

Seal Rock [SAN FRANCISCO]: *island,* 600 feet long, 600 feet south of South Farallon (lat. 37°41'35" N, long. 123°00'10" W). Named on Farallon Islands (1988) 7.5' quadrangle. G.D. Hanna (p. 303) gave the designation "Sea Lion or Saddle Rock" for the feature.

Seal Rock [SAN MATEO]: *island,* 600 feet long, 5 miles south of downtown Half Moon Bay and 450 feet offshore (lat. 37°23'30" N, long. 122°25'25" W). Named on Half Moon Bay (1961) 7.5' quadrangle. The feature also has been called Sea Lion Rock (Brown, p. 87).

Seal Rock: see **Sail Rock** [SAN MATEO].

Seal Rocks [SAN FRANCISCO]: *rocks,* 0.25 mile south-southwest of Point Lobos, and 500 feet offshore (lat. 37°46'40" N, long. 122°30'55" W). Named on San Francisco North (1956) 7.5' quadrangle.

Seal Slough [SAN MATEO]: *water feature,* between Brewer Island and the mainland, joins San Francisco Bay nearly 2 miles east of downtown San Mateo (lat. 37°34'15" N, long. 122°17'35" W). Named on San Mateo (1956) 7.5' quadrangle. Called Seal Creek on San Mateo (1947) 7.5' quadrangle, but United States Board on Geographic Names (1961b, p. 16) rejected the names "Seal Creek," "Angelo Slough," and "San Mateo Slough" for the feature.

Searsville: see **Searsville Lake** [SAN MATEO].

Searsville Lake [SAN MATEO]: *lake,* 0.5 mile long, behind a dam on San Francisquito Creek 5.25 miles south of downtown Redwood City (lat. 37°24'25" N, long. 122°14'10" W). Named on Palo Alto (1961) 7.5' quadrangle. John H. Sears built a house at the site in 1854, and later the building was used as a hotel— the village of Searsville grew around the hotel (Hoover, Rensch, and Rensch, p. 400). Postal authorities established Searsville post office in 1858 and discontinued it in 1893 (Frickstad, p. 169). Water of the lake encroached on the site of the village of Searsville in 1890 (Brown, p. 87).

Second Mallard Branch [SOLANO]: *water feature,* joins Cutoff Slough nearly 5 miles southsoutheast of Fairfield (lat. 38°11' N, long. 122°00'45" W). Named on Fairfield South (1949) 7.5' quadrangle.

Seeboy Ridge [SANTA CLARA]: *ridge,* northto northwest-trending, 2.5 miles long, 5 miles northwest of Isabel Valley (lat. 37°22'30" N, long. 121°35'40" W). Named on Eylar Mountain (1955) and Isabel Valley (1955) 7.5' quadrangles.

Segunda Creek: see **Dry Creek** [ALAMEDA] (1).

Selby [CONTRA COSTA]: *locality,* 6.5 miles west-northwest of Martinez along Southern Pacific Railroad (lat. 38°03'25" N, long. 122°14'35" W). Named on Benicia (1959) 7.5' quadrangle. Postal authorities established Selby post office in 1886 and discontinued it in 1967; the name is for Prentiss Selby, first postmaster (Salley, p. 201). Ringgold's (1850a) map has the name "Pyramid Pt." near present Selby.

Semple Point [SOLANO]: *promontory,* 3 miles south-southeast of downtown Vallejo along Carquinez Strait (lat. 38°03'55" N, long. 122°13'35" W). Named on Benicia (1959) 7.5' quadrangle. Called Pt. Semple on Ringgold's (1850a) map.

Seneca Reservoir [ALAMEDA]: *lake,* 550 feet long, 7 miles east-southeast of downtown Oakland (lat. 37°45'20" N, long. 122°09'20" W). Named on Oakland East (1959) 7.5' quadrangle. The reservoir was built in 1950 and named for Seneca Street, where it is located (Mosier and Mosier, p. 80).

Serpentine Point [MARIN]: *peak,* 5 miles westsouthwest of downtown San Rafael (lat. 37°56'15" N, long. 122°36'45" W). Named on San Rafael (1954) 7.5' quadrangle.

Serpents Slough [CONTRA COSTA]: *water feature,* 3.5 miles north of the settlement of Bethel Island on Webb Tract (lat. 38°03'50" N, long. 121°38'15" W). Named on Jersey Island (1952) 7.5' quadrangle. Called Serpent Slough on Jersey (1910) 7.5' quadrangle.

Serrito de San Antonio: see **Albany Hill** [ALAMEDA].

Seven Mile Beach: see **Mussel Rock** [SAN MATEO] (1).

Seven Mile House: see **Edenvale** [SANTA CLARA].

Seven Sisters: see **Black Mountain** [MARIN].

Shadow Spring [SANTA CLARA]: *spring*, 2 miles southwest of Pacheco Pass (lat. 37°02'25" N, long. 121°13'40" W). Named on Pacheco Pass (1955) 7.5' quadrangle.

Shaeirn Lake [SANTA CLARA]: *lake*, 600 feet long, 8.5 miles east of Gilroy Hot Springs (lat. 37°05'30" N, long. 121°19'10" W; sec. 4, T 10 S, R 6 E). Named on Pacheco Peak (1955) 7.5' quadrangle, which also shows Shaeirn ranch situated 1 mile west of the lake. Called Sharon Lake on Gilroy Hot Springs (1921) 15' quadrangle.

Shafer Creek [ALAMEDA]: *stream*, flows 1.25 miles to Trout Creek 5.5 miles south-southwest of Mendenhall Springs (lat. 37°30'45" N, long. 121°40'50" W; near W line sec. 8, T 5 S, R 3 E); the stream heads at Shafer Flat. Named on Mendenhall Springs (1956) 7.5' quadrangle.

Shafer Flat [ALAMEDA]: *area*, 5 miles south-southwest of Mendenhall Springs (lat. 37°31'40" N, long. 121°41'45" W; sec. 6, T 5 S, R 3 E). Named on Mendenhall Springs (1956) 7.5' quadrangle. The misspelled name commemorates Louis Schaffer, landowner at the site (Mosier and Mosier, p. 80-81).

Shafter [MARIN]: *locality*, 10.5 miles southwest of downtown Novato (lat. 38°00'20" N, long. 122°42'50" W). Named on San Geronimo (1954) 7.5' quadrangle. Petaluma (1914) 15' quadrangle shows the place along Northwestern Pacific Railroad.

Shag Rock [SAN FRANCISCO]: *rock*, in San Francisco Bay 5 miles east-southeast of Mount Davidson, and 2000 feet south of Hunters Point.(lat. 37°43' N, long. 122°22' W). Named on San Mateo (1915) 15' quadrangle.

Shag Rock: see **Shag Rocks** [SAN FRANCISCO].

Shag Rocks [SAN FRANCISCO]: *rocks*, 2.25 miles northwest of North Point in San Francisco Bay (lat. 37°50'05" N, long. 122°26'20" W). Named on San Francisco North (1956) 7.5' quadrangle. Called Shag Rock on San Francisco (1899, reprinted 1913) 15' quadrangle.

Shag Slough [SOLANO]: *water feature*, partly in Yolo County, joins Cache Slough 7 miles north of Rio Vista (lat. 38°15'35" N, long. 121°41'25" W). Named on Liberty Island (1978) 7.5' quadrangle. Cache Slough (1916) 7.5' quadrangle shows the feature before it was modified.

Shallow Beach [MARIN]: *beach*, 5.5 miles northwest of Point Reyes Station on the southwest side of Tomales Bay (lat. 38°07'25" N, long. 122°52'50" W). Named on Drakes Bay (1953) 7.5' quadrangle.

Shannon [SANTA CLARA]: *locality*, 1 mile west-northwest of downtown Los Gatos (lat. 37°13'50" N, long. 121°58' W). Named on Los Gatos (1919) 15' quadrangle.

Shanti Ashrama [SANTA CLARA]: *locality*, 3.5 miles west-southwest of Mount Stakes in Upper San Antonio Valley (lat. 37°18'30" N, long. 121°28'10" W; sec. 19, T 7 S, R 5 E). Named on Mount Stakes (1955) 7.5' quadrangle.

Sharon Lake: see **Shaeirn Lake** [SANTA CLARA].

Sharp Park [SAN MATEO]: *district*, 4.5 miles west-southwest of downtown South San Francisco near the coast (lat. 37°38'05" N, long. 122°29'20" W). Named on San Francisco South (1956) 7.5' quadrangle. Called Salada on San Mateo (1915) 15' quadrangle—the place is north of Laguna Salada. The community developed in 1905 with the name "Salada Beach" after nearby Laguna Salada (Gudde, 1949, p. 327). Salada Beach and Brighton Beach subdivision combined in 1935 to form the town of Sharp Park, named for land south of the place that the Sharp family donated to San Francisco for a park (Brown, p. 78-79). Residents of the town of Sharp Park voted in 1957 to join neighboring communities and form the new city of Pacifica. Postal authorities established Salada Beach post office in 1907, changed the name to Sharp Park in 1935, and discontinued it in 1959 (Salley, p. 191, 202).

Shaw Gulch [SAN MATEO]: *canyon*, 1 mile long, 6 miles west-southwest of La Honda (lat. 37°16'35" N, long. 122°21'55" W; sec. 35, T 7 S, R 5 W). Named on La Honda (1961) 7.5' quadrangle. The name commemorates the Shaw family, who had a ranch in the canyon after about 1870 (Brown, p. 88).

Sheep Island: see **Brooks Island** [CONTRA COSTA].

Sheep Ridge [SANTA CLARA]: *ridge*, northwest-trending, 2.5 miles long, 5.5 miles east of San Martin (lat. 37°06' N, long. 121°30'30" W). Named on Gilroy (1955) and Gilroy Hot Springs (1955) 7.5' quadrangles.

Sheep Slough [CONTRA COSTA]: *water feature*, 3.25 miles east of the settlement of Bouldin Island between Quimby Island and Holland Tract (lat. 38°01'15" N, long. 121°34'45" W). Named on Bouldin Island (1978) 7.5' quadrangle.

Sheldrake Slough [SOLANO]: *water feature*, joins Suisun Slough 3.5 miles south of Fairfield (lat. 38°11'50" N, long. 122°02'45" W). Named on Fairfield South (1949) 7.5' quadrangle.

Shell Beach [MARIN]: *beach*, 5 miles northwest of Point Reyes Station on the southwest side of Tomales Bay (lat. 38°07'05" N, long. 122°52'25" W). Named on Inverness (1954) 7.5' quadrangle.

Shell Mound [ALAMEDA]: *locality*, 2.5 miles north-northwest of downtown Oakland along Southern Pacific Railroad in Emeryville (lat. 37°50'05" N, long. 122°17'30" W). Named on San Francisco (1899) 15' quadrangle.

Nelson's (1909) map shows the place situated near the site of a well-known Indian shell mound.

Shell Ridge [CONTRA COSTA]: *ridge,* west-northwest-trending, 3.5 miles long, center 3 miles east of Walnut Creek civic center (lat. 37°53'35" N, long. 122°00'30" W). Named on Clayton (1953) and Walnut Creek (1959) 7.5' quadrangles.

Shelter Cove [SAN MATEO]: *settlement,* 3 miles north-northwest of Montara Knob near the coast (lat. 37°35'50" N, long. 122°23'15" W). Named on Montara Mountain (1956) 7.5' quadrangle. The settlement began as a resort in the late 1930's; the embayment at the place was called Pirate's Cove for rum-running activity there during Prohibition times (Brown, p. 88). San Mateo (1942) 15' quadrangle has the name "Shelter Cove" for the embayment.

Shepard Creek: see **Shephard Creek** [ALAMEDA].

Shephard Creek [ALAMEDA]: *stream,* flows 1.5 miles to join Palo Seco Creek and form Sausal Creek 3.5 miles east-northeast of downtown Oakland (lat. 37°49'10" N, long. 122°12'25" W). Named on Oakland East (1959) 7.5' quadrangle. Called Shepard Creek on Concord (1897) 15' quadrangle. The misspelled name is for William Joseph Shepherd, who owned land along the stream; the canyon of the creek is called Shepherd Canyon (Mosier and Mosier, p. 81).

Shepherd Canyon: see **Shephard Creek** [ALAMEDA].

Sherburne Hills [CONTRA COSTA]: *ridge,* northwest-trending, 3 miles long, 3 miles east-southeast of Danville (lat. 37°47'55" N, long. 121°56'50" W). Named on Diablo (1953) 7.5' quadrangle.

Sheridan Creek [ALAMEDA]: *stream,* flows 3 miles to Alameda Creek 1.25 miles south-southeast of Sunol (lat. 37°34'40" N, long. 121°52'35" W). Named on Niles (1961) 7.5' quadrangle. The stream was named in 1906 for Sheridan school, which was near the creek; the canyon of the stream was called Lleguas Valley (Mosier and Mosier, p. 81).

Sherman: see **Madrone** [SANTA CLARA]; **Point Sherman**, under **Port Chicago** [CONTRA COSTA].

Sherman Flats [SANTA CLARA]: *area,* 2 miles west-southwest of Eylar Mountain (lat. 37°27'40" N, long. 121°34'45" W). Named on Eylar Mountain (1955) 7.5' quadrangle.

Shingle Valley [SANTA CLARA]: *valley,* drained by a stream that joins Animas Creek 4.25 miles east of Coyote (lat. 37°12'35" N, long. 121°39'40" W). Named on Morgan Hill (1955) 7.5' quadrangle.

Shinn [ALAMEDA]: *locality,* 1.25 miles northwest of Fremont civic center along Southern Pacific Railroad (lat. 37°34' N, long. 121°58'55" W; sec. 21, T 4 S, R 1 W). Named on Niles (1961) 7.5' quadrangle. The name

commemorates James Shinn, who settled at the place in 1856 (Mosier and Mosier, p. 81).

Ship Channel: see **Sacramento River Deep Water Ship Channel** [SOLANO].

Shoal Point: see **Point Potrero** [CONTRA COSTA].

Shoemaker: see **Camp Shoemaker**, under **Camp Parks** [ALAMEDA-CONTRA COSTA].

Shoquel Augmentation [SANTA CLARA]: *land grant,* mainly in Santa Cruz County, but extends over the crest of Santa Cruz Mountains into Santa Clara County 9 miles south-southeast of Los Gatos. Named on Laurel (1955) and Los Gatos (1953) 7.5' quadrangles. Martina Castro received the land in 1844 as an addition to her Soquel grant in present Santa Cruz County; she claimed 32,702 acres patented in 1860 (Arbuckle, p. 35; Arbuckle called the grant Soquel Augmentacion). The name "Soquel" is from an Indian village (Kroeber, p. 59).

Shore Acres [CONTRA COSTA]: *town,* 4.5 miles west of Pittsburg (lat. 38°02'10" N, long. 121°57'50" W). Named on Honker Bay (1953) 7.5' quadrangle.

Short Ridge [CONTRA COSTA]: *ridge,* west-northwest-trending, 2 miles long, 2 miles east of Danville (lat. 37°49'20" N, long. 121° 58' W). Named on Diablo (1953) 7.5' quadrangle.

Short Slough [CONTRA COSTA]: *water feature,* 3 miles north of the settlement of Bethel Island on Webb Tract (lat. 38°03'30" N, long. 121°37'45" W). Named on Bouldin Island (1978) and Jersey Island (1952) 7.5' quadrangles.

Shotgun Bend [SANTA CLARA]: *locality,* 2.5 miles northwest of Black Mountain (1), where Page Mill Road makes a sharp turn (lat. 37°20'45" N, long. 121°10'45" W). Named on Mindego Hill (1961) 7.5' quadrangle.

Shroyer Mountain [MARIN]: *peak,* 6.25 miles west-southwest of downtown Novato (lat. 38°03'55" N, long. 122°40'10" W). Altitude 1458 feet. Named on San Geronimo (1954) 7.5' quadrangle. Teather (p. 72) associated the name with Aaron Schroyer, who was justice of the peace for Nicasio from 1863 until 1873.

Shubrick Point: see **Southeast Farallon** [SAN FRANCISCO].

Sidney Flat [CONTRA COSTA]: *area,* 7 miles north-northeast of Mount Diablo in Markely Canyon (lat. 37°58'15" N, long. 121°51'45" W; near SE cor. sec. 33, T 2 N, R 1 E). Named on Antioch South (1953) 7.5' quadrangle.

Sierra Azul [SANTA CLARA]: *ridge,* northwest-trending, 8 miles long, in Santa Cruz Mountains northwest of Loma Prieta. Named on Loma Prieta (1955), Los Gatos (1953), and Santa Teresa Hills (1953) 7.5' quadrangles. *Sierra azul* means "blue mountain" in Spanish. According to testimony of James Alexander Forbes in 1857 (United States Supreme Court, p. 44), "The whole ridge from a considerable distance to the southeast, towards Monterey, up to the west of Santa Clara, is called the Sierra Azul, and sometimes the Santa Cruz mountains." Lyman (p. 270) noted that New Almaden mine is "in one of the ridges of Sierra Azul mountain."

Sierra Creek [SANTA CLARA]: *stream,* flows nearly 1 mile to lowlands 1.25 miles northeast of Berryessa (lat. 37°24' N, long. 121°50'30" W), and extends through lowlands in an artificial watercourse. Named on Calaveras Reservoir (1961) 7.5' quadrangle.

Sierra de Bolbones: see **Arroyo de las Nueces y Sierra de Bolbones**, under **Arroyo de las Nueces y Bolbones** [CONTRA COSTA].

Sierra de la Santa Cruz: see **Santa Cruz Mountains** [SAN MATEO-SANTA CLARA].

Sierra del Encino: see **New Almaden** [SANTA CLARA].

Sierra del Monte Diablo: see **Diablo Range** [ALAMEDA-CONTRA COSTA-SANTA CLARA].

Sierra de los Bolbones: see **Mount Diablo** [CONTRA COSTA].

Sierra de San Bruno: see **San Bruno Mountain** [SAN MATEO].

Sierra de San Pedro: see **San Pedro Mountain** [SAN MATEO].

Sierra de Santa Clara: see **San Pedro Mountain** [SAN MATEO].

Sierra Morena [SAN MATEO]: *peak,* 850 feet west of Skeggs Point (lat. 37°24'35" N, long. 122°18'25" W; sec. 16, T 6 S, R 4 W). Altitude 2417 feet. Named on Woodside (1961) 7.5' quadrangle. In Spanish times, the name applied to the entire ridge on which this peak is a prominence—*sierra morena* means "dark mountain" in Spanish (Brown, p. 58). Irelan (p. 533) referred to the entire north part of Santa Cruz Mountains as Sierra Moreno.

Sierra Point [SAN MATEO]: *promontory,* 2 miles northeast of downtown South San Francisco along San Francisco Bay (lat. 37° 40'30" N, long. 122°23'15" W). Named on San Francisco South (1947) 7.5' quadrangle. The feature now protrudes into landfill. The embayment north of Sierra Point is called Candlestick Cove, from Candlestick Point [SAN FRANCISCO]; the causeway built to carry a highway across the cove forms a body of water called Brisbane Lagoon (Brown, p. 16).

Siesta Valley [CONTRA COSTA]: *canyon,* 1.5 miles west-southwest of Orinda (lat. 37°52'20" N, long. 122°12'20" W). Named on Briones Valley (1959) and Oakland East (1959) 7.5' quadrangles.

Signal Hill [SOLANO]: *peak,* 2 miles south-southeast of Mount Vaca on Napa-Solano county line (lat. 38°22'35" N, long. 122°05' W; near S line sec. 9, T 6 N, R 2 W). Altitude 2394 feet. Named on Fairfield North (1951) and Mount Vaca (1951) 7.5' quadrangles.

Signal Hill: see **Albany Hill** [ALAMEDA]; **Telegraph Hill** [SAN FRANCISCO].

Silva Island [MARIN]: *island,* 0.25 mile long, 6 miles south of downtown San Rafael in Richardsons Bay (lat. 37°53'15" N, long. 122°30'55" W). Named on San Rafael (1954) 7.5' quadrangle. The feature now is connected to land.

Silver Creek [SANTA CLARA]: *stream,* flows 14 miles to Miguelita Creek 2.5 miles northeast of downtown San Jose (lat. 37°21'35" N, long. 121°51'45" W). Named on Lick Observatory (1955), Morgan Hill (1955), and San Jose East (1961) 7.5' quadrangles. San Jose (1899) 15' quadrangle shows the stream ending in marsh less than 2 miles northwest of Evergreen.

Silveyville: see **Dixon** [SOLANO].

Simla: see **Monta Vista** [SANTA CLARA].

Simmons Island [SOLANO]: *island,* 7 miles west-southwest of Birds Landing (2) between Honker Bay and Suisun Bay (lat. 38°05'45" N, long. 121°59'15" W). Named on Honker Bay (1953) and Vine Hill (1959) 7.5' quadrangles. United States Board on Geographic Names (1933, p. 694) rejected the names "Ead's Island" and "Richs Island" for the feature. Later the Board (1988b, p. 4) approved the name "Andy Mason Slough" for a water passage, 0.4 mile long, that extends south from Grizzly Bay through Simmons Island to Suisun Cutoff (lat. 38°05'38" N, long. 122°00'45" W, at S end).

Simmons Point [SOLANO]: *promontory,* 6.25 miles south-southwest of Birds Landing (2) at the west end of Chipps Island (lat. 38°03'15" N, long. 121°56' W). Named on Honker Bay (1953) 7.5' quadrangle. Called Pt. Simmons on Ringgold's (1850c) map.

Simms Island [MARIN]: *hill,* 1.5 miles southeast of downtown San Rafael (lat. 37°57'30" N, long. 122°30'15" W). Named on San Rafael (1954) 7.5' quadrangle.

Simpson's: see **Melrose** [ALAMEDA].

Simpson's Landing: see **Hayward Landing** [ALAMEDA].

Simpton Point [MARIN]: *promontory,* on the north side of Angel Island (lat. 37°52'10" N, long. 122°25'25" W). Named on San Francisco North (1956) 7.5' quadrangle. United States Board on Geographic Names (1980, p. 4) approved the name "Point Simpton" for the feature. The Board at the same time approved the name "Winslow Cove" for the embayment just west of the promontory (lat. 37°52'15" N, long. 122°25'33" W). This feature was called China Cove after United States Immigration Service established a station there in 1910; the name "Winslow" is for Charles A. Winslow, a leader in making Angel Island a state park (Teather, p. 16).

Sinbad Creek [ALAMEDA]: *stream,* flows 7 miles to Sunol Valley at Sunol (lat. 37°35'40" N, long. 121°53'15" W; sec. 8, T 4 S, R 1 E). Named on Dublin (1961) and Niles (1961) 7.5' quadrangles. The stream first was called

Batchelder Creek for Thomas Farwell Batchelder, who lived in the neighborhood in the 1870's (Mosier and Mosier, p. 82).

Sindicich Lagoons [CONTRA COSTA]: *lakes,* two, largest 325 feet long, 5 miles north-north-east of Orinda (lat. 37°56'40" N, long. 122°08'25" W). Named on Briones Valley (1959) 7.5' quadrangle.

Sir Francis Drake's Bay: see **Drakes Bay** [MARIN].

Sisters: see **The Sisters** [MARIN].

Sitio de la Brea: see **Las Animas** [SANTA CLARA].

Sizer: see **Mount Sizer** [SANTA CLARA].

Sizer Flat [SANTA CLARA]: *area,* 4 miles west-northwest of Mount Sizer (lat. 37°13'50" N, long. 121°34'45" W). Named on Mount Sizer (1955) 7.5' quadrangle.

Skeggs Point [SAN MATEO]: *locality;* view-point 7.5 miles east-southeast of the town of Half Moon Bay (lat. 37°24'40" N, long. 122°18'20" W). Named on Woodside (1961) 7.5' quadrangle. California Division of High-ways officials named the place in 1928 for John H. Skeggs, highway engineer, who was largely responsible for the road to the site (Brown, p. 89).

Skillet Creek: see **Llagas Creek** [SANTA CLARA].

Skunk Hill: see **Albany Hill** [ALAMEDA].

Skunk Hollow: see **Grizzly Creek** [SANTA CLARA]; **Skunk Hollow Gulch** [SANTA CLARA].

Skunk Hollow Gulch [SANTA CLARA]: *can-yon,* 1 mile long, opens into an unnamed can-yon 5 miles southeast of Mount Stakes (lat. 37°15'45" N, long. 121°27'50" W). Named on Mount Stakes (1955) 7.5' quadrangle. Called Skunk Hollow on Mount Boardman (1942) 15' quadrangle.

Sky Campground [MARIN]: *locality,* 2.25 miles south-southwest of Point Reyes Station on Inverness Ridge (lat. 38°02'25" N, long. 122°49'40" W). Named on Inverness (1954, photorevised 1971) 7.5' quadrangle.

Skyland: see **Wrights** [SANTA CLARA].

Sky Londa [SAN MATEO]: *settlement,* 3 miles southeast of Skeggs Point along La Honda Creek (lat. 37°23' N, long. 122°15'45" W). Named on Woodside (1961) 7.5' quadrangle.

Sky Valley [SOLANO]: *canyon,* 4.5 miles long, along Sulphur Springs Creek above a point 3.5 miles north of Benicia (lat. 38° 06' N, long. 122°09'40" W; near S line sec. 14, T 3 N, R 3 W). Named on Benicia (1959) and Cordelia (1951) 7.5' quadrangles.

Slate Creek [SAN MATEO]: *stream,* flows nearly 4 miles to Pescadero Creek 5 miles south-southeast of Mindego Hill (lat. 37°14'20" N, long. 122°12'10" W; sec. 16,T 8 S, R 3 W). Named on Big Basin (1955) and Mindego Hill (1961) 7.5' quadrangles. Stanger (1967, p. 93) gave the name "Rock Creek" as an alternate.

Slaughterhouse Point [SOLANO]: *promontory,* 4 miles north-northwest of downtown Vallejo on the east side of Napa River (lat. 38° 09'15" N, long. 122°17'20" W; sec. 34, T 4 N, R 4 W). Named on Cuttings Wharf (1949) 7.5' quadrangle.

Sleepy Hollow [CONTRA COSTA]: *valley,* 2 miles north of Orinda along Lauterwasser Creek (lat. 37°54'25" N, long. 122°11'10" W). Named on Briones Valley (1959) 7.5' quad-rangle.

Sleepy Hollow [MARIN]: *valley,* 7 miles south of downtown Novato (lat. 38°00'30" N, long. 122°34'45" W). Named on Novato (1954) 7.5' quadrangle.

Sleepy Hollow Creek [MARIN]: *stream,* flows 3.5 miles to San Anselmo Creek 2.25 miles west-northwest of downtown San Rafael (lat. 37°58'50" N, long. 122°34'10" W); the stream drains Sleepy Hollow. Named on San Rafael (1954) 7.5' quadrangle.

Smith: see **Point Smith**, under **Quarry Point** [MARIN].

Smith Creek [SANTA CLARA]:
(1) *stream,* flows nearly 3 miles to San Tomas Aquinas Creek 1.25 miles west-southwest of downtown Campbell (lat. 37°16'35" N, long. 121°58'10" W). Named on San Jose West (1961) 7.5' quadrangle.
(2) *stream,* flows 14 miles to join Isabel Creek and form Arroyo Hondo 1.5 miles south of Mount Day (lat. 37°23' N, long. 121°41'30" W; sec. 30, T 6 S, R 3 E). Named on Isabel Valley (1955), Lick Observatory (1955), and Mount Day (1955) 7.5' quadrangles.

Smith Gulch [ALAMEDA]: *canyon,* drained by a stream that flows 1.25 miles to Arroyo Mocho 6.5 miles southeast of Cedar Mount-ain (lat. 37°29' N, long. 121°31'50" W; sec. 21, T 5 S, R 4 E). Named on Eylar Mountain (1955) 7.5' quadrangle. The name commemo-rates Elmer Smith, who owned the canyon before 1917 (Mosier and Mosier, p. 82).

Smith Gulch: see **Bull Run Creek** [SAN MATEO].

Smiths Landing [MARIN]: *locality,* 3 miles west-southwest of Tomales on the northeast side of Tomales Bay (lat. 38°14'10" N, long. 122°57'30" W). Named on Point Reyes (1918) 15' quadrangle.

Smith's Landing: see **Antioch** [CONTRA COSTA].

Smith Slough [SAN MATEO]: *water feature,* extends 1.5 miles from Redwood Creek to Steinberger Slough nearly 2 miles north-northwest of downtown Redwood City (lat. 37°30'30" N, long. 122°14'35" W). Named on Redwood Point (1959) 7.5' quadrangle. The name commemorates William C.R. Smith, who built a landing along the slough in the 1850's (Brown, p. 90).

Smith Slough: see **Steinberger Slough** [SAN MATEO].

Snag Island [SOLANO]: *island,* 7 miles southwest of Birds Landing (2) in Suisun Bay (lat. 38°04'20" N, long. 121°58'30" W). Named on Honker Bay (1953) 7.5' quadrangle. Called Palo Alto Id. on Ringgold's (1850c) map, which shows Palo Alto Pt. at the east end.

Snake's Head: see **Pillar Point** [SAN MATEO].

Snoboy [ALAMEDA]: *locality,* 3 miles southeast of Fremont civic center along Southern Pacific Railroad (lat. 37°30'40" N, long. 121°56'35" W). Named on Niles (1961) 7.5' quadrangle.

Sobey Creek [SANTA CLARA]: *stream,* flows 2 miles to Wildcat Creek nearly 3 miles west-southwest of downtown Campbell (lat. 37°16'05" N, long. 121°59'35" W). Named on Cupertino (1961, photorevised 1968 and 1973) and San Jose West (1961, photorevised 1968 and 1973) 7.5' quadrangles. Called Vasona Creek on Cupertino (1961) and San Jose West (1961) 7.5' quadrangles. United States Board on Geographic Names (1972, p. 3) gave the name "Vasona Creek" as a variant.

Sobrante [CONTRA COSTA]: *locality,* 1 mile southeast of Pinole Point along Southern Pacific Railroad (lat. 38°00'10" N, long. 122° 20'50" W). Named on Mare Island (1959) 7.5' quadrangle.

Sobrante: see **El Sobrante** [CONTRA COSTA] (2).

Sobrante Ridge [CONTRA COSTA]: *ridge,* northwest-trending, 7.5 miles long, center 6.25 miles northwest of Orinda (lat. 37°57'15" N, long. 122°14'45" W). Named on Briones Valley (1959) and Richmond (1959) 7.5' quadrangles.

Socayre: see **Yerba Buena** [SANTA CLARA].

Soda Gulch [SAN MATEO]: *canyon,* drained by a stream that flows less than 1 mile to Purisima Creek 2.5 miles northwest of Skeggs Point (lat. 37°26' N, long. 122°20'35" W; near S line sec. 6, T 6 S, R 4 W). Named on Woodside (1961) 7.5' quadrangle. The name is from the numerous springs of sulfurous water in the canyon; the feature was called Underwood Gulch in the 1860's—Joshua Underwood lived there in the late 1850's (Brown, p. 90).

Soda Spring Canyon [SANTA CLARA]: *canyon,* drained by a stream that flows 4.25 miles to Lexington Reservoir nearly 3 miles south of downtown Los Gatos (lat. 37°11'05" N, long. 121°58'40" W). Named on Los Gatos (1953) 7.5' quadrangle. Franke (p. 16) referred to this canyon when he noted a small carbonated spring called Alma Soda Spring "in Cavanaugh Gulch, about a mile from Alma Station." The canyon was known as Conyer Gulch in the 1860's, for a man who camped on the flat at its mouth; later John Cavance came to the canyon, and the name "Cavanaugh" is a misspelling of the word "Cavance" (Young, p. 125).

Soda Springs Canyon [SANTA CLARA]: *can-*

yon, drained by a stream that flows 4 miles to Coyote Creek 3 miles south-southeast of Mount Sizer (lat. 37°10'15" N, long. 121°29'50" W); Madrone Soda Springs is in the canyon. Named on Mount Sizer (1955) 7.5' quadrangle.

Soda Springs Creek [SOLANO]: *stream,* flows 2.5 miles to Laurel Creek 3.25 miles northeast of Fairfield (lat. 38°17'40" N, long. 122°01'20" W; near W line sec. 7, T 5 N, R 1 W); the creek goes past Tolenas Springs. Named on Fairfield North (1951) 7.5' quadrangle.

Solano City [SOLANO]: *locality,* 1.5 miles east of Denverton along Oakland Antioch and Eastern Railroad (lat. 38°13'35" N, long. 121°52'15" W). Named on Birds Landing (1918) 7.5' quadrangle.

Solar en Santa Clara: see **Bennett Tract** [SANTA CLARA].

Solis [SANTA CLARA]: *land grant,* west of Gilroy. Named on Gilroy (1955) and Mount Madonna (1955) 7.5' quadrangles. Mariano Castro received the land in 1835; Rufino Castro and others claimed 8875 acres patented in 1859 (Cowan, p. 99). According to Arbuckle (p. 34-35), Solis is a family name.

Somersville [CONTRA COSTA]: *locality,* 6 miles north-northeast of Mount Diablo in Markley Canyon (lat. 37°57'25" N, long. 121°51'45" W; sec. 4, T 1 N, R 1 E). Site named on Antioch South (1953) 7.5' quadrangle. Postal authorities established Somersville post office in 1863 and discontinued it in 1910 (Frickstad, p. 23); the name commemorates Francis Somers, who started coal mines near the place (Mosier, p. 7). United States Board on Geographic Names (1933, p. 706) rejected the forms "Sommerville" and "Summerville" for the name.

Sommerville: see **Somersville** [CONTRA COSTA].

Soquel Augmentacion: see **Shoquel Augmentation** [SANTA CLARA].

Sorenson [ALAMEDA]: *locality,* 2 miles southsoutheast of Hayward along Western Pacific Railroad (lat. 37°38'35" N, long. 122° 04' W). Named on Hayward (1915) 15' quadrangle. The misspelled name commemorates Hansen Sorensen, a landowner who came to Hayward in 1881 (Mosier and Mosier, p. 82).

Sorosis: see **Champaign Fountain** [SANTA CLARA].

Soulafate: see **Soulajule** [MARIN] (1).

Soulajule [MARIN]:

(1) *land grant,* 8 miles southeast of Tomales. Named on Point Reyes NE (1954) 7.5' quadrangle. Ramon Mesa received 20 leagues in 1844; J.S. Brackett claimed 2492 acres patented in 1879 (Cowan, p. 100; Cowan listed this and the other Soulajule grants under the designation "Soulajule, or Soulafate"). The name appears to be from an Indian word (Kroeber, p. 60).

(2) *land grant,* 9.5 miles west of downtown Novato. Named on Inverness (1954), Petaluma (1953), and Point Reyes NE (1954) 7.5' quadrangles. Ramon Mesa received 20 leagues in 1844; G.N. Cornwall claimed 919 acres patented in 1879 (Cowan, p. 100).

(3) *land grant,* 10 miles southeast of Tomales. Named on Inverness (1954) and Point Reyes NE (1954) 7.5' quadrangles. Ramon Mesa received 20 leagues in 1844; M.F. Gormley claimed 2266 acres patented in 1879 (Cowan, p. 100).

(4) *land grant,* 5.5 miles southeast of Tomales. Named on Point Reyes NE (1954) 7.5' quadrangle. Ramon Mesa received 20 leagues in 1844; P.J. Vasquez claimed 3774 acres patented in 1879 (Cowan, p. 100).

(5) *land grant,* 10 miles west-northwest of downtown Novato. Named on Petaluma (1953) and Point Reyes NE (1954) 7.5' quadrangles. Ramon Mesa received 20 leagues in 1844; L.D. Watkins claimed 1447 acres patented in 1879 (Cowan, p. 100).

Soup Bowl Creek [SANTA CLARA]: *stream,* flows 2.25 miles to Middle Fork Coyote Creek nearly 5 miles south-southwest of Isabel Valley (lat. 37°15'10" N, long. 121°34'45" W). Named on Isabel Valley (1955) 7.5' quadrangle.

Southampton Bay [SOLANO]: *embayment,* 2 miles northwest of downtown Benicia along Carquinez Strait (lat. 38°04' N, long. 122°11'15" W). Named on Benicia (1959) 7.5' quadrangle. Cañizares called the feature Puerto de la Asunta in 1775 because he found it on the day of that feast—*Puerto de la Asunta* means "Asumption Harbor" in Spanish (Galvin, p. 96, 105). The present name is for the navy storeship *Southampton* that Commodore Thomas ap Catesby Jones brought to Benicia in 1849 (Bancroft, 1888, p. 473; Dillon, p. 31).

Southampton Shoal [SAN FRANCISCO]: *shoal,* 6 miles north of North Point in San Francisco Bay (lat. 37°53'30" N, long. 122°24'20" W). Named on San Quentin (1959) 7.5' quadrangle. The name is from the ship for which Southampton Bay was named (Dillon, p. 31).

Southampton Shoal Channel [SAN FRANCISCO]: *channel,* 7.5 miles north of North Point in San Francisco Bay (lat. 37°54'45" N, long. 122°25'20" W); the feature is north-northwest of Southampton Shoal. Named on San Quentin (1959) 7.5' quadrangle.

South Babb Creek [SANTA CLARA]: *stream,* flows 5 miles to Silver Creek 3.25 miles northwest of Evergreen (lat. 37°20'55" N, long. 121°49'05" W). Named on San Jose East (1961) 7.5' quadrangle.

South Basin [SAN FRANCISCO]: *embayment,* 4.25 miles east-southeast of Mount Davidson along San Francisco Bay (lat. 37°43'15" N, long. 122°22'45" W); the feature is on the south side of Hunters Point. Named on San Francisco South (1956) 7.5' quadrangle.

South Bay [SAN FRANCISCO]: *embayment,* along the coast 1.5 miles south-southwest of Fort Point (lat. 37°47'35" N, long. 122°29'30" W). Named on San Francisco North (1956) 7.5' quadrangle.

South Berkeley: see **Lorin** [ALAMEDA].

South Channel: see **Oakland Inner Harbor** [ALAMEDA].

South City: see **South San Francisco** [SAN MATEO].

South Coyote [SANTA CLARA]: *settlement,* 1.5 miles southeast of Coyote (lat. 37°12' N, long. 121°43'15" W). Named on Morgan Hill (1955) 7.5' quadrangle.

South Coyote Slough: see **Coyote Creek** [ALAMEDA-SANTA CLARA].

Southeast Farallon [SAN FRANCISCO]: *island,* about 4300 feet long, 30 miles west-southwest of the Golden Gate (lat. 37°41'55" N, long. 123°05' W); the feature is the largest of Farallon Islands. Named on Farallon Islands (1988) 7.5' quadrangle. Ringgold (p. 11) referred to South or Great Farallon. The island is believed to be the one that Vizcaino in 1603 called Isle Hendida (Hoover, p. 3). Hoover (frontispiece map) used the name "Shubrick Point" for a promontory at the east end of the island, and used the name "East Landing" at a narrow embayment at the southeast corner of the island.

Southeast Reef: see **Wash Rock** [SAN MATEO].

Southern Heights Ridge [MARIN]: *ridge,* southeast- to east-trending, 1.25 miles long, 1.5 miles south-southeast of downtown San Rafael (lat. 37°57'15" N, long. 122°31'10" W). Named on San Rafael (1954) 7.5' quadrangle.

Southern Pacific Basin: see **Oakland Middle Harbor** [ALAMEDA].

South Farallon: see **Southeast Farallon** [SAN FRANCISCO].

South Fork [SANTA CLARA]: *canyon,* drained by a stream that flows nearly 1 mile to lowlands 2 miles southwest of Gilroy (lat. 36°59' N, long. 121°35'10" W). Named on Chittenden (1955) 7.5' quadrangle.

South Granada: see **El Granada** [SAN MATEO].

South Lake [SAN FRANCISCO]: *lake,* 350 feet long, 1.25 miles southeast of Point Lobos (lat. 37°45'55" N, long. 122°29'55" W). Named on San Francisco North (1956) 7.5' quadrangle.

South Palo Alto: see **Mayfield** [SANTA CLARA].

South Panther Creek: see **Llagas Creek** [SANTA CLARA].

South Peak [SAN MATEO]: *peak,* 0.25 mile east-southeast of Montara Knob on Montara Mountain (lat. 37°33'20" N, long. 122°28'45" W; sec. 26, T 4 S, R 6 W); the feature is nearly 0.5 mile south-southwest of North Peak. Altitude 1833 feet. Named on Montara Mountain (1956) 7.5' quadrangle.

South Pocket [SANTA CLARA]: *canyon,* drained by a stream that flows 1.5 miles to Arroyo Mocho 2.5 miles southeast of Eylar Mountain (lat. 37°27'05" N, long. 121°30'50" W; sec. 34, T 5 S, R 4 E). Named on Eylar Mountain (1955) and Mount Boardman (1955) 7.5' quadrangles. Called Blackbird Valley on Mount Hamilton (1897) 15' quadrangle.

South San Francisco [SAN MATEO]: *city,* 15 miles northwest of downtown Redwood City (city hall near lat. 37°39'20" N, long. 122°24'45" W). Named on San Francisco South (1956) and San Leandro (1959) 7.5' quadrangles. G.F. Swift gave the name "South San Francisco" to the industrial development that he started along San Francisco Bay east of the center of the present city; the residential and business district of the community originally was called Baden, from nearby Baden dairy farm (Brown, p. 90; Gudde, 1949, p. 20). Postal authorities established South San Francisco post office in 1892, discontinued it when they moved the post office to Baden Station in 1895, and reestablished it in 1897 (Salley, p. 209). The city incorporated in 1908. The place commonly is called South City (Brown, p. 91).

South San Ramon Creek [ALAMEDA-CONTRA COSTA]: *stream,* heads in Contra Costa County and flows 5 miles to a canal located 1 mile east of Dublin in Alameda County (lat. 37°42'05" N, long. 121°55'05" W); the stream drains the south part of San Ramon Valley. Named on Diablo (1953) and Dublin (1961) 7.5' quadrangles. Dublin (1961, photorevised 1980) 7.5' quadrangle shows the stream in an artificial watercourse in Alameda County.

South Slough [SOLANO]: *water feature,* on Napa-Solano county line, joins Napa River 3.25 miles north-northwest of downtown Vallejo (lat. 38°09'40" N, long. 122°17'15" W; sec. 34, T 4 N, R 4 W). Named on Cuttings Wharf (1949) 7.5' quadrangle.

South Vallejo [SOLANO]: *district,* 1 mile southeast of downtown Vallejo (lat. 38°05'10" N, long. 122°14'35" W). Named on Karquines (1898) 15' quadrangle. Postal authorities established South Vallejo post office 2 miles south of Vallejo in 1870 and discontinued it in 1872 (Salley, p. 209).

Spanish Anchorage: see **Old Spanish Anchorage,** under **Fort Point** [SAN FRANCISCO].

Spanish Peak: see **Scarper Peak** [SAN MATEO].

Spanish Ranch Creek [SAN MATEO]: *stream,* flows 0.5 mile to Weeks Creek 2 miles north of La Honda (lat. 37°20'55" N, long. 122°16'05" W; sec. 2, T 7 S, R 4 W). Named on La Honda (1961) 7.5' quadrangle.

Spanish Town: see **Half Moon Bay** [SAN MATEO] (2).

Spanishtown: see **Mexican Camp** [SANTA CLARA].

Sparkel [CONTRA COSTA]: *locality,* nearly 2 miles north of Walnut Creek civic center along Sacramento Northern Railroad (lat. 37°55'50" N, long. 122°03'15" W). Named on Walnut Creek (1959) 7.5' quadrangle.

Spear Point: see **Mare Island** [SOLANO].

Spike Buck Creek [MARIN]: *stream,* flows 1.25 miles to Rattlesnake Creek 5.5 miles southsouthwest of downtown San Rafael (lat. 37°54'15" N, long. 122°35'20" W). Named on San Rafael (1954) 7.5' quadrangle.

Spinner Island [SOLANO]: *island,* 3400 feet long, along Montezuma Slough 4.25 miles south of Birds Landing (2) (lat. 38°04'10" N, long. 121°52'05" W). Named on Antioch North (1978) 7.5' quadrangle.

Spoonbill [SOLANO]: *locality,* 5.25 miles south-southwest of Birds Landing (2) along Sacramento Northern Railroad on Van Sickle Island (lat. 38°03'05" N, long. 121°54'10" W); the place is along Spoonbill Creek. Named on Honker Bay (1953) 7.5' quadrangle.

Spoonbill Creek [SOLANO]: *water feature,* extends from Suisun Bay to Honker Bay between Chipps Island and Van Sickle Island; joins Honker Bay 5 miles south-southwest of Birds Landing (2) (lat. 38°04'20" N, long. 121°54'35" W). Named on Honker Bay (1953) 7.5' quadrangle.

Spreckels Lake [SAN FRANCISCO]: *lake,* 900 feet long, 1.25 miles east-southeast of Point Lobos (lat. 37°46'15" N, long. 122°29'35" W). Named on San Francisco North (1956) 7.5' quadrangle.

Sprig Lake [SANTA CLARA]: *lake,* 250 feet long, nearly 1.5 miles east-southeast of Mount Madonna (lat. 37°00'15" N, long. 121°40'50" W). Named on Mount Madonna (1955) 7.5' quadrangle.

Spring Branch [SOLANO]: *stream,* flows 4.5 miles to First Mallard Branch 3.25 miles south-southeast of Fairfield (lat. 38°12'20" N, long. 122°01'40" W). Named on Denverton (1953) and Fairfield South (1949) 7.5' quadrangles. Called Spring Brook on Carquinez (1938) 15' quadrangle, and called Spring Branch Cr. on Carquinez Strait (1940) 15' quadrangle.

Spring Branch Creek: see **Spring Branch** [SOLANO].

Spring Bridge Gulch [SAN MATEO]: *canyon,* drained by a stream that flows 1 mile to the sea nearly 2 miles north-northwest of Pigeon Point (lat. 37°12'20" N, long. 122°24'15" W). Named on Pigeon Point (1955) 7.5' quadrangle. Brown (p. 34) gave the name "Foam Gulch" as an early designation for the canyon—this name was from a bridge that was called Foam Bridge because sea foam blew over the road there.

Spring Brook: see **Spring Branch** [SOLANO].

Spring Canyon [SANTA CLARA]: *canyon,*

drained by a stream that flows 2 miles to Arroyo Valle 5 miles south-southwest of Eylar Mountain (lat. 37°24'30" N, long. 121°34'45" W; sec. 18, T 6 S, R 4 E). Named on Eylar Mountain (1955) 7.5' quadrangle.

Spring Ridge: see Windy Hill [SAN MATEO].

Springtowne: see Vallejo [SOLANO].

Spring Valley: see Chinatown [SAN FRANCISCO].

Spring Valley Creek: see Spring Valley Ridge [SAN MATEO].

Spring Valley Lakes: see Lower Crystal Springs Reservoir [SAN MATEO].

Spring Valley Ridge [SAN MATEO]: ridge, southeast-trending, 2 miles long, 2.5 miles east of Montara Knob (lat. 37°33'45" N, long. 122°26'05" W). Named on Montara Mountain (1956) 7.5' quadrangle. The name is from Spring Valley Water Company (Brown, p. 91). Brown, (p. 91) used the name "Spring Valley Creek" for the stream on the northeast side of the ridge.

Squattersville: see San Lorenzo [ALAMEDA] (3).

Squealer Gulch [SAN MATEO]: canyon, drained by a stream that flows 2.25 miles to West Union Creek 2 miles north-northeast of Skeggs Point (lat. 37°26'40" N, long. 122°17'25" W). Named on Woodside (1961) 7.5' quadrangle. According to Stanger (1967, p. 133), the name probably is for an early settler called Squealer Sam Alwell because of his high voice.

Stafford Lake [MARIN]: lake, 3700 feet long, behind a dam on Novato Creek nearly 4 miles west of downtown Novato (lat. 38°07'05" N, long. 122°38'10" W). Named on San Geronimo (1954) 7.5' quadrangle. The name commemorates Dr. Charles Stafford, veterinarian and board member of North Marin County Water District (Teather, p. 73).

Stake Point [CONTRA COSTA]: promontory, 4 miles west-northwest of Pittsburg along Suisun Bay (lat. 38°03'05" N, long. 121°56'55" W). Named on Honker Bay (1953) 7.5' quadrangle. Called Pt. Picket on Ringgold's (1850b) map.

Stakes: see Mount Stakes [SANTA CLARA].

Stancos Creek: see Los Trancos Creek [SAN MATEO-SANTA CLARA].

Star Canyon [SANTA CLARA]: canyon, drained by a stream that flows nearly 1 mile to Hoover Creek 3.5 miles west-southwest of Mount Sizer (lat. 37°11'25" N, long. 121°34'05" W). Named on Mount Sizer (1955) 7.5' quadrangle.

Star Creek [SANTA CLARA]: stream, flows nearly 1.5 miles to Pescadero Creek 5.5 miles southwest of Gilroy (lat. 36°56'20" N, long. 121°37'20" W). Named on Watsonville East (1955) 7.5' quadrangle.

Steamboat Point [SAN FRANCISCO]: promontory, 0.5 mile south of Rincon Point along San Francisco Bay on the north side of present

China Basin (lat. 37°46'40" N, long. 122°23'20" W). Named on San Francisco (1915) 15' quadrangle.

Steamboat Slough [SOLANO]: water feature, joins Cache Slough 2.5 miles northeast of Rio Vista (lat. 38°10'55" N, long. 121°39'30" W). Named on Courtland (1978), Isleton (1978), and Rio Vista (1978) 7.5' quadrangles. Called Middle Fork [Sacramento River] on Ringgold's (1850c) map, which shows Pt. Chapman along Sacramento River opposite the mouth of present Steamboat Slough.

Steamboat Slough: see Alviso Slough [SANTA CLARA].

Steele: see Año Nuevo Bay [SAN MATEO].

Steeple Rock: see Sail Rock [SAN MATEO].

Steep Ravine Canyon [MARIN]: canyon, along Webb Creek, which flows 2.25 miles to Bolinas Bay 3.5 miles east-southeast of Bolinas (lat. 37°53'05" N, long. 122°37'40" W). Named on San Rafael (1954) 7.5' quadrangle.

Stege [CONTRA COSTA]: locality, 1.5 miles south-southeast of Richmond civic center along Southern Pacific Railroad (lat. 37° 55' N, long. 122°19'35" W). Named on Richmond (1959) 7.5' quadrangle. Called Steige on Smith and Elliott's (1879) map. Postal authorities established Stege post office in 1889 and discontinued it in 1935 (Frickstad, p. 23). The name commemorates Richard Stege, who settled on a farm at the place about 1890 (Gudde, 1949, p. 343). Postal authorities established Schmidtville post office 2 miles northeast of Stege in 1900 and discontinued it in 1901 (Salley, p. 199).

Steige: see Stege [CONTRA COSTA].

Steiger Hill [SOLANO]: peak, 5.5 miles east of Mount Vaca (lat. 38° 23'55" N, long. 122°00'10" W). Named on Mount Vaca (1951) 7.5' quadrangle.

Steinbergen Creek: see Steinberger Slough [SAN MATEO].

Steinbergens Slough: see Steinberger Slough [SAN MATEO].

Steinberger Creek [SAN MATEO]: see Steinberger Slough [SAN MATEO].

Steinbergers: see Redwood City [SAN MATEO].

Steinberger Slough [SAN MATEO]: water feature, opens into San Francisco Bay 4 miles north of downtown Redwood City (lat. 37° 32'40" N, long. 122°13'20" W). Named on Redwood Point (1959) 7.5' quadrangle. Called Steinberger Creek on Hayward (1915) 15' quadrangle, but United States Board on Geographic Names (1961b, p. 16) rejected this name, and the names "Steinbergens Slough," "Steinberger's Slough," "Steinbergen Slough," "Steinbergen Creek," and "Smith Slough" for the feature.

Stemple Creek [MARIN]: stream, heads in Sonoma County and flows 15 miles to Estero de San Antonio 1.5 miles north of Tomales in Marin County (lat. 38°16'15" N, long.

122°54'20" W). Named on Cotati (1954), Two Rock (1954) and Valley Ford (1954) 7.5' quadrangles. Teather (p. 75) associated the name with Henry M. Stemple, a rancher in the region. United States Board on Geographic Names (1943, p. 13) rejected the names "Aurora Creek," "Estero de San Antonio," and "Two Rock Creek" for the stream, or for any part of it.

Stemple Creek: see **Estero de San Antonio** [MARIN].

Stephens: see **Point Stephens**, under **Point Richmond** [CONTRA COSTA] (1).

Stephens Creek: see **Stevens Creek** [SANTA CLARA].

Stephenson: see **Point Stephenson**, under **Middle Point** [CONTRA COSTA].

Stevens Creek [SANTA CLARA]: *stream,* flows 21 miles to mud flats along San Francisco Bay 4 miles north-northeast of downtown Mountain View (lat. 37°26'45" N, long. 122°03'45" W). Named on Cupertino (1961), Mindego Hill (1961), and Mountain View (1961) 7.5' quadrangles. Members of the Anza expedition gave the name "Arroyo de San Jose Cupertino" to the stream in 1776 (Hoover, Rensch, and Rensch, p. 459). Called Cupertino Creek on Healy's (1866) map, and called Stephens Cr. on Hare's (1872) map. The modern name honors Elisha Stevens, who came overland to California in 1844 and settled by the stream in 1848 (Butler, p. 108). United States Board on Geographic Names (1933, p. 721) rejected the names "Cupertino Creek" and "Steven's Creek" for the stream, and later the Board (1968b, p. 9) rejected the names "Whishman Slough" and "Whisman Slough" for it.

Stevens Creek Reservoir [SANTA CLARA]: *lake,* 1.25 miles long, behind a dam on Stevens Creek 3 miles southwest of downtown Cupertino (lat. 37°17'55" N, long. 122°04'30" W; on W line sec. 27, T 7 S, R 2 W). Named on Cupertino (1961) 7.5' quadrangle.

Stewart Point [MARIN]: *ridge,* east-southeast-to southeast-trending, 1 mile long, 2.25 miles northwest of Bolinas (lat. 37°55'45" N, long. 122°42'55" W). Named on Bolinas (1954) 7.5' quadrangle.

Stewartville [CONTRA COSTA]: *locality,* 6 miles northeast of Mount Diablo (lat. 37°56'50" N, long. 121°50'55" W; sec. 10, T 1 N, R 1 E). Site named on Antioch South (1953) 7.5' quadrangle. Postal authorities established Stewartville post office in 1882 and discontinued it in 1902 (Frickstad, p. 24). The name was for William Stewart, owner of a coal mine at the place (Mosier, p. 7; Mosier called the place Stewartsville). Postal authorities established Judsonville post office 3 miles northeast of Stewartville in 1878, discontinued it for a time in 1879, and discontinued it finally in 1883 (Salley, p. 108). Judsonville was a coal-mine town named for Egbert

Judson, a stockholder in the mine there (Mosier, p. 6).

Still Island: see **Belvedere Island** [MARIN].

Stillwater Bay: see **Belvedere Cove** [MARIN].

Stinson Beach [MARIN]: *town,* 2.5 miles east-southeast of Bolinas along Bolinas Bay (lat. 37°53'55" N, long. 122°38'20" W). Named on Bolinas (1954) 7.5' quadrangle. Postal authorities established Stinson Beach post office in 1916 (Frickstad, p. 89). The name "Stinson" commemorates Nathan H. Stinson, who bought land at the site in 1866 (Hanna, P.T., p. 316).

Stinson Gulch [MARIN]: *canyon,* drained by a stream that flows 1.25 miles to Bolinas Lagoon 2 miles east of Bolinas (lat. 37° 54'25" N, long. 122°39'05" W); the canyon is north of Stinson Beach. Named on Bolinas (1954) 7.5' quadrangle.

Stivers Lagoon [ALAMEDA]: *marsh,* center 0.5 mile southeast of present Fremont civic center (lat. 37°32'45" N, long. 121°57'35" W; in and near sec. 34, T 4 S, R 1 W). Named on Livermore (1961) 15' quadrangle. Called The Lagoon on Pleasanton (1906) 15' quadrangle, which shows a lake in the marsh. The name "Stivers" is for Simon Stivers, who settled at the place in 1850; the feature originally was called La Laguna, and it also was called Tule Pond for the vegetation there; a lake created from the marsh in 1968 is called Lake Elizabeth for Fremont's sister city, Elizabeth, Australia (Mosier and Mosier, p. 49).

Stockton Pass: see **Mission Pass** [ALAMEDA].

Stockyards: see **Emeryville** [ALAMEDA].

Stokes Landing: see **Mount Eden** [ALAMEDA].

Stone Dam Reservoir [SAN MATEO]: *lake,* 500 feet long, behind a dam on Pilarcitos Creek 5.25 miles east-southeast of Montara Knob (lat. 37°31'35" N, long. 122°23'50" W; sec. 3, T 5 S, R 5 W). Named on Montara Mountain (1956) 7.5' quadrangle.

Stoneman: see **Camp Stoneman** [CONTRA COSTA].

Stone Valley [CONTRA COSTA]: *valley,* 2.5 miles north-northwest of Danville (lat. 37°51'20" N, long. 122°01' W). Named on Las Trampas Ridge (1959) 7.5' quadrangle. The name commemorates Albert W. Stone, a settler in the valley (Hoover, Rensch, and Rensch, p. 58).

Stonybrook: see **Farwell** [ALAMEDA].

Stonybrook Canyon [ALAMEDA]: *canyon,* drained by a stream that flows 5 miles to Alameda Creek 3.5 miles north-northeast of Fremont civic center (lat. 37°35'55" N, long. 121°56'45" W; sec. 11, T 4 S, R 1 W). Named on Dublin (1961) and Niles (1961) 7.5' quadrangles. The name, which originally had the form "Stony Brook Canyon," is from large stones in the stream in the canyon—the stream is called Stonybrook Creek (Mosier and Mosier, p. 84).

Stonybrook Creek: see **Stonybrook Canyon** [ALAMEDA].

Storehouse Rock: see **Pigeon Point** [SAN MATEO].

Stow Lake [SAN FRANCISCO]: *lake,* 1800 feet long, 2.25 miles east-southeast of Point Lobos (lat. 37°46'10" N, long. 122°28'25" W). Named on San Francisco North (1956) 7.5' quadrangle.

Strait of Napa: see **Mare Island Strait** [SOLANO].

Straits of Carquines: see **Carquinez Strait** [CONTRA COSTA].

Straits of San Pablo: see **San Pablo Strait** [MARIN].

Strawberry Canyon: see **Strawberry Creek** [ALAMEDA].

Strawberry Creek [ALAMEDA]: *stream,* flows 1.5 miles to lowlands 4.5 miles north of downtown Oakland (lat. 37°52'20" N, long. 122°15'10" W). Named on Briones Valley (1959), Oakland East (1959), and Oakland West (1959) 7.5' quadrangles. The stream also was called Alta Creek; Crespi called the canyon of the creek Arroyo de la Bocana in 1772—*bocana* means "mouth" in Spanish; the canyon also is called Strawberry Canyon, and in the 1860's it was known as Blake's Ravine for George Mansfield Blake, who owned land there (Mosier and Mosier, p. 84).

Strawberry Flat [SANTA CLARA]: *area,* 2.5 miles south-southeast of Eylar Mountain (lat. 37°26'35" N, long. 121°31'25" W; sec. 3, T 6 S, R 4 E). Named on Eylar Mountain (1955) 7.5' quadrangle.

Strawberry Hill [SAN FRANCISCO]: *island,* 1050 feet long, 2.25 miles east-southeast of Point Lobos in Stow Lake (lat. 37°46'10" N, long. 122°28'25" W). Named on San Francisco North (1956) 7.5' quadrangle.

Strawberry Point [MARIN]: *peninsula,* 6 miles south-southeast of downtown San Rafael along Richardson Bay (lat. 37°53'15" N, long. 122°30'20" W). Named on San Quentin (1959) and San Rafael (1954) 7.5' quadrangles. Postal authorities established Strawberry Point post office in 1960 and discontinued it in 1961 (Salley, p. 214).

Striped Rock: see **Devils Slide** [SAN MATEO].

Stuart Camp [SANTA CLARA]: *locality,* nearly 3 miles east-northeast of Bielawski Mountain (lat. 37°13'55" N, long. 122°02'30" W). Named on Castle Rock Ridge (1955) 7.5' quadrangle.

Stuart Point [MARIN]: *promontory,* on the west side of Angel Island (lat. 37°51'40" N, long. 122°26'45" W). Named on San Francisco North (1956) 7.5' quadrangle. United States Board on Geographic Names (1980, p. 4) approved the name "Point Stuart" for the feature. The name commemorates Frederick D. Stuart, hydrographer with Cadwalader Ringgold's expedition of 1849 (Teather, p. 2).

Subeet [SOLANO]: *locality,* 2.5 miles southwest of Fairfield along Southern Pacific Railroad (lat. 38°13'40" N, long. 122°04'55" W). Named on Fairfield South (1949) 7.5' quadrangle. The name is from words "sugar" and "beet," and is for the location of the place in a sugar-beet raising territory (Gannett, p. 292).

Sucro [SOLANO]: *locality,* nearly 2 miles north-northeast of Dixon along Southern Pacific Railroad (lat. 38°28'10" N, long. 121°48'10" W; at W line sec. 7, T 7 N, R 2 E). Named on Dixon (1952) 7.5' quadrangle.

Sugar Loaf: see **Sugarloaf Butte** [ALAMEDA].

Sugarloaf [MARIN]: *peak,* 3 miles west of Tomales near Dillon Beach (lat. 38°15'10" N, long. 122°57'30" W). Named on Valley Ford (1954) 7.5' quadrangle. Point Reyes (1918) 15' quadrangle has the name "Sugarloaf Hill" at or near this peak.

Sugarloaf Butte [ALAMEDA]: *peak,* 1.5 miles south-southwest of Cedar Mountain (lat. 37°32'10" N, long. 121°37' W; sec. 35, T 4 S, R 3 E). Altitude 2726 feet. Named on Cedar Mountain (1956) 7.5' quadrangle. Called Sugar Loaf on California Mining Bureau's (1917b) map, and called Sugar Loaf Peak on Thompson and West's (1878) map

Sugarloaf Hill [CONTRA COSTA]: *ridge,* northwest-trending, 2 miles long, 3 miles north-northwest of Danville (lat. 37°52'05" N, long. 122°02'05" W). Named on Las Trampas Ridge (1959) and Walnut Creek (1959) 7.5' quadrangles.

Sugarloaf Hill: see **Sugarloaf** [MARIN].

Sugarloaf Mountain [SANTA CLARA]: *peak,* 2.5 miles north-northwest of Isabel Valley (lat. 37°20'50" N, long. 121°33'45" W; sec. 8, T 7 S, R 4 E). Altitude 2798 feet. Named on Isabel Valley (1955) 7.5' quadrangle.

Sugar Loaf Peak: see **Las Trampas Peak** [CONTRA COSTA]; **Sugarloaf Butte** [ALAMEDA].

Suisun [SOLANO]: *land grant,* at and west of Fairfield. Named on Cordelia (1951), Fairfield North (1951), Fairfield South (1949), and Mount George (1951) 7.5' quadrangles. Francisco Solano, an Indian, received 4 leagues in 1842; Archibald A. Ritchie claimed 17,755 acres patented in 1857, and J.H. Fine claimed 482 acres patented in 1882 (Cowan, p. 100).

Suisun: see **Suisun City** [SOLANO].

Suisun Bay [CONTRA COSTA-SOLANO]: *bay,* extends for 14 miles west along Contra Costa-Solano county line from the confluence of Sacramento River and San Joaquin River to Carquinez Strait. Named on Antioch North (1978), Honker Bay (1953), and Vine Hill (1959) 7.5' quadrangles. Called Middle Fork [Sacramento River] on Ringgold's (1850c) map, and the easternmost part of the bay is considered part of Sacramento River on Honker Bay (1918) 7.5' quadrangle. The feature had the early names "Puerto Dulce" and "Freshwater Bay" (Gudde, 1949, p. 346). Ringgold (p. 27) used the designation "Bay of Suisun." The name "Suisun" is from an Indian tribe or village (Kroeber, p. 60).

Suisun City [SOLANO]: *town,* less than 1 mile south of downtown Fairfield at the head of Suisun Slough (lat. 38°14'20" N, long. 122°02'20" W). Named on Fairfield South (1949) 7.5' quadrangle. Called Suisun on Suisun (1918) special quadrangle. Postal authorities established Suisun post office in 1854 and changed the name to Suisun City in 1857 (Salley, p. 215). The town incorporated in 1868. Postal authorities established Barton's Store post office in 1857 when they split it off from Suisun City post office, and discontinued it in 1858; the name was for John W. Barton, store owner and first postmaster (Salley, p. 15). Captain Josiah Wing and John Owen laid out the town of Suisun near a shipping point already in use (Hoover, Rensch, and Rensch, p. 521).

Suisun City: see **Rio Vista** [SOLANO].

Suisun Creek [SOLANO]: *stream,* heads in Napa County and flows 20 miles, including through Lake Curry, to marsh 5 miles southwest of Fairfield in Solano County (lat. 38°11'35" N, long. 122°06'10" W). Named on Capell Valley (1951), Fairfield North (1951), Fairfield South (1949), and Mount George (1951) 7.5' quadrangles.

Suisun Creek: see **Suisun Slough** [SOLANO].

Suisun Cutoff [SOLANO]: *water feature,* extends between Simmons Island and Ryer Island (2) from Suisun Bay to Grizzly Bay 8 miles east-northeast of Benicia (lat. 38°05'40" N, long. 122°01'15" W). Named on Honker Bay (1953) and Vine Hill (1959) 7.5' quadrangles.

Suisun Hill [SOLANO]: *peak,* 2.5 miles southsoutheast of Fairfield (lat. 38°12'55" N, long. 122°01'05" W; near S line sec. 6, T 4 N, R 1 W). Altitude 212 feet. Named on Fairfield South (1949) 7.5' quadrangle.

Suisun Point [CONTRA COSTA]: *promontory,* 1.5 miles north-northeast of Martinez at the west end of Suisun Bay (lat. 38°02'05" N, long. 122°07'05" W). Named on Vine Hill (1959) 7.5' quadrangle.

Suisun Reservoir [SOLANO]: *lake,* 1000 feet long, 6.5 miles west-northwest of Fairfield (lat. 38°17'55" N, long. 122°08'40" W; sec. 12, T 5 N, R 3 W). Named on Mount George (1951) 7.5' quadrangle.

Suisun Slough [SOLANO]: *water feature,* extends from Suisun City to Grizzly Bay 9 miles south of Fairfield (lat. 38°07'15" N, long. 122°03'50" W). Named on Fairfield South (1949) and Vine Hill (1959) 7.5' quadrangles. Called Suisun Creek on Ringgold's (1850c) map, but United States Board on Geographic Names (1943, p. 13) rejected this name for the feature.

Suisun Valley [SOLANO]: *valley,* 6 miles northwest of Fairfield along Suisun Creek, mainly in Solano County, but extends north into Napa

County (lat. 38°18'45" N, long. 122°07'30" W). Named on Fairfield North (1951) and Mount George (1951) 7.5' quadrangles.

Sulfur Creek [SANTA CLARA]: *stream,* flows 2.5 miles to San Benito County 13 miles eastsoutheast of Gilroy (lat. 36°57'35" N, long. 121°20'40" W). Named on Three Sisters (1954) 7.5' quadrangle.

Sulphur Creek [ALAMEDA]: *stream,* flows 3.5 miles to San Francisco Bay nearly 5 miles south of downtown San Leandro (lat. 37°39'20" N, long. 122°09'25" W). Named on Hayward (1959) and San Leandro (1959) 7.5' quadrangles. Captain John Chisholm built Chisholm Landing at the mouth of Sulphur Creek after he landed there in 1851 (Mosier and Mosier, p. 22-23).

Sulphur Creek [SANTA CLARA]:
(1) *stream,* flows nearly 5 miles to Smith Creek 1.5 miles south-southwest of Mount Hamilton (lat. 37°19'15" N, long. 121°39'20" W; sec. 16, T 7 S, R 3 E). Named on Isabel Valley (1955) and Lick Observatory (1955) 7.5' quadrangles.
(2) *stream,* flows 1.25 miles to Middle Fork Coyote Creek 4 miles northwest of Mount Sizer (lat. 37°14'45" N, long. 121°34'25" W; sec. 7, T 8 S, R 4 E). Named on Mount Sizer (1955) 7.5' quadrangle.

Sulphur Creek: see **Ward Creek** [ALAMEDA].

Sulphur Gulch [SANTA CLARA]: *canyon,* drained by a stream that flows 3.5 miles to Arroyo Valle 4.25 miles south-southwest of Eylar Mountain (lat. 37°25'05" N, long. 121°34'30" W; sec. 18, T 6 S, R 4 E). Named on Eylar Mountain (1955) 7.5' quadrangle.

Sulphur Spring [CONTRA COSTA]: *spring,* 4.25 miles west of Mount Diablo in Pine Canyon (lat. 37°53'10" N, long. 121°59'25" W). Named on Clayton (1953) 7.5' quadrangle.

Sulphur Spring Canyon [ALAMEDA-CONTRA COSTA]: *canyon,* 1.5 miles long, 3 miles east-northeast of Cedar Mountain on Alameda-Contra Costa county line (lat. 37°34'35" N, long. 121°33'15" W). Named on Cedar Mountain (1956) 7.5' quadrangle.

Sulphur Spring Creek: see **Sulphur Springs Creek** [SANTA CLARA]; **Ward Creek** [ALAMEDA].

Sulphur Spring Gulch [SANTA CLARA]: *canyon,* drained by a stream that flows nearly 1 mile to San Antonio Creek 6.5 miles southsoutheast of Eylar Mountain (lat. 37°23'05" N, long. 121°30'25" W; sec. 26, T 6 S, R 4 E). Named on Eylar Mountain (1955) 7.5' quadrangle.

Sulphur Springs [SOLANO]: *locality,* 4 miles east-northeast of downtown Vallejo (lat. 38°07'25" N, long. 122°11'25" W; near NW cor. sec. 10, T 3 N, R 3 W). Named on Karquines (1898) 15' quadrangle. Benicia (1959) 7.5' quadrangle shows the site in a place called Blue Rock Springs Park. A resort at the place was called Vallejo White Sulphur Springs, White Sulphur Springs, Vallejo Sulphur Springs (Bradley, p. 310), and Blue Rock Springs (Laizure, 1927b, p. 209).

Sulphur Springs Creek [SANTA CLARA]: *stream,* flows 3.5 miles to Beauregard Creek 7.25 miles south of Mount Boardman (lat. 37° 22'35" N, long. 121°29'10" W; near S line sec. 25, T 6 S, R 4 E). Named on Eylar Mountain (1955) and Mount Boardman (1955) 7.5' quadrangles. Called Sulphur Spring Creek on Mount Hamilton (1897) 15' quadrangle, where the name applies also to present Day Creek (2), a tributary of present Sulphur Springs Creek.

Sulphur Springs Creek [SOLANO]: *stream,* flows 5 miles to Carquinez Strait 2 miles east-northeast of Benicia (lat. 38°03'35" N, long. 122°07'15" W); the stream passes east of Sulphur Springs Mountain. Named on Benicia (1959) 7.5' quadrangle. Called Sulphur Springs Valley Creek on Karquines (1898) 15' quadrangle.

Sulphur Springs Creek: see **Blue Rock Springs Creek** [SOLANO].

Sulphur Springs Mountain [SOLANO]: *ridge,* south-southeast to south-trending, 4.5 miles long, 6 miles south-southwest of Cordelia (lat. 38°08' N, long. 122°10'50" W); the north end of the ridge is in Napa County. Named on Benicia (1959) and Cordelia (1951) 7.5' quadrangles.

Sulphur Springs Valley Creek: see **Sulphur Springs Creek** [SOLANO].

Summerville: see **Somersville** [CONTRA COSTA].

Summit: see **The Summit**, under **Altamont** [ALAMEDA].

Summit Reservoir [ALAMEDA-CONTRA COSTA]: *lake,* 750 feet long, 4.5 miles east-southeast of Richmond civic center on Alameda-Contra Costa county line (lat. 37°54'20" N, long. 120°16'10" W). Named on Richmond (1959) 7.5' quadrangle.

Summit Rock [SANTA CLARA]: *peak,* 1.25 miles north-northwest of Bielawski Mountain (lat. 37°14'25" N, long. 122°05'50" W; sec. 17, T 8 S, R 2 W). Named on Castle Rock Ridge (1955) 7.5' quadrangle.

Summit Spring [SAN MATEO]: *spring,* 1 mile north of Skeggs Point (lat. 37°25'35" N, long. 122°18'20" W). Named on Woodside (1961) 7.5' quadrangle. A travellers stop called Summit Springs House was built by the spring in the 1860's, and the village that grew around the hostelry was called Summit Springs—the village was gone by the 1880's (Brown, p. 93).

Summit Springs: see **Summit Spring** [SAN MATEO].

Summit Springs House: see **Summit Spring** [SAN MATEO].

Sundburg Creek: see **Patterson Creek** [ALAMEDA].

Sundburg Landing: see **Patterson Landing** [ALAMEDA].

Sunnyside: see **Ross** [MARIN].

Sunnyvale [SANTA CLARA]: *city,* 9 miles west-northwest of downtown San Jose (lat. 37°22'15" N, long. 122°02'15" W). Named on Cupertino (1961), Milpitas (1961), Mountain View (1961), and San Jose West (1961) 7.5' quadrangles. W.E. Crossman bought 200 acres from Patrick Murphy in 1898 and subdivided the land into lots for a town that first he called Encinal, and later called Sunnyvale (Butler, p. 36). Postal authorities established Encinal post office in 1897 and changed the name to Sunnyvale in 1901 (Frickstad, p. 173). The city incorporated in 1912. Palo Alto (1899) 15' quadrangle shows a place called Murphy located along Southern Pacific Railroad in present Sunnyvale (lat. 37°22'35" N, long. 122°01'45" W). The name was for Martin Murphy, Jr., who owned land at the site (Rambo, 1973, p. 44).

Sunnyvale West Outfall Channel: see **Moffett Channel** [SANTA CLARA].

Sunol [ALAMEDA]: *town,* 5.5 miles northeast of Fremont civic center (lat. 37°35'40" N, long. 121°53'05" W; near S line sec. 8, T 4 S, R 1 E); the town is in Sunol Valley. Named on Niles (1961) 7.5' quadrangle. Pleasanton (1906) 15' quadrangle has both the names "Sunol" and "Sunolglen P.O." at the place. The name "Sunol" commemorates Antonio Sunol, part owner of El Valle de San Jose grant (Gudde, 1949, p. 347). Postal authorities established Sunol post office in 1871, changed the name to Sunolglen the same year, and changed it back to Sunol in 1920 (Frickstad, p. 3). Idlwood, a station of Western Pacific Railroad, is situated west of Sunol (Mosier and Mosier, p. 45).

Sunolglen: see **Sunol** [ALAMEDA].

Sunol Ridge [ALAMEDA]: *ridge,* northwest-trending, nearly 7 miles long, center 4.5 miles south of Dublin (lat. 37°38'20" N, long. 121° 56'05" W); the ridge extends northwest from Sunol. Named on Dublin (1961) and Niles (1961) 7.5' quadrangles.

Sunol Valley [ALAMEDA]: *valley,* at and southeast of Sunol along Alameda Creek (lat. 37°35' N, long. 121°52'30" W). Named on La Costa Valley (1960) and Niles (1961) 7.5' quadrangles.

Sunset District [SAN FRANCISCO]: *district,* 4 miles southwest of San Francisco civic center (lat. 37°45' N, long. 122°29' W). Named on San Francisco North (1956) and San Francisco South (1956) 7.5' quadrangles.

Sunset Reservoir [SAN FRANCISCO]: *lake,* 1050 feet long, 1.5 miles west-southwest of Mount Sutro (lat. 37°45'05" N, long. 122°28'55" W); the feature is in Sunset District. Named on San Francisco North (1956) 7.5' quadrangle.

Sunshine Camp [CONTRA COSTA]: *locality,* 3 miles east-northeast of Mount Diablo (lat. 37°54' N, long. 121°51'50" W: sec. 28, T 1 N,

R 1 E). Named on Antioch South (1953) 7.5' quadrangle.

Sun Valley [MARIN]: *valley,* less than 1 mile northwest of downtown San Rafael (lat. 37°58'50" N, long. 122°32'35" W). Named on San Rafael (1954) 7.5' quadrangle.

Surveyor's Gulch: see **Yankee Jim Gulch** [SAN MATEO].

Sutro: see **Mount Sutro** [SAN FRANCISCO].

Sutro Crest: see **Mount Sutro** [SAN FRANCISCO].

Sutter Bank: see **Cordell Bank** [MARIN].

Sutter Island: see **Ryer Island** [SOLANO] (1).

Sutter Slough [SOLANO]: *water feature,* extends for 4.5 miles along Solano-Sacramento county line to Steamboat Slough 8 miles northeast of Rio Vista (lat. 38°15'15" N, long. 121°36' W). Named on Courtland (1978) 7.5' quadrangle. Called West Fork [Sacramento River] on Ringgold's (1850d) map.

Suval [SOLANO]: *locality,* 2 miles west of downtown Fairfield along Sacramento Northern Railroad (lat. 38°14'50" N, long. 122°04'40" W). Named on Fairfield South (1949) 7.5' quadrangle.

Sveadal [SANTA CLARA]: *settlement,* 3.5 miles east-southeast of Loma Prieta along Uvas Creek (lat. 37°05'05" N, long. 121°47'15" W; near SE cor. sec. 6, T 10 S, R 2 E). Named on Loma Prieta (1955) 7.5' quadrangle. United States Board on Geographic Names (1983d, p. 4) approved the name "Crystal Peak" for a peak located 3.3 miles northwest of Sveadal (lat. 37°06'48" N, long. 121°50'05" W; sec. 35, T 9 S, R 1 E); the name is for a radio facility on the peak, and also for commemoration of early crystal-radio development.

Swanson Canyon [SANTA CLARA]: *canyon,* drained by a stream that flows nearly 1.5 miles to Uvas Creek 3.25 miles east-southeast of Loma Prieta (lat. 37°05'10" N, long. 121°47'30" W; sec. 6, T 10 S, R 2 E). Named on Loma Prieta (1955) 7.5' quadrangle.

Swanzy Lake: see **Swanzy Reservoir** [SOLANO].

Swanzy Reservoir [SOLANO]: *lake,* 950 feet long, 2.5 miles southeast of downtown Vallejo (lat. 38°04'35" N, long. 122°13'30" W). Named on Benicia (1959) 7.5' quadrangle. United States Board on Geographic Names (1962, p. 17) rejected the names "Swanzy Lake" and "Vallejo Reservoir" for the feature.

Sweany Creek [SOLANO]: *stream,* flows 6 miles to lowlands 1 mile west of Allendale (lat. 38°26'40" N, long. 121°57'30" W). Named on Allendale (1953), Dixon (1952), and Mount Vaca (1951) 7.5' quadrangles. Called Sweeny Creek on Napa (1902) 30' quadrangle, and called Sweeney Creek on Vacaville (1953) 15' quadrangle, which shows the stream extending through lowlands to Ulatis Creek 3.5 miles east of Elmira.

Swede George Canyon: see **Swede George Creek** [MARIN].

Swede George Creek [MARIN]: *stream,* flows 1.25 miles to Alpine Lake nearly 4 miles northeast of Bolinas (lat. 37°56'25" N, long. 122°37'35" W). Named on San Rafael (1954) 7.5' quadrangle. East Fork enters from the east near the mouth of the main stream and is 1.5 miles long. West Fork enters 0.25 mile from the mouth of the main stream and is nearly 1 mile long. Both forks are named on San Rafael (1954) 7.5' quadrangle. Mount Tamalpais (1950) 15' quadrangle has the name "Swede George Canyon" for the canyon of the stream.

Sweeney: see **East Palo Alto** [SAN MATEO].

Sweeney Creek: see **Sweany Creek** [SOLANO].

Sweeney Ridge [SAN MATEO]: *ridge,* northwest- to north-trending, 2 miles long, 3.5 miles north-northeast of Montara Knob (lat. 37° 36'10" N, long. 122°27'20" W). Named on Montara Mountain (1956) 7.5' quadrangle. The name is from Sweeney ranch, which was on the ridge in the 1880's; the feature also was called Irish Ridge (Brown, p. 93).

Sweeny Creek: see **Sweany Creek** [SOLANO].

Sweet Springs [ALAMEDA]: *springs,* 2.25 miles southeast of Cedar Mountain (lat. 37°32'20" N, long. 121°34'20" W; sec. 31, T 4 S, R 4 E). Named on Cedar Mountain (1956) 7.5' quadrangle. Water that comes from fourteen springs has a distinctly sweet taste (Waring, p. 310).

Sweetwater Creek [SANTA CLARA]: *stream,* flows 3.5 miles to Sulphur Springs Creek 7 miles south-southwest of Mount Boardman (lat. 37°23' N, long. 121°29'45" W; sec. 26, T 6 S, R 4 E). Named on Eylar Mountain (1955) and Mount Boardman (1955) 7.5' quadrangles.

Sweigert Creek [SANTA CLARA]: *stream,* flows 0.5 mile to lowlands 2.25 miles north-northeast of Berryessa (lat. 37°24'55" N, long. 121°50'30" W). Named on Calaveras Reservoir (1961, photorevised 1968 and 1973) 7.5' quadrangle. Called Cropley Creek on Calaveras Reservoir (1961) 7.5' quadrangle. United States Board on Geographic Names (1972, p. 3) approved the name "Sweigert Creek" for the stream, and listed the name "Cropley Creek" as a variant.

Swiss Creek [SANTA CLARA]: *stream,* flows 2.5 miles to Stevens Creek 3.5 miles northwest of downtown Saratoga in Stevens Creek Reservoir (lat. 37°17'45" N, long. 122°04'45" W; sec. 28, T 7 S, R 2 W). Named on Cupertino (1961) 7.5' quadrangle.

Sycamore: see **Camp Sycamore** [SANTA CLARA].

Sycamore Canyon [SANTA CLARA]: *canyon,* drained by a stream that flows nearly 1 mile to Soda Springs Canyon 3.5 miles south of Mount Sizer (lat. 37°10' N, long. 121°30'45" W; sec. 10, T 9 S, R 4 E). Named on Mount Sizer (1955) 7.5' quadrangle.

Sycamore Creek [CONTRA COSTA]: (1) *stream,* formed by the confluence of East Fork and West Fork, flows nearly 7 miles to San Ramon Creek 1 mile southeast of Danville (lat. 37°48'40" N, long. 121°59' W); the stream goes through Sycamore Valley. Named on Diablo (1953) 7.5' quadrangle. East Fork is 1 mile long and West Fork is 1.25 miles long; both forks are named on Diablo (1953) 7.5' quadrangle.

(2) *stream,* flows nearly 4 miles through Hog Canyon to Marsh Creek 5.5 miles east of Mount Diablo (lat. 37°53'10" N, long. 121° 48'40" W; sec. 36, T 1 N, R 1 E). Named on Antioch South (1953) and Tassajara (1953) 7.5' quadrangles.

Sycamore Creek [SANTA CLARA]:
(1) *stream,* flows 3.5 miles to Arroyo Valle 3.5 miles west-southwest of Eylar Mountain (lat. 37°27'05" N, long. 121°36'10" W; sec. 36, T 5 S, R 3 E). Named on Eylar Mountain (1955) and Mount Day (1955) 7.5' quadrangles.
(2) *stream,* flows 2 miles to Uvas Creek nearly 4 miles northeast of Mount Madonna (lat. 37°03'20" N, long. 121°39'50" W). Named on Mount Madonna (1955, photorevised 1968 and 1973) 7.5' quadrangle. The name is for the many sycamore trees on the banks of the stream (United States Board on Geographic Names, 1973a, p. 3).

Sycamore Slough [SOLANO]: *water feature,* 9.5 miles north of Rio Vista near Hass Slough (lat. 38°17'50" N, long. 121°43'25" W). Named on Liberty Island (1978) 7.5' quadrangle.

Sycamore Spring [ALAMEDA]: *spring,* 7 miles south of Sunol (lat. 37°29'45" N, long. 121°51'05" W; sec. 15, T 5 S, R 1 E). Named on Calaveras Reservoir (1961) 7.5' quadrangle.

Sycamore Spring [CONTRA COSTA]:
(1) *spring,* less than 1 mile northeast of Mount Diablo (lat. 37°53'15" N, long. 121°54'05" W; sec. 31, T 1 N, R 1 E). Named on Clayton (1953) 7.5' quadrangle.
(2) *spring,* 5.5 miles east-southeast of Mount Diablo (lat. 37°51'35" N, long. 121°48'50" W; sec. 12, T 1 S, R 1 E); the spring is near Sycamore Creek (2). Named on Tassajara (1953) 7.5' quadrangle.

Sycamore Valley [CONTRA COSTA]: *valley,* 3 miles east-southeast of Danville (lat. 37°48'30" N, long. 121°57' W); the valley is along Sycamore Creek (1). Named on Diablo (1953) 7.5' quadrangle.

Sykes Slough [SOLANO]: *water feature,* 8 miles northeast of Dixon between Putah Creek and South Fork Putah Creek (lat. 38°31'35" N, long. 121°43'50" W). Named on Swingle (1915) 7.5' quadrangle.

— T —

Table Butte: see **Mount Tamalpais** [MARIN].
Table Hill: see **Mount Tamalpais** [MARIN].

Table Mountain [SANTA CLARA]:
(1) *peak,* 2 miles south-southeast of Black Mountain (1) (lat. 37°17'20" N, long. 122°08'20" W; sec. 25, T 7 S, R 3 W). Altitude 1852 feet. Named on Mindego Hill (1961) 7.5' quadrangle.
(2) *ridge,* east-trending, 1 mile long, 3 miles west of Saratoga (lat. 37°15'35" N, long. 122°04'40" W). Named on Cupertino (1961) 7.5' quadrangle.

Table Mountain: see **Mount Tamalpais** [MARIN].

Tahana Gulch [SAN MATEO]: *canyon,* drained by a stream that flows 1.5 miles to Bradley Creek 3 miles south of the village of San Gregorio (lat. 37°17'05" N, long. 122°22'45" W). Named on La Honda (1961) 7.5' quadrangle.

Tamal: see **San Quentin** [MARIN].

Tamalpais: see **Kentfield** [MARIN]; **Mill Valley** [MARIN] (2); **Mount Tamalpais** [MARIN].

Tamalpais Creek [MARIN]: *stream,* flows 1.25 miles to Corte Madera Creek 2 miles southsouthwest of downtown San Rafael (lat. 37°56'55" N, long. 122°32'40" W). Named on San Rafael (1954) 7.5' quadrangle. The name was given to a previously unnamed stream during World War II so that a navy oiler ship constructed near Saucelito could have the name "Tamalpais"—the navy customarily named oilers for streams (Teather, p. 77).

Tamalpais Valley [MARIN]: *valley,* 6.5 miles south of downtown San Rafael along Coyote Creek (lat. 37°52'45" N, long. 122° 32' W). Named on San Rafael (1954) 7.5' quadrangle. Called Coyote Valley on a county map of 1873 (Teather, p. 79).

Tamalpais Valley: see **Tamalpais**, under **Mill Valley** [MARIN] (2).

Tamalpais Valley Junction [MARIN]: *locality,* 6.25 miles south of downtown San Rafael (lat. 37°52'55" N, long. 122°31'25" W); the place is near the mouth of Tamalpais Valley. Named on San Rafael (1954) 7.5' quadrangle.

Tanforan: see **San Bruno** [SAN MATEO].

Tar Creek [SANTA CLARA]: *stream,* flows 8 miles to Carnadero Creek 5.5 miles southsoutheast of Gilroy (lat. 36°55'50" N, long. 121°32'30" W). Named on Chittenden (1955) 7.5' quadrangle. Called La Brea Creek on San Juan Bautista (1917) 15' quadrangle. Goodyear (1888, p. 94) called the stream Tar Spring Creek, and described "copious seepages of black tar" along it.

Tar Creek: see **Tarwater Creek** [SAN MATEO].

Tarraville Canyon: see **Tarraville Creek** [ALAMEDA].

Tarraville Creek [ALAMEDA]: *stream,* flows 4 miles to Arroyo Mocho 6 miles southeast of Cedar Mountain (lat. 37°30' N, long. 121°32'10" W; sec. 16, T 5 S, R 4 E). Named on Eylar Mountain (1955) 7.5' quadrangle.

On Mount Boardman (1955) 7.5' quadrangle, the canyon of the creek has the name "Tarraville Canyon."

Tar Spring Creek: see **Tar Creek** [SANTA CLARA].

Tarwater Creek [SAN MATEO]: *stream,* flows 2.25 miles to Pescadero Creek 3.5 miles south of Mindego Hill (lat. 37°15'40" N, long. 122°14'25" W; sec. 6, T 8 S, R 3 W). Named on Mindego Hill (1961) 7.5' quadrangle. Brown (p. 6, 93) used the name "Tar Creek" for the stream, and noted that asphalt and oil seep into the water; Brown also mentioned that the east branch of the stream was called Bear Creek

Tasajero: see **Tassajara** [CONTRA COSTA].

Tasajero Creek: see **Tassajara Creek** [CONTRA COSTA].

Tassajara [CONTRA COSTA]: *locality,* 6.5 miles south-southeast of Mount Diablo (lat. 37°47'45" N, long. 121°51'45" W; near S line sec. 33, T 1 S, R 1 E); the place is along Tassajara Creek. Named on Tassajara (1953) 7.5' quadrangle. Called Tassajero on Mount Diablo (1898) 15' quadrangle. United States Board on Geographic Names (1933, p. 745) first approved the name "Tassajero," and rejected the names "Tasajero" and "Tassajera" for the place; later the Board (1960a, p. 18) approved the name "Tassajara," and rejected the name "Tassajero." Postal authorities established Tassajara post office in 1896 and discontinued it in 1922 (Frickstad, p. 24). The name is from a Spanish-American term for a place where meat is cut in strips and dried in the sun (Gudde, 1949, p. 354).

Tassajara Creek [ALAMEDA-CONTRA COSTA]: *stream,* heads in Contra Costa County and flows 10.5 miles to lowlands 6.25 miles west-northwest of Livermore in Alameda County (lat. 37°42'50" N, long. 121°52'30" W). Named on Dublin (1961), Livermore (1961), and Tassajara (1953) 7.5' quadrangles. Called Tassajero Creek on Mount Diablo (1898) and Pleasanton (1906) 15' quadrangles. United States Board on Geographic Names (1933, p. 745) first approved the form "Tassajero," and rejected the forms "Tasajero" and "Tassajera" for the name; later the Board (1960a, p. 18) approved the form "Tassajara" and rejected the forms "Tassajero" and (1967c, p. 5) "Tassajera."

Tassajera: see **Tassajara** [CONTRA COSTA].

Tassajera Creek: see **Tassajara Creek** [ALAMEDA-CONTRA COSTA].

Tassajero: see **Tassajara** [CONTRA COSTA].

Tassajero Creek: see **Tassajara Creek** [ALAMEDA-CONTRA COSTA].

Taylor: see **Camp Taylor** [MARIN].

Taylor Island: see **Ryer Island** [SOLANO] (1).

Taylor Slough [CONTRA COSTA]: *water feature,* extends for nearly 5 miles between Bethel Island (1) and Jersey Island from Piper Slough to Dutch Slough at the settlement of Bethel Island (lat. 38° 00'50" N, long. 121°38'45" W). Named on Jersey Island (1978) 7.5' quadrangle.

Taylorville [MARIN]: *locality,* 11 miles west-southwest of downtown Novato along Northwestern Pacific Railroad (lat. 38°01'45" N, long. 122°44'20" W); the place is 1 mile northwest of Camp Taylor. Named on Petaluma (1914) 15' quadrangle. The name is for Samuel P. Taylor, who built the first paper mill on the Pacific Coast (Gudde, 1949, p. 354).

Teachers Beach [MARIN]: *beach,* 4.5 miles northwest of Point Reyes Station on the southwest side of Tomales Bay (lat. 38°06'50" N, long. 122°52'05" W). Named on Inverness (1954) 7.5' quadrangle.

Teague Hill [SAN MATEO]: *peak,* nearly 1 mile north-northeast of Skeggs Point (lat. 37°25'15" N, long. 122°17'50" W). Named on Woodside (1961) 7.5' quadrangle. Andrew Teague lived at the place from 1854 until 1860 (Brown, p. 94).

Teal [SOLANO]: *locality,* 5.5 miles south-southwest of Fairfield along Southern Pacific Railroad (lat. 38°10'25" N, long. 122°04'40" W). Named on Fairfield South (1949) 7.5' quadrangle.

Tehan Canyon [ALAMEDA]: *canyon,* drained by a stream that flows 1.5 miles to Amador Valley 1.5 miles south-southeast of Dublin (lat. 37°40'50" N, long. 121°55'25" W). Named on Dublin (1961) 7.5' quadrangle. The name is for William Tehan, who settled at the place in the 1860's—the stream in the canyon is called Tehan Creek (Mosier and Mosier, p. 86).

Tehan Creek: see **Tehan Canyon** [ALAMEDA].

Tehan Falls [ALAMEDA]: *waterfall,* 2 miles south of Dublin (lat. 37°40'25" N, long. 121°56'20" W; sec. 14, T 3 S, R 1 W); the feature is in Tehan Canyon. Named on Dublin (1961) 7.5' quadrangle.

Telegraph Canyon [ALAMEDA]: *canyon,* drained by a stream that flows 0.5 mile to Claremont Creek 5 miles north-northeast of downtown Oakland (lat. 37°52'10" N, long. 122°13'25" W). Named on Oakland East (1959) 7.5' quadrangle. A transcontinental telegraph line was built through the canyon in 1858; the canyon of present Claremont Creek was called Telegraph Canyon until 1886 or 1887 (Mosier and Mosier, p. 87).

Telegraph Hill [SAN FRANCISCO]: *hill,* 0.5 mile southeast of North Point (lat. 37°48'10" N, long. 122°24'20" W). Named on San Francisco North (1956) 7.5' quadrangle. Spaniards called the hill Loma Alta, but as early as 1849 it sometimes was called Signal Hill because it was used as a lookout for incoming ships; by 1853 it was called Inner Signal Station and was connected by telegraph to Outer Signal Station located near Point Lobos, where ships were sighted before they entered the Golden Gate (Hoover, Rensch, and Rensch, p. 362-

363). The promontory formed by the south-east shoulder of the hill—which came to the edge of San Francisco Bay before landfill modified the shoreline—was called Punta de la Loma Alta and Punta del Embarcadero in Spanish days; later the promontory was known as Clark's Point for William S. Clark, who took land there as a squatter in 1848 (Hoover, Rensch, and Rensch, p. 357). The same promontory is called Pt. Montgomery on Ringgold's (1850a) map—Captain John Berrien Montgomery, commander of United States sloop *Portsmouth*, set up a gun battery called Fort Montgomery at the point in 1846 (Frazer, p. 27; Whiting and Whiting, p. 56). The embayment, now filled, that extended southeast from Clark's Point to Rincon Point was called Yerba Buena Cove (Soule, Gihon, and Nisbet, p. 157); the feature also was known as Loma Alta Cove (Davis, W.H., p. 2)—Soule, Gihon, and Nisbet's (1855) map shows the shoreline before the cove was filled. According to Bancroft (1886. p. 590), the name "Yerba Buena" applied before 1827 to an anchorage west of present North Point. The name no doubt is from mint that grew in abundance near the cove—*yerba buena* means "good herb" in Spanish (Soule, Gihon, and Nisbet, p. 157).

Telmat: see **Hamlet** [MARIN].

Temescal [ALAMEDA]: *locality,* 2 miles north-northeast of downtown Oakland (lat. 37°49'50" N, long. 122°15'50" W); the place is near Temescal Creek. Named on San Francisco (1899) 15' quadrangle.

Temescal: see **North Temescal**, under **Oakland** [ALAMEDA].

Temescal Creek [ALAMEDA]: *stream,* flows 3 miles to lowlands 3 miles north-northeast of downtown Oakland (lat. 37°51' N, long. 122°14'15" W). Named on Oakland East (1959) and Oakland West (1959) 7.5' quadrangles. Called Kohler Creek on Concord (1897) 15' quadrangle. The name apparently is from an Indian sweat house near the stream—*temescal* means "sweat house" in Spanish (Hoover, Rensch, and Rensch, p. 3). The name "Kohler" recalls Andrew Kohler, who owned land in the neighborhood in the 1880's (Mosier and Mosier, p. 48).

Temescal Lake: see **Lake Temescal** [ALAMEDA].

Tenderfoot Flat [CONTRA COSTA]: *area,* 2.5 miles west-northwest of Mount Diablo (lat. 37°53'35" N, long. 121°57'25" W; sec. 34, T 1 N, R 1 W). Named on Clayton (1953) 7.5' quadrangle.

Ten Mile Beach: see **Point Reyes Beach** [MARIN].

Tennant [SANTA CLARA]: *locality,* 1.5 miles southeast of Morgan Hill along Southern Pacific Railroad (lat. 37°06'55" N, long. 121° 38' W). Named on Morgan Hill (1917) 15' quadrangle. The place was near the site of Twenty-one Mile House—named for the distance from San Jose—built in 1852, burned down in 1853, and soon rebuilt by William Tennant (*San Jose Mercury-News, California Today Magazine,* October 23, 1977). Postal authorities established Tennant post office in 1871, discontinued it for a time in 1879, and discontinued it finally in 1887 (Frickstad, p. 175).

Tennessee Cove [MARIN]: *embayment,* 2 miles northwest of Point Bonita along the coast (lat. 37°50'25" N, long. 122°33'05" W); the feature is at the mouth of Tennessee Valley. Named on Point Bonita (1954) 7.5' quadrangle. The name is from the steamer *Tennessee,* which went aground at the place in 1853 (Hoover, Rensch, and Rensch, p. 186). The feature also had the names "Indian Cove" and "Potatoe Cove" before application of the present name—the embayment is near Potato Patch Shoal (Teather, p. 79).

Tennessee Point [MARIN]: *promontory,* 1.5 miles northwest of Point Bonita along the coast (lat. 37°50'05" N, long. 122°32'55" W). Named on Point Bonita (1954) 7.5' quadrangle.

Tennessee Valley [MARIN]: *canyon,* drained by a stream that flows 2 miles to the sea 2.25 miles northwest of Point Bonita at Tennessee Cove (lat. 37°50'30" N, long. 122°33'05" W). Named on Point Bonita (1954) 7.5' quadrangle. Called Elk Valley on Tamalpais (1897) 15' quadrangle, but United States Board on Geographic Names (1962, p. 17) rejected this name.

Tequisquite: see **Llano del Tequisquita** [SANTA CLARA].

Terra Linda: see **San Rafael** [MARIN].

Tesla [ALAMEDA]: *locality,* 5.5 miles south-southwest of Midway in Corral Hollow (lat. 37°38'25" N, long. 121°36' W; sec. 25, T 3 S, R 3 E). Site named on Midway (1953) 7.5' quadrangle. John Treadwell and James Treadwell founded a town at the place in 1890 for workers of nearby coal mines; they named the town for Nikola Tesla, a famous inventor of electrical devices (Mosier, p. 7). Postal authorities established Tesla post office in 1898 and discontinued it in 1915 (Frickstad, p. 3).

Thayer: see **Mount Thayer** [SANTA CLARA].

The Big Coyote: see **Coyote Point** [SAN MATEO].

The Big Ditch [SOLANO]: *stream,* flows 9.5 miles to an intermittent lake 10 miles southeast of Elmira (lat. 38°15'10" N, long. 121°46'05" W). Named on Birds Landing (1953) and Dozier (1952) 7.5' quadrangles.

The Brothers [CONTRA COSTA]: *islands,* two, each 350 feet long, less than 0.5 mile west-southwest of Point San Pablo in San Francisco Bay (lat. 37°57'45" N, long. 122°26' W). Named on San Quentin (1959) 7.5' quadrangle. Buffum (p. 28) used the name "Two Brothers" for the islands.

The Coyote: see **Coyote Point** [SAN MATEO].

The Cut: see **Bay Slough** [SAN MATEO].

The Cutoff: see **Bay Slough** [SAN MATEO].

The Family Farm [SAN MATEO]: *settlement,* 7 miles south of downtown Redwood City in present Portola Valley (1) (lat. 37°23'15" N, long. 122°14' W). Named on Palo Alto (1953) 7.5' quadrangle.

The Great Beach: see **Point Reyes Beach** [MARIN].

The Knife [ALAMEDA-CONTRA COSTA]: *ridge,* northwest-trending, 1 mile long, 5.5 miles south of Danville on Alameda-Contra Costa county line (lat. 37°44'30" N, long. 122°00'15" W). Named on Hayward (1959) 7.5' quadrangle.

The Lagoon: see **Stivers Lagoon** [ALAMEDA].

The Laguna: see **Upper Crystal Springs Reservoir** [SAN MATEO].

The Mesa [SAN MATEO]: *relief feature,* 2 miles north-northeast of Pigeon Point (lat. 37°12'20" N, long. 122°22'30" W). Named on Franklin Point (1955) and Pigeon Point (1955) 7.5' quadrangles.

The Narrows [SANTA CLARA]: *narrows,* 4.5 miles south-southwest of Eylar Mountain along Arroyo Valle (lat. 37°24'45" N, long. 121°34'50" W). Named on Eylar Mountain (1955) 7.5' quadrangle.

The Peak [SANTA CLARA]: *peak,* 1.25 miles east-southeast of Bielawski Mountain on Santa Clara-Santa Cruz county line (lat. 37°13'10" N, long. 122°04'15" W; sec. 22, T 8 S, R 2 W). Altitude 2886 feet. Named on Castle Rock Ridge (1955) 7.5' quadrangle.

The Potato Patch [SAN MATEO]: *area,* 3.5 miles southwest of La Honda along Pomponio Creek (lat. 37°17'25" N, long. 122°19'15" W; sec. 29, T 7 S, R 4 W). Named on La Honda (1961) 7.5' quadrangle.

The Sisters [MARIN]: *islands,* two, largest 200 feet long, 1800 feet northeast of Point San Pedro in San Pablo Bay (lat. 37°59'20" N, long. 120°26'30" W). Named on San Quentin (1959) 7.5' quadrangle.

The Summit: see **Altamont** [ALAMEDA].

The Tunnel: see **Wrights** [SANTA CLARA].

The Willows: see **Willow Glen** [SANTA CLARA].

Thomasson [SOLANO]: *locality,* 4.25 miles southwest of Fairfield along Southern Pacific Railroad (lat. 38°13' N, long. 122°06'25" W). Named on Fairfield South (1949) 7.5' quadrangle. Postal authorities established Thomasson post office in 1907 and discontinued it in 1913; the name is for a rancher who used the place as a shipping point (Salley, p. 221).

Thompson: see **Point Thompson**, under **Mare Island** [SOLANO].

Thompson Creek [SANTA CLARA]: *stream,* flows 9 miles to Silver Creek 4.25 miles east-southeast of downtown San Jose (lat. 37° 19'35" N, long. 121°48'35" W). Named on

Lick Observatory (1955) and San Jose East (1961) 7.5' quadrangles. On San Jose East (1961, photorevised 1968 and 1973) 7.5' quadrangle, the stream ends before it reaches Silver Creek. Called Dry Creek on San Jose (1899) 15' quadrangle, which shows the stream ending in a marsh.

Thompson's Landing: see **Roberts Landing** [ALAMEDA].

Thona: see **New Almaden Station** [SANTA CLARA].

Thornhill [ALAMEDA]: *locality,* 3 miles east-northeast of downtown Oakland along Oakland Antioch and Eastern Railroad (lat. 37°49'50" N, long. 122°13' W). Named on Concord (1915) 15' quadrangle. Concord (1943) 15' quadrangle shows a place called Monclair situated at or near the site. Thornhill railroad station was established in 1913; the name commemorates Hiram Thorne, who was in the neighborhood in the 1850's (Mosier and Mosier, p. 88).

Thornton [SAN MATEO]: *locality,* 5.5 miles west-northwest of downtown South San Francisco along Ocean Shore Railroad (lat. 37°41'45" N, long. 122°29'50" W). Named on San Mateo (1915) 15' quadrangle. The name is for R.S. Thornton, an early settler in the neighborhood (Brown, p. 94). J.R. Wagner (p. 52) gave the name "Ocean View" as an alternate.

Three Fathom Shoal: see **Benicia Shoals** [SOLANO].

Three Peaks [MARIN]: *peak,* 9.5 miles southeast of Tomales (lat. 37°08'15" N, long. 122°48'05" W). Altitude 1161 feet. Named on Point Reyes NE (1954) 7.5' quadrangle.

Three Rocks [SAN MATEO]: *rocks,* 2.25 miles south-southwest of downtown Half Moon Bay off Miramontes Point (lat. 37°25'55" N, long. 122°26'35" W). Named on Half Moon Bay (1961) 7.5' quadrangle.

Tiburon [MARIN]: *town,* 2 miles east-northeast of downtown Sausalito (lat. 37°52'30" N, long. 122°27'15" W); the town is at the southeast end of Tiburon Peninsula. Named on San Francisco North (1956) and San Quentin (1959) 7.5' quadrangles. Postal authorities established Tiburon post office in 1884 (Frickstad, p. 89), and the town incorporated in 1964.

Tiburon: see **Point Tiburon** [MARIN].

Tiburon Peninsula [MARIN]: *peninsula,* extends 4.5 miles southeast between San Francisco Bay and Richardson Bay; center 5 miles south-southeast of downtown San Rafael (lat. 37°54' N, long. 122° 28'45" W). Named on San Quentin (1959) and San Rafael (1954) 7.5' quadrangles.

Tice Creek [CONTRA COSTA]: *stream,* flows 4 miles to Las Trampas Creek 0.5 mile south of Walnut Creek civic center (lat. 37°53'40" N, long. 122°03'30" W); the stream drains Tice Valley. Named on Las Trampas Ridge (1959)

and Walnut Creek (1959) 7.5' quadrangles.

Tice Valley [CONTRA COSTA]: *valley,* 5 miles northwest of Danville (lat. 37°52' N, long. 122°04'10" W); the valley is along Tice Creek. Named on Las Trampas Ridge (1959) 7.5' quadrangle. The name commemorates James Tice, a landowner in the neighborhood (Hoover, Rensch, and Rensch, p. 58).

Tick Creek [SANTA CLARA]: *stream,* flows 3.25 miles to Carnadero Creek 5.25 miles south-southeast of Gilroy (lat. 36°55'55" N, long. 120°32'30" W). Named on Chittenden (1955) 7.5' quadrangle.

Tidal Canal [ALAMEDA]: *water feature,* extends for 1.5 miles between Oakland and Alameda from Oakland Inner Harbor to San Leandro Bay 4 miles southeast of downtown Oakland (lat. 37°45'30" N, long. 122°13'25" W). Named on Oakland East (1959) 7.5' quadrangle.

Timber Ridge [SANTA CLARA]: *ridge,* north-northwest-trending, 2.5 miles long, 5.25 miles east of San Martin (lat. 37°05'30" N, long. 121°30'50" W). Named on Gilroy (1955) 7.5' quadrangle.

Tindle Spring [SOLANO]: *spring,* 7.5 miles northwest of Fairfield (lat. 38°18'30" N, long. 122°09'20" W; sec. 2, T 5 N, R 3 W). Named on Mount George (1951) 7.5' quadrangle.

Tito: see **Quito** [SANTA CLARA].

Tobin: see **Pedro Valley** [SAN MATEO].

Tocaloma [MARIN]: *locality,* 3 miles east-southeast of Point Reyes Station along Lagunitas Creek (lat. 38°03' N, long. 122°45'30" W). Named on Inverness (1954) 7.5' quadrangle. Point Reyes (1918) 15' quadrangle shows the place located along Northwestern Pacific Railroad. Postal authorities established Tocaloma post office in 1891 and discontinued it in 1919 (Frickstad, p. 89). The name probably is from an Indian word (Kroeber, p. 62-63).

Todd Creek [SANTA CLARA]: *stream,* flows 1.5 miles to Bonjetti Creek nearly 2 miles northeast of Bielawski Mountain (lat. 37°14'35" N, long. 122°04'10" W; sec. 10, T 8 S, R 2 W). Named on Castle Rock Ridge (1955) 7.5' quadrangle.

Todos Santos: see **Concord** [CONTRA COSTA].

Toe Drain [SOLANO]: *water feature,* artificial waterway in Yolo Bypass that parallels the west side of Sacramento River Deep Water Ship Channel; extends from Yolo County into Solano County as far as Prospect Slough 9 miles north of Rio Vista (lat. 38°17'15" N, long. 121°39'45" W). Named on Liberty Island (1978) 7.5' quadrangle.

Toland Landing [SOLANO]: *locality,* 6 miles south-southwest of Rio Vista along Sacramento River (lat. 38°05'15" N, long. 121°45'05" W); the place is on Los Ulpinos grant. Named on Antioch North (1978) 7.5' quadrangle. The name commemorates Dr.

Hugh Hugar Toland, founder of University of California Medical School, and owner of 11,800 acres of Los Ulpinos grant (Hoover, Rensch, and Rensch, p. 524).

Tolenas [SOLANO]:

(1) *land grant,* northeast of Fairfield. Named on Denverton (1953), Elmira (1953), Fairfield North (1951), Fairfield South (1949), and Mount George (1951) 7.5' quadrangles. Jose F. Armijo received 3 leagues in 1840 and claimed 13,316 acres patented in 1868 (Cowan, p. 103-104). The name apparently is from an Indian village (Kroeber, p. 63).

(2) *locality,* 2.25 miles east-northeast of downtown Fairfield along Southern Pacific Railroad (lat. 38°16' N, long. 122°00'05" W; sec. 20, T 5 N, R 1 W); the place is on Tolenas grant. Named on Fairfield North (1951) 7.5' quadrangle. Postal authorities established Tolenas post office in 1872, discontinued it in the same year, reestablished it in 1913, and discontinued it in 1914 (Frickstad, p. 193).

Tolenas Springs [SOLANO]: *springs,* 4 miles north of Fairfield (lat. 38°18'35" N, long. 122°03'10" W); the springs are on Tolenas grant. Named on Fairfield North (1951) 7.5' quadrangle. Nineteen springs at the site were the basis of a resort (Anderson, Winslow, p. 255-256).

Toll Gate: see **Saratoga** [SANTA CLARA].

Tollhouse Creek: see **Nuff Creek** [SAN MATEO].

Tolman Peak [ALAMEDA]: *peak,* 4.5 miles north-northwest of Fremont civic center (lat. 37°36'50" N, long. 121°59'25" W). Named on Niles (1961) 7.5' quadrangle. The name commemorates Professor Cyrus Fisher Tolman of Stanford University, who frequently brought geology students to the place (United States Board on Geographic Names, 1959a, p. 3).

Tomales [MARIN]: *village,* 21 miles west-north-west of downtown Novato near Keyes Creek (lat. 38°14'45" N, long. 122°54'15" W). Named on Tomales (1954) and Valley Ford (1954) 7.5' quadrangles. Postal authorities established Tomalles post office in 1854 and changed the name to Tomales before 1879 (Salley, p. 223). John Keys arrived at the place in 1850, when present Keyes Creek was navigable, and built a home, stores, and a wharf called Keys Embarcadero (Donnelly, p. 48).

Tomales: see **Camp Tomales** [MARIN].

Tomales Bay [MARIN]: *bay,* extends southeast for 13 miles from Bodega Bay; the mouth of Tomales Bay is 4 miles west-southwest of Tomales (lat. 38°14' N, long. 122°58'30" W). Named on Drakes Bay (1953), Inverness (1954), Point Reyes NE (1954), and Tomales (1954) 7.5' quadrangles. Called Estero Americano on Ringgold's (1850b) map. Members of the Vizcaino expedition found the bay in 1603 and called it Rio Grande de San Sebasitan (Wagner, H.R., p. 419). The name "Tomales" comes from an Indian word that means "bay" (Kroeber, p. 63).

Tomales Bluff [MARIN]: *promontory,* 5 miles west of Tomales at the northwest end of Tomales Point (lat. 38°14'25" N, long. 122° 59'40" W). Named on Tomales (1954) 7.5' quadrangle. Called Pt. Bodega on Ringgold's (1850b) map.

Tomales Creek: see **Estero de San Antonio** [MARIN].

Tomales Point [MARIN]: *peninsula,* 4.25 miles west-southwest of Tomales (lat. 38°13'15" N, long. 122°58'30" W); the feature is southwest of the mouth of Tomales Bay. Named on Tomales (1954) 7.5' quadrangle. The place also is called Pierce Point for Solomon Pierce, who bought land there in 1858 (Mason, 1976a, p. 149).

Tomales y Baulines [MARIN]:

(1) *land grant,* 6 miles north-northwest of Bolinas. Named on Bolinas (1954), Double Point (1954), Inverness (1954), and San Geronimo (1954) 7.5' quadrangles. Called Tomales y Bolinas on Point Reyes (1918) 15' quadrangle. Rafael Garcia received 5 leagues in 1836 and claimed 9468 acres patented in 1883 (Cowan, p. 104).

(2) *land grant,* extends for 9 miles northwest from Mount Tamalpais. Named on Bolinas (1954), San Geronimo (1954), and San Rafael (1954) 7.5' quadrangles. Rafael Garcia received 5 leagues in 1836; Bethuel Phelps claimed 13,316 acres patented in 1866 (Cowan, p. 104).

Tomales y Bolinas: see **Tomales y Baulines** [MARIN] (1).

Tomalles: see **Tomales** [MARIN].

Tomasini Canyon [MARIN]: *canyon,* drained by a stream that flows 4 miles to lowlands along Tomales Bay near Point Reyes Station (lat. 38°04'15" N, long. 122°48'30" W). Named on Inverness (1954) 7.5' quadrangle. The name commemorates Battista Tomasini, who bought 830 acres in the neighborhood in 1880 (Mason, 1976a, p. 150).

Toms Point [MARIN]: *promontory,* 3.5 miles southwest of Tomales on the northeast side of Tomales Bay (lat. 38°12'50" N, long. 122° 57'05" W). Named on Tomales (1954) 7.5' quadrangle. The name commemorates Tom Wood, who deserted from the United States navy ship *Warren* in 1844 and lived among Indians of Tomales Bay (Mason, 1976b, p. 106).

Tonquin Point: see **Black Point** [SAN FRANCISCO].

Torello Canyon: see **San Vicente Creek** [SAN MATEO].

Tormey [CONTRA COSTA]: *locality,* 6.5 miles west-northwest of Martinez near the mouth of Cañada del Cierbo (lat. 38°03' N, long. 122°14'55" W). Named on Benicia (1959) 7.5' quadrangle. Called El Cierbo on Karquines (1898) 15' quadrangle. Postal authorities established Tormey post office in 1891 and dis-

continued it in 1892 (Frickstad, p. 24). The name is for John and Patrick Tormey, who bought part of Pinole grant in 1867 (Gudde, 1949, p. 366).

Toroges Creek [ALAMEDA]: *stream,* flows 2 miles to lowlands 6 miles southeast of Fremont civic center (lat. 37°29' N, long. 121° 54'45" W). Named on Milpitas (1961) 7.5' quadrangle.

Torquay: see **Pescadero** [SAN MATEO].

Tower Rocks: see **Cave Point** [CONTRA COSTA].

Toyon Camp [CONTRA COSTA]: *locality,* 1 mile south-southwest of Mount Diablo (lat. 37°52' N, long. 121°55'25" W; sec. 12, T 1 S, R 1 W). Named on Diablo (1953) 7.5' quadrangle.

Trail Canyon [SANTA CLARA]: *canyon,* drained by a stream that flows nearly 1 mile to San Antonio Creek 6.5 miles south-southeast of Eylar Mountain (lat. 37°23'10" N, long. 121°30'20" W). Named on Eylar Mountain (1955) 7.5' quadrangle.

Trancas Creek: see **Corinda Los Trancos Creek** [SAN MATEO].

Travis Air Force Base [SOLANO]: *military installation,* 7 miles south-southeast of Vacaville (lat. 38°15'45" N, long. 121°56'15" W). Named on Denverton (1953) and Elmira (1953) 7.5' quadrangles. Elmira (1953) 7.5' quadrangle also has the name "Travis Field" at the place. The name "Travis" honors Brigadier General Robert F. Travis, who was killed in an airplane accident at the site in 1950 (Hoover, Rensch, and Rensch, p. 523). Postal authorities established Fairfield Unit Number 1 post office in 1943, changed the name to Air Base in 1945, and changed it to Travis Air Force Base in 1950 (Salley, p. 2, 72).

Travis Field: see **Travis Air Force Base** [SOLANO].

Treasure Island [SAN FRANCISCO]: *island,* about 1 mile long, 2.25 miles east-northeast of North Point in San Francisco Bay (lat. 37° 49'30" N, long. 122°22'15" W); the feature is connected to Yerba Buena Island by a causeway. Named on Oakland West (1959) and San Francisco North (1956) 7.5' quadrangles. The island was built from 1936 to 1938 by pumping sand and mud dredged from the bay into an enclosure formed by a rock retaining wall; it was used for Golden Gate International Exposition in 1939 and 1940, and it became a navy installation during World War II (Bowen, p. 338-339).

Treasure Rock: see **Red Rock** [CONTRA COSTA-MARIN-SAN FRANCISCO].

Tree Slough [SOLANO]: *water feature,* on Grizzly Island, joins Montezuma Slough 6 miles west-southwest of Denverton (lat. 38° 10'45" N, long. 121°59'40" W). Named on Denverton (1953) and Fairfield South (1949) 7.5' quadrangles. Called Land Slough on Denverton (1918) 7.5' quadrangle.

Tremont [SOLANO]: *locality,* 4 miles northeast of Dixon along Southern Pacific Railroad (lat. 38°29'45" N, long. 121°46'45" W). Named on Dixon (1952) 7.5' quadrangle. Postal authorities established Tremont post office in 1876, discontinued it in 1878, reestablished it in 1889, discontinued it for a time in 1891, and discontinued it finally in 1896; the name is from a place in New York (Salley, p. 224).

Trestle Glen: see **Indian Gulch** [ALAMEDA].

Trevarno [ALAMEDA]: *locality,* 6 miles southwest of Altamont (lat. 37°41'25" N, long. 121°44'45" W). Named on Altamont (1953) 7.5' quadrangle. Officials of Coast Manufacturing and Supply Company named the place after George Bickford's home in England; the company made safety fuses invented by William Bickford, George's father (Gudde, 1949, p. 368).

Tripp Creek: see **West Union Creek** [SAN MATEO].

Tripp Gulch [SAN MATEO]: *canyon,* drained by a stream that flows 1.25 miles to West Union Creek 2 miles northeast of Skeggs Point (lat. 37°25'50" N, long. 122°16'30" W). Named on Woodside (1961) 7.5' quadrangle. Dr. R.C. Tripp opened Woodside store near the mouth of the canyon in 1851 (Brown, p. 95).

Trout Creek [ALAMEDA]: *stream,* flows 4.25 miles to Arroyo Valle about 5.5 miles south of Mendenhall Springs (lat. 37°30'35" N, long. 121°38' W; sec. 10, T 5 S, R 3 E). Named on Mendenhall Springs (1956) 7.5' quadrangle. South Fork enters from the south 1.5 miles upstream from the mouth of the main creek; it is 1.5 miles long and is named on Mendenhall Springs (1956) and Mount Day (1955) 7.5' quadrangles.

Trout Creek [SANTA CLARA]: *stream,* flows 2 miles to the canyon of Los Gatos Creek 1.5 miles south-southwest of downtown Los Gatos (lat. 37°12'10" N, long. 121°59'30" W; sec. 29, T 8 S, R 1 W). Named on Castle Rock Ridge (1955) and Los Gatos (1953) 7.5' quadrangles. According to Young (p. 122-123), the name recalls a Greek fish peddler of the 1850's who had the nickname "Trout."

Tularcitos [SANTA CLARA]: *land grant,* northeast of the city of Milpitas. Named on Calaveras Reservoir (1961) and Milpitas (1961) 7.5' quadrangles. Jose Higuera received 2 leagues in 1821, and he or his son claimed 4394 acres patented in 1870 (Cowan, p. 105). According to Perez (p. 103), Jose Higuera was the grantee in 1839, and his heirs were the patentees in 1870.

Tularcitos Creek [SANTA CLARA]: *stream,* flows 1 mile to lowlands nearly 2 miles northeast of downtown Milpitas (lat. 37°26'50" N, long. 121°52'50" W); the stream is on Tularcitos grant. Named on Milpitas (1961) 7.5' quadrangle. South Branch Tularcitos Creek flows 1 mile to lowlands 10.5 mile east-

southeast of the entrance of Tularcitos Creek to lowlands; it is named on Calaveras Reservoir (1961) 7.5' quadrangle. Tularcitos Creek and South Branch Tularcitos Creek are unconnected on the maps.

Tulare Hill [SANTA CLARA]: *hill,* 1 mile westnorthwest of Coyote (lat. 37°13'15" N, long. 121°45'15" W). Altitude 565 feet. Named on Santa Teresa Hills (1953) 7.5' quadrangle.

Tule Lake [SANTA CLARA]: *lake,* 175 feet long, 6 miles west-southwest of Mount Sizer (lat. 37°10'45" N, long. 121°36'50" W). Named on Mount Sizer (1955) 7.5' quadrangle.

Tule Pond [ALAMEDA]: *intermittent lake,* 1800 feet long, 0.5 mile north-northwest of Fremont civic center (lat. 37°33'30" N, long. 121°58'25" W; sec. 28, T 4 S, R 1 W). Named on Niles (1961) 7.5' quadrangle. Cluff and Bolt (p. 61) gave the alternate name "Tysons Lagoon" for the feature.

Tule Pond: see **Stivers Lagoon** [ALAMEDA].

Tunitas [SAN MATEO]: *locality,* 6 miles southsoutheast of the town of Half Moon Bay (lat. 37°22'50" N, long. 122°23'25" W); the place is on the divide between Tunitas Creek and Lobitos Creek. Named on Halfmoon Bay (1940) 15' quadrangle. Half Moon Bay (1961) 7.5' quadrangle shows Tunitas Sch. at the place.

Tunitas Beach [SAN MATEO]: *beach,* 2.25 miles north-northwest of the village of San Gregorio along the coast (lat. 37°21'25" N, long. 122°23'55" W); the beach is at the mouth of Tunitas Creek. Named on San Gregorio (1961) 7.5' quadrangle. The place first was called Potter's Beach for T.F. Potter ranch, which was near the beach in the 1860's and 1870's (Brown, p. 95).

Tunitas Creek [SAN MATEO]: *stream,* flows 6.5 miles to the sea 2.25 miles north-northwest of the village of San Gregorio (lat. 37° 21'25" N, long. 122°23'55" W). Named on Half Moon Bay (1961), San Gregorio (1961), and Woodside (1961) 7.5' quadrangles. The stream was called Arroyo de las Tunitas in Spanish times; *tunita* is the diminutive of *tuna,* the Spanish term for the fruit of a plant sometimes called the beach apple—the plant is abundant near the mouth of the stream (Gudde, 1949, p. 372; Brown, p. 95-96). East Fork enters from the east 2.25 miles upstream from the mouth of the main creek; it is 2.5 miles long and is named on Woodside (1961) 7.5' quadrangle. The railroad stop near the creek about 1910 was called Long Bridge for a structure built across the stream in 1869 (Brown, p. 49). Alexander Gordon built Gordon's Chute near the mouth of Tunitas Creek in the 1870's to load farm produce and lumber from a high bluff onto ships anchored just offshore (Stanger, 1963, p. 133).

Tunnel: see **The Tunnel**, under **Wrights** [SANTA CLARA]

Tunnel Creek [ALAMEDA]: *stream*, flows 2 miles to Arroyo Mocho 2 miles north-north-west of Cedar Mountain (lat. 37°35' N, long. 121°37'25" W; at W line sec. 14, T 4 S, R 3 E). Named on Cedar Mountain (1956) 7.5' quadrangle. A tunnel to carry water was dug near the mouth of the stream before 1921 (Mosier and Mosier, p. 89).

Tunnel Ridge: see **Sawyer Ridge** [SAN MATEO].

Turkey Flat [SANTA CLARA]: *area*, 5 miles north of Pacheco Peak along North Fork Pacheco Creek (lat. 37°04'50" N, long. 121°17'20" W). Named on Pacheco Peak (1955) 7.5' quadrangle.

Turk Island [ALAMEDA]: *hill*, 4.5 miles north-west of downtown Newark (lat. 37°34'20" N, long. 122°06'10" W). Altitude 116 feet. Named on Newark (1959) 7.5' quadrangle. The feature is unnamed on Haywards (1899) 15' quadrangle, which shows it as an island in marsh along San Francisco Bay. E.H. Dyer named the feature Peruvian Island in the 1850's, and W.J. Lewis named it Brown Island in 1860 for the owner, Charles Brown; John A. Plummer and sons established their Turk's Island Salt Works there in 1869 (Mosier and Mosier, p. 89).

Turner Gulch [SANTA CLARA]: *canyon*, drained by a stream that flows nearly 2 miles to Arroyo Mocho 1.5 miles east-southeast of Eylar Mountain (lat. 37°28'05" N, long. 121°31'10" W). Named on Eylar Mountain (1955) and Mount Boardman (1955) 7.5' quadrangles.

Turtle Rock [CONTRA COSTA]: *relief feature*, 2 miles west-southwest of Mount Diablo (lat. 37°52' N, long. 121°56'45" W). Named on Diablo (1953) 7.5' quadrangle.

Twelve Mile Creek: see **Colma Creek** [SAN MATEO].

Twelvemile Creek [SAN MATEO]: *stream*, flows 2.25 miles to Colma Creek nearly 1 mile west of downtown South San Francisco (lat. 37°39'25" N, long. 122°25'45" W). Named on San Francisco South (1956) 7.5' quadrangle. The name is for Twelve Mile House, established in 1851 near the creek; the stream also was called Baden Creek for the nearby community of Baden (Brown, p. 4), which now is part of South San Francisco.

Twelve Mile House: see **Coyote** [SANTA CLARA]; **Twelvemile Creek** [SAN MATEO].

Twenty-one Mile House: see **Tennant** [SANTA CLARA].

Twenty-one Mile Peak: see **El Toro** [SANTA CLARA].

Twin Creeks [SANTA CLARA]: *settlement*, nearly 2 miles southwest of New Almaden at the entrance of Alamitos Creek into Barret Canyon (lat. 37°09'20" N, long. 121°50'35" W; near NE cor. sec. 15, T 9 S, R 1 E). Named on Santa Teresa Hills (1953) 7.5' quadrangle.

Los Gatos (1919) 15' quadrangle shows a place called Lovely Glen Resort at or near the site.

Twin Fall Creek [SANTA CLARA]: *stream*, flows 2 miles to Llagas Creek 3.5 miles south-southeast of New Almaden (lat. 37°07'50" N, long. 121°47'35" W). Named on Loma Prieta (1955) and Santa Teresa Hills (1953) 7.5' quadrangles.

Twin Lakes [SANTA CLARA]: *lakes*, two, largest 400 feet long, nearly 6 miles west-south-west of Mount Sizer (lat. 37°10'50" N, long. 121°36'40" W). Named on Mount Sizer (1955) 7.5' quadrangle.

Twin Peaks [CONTRA COSTA]: *peaks*, 2.25 miles north-northwest of Mount Diablo (lat. 37°54'40" N, long. 121°56'10" W; sec. 26, T 1 N, R 1 W). Named on Clayton (1953) 7.5' quadrangle.

Twin Peaks [SAN FRANCISCO]: *peaks*, two, 0.5 mile southeast of Mount Sutro (lat. 37°45'10" N, long. 122°26'45" W). Altitude of highest is 922 feet. Named on San Francisco North (1956) 7.5' quadrangle. The peaks were called Las Papas in Spanish times—*las papas* means "the potatoes" in Spanish; they were called Twin Sisters and Mission Peaks in later times (Gudde, 1949, p. 218, 373). The south end of the ridge on which the peaks lie is called Las Papas Hill on San Mateo (1899) 15' quadrangle. The range that includes present Twin Peaks has the name "Mission Mountains" on Wackenreuder's (1861) map.

Twin Peaks [SANTA CLARA]: *peaks*, two, nearly 5 miles north-northeast of Mount Madonna (lat. 37°04'45" N, long. 121°41'15" W). Named on Mount Madonna (1955) 7.5' quadrangle.

Twin Sisters [SOLANO]: *peaks*, two, 8 miles west-northwest of Fairfield (lat. 38°18'20" N, long. 122°10'10" W; sec. 2, 3, T 5 N, R 3 W). Altitudes 2177 and 2259 feet. Named on Mount George (1951) 7.5' quadrangle.

Twin Sisters: see **Twin Peaks** [SAN FRANCISCO].

Twin Sloughs [SOLANO]: *water features*, 4.5 miles south of Fairfield in marsh (lat. 38°11'05" N, long. 122°03'20" W). Named on Fairfield South (1949) 7.5' quadrangle.

Twin Trees Station: see **Palo Alto** [SANTA CLARA].

Two Brothers: see **The Brothers** [CONTRA COSTA].

Two Rock Creek: see **Stemple Creek** [MARIN].

Two Rock Ranch Station Military Reservation [MARIN]: *military installation*, 5.5 miles southeast of Bloomfield near the village of Two Rock (lat. 38°15' N, long. 122°47'30" W). Named on Point Reyes NE (1954) and Two Rock (1954) 7.5' quadrangles. The installation is mainly in Sonoma County, but extends southwest into Marin County 6 miles east of Tomales.

Tyson Lake [ALAMEDA]: *lake,* 425 feet long, 3 miles east-northeast of downtown Oakland (lat. 37°49'20" N, long. 122°13'05" W). Named on Oakland East (1959) 7.5' quadrangle. The name is for Dr. James Tyson, whose estate was near the lake (Mosier and Mosier, p. 89-90).

Tysons Lagoon: see **Tule Pond** [ALAMEDA].

– U –

Ualtis Creek: see **Ulatis Creek** [SOLANO].

Ulatis Creek [SOLANO]: *stream,* flows 11 miles to lowlands 1.5 miles east of downtown Vacaville (lat. 38°21'20" N, long. 121°57'55" W). Named on Allendale (1953), Elmira (1953), and Mount Vaca (1951) 7.5' quadrangles. United States Board on Geographic Names (1933, p. 780) rejected the name "Ualtis Creek" for the feature. The name "Ulatis" evidently is from the designation of Indians who lived in the neighborhood (Kroeber, p. 65).

Ulistac [SANTA CLARA]: *land grant,* 2 miles south-southeast of Alviso. Named on Milpitas (1961) 7.5' quadrangle. Marcelo Pico and an Indian called Cristobal received 0.5 league in 1845; J.D. Hoppe claimed 2217 acres patented in 1868 (Cowan, p. 106). Kroeber (p. 65) considered the name "Ulistac" to be of Indian origin.

Ulmar [ALAMEDA]: *locality,* 4 miles southwest of Altamont along Southern Pacific Railroad (lat. 37°42'10" N, long. 121°42'50" W). Named on Altamont (1953) 7.5' quadrangle.

Umunhum: see **Mount Umunhum** [SANTA CLARA].

Uncle Sam Canyon [CONTRA COSTA]: *canyon,* drained by a stream that flows less than 1 mile to Mitchell Creek nearly 3 miles northwest of Mount Diablo (lat. 37°54'40" N, long. 121°56'50" W; near NW cor. sec. 26, T 1 N, R 1 W). Named on Clayton (1953) 7.5' quadrangle.

Uncle Sam Rock: see **Colorado Reef**, under **Point Montara** [SAN MATEO].

Underwood Gulch: see **Soda Gulch** [SAN MATEO].

Union: see **Unon City** [ALAMEDA].

Union Avenue: see **Campbell** [SANTA CLARA].

Union City [ALAMEDA]: *city,* 5 miles north of downtown Newark (lat. 37°36' N, long. 122°03' W). Named on Newark (1959) 7.5' quadrangle. Newark (1948) 7.5' quadrangle has the name "Union City" on a small community near the west edge of present Union City (lat. 37°35'45" N, long. 122°05'20" W). According to Hoover, Rensch, and Rensch (p. 17), John M. Horner bought 110 acres in 1850 and laid out a town that he called Union City; then Henry C. Smith bought 465 acres next to Horner's Union City and began selling lots in 1851 in his own town of New Haven; finally Strode and Jones bought 750 acres south and west of the first two towns and laid out the town of Alvarado in 1852. Horner took the name "Union" from a river steamer, *The Union,* that he purchased and used to carry agricultural produce from Union City to San Francisco; the steamer was made in Union City, New Jersey (Mosier and Mosier, p. 90). In 1853 New Haven took the name of neighboring Alvarado, and in 1958 Alvarado and Decoto consolidated to form a new city that took the name "Union City" (Hoover, Rensch, and Rensch, p. 17). Postal authorities established Union post office 20 miles south of Oakland in 1851 and discontinued it in 1853; they established Union City post office in 1959 (Salley, p. 227), the year that Union City incorporated.

Union Creek [SOLANO]: *stream,* flows 4 miles to marsh 4.25 miles west of Denverton (lat. 38°13'45" N, long. 121°58'30" W). Named on Denverton (1953) and Elmira (1953) 7.5' quadrangles.

Union Creek: see **West Union Creek** [SAN MATEO].

University Avenue: see **West Berkeley** [ALAMEDA].

University Park: see **Palo Alto** [SANTA CLARA].

Upper Bean Hollow Lake: ee **Bean Hollow Lake** [SAN MATEO].

Upper Crystal Springs Reservoir [SAN MATEO]: *lake,* 2.5 miles long, center 5 miles south of downtown San Mateo (lat. 37°29'45" N, long. 122°20' W); the lake is southwest of Lower Crystal Springs Reservoir, and separated from it by a low dam that forms a causeway. Named on San Mateo (1956) and Woodside (1961) 7.5' quadrangles. Upper Crystal Springs Reservoir and Lower Crystal Springs Reservoir together are called Crystal Springs Lake on San Mateo (1915) 15' quadrangle. The lake that occupied the lower part of present Upper Crystal Springs Reservoir before 1877 was referred to in early times at Laguna de Raimundo, Laguna Grande, Harrington's Pond, Byrnes' Lake, and The Laguna (Brown, p. 74). The valley around and for about 2 miles southeast of this earlier lake was called Cañada de Raimundo in Spanish times; the stream in the valley is called Cañada Raimundo Creek (Brown, p. 16, 74).

Upper Emerald Lake [SAN MATEO]: *lake,* 550 feet long, 2.5 miles southwest of downtown Redwood City (lat. 37°27'35" N, long. 122°15'30" W); the lake is 0.5 mile southsoutheast of Lower Emerald Lake. Named on Woodside (1961) 7.5' quadrangle.

Upper Penitencia Creek [SANTA CLARA]: *stream,* flows 11 miles to Coyote Creek 2.5 miles north-northeast of downtown San Jose (lat. 37°22'05" N, long. 121°52'45" W).

SAN FRANCISCO BAY AREA

Named on Calaveras Reservoir (1961), Mount Day (1955), San Jose East (1961), and San Jose West (1961) 7.5' quadrangles. Hare's (1872) map has the name "Penetencia Creek." Both Upper Penitencia Creek and Lower Penitencia Creek are called Penitencia Creek on San Jose (1899) 15' quadrangle, although they are shown as separate streams—United States Board on Geographic Names (1962, p. 13, 18) rejected the name "Penitencia Creek" for both streams. Gudde (1949, p. 257) noted that the name "Arroyo de la Penitencia" appears on a map of 1840. Whitney (p. 51) mentioned that Arroyo de la Penitencia also is called Arroyo Aguage.

Upper San Antonio Valley [SANTA CLARA]: *valley,* 3.5 miles west of Mount Stakes on upper reaches of Jumpoff Creek (lat. 37°19' N, long. 121°28'15" W); the valley is south of San Antonio Valley. Named on Mount Stakes (1955) 7.5' quadrangle.

Upper San Leandro Reservoir [ALAMEDA-CONTRA COSTA]: *lake,* on Alameda-Contra Costa county line, behind a dam on San Leandro Creek 10 miles east-southeast of downtown Oakland (lat. 37°45'50" N, long. 122°05'45" W). Named on Las Trampas Ridge (1959) and Oakland East (1959) 7.5' quadrangles.

Uval Creek: see **Bull Run Creek** [SAN MATEO].

Uvas: see **Bradleys Store** [SANTA CLARA].

Uvas Creek [SANTA CLARA]: *stream,* flows 25 miles to a point 3 miles south-southeast of Gilroy, beyond which the stream is called Carnadero Creek. Named on Chittenden (1955), Gilroy (1955), Loma Prieta (1955), and Mount Madonna (1955) 7.5' quadrangles. On Morgan Hill (1917) 15' quadrangle, Uvas Creek appears to join Bodfish Creek to form Carnadero Creek 3 miles west of Gilroy, but the relation of the three streams is unclear on the map.

Uvas Creek: see **Little Uvas Creek** [SANTA CLARA].

Uvas Reservoir [SANTA CLARA]: *lake,* 2 miles long, behind a dam on Uvas Creek nearly 4 miles north-northeast of Mount Madonna (lat. 37°03'55" N, long. 121°41'25" W). Named on Mount Madonna (1955, photorevised 1968 and 1973) 7.5' quadrangle.

— V —

Vaca: see **Elmira** [SOLANO]; **Mount Vaca** [SOLANO].

Vaca Canyon [CONTRA COSTA]: *canyon,* 2 miles long, opens into Alhambra Valley 6.25 miles north-northeast of Orinda (lat. 37°57'55" N, long. 122°08'50" W). Named on Briones Valley (1959) 7.5' quadrangle. Waring (p. 208) noted that two springs, called Ferndale Springs, were located in Vaca Can-

yon and provided water to a bottling works; the water was noticeably carbonated.

Vaca Mountains [SOLANO]: *range,* south of Putah Creek on Napa-Solano county line; Blue Ridge (2) is at the crest of the range. Named on Capell Valley (1951), Fairfield North (1951), Monticello Dam (1959), and Mount Vaca (1951) 7.5' quadrangles. United States Board on Geographic Names (1970a, p. 3) gave the name "Blue Mountains" as a variant, and noted that the name "Vaca" commemorates the Vaca family, early residents of the region.

Vaca Peak: see **Mount Vaca** [SOLANO].

Vaca Valley [SOLANO]: *valley,* at and northwest of Vacaville. Named on Allendale (1953), Elmira (1953), Fairfield North (1951), and Mount Vaca (1951) 7.5' quadrangles.

Vacaville [SOLANO]: *city,* 8 miles north-northeast of Fairfield (lat. 38°21'05" N, long. 121°59'35" W). Named on Elmira (1953) and Fairfield North (1951, photorevised 1968 and 1973) 7.5' quadrangles. Postal authorities established Vacaville post office in 1854 (Frickstad, p. 193), and the city incorporated in 1892. Manuel Vaca deeded 9 square miles of his Los Putos grant to William McDaniel in 1850 with the understanding that McDaniel would lay out a town on one of the square miles, give Vaca certain town lots, and name the place Vacaville; the town plat was filed in 1851 (Hoover, Rensch, and Rensch, p. 522-523). Postal authorities established Nut Tree post office 2.5 miles northeast of Vacaville post office in 1962 at a roadside attraction that Edwin Power started in 1921 when he set up a stand under a huge black-walnut tree (Salley, p. 157).

Vacaville Junction [SOLANO]: *locality,* 4 miles south-southeast of Vacaville along Sacramento Northern Railroad (lat. 38°17'50" N, long. 121°57'50" W; sec. 10, T 5 N, R 1 W). Named on Elmira (1953) 7.5' quadrangle.

Vale [SOLANO]: *locality,* 7 miles east-southeast of Elmira along Sacramento Northern Railroad (lat. 38°19'15" N, long. 121°47'05" W; near W line sec. 32, T 6 N, R 2 E); nearly 2 miles west-northwest of the site of Maine Prairie. Named on Dozier (1952) 7.5' quadrangle. Called Maine Prairie Sta. on Maine Prairie (1916) 7.5' quadrangle, which shows the place along Oakland Antioch and Eastern Railroad.

Vallecitos Creek [ALAMEDA]: *stream,* flows 5 miles to Arroyo de la Laguna at Sunol (lat. 37°35'40" N, long. 121°53' W); the stream drains Vallecitos Valley. Named on La Costa Valley (1960) 7.5' quadrangle.

Vallecitos Valley [ALAMEDA]: *valley,* 2 miles east of Sunol along Vallecitos Creek (lat. 37°36' N, long., 121°53'30" W). Named on La Costa Valley (1960) 7.5' quadrangle.

Valle de San Jose [ALAMEDA]: *land grant,* at and northeast of Sunol. Named on Altamont

(1953), Dublin (1961), La Costa Valley (1960), Livermore (1961), Mendenhall Springs (1956), and Niles (1961) 7.5' quadrangles. Antonio Maria Pico and Antonio Maria Sunol received the land in 1839; Sunol and Bernal claimed 48,436 acres patented in 1865 (Cowan, p. 80).

Vallejo [SOLANO]: *city,* 15 miles southwest of Fairfield along Mare Island Strait (downtown near lat. 38°06'10" N, long. 122°15'20" W). Named on Benicia (1959), Cordelia (1951), Cuttings Wharf (1949), and Mare Island (1959) 7.5' quadrangles. Postal authorities established Vallejo post office in 1851, discontinued it in 1853, and reestablished it in 1855 (Frickstad, p. 193). The city incorporated in 1868. Mariano G. Vallejo founded the town in 1850 and offered land and money to the state legislature for public buildings if the state capital were moved to the place; the legislature moved to Vallejo early in 1852, but left almost immediately (Hoover, Rensch, and Rensch, p. 521-522). Postal authorities established East Vallejo post office in 1951 and changed the name to Springtowne in 1962 (Salley, p. 64). They established Federal Terrace post office as a branch of Vallejo post office in 1944 at a federal housing tract; they established Hillside post office as a branch of Vallejo post office at a wartime housing project in 1945, and discontinued it in 1946 (Salley, p. 73, 98).

Vallejo: see **East Valllejo**, under **Vallejo** [SOLANO]; **South Vallejo** [SOLANO].

Vallejo Bay: see **Carquinez Strait** [CONTRA COSTA-SOLANO].

Vallejo Beach [SAN MATEO]: *beach,* 3 miles northwest of downtown Half Moon Bay along the coast (lat. 37°29'45" N, long. 122° 27'45" W. Named on Half Moon Bay (1961) 7.5' quadrangle.

Vallejo Heights [SOLANO]: *ridge,* northwest-trending, less than 1 mile long, 1 mile north-northwest of downtown Vallejo (lat. 38° 07' N, long. 122°15'50" W). Named on Mare Island (1959) 7.5' quadrangle. Called Vallejo Hill on Mare Island (1916) 15' quadrangle.

Vallejo Hill: see **Vallejo Heights** [SOLANO].

Vallejo Junction [CONTRA COSTA]: *locality,* 6 miles west-northwest of Martinez at the south terminus of a railroad ferry across Carquinez Strait to Vallejo [SOLANO] (lat. 38°03'15" N, long. 122° 13'45" W). Named on Karquines (1898) 15' quadrangle.

Vallejo Reservoir: see **Swanzy Reservoir** [SOLANO].

Vallejo's Mills: see **Niles District** [ALAMEDA].

Vallejo Sulphur Springs: see **Sulphur Springs** [SOLANO].

Vallejo White Sulphur Springs: see **Sulphur Springs** [SOLANO].

Vallemar [SAN MATEO]: *district,* 4 miles north of Montara Knob in Calera Valley (lat. 37°36'45" N, long. 122°28'45" W). Named

on Montara Mountain (1956) 7.5' quadrangle. Residents of the place voted in 1957 to join neighboring communities and form the new city of Pacifica.

Valle Vista [CONTRA COSTA]: *locality,* 4.5 miles south-southeast of Orinda (lat. 37°49'20" N, long. 122°08' W; near NE cor. sec. 25, T 1 S, R 3 W). Named on Oakland East (1959) 7.5' quadrangle. Concord (1915) 15' quadrangle shows the place located along Oakland Antioch and Eastern Railroad.

Valley of San Jose: see **Santa Clara Valley** [SANTA CLARA].

Valona [CONTRA COSTA]: *town,* 5.5 miles west-northwest of Martinez (lat. 38°03'10" N, long. 122°13'20" W). Named on Benicia (1959) 7.5' quadrangle.

Valpe Creek [ALAMEDA-SANTA CLARA]: *stream,* heads in Alameda County and flows 5.5 miles to Alameda Creek 3.25 miles northeast of Mount Day in Santa Clara County (lat. 37°27'20" N, long. 121°39'30" W; sec. 33, T 5 S, R 3 E); the stream heads on Valpe Ridge. Named on Mendenhall Springs (1956) and Mount Day (1955) 7.5' quadrangles.

Valpe Ridge [ALAMEDA-SANTA CLARA]: *ridge,* north- to west-trending, 14 miles long, 5 miles north-northeast of Mount Day (lat. 37°29' N, long. 121°39'30" W); mainly in Santa Clara County, but extends northwest for 7.5 miles into Alameda County. Named on Eylar Mountain (1955), La Costa Valley (1960), Mendenhall Springs (1956), and Mount Day (1955) 7.5' quadrangles. Pleasanton (1906) 15' quadrangle shows Valpe Ridge extending northwest to include present Apperson Ridge. The misspelled name commemorates Calvin Valpey, who settled at the ridge in 1850; the feature first was called Pine Ridge (Mosier and Mosier, p. 91).

Valta: see **Elmira** [SOLANO].

Vance Canyon [SANTA CLARA]: *canyon,* drained by a stream that flows 1.5 miles to Packwood Valley 4.5 miles west of Mount Sizer (lat. 37°12'25" N, long. 121°35'45" W; sec. 25, T 8 S, R 3 E). Named on Mount Sizer (1955) 7.5' quadrangle.

Van Court's Hill: see **Belmont Hill** [SAN MATEO].

Vanden [SOLANO]: *locality,* 4.5 miles south-southeast of Vacaville along Southern Pacific Railroad (lat. 38°17'10" N, long. 121° 58' W). Named on Elmira (1917) 7.5' quadrangle. Postal authorities established Vanden post office in 1897 and discontinued it in 1899 (Frickstad, p. 193).

Van Horn Flats [SANTA CLARA]: *area,* 1.5 miles west of Mount Day (lat. 37°25'15" N, long. 121°43'30" W; sec. 11, T 6 S, R 2 E). Named on Mount Day (1955) 7.5' quadrangle.

Van Sickle Island [SOLANO]: *island,* 4.5 miles south-southwest of Birds Landing (2) along Suisun Bay between Montezuma Slough and Spoonbill Creek (lat. 38°04'15" N, long.

121°53'30" W). Named on Antioch North (1978) and Honker Bay (1953) 7.5' quadrangles. Called Jones I. on Ringgold's (1850c) map, which shows Pt. Hansen at the east end of the island. United States Board on Geographic Names (1933, p. 787) rejected the form "Van Sickle's Island" for the name.

Van Wych Canyon: see **Van Wyck Creek** [MARIN].

Van Wyck Camp [MARIN]: *locality,* 5.5 miles southwest of downtown San Rafael (lat. 37°54'30" N, long. 122°35'45" W). Named on San Rafael (1954) 7.5' quadrangle.

Van Wyck Creek [MARIN]: *stream,* flows 1.25 miles to Alpine Lake 5.25 miles west-southwest of downtown San Rafael (lat. 37° 56'50" N, long. 122°37'20" W). Named on San Rafael (1954) 7.5' quadrangle. The canyon of the stream is called Van Wych Canyon on Mount Tamalpais (1950) 15' quadrangle. Teather (p. 85) associated the name with Sidney M. Van Wyck, Jr., who was a leader in the creation of Mount Tamalpais state park.

Vasona: see **Vasona Junction** [SANTA CLARA].

Vasona Creek [SANTA CLARA]: *stream,* flows nearly 1.5 miles to end in lowlands 1.25 miles east-northeast of Saratoga (lat. 37°15'55" N, long. 122°00'15" W). Named on Cupertino (1961, photorevised 1968 and 1973) 7.5' quadrangle. On Cupertino (1961) and San Jose West (1961) 7.5' quadrangles, present Sobey Creek is called Vasona Creek; United States Board on Geographic Names (1972, p. 3) listed the variant name "Vasona Creek" for Sobey Creek.

Vasona Junction [SANTA CLARA]: *locality,* 1.5 miles north-northeast of downtown Los Gatos along Southern Pacific Railroad, where two rail lines meet (lat. 37°15'25" N, long. 121°57'50" W). Named on San Jose West (1961) 7.5' quadrangle. Called Vasona on California Mining Bureau's (1917b) map. According to Patricia Loomis (*San Jose Mercury,* February 2, 1981), Albert August Vollmer asked officials of Southern Pacific Railroad about 1900 to put a flag stop near his home; when the officials agreed, they told Vollmer to name the stop, and he called it Vasona for a pony that he had owned.

Vasona Reservoir [SANTA CLARA]: *lake,* nearly 1 mile long, behind a dam on Los Gatos Creek 2 miles north-northeast of downtown Los Gatos (lat. 37°14'50" N, long. 121°57'50" W). Named on Los Gatos (1953) 7.5' quadrangle.

Vasquez Peak [SANTA CLARA]: *peak,* 4.5 miles east-southeast of Gilroy Hot Springs (lat. 37°04'50" N, long. 121°24' W; near W line sec. 11, T 10 S, R 5 E). Altitude 2210 feet. Named on Gilroy Hot Springs (1955) 7.5' quadrangle.

Veale Tract [CONTRA COSTA]: *area,* 4 miles east-northeast of Brentwood (lat. 37°58' N,

long. 121°37' W). Named on Brentwood (1978) and Woodward Island (1978) 7.5' quadrangles.

Venice Beach [SAN MATEO]: *beach,* 1.5 miles northwest of downtown Half Moon Bay along the coast (lat. 37°28'50" N, long. 122° 27'05" W). Named on Half Moon Bay (1961) 7.5' quadrangle.

Verde Canyon [MARIN]: *canyon,* drained by a stream that flows 2.5 miles to Walker Creek 7.5 miles southeast of Tomales (lat. 38° 10' N, long. 122°48'40" W). Named on Point Reyes NE (1954) 7.5' quadrangle.

Verona [ALAMEDA]: *locality,* 2.25 miles north of Sunol along Western Pacific Railroad and Southern Pacific Railroad (lat. 37°37'45" N, long. 121°52'50" W). Named on Pleasanton (1906) 15' quadrangle. The place was the station for Phoebe Hurst's estate, La Hacienda del Pozo de Verona, for which it was named (Mosier and Mosier, p. 91).

Vicente Creek: see **San Vicente Creek** [SAN MATEO].

Vichy Spring: see **New Almaden** [SANTA CLARA].

Vincent Landing [MARIN]: *locality,* 2.5 miles southwest of Tomales along the northeast side of Tomales Bay (lat. 38°13'05" N, long. 122°56'20" W). Named on Tomales (1954) 7.5' quadrangle.

Vine Hill [CONTRA COSTA]: *district,* 2.25 miles east of downtown Martinez (lat. 38°00'30" N, long. 122°05'40" W). Named on Vine Hill (1959) 7.5' quadrangle.

Violet [SOLANO]: *locality,* 4.5 miles south-southwest of Allendale along Southern Pacific Railroad (lat. 38°23' N, long. 121°58'15" W). Named on Wolfskill (1917) 7.5' quadrangle.

Vision: see **Mount Vision** [MARIN].

Vision Hill: see **Mount Vision** [MARIN].

Visitacion: see **Brisbane** [SAN MATEO].

Visitacion City: see **Brisbane** [SAN MATEO].

Visitacion Point [SAN MATEO]: *promontory,* 2.5 miles north-northeast of downtown South San Francisco along San Francisco Bay (lat. 37°41'35" N, long. 122°23'55" W). Named on San Francisco South (1947) 7.5' quadrangle. Called Visitation Pt. on San Mateo (1915) 15' quadrangle, but United States Board on Geographic Names (1949a, p. 4) rejected this form of the name; the Board pointed out that the name is from Cañada de Guadalupe y la Visitacion grant, where the promontory is located. The feature now protrudes into landfill. San Mateo (1899) 15' quadrangle has the name "Visitation Pt." at a place about 0.5 mile farther south-southeast on the south side of the mouth of Guadalupe Valley.

Visitacion Valley [SAN FRANCISCO-SAN MATEO]: *valley,* 3 miles southeast of Mount Davidson on San Francisco-San Mateo county line (lat. 37°42'30" N, long. 122°24'50" W). Named on San Francisco South (1956) 7.5' quadrangle. Called Visitation Valley on San Mateo (1915) 15' quadrangle, but United States Board on Geographic Names (1949a, p. 14) rejected this form of the name. The feature also was called Schwerin Valley for Henry Schwerin, a dairyman who lived there in the 1850's (Brown, p. 98).

Visitation Point: see **Visitacion Point** [SAN MATEO].

Visitation Valley: see **Visitacion Valley** [SAN FRANCISCO-SAN MATEO].

Vista Grande: see **Daly City** [SAN MATEO].

Volanti Slough [SOLANO]: *water feature,* joins Suisun Slough 4.5 miles south of Fairfield (lat. 38°10'50" N, long. 122°02'45" W). Named on Fairfield South (1949) 7.5' quadrangle. United States Board on Geographic Names (1983c, p. 6) approved the name "Navy Point" for a promontory on the west shore of Suisun Slough opposite the mouth of Volanti Slough (lat. 38°10'45" N, long. 122° 02'51" W).

Volimer Peak [CONTRA COSTA]: *peak,* 2.25 miles west of Orinda on San Pablo Ridge (lat. 37°53' N, long. 122°13'15" W). Altitude 1905 feet. Named on Briones Valley (1959) 7.5' quadrangle. Called Bald Peak on Concord (1897) 15' quadrangle, but United States Board on Geographic Names (1960b, p. 19) rejected this designation for the feature.

— W —

Waddell Beach: see **Año Nuevo Creek** [SAN MATEO].

Waddell Creek: see **West Waddell Creek** [SAN MATEO].

Waddell's Landing: see **Waddell Beach**, under **Año Nuevo Creek** [SAN MATEO].

Waddell's Wharf: see **Waddell Beach**, under **Año Nuevo Creek** [SAN MATEO].

Wagoner Field: see **Livermore Naval Air Station**, under **Livermore** [ALAMEDA].

Walden: see **Locust** [CONTRA COSTA].

Walden Spur: see **Pottery** [ALAMEDA].

Waldo [MARIN]: *locality,* 1.25 miles northwest of downtown Sausalito along Western Pacific Railroad (lat. 37°52'20" N, long. 122° 30'10" W). Named on Point Bonita (1954) 7.5' quadrangle.

Waldo Point [MARIN]: *promontory,* 7 miles south-southeast of downtown San Rafael along Richardson Bay (lat. 37°52'15" N, long. 122°30'15" W). Named on Tamalpais (1897) 15' quadrangle.

Walker Canyon [CONTRA COSTA]: *canyon,* drained by a stream that flows 1.25 miles to Ygnacio Valley 4.5 miles west-northwest of Mount Diablo (lat. 37°54'15" N, long. 121°59'20" W). Named on Clayton (1953) 7.5' quadrangle.

Walker Creek [MARIN]: *stream,* formed by the confluence of Arroyo Sausal and Salmon Creek, flows 15 miles to Tomales Bay 2 miles south-southwest of Tomales (lat. 38°13'20" N, long. 122° 55'15" W). Named on Point Reyes NE (1954) and Tomales (1954) 7.5' quadrangles. United States Board on Geographic Names (1943, p. 14) rejected the names "Arroyo San Antonio," "Arroyo Sausal," "Keyes Creek," "Keys Creek," and "Salmon Creek" for the stream, or for any part of it. The name "Walker" commemorates the family of Lewis W. Walker, an early landowner in the neighborhood (Mason, 1976b, p. 153).

Walker Gulch [SAN MATEO]: *canyon,* drained by a stream that flows 1 mile to Purisima Creek 4 miles west-northwest of Skeggs Point (lat. 37°26'15" N, long. 122°22'05" W). Named on Woodside (1961) 7.5' quadrangle.

Wallace: see **Mount Wallace** [ALAMEDA].

Wall Point [CONTRA COSTA]: *peak,* 2.5 miles southwest of Mount Diablo (lat. 37°51'25" N, long. 121°57'10" W; sec. 10, T 1 S, R 1 W). Named on Diablo (1953) 7.5' quadrangle.

Wall Point: see **Point Wall** [SOLANO].

Walnut Creek [CONTRA COSTA]:
(1) *stream,* formed by the confluence of San Ramon Creek and Las Trampas Creek, flows 10 miles to Pacheco Creek 3.5 miles east of Martinez (lat. 38°01'25" N, long. 122°04'10" W); the stream heads in the city of Walnut Creek. Named on Vine Hill (1959) and Walnut Creek (1959) 7.5' quadrangles. Called Arroyo de las Nueces on a diseño of Arroyo de las Nueces y Bolbones grant made in 1834 (Becker, 1969). The stream also was called Arroyo de los Nogales in the early days because of black-walnut trees that grew along it—*nogales* means "walnuts" in Spanish, and *nueces* means "nuts" (Gudde, 1949, p. 382).
(2) *city,* 8 miles west of Mount Diablo (civic center near lat. 37°54'10" N, long. 122°03'30" W); the city is along Walnut Creek (1). Named on Walnut Creek (1959) 7.5' quadrangle. Postal authorities established Walnut Creek post office in 1862 (Frickstad, p. 24), and the city incorporated in 1914.

Walpert Ridge [ALAMEDA]: *ridge,* southeast-to south-trending, 6.5 miles long, center 5 miles south-southwest of Dublin (lat. 37°38'20" N, long. 121°59'10" W). Named on Dublin (1961), Hayward (1959), and Niles (1961) 7.5' quadrangles. The name commemorates John Walpert, who owned land on the ridge (Mosier and Mosier, p. 91-92).

Walshs Pocket [ALAMEDA]: *canyon,* drained by a stream that flows 0.5 mile to Martin Canyon 1.5 miles west-northwest of Dublin (lat. 37°42'50" N, long. 121°57'45" W; sec. 34, T 2 S, R 1 W). Named on Dublin (1961) 7.5' quadrangle. The name commemorates James Walsh, a local farmer (Mosier and Mosier, p. 92).

Walwood [CONTRA COSTA]: *locality,* 3 miles east of the present Walnut Creek civic center at the end of a branch of Oakland Antioch and Eastern Railroad (lat. 37°54'15" N, long.

122°00'25" W). Named on Concord (1915) 15' quadrangle.

Wanda: see **Mount Wanda**, under **Martinez** [CONTRA COSTA].

Ward Creek [ALAMEDA]: *stream,* flows 3.5 miles to lowlands 0.5 mile southeast of downtown Hayward (lat. 37°39'55" N, long. 122° 04'35" W). Named on Hayward (1959) and Newark (1959) 7.5' quadrangles. The name commemorates Charles Trobridge Ward, who owned land along the upper part of the creek in the early 1870's; the stream originally was called Sulphur Spring Creek, but the upper part was renamed Ward Creek, and the lower part retains the name "Sulphur Creek" (Mosier and Mosier, p. 92).

Warm Springs [ALAMEDA]: *springs,* 4.5 miles southeast of Fremont civic center (lat. 37°30'10" N, long. 121°54'25" W); the springs are near Agua Caliente Creek. Named on Niles (1961) 7.5' quadrangle. Berkstresser (p. A-3) gave the names "Alameda Warm Springs" and "Mission San Jose Hot Springs" as alternates.

Warm Springs: see **Warm Springs District** [ALAMEDA].

Warm Springs Creek: see **Agua Caliente Creek** [ALAMEDA].

Warm Springs District [ALAMEDA]: *district,* 5 miles south-southeast of Fremont civic center in Fremont (lat. 37°29'15" N, long. 121°55'35" W). Named on Milpitas (1961) 7.5' quadrangle. San Jose (1899) 15' quadrangle has the name "Warm Springs" for the community that joined in 1956 with neighboring communities to form the new city of Fremont. The springs called Warm Springs are in the district. Thompson and West (1878, p. 27) noted a hamlet called Harrisburg, or Peacock's, that was located a short distance east of Warm Springs railroad station. Postal authorities established Harrisburgh post office in 1865 and changed the post office name to Warm Springs in 1885; the name "Harrisburgh" was for Abram Harris, who settled at the site in 1858—George W. Peacock was the first postmaster (Salley, p. 94). Postal authorities changed the name of Warm Springs post office to Warmsprings in 1895 and back to Warm Springs in 1950 (Salley, p. 234).

Warm Springs Landing: see **Mud Slough** [ALAMEDA].

Warner Canyon [MARIN]: *canyon,* 1.5 miles long, 4 miles south of downtown San Rafael (lat. 37°54'50" N, long. 122°32'05" W). Named on San Rafael (1954) 7.5' quadrangle. Dr. Alexander Warner of San Francisco had a house and tent platforms in the canyon for use during his summer visits (Teather, p. 85).

Warrington Island: see **Wheeler Island** [SOLANO].

Washerwoman's Lagoon: see **Marina District** [SAN FRANCISCO].

Washington Corners: see **Irvington District** [ALAMEDA].

Washington Slough: see **False River** [CONTRA COSTA].

Wash Rock [SAN MATEO]: *rock,* 2.5 miles west of downtown Half Moon Bay, and 2.25 miles south-southeast of Pillar Point (lat. 37° 28'05" N, long. 122°28'30" W). Named on Half Moon Bay (1961) 7.5' quadrangle. The rock is a high point on an underwater feature called Southeast Reef (United States Coast and Geodetic Survey, p. 122).

Water Gulch [SANTA CLARA]: *canyon,* drained by a stream that flows 3.5 miles to East Fork Coyote Creek 2.25 miles southwest of Bear Mountain (lat. 37°12'15" N, long. 121°27'35" W; sec. 29, T 8 S, R 5 E). Named on Mississippi Creek (1955) and Mount Sizer (1955) 7.5' quadrangles.

Waterman Creek [SAN MATEO]: *stream,* flows 3 miles to Pescadero Creek 7 miles south-southeast of Mindego Hill just inside of Santa Cruz County (lat. 37°12'50" N, long. 122°10'30" W; near N line sec. 27, T 8 S, R 3 W). Named on Big Basin (1955) 7.5' quadrangle.

Waterman Park: see **Fairfield** [SOLANO].

Watson Canyon [CONTRA COSTA]: *canyon,* drained by a stream that flows 1.5 miles to San Ramon Valley 4.25 miles southeast of Danville (lat. 37°46'20" N, long. 121°57'10" W). Named on Diablo (1953) 7.5' quadrangle.

Watson Hollow [SOLANO]: *valley,* 3 miles north-northwest of Rio Vista (lat. 38°11'40" N, long. 121°42'40" W). Named on Rio Vista (1978) 7.5' quadrangle.

Wauhab Ridge [ALAMEDA]: *ridge,* west- to northwest-trending, 6 miles long, 8 miles east-southeast of Sunol (lat. 38°32' N, long. 121°45'30" W). Named on La Costa Valley (1960) and Mendenhall Springs (1956) 7.5' quadrangles. The name commemorates Joshua W. Wauhab, who settled at the site in 1851 (Mosier and Mosier, p. 93).

Wayne [SANTA CLARA]: *locality,* 3 miles south of downtown Milpitas along Southern Pacific Railroad (lat. 37°23'10" N, long. 121° 53'50" W). Named on Milpitas (1961) 7.5' quadrangle.

Webb Creek [MARIN]: *stream,* flows 2.25 miles to Bolinas Bay 3.5 miles east-southeast of Bolinas (lat. 37°53'05" N, long. 122°37'40" W). Named on Bolinas (1954) and San Rafael (1954) 7.5' quadrangles. The name commemorates Johnathan E. Webb, a conservationist interested in preserving Mount Tamalpais and vicinity (Teather, p. 87).

Webb Point [CONTRA COSTA]: *promontory,* 6.25 miles north-northeast of the settlement of Bethel Island (lat. 38°05'30" N, long. 121°34'40" W); the feature is at the northeast corner of Webb Tract. Named on Bouldin Island (1978) 7.5' quadrangle.

Webb Reach [CONTRA COSTA]: *water fea-*

ture, part of San Joaquin River 6.5 miles north-northeast of the settlement of Bouldin Island (lat. 38°06' N, long. 121°35'45" W); the feature is north of Webb Tract. Named on Bouldin Island (1978) 7.5' quadrangle.

Webb's Landing: see **Webb Tract** [CONTRA COSTA].

Webb Tract [CONTRA COSTA]: *island,* 4.5 miles long, 4.5 miles north-northeast of the settlement of Bethel Island between San Joaquin River, Old River, False River, and Fishermans Cut (lat. 38°04'30" N, long. 121°36'45" W). Named on Bouldin Island (1978) and Jersey Island (1978) 7.5' quadrangles. Postal authorities established Webb's Landing post office on Webb Tract (NW quarter sec. 19, T 3 N, R 4 E) in 1873 and discontinued in 1879 (Salley, p. 236).

Weeks Creek [SAN MATEO]: *stream,* flows 1.5 miles to La Honda Creek 2 miles north of La Honda (lat. 37°20'45" N, long. 122°16'25" W; near S line sec. 2, T 7 S, R 4 W). Named on La Honda (1961) 7.5' quadrangle. The name is from Robinson J. Weeks ranch, the first American establishment in the neighborhood (Brown, p. 99).

Welch Creek [ALAMEDA]: *stream,* flows 3 miles to Alameda Creek 4 miles south of Sunol (lat. 37°32'05" N, long. 121°51'05" W; at N line sec. 3, T 5 S, R 1 E). Named on La Costa Valley (1960) 7.5' quadrangle. The name is for a ranch owner (Mosier and Mosier, p. 93).

Weldon Canyon [SOLANO]: see **Mix Canyon** [SOLANO].

Wells Slough [SOLANO]: *water feature,* joins Suisun Slough 5.5 miles south-southwest of Fairfield (lat. 38°10'20" N, long. 122°03'45" W). Named on Fairfield South (1949) 7.5' quadrangle.

Werner [CONTRA COSTA]: *locality,* 5 miles east of Brentwood along Atchison, Topeka and Santa Fe Railroad (lat. 37°56'25" N, long. 121°36'25" W). Named on Woodward Island (1978) 7.5' quadrangle.

West Berkeley [ALAMEDA]: *district,* 3 miles north-northwest of downtown Oakland near San Francisco Bay (lat. 37°52' N, long. 122°18' W). Named on San Francisco (1899) 15' quadrangle. The station along Southern Pacific Railroad in West Berkeley had the name "University Avenue" (Diller and others, p. 83).

West End: see **Alameda** [ALAMEDA].

Western Addition [SAN FRANCISCO]: *district,* 1.5 miles west-northwest of San Francisco civic center (lat. 37°47' N, long. 122°26'45" W). Named on San Francisco North (1956) 7.5' quadrangle.

West Hartley [CONTRA COSTA]: *locality,* 7 miles northeast of Mount Diablo (lat. 37°56'25" N, long. 121°48'45" W; near S line sec. 12, T 1 N, R 1 E). Site named on Antioch South (1953) 7.5' quadrangle. The place was

a coal-mine town founded in the late 1880's; the name is from the famous West Hartley coal mine in England (Mosier, p. 7).

Westlake [SAN MATEO]: *district,* 5 miles northwest of downtown South San Francisco (lat. 37°41'55" N, long. 122°29'10" W). Named on San Francisco South (1956) 7.5' quadrangle.

West Marin Island [MARIN]: *island,* 700 feet long, 400 feet west-northwest of East Marin Island in San Rafael Bay (lat. 37°57'55" N, long. 122°28'20" W). Named on San Quentin (1959) 7.5' quadrangle. This island and East Marin Island together have the name "Marin Is." on San Francisco (1915) 15' quadrangle.

West Oakland: see **Oakland** [ALAMEDA].

West Peak [MARIN]: *peak,* 5 miles southwest of downtown San Rafael on Mount Tamalpais (lat. 37°55'25" N, long. 122°35'45" W). Named on San Rafael (1954) 7.5' quadrangle.

West Pittsburg [CONTRA COSTA]: *locality,* 3 miles west of Pittsburg (lat. 38°01'40" N, long. 121°56' W). Named on Honker Bay (1953) 7.5' quadrangle. Honker Bay (1918) 7.5' quadrangle has the name "West Pittsburg" at a place located 5 miles farther east along Oakland Antioch and Eastern Railroad.

West Point [MARIN]: *locality,* 5 miles southwest of downtown San Rafael on the southeast side of Mount Tamalpais (lat. 37°55' N, long. 122°35'35" W). Named on San Rafael (1954) 7.5' quadrangle.

West Point: see **Ravenswood Point** [SAN MATEO].

Westpoint Creek: see **Westpoint Slough** [SAN MATEO].

Westpoint Slough [SAN MATEO]: *water feature,* extends for 3.5 miles from Ravenswood Slough to Redwood Creek 2.5 miles northnortheast of downtown Redwood City (lat. 37°31'05" N, long. 122°12'10" W). Named on Palo Alto (1961) and Redwood Point (1959) 7.5' quadrangles. Called Westpoint Creek on Hayward (1915) 15' quadrangle.

West San Leandro [ALAMEDA]: *locality,* 1.5 miles southwest of downtown San Leandro along Southern Pacific Railroad (lat. 37°42'15" N, long. 122°10'35" W). Named on Haywards (1899) 15' quadrangle. The railroad station at the place was called Mulford, for Mulford Landing, until 1887 (Mosier and Mosier, p. 94).

West San Lorenzo [ALAMEDA]: *locality,* 3.25 miles south of downtown San Leandro along Southern Pacific Railroad (lat. 37°40'35" N, long. 122°09'20" W); the place is 1.5 miles west-southwest of San Lorenzo. Named on Haywards (1899) 15' quadrangle.

West Side: see **Cupertino** [SANTA CLARA].

West Union Creek [SAN MATEO]: *stream,* flows 4.25 miles to Bear Creek (2) 2.25 miles east-northeast of Skeggs Point (lat. 37°25'30" N, long. 122°15'55" W). Named on Woodside (1961) 7.5' quadrangle. West Union sawmill was built along the creek in the 1850's; other names for the stream were Tripp Creek, for Dr. R.O. Tripp, and Greer's Creek, for John Greer, who lived by the stream in the 1850's (Brown, p. 99-100).

West Waddell Creek [SAN MATEO]: *stream*, flows 1.25 miles to Santa Cruz County 8.5 miles south of Mindego Hill (lat. 37°11'25" N, long. 122°14'50" W; at S line sec. 36, T 8 S, R 4 W). Named on Big Basin (1955) 7.5' quadrangle. The name commemorates William W. Waddell, who had a sawmill in the neighborhood (Hoover, Rensch, and Rensch, p. 476).

Whaler's Harbor: see **Richardson Bay** [MARIN].

Wheeler Island [SOLANO]: *island*, 5 miles southwest of Birds Landing (2) along Suisun Bay (lat. 38°05' N, long. 121°56'30" W). Named on Honker Bay (1953) 7.5' quadrangle. Shown as part of Warrington Island on Ringgold's (1850c) map.

Whishman Slough: see **Stevens Creek** [SANTA CLARA].

Whiskey Flat [SANTA CLARA]: *area*, 2.25 miles southwest of Pacheco Pass (lat. 37°02'25" N, long. 121°14'05" W). Named on Pacheco Pass (1955) 7.5' quadrangle.

Whiskey Hill: see **Woodside** [SAN MATEO].

Whisman Slough: see **Jagel Slough** [SANTA CLARA]; **Stevens Creek** [SANTA CLARA].

White Canyon [CONTRA COSTA]: *canyon*, drained by a stream that flows nearly 1 mile to Mitchell Creek 2.5 miles northwest of Mount Diablo (lat. 37°54'30" N, long. 121°56'55" W; near W line sec. 26, T 1 N, R 1 W). Named on Clayton (1953) 7.5' quadrangle.

White Cliff Point: see **Fort Point** [SAN FRANCISCO].

White Gulch [MARIN]: *canyon*, 0.5 mile long, 4.25 miles southwest of Tomales on the west side of Tomales Bay (lat. 38°11'50" N, long. 122°57'10" W). Named on Tomales (1954) 7.5' quadrangle. On Point Reyes (1918) 15' quadrangle, the name applies to the flooded lower part of the canyon.

White Hill [MARIN]: *peak*, 6.5 miles north-northwest of Bolinas (lat. 37°59'40" N, long. 122°37'35" W). Altitude 1430 feet. Named on Bolinas (1954) and San Rafael (1954) 7.5' quadrangles.

Whitehouse Creek [SAN MATEO]: *stream*, heads in Santa Cruz County and flows 5 miles to the sea less than 1 mile east-southeast of Franklin Point (lat. 37°08'45" N, long. 122°20'45" W). Named on Franklin Point (1955) 7.5' quadrangle. The name is for a white prefabricated building that was shipped around Cape Horn and erected near the stream in 1852; the creek was called Arroyo de Soto in the 1840's for Eugenio Soto, who lived near it (Brown, p. 100-101; Brown used the form "White House Creek" for the name).

White House Pool [MARIN]: *water feature*, less

than 1 mile west-southwest of Point Reyes Station along Lagunitas Creek (lat. 38° 03'50" N, long. 122°49'10" W). Named on Inverness (1954) 7.5' quadrangle. A white house stood by the place until 1969 (Teather, p. 87).

White Island: see **Alcatraz Island** [SAN FRANCISCO].

White Slough [SOLANO]: *water feature*, joins Napa River 2.25 miles north-northwest of downtown Vallejo (lat. 38°08'05" N, long. 122°16'05" W; sec. 2, T 3 N, R 4 W). Named on Cuttings Wharf (1949) and Mare Island (1959) 7.5' quadrangles.

White Sulphur Springs: see **Sulphur Springs** [SOLANO].

Whiting Ridge [SAN MATEO]: *ridge*, west-southwest-trending, 1.5 miles long, 1.5 miles east-northeast of Montara Knob (lat. 37°34'05" N, long. 122°27'25" W). Named on Montara Mountain (1956) 7.5' quadrangle. Willard J. Whiting settled on the ridge about 1860 (Brown, p. 101).

Whiting Rock [CONTRA COSTA]: *rock*, 0.5 mile southwest of Point San Pablo in San Francisco Bay (lat. 37°57'35" N, long. 122°26'10" W). Named on San Quentin (1959) 7.5' quadrangle.

Whitlock Creek [ALAMEDA]: *stream*, flows 3 miles to Alameda Creek 10 miles southeast of Sunol (lat. 37°29'30" N, long. 121°44'55" W; near S line sec. 15, T 5 S, R 2 E). Named on Mendenhall Springs (1956) and Mount Day (1955) 7.5' quadrangles. Mount Hamilton (1897) 15' quadrangle has the name "Whitlock Gulch" for the canyon of the stream. The name commemorates Oscar Whitlock and Herman Whitlock, who settled along the stream in the 1870's (Mosier and Mosier, p. 94).

Whitlock Gulch: see **Whitlock Creek** [ALAMEDA].

Whitman [CONTRA COSTA]: *locality*, 3 miles northeast of present Walnut Creek civic center along a branch of Oakland Antioch and Eastern Railroad (lat. 37°56' N, long. 122°01'10" W). Named on Concord (1915) 15' quadrangle.

Whittemore Gulch [SAN MATEO]: *canyon*, drained by a stream that flows nearly 2 miles to Purisima Creek 4 miles west-northwest of Skeggs Point (lat. 37°26'15" N, long. 122°22'05" W; sec. 2, T 6 S, R 5 W). Named on Woodside (1961) 7.5' quadrangle. Richard Whittemore settled at the place about 1860 (Brown, p. 101).

Wicks Landing: see **Mulford Landing** [ALAMEDA].

Widow Reed Creek: see **Arroyo Corte Madera Del Presidio** [MARIN].

Wiedman Hill [CONTRA COSTA]: *peak*, 6 miles south of Danville (lat. 37°44'15" N, long. 121°59'35" W; near S line sec. 20, T 2 S, R 1 W). Altitude 1854 feet. Named on Dublin (1961) 7.5' quadrangle.

Wilbur's Creek: see **Mindego Creek** [SAN MATEO].

Wildcat Canyon [SANTA CLARA]:
(1) *canyon*, drained by a stream that flows nearly 1 mile to Castro Valley 3.25 miles southwest of Gilroy (lat. 36°58'10" N, long. 121° 36'05" W). Named on Chittenden (1955) 7.5' quadrangle.
(2) *canyon*, drained by a stream that heads in San Benito County and flows 3.5 miles to South Fork Pacheco Creek 7 miles south-southwest of Pacheco Pass (lat. 36°58'15" N, long. 121°15'30" W; near S line sec. 13, T 11 S, R 6 E). Named on Mariposa Peak (1969) 7.5' quadrangle.

Wildcat Creek [CONTRA COSTA]: *stream*, flows 12 miles to Castro Creek 2.25 miles east-southeast of Point San Pablo (lat. 37°57'10" N, long. 121°23'15" W). Named on Briones Valley (1959), Richmond (1959), and San Quentin (1959) 7.5' quadrangles. Whitney (p. 15) used the form "Wild Cat Creek" for the name.

Wildcat Creek [SANTA CLARA]: *stream*, flows 4 miles to San Tomas Aquinas Creek 2.5 miles north-northwest of downtown Los Gatos (lat. 37°16'15" N, long. 121°59'25" W). Named on Castle Rock Ridge (1955), Cupertino (1961), and San Jose West (1961) 7.5' quadrangles.

Wildcat Lake [MARIN]: *lake*, 1050 feet long, 1.25 miles north of Double Point (lat. 37°58'05" N, long. 122°47'05" W). Named on Double Point (1954) 7.5' quadrangle.

Wild Horse Canyon [SOLANO]: *canyon*, drained by a stream that flows 6.25 miles to Cold Canyon 6.5 miles north of Mount Vaca (lat. 38°29'50" N, long. 122°05'55" W; sec. 32, T 8 N, R 2 W). Named on Mount Vaca (1951) 7.5' quadrangle.

Wild Horse Creek [SOLANO]: *stream*, flows 3.25 miles to Green Valley Creek 7 miles west of Fairfield in Green Valley (lat. 38°15'40" N, long. 122°09'55" W; sec. 23, T 5 N, R 3 W). Named on Mount George (1951) 7.5' quadrangle.

Wild Horse Valley [SOLANO]: *valley*, 8 miles southwest of Mount Vaca on Napa-Solano county line (lat. 38°19' N, long. 122° 11'45" W; on S line sec. 33, T 6 N, R 3 W). Named on Mount George (1951) 7.5' quadrangle.

Wild Oat Canyon [CONTRA COSTA]: *canyon*, drained by a stream that flows 0.5 mile to Donner Canyon 1.25 miles north of Mount Diablo (lat. 37°54' N, long. 121°54'45" W; near SE cor. sec. 25, T 1 N, R 1 W). Named on Clayton (1953) 7.5;' quadrangle.

Wilkins Gulch [MARIN]: *canyon*, drained by a stream that flows 1.5 miles to Bolinas Lagoon nearly 2 miles north-northwest of Bolinas (lat. 37°56'05" N, long. 122°41'45" W). Named on Bolinas (1954) 7.5' quadrangle. Teather (p. 88) associated the name with William Wallace Wilkins, who bought a ranch in the neighborhood in 1869.

William Rust Summit: see **Camp Herms** [CONTRA COSTA].

Williams: see **Bill Williams Creek** [MARIN].

Williams Gulch [ALAMEDA]: *canyon*, drained by a stream that flows 6.5 miles to San Antonio Creek 6.5 miles east of Sunol (lat. 37°34'30" N, long. 121°46'05" W; sec. 21, T 4 S, R 2 E). Named on La Costa Valley (1960) and Mendenhall Springs (1956) 7.5' quadrangles.

Williams Reservoir [SANTA CLARA]: *lake*, 2000 feet long, behind a dam on Los Gatos Creek nearly 3 miles south of Mount Umunhum (lat. 37°07'15" N, long. 121°54'20" W). Named on Laurel (1955) 7.5' quadrangle.

Willota [SOLANO]: *locality*, 3.5 miles west of Fairfield along Sacramento Northern Railroad (lat. 38°14'35" N, long. 122°06'20" W). Named on Fairfield South (1949) 7.5' quadrangle.

Willow Creek [CONTRA COSTA]: *water feature*, enters Sacramento River (present Suisun Bay) 1.5 miles west-northwest of Pittsburg (lat. 38°02'25" N, long. 121°54'25" W). Named on Honker Bay (1918) 7.5' quadrangle.

Willow Creek: see **Bull Run Creek** [SAN MATEO].

Willow Glen [SANTA CLARA]: *district*, 1.5 miles south of downtown San Jose (lat. 37°18'30" N, long. 121°53'45" W). Named on San Jose West (1961) 7.5' quadrangle. The place first was called The Willows because of a thick growth of willows there in the 1860's (Fox, p. 10). Postal authorities established Kensington post office in 1893, changed the name to Willowglen in 1895, and discontinued it in 1900, when they changed the name to San Jose Station No. 2 (Salley, p. 110, 241). United States Board on Geographic Names (1933, p. 820) rejected the form "Willowglen" for the name of the district.

Willow Marsh: see **Amador Valley** [ALAMEDA].

Willow Point [MARIN]: *promontory*, 2.5 miles northwest of Point Reyes Station on the southwest side of Tomales Bay (lat. 38°05'25" N, long. 122°50'30" W). Named on Inverness (1954) 7.5' quadrangle. The feature also is called Giubbini Point for a Swiss dairyman who lived there (Mason, 1976a, p. 150).

Willow Ridge [SANTA CLARA]: *ridge*, north-trending, 1.5 miles long, 5 miles north-northeast of Gilroy Hot Springs (lat. 37°11'05" N, long. 121°27'40" W). Named on Mississippi Creek (1955) 7.5' quadrangle.

Willows: see **The Willows**, under **Willow Glen** [SANTA CLARA].

Willow Slough [CONTRA COSTA]: *water feature*, 3 miles east-northeast of the present settlement of Bethel Island (lat. 38°02' N, long. 121°35'45" W). Named on Bouldin (1910) 7.5' quadrangle.

Willow Spring [SANTA CLARA]: *spring,* 3.25 miles west-northwest of Mount Sizer (lat. 37°14' N, long. 121°34' W; near W line sec. 17, T 8 S, R 4 E). Named on Mount Sizer (1955) 7.5' quadrangle.

Willow Springs Canyon [SANTA CLARA]: *canyon,* drained by a stream that flows 1.5 miles to lowlands 2.25 miles northwest of Morgan Hill (lat. 37°09' N, long, 121°41'15" W). Named on Morgan Hill (1955) 7.5' quadrangle.

Wilson Gulch [SAN MATEO]: *canyon,* drained by a stream that heads in Santa Cruz County and flows less than 1 mile to the sea 2 miles east of Año Nuevo Point (present Point Año Nuevo) at San Mateo-Santa Cruz county line (lat. 37°06'25" N, long. 122°17'30" W). Named on Año Nuevo (1955) 7.5' quadrangle.

Wilson Peak [SANTA CLARA]: *peak,* 2.5 miles east-southeast of Gilroy Hot Springs (lat. 37°05'40" N, long. 121°26'05" W; sec. 4, T 10 S, R 5 E). Altitude 2651 feet. Named on Gilroy Hot Springs (1955) 7.5' quadrangle.

Wilson Point [CONTRA COSTA]: *promontory,* 2.5 miles east of Pinole Point along San Pablo Bay (lat. 38°00'40" N, long. 122°18'55" W). Named on Mare Island (1959) 7.5' quadrangle.

Windmill Gulch [SAN MATEO]: *canyon,* drained by a stream that flows 0.5 mile to Honsinger Creek 6.5 miles southwest of La Honda (lat. 37°15'35" N, long. 122°21'35" W; near S line sec. 2, T 8 S, R 5 W). Named on La Honda (1961) 7.5' quadrangle.

Windy Gap [MARIN]: *pass,* 4.5 miles southwest of Tomales near the southeast end of Tomales Point (lat. 38°11'55" N, long. 122°57'40" W). Named on Tomales (1954) 7.5' quadrangle.

Windy Hill [SAN MATEO]: *peak,* 4 miles north-northwest of Mindego Hill (lat. 37°21'50" N, long. 122°14'45" W; sec. 36, T 6 S, R 4 W). Named on Mindego Hill (1961) 7.5' quadrangle. United States Board on Geographic Names (1975a, p. 11-12) approved the name "Spring Ridge" for the ridge on which Windy Hill is the high point.

Windy Point [CONTRA COSTA]: *peak,* 3 miles southeast of Mount Diablo (lat. 37°51'10" N, long. 121°52'30" W; on S line sec. 9, T 1 S, R 1 E). Altitude 2112 feet. Named on Diablo (1953) and Tassajara (1953) 7.5' quadrangles.

Windy Ridge [MARIN]: *ridge,* north-northwest-trending, 1 mile long, 3 miles southwest of downtown San Rafael (lat. 37°56'35" N, long. 122°34'05" W). Named on San Rafael (1954) 7.5' quadrangle.

Winehaven [CONTRA COSTA]: *locality,* 1 mile south-southeast of Point San Pablo (lat. 37°57' N, long. 122°25' W). Named on San Francisco (1915) 15' quadrangle. Postal authorities established Winehaven post office in 1910 and discontinued it in 1925 (Salley, p. 241).

Winfield Scott: see **Fort Winfield Scot**t, under **Fort Point** [SAN FRANCISCO].

Winslow Cove: see **Simpton Point** [MARIN].

Winter Island [CONTRA COSTA]: *island,* 2.25 miles long, 3 miles northwest of Antioch (lat. 38°02'45" N, long. 121°51' W). Named on Antioch North (1978) 7.5' quadrangle, which shows the feature as mainly marsh and water. Called Ruckels I. on Ringgold's (1850b) map.

Wise: see **Point Wise** [SOLANO].

Wisener Creek: see **Norris Creek** [ALAMEDA].

Wittenberg: see **Mount Wittenberg** [MARIN].

Wittenberg Hill: see **Mount Wittenberg** [MARIN].

Wolf Ridge [MARIN]: *ridge,* west-trending, 1.5 miles long, 2 miles north of Point Bonita (lat. 37°50'35" N, long. 122°32'05" W). Named on Point Bonita (1954) 7.5' quadrangle.

Wolfskill [SOLANO]: *locality,* 3.5 miles north of Allendale along Southern Pacific Railroad (lat. 38°29'50" N, long. 121°57'10" W); the place is on Rio de los Putos grant, which William Wolfskill owned. Named on Wolfskill (1917) 7.5' quadrangle.

Woodacre [MARIN]: *settlement,* 8 miles south-southwest of downtown Novato (lat. 38°00'30" N, long. 122°38'15" W). Named on San Geronimo (1954) 7.5' quadrangle. Promoters began a subdivision at the place in 1912, and postal authorities established Woodacre post office there in 1925 (Salley, p. 242)

Woodhams Creek [SAN MATEO]: *stream,* flows 2 miles to La Honda Creek near the north edge of La Honda (lat. 37°19'25" N, long. 122°16'15" W; sec. 14, T 7 S, R 4 W). Named on La Honda (1961) and Mindego Hill (1961) 7.5' quadrangles. Mr. A. Woodham had a dairy along the stream about 1860 (Brown, p. 102).

Woodhaven Camp [SAN MATEO]: *locality,* 3 miles north of La Honda (lat. 37°21'40" N, long. 122°15'40" W; near SE cor. sec. 35, T 6 S, R 4 W). Named on La Honda (1961) 7.5' quadrangle.

Wood Island [MARIN]: *hill,* 2.25 miles south-southeast of downtown San Rafael (lat. 37°56'40" N, long. 122°30'40" W). Named on San Rafael (1954) 7.5' quadrangle. The feature had the local name "Dean's Island" in the early 1920's (Teather, p. 89).

Wood Island: see **Yerba Buena Island** [SAN FRANCISCO].

Woodruff Creek [SAN MATEO]: *stream,* flows 3 miles to La Honda Creek 1.25 miles north of La Honda (lat. 37°20'15" N, long. 122°16'05" W; sec. 11, T 7 S, R 4 W). Named on La Honda (1961) and Mindego Hill (1961) 7.5' quadrangles. Charles E. Woodruff had a ranch along the stream after about 1862 (Brown, p. 102).

Woods Creek: see **Mills Creek** [SAN MATEO] (2).

Woodside [SAN MATEO]: *town,* 4 miles south-southwest of downtown Redwood City (lat.

37°25'45" N, long. 122°15'30" W). Named on La Honda (1961), Palo Alto (1961), and Woodside (1961) 7.5' quadrangles. Parkhurst, Ellis, and Tripp had a lumber camp at the place as early as 1849, and in 1851 Tripp opened a store there that housed Woodside post office in 1854—the name "Woodside" then was used for the community near the store; in the early 1860's a new business center called Greersburg was started farther east at Adobe Corner, but by the 1870's the name "Woodside" applied to both places (Brown, p. 102). The name "Greersburg" was for the Greer family, owners of Cañada de Raymundo grant (Hoover, Rensch, and Rensch, p. 399). A group of saloons frequented by teamsters in the 1880's was located a little east of the first two settlements, and was called Whiskey Hill; the settlement that developed at Whiskey Hill took the name "Haakerville" for William Haaker, owner of a store there, but again use of the name "Woodside" was extended to apply to Haakerville (Brown, p. 100, 102). Postal authorities established Woodside post office in 1854, moved it 1.25 miles east in 1909, discontinued it in 1915, and reestablished it in 1949 (Salley, p. 243). The town incorporated in 1856.

Woodside Glens [SAN MATEO]: *district,* 3.25 miles south-southwest of downtown Redwood City (lat. 37°26'25" N, long. 122°15'20" W); the place is in Woodside. Named on Woodside (1961) 7.5' quadrangle.

Woodstock: see **Alameda** [ALAMEDA].

Woodville [MARIN]: *locality,* 2.5 miles north-northwest of Bolinas (lat. 37°56'40" N, long. 122°42'20" W). Named on Bolinas (1954) 7.5' quadrangle. The place first was called Dogtown (Laizure, 1926, p. 320).

Worley Flat [SAN MATEO]: *area,* 3 miles south of La Honda along Pescadero Creek (lat. 37°16'30" N, long. 122°16'15" W; sec. 35, T 7 S, R 4 W). Named on La Honda (1961) 7.5' quadrangle.

Wright Cut [SOLANO]: *water feature,* joins Lindsey Slough 6.25 miles north of Rio Vista (lat. 38°14'50" N, long. 121°41'40" W). Named on Liberty Island (1978) and Rio Vista (1978) 7.5' quadrangles.

Wrights [SANTA CLARA]: *village,* 6.25 miles south-southeast of downtown Los Gatos along Los Gatos Creek (lat. 37°08'20" N, long. 121°56'45" W; sec. 23, T 9 S, R 1 W). Named on Los Gatos (1919) 15' quadrangle; the site is named on Los Gatos (1953) 7.5' quadrangle. The place began in 1877, when railroad construction reached the north portal of a tunnel there; it first was known as The Tunnel, and in 1880 as Wright's Station (Young, p. 42-43) for John Vincent Wright, son of James Richard Wright, the hotel operator at Burrell (Hoover, Rensch, and Rensch, p. 456). The settlement of Burrell was near the summit of Santa Cruz Mountains and was named for Lyman John Burrell, who lived there in the early 1850's (Hoover, Rensch, and Rensch, p. 455). Laurel (1955) 7.5' quadrangle has the label "Burrell Sch. (Abandoned)"—the principal evidence of Burrell on the map—at a point 1.5 miles south-southeast of the site of Wrights. Postal authorities established Wrights post office in 1879 and discontinued it in 1938 (Frickstad, p. 175). Postal Route (1884) map shows a place called Skyland situated 2 miles east of Wrights near Santa Clara-Santa Cruz county line; postal authorities established Skyland post office in 1884 and discontinued it in 1886 (Frickstad, p. 175). A place called Patchin was located 2 miles west-northwest of the site of Wrights at the junction of present Mountain Charley Road and the old Santa Cruz Highway; the place is said to have been named for a famous race horse, George M. Patchen (Hoover, Rensch, and Rensch, p. 456). Postal authorities established Patchin post office in 1872, discontinued it in 1895, reestablished it in 1897, and discontinued it in 1925 (Frickstad, p. 174). United States Board on Geographic Names (1979b, p. 5) approved the name "Patchen Pass" for the pass at the crest of Santa Cruz Mountains, near the site of Patchin, that is traversed by the main highway from Los Gatos to the coast. The Board at the same time approved the name "Cuesta de los Gatos" for the ridge, less than 2 miles long, where the pass is situated. The Board noted that city officials of Los Gatos proposed the name for the pass in 1976 to commemorate the community of Patchen (or Patchin); the name for the ridge was in use locally before 1831.

Wright's Station: see **Wrights** [SANTA CLARA].

— X - Y —

Yacht Harbor [SAN FRANCISCO]: *water feature,* 2 miles east of Fort Point along San Francisco Bay in Marina District (lat. 37°48'25" N, long. 122°26'35" W). Named on San Francisco North (1956) 7.5' quadrangle. The site was called Harbor View in the 1870's (O'Brien, p. 192).

Yankee Jim Gulch [SAN MATEO]: *canyon,* drained by a stream that flows 1.5 miles to the sea less than 1 mile north-northwest of Pigeon Point (lat. 37°11'35" N, long. 122°23'50" W). Named on Franklin Point (1955) and Pigeon Point (1955) 7.5' quadrangles. The canyon was called Arroyo de la Ballena in Spanish times, and was called Surveyor's Gulch in the 1850's (Brown, p. 103).

Yeguas Creek: see **Adobe Creek** [SANTA CLARA].

Yellow Bluff [MARIN]: *promontory,* 1.5 miles south-southeast of downtown Sausalito along

San Francisco Bay (lat. 37°50'10" N, long. 122°28'15" W). Named on San Francisco North (1956) 7.5' quadrangle.

Yerba Buena [SANTA CLARA]: *land grant,* 5 miles southeast of downtown San Jose. Named on Lick Observatory (1955), Morgan Hill (1955), San Jose East (1961), and Santa Teresa Hills (1953) 7.5' quadrangles. Thompson and West's (1876) map has the name "Yerba Buena y Socayre" for the grant. Antonio Chabolla received the land in 1833 and claimed 24,332 acres patented in 1859; the grant also was called Socayre (Cowan, p. 108). According to Perez (p. 104), the grant was made in 1840.

Yerba Buena: see **San Francisco** [SAN FRANCISCO].

Yerba Buena Cove: see **Telegraph Hill** [SAN FRANCISCO].

Yerba Buena Creek [SANTA CLARA]: *stream,* flows nearly 3.5 miles to Thompson Creek 1 mile southeast of Evergreen (lat. 37° 17'55" N, long. 121°46'15" W); the stream is on Yerba Buena grant. Named on San Jose East (1961) 7.5' quadrangle.

Yerba Buena Island [SAN FRANCISCO]: *island,* 4300 feet long, 2.25 miles east-northeast of North Point in San Francisco Bay (lat. 37°48'40" N, long. 122°21'50" W). Named on Oakland West (1959) 7.5' quadrangle. Called Goat Id. on San Francisco (1899, reprinted 1913) 15' quadrangle, but United States Board on Geographic Names (1933, p. 829) rejected this name and noted that the California legislature restored the old Spanish name "Yerba Buena" to the island in 1931. The name "Goat Island" was from the goats turned loose to multiply on the island in the 1840's (Davis, W.H., p. 140). Ayala named the feature Isla de Alcatraces in 1775 for the abundance of pelicans there (Gudde, 1949, p. 6). It was known as Wood Island in the early nineteenth century (Wagner, H.R., p. 422).

Yerba Buena y Socayre: see **Yerba Buena** [SANTA CLARA].

Ygnacio Valley [CONTRA COSTA]: *valley,* 3 miles northeast of Walnut Creek civic center (lat. 37°55'30" N, long. 122°01' W). Named on Clayton (1953) and Walnut Creek (1959) 7.5' quadrangles.

Yolanda: see **San Anselmo** [MARIN].

Yolano [SOLANO]: *locality,* 7 miles east-southeast of Dixon along Sacramento Northern Railroad (lat. 38°24'35" N, long. 121°42'15' W; sec. 36, T 7 N, R 2 E). Named on Saxon (1952) 7.5' quadrangle. Railroad officials coined the name from the words "Yolo" and "Solano"—the place is near Solano-Yolo county line (Hanna, P.T., p. 361).

Yolo Basin: see **Yolo Bypass** [SOLANO].

Yolo Bypass [SOLANO]: *area,* lowlands west of Sacramento River, mainly in Yolo County, but extends south nearly to Rio Vista in Solano County. Named on Liberty Island (1978) and Rio Vista (1978) 7.5' quadrangles. Called Yolo Basin on Cache Slough (1916) and Rio Vista (1910) 7.5' quadrangles, which show the feature as marsh and water.

Yolo Landing [SOLANO]: *locality,* 2.5 miles west-southwest of Birds Landing (2) along Montezuma Slough (lat. 38°07'25" N, long. 121°54'50" W). Named on Honker Bay (1918) 7.5' quadrangle.

York Island [CONTRA COSTA]: *island,* 1 mile northwest of Pittsburg in present Suisun Bay (lat. 38°02'35" N, long. 121°53'50" W). Named on Honker Bay (1918) 7.5' quadrangle.

– Z –

Zimmerman's Mountain House: see **Mountain House** [ALAMEDA].

Zion: see **Mount Zion** [CONTRA COSTA].

REFERENCES CITED

BOOKS AND ARTICLES

Agassiz, L. 1853. "Extraordinary fishes from California, constituting a new family." *American Journal of Science and Arts* (series 2), v. 16, no. 48, p. 380-390.

Anderson, F.M. 1899. "The geology of Point Reyes Peninsula." *University of California, Bulletin of the Department of Geology,* v. 2, no. 5, p. 119-153.

Anderson, Winslow. 1892. *Mineral springs and health resorts of California.* San Francisco: The Bancroft Company, 347 p.

Antisell, Thomas. 1856. "Geological report." *Reports of explorations and surveys, to ascertain the most practicable and economical route for a railroad from the Mississippi River to the Pacific Ocean.* Volume VII, Part II. (33d Cong., 2d Sess., Sen. Ex. Doc. No. 78.) Washington: Beverley Tucker, Printer, 204 p.

Arbuckle, Clyde. 1968. *Santa Clara Co. Ranchos.* San Jose, California: The Rosicrucian Press, Ltd., 46 p.

Bancroft, Hubert Howe. 1886. *History of California, Volume II, 1801-1824.* San Francisco: The History Company, Publishers, 795 p.

———1888. *History of California, Volume VI, 1848-1859.* San Francisco: The History Company, Publishers, 787 p.

Becker, Robert H. 1964. *Diseños of California ranchos.* San Francisco: The Book Club of California, (no pagination).

———1969. *Designs on the land.* San Francisco: The Book Club of California, (no pagination).

Berkstresser, C.F., Jr. 1968. *Data for springs in the Southern Coast, Transverse, and Peninsular Ranges of California.* (United States Geological Survey, Water Resources Division, Open-file report.) Menlo Park, California, 21 p. + appendices.

Bidwell, John. 1964. *A journey to California, 1841, The first emigrant party to California by wagon train, The journal of John Bidwell.* Berkeley, California: The Friends of the Bancroft Library, 55 p. + 32 p.

Blake, W.P. 1854. "Quicksilver mine of Almaden, California." *American Journal of Science and Arts* (series 2), v. 17, no. 51, p. 438-440.

———1856. "Observations on the physical geography and geology of the coast of California, from Bodega bay to San Diego." *United States Coast Survey, Report of the Superintendent 1855.* (34th Cong., 1st Sess., Sen. Ex. Doc. 22.) Appendix 65, p. 376-398.

Bolton, Herbert Eugene. 1931. *Outpost of empire.* New York: Alfred A. Knopf, 334 p.

Bowen, Oliver E., Jr. 1951. "Highways and byways of particular geologic interest." *Geologic guidebook of the San Francisco Bay Counties.* (California Division of Mines Bulletin 154.) San Francisco: Division of Mines, p. 315-379.

Bradley, Walter W. 1915. "The counties of Colusa, Glenn, Lake, Marin, Napa, Solano, Sonoma, Yolo." *Report XIV of the State Mineralogist.* Sacramento: California State Mining Bureau, p. 173-370.

Brewer, William H. 1949. *Up and down California in 1860-1864.* (Edited by Francis P. Farquhar.) Berkeley and Los Angeles: University of California Press, 583 p.

Brown, Alan K. 1975. *Place names of San Mateo County.* San Mateo, California: San Mateo County Historical Association, 118 p.

Bruntz, George G. 1971. *The history of Los Gatos, gem of the foothills.* Fresno, California: Valley Publishers, 173 p.

Buffum, E. Gould. 1850. *Six months in the gold mines; From a journal of three years' residence in Upper and Lower California, 1847-8-9.* Philadelphia: Lea and Blanchard, 172 p.

Butler, Phyllis Filiberti. 1975. *The valley of Santa Clara, Historic buildings, 1792-1920.* San Jose, California: Junior League of San Jose, Inc., 192 p.

California Division of Highways. 1934. *California highway transportation survey, 1934.* Sacramento: Department of Public Works, Division of Highways, 130 p. + appendices.

Carey, E.P, and Miller, W.J. 1907. "The crystalline rocks of the Oak Hill area near San Jose, California." *Journal of Geology,* v. 15, no. 2, p. 152-169.

Clark, Donald Thomas. 1986. *Santa Cruz County place names.* Santa Cruz: Santa Cruz Historical Society, 552 p.

Clark, William O. 1924. *Ground water in Santa Clara Valley, California.* (United States Geological Survey Water-Supply Paper 519.) Washington: Government Printing Office, 209 p.

Cluff, Lloyd S., and Bolt, Bruce A. 1969. "Risk from earthquakes in the modern urban environment, with special emphasis on the San Francisco Bay area." *Urban environmental geology in the San Francisco Bay region.* San Francisco: Association of Engineering Geologists, San Francisco Section, p. 25-64.

Cowan, Robert G. 1956. *Ranchos of California.* Fresno, California: Academy Library Guild, 151 p.

Coy, Owen C. 1923. *California county boundaries.* Berkeley: California Historical Survey Commission, 335 p.

Crawford, J.J. 1894. "Report of the State Mineralogist." *Twelfth report of the State Mineralogist, (Second Biennial,) two years ending September 15, 1894.* Sacramento: California State Mining Bureau, p. 8-412.

_____1896. "Report of the State Mineralogist." *Thirteenth report (Third Biennial) of the State Mineralogist for the two years ending September 15, 1896.* Sacramento: California State Mining Bureau, p. 10-646.

Cunningham, Florence R. 1967. *Saratoga's first hundred years.* Fresno, California: Valley Publishers, 367 p.

Curtis, James R. 1978. "Whatever happened to Port San Jose?" *The California Geographer,* v. 18, p. 35-42.

Dall, William Healey, and Harris, Gilbert Dennison. 1892. *Correlation papers, Neocene.* (United States Geological Survey Bulletin 84.) Washington: Government Printing Office, 349 p.

Dana, James D. 1849. "Notes on Upper California." *American Journal of Science and Arts,* (series 2), v. 7, no. 20, p. 247-264.

Davidson, George. 1907. "The discovery of the Bay of San Francisco and the rediscovery of the Port of Monterey." *Transactions and Proceedings of the Geographical Society of the Pacific* (series. 2), v. 4, p. 1-153.

Davis, Fenelon F., and Goldman, Harold B. 1958. "Mines and mineral resources of Contra Costa County, California." *California Journal of Mines and Geology,* v. 54, no. 4, p. 501-581.

Davis, Fenelon F., and Jennings, Charles W. 1954. "Mines and mineral resources of Santa Clara County, California." *California Journal of Mines and Geology,* v. 50, no. 2, p. 321-430.

Davis, Fenelon F., and Vernon, James W. 1951. "Mines and mineral resources of Contra Costa County." *California Journal of Mines and Geology,* v. 47, no. 4, p. 561-617.

Davis, William Heath. 1962. *Seventy-five years in California.* San Francisco, California: John Howell—Books, 345 p.

Delavan, James. 1956. *Notes on California and the placers, How to get there, and what to do afterwards.* Oakland, California: Biobooks, 156 p.

Diller, J.S., and others. 1915. *Guidebook of the Western United States, Part D. The Shasta Route and Coast Line.* (United States. Geological Survey Bulletin 614.) Washington: Government Printing Office, 142 p.

Dillon, Richard. 1980. *Great expectations, The story of Benicia, California.* (No place): Benicia Heritage Book, Inc., 241 p.

Donnelly, Florence G. 1960. *Early days in Marin.* San Rafael, California: Marin County Savings and Loan Association, 63 p.

Eckel, Edwin C. 1933. "Limestone deposits of the San Francisco region." *California Journal of Mines and Geology,* v. 29, no. 3-4, p. 348-361.

Fairley, Lincoln. 1985. "Mt. Tamalpais: Man and a mountain's resources." *The Californians,* v. 3, no. 1, p. 33-39.

_____1987. *Mount Tamalpais.* San Francisco, California: Scottwall Associates, 201 p.

Fava, Florence M. 1976. *Los Altos Hills.* Woodside, California: Gilbert Richards Publications, 135 p.

Fox, Frances L. 1978. *Land grant to landmark..* San Jose, California: The Pied Piper Publishers, 131 p.

Franke, Herbert A. 1930. "Santa Clara County." *Mining in California,* v. 26, no. 1, p. 2-39.

Frazer, Robert W. 1965. *Forts of the West.* Norman: University of Oklahoma Press, 246 p.

Fremont, John Charles. 1964. *Geographical memoir upon Upper California in illustration of his map of Oregon and California, newly reprinted from the edition of 1848.* San Francisco: The Book Club of California, 65 p.

Frickstad, Walter N. 1955. *A century of California post offices, 1848 to 1954.* Oakland, California: Philatelic Research Society, 395 p.

Galvin, John (editor). 1971. *The first Spanish entry into San Francisco Bay, 1775.* San Francisco, California: John Howell—Books, 130 p.

Gannett, Henry. 1905. *The origin of certain place names in the United States.* (Second edition.) (United States Geological Survey Bulletin No. 258.) Washington: Government Printing Office, 334 p.

Gilliam, Harold. 1962. *Island in time, The Point Reyes Peninsula.* San Francisco: Sierra Club, 87 p.

Gleason, Duncan. 1958. *The islands and ports of California.* New York: The Devin-Adair Company, 201 p.

Goodyear, W.A. 1888. "Petroleum, asphaltum, and natural gas." *Seventh annual report of the State Mineralogist, for the year ending October 1, 1887.* Sacramento: California State Mining Bureau, p. 63-114.

Grant, U.S., IV, and Gale, Hoyt Rodney. 1931. *Catalogue of the marine Pliocene and Pleistocene Mollusca of California and adjacent regions.* (San Diego Society of Natural History Memoirs, Volume I.) San Diego, California: San Diego Society of Natural History, 1036 p.

Gudde, Erwin G. 1949. *California place names.* Berkeley and Los Angeles: University of California Press, 431 p.

_____1969. *California place names.* Berkeley and Los Angeles: University of California Press, 416 p.

Hanna, G. Dallas. 1951. "Geology of the Farallon Islands." *Geologic guidebook of the San Francisco Bay counties.* (California Division of Mines Bulletin 154.) San Francisco, California: Division of Mines, p. 301-310.

Hanna, Phil Townsend. 1951. *The dictionary of California land names.* Los Angeles: The Automobile Club of Southern California, 392 p.

Hanna, Warren L. 1979. *Lost harbor, The controversy over Drake's California anchorage.* Berkeley, Los Angeles, London: University of California Press, 459 p.

Hansen, Gladys, and Condon, Emmet. 1989. *Denial of disaster.* San Francisco: Cameron and Company, 160 p.

Harlow, Neal. 1950. *The maps of San Francisco Bay, from the Spanish discovery in 1769 to the American occupation.* The Book Club of California, 140 p.

Hart, James D. 1978. *A companion to California.* New York: Oxford University Press, 504 p.

Hildebrand, George H. 1982. *Borax pioneer: Francis Marion Smith.* San Diego, California: Howell North Books, 318 p.

Hillman, Raymond W., and Covello, Leonard A. 1985. *Cities and towns of San Joaquin County since 1847.* Fresno, California: Panorama West Books, 248 p.

Holmes, Kenneth L. (editor). 1983. *Covered wagon women, Diaries & letters from the western trails, 1840-1890, Volume I, 1840-1848.* Glendale, California: The Arthur H. Clark Company, 272 p.

Hoover, Mildred Brooke. 1932. *The Farallon Islands, California.* Stanford University, California: Stanford University Press, 18 p.

Hoover, Mildred Brooke, Rensch, Hero Eugene, and Rensch, Ethel Grace. 1966. *Historic spots in California.* (Third edition, revised by William N. Abeloe.) Stanford, California: Stanford University Press, 642 p.

Hynding, Alan. 1982. *From frontier to suburb, The story of the San Mateo peninsula.* Belmont, California: Star Publishing Company, 343 p.

Irelan, William, Jr. 1888. "Report of the State Mineralogist." *Eighth annual report of the State Mineralogist for the year ending October 1, 1888.* Sacramento: California State Mining Bureau, p. 12-695.

Johnson, Kenneth M. 1963. *The New Almaden quicksilver mine.* Georgetown, California: The Talisman Press, 115 p.

Kelly, William. 1950. *A stroll through the diggings of California.* Oakland, California: Biobooks, 206 p.

Kroeber, A.L. 1916. "California place names of Indian origin." *University of California Publications in American Archaeology and Ethnology,* v. 12, no. 2, p. 31-69.

Laizure, C. McK. 1926. "San Francisco field division (Marin County)." *Mining in California,* v. 22, no. 3, p. 314-365.

_____1927a. "San Francisco field division (Contra Costa County)." *Mining in California,* v. 23, no. 1, p. 2-31.

_____1927b. "San Francisco field division (Solano County)." *Mining in California,* v. 23, no. 2, p. 203-213.

Lanyon, Milton, and Bulmore, Laurence. 1967. *Cinnabar Hills.* (Authors), 128 p.

Latta, Frank F. 1949. *Black gold in the Joaquin.* Caldwell, Idaho: The Caxton Printers, 344 p.

_____1976. *Saga of Rancho El Tejon.* Santa Cruz, California: Bear State Books, 293 p.

Lewis, Oscar. 1954. *George Davidson, Pioneer West Coast scientist.* Berkeley and Los Angeles: University of California Press, 146 p.

Lyman, C.S. 1848. "Mines of cinnabar in Upper California." *American Journal of Science and Arts* (series 2), v. 6, no. 17, p. 270-271.

MacGregor, Bruce A. 1968. *South Pacific Coast, An illustrated history of the narrow gauge South Pacific Coast Railroad.* Berkeley, California: Howell-North Books, 280 p.

MacMullen, Jerry. 1944. *Paddle-wheel days in California.* Stanford, California: Stanford University Press, 157 p.

Mason, Jack. 1972. *Point Reyes, The solemn land.* (Second edition.) Inverness, California: North Shore Books, 198 p.

_____1976a. *Earthquake Bay, A history of Tomales Bay, California.* Inverness, California: North Shore Books, 166 p.

_____1976b. *Early Marin.* (Second revised edition.) Inverness, California: North Shore Books, 228 p.

Mendenhall, Walter C. 1908. *Preliminary report on the ground waters of San Joaquin Valley, California.* (United States Geological Survey Water-Supply Paper 222.) Washington: Government Printing Office, 52 p.

Miller, Robert C. 1958. "The relict fauna of Lake Merced, San Francisco." *Journal of Marine Research,* v. 17, p. 375-382.

Morrall, June. 1978. *Half Moon Bay memories.* El Granada, California: Moonbeam Press, 176 p.

Mosier, Dan L. 1979. *California coal towns, coaling stations, & landings.* San Leandro, California: Mines Road Books, 8 p.

Mosier, Dan, and Finney, Page. 1980. *Dublin gold, The story of Gold Creek.* San Leandro, California: Mines Road Books, 17 p.

Mosier, Page, and Mosier, Dan. 1986. *Alameda County place names.* Fremont, California: Mines Road Books, 105 p.

Nelson, N.C. 1909. "Shellmounds of the San Francisco Bay region." *University of California Publications in American Archaeology and Ethnology,* v. 7, no. 4, p. 309-356.

Newhall, Ruth Waldo. 1958. *The Newhall ranch.* San Marino, California: The Huntington Library, 120 p.

O'Brien, Robert. 1948. *This is San Francisco.* San Carlos, California: Nourse Publishing Company, 351 p.

Parke, John G. 1857. "General report." *Reports of explorations and surveys, to ascertain the most practicable and economical route for a railroad from the Mississippi River to the Pacific Ocean.* Volume VII. (33d Cong., 2d Sess., Sen. Ex. Doc. No. 78.) Washington: Beverley Tucker, Printer, 42 p.

Perez, Crisostomo N. 1996. *Land grants in Alta*

California. Rancho Cordova, California: Landmark Enterprises, 264 p.

Pierce, Marjorie. 1977. *East of the Gabilans.* Fresno: Valley Publishers, 194 p.

Rambo, F. Ralph, 1964. *Almost forgotten.* (Author), 48 p.

_____1973. *Pioneer blue book of the old Santa Clara Valley.* San Jose, California: The Rosicrucian Press, Ltd., 48 p.

Reinstedt, Randall A. 1975. *Shipwrecks & sea monsters of California's central coast.* Carmel, California: Ghost Town Publications, 168 p.

Revere, Joseph Warren. 1947. *Naval duty in California.* Oakland, California: Biobooks, 245 p.

Ringgold, Cadwalader. 1852. *A series of charts, with sailing directions, embracing surveys of the Farallones, entrance to the Bay of San Francisco, Bays of San Francisco and San Pablo, Straits of Carquines and Suisun Bay, confluence and deltaic branches of the Sacramento and San Joaquin Rivers, and the Sacramento River (with the Middle Fork) to the American River, including the cities of Sacramento and Boston, State of California.* (Fourth edition, with additions.) Washington: Jno. T. Towers, 48 p.

Salley, H.E. 1977. *History of California post offices, 1849-1976.* La Mesa, California: Postal History Associates, Inc., 300 p.

Sawyer, Eugene T. 1922. *History of Santa Clara County, California.* Los Angeles, California: Historic Record Company, 310 p.

Schwartz, Harvey. 1979. "Fort Ross, California, Imperial Russian outpost on America's western frontier, 1812-1841." *Journal of the West,* v. 18, no. 2, p. 35-48.

Shanks, Ralph C., Jr., and Shanks, Janetta Thompson. 1976. *Lighthouses of San Francisco Bay.* San Anselmo, California: Costaño Books, 125 p.

Shumate, Albert. 1977. *Francisco Pacheco of Pacheco Pass.* Stockton, California: University of the Pacific, 47 p.

Smith and Elliott. 1979. *Facsimile reproduction of Illustrations of Contra Costa Co., California, with historical sketch, 1879, Smith & Elliott.* Fresno: Valley Publishers, 57 p.

Smith, Persifor F. 1850. "Report of General Persifor F. Smith." *Report of the Secretary of War, communicating information in relation to the geology and topographiy of California.* (31st Cong., 1st Sess., Sen. Ex. Doc. No. 47.) Washington: Government Printing Office, p. 75-108.

Soule, Frank, Gihon, John H., and Nisbet, James. 1855. *The annals of San Francisco.* New York: D. Appleton & Company, 852 p.

Spence, Mary Lee, and Jackson, Donald (editors). 1973. *The expeditions of John Charles Frémont, Volume 2, The Bear Flag revolt and the court-martial.* Urbana, Chicago, and London: University of Illinois Press, 519 p.

Stanger, Frank M. 1963. *South from San Francisco, San Mateo County, California, Its history and heritage.* San Mateo, California: San Mateo County Historical Association, 214 p.

_____1967. *Sawmills in the redwoods, Logging on the San Francisco peninsula, 1849-1967.* San Mateo, California: San Mateo County Historical Association, 160 p.

Stanger, Frank M., and Brown, Alan K. 1969. *Who discovered the Golden Gate?* San Mateo, California: San Mateo County Historical Association, 173 p.

Stanton, Timothy W. 1896. "The faunal relations of the Eocene and Upper Cretaceous of the Pacific Coast." *Seventeenth Annual Report of the United States Geological Survey to the Secretary of the Interior, Part III, Mineral resources of the United States, 1895.* Washington: Government Printing Office, p. 1005-1060.

Taylor, Bayard. 1850. *Eldorado, or Adventures in the path of empire.* New York: George P. Putnam, (two volumes) 251 p + 247 p.

Teather, Louise. 1986. *Place names of Marin.* San Francisco, California: Scottwall Associates, 96 p.

Thompson & West. 1876. *Historical atlas map of Santa Clara County, California.* San Francisco, California: Thompson & West, 119 p.

_____1878. *Official and historical atlas map of Alameda County, California.* Oakland, California: Thompson & West, 171 p.

_____1879. *History of San Joaquin County, California.* Oakland, California: Thompson & West, 142 p.

Treutlein, Theodore E. 1968. *San Francisco Bay, Discovery and colonization, 1769-1776.* San Francisco: California Historical Society, 152 p.

Tyson, James L. 1955. *Diary of a physician in California.* Oakland, California: Biobooks, 124 p.

Tyson, Philip T. 1850. "Report of P.T. Tyson, esq., upon the geology of California." *Report of the Secretary of War, communicating information in relation to the geology and topography of California.* (31st Cong., 1st Sess., Sen. Ex. Doc. No. 47.) Washington: Government Printing Office, p. 3-74.

United States Board on Geographic Names. 1901. *Second report of the United States Board on Geographic Names, 1890-1899.* Washington: Government Printing Office, 150 p.

_____(under name "United States Geographic Board"). 1933. *Sixth report of the United States Geographic Board, 1890 to 1932.* Washington: Government Printing Office, 834 p.

_____(under name "United States Geographic Board"). 1934. *Decisions of the United States Geographic Board, No. 41—May 2, 1934.* Washington: Government Printing Office, 4 p.

_____(under name "United States Board on Geographical Names"). 1939. *Decisions of the United States Board on Geographical*

Names, Decisions rendered between July 1, 1938, and June 30, 1939. Washington: Government Printing Office, 41 p.

_____(under name "United States Board on Geographical Names"). 1943. Decisions rendered between July 1, 1941, and June 30, 1943. Washington: Department of the Interior, 104 p.

_____1948. Decision lists nos. 4801-4806, January-June, 1948. Washington: Department of the Interior, 25 p.

_____1949a. Decision list no. 4903, March 1949. Washington: Department of the Interior. 26 p.

_____1949b. Decision lists nos. 4905, 4906, May, June, 1949. Washington: Department of the Interior, 10 p.

_____1950. Decisions on names in the United States and Alaska rendered during April, May, and June 1950. (Decision list no. 5006.) Washington: Department of the Interior, 47 p.

_____1954. Decisions on names in the United States, Alaska and Puerto Rico, Decisions rendered from July 1950 to May 1954. (Decision list no. 5401.) Washington: Department of the Interior, 115 p.

_____1959a. Decisions on names in the United States, Puerto Rico and the Virgin Islands, Decisions rendered from April 1957 through December 1958. (Decision list no. 5901.) Washington: Department of the Interior, 100 p.

_____1959b. Decisions on names in the United States, Decisions rendered from January, 1959 through April, 1959. (Decision list no. 5902.) Washington: Department of the Interior, 49 p.

_____1960a. Decisions on names in the United States and Puerto Rico, Decisions rendered in May, June, July, and August, 1959. (Decision list no. 5903.) Washington: Department of the Interior, 79 p.

_____1960b. Decisions on names in the United States, Puerto Rico and the Virgin Islands, Decisions rendered from January through April 1960. (Decision list no. 6001.) Washington: Department of the Interior, 79 p.

_____1961a. Decisions on names in the United States, Decisions rendered from September through December 1960. (Decision List No. 6003.) Washington: Department of the Interior, 73 p.

_____1961b. Decisions on names in the United States, Decisions rendered from May through August 1961. (Decision list no. 6102.) Washington: Department of the Interior, 81 p.

_____1962. Decisions on names in the United States, Decisions rendered from September through December 1961. (Decision list no. 6103.) Washington: Department of the Interior, 75 p.

_____1964. Decisions on geographic names in the United States, January through April 1964. (Decision list no. 6401.) Washington: Department of the Interior, 74 p.

_____1967a. Decisions on geographic names in the United States, January through March 1967. (Decision list no. 6701.) Washington: Department of the Interior, 20 p.

_____1967b. Decisions on geographic names in the United States, April through June 1967. (Decision list no. 6702.) Washington: Department of the Interior, 26 p.

_____1967c. Decisions on geographic names in the United States, July through September 1967. (Decision list no. 6703.) Washington: Department of the Interior, 29 p.

_____1968a. Decisions on geographic names in the United States, October through December 1967. (Decision list no. 6704.) Washington: Department of the Interior, 46 p.

_____1968b. Decisions on geographic names in the United States, January through March 1968. (Decision list no. 6801.) Washington: Department of the Interior, 51 p.

_____1969. Decisions on geographic names in the United States, July through September 1969. (Decision list no. 6903.) Washington: Department of the Interior, 36 p.

_____1970a. Decisions on geographic names in the United States, April through June 1970. (Decision list no. 7002.) Washington: Department of the Interior, 20 p.

_____1970b. Decisions on geographic names in the United States, July through September 1970. (Decision list no. 7003.) Washington: Department of the Interior, 15 p.

_____1972. Decisions on geographic names in the United States, April through June 1972. (Decision list no. 7202.) Washington: Department of the Interior, 30 p.

_____1973a. Decisions on geographic names in the United States, October through December 1972. (Decision list no. 7204.) Washington: Department of the Interior, 15 p.

_____1973b. Decisions on geographic names in the United States, April through June 1973. (Decision list no. 7302.) Washington: Department of the Interior, 16 p.

_____1974. Decisions on geographic names in the United States, July through September 1974. (Decision list no. 7403.) Washington: Department of the Interior, 34 p.

_____1975a. Decisions on geographic names in the United States, January through March 1975. (Decision list no. 7501.) Washington: Department of the Interior, 36 p.

_____1975b Decisions on geographic names in the United States, July through September 1975. (Decision list no. 7503.) Washington: Department of the Interior, 33 p.

_____1976a. Decisions on geographic names in the United States, October through December 1975. (Decision list no. 7504.) Washington: Department of the Interior, 45 p.

_____1976b. Decisions on geographic names in the United States, April through June 1976. (Decision list no. 7602.) Washington: Department of the Interior, 26 p.

_____1977. *Decisions on geographic names in the United States, July through September 1977.* (Decision List No. 7703.) Washington: Department of the Interior, 25 p.

_____1978. *Decisions on geographic names in the United States, October through December 1977.* (Decision list no. 7704.) Washington: Department of the Interior, 29 p.

_____1979a. *Decisions on geographic names in the United States, April through June 1979.* (Decision list no. 7902.) Washington: Department of the Interior, 33 p.

_____1979b. *Decisions on geographic names in the United States, July through September 1979.* (Decision list no. 7903.) Washington: Department of the Interior, 38 p.

_____1980. *Decisions on geographic names in the United States, January through March 1980.* (Decision list no. 8001.) Washington: Department of the Interior, 23 p.

_____1981a. *Decisions on geographic names in the United States, October through December 1980.* (Decision list no. 8004.) Washington: Department of the Interior, 21 p.

_____1981b. *Decisions on geographic names in the United States, January through March 1981.* (Decision list no. 8101.) Washington: Department of the Interior, 23 p.

_____1983a. *Decisions on geographic names in the United States, July through September 1982.* (Decision list no. 8203.) Washington: Department of the Interior, 25 p.

_____1983b. *Decisions on geographic names in the United States, January through March 1983.* (Decision list no. 8301.) Washington: Department of the Interior, 33 p.

_____1983c. *Decisions on geographic names in the United States, April through June 1983.* (Decision list no. 8302.) Washington: Department of the Interior, 29 p.

_____1983d. *Decisions on geographic names in the United States, July through September 1983.* (Decision list no. 8303.) Washington: Department of the Interior, 26 p.

_____1983e. *Decisions on geographic names in the United States, October through December 1983.* (Decision list no. 8304.) Washington: Department of the Interior, 20 p.

_____1984a. *Decisions on geographic names in the United States, January through March 1984.* (Decision list no. 8401.) Washington: Department of the Interior, 29 p.

_____1984b. *Decisions on geographic names in the United States, October through December 1984.* (Decision list no. 8404.) Washington: Department of the Interior, 18 p.

_____1985a. *Decisions on geographic names in the United States, January through March 1985.* (Decision list no. 8501.) Washington: Department of the Interior, 18 p.

_____1985b. *Decisions on geographic names in the United States, October through December 1985.* (Decision list no. 8504.) Washington: Department of the Interior, 12 p.

_____1988a. *Decisions on geographic names in the United States, April through June 1988.* (Decision list no. 8802.) Washington: Department of the Interior, 19 p.

_____1988b. *Decisions on geographic names in the United States, October through December 1988.* (Decision list no. 8804.) Washington: Department of the Interior, 20 p.

_____1989. *Decisions on geographic names in the United States, January through March 1989.* (Decision list no. 8901.) Washington: Department of the Interior, 9 p.

_____1995. *Decisions on geographic names in the United States.* (Decision list 1995.) Washington: Department of the Interior, 19 p.

United States Coast and Geodetic Survey. 1963. *United States Coast Pilot 7, Pacific Coast, California, Oregon, Washington, and Hawaii.* (Ninth edition.) Washington: United States Government Printing Office, 336 p.

United States Supreme Court. 1857. *The United States, Appellants, vs. The Guadalupe Mining Company.* (Sen. Ex. Doc. 78.) 158 p.

Wagner, Henry R. 1968. *The cartography of the Northwest Coast of America to the year 1800.* (One-volume reprint of the 1937 edition.) Amsterdam: N. Israel, 543 p.

Wagner, Jack R. 1974. *The last whistle (Ocean Shore Railroad).* Berkeley, California: Howell-North Books, 135 p.

Waring, Gerald A. 1915. *Springs of California.* (United States Geological Survey Water-Supply Paper 338.) Washington: Government Printing Office, 410 p.

White, Philo. 1965. *Philo White's narrative of a cruize in the Pacific to South America and California on the U.S. Sloop-of-War "Dale," 1841-1843.* Denver, Colorado: Old West Publishing Company, 84 p.

Whiting, J.S., and Whiting, Richard J. 1960. *Forts of the State of California.* (Authors), 90 p.

Whitney, J.D. 1865. *Report of progress and synopsis of the field-work from 1860 to 1864.* (Geological Survey of California, Geology, Volume I.) Published by authority of the Legislature of California, 498 p.

Wilkes, Charles. 1958. *Columbia River to the Sacramento.* Oakland, California: Biobooks, 140 p.

Williamson, R.S. 1855. "Report." *Reports of explorations and surveys, to ascertain the most practicable and economical route for a railroad from the Mississippi River to the Pacific Ocean.* Volume V, part I. (33d Cong., 2d Sess., Sen. Ex. Doc. No. 78) Washington: Beverley Tucker, Printer, 43 p.

_____1857. "General report." *Reports of explorations and surveys, to ascertain the most practicable and economincal route for a railroad from the Mississippi River to the Pacific Ocean.* Volume VI, part I. (33d Cong., 2d Sess., Sen. Ex. Doc. No. 78.) Washington: Beverly Tucker, Printer, 134 p.

Wyman, Beth. 1983. *Hiram Morgan Hill.* (Author), 50 p.

Young, John V. 1979. *Ghost towns of the Santa Cruz Mountains*. Santa Cruz, California: Paper Vision Press, 156 p.

MISCELLANEOUS MAPS

Baker. 1855. "Map of the mining region, of California." Drawn by Geo. H. Baker.

Bancroft. 1864. "Bancroft's map of the Pacific States." Compiled by Wm. H. Knight. Published by H.H. Bancroft & Co., Booksellers and Stationers, San Francisco, Cal.

Beechey. 1827-1828. "The harbor of San Francisco, Nueva California." By Captn. F.W. Beechey, R.N.F.R.S.

California Division of Highways. 1934. (Appendix "A" *of* California Division of Highways.)

California Mining Bureau. 1909a. "Sonoma, Marin, Napa, Yolo, and Solano Counties." (*In* California Mining Bureau Bulletin 56.)

_____1909b. "San Francisco, San Mateo, Contra Costa, Alameda, Santa Clara, and Santa Cruz Counties." (*In* California Mining Bureau Bulletin 56.)

_____1917a. (Untitled map *in* California Mining Bureau Bulletin 74, p. 164.)

_____1917b. (Untitled map in California Mining Bureau Bulletin 74, p. 166.)

Clark. 1924. "Map of the drainage basin of Alameda Creek and adjacent area." (Plate III *in* W.O. Clark.)

Costanso. 1771. "Carta reducida del Oceano Asiatico o mar del Sur." (Reproduced *in* Harlow.)

Crespi. 1772. "Mapa de lo substancial del famoso Puerto y Rio de San Francisco explorado por tierra en el mes de morzo del presente año de 1772." (Reproduced *in* Harlow.)

Dalrymple. 1789. "Plan of Port Sn francisco on the west coast of California." (Reproduced *in* Harlow.)

Davis and Vernon. 1951. "Mines and mineral deposits of Contra Costa County, California" (Plate 42 *in* Davis and Vernon.)

Derby. 1850. "Reconnaissance of the Tulares Valley." Lieut. G.H. Derby, Topl. Engrs., April and May, 1850.

Diller and others. 1915. "Geologic and topographic map of the Shasta route from Seattle, Washington, to San Francisco, California." (*In* Diller and others.)

Eddy. 1854. "Approved and declared to be the official map of the State of California by an act of the Legislature passed March 25th 1853." Compiled by W. M. Eddy, State Surveyor General. Published for R. A. Eddy, Marysville, California, by J. H. Colton, New York.

Font. 1777. "Plan, o mapa del viage que bicimos desde Monterey al Puerto de Sn. francisco". (Reproduced *in* Harlow.)

Fremont. 1845. "Map of an exploring expedition to the Rocky Mountains in the year 1842 and to Oregon & North California in the years 1843-44." By Brevet Capt. J.C. Frémont.

_____1848. "Map of Oregon and Upper California from the surveys of John Charles Frémont, and other authorities." Drawn by Charles Preuss. Washington City.

Goddard. 1857. "Britton & Rey's map of the State of California." By George H. Goddard.

Hare. 1872. "Map of vicinity of San Jose." Published by Geo. H. Hare, Book Dealer, San Jose.

Healy. 1866. (Untitled part of a map by Charles T. Healy, reproduced *in* Fava, p. 33.)

Jefferson. 1849. "Map of the emigrant road from Independence Mo. to St. Francisco, California." By T.H. Jefferson.

Mendenhall. 1908. "Artesian areas and groundwater levels in the San Joaquin Valley, California." (Plate I *in* Mendenhall.)

Mitchell. 1856. "Mitchell's new national map." Published by S. Augustus Mitchell.

Nelson. 1909. "Map of San Francisco Bay region showing distribution of shell heaps." (Map I *in* Nelson.)

Parke. 1854-1855. "Map No. 1, San Francisco Bay to the plains of Los Angeles." From explorations and surveys made by Lieut. John G. Parke. Constructed and drawn by H. Custer. (In *Reports of explorations and surveys, to ascertain the most practicable and economical route for a railroad from the Mississippi River to the Pacific Ocean*. Volume XI. 1861.)

Peninsular Railway Company. 1912. (Map showing interurban lines of Peninsular Railway Company, reproduced in *San Jose Mercury,* January 2, 1964.)

Postal Route. 1884. (Map reproduced in *Early California, Northern Edition*. Corvalis, Oregon: Western Guide Publishers, p. 34-43.)

Ringgold. 1850a. "Chart of the Bay of San Pablo, Straits of Carquines, and part of the Bay of San Francisco, California." By Cadwalader Ringgold, Commander, U.S. Navy, Assisted by Simon F. Blunt, Lieut. U.S.N. 1850.

_____1850b. "Chart of Suisun & Vallejo Bays, with the confluence of the Rivers Sacramento and San Joaquin, California." By Cadwalader Ringgold, Commander U.S. Navy, Assisted by Sam. R. Knox, Lieut. U.S.N., and Wm. P. Humphreys & J.H. Rowe Engineers. 1850.

_____1850c. "General chart embracing survey of the Farallones entrance to the Bay of San Francisco, Bays of San Francisco and San Pablo, Straits of Carquines and Suisun Bay, and the Sacramento and San Joaquin Rivers to the cities of Sacramento and San Joaquin, California." By Cadwalader Ringgold, Commander, U.S. Navy. 1850.

_____1850d. "Chart of the Sacramento River from Suisun City to the American River, California." By Cadwalader Ringgold, Commander, U.S. Navy, Assisted by Edwin Cullberg, Lieut. of the Hydrotechnic Corps, Swedish

Navy, and T.A. Emmet, Civil Engineer. 1850.
_____1850e. "Straits of Carquines and Vallejo Bay." By Cadwalader Ringgold, U.S. N. 1850.

Rogers and Johnston (1857). "State of California." By Prof. H.D. Rogers & A. Keith Johnston.

Sage. 1846. "Map of Oregon, California, New Mexico, N.W. Texas, & the proposed Territory of Ne-Bras-ka." By Rufus B. Sage.

Smith and Elliott. 1879. "Map of Contra Costa and part of Alameda County." Published by Smith & Elliott, Engravers and lithographers, Oakland, Cal. (*In* Smith and Elliott.)

Soule, Gihon, and Nisbet. 1855. "Map of San Francisco." (*In* Soule, Gihon, and Nisbet, p. 20.)

Thompson and West. 1876. (Maps *in* Thompson and West, 1876.)
_____1878. (Maps *in* Thompson and West, 1878.)
_____1879. (Maps *in* Thompson and West, 1879.)

Trask. 1853. "Topographical map of the mineral districts of California." Being the first map ever published from actual survey. By John B. Trask. Lithog. and Published by Britton & Rey. San Francisco.

Wackenreuder. 1861. "City and County of San Francisco." Drawn by V. Wackenreuder, C.E. Published by Henry G. Langley for the San Francisco directory.

Wilkes. 1841. "Map of Upper California." By the U.S. Ex. Ex. and best authorities.
_____1849. "Map of Upper California." By the best authorities.

Williamson. 1853. "General map of explorations and surveys in California." By Lieut. R.S. Williamson, Topl. Engr., assisted by Lieut. J.G. Parke, Topl. Engr., and Mr. Isaac William Smith, Civ. Engr. (In *Reports of explorations and surveys, to ascertain the most practicable and economical route for a railroad from the Mississippi River to the Pacific Ocean.* Volume XI. 1861.)

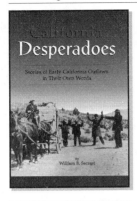

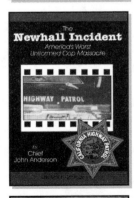

About the Author

Many years ago in connection with his more than three-decade-long career as a geologist with the United States Geological Survey, David L. Durham often needed to know the whereabouts of some obscure or vanished place in California. He searched for a suitable gazetteer to help him locate these features but found no such volume. To meet his needs he began compiling his own gazetteer for part of the state and, as his interests expanded, so did his gazetteer.

For the first twelve years of his retirement, Mr. Durham compiled information for the gazetteer nearly full-time. Eventually he extended coverage to all of California. The definitive gazetteer of California, *California's Geographic Names: A Gazetteer of Historic and Modern Names of the State* is the result. The Durham's Place-Names of California series, of which this volume is one, contains the same information as *California's Geographic Names* but in thirteen regional divisions.

Mr. Durham was born in California, served as an infantryman in France and Germany during World War II and holds a Bachelor of Science degree from the California Institute of Technology. He and his wife Nancy have two grown children.